T0398519

The Singing of the Strasbourg Protestants, 1523–1541

To my grandmother

The Singing of the Strasbourg Protestants, 1523–1541

DANIEL TROCMÉ-LATTER

Homerton College, Cambridge, UK

LONDON AND NEW YORK

First published 2015 by Ashgate Publishing

Published 2016 by Routledge
2 Park Square, Milton Park, Abingdon, Oxon OX14 4RN
711 Third Avenue, New York, NY 10017, USA

Routledge is an imprint of the Taylor & Francis Group, an informa business

British Library Cataloguing in Publication Data
A catalogue record for this book is available from the British Library.

The Library of Congress has cataloged the printed edition as follows:
Trocmé-Latter, Daniel.
The singing of the Strasbourg Protestants, 1523–1541 / by Daniel Trocmé-Latter.
pages cm. – (St Andrews studies in Reformation history)
Includes bibliographical references and index.
ISBN 978-1-4724-3206-3 (hardcover : alk. paper)
1. Church music–France–
Strasbourg–16th century. 2. Church music–Protestant churches–16th century.
3. Reformation–France–Strasbourg. I. Title.
ML3127.8.S87T76 2015
264'.2309443954–dc23

2014037442

ISBN 9781472432063 (hbk)

Contents

List of Figures

List of Tables and Music Examples

Tables

Music Examples

Notes on Style and Language

The dialect of most German quotations is *Frühneuhochdeutsch* (Early New High German).

Manuscript quotations are from original sources where these were available. Quotations from sixteenth-century printed sources are taken from the original publication, where possible.

Original spelling (as found in the source used) has been retained throughout, including the letters 'u', 'v', 'i', 'j'. The only exceptions are instances of the letter 'v' with either an umlaut or a superscript 'u'; these have been simplified as 'v'.

Shorthand abbreviations, both in manuscript and printed works, have been expanded (e.g. *Psalmē* has become *Psalme[n]*; *od'* has become *od[er]*).

Song titles retain their sixteenth-century spellings. Generally, the form in which a song title most commonly appears has been used. Where songs are discussed in the context of a particular publication, however, they will be spelt as found in that publication. This means that some song titles may be spelt in different ways at different points within this book. Titles of songs and poems are between inverted commas (e.g. 'Gott sey gelobet'), while publication titles are in italics (e.g. *Teütsch Kirchenampt*).

Line-breaks in book titles are usually only used in the bibliography in instances of clarification, e.g. to distinguish between two editions of the same book published in the same year.

Place names and personal names have been standardised, according to generally accepted modern-day spellings in English scholarship.

Biblical quotations (except when incorporated into a sixteenth-century text or otherwise specified) are from the New International Version (NIV), taken from http://www.biblegateway.com.

All manuscript classmarks refer to the collection of the Strasbourg Archives de la Ville et de la Communauté urbaine, unless otherwise stated. See p. 378 for a list of the collections consulted.

Dating of Sources

In Germany until 1544, although 1 January was considered the beginning of the historical year, the numbering of the new year in most places did not change until 25 March, the beginning of the civil year.[1] However, Strasbourg sources from the 1520s and 1530s often seem to change the numbering of the year before 25 March, which obviously poses a problem for the dating of sources from January to March each year. There therefore remains some ambiguity regarding the order of certain events as described in Chapters 2 and 3. Nevertheless, it is worth mentioning that some compilations of historical sources from Strasbourg[2] also treat 1 January as the beginning of the historical year. 1 January has therefore been taken as the beginning of the new calendar year for the purposes of this book.

[1] Every region of Europe had its own custom. Neighbouring Lorraine, for example, began the year on *both* 25 December *and* 25 March. See J. J. Bond, *Handy-Book of Rules and Tables for Verifying Dates with the Christian Era* (London: Bell & Sons, 1875), pp. 94, 97.

[2] For example, Hans Virck, et al., eds, *Politische Correspondenz der Stadt Strassburg im Zeitalter der Reformation*, 5 vols (Strasbourg: Trübner, 1882–1933).

List of Abbreviations

Library Sigla

CH SH	Schaffhausen, Stadtbibliothek
CH Zz	Zurich, Zentralbibliothek
D As	Augsburg, Staats- und Stadtbibliothek
D Bsb	Berlin, Staatsbibliothek (Preussischer Kulturbesitz)
D Dl	Dresden, Sächsische Landesbibliothek; Staats- und Universitätsbibliothek
D GOl	Gotha, Forschungsbibliothek
D Gs	Göttingen, Niedersächsische Staats- und Universitätsbibliothek
D HAu	Halle, Universitäts- und Landesbibliothek
D Iek	Isny, Württemberg, Bibliothek der evangelischen Stadtkirche
D Mbs	Munich, Bayerische Staatsbibliothek
D PA	Paderborn, Erzbischöfliche Akademische Bibliothek
D Rs	Regensburg, Staatliche Bibliothek
D Sl	Stuttgart, Württembergische Landesbibliothek
D WGp	Lutherstadt Wittenberg, Evangelisches Predigerseminar Bibliothek
D Z	Zwickau, Ratsschulbibliothek, Wissenschaftliche Bibliothek
DK Kk	Copenhagen, Kongelige Bibliotek

E Mn	Madrid, Biblioteca Nacional
F Sn	Strasbourg, Bibliothèque nationale et universitaire
F Ssp	Strasbourg, Médiathèque protestante (formerly the Bibliothèque du Séminaire protestant)
GB Cu	Cambridge, University Library
GB Lbl	London, British Library
GB Lkc	London, King's College Library
NL DHk	The Hague, Koninklijke Bibliotheek
RUS Mrg	Moscow, Rossiyskaya Gosudarstvennaya Biblioteka

Classmarks for the Bibliothèque Wilhelmitana (contained within F Ssp) are somewhat ambiguous, as there is no central catalogue for this library.

Other Abbreviations

AST	Archives du Chapitre Saint-Thomas, held in the AVS.
AVS	Archives de la Ville et de la Communauté urbaine, Strasbourg (formerly the Archives municipales de Strasbourg).
BDS	R. Stupperich and G. Seebass, eds, *Martini Buceri Opera Omnia: Deutsche Schriften*, 17 vols (Gütersloh: Gütersloh Verlagshaus G. Mohn, 1960–).
BMS	Bibliothèque municipale de Strasbourg.
BNUS	Bibliothèque nationale et universitaire de Strasbourg.
CCCC	Parker Library, Corpus Christi College, Cambridge.
COO	J. W. Baum et al., eds, *Ioannis Calvini opera quae supersunt omnia*, 59 vols (Brunswick: Schwetschke, 1863–1900).

COS	P. Barth and G. Niesel, eds, *Joannis Calvini opera selecta*, 5 vols (Munich: Kaiser, 1926–1936).
Church Mother	E. A. McKee, *Katharina Schütz Zell. Church Mother: The Writings of a Protestant Reformer in Sixteenth-Century Germany* (Chicago: University of Chicago Press, 2006).
CorrBucer	J. Rott et al., eds, *Correspondance de Martin Bucer*, 5 vols (Leiden: Brill, 1979–).
CorrCapito	E. Rummel, ed., with M. Kooistra, *The Correspondence of Wolfgang Capito*, 2 vols (Toronto: University of TorontoPress, 2005–).
DKL III	J. Stalmann et al., eds, *Das Deutsche Kirchenlied. Kritische Gesamtausgabe der Melodien*, Abteilung III (Kassel: Bärenreiter, 1993–).
Garside	C. Garside, Jr, 'The Origins of Calvin's Theology of Music: 1536–1543', *Transactions of the American Philosophical Society*, 69.4 (1979), pp. 1–35.
Hubert	F. Hubert, *Die Straßburger liturgischen Ordnungen imZeitalter der Reformation* (Göttingen: Vandenhoeck & Ruprecht, 1900).
KSZ	E. A. McKee, *Katharina Schütz Zell*, 2 vols (Leiden: Brill, 1999).
LW	J. Pelikan and T. Lehmann, eds, *Luther's Works: American Edition*, 55 vols (St Louis: Concordia; Philadelphia: Muehlenberg & Fortress, 1955–86).
MPGR	R. W. Oettinger, *Music as Propaganda in the German Reformation* (Aldershot: Ashgate, 2001).
PH	Pièces Historiques, Archives d'Etat de Genève.
RISM DKL	K. Ameln, M. Jenny, and W. Lipphardt, eds, *Das Deutsche Kirchenlied DKL*, Répertoire International des Sources Musicales, B/VIII/1–2 (Kassel: Bärenreiter, 1975 and 1980).

USTC	Universal Short Title Catalogue (online resource: www.ustc.ac.uk).
VD16	Bezzel, I, et al., eds, *Verzeichnis der im deutschen Sprachbereich erschienenen Drucke des 16. Jahrhunderts* (Stuttgart: Hiersemann, 1983–) (online resource: www.vd16.de).
WA	J. C. F. Knaake et al., eds, *D. Martin Luthers Werke: Kritische Gesamtausgabe*, 73 vols (Weimar: Böhlau, 1883–).
WA Br	J. C. F. Knaake et al., eds, *D. Martin Luthers Werke: Kritische Gesamtausgabe – Briefwechsel*, 17 vols (Weimar: Böhlau, 1930–1983).
Wackernagel DKL	P. Wackernagel, *Das deutsche Kirchenlied von der ältesten Zeit bis zu Anfang des XVII. Jahrhunderts*, 5 vols (Leipzig: Teubner, 1864–1877; repr. Hildesheim: Olms, 1964).
ZwBw	E. Egli et al., eds, *Zwinglis Briefwechsel*, 5 vols (Leipzig: Nachfolger, 1911–1935) (= *Huldreich Zwinglis Sämtliche Werke*, 14 vols [Berlin: Schwetschke; Leipzig: Nachfolger; Zurich: Berichthaus; Zurich: Theologischer Verlag, 1905–1956], vols 7–11).

Acknowledgements

I am indebted to various individuals who have given up a great deal of time to support me in this endeavour. This project lay somewhere in between the various areas of expertise of Iain Fenlon, Ulinka Rublack, and Geoffrey Webber, and I am grateful to them all for their guidance and encouragement. I would also like to thank Susan Rankin for agreeing to supervise a small project which I undertook on the Genevan Psalter in the year 2005–2006 and for encouraging me in the earliest stages of my interest in the music of the Reformation. My thanks also go to Robin Leaver and Gerald Hobbs for their advice on various sections of my writing, as well as to numerous others for being willing to answer questions related to my work. I have also received a great deal of advice and help with translating texts from family, friends, and friends of friends.

The institutions in Strasbourg that granted me access to their collections enabled me to undertake this project, and I am especially grateful to the staff at the Archives de la Ville et de la Communauté urbaine de Strasbourg, the staff at the Médiathèque protestante, and also to Catherine Donnadieu and the reading room staff at the Bibliothèque nationale et universitaire. My thanks go to my grandmother, Ann Trocmé, for accommodating me so readily and generously during my visits to Strasbourg. I dedicate this monograph to her. In addition, I am grateful to all the libraries that have allowed me to reproduce images in this book, as well as to Eric McFadden at Classical Numismatic Group.

Finally, thanks to Julia for her unending generosity, help, patience, and love, and for making it all worthwhile.

Double-page map of Strasbourg published in G. Braun, *Civitates Orbis Terrarum*, 6 vols (Cologne: Agrippina, 1572–1617), vol. 1, no. 33. E Mn – GMG.46(1), via Wikimedia Commons (http://commons.wikimedia.org/wiki/File:CivitatesOrbisTerrarum_Strasbourg.jpg).

Introduction

> Music… has been placed before and directed to God our Father, so that absolutely no song may be sung and no instrumentalising may take place except by and for Christian spiritual activities.[1]
>
> Martin Bucer, *Gesangbuch* (1541)

Most people would not instinctively associate the name Martin Bucer with ecclesiastical music. Since he is best known today in the English-speaking world as a German immigrant advisor to Thomas Cranmer, the statement that Bucer was one of the most important proponents of hymnody may come as something of a surprise. Yet this is exactly what he was. Likewise, the assertion that Strasbourg's reforms influenced German, Swiss, French, and English Protestantism is quite a claim. Nevertheless, it is also true.

Sixteenth-century Strasbourg was the gateway between the Holy Roman Empire and the rest of Western Europe. Home to a major printing press (and proud of its association with the father of printing, Johannes Gutenberg), the city was located along several key trade routes and was therefore well placed to both receive and disseminate knowledge. A Free Imperial City of the Holy Roman Empire, Strasbourg also boasted an advanced form of government for its time, electing an *Ammeister* each year and being ruled by magistrates and regulated by councils.[2] This structure of governance affected the way in which Strasbourg experienced the Protestant Reformation. Despite vociferous protests from many members of the clergy, churches ultimately fell under the authority of the city. This enabled the reformers, so long as they had supporters among the municipal authorities, to push through the changes they saw as necessary,

[1] 'die Music für andern dingen ist / zů Got vnserm Vater gerichtet vnd gestellet haben / also das kein Lied ůberal / kein seitenspil / anders dann von / vnd zů christlichen geistlichen hendelen gesungen vnd gebrauchet wůrde'. Martin Bucer, preface to *Gesangbuch / darinn begriffen sind / die aller fůrnemisten vnd besten Psalmen / Geistliche Lieder / vnd Chorgeseng / aus dem Wittembergischen / Strasburgischen / vnd anderer Kirchen Gesangbůchlin zůsamen bracht / vnd mit besonderem fleis corrigiert vnd gedrucket. Fůr Stett vnd Dorff Kirchen / Lateinische vnd Deudsche Schůler* (Strasbourg: Messerschmidt and Köpfel, 1541), fol. A3r; reproduced in R. Stupperich and G. Seebass, eds, *Martini Buceri Opera Omnia: Deutsche Schriften*, 17 vols (Gütersloh: Gütersloh Verlagshaus G. Mohn, 1960–) (hereafter: *BDS*), vol. 7, p. 579. Based on the translation in C. Garside, Jr, 'The Origins of Calvin's Theology of Music: 1536–1543', *Transactions of the American Philosophical Society*, 69.4 (1979) (hereafter: *Garside*), p. 30. See also Appendix H, p. 343.

[2] T. A. Brady, *Ruling Class, Regime and Reformation at Strasbourg, 1520–1555* (Leiden: Brill, 1978), pp. 163–5; L. J. Abray, *The People's Reformation: Magistrates, Clergy, and Commons in Strasbourg, 1500–1598* (Oxford: Blackwell, 1985), pp. 50–51.

not just for Strasbourg, but for the whole of Christendom. The bishop resided 50km away in Saverne, and being a Free City meant that Strasbourg had no royal representation to the emperor.

Key to these changes was Martin Bucer, a former Dominican monk, who arrived in Strasbourg in 1523 and almost immediately took the reins of the emerging reformist movement there. Though not a musician of any merit (if at all), Bucer was also key to the centrality of music within Strasbourg's early reforms. His writings, along with those of his colleague Wolfgang Capito, make numerous references to the importance of congregational singing, the use of the vernacular, and the immorality of priests, monks, and choir singers.

This book sets out to investigate the phenomenon of music within the context of German Reformation history – a relatively novel approach to the period in question. Music was, in some form or another, a pastime enjoyed by all in sixteenth-century society, from the lowliest of peasants to the noblest of lords. One of the most fundamental changes to people's lives during the Reformation occurred through music and as a result of it. In ecclesiastical life, hymns often formed the common person's main form of contact with the Scriptures.[3] Ecclesiastical music had previously been a professional activity; singing to God and to the saints had been done on behalf of the common people by a choir or by the clergy, and in Latin, which made it incomprehensible to the majority. The change for congregations, who were now singing for themselves, was therefore radical. Polemical song, too, was a crucial means of disseminating the Reformation message among the wider populace. In short, music was used as a method of educating the uneducated, both in spiritual and worldly matters relating to the Reformation.

As a historical 'tool', music has been underutilised in Reformation scholarship. This is in part due to the unfortunate popular perception during the last 200 years of the music of the Reformation, namely that the art prospered under the Lutherans and suffered under the Zwinglians and Calvinists. Hyperbolic references to Martin Luther's delight in music are common in nineteenth-century writings,[4] and myths about Jean Calvin's opposition to music are still promoted today. The 2005 *Oxford History of Western Music* claims that 'nowhere do the differences among the reformed churches show up more clearly than in their attitudes toward music' (something which is difficult to justify in light of, for example, the fundamental differences in their approach to the nature of the Eucharist), and reaches the surprising conclusion that Calvin was the 'most negative of all' reformers in his outlook on music.[5] It is undeniable, of

[3] C. B. Brown, *Singing the Gospel: Lutheran Hymns and the Success of the Reformation* (Cambridge, MA, and London: Harvard University Press, 2005), p. 15.

[4] For example, see such articles as 'On Luther's Love for and Knowledge of Music', 'by a German student', *The Musical Times and Singing Class Circular*, 1 (1845), pp. 82–3, 87.

[5] R. Taruskin, *The Oxford History of Western Music*, 6 vols (Oxford: Oxford University Press, 2005), vol. 1, p. 754. Taruskin's article on the Genevan Psalter is factually incorrect in several places.

course, that aspects of society, culture, and the arts were changed as a result of the Reformation. But broad generalisations are of little academic value. It must be borne in mind that what is known as the 'Reformation' was not one, but multiple, movements sweeping across Europe. At the beginning of this period, the multiplicity of differences in theological opinion was considerable, but reforming thought had yet to crystallise into the distinct camps we identify today. Each region or city approached reform in its own way, depending on its academics, politics, influence, and location.

It is important to note that many parts of supposedly Protestant lands, especially rural areas, often neglected to implement any reforms at all.[6] However, even within more urban areas, the process of reform cannot be said to have been immediate. Such a generalisation would be overconfident in its assertion that the Reformation was, first, understood by the people; second, desired by the people; and third, spread by means accessible to the people. Nevertheless, if the evidence from Strasbourg is to be believed, some effects were indeed immediate, or at least happened very quickly, such as the implementation of congregational hymns. A thorough investigation into music and approaches to music at the beginning of the Reformation is therefore essential if we are to understand properly the development of these Protestant confessions and their relationship to culture and society.

The influence and importance of Strasbourg during the Reformation era has already received scholarly attention from a number of sources. In particular, Patrice Veit has already identified Strasbourg's unique approach to church music under its first Protestant leaders.[7] Indeed, Martin Bucer and the other Strasbourg preachers recognised the immense value of communal singing in church, and noted the historical precedent for it in the Bible and in the early Church. They objected to the facts that church singing was done in Latin, and that the common people were not usually allowed to participate in it. Their solution was to ban choral singing and the choral institution and replace it with German psalms and spiritual songs designed for the laity. This approach differed considerably from that of Martin Luther, who also introduced vernacular congregational singing but maintained the role of the choir, as well as from that of Huldrych Zwingli, who removed all music from Zurich's churches.

The importance of music as a factor in the initial spread of the Reformation is gaining recognition by historians. Song can be said to have made a double impact, as an element of both print culture and oral culture, and Robert Scribner's work has acknowledged song to be a vital link between the oral and

6 See G. Strauss, *Luther's House of Learning: Indoctrination of the Young in the German Reformation* (Baltimore and London: Johns Hopkins University Press, 1978). However, one Strasbourg politician claimed that people flocked from rural areas to experience the new Protestant service. See below, p. 246.

7 P. Veit, *Das Kirchenlied in der Reformation Martin Luthers* (Stuttgart: Steiner, 1986), pp. 9–12.

the written.[8] Andrew Pettegree has identified four steps in the laypeople's process of understanding the Reformation: awareness, identification, understanding, and activism. The crucial first step, awareness, was reached by several means. The new ideas were heard in the marketplace, in taverns, in the theatre, and in church – through preaching, but also through song. In addition, these ideas were often printed in pamphlets and then read aloud by those able to do so (thereby reaching an illiterate audience).[9]

An increasing amount of attention has been paid to the cultural practices of the Reformation over the past few decades.[10] Jonathan Willis's recent investigation into church music in post-Reformation England[11] takes a fresh approach to music as a source for historical investigation and is an encouraging step in the right direction for Reformation music history. Joseph Herl's valuable study of music in Reformation and post-Reformation Germany provides a great deal of insight into the relationship between choir and congregation, but gives the impression that Germany was more homogeneous in its liturgical musical practices than was actually the case.[12] Demonstrating the importance of localised studies, Christopher Boyd Brown has produced a fascinating insight into reform in Joachimsthal (modern-day Jáchymov in the Czech Republic).[13]

[8] R. W. Scribner, 'Flugblatt und Analphabetentum. Wie kam der gemeine Mann zu reformatorischen Ideen?', in H. J. Köhler, ed., *Flugschriften als Massenmedium der Reformationszeit* (Stuttgart: Klett-Cotta, 1981), pp. 69–76. See, more generally, Scribner, *For the Sake of Simple Folk* (Oxford: Oxford University Press, 1981).

[9] A. Pettegree, *Reformation and the Culture of Persuasion* (Cambridge: Cambridge University Press, 2005), pp. 6–8.

[10] Hans-Christoph Rublack has investigated the relationship between song and society. See H.-C. Rublack, 'The Song of Contz Anahans: Communication and Revolt in Nördlingen, 1525', in R. P. Hsia, ed., *The German People and the Reformation* (Ithaca and London: Cornell University Press, 1988), pp. 102–20.

[11] J. Willis, *Church Music and Protestantism in Post-Reformation England: Discourses, Sites and Identities* (Farnham: Ashgate, 2010).

[12] J. Herl, *Worship Wars in Early Lutheranism: Choir, Congregation, and Three Centuries of Conflict* (Oxford: Oxford University Press, 2004). Other significant works include Robin Leaver's writing on the origins and spread of the metrical psalms: *'Goostly psalmes and spirituall songes': English and Dutch Metrical Psalms from Coverdale to Utenhove 1535–1566* (Oxford: Clarendon Press, 1991); K. H. Marcus, 'Hymnody and Hymnals in Basel, 1526–1606', *The Sixteenth-Century Journal*, 32 (2001), pp. 723–41; and C. Schalk, *Music in Early Lutheranism: Shaping the Tradition (1524–1672)* (St Louis: Concordia, 2001).

[13] Brown, *Singing the Gospel*. Brown uses musical sources to demonstrate that the Lutheran Reformation did have an effect on the common people of the sixteenth century. His study is in part a musicological reaction to the findings of Gerald Strauss, who in the 1970s argued that, in an attempt to educate the wider population, the Protestant reformers in Germany implemented methods that did not have a long-lasting effect and in many cases made no difference at all. Strauss concluded that the German people were not affected by the reforms in the long term and, to the infuriation of the Lutheran clergy, continued with many medieval practices (see Strauss, *Luther's House of Learning* and 'Success and Failure in the German Reformation', *Past & Present*, 67 (1975), pp. 30–63). He was criticized for applying his findings to the whole of Germany, without considering the effect of the Reformation at a local level. Lorna Abray, for example, notes that Strauss concentrates on

However, Joachimsthal was a small mining town established at the beginning of the sixteenth century. It was not a printing centre, nor was it especially distinct in terms of religion. Brown's study, therefore, is of limited value in adding to our knowledge of the reform of music in sixteenth-century Protestantism, although it lays an important foundation for studies of larger areas such as Strasbourg. Alexander Fisher likewise concentrates on one area of Germany, namely the Free Imperial City of Augsburg.[14] His study, however, much like Brown's, is set in a later period where confessional divisions had become less nuanced. Many other historical studies of the Reformation and music's involvement in it have appeared in articles that by their very nature are unable to encompass a detailed survey of the sources involved.[15] Even René Bornert's authoritative and monumental volume on Strasbourg's liturgical reforms[16] makes reference only to a fraction of the relevant archival material, leaving much of the wealth of knowledge contained in these archives untouched. It is high time, therefore, that Strasbourg's artistic reforms were given the attention they deserve.

Among the important questions raised in these studies is the extent to which a less Lutheran and more 'primitive' notion of Protestant theology of music can be established. At the beginning of the Reformation, Bucer did not consider himself to be 'Lutheran' or 'Zwinglian', but nevertheless he had very distinct views on the uses and abuses of music. Bucer was also an influential figure in Protestantism in other areas of Europe. His effect on the Church's policy towards music therefore deserves exploration as part of any such study. One of the most important pieces of scholarship in this regard is Charles Garside's article on Jean Calvin's theology of music.[17] In this piece, Garside traces the development of the Genevan reformer's attitudes to music, and identifies the clear connection with Bucer's own stance on music.

---

the effect of Lutheranism in rural areas, and that his results apply neither to Strasbourg nor to the peasants of Strasbourg's rural territories (Abray, *The People's Reformation*, p. 209, incl. n. 3). Brown's work covers hymns and hymnals, music's relationship with society, education, domestic life, and church life.

[14] A. J. Fisher, *Music and Religious Identity in Counter-Reformation Augsburg, 1580–1630* (Aldershot: Ashgate, 2004).

[15] See, for example, the highly informative but concise article by R. G. Hobbs, '"Quam Apposita Religioni Sit Musica": Martin Bucer and Music in the Liturgy', *Reformation and Renaissance Review*, 6 (2004), pp. 155–78. Patrice Veit's work on inventories and wills points to the fact that songbooks and hymnals were collected as household items and treasured by multiple generations. (Veit, 'Das Gesangbuch als Quelle lutherischer Frömmigkeit', *Archiv für Reformationsgeschichte*, 79 (1988), pp. 218). He also emphasises the links between songbooks, prayer books, devotional books, and bibles (pp. 206, 210).

[16] R. Bornert, *La Réforme protestante du culte à Strasbourg au XVIe siècle (1523–1598)* (Leiden: Brill, 1981).

[17] *Garside*, pp. 1–35.

The use of music as propaganda in the German Reformation is covered in some detail by Rebecca Wagner Oettinger,[18] who asserts that popular songs of the Reformation had a greater effect on the common people than did religious writings or sermons, and also recognises that hymnology, as well as propagandistic music, is often sidelined in musicology and other disciplines. As well as providing a great deal of useful data on Strasbourg's popular songs during the Reformation, Oettinger's monograph suggests the need for studies that investigate sacred and secular song alongside one another.[19] With this in mind, this book investigates music from both spheres of life in Strasbourg, while maintaining a distinction between the two: one type of song relating very closely to the liturgy itself and the unique context of ecclesiastical worship, and the other reflecting the discussions, politics, and sometimes aspirations of the public in everyday life. Chapter 4 demonstrates some of the issues with which popular songwriters were concerned. It also observes the decline in polemical songs during the 1530s and in popular songs in general throughout the early Reformation period. Finally, it analyses the extra-biblical texts[20] of the 'official' songs of the Church in Strasbourg – the hymns published from 1524 onwards.

Centrally located in the west of the European continent, but situated on the western edge of the Holy Roman Empire, late-medieval Strasbourg was an extremely wealthy city, with merchants from all over Europe selling their wares there or exporting wine and grain elsewhere. It was an important point of trade along the route of the river Rhine as well as by land, being linked by road to cities in all directions. The city was ruled by the *Magistrat* in an oligarchic regime.[21] The *Ammeister* was in overall control, and an election for this position took place each year. In addition, there were four *Stättmeister* in office, and various councils dealing with different aspects of government.[22] Apart from the clergy, all permanent members of the community were citizens, each having a degree of legal equality.[23] Guilds, open to both men and women, had a great deal of popular control. The humanist movement was beginning to gain a foothold

---

[18] R. W. Oettinger, *Music as Propaganda in the German Reformation* (Aldershot: Ashgate, 2001) (hereafter: *MPGR*); and Oettinger, 'Thomas Murner, Michael Stifel, and Songs as Polemic in the Early Reformation', *Journal of Musicological Research*, 22 (2003), pp. 45–100.

[19] Both sorts of song were often disseminated in the form of broadsheet prints, and then transmitted orally – an essential medium that deserves more attention from scholars, since at this time 'few could read but almost anyone could talk or sing' (*MPGR*, p. 12). In addition, Oettinger considers the significance of song in the Reformation period as a means of resistance against religious and political oppression and investigates the importance of contrafacta. Her work, however, contains several inaccuracies, and I have attempted here to untangle a problem with reference to one Strasbourg pamphlet in particular (see pp. 167–8, incl. n. 57).

[20] That is, those texts which are not directly from the Bible.

[21] Hereafter referred to as the 'council' or 'authorities'.

[22] H. Eells, *Martin Bucer* (New Haven: Yale University Press; London: Oxford University Press, 1931), pp. 19–20.

[23] Brady, *Ruling Class*, pp. 97–124.

here at the end of the fifteenth century, when a new group of educated men immigrated to Strasbourg, seeking employment in its churches and chapters.[24] At the beginning of the sixteenth century, the city was already a significant force in the printing trade, with only Leipzig and Nuremberg exceeding it in terms of print output.[25] German bibles had been in print in Strasbourg since 1466,[26] and missals may have been available in the vernacular by 1520.[27] Luther's writings were being published in the city from 1519.[28]

By the time Luther's opposition to the Roman Church was gaining momentum, the printing industry was producing a variety of material in Strasbourg. Religious writings dominated the market, however, and the printers were promoting the ever-growing debates of the Church.[29] In 1522, for example, Thomas Murner, a Franciscan friar and theologian, produced a book of satirical verse against Martin Luther.[30] This same year, he also published a book entitled *Ob der Künig usz engelland ein lügner sey oder der Luther* (the rather sarcastic and leading title translating as: *Whether the King of England, or Luther, is a liar*).[31] Similarly, in 1523, a translation of John Fisher's *Sermon Against the Pernicious Doctrine of Martin Luther* (1521) appeared in Strasbourg from the same press.[32] Clearly, there was a wide variety of information available

---

24 M. U. Chrisman, *Strasbourg and the Reform: A Study in the Process of Change* (New Haven and London: Yale University Press, 1967), p. 46.

25 M. U. Edwards, Jr, *Printing, Propaganda, and Martin Luther* (Berkeley and Los Angeles: University of California Press, 1994), p. 10.

26 The first to appear was in 1466, off the press of Johannes Mentelin (see Bornert, *Réforme protestante du culte*, p. 610). Although some vernacular bibles were printed, Miriam Chrisman estimates that there would not have been enough in circulation for every household to have owned one (see Chrisman, *Lay Culture, Learned Culture: Books and Social Change in Strasbourg, 1480–1599* (New Haven and London: Yale University Press, 1982), pp. 154–5).

27 This point was picked up on by Thomas Murner in his anti-Lutheran defence of the old Church in 1520, although no extant examples are known. See Abray, *The People's Reformation*, pp. 22–3.

28 Including *Ad Leonem X. Pontificem Maximvm: Resolutiones disputationum de uirtute indulgentiaru[m]* (Strasbourg: Schürer, 1519) and *Ein Sermon von dem Gebeet vnd Procession. yn der Creützwochen: auch sunst on allem gebet durch dz ga[n]tz Jar wie sich der me[n]sch darin halte[n] sol, allen christen me[n]sche[n] nützlich vnd selig zü wissen* (Strasbourg: Knobloch, 1519).

29 Chrisman, 'Printing and the Evolution of Lay Culture in Strasbourg 1480–1599', in Hsia, *The German People and the Reformation*, p. 84.

30 T. Murner, *Von dem grossen Lutherischen Narren wie in doctor Murner beschworen hat. &c.* (Strasbourg: Grüninger, 1522).

31 Strasbourg: Grüninger, 1522. This was a response to Henry VIII's 1521 defence of the seven sacraments of the Roman Church, against which Luther had written. For this piece of polemical writing, the King of England was awarded the title 'Defender of the Faith' by Pope Leo X.

32 J. Fisher, trans. J. Cochlaeus, *Uon dem hochgelerten vn[nd] geistlichen Bischoff Johannes von Roffa vß engeland / seynes großen nutzlichen bůchs CXXXIX. artickel wid[er] M. Luther sein hie verteütscht zů nutz dem christlichen volck zů bedencke[n] irer selen selikeit* (Strasbourg: Grüninger, 1523).

to the literate people of Strasbourg.[33] Printers who were producing polemical writings by Luther might have been working just doors away from rivals who were printing defences of the Catholic faith.

Miriam Chrisman has recognised the importance of the printing trade in the creation and dissemination of music for the Reformation.[34] Those publications from the beginning of the Reformation in Strasbourg that are listed in the *RISM Das Deutsche Kirchenlied* catalogue[35] demonstrate that a variety of religious music was published, including orders of worship with hymns interspersed into the liturgy, hymnals for use in church and in the home, polyphonic partbooks, and pamphlets with no apparent liturgical function but designed to be sung in instances of private devotion. Such publications are an underexplored aspect of the spread of the Reformation.

Although it is clear that books and pamphlets by figures such as Thomas Murner were being aimed at a wide spectrum of social levels (poetry in verse, for example, could easily have been accessed by the literate, and recited in taverns or in the marketplace to the illiterate), it must be remembered that the printed word was still harder for the common man to comprehend than pictures or song, both of which were more direct forms of communication for those who could not read. Jean Rott has established two broad categories of publications from the Reformation era: the first includes books aimed at the intellectual strata of society, including Latin bibles, law treatises, and books on medicine. The second includes books directed at nobles, merchants, and artisans with a limited education, such as German bibles, vernacular treatises, and grammar books.[36]

Hymnals and psalters would also have fallen into this latter category. Barring the earliest religious songbooks, which were essentially orders of service with an added song or two, these tomes were simple enough in design and concept to be of interest to the middle class: they were small, they were in German, and they were common. As demonstrated in Appendix A, the majority of those printed (in Strasbourg, at least) contained melodies. However, this should not necessarily be considered a hindrance to those who did not read music. In his book on the role of images in disseminating the Reformation message, Robert Scribner acknowledges that Reformation ideas may also have encouraged

[33] It is also worth noting that books were being produced in different sizes. A pocket-sized version of Luther's German translation of the Old Testament was published in Strasbourg by Johann Knobloch in 1524. The fact that the Bible was being produced in a handbook design, to be carried around, rather than simply placed on a library bookshelf, confirms the intention of the reformers to reach a wider audience. See Pettegree, *Reformation and the Culture of Persuasion*, p. 132.

[34] Chrisman, 'Printing and the Evolution of Lay Culture'; Chrisman, *Lay Culture, Learned Culture*.

[35] K. Ameln, M. Jenny, and W. Lipphardt, eds, *Das Deutsche Kirchenlied DKL*, Répertoire International des Sources Musicales, B/VIII/1–2 (Kassel, Basel, and London: Bärenreiter, 1975 and 1980) (hereafter: *RISM DKL*).

[36] J. Rott, 'Note sur l'imprimerie alsacienne aux XVe et XVIe siècles', *Revue d'Alsace*, 95 (1956), pp. 69–70.

the spread of literacy.[37] It is likely, then, that the Reformation also assisted in promoting musical literacy. It becomes necessary, of course, to define what constitutes being able to 'read' music. Is it being able to sing a melody perfectly and unaided? Or, more likely in the case of the Reformation, is it being able to judge approximately the pitch contours of a tune and sing along with others in a group? For those being asked to read hymn texts and tunes for the first time – a significant proportion of the population – the latter option is what reading music would have entailed. For those who purchased hymnals for themselves but who had not been educated in music, the melodies could have acted as an *aide-mémoire*, if nothing else, for those familiar tunes which they had heard or sung in church or around the town.

Brown makes the essential point that 'the study of Lutheran hymns has been left largely to hymnologists and musicologists, who have made the historian's task much easier through their labours in the bibliography of hymn printing and their critical research into texts and melodies'.[38] This book is the next step in the process of redressing the false dichotomy between historical and musicological studies through the simple process of treating music as a historical source. This will result in an analysis of the emergence and role of congregational singing at the beginning of the Reformation in Strasbourg, and an explanation of how music, as a transmitter of Christian doctrine, helped form the identity of the new Church. Strasbourg is the focus of this study, first and foremost because of its confessional ambiguity during the first few years of the Reformation. The effect this had on the stance on music of city and Church is unusual. Pettegree has stated that, of all the liturgical traditions outside Wittenberg, the 'most important by far was the largely independent liturgical tradition crafted in the Rhineland city of Strasbourg. The liturgy as it emerged from the years leading to the abolition of the Mass allowed a central role for congregational singing'.[39] Indeed, this is of vital importance: because Strasbourg led the way in the promotion of the service of the Lord's Supper (the Eucharistic alternative to the Roman Mass), it was thereby also a leader in the development of early Protestant congregational singing, alongside, if not ahead of, Wittenberg. Wandel has noted that in Strasbourg 'our knowledge of lived Christianity [is] among the best for sixteenth-century centers of reform'.[40] Strasbourg is today recognised as one of the most important centres of the Reformation; its significance as a hymn-printing centre is also of vital importance. Of approximately 50 towns involved in the printing of German Protestant hymns, Nuremberg, Leipzig, Wittenberg, and Strasbourg account for almost half of the nation's output in the

[37] Scribner, *Simple Folk*, p. 2. Brown observes that Scribner overlooks popular hymn texts that are associated with some of the images in his study (see Brown, *Singing the Gospel*, pp. 4–5).

[38] Brown, *Singing the Gospel*, p. 5.

[39] Pettegree, *Reformation and the Culture of Persuasion*, p. 47.

[40] L. P. Wandel, *Voracious Idols and Violent Hands: Iconoclasm in Reformation Zurich, Strasbourg, and Basel* (Cambridge: Cambridge University Press, 1994), p. 22.

sixteenth century.[41] There have been relatively few studies written exclusively about the part played by music in the spread of the Reformation. Song was initially studied by musicologists as a by-product of the Reformation, the beginnings of congregational singing as we know it today, and often viewed by liturgists merely as a noteworthy element of the new service.

However, rather than concentrating solely on music in the 'public' reforms, this study also answers questions about the 'private' role of music in the Reformation. Why did the reformers view music as essential to their cause? What did they believe was the Church's historical stance on music? Why and how were popular songs controlled in Strasbourg?

Secondary reasons for focusing on Strasbourg include its geographical position in Europe, and the influence that its reforms and reformers had elsewhere, most notably in Switzerland. In trade, politics, and religion, the river Rhine provided the key to Strasbourg's connections with the Swiss cities. It was only to be expected, therefore, that the Protestant reforms in the Swiss territories would share some common ground with those of Strasbourg.[42] Despite a meeting in 1518 between Martin Bucer, the city's future reformer, and Martin Luther, which resulted in Bucer's conversion to the Reformation cause, Bucer soon started erring on the more radical side of Protestantism that was emerging in Zurich. Indeed, Brady states that 'Strasbourg appeared in early 1524 to be the major free city sailing most nearly in Zurich's wake'.[43] Bucer's 1524 publication, *Grund und Ursach*,[44] aligns with the Zurich reformer Huldrych Zwingli on several points, especially in relation to the nature of the Eucharist, notions of the Mass as a sacrifice, and matters pertaining to vestments and the altar. When Bucer became Strasbourg's main reformer in 1524, he began implementing what was largely a Zwinglian-style reform in the city.[45] However, the city refused to abolish the Mass entirely until 1529, and this occurred only after intense lobbying from the city's reforming party. In 1530, Strasbourg was one of four cities that signed up to the Tetrapolitan Confession, a document that officially tied it into the non-Lutheran reforms happening in and around the Swiss territories.[46] Even as the city became less Zwinglian in its theology in later years, partly through pressure from Lutherans in Wittenberg, it took a long

[41] See Brown, *Singing the Gospel*, p. 2; also p. 7, calculating the number of editions catalogued by *RISM DKL*.

[42] See Bornert, *Réforme protestante du culte*, pp. 81–2.

[43] Brady, *Turning Swiss: Cities and Empire, 1450–1550* (Cambridge: Cambridge University Press, 1985), p. 162.

[44] Bucer, *Grund vn[nd] vrsach ausz gotlicher schrifft d[er] neüwerungen / an dem nachtmal des herren / so man die Mess nennet / Tauff / Feyrtagen / bildern vn[nd] gesang / in der gemein Christi / wan[n] die zůsamen kompt / durch vnnd auff das wort gottes / zů Straßburg fürgenomen* (Strasbourg: Köpfel, 1524). Text reproduced in *BDS*, 1, pp. 194–278.

[45] O. F. Cypris, 'Basic Principles: Translation and Commentary of Martin Bucer's *Grund und Ursach*, 1524' (PhD diss., Union Theological Seminary, New York, 1971), p. 3.

[46] The other three cities were Constance, Memmingen, and Lindau.

time to gain a reputation as a more 'Lutheran' city.[47] Crucially, however, there is one major element of Strasbourg's early reforms that makes it stand out from those of Zurich: its attitude towards music. Whereas Wittenberg had introduced vernacular congregational singing at the beginning of the Reformation, the policy in Zurich had been to remove all music from church services. Strasbourg, in its approach to music, was evidently more influenced by Luther than by Zwingli.[48] Because of the confessional ambiguity of Strasbourg during this period, this study tries to distance itself from terms such as 'Lutheran' and 'Zwinglian' in its description of the earliest hymns in Strasbourg, preferring instead to acknowledge the existence of a spectrum of musico-liturgical attitudes.

Music was on the agenda of the Strasbourg reforms from the dawn of the Reformation. Both Matthäus Zell and Martin Bucer spoke in depth of the role of music in church in their lengthy published tracts of 1523 and 1524 respectively.[49] Luther believed that the Church Fathers and prophets desired that the Word of God be sung to music, and both Bucer in Strasbourg and Calvin in Geneva adopted this philosophy.[50] For these reformers, God came to the people whenever the Scriptures were spoken or sung in an intelligible manner. Congregational singing was therefore in conformity with the Bible; but what was sung also had to have a scriptural basis.[51] Music in church, however, had to remain subordinate to the text, and could not serve a purely artistic purpose.[52]

This study makes use of four different types of document: songbooks and liturgical orders of service from 1524 to 1541 (including an analysis of their prefaces); chronicles of the Reformation; the published writings of the Strasbourg reformers, including documents such as Bucer's *Grund und Ursach*,[53] writings in favour of the abolition of the Mass, and the Tetrapolitan Confession and Apology; and unexplored archival material, mostly from the Archives de la Ville et de la Communauté urbaine, Strasbourg (AVS).[54] The publication of Bucer's

---

[47] See Abray, *The People's Reformation*, p. 177. It was not until the end of the Imperial Interim of the 1550s, during which Catholicism was briefly reintroduced, that a stable and recognisable sort of Lutheranism was really established in the city, under Johann Marbach's leadership.

[48] Wittenberg had also both kept the Latin language and given a prominent role to the choir. Strasbourg did not emulate Wittenberg to this extent under Bucer's leadership.

[49] M. Zell, *Christeliche vera[n]twortung M. Matthes Zell von Keyserßberg Pfarrherrs vnd predigers im Münster zů Straßburg / vber Artickel jm vom Bischöfflichem Fiscal daselbs entgegen gesetzt / vnnd im rechten vbergeben* (Strasbourg: Köpfel, 1523); Bucer, *Grund und Ursach*.

[50] Veit, *Kirchenlied in der Reformation*, pp. 28–9; citing J. C. F. Knaake et al., eds, *D. Martin Luthers Werke: Kritische Gesamtausgabe*, 73 vols (Weimar: Böhlau, 1883–) (hereafter: *WA*), vol. 50, pp. 371–2.

[51] Bornert, *Réforme protestante du culte*, p. 470.

[52] Ibid., p. 472. See Bucer, *S. Psalmorum libri quinque ad Ebraicam veritatem versi et familiari explanatione elucidati per Aretium Felinum* (Strasbourg: Ulricher, 1529), fol. 170r; and Bucer, preface to the 1541 *Gesangbuch* (reproduced in *BDS*, 7, pp. 577–82).

[53] See p. 10, n. 44.

[54] These manuscripts range from one-page letters between bishop and council, to financial records, to ironic dialogues (for example, 1 AST 183, 40), to tracts arguing for the abolition of

German writings,[55] for example, has gone some way to providing access to the manuscript texts of the Strasbourg Reformation, many of which are reproduced in the 17 volumes (to date) of this collection. It has also led to a greater interest in the study of Martin Bucer, and in the thoughts and opinions of those who led the Reformation in Strasbourg. However, many other documents relating to the Reformation have not yet been published, and therefore still cannot be accessed without visiting the Strasbourg archives themselves. The earliest major writings on music's role in worship appear from the year 1523. Christian Meyer has written that 'the year 1541 marks a cornerstone in the history of the Strasbourg liturgy',[56] in part because of the appearance of the great Strasbourg *Gesangbuch*. It is for these reasons that this study concentrates on the period 1523–1541.

Often in archival writings, singing was lumped together with other 'papist' excesses, even from those reformers who later spoke out in favour of musical reform (as opposed to musical abolition). A good example of this is a document in which Wolfgang Capito remarked that an array of things as eclectic as 'monks, nuns, priests, crockery, bell ringing, singing, the consecration of water and salt, the blessing of palms and herbs, the burning of candles … benefices, commemorations, and Mass endowments' were just a few of the signs of the Antichrist's grip on Christianity.[57] Music was not singled out as an abuse, but it

the Mass. The majority of these manuscripts are from the Archives du Chapitre Saint-Thomas (hereafter: AST), held at the Archives de la Ville et de la Communauté urbaine, Strasbourg (AVS), although others can be found in other libraries in Strasbourg, Germany, and Switzerland. Fortunately, the majority of Bucer's own manuscripts have been transcribed and published as *BDS* (one of Bucer's contemporaries commented that a 'conjuror rather than a reader' would be needed in order to decipher his handwriting (Letter from Edmund Grindal to Conrad Hubert, 23 May 1559, quoted in H. Robinson, ed., *The Zurich Letters (second series)* (Cambridge: Cambridge University Press, 1845), p. 18)). The AST are classified according to theme (to take an example at random, 1 AST 87 contains documents concerning the relationship of the Strasbourg reformers with the Catholic Church, between 1522 and 1646) and each document is numbered individually (1 AST 87, 5, for example, concerns clerical marriage). The AVS also contain other relevant collections, including those with the prefixes II, IV, V, VI, VIII, 6 R, and 1 MR, and 90 Z. All manuscripts discussed in this book are, unless otherwise stated, from the AVS.

[55] See p. 1, n. 1.

[56] C. Meyer, 'Gesangbuch, darin begriffen sind … Martin Bucer et le chant liturgique', in C. Krieger and M. Lienhard, eds, *Martin Bucer and Sixteenth Century Europe*, 2 vols (Leiden: Brill, 1993), vol. 2, p. 215.

[57] 'allein bedrachte vn[nd] vffsåtz der mensche[n] zů vnsern zeite[n] / wider frey vnd als billichen vorgehalten wirt / zergot das endtchristisch regiment / als munch / non[n] / pfaffen blatte[n] / gekleng / geseng / wasser vn[nd] saltz weihen / palme[n] vnd kreütter segen / liechter brenne[n] / … pfründen / jarzeit / vnd meß stifften'. W. Capito, *Verwarnung / der diener des worts / vnd der brüder zu Straßburg. An die Brůder von Landen vnd Stetten gemeiner Eidgnoßschafft. Wider die Gotslesterige Disputation Brůder Conradts Augustiner Ordens Prouincial* (Strasbourg: Köpfel, 1524), fol. Cij^v. An edition was also published in the same year in Augsburg, by Ulhart. The text is reprinted in B. Miles, 'Wolfgang Capito's *Warning of the ministers of the Word and the brethren at Strasbourg to the brethren of the regions and cities of the [Swiss] Confederation against the blasphemous disputation of Brother Konrad, provincial of the Augustinian Order*', in E. Rummel and M. Kooistra, eds, *Reformation Sources: The Letters of Wolfgang Capito and his*

was something that was deserving of reform. There are plenty of examples of Capito's later support of congregational singing.[58]

This is primarily a study of the music of the people; I have excluded from this study any detailed research into several unexplored avenues in the field of polyphony, since they deserve to have their own platform rather than to be condensed into part of a broader study.[59]

The apparent hesitation to approach the music of the Reformation directly, which can be seen in scholarship trends in the last few decades, is perhaps due to the uncertainty about whether monophonic hymns are a legitimate area of musicological study. As Oettinger has warned, 'one must be careful not to discount the importance of popular songs simply because they are monophonic'.[60] She has also noted the 'fluid boundary between the sacred and secular spheres'.[61] By extension, we can therefore add liturgical songs to the category of monophonic songs whose importance should not be discounted. Bringing congregational singing into mainstream historical study is a little-used process, albeit one with much potential. Christine Dempsey has written that the use of music and music books as historical sources is a unique means of undertaking such historical enquiry, and allows hymnody to become a historical source in its own right.[62] In this way, the music itself is treated not only as musicological analytical material, but also as primary evidence of cultural thinking and social reform. Hymnology can therefore be used to create a study that embraces both a historical understanding of this period (culturally, socially, and theologically) and an understanding of the musical genre involved. Music itself is thereby brought into mainstream historical study and made an approachable source, and reservations about the artistic value of the repertory become irrelevant.

Simultaneously, our understanding of church reform is broadened. Indeed, it is impossible for us to understand fully the history of such reforms without first understanding the reform of church music. For Bucer and Capito, introducing a vernacular liturgy was insufficient. Singing helped internalise the Word of God,

---

Fellow Reformers in Alsace and Switzerland (Toronto: Centre for Reformation and Renaissance Studies, 2007), pp. 177–200.

[58] See Chapters 2 and 3.

[59] For example, the *Cantiones quinque uocum selectissimae* (Strasbourg: Schöffer, 1539), which does not exist in a modern edition, and the *Epicedion Thomae Sporeri Musicorum Principis* (Strasbourg: Schöffer & Apiarius, 1534) (see Chapter 3) which still has not been studied in a musicological context and which as a book was only recently given any scholarly attention at all (S. Söll-Tauchert, *Hans Baldung Grien (1484/85–1545): Selbstbildnis und Selbstinszenierung* (Cologne: Böhlau, 2010), pp. 66–99). Equally, we are unaware of who the customers of such collections in Strasbourg were, or how widely this music would have been performed, given that Strasbourg at this time was otherwise lacking a supply of polyphonic music.

[60] *MPGR*, p. 34.

[61] Ibid., p. 21.

[62] C. A. Dempsey, '*Geistliche Gesangbuch, Geistreiche Gesangbuch*: The Development of Confessional Unity in the Evangelical Hymnbook 1524–1587' (PhD diss., University of Nebraska, 2003), pp. 11, 16.

yet this was a skill that had been devastatingly mistreated for hundreds of years. They saw the opportunity to return Christianity to the laypeople, and music was their means by which to achieve this.

CHAPTER 1

The Church and the 'Wonderful Art' of Music

During the Frankish reign of King Clovis I (c. 466–511), the Christians of Alsace led a pious and respectable life:

> All priests lived with their wives and children in the church … Before Communion a sermon was held; this was followed by a broad and general confession, and then the Absolution. After this, psalms were sung in the common tongue; hereafter the blessing was given and everyone went home.[1]

This is, at least, how the chronicle of Daniel Specklin, an architect born in Strasbourg in 1536, reads. It is a document that betrays the bias of retrospect, not least in its naïve-sounding assurances that the clergy all abided with their nuclear families, and everyone attended church to sing the Psalms, translated into the vernacular. The chronicle also reports that Frankish priests read the Holy Gospels and the Psalms in all churches. On Maundy Thursday, Good Friday, and at Easter and other holy festivals, everyone dressed in white and processed to the church while singing 'Christian songs' (*christlichen gesangen*).[2] However, even if this seems to be something of a rose-tinted reminiscence, this same sentiment and conviction that the Church was once both purer and more community orientated is clearly prevalent in the Protestant reformers' own longing for the halcyon days of the Church Fathers.

It was the view of the sixteenth-century reformers that liturgical practices and ecclesiastical traditions had strayed so far from the intentions of the early Church as to be almost unrecognisable.[3] The earliest Christian hymns, for example, had

[1] 'Alle prister mit weib und kind wohneten ahn den kirchen … Vor der cumunion geschahe ein predig, daruff ein breicht und offne beicht, doruff die absolution. Hernach sange man psalmen in gemeiner sprach, hernoch gab man den segen und ging iederman heim'. *Fragments des anciennes chroniques d'Alsace*, II (1890), no. 619.

[2] 'Der konig Clodoveus ordnet auch allen bischoffen und pristern ihr narung vir weib und kind. Er liesz auch in alle kirchen die Evangelia schreyben, das gleichen auff die psalmen, der wahren numen zwelff … In der ostern, pfinsten und carfritag oder sunst etwan heiligen festen, ist alles volck in weyssen kleydern und liechtern mit christlichen gesangen aum [*sic*] mitternacht zu den kirchen gangen'. *Fragments des anciennes chroniques d'Alsace*, II (1890), no. 619. See also nos 627 and 628.

[3] As demonstrated below, this view seems to have been reached through a combination of guesswork and historical accounts.

given way to plainchant, and the role of the congregation gradually declined. In the Carolingian Empire during the eighth and ninth centuries, Gregorian chant became the staple musical ingredient of the liturgy.[4] Furthermore, as musical notation was developed, new polyphonic styles gradually began to be heard alongside plainchant.[5] By the middle of the fifteenth century, polyphonic settings of the complete text of the Mass Ordinary had become commonplace. Other elements of the liturgy were also often set to music, including introits, graduals, and anthems.[6] The Protestant reformers, therefore, inherited an ever-flourishing tradition of choral polyphony, which they did not deem to be fit for use in worship. Music, they decided, had become too elaborate, and often concealed the text being sung. Sometimes, profane melodies were used,[7] which some felt carried connotations with inappropriate texts. Furthermore, the Latin language was not comprehensible to the common people, and there was usually little, if any, room for congregational participation, as choirs sang on behalf of the people.[8] During the thirteenth and fourteenth centuries, for example, St Thomas's Church in Strasbourg had employed 15 'summissaries' to sing Masses at the high altar, as well as two *Seelmessern* to sing Requiem Masses for the souls of the departed. Likewise, the Church of St Peter the Young employed 14 choral vicars to sing the offices with the canons.[9] In 1429 the city established an annual Mass to be sung 'to praise and thank Almighty God, his worthy mother Mary, and all the saints'.[10] Congregations, on the other hand, would sing only in processions and on some feast days.[11] Prior to the Reformation, there had been various conciliar recommendations concerning music and other liturgical

[4] For a background to Gregorian chant and its dissemination, see in particular S. Boynton, 'Plainsong', and M. McGrade, 'Enriching the Gregorian heritage', in M. Everist, ed., *The Cambridge Companion to Medieval Music* (Cambridge: Cambridge University Press, 2011), pp. 9–25 and 26–45 respectively.

[5] On early polyphonic styles, see Everist, 'The thirteenth century', in Everist, ed., *The Cambridge Companion to Medieval Music*, pp. 67–86.

[6] For a detailed explanation of the texts of the Mass, see J. Harper, *The Forms and Orders of Western Liturgy from the Tenth to the Eighteenth Century* (Oxford: Oxford University Press, 1991).

[7] See the complaint made by Bucer in 1529 in *S. psalmorum libri quinque*, fol. 170r.

[8] See J. Janota, *Studien zu Funktion und Typus des deutschen geistlichen Liedes im Mittelalter* (Munich: Beck, 1968). See also R. Bornert, *La Réforme protestante du culte à Strasbourg au XVIe siècle (1523–1598)* (Leiden: Brill, 1981), pp. 472–3; A. Pettegree, *Reformation and the Culture of Persuasion* (Cambridge: Cambridge University Press, 2005), p. 42.

[9] F. Rapp, *Réformes et Réformation à Strasbourg : Église et société dans le diocèse de Strasbourg (1450–1525)* (Paris: Ophrys, 1974), p. 86.

[10] 'ewiglich zu singen in Unser Frauencapellen allzeit auf den nechsten Montag vor *Nativitatis Mariae*, zu lob und danck dem allmechtigen Gott, seiner würdigen mutter Maria und allen heyligen um gnedige vorsehung der Statt'. *Fragments des anciennes chroniques d'Alsace*, IV (1901), no 3939.

[11] See the elaborate description of pre-Reformation processions during Holy Week and Easter in A. Straub, *Geschichtskalender des Hochstiftes und des Münsters von Strassburg* (Rixheim: Sutter, 1891), pp. 69–70.

practices, although such advice had tended to fall on deaf ears.[12] The reformers argued that radical change was required.

Since the early centuries of the first millennium, the terms *psalmus* and *hymnus* had both referred to a spiritual song used in worship. Unlike the Psalms, the texts of hymns were often not purely scriptural. By the eleventh century, a canon of between 200 and 300 hymns existed,[13] intended for use in the Divine Office and during processions on festivals and on other occasions. Although it is not known precisely how hymns were performed during the times of the Church Fathers, the reformers attempted to return to what they believed was a more ancient and therefore more authentic model of worship, and one that permitted the congregation to sing.

The origins of the Christian hymn can be found in the legend of St Ambrose (c. 340–397) who as Bishop of Milan introduced songs for his congregation to sing. Others, including Aurelius Prudentius (d. c. 413), St Gregory of Nazianzus (d. 390), and St Hilary of Poitiers (d. 368) also tried their hand at hymn-writing.[14] Over years and centuries the function and definition of the hymn varied. Hymns became especially important in early monastic liturgies, for which a vast repertoire came to be written. Serving as a congregational song from the fourth century onwards, the hymn continued to undergo modification in the following centuries. By the eighth century – and perhaps earlier – it had become the responsibility of the choir to perform hymns on behalf of the congregation, and during the tenth, eleventh, and twelfth centuries, choral performance was the normal custom.[15] Over time, many people became disillusioned with the part that music played in divine worship,[16] and, approaching the time of the Reformation, this opposition started becoming more serious. By the end of the fifteenth century, although there was a range of worship songs in existence for special occasions at which the congregation might be expected to participate, congregational singing played no essential role in the liturgy of the Mass. As in all cities in the early modern era, music was a regular pastime in Strasbourg. Special celebrations as well as informal gatherings involved singing, playing, and dancing. People sang at home and at work. Yet ironically, as observed by

[12] For example, the Council of Basel in 1503 addressed the issue of early curtailment and use of secular melodies in the Nicene Creed. The 1528 Council of Paris had also addressed church music. See K. G. Fellerer, trans., M. Hadas, 'Church Music and the Council of Trent', *The Musical Quarterly*, 39 (1953), p. 578.

[13] P. Wilton, 'Hymn', in A. Latham, ed., *The Oxford Companion to Music* (www.oxfordmusiconline.com) (accessed 23 March 2010).

[14] C. Blume, 'Hymnody and Hymnology', in *The Catholic Encyclopedia (Online)* (www.newadvent.org/cathen/07596a.htm) (accessed 20 March 2011).

[15] W. Anderson et al., 'Hymn', in D. Root, ed., *Grove Music Online* (www.oxfordmusiconline.com) (accessed 23 March 2010).

[16] See, for example, J. Angerer, *Die liturgisch-musikalische Erneuerung der Melker Reform. Studien zur Erforschung der Musikpraxis in den Benediktinerklöstern des 15. Jahrhunderts* (Vienna: Verlag der Österreichischen Akademie der Wissenschaften, 1974).

Andrew Pettegree, the church would have been one of the few places where the populace did not regularly engage in music-making.[17] 'If the reformers invested such hopes in music, it was partly because singing was such a ubiquitous part of pre-industrial society'.[18]

An early prelude to the Reformation stance on music can be seen in the tract of the fourteenth-century English preacher, John Wycliffe, *Opus Evangelicum*. This includes a lengthy quote from St Chrysostom (c. 347–407), who felt that private prayer was immensely preferable to a public petition to God. By audibly expressing one's thoughts, one prayed in a disorderly fashion. If other people were around, not only would an audible prayer not be heard by God, it would be mocked by those others who had heard the secrets of the petitioner.[19] Chrysostom also asserted that those who prayed out loud could not believe in God's ubiquity and ability to hear hidden things (*absconsa*).[20] By praying audibly, one also impeded the prayers of those around.[21]

Wycliffe concluded that Chrysostom's statement equated to a condemnation of 'elaborate singing' (*cantus organicus*), 'because it distracts both the singer and also the people listening from mental consideration of heavenly things … [therefore] it seems that this type [of prayer] was introduced by the planning of the devil'.[22] Wycliffe noted that ancient precedent did not justify modern-day usage of music: 'For it does not follow that because the Old Testament Fathers played on various instruments in the Temple of Solomon, Christians should today thus sing'. Likewise, if some laymen had in the past found the ringing of bells or the singing of choirs helpful in their devotion, it did not mean that these were necessarily useful tools, because they are an obstacle for most people.[23]

---

17 Pettegree, *Reformation and the Culture of Persuasion*, p. 42.

18 Ibid., p. 41.

19 J. Wycliffe, ed. J. Loserth, *Opus Evangelicum*, 4 vols (London: Trübner, 1895–96), vol. 2, p. 261. Bucer also noted Chrysostom's position in his 'Florilegium Patristicum' (Parker Library, Corpus Christi College, Cambridge [hereafter: CCCC], ms. 418, p. 138; reproduced in M. Bucer and M. Parker, ed. P. Fraenkel, *Florilegium Patristicum* (Leiden: Brill, 1988), p. 56).

20 'Nam ex clamosa oracione multa mala nascuntur, maxime hec tria, primum quia qui clamose orat non Deum ubique credit esse et absconsa audire; et ideo Deum honorat qui absconse orat, primo quia orat, secundo quia credit Deum absconsa audire, sicut et audit. Nam Deus voce non clamosa audire, sicut et audit. Nam Deus voca non clamosa pulsandus est, quia non est vocis auditor sed cordis'. Wycliffe, *Opus Evangelicum*, vol. 2, p. 261.

21 Ibid.

22 'Videtur istum sanctum parum vel nichil commendare cantum organicum vel subtilem sed pocius condempnare, quia distrahit a cogitacione mentali supracelestium tam cantantem quam eciam populum audientem; et cum non fundatur in fide scripture sed evidencius eius oppositum, videtur quod iste modus fuit ex cautela diaboli introductus'. Ibid.

23 'Patres legis veteris canebant in diversis organis in templo Salomonis, ergo christiani debent hodie sic cantare; nec sequitur: Si rudes distantes laici per hoc quandoque excitantur ad devocionem, ergo modus ille est adeo observandus; et sic dicitur de pulsibus campanarum, de cantibus chororum et multis aliis ut fides hodie introductis, de quibus est probabile quod per accidens quandoque proficiunt, sed est evidencius quod pluribus viantibus magis obsunt'. Ibid., 260–61. Such views are reminiscent of Huldrych Zwingli's interpretation of the phrase 'in your hearts' (which features in

Girolamo Savonarola was another proto-reformer who attacked polyphonic music and organ playing, as well as secular songs. At the end of 1494, the Florentine friar complained that 'we today have converted these divine praises into something secular, with music and songs that delight the sense and the ear but not the spirit; and this is not to the honour of God'.[24] At the beginning of the following year, in his sermon on the Book of Psalms, Savonarola recommended the use of 'interior' worship, as emphasised by the early Church, rather than 'exterior' worship, in which category he included elaborate singing. Time and again, he renewed his attack on polyphony, at times going so far as to attribute its invention to the devil, who created it to distract people so that they might not pray inwardly.[25] He also felt that intelligibility was compromised in polyphony, complaining: 'there stands a singer with a large voice like a calf's, and the others howl around him like dogs, and no one understands what they are saying. Let figural music go, and sing the plainchant ordered by the [early] church!'.[26] To Savonarola, polyphonic music was inextricably linked with the financial abuses of the Church, and he accused priests of luring almsgivers into churches with sweet-sounding music.[27]

Savonarola, though, much like his German counterparts three decades later, was not opposed to the use of music, but he was adamant that it be reformed. In March 1496 he addressed the adolescent boy singers of the city (the *fanciulli*), congratulating them on their performance of *laude* (simple vernacular sacred songs),[28] but not without alerting them to room for further improvement:

> [Y]ou sing laude in the morning, and this is good; but I would like it if sometimes you would sing songs of the Church such as *Ave Maris Stella*, or *Veni Creator Spiritus*, and nor would it be such a bad thing if the rest of the congregation were to join in.

passages such as Ephes. 5:19 and Col. 3:16) which the Swiss reformer argued was a commandment to pray silently, a claim that underpinned his call for worship without song (see below, p. 100).

24 'Ma noi oggidì abbiamo convertite queste laude divine in cose seculari e in musiche e canti che delettino el senso e l'orecchio e non lo spirito; e questo non è onore di Dio'. G. Savonarola, ed. L. Firpo, *Prediche sopra Aggeo* (Rome: Belardetti, 1965), p. 115 (30 Nov 1494); translated in P. Macey, *Bonfire Songs: Savonarola's Musical Legacy* (Oxford: Clarendon Press, 1998), p. 93.

25 Savonarola, ed. V. Romano, *Prediche sopra i Salmi*, 2 vols (Rome: Belardetti, 1969–74), vol. 1, pp. 89–90 (January 1495). See also Macey, *Bonfire Songs*, p. 94.

26 'vi sta là un cantore con una voce grossa che pare un vitello e li altri gli cridono atorno come cani e non s'intende cosa che dichino. Lasciate andare e' canti figurati, e cantate e' cantri fermi ordinati dalla Chiesa'. Savonarola, ed. P. Ghiglieri, *Prediche sopra Amos e Zaccaria*, 3 vols (Rome: Belardetti, 1971–72), vol. 2, p. 23 (7 March 1496); translated in I. A. Fenlon, 'Music and Reform in Sixteenth-Century Italy', in R. De Maio et al., eds, *Bellarmino e la controriforma* (Sora: Centro di studi sorani 'Vincenzo Patriarca', 1990), p. 868.

27 Savonarola, ed. R. Ridolfi, *Prediche sopra Giobbe*, 2 vols (Rome: Belardetti, 1957), vol. 2, p. 446 (April 1495); Macey, *Bonfire Songs*, pp. 94–5.

28 On the origins of the *lauda*, see Fenlon, 'Music and Reform', pp. 864–6.

> And if, as I came into the pulpit, you were singing *Ave Maris Stella*, perhaps I also would sing with you.[29]

This comment is significant, as it demonstrates favour towards congregational singing. By choosing to sing something which was not only pure in spirit (even if not biblical), but well known by the public (and therefore more likely to be a text understood by those listening), the *fanciulli* would have enabled worshippers around them to voice their praises to God through song.

Choral singing did have a role to play in Strasbourg's churches before the Reformation (see Figure 1.1).[30] However, despite the lack of opportunity for congregational singing at the turn of the century, presses in the city were already publishing books of psalms, hymns, and other spiritual songs. Although many are now no longer traceable, we are aware of their existence largely thanks to such works as Miriam Chrisman's *Bibliography of Strasbourg Imprints* and, more recently, the Universal Short Title Catalogue from the University of St Andrews.[31] These record the first appearance of such publications in the city as early as the 1480s.[32] One pair of books from 1513 (the first volume entitled *Sequentiarum luculenta interpretatio*,[33] and the second entitled *Hymni de tempore & de sanctis*[34]), suggested that even before the Protestant Reformation had begun, there was some movement among religious and educational circles towards embracing the historical role of the hymn. Johann Adolph Mülich (also known as Johannes Adelphus) wrote the first volume, and may also have been

29 'voi cantate qua delle laude la mattina e sta bene; ma io vorrei ancora che voi cantassi qualche volta de' canti della Chiesa come è *Ave maris stella*, o *Veni creator Spiritus*, e non saria anche male nessuno che il popolo rispondesse; e quando io vengo in pergamo, se io trovassi che voi cantassi quella *Ave maris stella*, canterei forse ancora io'. Savonarola, *Prediche sopra Amos e Zaccaria*, vol. 2, pp. 80–81 (7 March 1496); translated in Macey, *Bonfire Songs*, p. 98. See also Fenlon, 'Music and Reform', p. 872.

30 Beat Föllmi provides a detailed account of Strasbourg's medieval Palm Sunday procession, but unfortunately does not cite his sources (see 'Rupture and Transformation of Collective Musical Memory among Urban Populations at the Time of the Reformation: The Case of Strasbourg', in T. Marković and V. Mikić, eds, *Musical Culture & Memory* (Belgrade: Belgrade University of Arts Press, 2008), pp. 16–25).

31 Available online at www.ustc.ac.uk.

32 Most notable of these is Spechtshart's *Flores musicae*, first printed in 1488 by Prüss, and printed many times thereafter.

33 J. Adelphus, *Seque[n]tiarum lucule[n]ta interpretatio: nedu[m] scholasticis / sed & ecclesiasticis cognitu necessaria* (Strasbourg: Schürer, 1513; repr. Knobloch, 1519) (*Containing an interpretation of sequences, the knowledge of which is necessary not only for scholars but also ecclesiastics*).

34 *Hymni de tempore & de sanctis: in ea[m] forma[m] qua a suis autoribus scripti sunt denuo redacti: & [secundu]m legem carminis dilige[n]ter emendati atque interpretati* (Strasbourg: Knobloch, 1513; repr. 1516, 1518). The title can be translated as *Hymns for ordinary time and for holy days: collected again in the same form in which they were written by the authors, and following the law of songs diligently amended and interpreted.* Regarding the pairing of these two volumes, see C. G. A. Schmidt, *Histoire littéraire de l'Alsace à la fin du XVe et au commencement du XVIe siècle*, 2 vols (Paris: Sandoz & Fischbacher, 1879), vol. 2, p. 328.

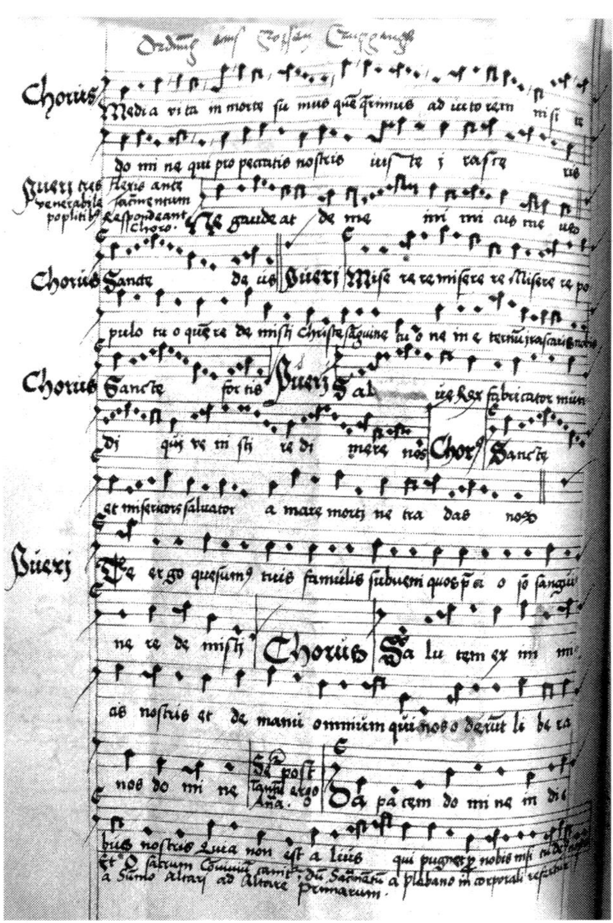

Figure 1.1 A page from the *Protocollum Wurmserianum*, AVS, 1 AST 192, 1523, fol. 6v. This manuscript gives us an idea of the sort of music being sung in Strasbourg before the Reformation, to which there is very little written reference. The text here is *Media vita in morte sumus* ('In the midst of life we are in death'), a Latin antiphon, sung at the 'great cloisters' (*grossen Crutzgang*) of Strasbourg. Alternate lines were sung by the choir and a group of boys. The notation is *Hufnagelschrift*, a form very common in this part of Germany (see D. Hiley and J. Szendrei, 'Notation, §III, 1: History of Western notation: Plainchant', in D. Root, ed., *Grove Music Online* (www.oxfordmusiconline.com) (accessed 20 September 2011). Reproduced by permission of the Archives de la Ville et de la Communauté urbaine de Strasbourg

the author of the second, although the name of the Alsatian humanist Jakob Wimpheling occurs a great deal within the book and it therefore seems likely that he was responsible for it.

The two books are essentially collections of sequences[35] and hymns respectively (without musical notation), with prefatory explanations that reveal that the authors had an interest in the history of the early Church. Their function was to enable further understanding of the history of hymns and sequences in the Church, and their modern application. In the 'Preambulum' of *Hymni de tempore & de sanctis*, a hymn was defined as 'praise to God with singing'.[36] The main writers of early hymns were listed as being St Gregory (of Nazianzus), Prudentius, St Ambrose, Sedulius, and St Hilary of Poitiers. St Hilary was credited with editing a collection of hymns into a 'brief and useful compendium'.[37] This enabled observations to be made about which hymns would be sung on holy days.[38] There were hymns, the writer continues, for all times of day, all with different function. Those for the middle of the night, for example, existed so that 'one may expel from oneself the shadows of ignorance and vice'.[39] St Hilary had sung hymns in the light of the day in order to pray, so that God, 'in the same way he illuminates the body with his clarity and splendour through the sun, might also illuminate our spirit with his holy grace'.[40]

In a section entitled 'On the Origin of Hymns' (*De origine hymno[rum]*), the *Confessions of St Augustine* were cited:

> Ambrose, bishop of Milan, began the singing of hymns in the Church of God. Augustine, [writes] in book 9 of his *Confessions*: 'Once, Justina, mother of the boy-king Valentinian, was persecuting Ambrose because of her heresy, to which she was seduced by the Arians. The pious common people kept watch in the church, prepared to die with their bishop. Therefore it was instituted that hymns and psalms be sung according to the traditions of the eastern regions, lest the people should collapse through the fatigue of sorrow, and from that time the tradition has been retained'.[41]

---

35 The Sequence is a short text traditionally said or sung immediately before the Gospel reading.

36 'Hymnus … laus Dei est cu[m] cantico'. *Hymni de tempore*, fol. Ciij^{v}.

37 'vnu[m] breue[m] & vtile[m] tractatu[m] colligere co[m]pendiose'. *Hymni de tempore*, fol. Ciij^{v}.

38 'Prima hui[us] intentio fuit describere illos [quos] cantant in prima feria: & sic deinceps [secundu]m ordine[m]'. *Hymni de tempore*, fol. Ciij^{v}.

39 'vt sc[ilicet] expellat a nobis tenebras ignora[n]tie & vitio[rum]'. *Hymni de tempore*, fol. Ciij^{v}.

40 'vt que[m]admodu[m] illuminat sua claritate & sple[n]dore solis in corpore: sic illuminet nos sanctis p[i]us gratia in mente'. *Hymni de tempore*, fol. Ciij^{v}.

41 'Ambrosius Hediolanensis episcopus incepit canere hymnos in ecclesia dei. Un[de] Augstinus lib[er] .ix. co[n]fessio. Cum Justina Valentiniani reg[is] pueri mater Ambrosiu[m] p[er] sequeret heresies sue causa: qua fuerat seducta ab Arrianis: excubabat pia plebs in eccl[es]a mori parata cu[m] episcopo suo. tu[n]c hymni & psalmi vt canerent[ur] [secundu]m morem orientaliu[m] partiu[m]: ne p[o]p[u]l[i]s meroris tedio co[n]tabescerer : institutu[m] est : & ex illo in hodiernu[m] retentu[m]'. *Hymni de tempore*, fol. Cij^{r}; citing Augustine's *Confessions* (see M. Skutella, ed., *S. Aureli Augustini Confessionum* (Stuttgart: Teubner, 1981), pp. 191–3). Bucer used the same story to illustrate patristic use of hymnody in CCCC, ms. 418, p. 138 (*Florilegium Patristicum*, p. 56).

Singing, therefore, according to this myth, had been instituted in the Church to raise the spirits of the faithful during times of persecution or trouble. The next section, on the use of hymns, stated that some did not condone the use of hymns because they were the work of humans rather than of the Spirit.[42] On the contrary, there were no words of the *Hymnus Angelicus* (the Great Doxology)[43] that were earthly or human, and this formula was in accepted usage because 'the Church received these words not only in both Testaments,[44] but also in the writings of the Fathers'.[45]

A preface, addressed by Wimpheling to 'the ordinary, very vigilant reader' (*ordinario lectori vigilantissimo*), features in the book. The fact that the book was written in Latin, of course, indicates that it was intended for an educated audience – a very particular sort of 'ordinary' reader. The preface was also addressed, among others, to the priests at the Heidelberg Gymnasium. That this volume should be destined for the education of young scholars should not be a surprise, given Wimpheling's interest in pedagogy, especially if he were indeed involved in the production of both volumes.[46] The preface strongly advocated the need for the young to be educated in Christian verse, rather than studying the work of 'gentile poets'. This comment reveals some degree of tension with the growing popularity of humanist studies: Wimpheling (himself of 'humanist' leanings) complained that the songs sung by the youth should instead be those of St Gregory, St Ambrose, St Catherine, Darsilius, and others, as those were morally edifying and beneficial to the community. Christian poetry, in the form of hymns, was here contrasted favourably with that of ancient Greek and Roman poets, both in subject matter and in compositional skill. He concluded:

> This book of songs is of that type which is made from hymns, to reveal to our young people that they may surely move on from the songs of gentile poets to Christian verse, which is both purified and civic-minded. So that they may at least read hymns correctly as initiates, that they may most easily understand, that they may most certainly reprove, that they may handle with greatest devotion those poems which were toiled over by Ambrose and Prudentius and other Christian poets with such labour, such diligence, such accuracy of syllabic measurement.[47]

---

42 'tan[que] humano studio co[m]positos'. *Hymni de tempore*, fol. Cij^r. This tension between Scripture and 'the work of humans' had been long-standing in the Church, and it resurfaced to varying degrees during the Protestant reforms of the sixteenth century.

43 'Glory to God in the Highest', etc.

44 It is not clear where such words may be found in the Old Testament.

45 'Un[de] eccl[es]ia no[n] solu[m] recipit verba vtrius[que] testame[n]ti: sed etia[m] sc[rip]toru[m] patru[m]'. *Hymni de tempore*, fol. Cij^r.

46 His work, *Adolescentia* (Strasbourg: Flach, 1500), spoke of the need to educate the young in a good way, something that would in turn solve current problems in ecclesiastical life.

47 'adolesce[n]tibus[que] nostris indicare liber carminis genus quo quis[que] hymno[rum] co[n]textus est. Ut vel six a carminib[us] gentiliu[m] poeta[um] ad christianos versus eque terson at[que] polítos transferant[ur]. vt sacris tande[m] initiati rectius hymnos legant: plani[us] intelligant: certius castigent: maiori[que] deuotione afficiant[ur] eis poematib[us] que ab Ambrosio & Prudentio

What is made clear from this book is that, even before the Reformation, scholars in Strasbourg and other parts of the Holy Roman Empire were stressing the need to reform the practice of hymn-singing. Although these volumes did not go as far as the reformers did in revising the practice (both in terms of intended readership, and also in that no suggestions were made regarding the musical manner in which the hymns should be sung), the appearance of such books in Strasbourg in 1513, and the fact that they were subsequently reprinted, may go some way towards explaining the interest taken by the Strasbourg reformers (none of whom were particularly noteworthy musicians[48]) in the history of hymns and congregational singing. The contributors to the volumes were clear that, because perfectly decent and pious hymns had been composed for the Church in the early centuries of Christianity, it was those that should be studied and used, rather than any secular poems currently in circulation.

Hymni de tempore & de sanctis emphasises a connection between praying, singing, and well-being. If a hymn was a sung prayer to God, and praising God was a good and necessary thing, it followed that this was also an activity in which everyone should partake. The benefits reaped were clear: sacred hymns replaced the poems of 'gentile poets', leading to the improvement of understanding, learning, and devotion.[49]

Those who attempted ecclesiastical reform in Strasbourg before the 1520s made great criticisms of the Church's morals and unethical practices. Such abuses were no secret: the laity complained about 'clerical greed, clerical laziness, clerical immorality, clerical ignorance, clerical contempt for the laity', as well as clerical absence.[50] Bishop Wilhelm von Hohnstein (r. 1506–41) issued various decrees against the conduct of the clergy, but with little effect.[51] According to some descriptions, the conduct of the laity was not always much better, with various corrupted customs being conflated with church feasts. The late Middle Ages saw a tradition of wanton songs and rude jokes around

ceretis[que] christianis poetis ta[n]to nisu: tanta diligentia: tam accurata syllaba[rum] me[n]sura sunt elucubrata'. *Hymni de tempore*, fol. Cj'.

48 The one possible exception is Symphorianus Pollio, whom Théodore Gérold describes as a gifted amateur. See T. Gérold, *Les plus anciennes mélodies de l'Eglise protestante de Strasbourg et leurs auteurs* (Paris: Alcan, 1928), pp. 32–3.

49 The printing industry had been useful in disseminating vernacular devotional material even before the beginning of the Reformation. In 1516, for example, an exegesis in German on the Ten Commandments was published in Strasbourg, taking the form of a conversation between a boy and his teacher: *Die zehe[n] gebot in disem büch erclert vnd vßgelegt durch etlich hochberümbte lerer* (Strasbourg: Grüninger, 1516). A facsimile can be found in J. W. van Maren, *Marquard von Lindau – Die Zehe Gebot (Straßburg 1516 und 1520)* (Amsterdam: Rodophi, 1980). See also J. B. Riederer, *Nachrichten zur Kirchen- Gelehrten- und Bůcher-Geschichte; aus gedruckten und ungedruckten Schriften*, 4 vols (Altdorf: Schüpfel, 1763–68), vol. 1, pp. 310–18.

50 L. J. Abray, *The People's Reformation: Magistrates, Clergy, and Commons in Strasbourg, 1500–1598* (Oxford: Blackwell, 1985), p. 25.

51 Ibid., p. 27; D. C. Steinmetz, *Reformers in the Wings: From Geiler von Kaysersberg to Theodore Beza*, 2nd edn (Oxford: Oxford University Press, 2001), pp. 13–14.

Pentecost, and during the days following Christmas a boy would be chosen to be 'bishop', dressing in episcopal vestments and conducting services in the cathedral. Such behaviour was in many cases encouraged by the clergy, who often joined in with the festivities. Other feasts involved barrels of wine being brought into the cathedral and carnivals being held in the cathedral grounds.[52] Among those who spoke out in favour of moral reform were Johann Geiler von Kaysersberg and Sebastian Brant. These men preached from pulpits in churches throughout the city, admonishing the people, as well as reprimanding the clergy for their immoral lives. Geiler was a secular priest and a close ally of the humanists of Strasbourg who were led by Jakob Wimpheling. However, Geiler differed fundamentally from the later reformers in his approach to Christianity, most strikingly by forbidding the laity from reading the Bible in the vernacular, warning people about making their own interpretations of the Scriptures, and commenting that it was 'as dangerous as permitting infants to cut their own bread'.[53]

Geiler had encountered Sebastian Brant in Basel during the 1470s. Brant, who was well known in humanist circles, is perhaps most famous for his satires, including *Das Narrenschiff*, first published in 1494, which tells the story of a ship of fools – a book which Brant himself described as being 'for the profit, salutary instruction, admonition and pursuit of wisdom, common sense and good manners; also for the condemnation and reproach of folly, blindness, error and stupidity'.[54] In the book, Brant warned against many foolish traits and habits, many of which related to aspects of late-medieval religion, including blasphemy and losing one's fear of God because of unpunished sins,[55] those who made noise during church services,[56] and the celebration of the Mass by those who ought 'nevermore go near the altar'.[57] Brant also commented that 'I fear the

---

52 T. W. Röhrich, *Geschichte der Reformation im Elsass und besonders in Strassburg: nach gleichzeitigen Quellen bearbeitet*, 3 vols (Strasbourg: Heitz, 1830–32), vol. 1, pp. 52–3. Part of the Pentecost celebrations centred around the so-called *Roraffen*, grotesque figures placed above the cathedral organ. Geiler von Kaysersberg requested that the city council abolish these abuses in 1501 (*Fragments des anciennes chroniques d'Alsace*, III (1892), no. 2994; see also the chronicle in Straub, *Geschichtskalender*, pp. 121–2).

53 'Infantibus periculosum est: si sibi comedendi panis incisio est'. Quoted in E. J. D. Douglass, *Justification in Late Medieval Preaching: A Study of John Geiler of Keisersberg* (Leiden: Brill, 1966), p. 76, incl. n. 3. Erasmus, too, later came to the conclusion that translating the Scriptures was a dangerous move (see P. S. Allen and H. M. Allen, eds, *Opus epistolarum Des. Erasmi Roterdami*, 12 vols (Oxford: Clarendon Press, 1906–58; repr. 1992), vol. 6, p. 85).

54 'So zů nutz heilsamer ler / ermanug [*sic*] / vnd eruolgung / der wißheit / vernunfft / vnd gůter sytten / Och zů verachtung / vnd stroff der narrheyt / blintheit Jrrsal / vnd dorheit'. S. Brant, *Das Narrenschiff* (Basel: Olpe, 1494), fol. v iv[v]; translated in Brant, trans. W. Gillis, *The Ship of Fools* (London: Folio Society, 1971), p. 325.

55 Brant, *Das Narrenschiff*, chapters 86–88.

56 Brant, *Das Narrenschiff*, chapter 44.

57 'Do weger wer er lyeß dar von | Vnd růrt den altter nyemer an'. Brant, *Das Narrenschiff*, fol. m vij[v]; translated in Brant, trans. Gillis, *The Ship of Fools*, p. 190.

days are close at hand | When men shall hear newfangled tales | And know that heresy prevails'.[58] He lamented the current state of the Roman Church, while unknowingly anticipating the blow the institution would be dealt by Luther a quarter of a century later.

Interestingly, though, unlike in the sermons of Savonarola, the practice of music was not a prominent feature on the agenda either of Geiler or of Brant. Only occasional references are to be found. In one sermon, Geiler explained that those who do not know how to pray could instead 'listen to the singing, notice the liturgical vestments and pictures on the walls, and ponder what they signify'.[59] Such a comment is striking in its distance from the Reformed Protestant view, which held that images were a distraction, vestments meaningless, and choir singing incomprehensible and useless. Geiler also complained, however, that the clerics often sang either badly or not at all, and urged Wimpheling to undertake a correction of the hymn repertory (Geiler considered many songs to have been badly spoilt over the years by ignorant copyists).[60] If *Sequentiarum luculenta interpretatio* and *Hymni de tempore & de sanctis* were indeed by Wimpheling, it is highly likely that they formed a part or all of his response to Geiler's complaints. It has even been suggested that there may be a connection between Geiler's efforts to improve liturgical choir singing and the reformers' attempts to introduce congregational singing,[61] although it needs to be remembered that the aims of the reformers and those of Geiler were very different.

Brant was perhaps the first to publish broadsides of sacred songs in the German tongue, sometimes also printed with the music.[62] He also pre-empted the Protestant reformers in complaining about the conduct of the choir. In *Das Narrenschiff*, he criticised those who gathered in the choirstalls, swapping useless gossip and advice.[63] The writings of the Strasbourg reformers, too, were littered with criticism of the singers of the Roman Church, one of their main points of objection being the singers' concern about their earning potential.[64] Brant agreed: they came only for gold, before finding the door and leaving.[65] Another of the reformers' complaints focused on the speed at which the

58 'Jch voͤrcht / es kumen bald die tag | Das man me nuwer maͤr werd jnn | Dann vns gefall vnd syg zuͤ synn'. Brant, *Das Narrenschiff*, fol. b viii^r; translated in Brant, trans. Gillis, *The Ship of Fools*, p. 31.

59 'Attende cantum: vestes sacras: saltem picturas in parietibus intuearis: et quid significent cogita'. Quoted in Douglass, *John Geiler of Keisersberg*, p. 144.

60 Schmidt, *Histoire littéraire de l'Alsace*, vol. 1, pp. 361–2, 371, 444.

61 Douglass, *John Geiler of Keisersberg*, p. 207.

62 *MPGR*, pp. 90–92.

63 Brant, *Das Narrenschiff*, fol. q^r.

64 See Chapters 2 and 3.

65 'Vnd das man gelt geb jn dem chor … Treffen doch bald wyder die tuͤren'. Brant, *Das Narrenschiff*, fol. q^v.

Psalms were recited in church;[66] again, Brant had already made this point in *Das Narrenschiff*.[67]

The Roman clergy in Strasbourg formed its own social and political group with its own system of organisation.[68] The bishop, who resided in Saverne,[69] to the north-west of Strasbourg, was represented in Strasbourg itself by the cathedral chapter. Four other chapters were also in existence at this time: those of St Thomas, St Peter the Young, St Peter the Old, and All Saints. Below the chapters in this hierarchy were the parish churches,[70] four of which were financially dependent on the chapters. Almost all the monastic orders had a presence in the city, as did two noble orders: the Teutonic Knights and the Knights of St John.[71] There were at least 19 convents within the city, and also about 180 chapels.[72]

Chrisman comments that, in Strasbourg, as in many late medieval towns and cities, the Church 'formed a state within a state', and that there was a conflict between city and Church.[73] However, this growing sense of resentment towards the clergy and religious orders in the years prior to the Reformation not only existed among preachers such as Brant and Geiler,[74] but was also active within the population at large. For example, in 1523, on the eve of Strasbourg's Reformation, Bishop Hohnstein wrote to the city council requesting that they ensure that peace and unity prevailed on the day of a religious procession through the city.[75] This suggests that the city folk were of a mind to disrupt what they deemed to be overtly pompous practices. In obedient response, the city council instructed 'that every man, young or old, [behave] with modesty and with devotion' during the Lady Day festivities.[76]

Representatives of the cathedral chapter in Strasbourg were drawn from members of the most noble families in Germany. It has often been said that

---

66 1 AST 170, 4, fol. 33v. See below, pp. 68–9.

67 Brant, 'Fur wissenheyt gottes', in *Das Narrenschiff*, fols. i vj^{v}–i viij^{r}.

68 M. U. Chrisman, *Strasbourg and the Reform: A Study in the Process of Change* (New Haven and London: Yale University Press, 1967), p. 32.

69 This situation had been the result of a conflict between church and state at the end of the fourteenth century.

70 Thomas Brady, relying on the Specklin chronicle, counts seven parish churches (T. A. Brady, *Ruling Class, Regime and Reformation at Strasbourg, 1520–1555* (Leiden: Brill, 1978), p. 217; *Fragments des anciennes chroniques d'Alsace*, II (1890), nos 2135 and 2136) but Miriam Chrisman believes there were nine (Chrisman, *Strasbourg and the Reform*, p. 32).

71 Chrisman, *Strasbourg and the Reform*, p. 33.

72 Brady, *Ruling Class*, p. 217.

73 Chrisman, *Strasbourg and the Reform*, p. 34.

74 See Schmidt, *Histoire littéraire de l'Alsace*, vol. 1, pp. 440–49.

75 1 MR 3, fol. 111r.

76 'Do beuelhen vnser hern Meister vnd Ratt diser stat Straßburg das ein jedas mensch jung oder alt zuchtiglich vnd mit andacht nach dem heyligen ampt dem Creutz gang jn ferner pfar oder der kirchen do er ist nachgang vnd got dem almechtig[e]n vmb fryd. son. vnd Einigkeÿt helffen anrüffn vnd byten. deß wyß sich menglich zuhalt[e]n'. 1 MR 3, fol. 112r.

Erasmus commented sarcastically that not even Jesus would have managed to gain access to the Strasbourg cathedral chapter, owing to a lack of sufficient personal wealth.[77] Members of the clergy were infamous for being absent and neglecting their duties. Often, a priest would obtain posts at several churches, attending to his duties at only the best paid, and sending deputies to take his place at the others.[78] Brant's *Narrenschiff* warned that 'many livings ... Can leave a man with both eyes blind ... Who gathers livings, living well, | Will find his last one waits in hell'.[79] In 1515, Wimpheling complained[80] that many benefices in Germany were given to Italians and to men who were 'unworthy' (*indigni*) of them.[81] Since they held so many different posts they did not recognise their parishioners' faces and neglected their pastoral duties. Pursuit of several simultaneous benefices, he continued, was encouraged, and corrupt legal action was employed in order to secure posts. Simony was used to procure some benefices, while others remained vacant.[82] The trail of these corrupt practices, he suggested, often led back to Rome.

> Candidates for benefices should not with impunity pass themselves off as the pope's familiars. Such people must not receive preferential treatment in the assignment of benefices, for this practice works to the disadvantage of the sons of our own princes. Sixtus IV explicitly forbade the custom of granting expectancies to German benefices to non-Germans ... No-one ought to hold two or three prebends at several collegiate churches in the same city, as well as the vicariate of the cathedral church, thus excluding learned and able candidates from nearly all positions, dignities, parish posts, and pensions.[83]

[77] Brady, *Ruling Class*, p. 221; Chrisman, *Strasbourg and the Reform*, p. 32; Chrisman, *Lay Culture, Learned Culture: Books and Social Change in Strasbourg, 1480–1599* (New Haven and London: Yale University Press, 1982), p. xxiii.

[78] Bornert, *Réforme protestante du culte*, p. 70.

[79] 'Dann wo er noch eyn dar zů nynnt | Wurt er an beiden ougen blynt ... Merck wer vil pfrůnden haben well | Der letsten wart er jnn der hell'. Brant, *Das Narrenschiff*, fol. e vii^r; translated in Brant, trans. Gillis, *The Ship of Fools*, p. 77.

[80] Wimpheling's *Responsa et replice ad Eneam Silvium*, in E. S. Piccolomini (Pope Pius II) and J. Wimpheling, *Germania Enee Silvij, in qua, candide lector, continentur. Grauamina germanicę nationis. Confutatio eorundem cum replicis* (Strasbourg: Beck, 1515). A modern edition exists in A. Schmidt, ed., *Aeneas Silvius: Germania, und Jakob Wimpfeling 'Responsa et replicae ad Eneam Silvium'* (Cologne: Böhlau, 1962).

[81] This complaint had its roots in the Investiture Controversy of the eleventh and twelfth centuries, in which the pope claimed that nations had too much control over the appointment of church officials. The problem was especially pronounced between the papacy and the Holy Roman Empire. See U.-R. Blumenthal, *The Investiture Controversy: Church and Monarchy from the Ninth to the Twelfth Century* (Philadelphia: University of Pennsylvania Press, 1988).

[82] G. Strauss, *Manifestations of Discontent in Germany on the Eve of the Reformation* (Bloomington and London: Indiana University Press, 1971), p. 44. For the Latin text, see Schmidt, *Aeneas Silvius*, p. 134.

[83] 'Impetret quoque nacio nostra, ne familiares fuisse impune mentiri liceat eos, qui nunquam fuerunt, ne nostrates graciis et privilegiis proximorum sedis aut pontificis familiarium et alienigenarum

Much to the dismay of many in the Holy Roman Empire, however, these practices continued unhindered. The German desire for political independence from Rome continued to intensify, and at the 1521 Diet of Worms, at which Luther was present, a similar complaint – this time more forcefully worded, and with a marked political edge – was recorded:

> Rome awards German benefices to unqualified, unlearned, and unfit persons such as gunners, falconers, bakers, donkey drivers, stable grooms, and so on, most of whom know not a word of German and never assume their duties connected with their benefices, shifting them instead to worthless vicars who are content with a pittance in pay. Thus the German laity receives neither spiritual care nor worldly counsel from the Church, while a hoard of money flows yearly to Italy with no return to us, least of all gratitude. We think that German benefices should be awarded to native Germans only and that beneficed persons ought to be required to reside in the place to which they are assigned.[84]

The Diet also noted that monks begged – in violation of their own rules – and that some priests were known to shame the poor into paying for Masses for their deceased relatives.[85]

It might be said that in the late medieval Church there was an imbalance between spiritualism and capitalism. The clergy earned their income through endowments, indulgences, and other fees, and it was in their financial interest to increase church attendance and encourage the laity to have services celebrated for family members. Thomas Brady believes it to be 'highly probable' that every upper-class family in Strasbourg 'had established Mass stipends in one or

innixi principum (eciam electorum) filios in assequendis prebendis antecedant, cum non oriundos ex Germania Sixtus IIII. ad Germaniam habere expectativas prohibuerit … ne quisquam duos aut tris canonicatus in diversis unius et eiusdem urbis collegiis et in cathedrali vicariam simul omnium corpora rapiens et absorbens (propterea nullum locum pro pensione alteri quantamvis docto et bono cessurus) seclusis officiis, dignitatibus, parochiis, capellaniis, pensionibus'. Quoted in Schmidt, *Aeneas Silvius*, p. 143. Translated in Strauss, *Manifestations of Discontent*, pp. 46–7.

84 'Item es werden die pfronden Teutscher nation zu Rom etwan buchsenmaistern, falknern, pfistern, eseltreibern, stallknechten und andern untuglichen, ungelärten und ungeschigkten personen verlihen und zu zeiten denen, die nit Teutsch gezungs seien; daraus erwechst, das sie ir pfronden nit selbs versehen und andern notdurftigen, armen priestern, die sich mit wennig benugen lassen und vil von inen absenz geben, zu versehen bevelhen; dardurch die armen laien jedes orts, zusambt mangel gaistlicher versehung, auch in zeitlichen hendeln von irem pfarrer alles trosts beraubt und also ain jarlich gult den Welschen personen aus Teutschen landen geraicht, davon in ewigkait Teutscher nation nichts wider zukombt, auch kain dank erzaigt wurdet. Wer billich, das allain gebornen Teutschen die pfrunden Teutscher nation verlihen wurden und dieselben auch residirten'. *Deutsche Reichstagsakten: jüngere Reihe*, 19 vols (Gotha: Perthes; Göttingen: Vandenhoeck & Ruprecht; Munich: Oldenbourg, 1893–), vol. 2, pp. 673–4. Translated in Strauss, *Manifestations of Discontent*, p. 54.

85 See *Deutsche Reichstagsakten: jüngere Reihe*, vol. 2, p. 690. Translated in Strauss, *Manifestations of Discontent*, pp. 59–60.

more churches and convents into whose necrologies their dead were entered'.[86] Such stipends were also the way in which church musicians (who were often also priests or deacons) made their living. A typical example of this happening in pre-Reformation Strasbourg is found in a letter from the bishop to the chapter of St Thomas. In 1515 the chapter had written to the Bishop of Strasbourg regarding the payment of the new organist, following the completed renovation of the organ in the church. The bishop replied in agreement that in order for the money to be made available, the ancient vicary of St Peter and St Paul would be suppressed, and the income from it would be used to pay an organist. It was stipulated that the organist should already be a priest, or else be less than a year away from ordination. The post-holder would also be permitted to sing in the choir when he was not playing the organ and earn the *Präsenz* (a payment received by singers on an individual basis for being present at a service to sing) on top of his normal salary.[87] The letter paraphrases Psalm 150 in claiming that

> God, the creator of the universe, is to be honoured, praised, and venerated in his saints and in his virtues, with manifold praise and the musical harmony, sounding out of different sonorities and instruments, and he ought to be praised with strings and the organ.[88]

The chapter had also complained to the bishop that the previous organ had been damaged because of the sheer number of people playing it (the implication being that they were not always very careful with the instrument), rather than having employed a fixed organist, who would have had a 'dutiful obedience to care for the organ' (*qui eis debita obedientia subsit organo prouideatur*). Unless there was a future provision for a fixed post, the concern was that the same would happen again.[89] Otto Nachtgall (or Luscinus) was the first organist to be appointed under this new arrangement, and he remained in the post until 1520. He was succeeded by Christoph von Konstanz, who was in turn succeeded in 1521 by Wolfgang Dachstein, a priest and Dominican monk.[90]

A significant amount of biographical material has survived for Wolfgang Dachstein and his colleague Matthias Greiter. Greiter, probably the most

---

86 Brady, *Ruling Class*, p. 228.

87 B II 62, 2 (in 1 AST-C 187); 1 AST 635, fol. CCix^{v}; 90 Z 14, pp. 681–2.

88 'Et Jpsi pluribus desuper prehabit[is] tractatibus, et maturis deliberationibus perpenderiut, Exhortatio[n]em diuinissimi prophete Dauid psalmo Centesimo quinquagesimo, deum et creatorem vniuersi Jn sanctis et virtutibus suis multiplici laude et Musica harmonia diuersorum sonorum et Instr[ument]orum concrepante decorand[um], collandand[um] et venerandum esse. ac laudari debere Jn chordis et Organo'. B II 62, 2 (in 1 AST-C 187); 1 AST 635, fol. CCix^{r}; 90 Z 14, pp. 679–80.

89 B II 62, 2; 1 AST 635, fol. CCix^{r}; 90 Z 14, pp. 680–81.

90 See H.-G. Rott, 'Probleme der Straßburger Historiographie des 16. Jahrhunderts: Dr. Nikolaus Wurmser, Dekan des St. Thomaskapitels, und sein Protokoll (1513–1524), in K. Andermann, ed., *Historiographie am Oberrhein im Späten Mittelalter und in der Frühen Neuzeit* (Sigmaringen: Thorbecke, 1988), p. 196. See also 90 Z 13, p. 3; 90 Z 14, pp. 648–720.

important musician in Strasbourg at this time, was a monk and ordained priest who had moved to Strasbourg by 1522,[91] and was in the same year appointed cathedral cantor.[92] In 1524, at the beginning of the Reformation, both Greiter and Dachstein left their monasteries and married Strasbourgeoise women, in doing so receiving citizenship of the city.[93] The two men were then given the task of composing new melodies for the congregation to sing. Apart from his post at the cathedral, Greiter at one point in his career held benefices from three churches in Strasbourg,[94] although it is unclear whether he performed regular tasks at each. He also began teaching music at the newly founded Gymnasium in 1538.[95] He was frequently writing to the authorities to request a pay rise to support his ever-growing family. In 1540, for example, he wrote requesting a higher salary in order to be able to support his wife and – by now – ten children.[96] The reformers and Strasbourg town council must have felt that he deserved and required these various sources of income, as he managed to retain his employment in the city despite being convicted, on various occasions, of being absent from the Lord's Supper, reading to himself during the sermon, a lack of diligence in his schoolteaching,[97] and having an adulterous affair.[98] In addition, he composed not only psalm tunes for use in church but also popular songs, something which may not have gained him any favour with the reformers.[99] With the return of Catholicism to Strasbourg, in 1549, he renounced Protestantism, thereby managing to retain his job at the cathedral.[100]

Dachstein also encountered problems with the city and church authorities in Strasbourg. Having apparently stayed out of trouble until the return of Catholicism to the city in 1549, he then seems to have asked for money several times to support his family. In 1550 he complained that he was being paid less than his predecessors, as well as separately being accused of having published inflammatory pamphlets against the council. He was also charged with failing

[91] M. H. Schmid, *Mathias Greiter: Das Schicksal eines Deutschen Musikers zur Reformationszeit* (Aichach: Mayer & Söhne, 1976), p. 37.

[92] *Fragments des anciennes chroniques d'Alsace*, III (1892), no. 2657.

[93] C. W. Young, 'School Music in Sixteenth-Century Strasbourg', *Journal of Research in Music Education*, 10.2 (1962), p. 130.

[94] The churches of St Martin, St Stephen and St Peter the Old. See Schmid, *Mathias Greiter*, pp. 125–32.

[95] Bornert, *Réforme protestante du culte*, p. 480.

[96] 'Aber Gott vnser vatter hatt mich mit grossem segen, das ist mit vil kinden begabet, also das ich selb xij bin, nämlich vj sün vnd iiij töchtern hab'. 1 AST 74, 189, fol. 214r; 90 Z 13, p. 304.

[97] Schmid, *Mathias Greiter*, p. 156–8; 1 AST 109, 36, pp. 4–5.

[98] Young, 'School Music in Sixteenth-Century Strasbourg', p. 131.

[99] These include such titles as 'Ich weiß ein hübsche Graserin' ('I know a pretty grazer, who grazes in my garden'), 'Des spils ich gar keyn glück' ('In games I have no luck'), and 'Es wolt ein jäger jagen' ('A hunter wants to hunt').

[100] H.-C. Müller and S. Davies, 'Greiter, Matthias', in Root, ed., *Grove Music Online* (www.oxfordmusiconline.com) (accessed 28 January 2011).

to give his music lessons.[101] Despite their apparent moral shortcomings, these two men provided Strasbourg with the majority of its Reformation hymn and psalm tunes.

References to music in pre-Reformation manuscripts are usually notes relating to specific church musicians[102] rather than to be calls to reform or rethink musical practice. However, two manuscripts in particular from before 1520 reveal the city's stance on music and dancing in the years before the Reformation. Both are in the hand of Sebastian Brant, who held several positions of authority in the Strasbourg government until his death in 1521. The first of these notices, dating from 1518,[103] relates to an outbreak of what is today thought to have been Sydenham's chorea (also known as St Vitus's dance), which caused involuntary movements in the sufferer, making him or her appear to be dancing. During the summer heat of July 1518, a woman stepped outside her house and began to 'dance'. She continued for many hours before collapsing from exhaustion, but recommenced her routine a few hours later. This continued until she was removed and taken to the shrine of St Vitus, patron saint of dancing, in the Vosges mountains close to Saverne. Within days, however, many others had started to dance, and by August the situation had turned into an epidemic. Not until late August or early September did the dancing craze diminish, by which time it is believed that hundreds of people across the social spectrum had died of their wounds and exhaustion.[104] The authorities tried a variety of methods to quell the epidemic. The first attempted solution was more dancing, accompanied by 'drumming and piping' (*trummen und pfeiffen*), as well as robust men to encourage the diseased in the movements and to dance with them.[105] It was believed that only through more dancing could the disease, or curse, be expelled. The second method was the complete opposite: Brant's manuscript, written in the midst of the crisis on 3 August, announced that dancing had been banned because of the diseases occurring from it. Only honest, upstanding people would be permitted to dance, on such occasions as celebrations of first Mass, but only in their homes, and without the use of drums (*boccken*). However, they were permitted to use string instruments (*seiten spiele[n]*) which were thought less

[101] Gérold, *Les plus anciennes mélodies*, pp. 27–30.

[102] For example, 1 AST 16, 1 (1 March 1520), regarding the retirement of 'Dr. Othomar' (presumably Otto Nachtgall), and 1 AST 16, 6 (10 November 1520), in which Brant recommends a young man to join the choir of St Thomas.

[103] 1 MR 3, fol. 72r. See also Brant's annals, in *Fragments des anciennes chroniques d'Alsace*, III (1892), no. 3443.

[104] See H. C. E. Midelfort, *A History of Madness in Sixteenth-Century Germany* (Stanford: Stanford University Press, 1999), pp. 33–5; and J. Waller, *A Time to Dance, a Time to Die – The Extraordinary Story of the Dancing Plage of 1518* (Royston, Herts: Icon Books, 2008), pp. 1–4.

[105] Waller, *A Time to Dance, a Time to Die*, pp. 112–26; *Fragments des anciennes chroniques d'Alsace*, II (1890), no. 2216.

likely to incite hysteria.[106] The third solution involved holding Masses for the sick, and taking all the afflicted to the St Vitus shrine.[107]

In the second of these manuscripts, dated 1519, Brant prohibited the singing of a puerile (*bübisch*) song entitled 'Bopperle Bopp'.[108] The song, he complained, was contrary to God, and certainly not suitable to be sung in front of women or young children. Singing it was banned in the city and suburbs of Strasbourg, and anyone who disobeyed would be locked in the tower (*will man jn torn begen*).[109] Complaints about this and other shameful songs also appeared in Brant's annals. One entry explains that a decree was made in 1515 to collect and burn all 'tales and songs printed against the confederates', and that no such poems or songs were to be printed without the permission of the *Ammeister* or a doctor of the chancel.[110] Another, from 1515, stated

> that shameful songs should be prohibited, [on pain of a fine] of 30 shillings, especially the 'Bopperle Bopp', and that our lords will seek out the printers [of such songs].[111]

In 1516, the printers of Strasbourg were interrogated over the printing of the so-called 'Würtembergisch Lied'. Martin Flach confessed to being the publisher of this song, but claimed he was unaware of the process of approval for such songs, and asked for mercy. Other printers were required to swear that they had no other such songs waiting to be published.[112]

These cases are among some of the first attempts at song censorship in Strasbourg.[113] They reveal that the regulation of activities such as dancing and music-making was deemed necessary by the authorities a considerable length of time before the Reformation had taken hold in Strasbourg. Official action was being taken (although we do not know how successful it may have been) to prevent people from singing songs that were lascivious or unchristian, or in some way immoral. The idea that the Reformation was responsible for launching this attack on unchristian music-making would therefore be a mistaken assumption. Although certain reformers, including those of Strasbourg, attacked such songs

---

[106] 1 MR 3, fol. 72r. Translated in Midelfort, *A History of Madness*, p. 35. Brant had warned of the moral dangers of dancing in *Das Narrenschiff*, chapter 61.

[107] Midelfort, *A History of Madness*, pp. 35–7; Waller, *A Time to Dance, a Time to Die*, pp. 143–54.

[108] There is no known record of the words of this song, nor any indication as to why its contents may have been so objectionable.

[109] 1 MR 3, fol. 86r.

[110] *Fragments des anciennes chroniques d'Alsace*, III (1892), no. 3418.

[111] 'Item die schampern lieder soll man bey 30 ß p verbieten und besonders das Bopperlebopp und hh. by den truckern suchen lassen. *Fragments des anciennes chroniques d'Alsace*, III (1892), no. 3414; Röhrich, *Mitteheilungen aus der Geschichte der evangelischen Kirche des Elsasses*, 3 vols (Paris and Strasbourg: Treuttel und Würtz, 1855), vol. 1, p. 395, n. 1.

[112] *Fragments des anciennes chroniques d'Alsace*, III (1892), no. 3423.

[113] Chrisman, *Lay Culture, Learned Culture*, p. 268, n. 35.

time and time again and fought for their abolition, they were by no means solely responsible for establishing an authoritarian stance on such pastimes.[114]

Strasbourg was one of the most receptive audiences for Martin Luther's early teachings. The reformer's writings first reached the city during 1518, and one chronicle tells of how, in emulation of the action supposedly taken by Luther at the Castle Church in Wittenberg one year earlier, his 95 theses were attached to the door of the cathedral and to several churches in Strasbourg.[115] Regardless of whether or not this actually took place, the story gives some indication of the popular reception of Luther's writings in Strasbourg. The initiative for reform in Strasbourg was taken by Matthäus Zell, preacher of St Laurence's Chapel in the cathedral. He defended Luther against his critics, and soon began preaching Luther's message to popular acclaim. Soon he was joined in his preaching by Wolfgang Capito, the third most senior clerical figure in Strasbourg and provost of St Thomas's Church, as well as other figures including Caspar Hedio and Anton Firn.[116] Before long, the reforming movement had attracted a selection of powerful local allies, including *Ammeister* past and future, noblemen, and merchants.[117]

Martin Bucer was born in modern-day Sélestat (at that time Schlettstadt) on 11 November 1491, and attended the city's school before joining the Dominican order to train as a monk. It was here that his interest in philosophy, especially the works of Aristotle, was kindled. The Dominicans viewed the study of Aristotle as a means leading to the study of theology.[118] Having been sent to the Dominican monastery in Heidelberg in 1512, he studied there and in Mainz for several years, before enrolling in his doctoral degree at the end of the decade. His library contained editions of Thomas Aquinas alongside humanist volumes, including titles by Erasmus as well as a book by Heinrich Bebel[119] that recommended many ancient authors in the study of rhetoric.[120] Bucer's early writings betray an emphasis not only on faith through Christ, but on the ethical values which are to be obtained therein.[121] His interest in Luther's theology grew, and in 1518 he attended the Heidelberg Disputation organised by Luther at the General

---

114 Erasmus, for example, was scathing about 'modern songs' to which 'young girls dance'. See C. A. Miller, 'Erasmus on Music', *The Musical Quarterly*, 56 (1966), p. 348; and H.-A. Kim, 'Erasmus on Sacred Music', *Reformation and Renaissance Review*, 8 (2006), pp. 285–6. For more on popular songs and the Reformation, see Chapter 4.

115 *Fragments des anciennes chroniques d'Alsace*, III (1892), no. 3010.

116 Pettegree, *Reformation and the Culture of Persuasion*, pp. 29–30; Chrisman, *Strasbourg and the Reform*, pp. 100–111; Abray, *The People's Reformation*, pp. 32–3.

117 Brady, *Turning Swiss*, p. 162.

118 M. Greschat, trans. S. E. Buckwalter, *Martin Bucer – A Reformer and His Times* (Louisville and London: Westminster John Knox Press, 2004), pp. 16–17.

119 Professor of rhetoric and poetry at the University of Tübingen.

120 Greschat, *Martin Bucer*, pp. 18–19.

121 Ibid., pp. 27–8.

Chapter of the Augustinians.[122] Bucer wrote of the event to the humanist Beatus Rhenanus, who was based in Strasbourg:

> Although our chief men refuted him with all their might, their wiles were unable to make him move an inch from his propositions. His sweetness in answering is remarkable, his patience in listening is incomparable … He agrees with Erasmus in all things, but with this difference in his favour, that what Erasmus only insinuates, he teaches openly and freely.[123]

Luther, in return, seemed taken with the young Dominican. He described Bucer as 'a young brother who almost alone in his order gives some promise. At Heidelberg he received me eagerly and simply, and conversed with me showing himself worthy of love and trust, and also of hope'.[124] Fascinatingly, Luther and Bucer seemed to have identified themselves as respective teacher and pupil. Although not a relationship which would persevere, it was crucial in forming Bucer's initial appreciation of the need for ecclesiastical reform, and was therefore also of significance to the direction taken by Strasbourg during the 1520s. Equally intriguing is Bucer's comparison of Luther with Erasmus;[125] he saw the two as equally important, but the former, in Bucer's estimation, being willing to go a degree further in his teaching than the latter.

Luther's own desire to reform the liturgy led him to consider the role of music in church services. He was a skilled musician, having received formal training in music, and he continued to make music as an adult.[126] Music, to Luther, was 'a beautiful, lovely gift of God' (*eine schöne, liebliche Gabe Gottes*),[127] and hymns

---

[122] D. F. Wright, ed., *Common Places of Martin Bucer* (Appleford, Abingdon: Sutton Courtenay Press, 1972), p. 19.

[123] 'ad Martinum illum Lutherium redeo, ut summa quidem vi nostri primores amolirentur, ne latum unguem (quidem) tamen ab instituto dimovere suis argutiis. Mira in respondendo suavitas, in audiendo incomparabilis longanimitas … Cum Erasmo illi conveniunt omnia, quin uno hoc praestare videtur, quod quae ille duntaxat insinuat, hic aperte docet et libere'. Quoted in A. Horawitz and K. Hartfelder, eds, *Briefwechsel des Beatus Rhenanus* (Leipzig: Teubner, 1886), p. 107. Translated in Wright, *Common Places of Martin Bucer*, pp. 19–20.

[124] 'Habes Epistolam Buccrianam fratris vel solius in ista secta candidi & optimę spei Iuuenis, qui me Haidelbergę & auide & simpliciter excepit atque conuersatus fuit, dignus amore & fide, Sed & spe'. J. C. F. Knaake et al., eds, *D. Martin Luthers Werke: Kritische Gesamtausgabe – Briefwechsel*, 17 vols (Weimar: Böhlau, 1930–83) (hereafter: *WA Br*), vol. 2, p. 39. Translated in Wright, *Common Places of Martin Bucer*, p. 20, n. 17.

[125] This comparison, incidentally, would not have been popular with Erasmus, who later referred to the 'Lutheran tragedy' (*Lutherana tragoedia*). See J. C. Olin, ed., *Christian Humanism and the Reformation – Selected Writings of Erasmus*, 2nd edn (New York: Fordham University Press, 1975), p. 6, incl. n. 5.

[126] R. A. Leaver, *Luther's Liturgical Music: Principles and Implications* (Grand Rapids and Cambridge: Eerdmans, 2007), pp. 102–3.

[127] J. G. Plochmann et al., eds, *Dr. Martin Luther's sämmtliche Werke*, 67 vols (Frankfurt am Main and Erlangen: Heyder & Zimmer, 1826–57), vol. 62, p. 111. See also Leaver, *Luther's Liturgical Music*, p. 70.

were an important way in which to disseminate the doctrine of the Church. In a letter to Georg Spalatin (reformer in Saxony and secretary to Frederick the Wise, Elector of Saxony) in 1523, he announced that he wanted the Word of God to be 'among the people' in the form of song.[128] From an early stage, therefore, Luther understood communal singing as theology for the people in musical form,[129] as well as a vehicle for dissemination of doctrine among the general population. Luther held several ancient hymns in high esteem, including the passion hymns *Patris sapientia* and *Rex Christe, factor omnium.*[130]

Bucer arrived in Strasbourg in May 1523. He had fled the monastery in Heidelberg at the beginning of 1521, being released from his monastic vows in April of that year,[131] and getting married the following year. After then preaching a series of sermons in Wissembourg (about 65 kilometres north of Strasbourg) he was forced to leave when fighting broke out, and he made his way to Strasbourg.[132] Within a matter of months he had been granted citizenship, and by 1524 he had emerged as the leader of the Strasbourg evangelical reforms.[133]

Strasbourg's first liturgical reform took place on 16 February 1524, when Diobald Schwarz, assistant to Matthäus Zell, celebrated Low Mass in German[134] in the chapel of St John the Baptist in the cathedral (see Figure 1.2). This Mass was based on the existing rite used in Strasbourg[135] but references to the Mass as a sacrifice were omitted, and Communion was distributed in both kinds.[136] Although, being a Low Mass, it seems unlikely that much, if any, music was used in this service, musical developments in the liturgy occurred very soon after. The first reference to music in the new German service appeared in one

[128] 'quo verbum dei vel cantu inter populos maneat'. *WA Br*, 3, p. 220. Translated in J. Pelikan and T. Lehmann, eds, *Luther's Works: American Edition*, 55 vols (St Louis: Concordia; Philadelphia: Muehlenberg & Fortress, 1955–86) (hereafter: *LW*), vol. 49, p. 68.

[129] Leaver, *Luther's Liturgical Music*, p. 19.

[130] Plochmann, *Dr. Martin Luther's sämmtliche Werke*, vol. 62, pp. 111–12. Both melodies, among others, were adapted into Lutheran hymns and subsequently used by J. S. Bach in his chorale preludes.

[131] Greschat, *Martin Bucer*, p. 34. See *BDS*, 1, pp. 285–90 for the text of the release from his vows.

[132] Steinmetz, *Reformers in the Wings*, p. 86.

[133] Wright, *Common Places of Martin Bucer*, p. 23.

[134] 1 AST 80, 2. See F. Hubert, *Die Straßburger liturgischen Ordnungen im Zeitalter der Reformation* (Göttingen, Vandenhoeck & Ruprecht, 1900) (hereafter: *Hubert*), pp. 57–75.

[135] See, for example, the *Breviarium Argentinense* (Strasbourg: Reyser, 1478; Grüninger, 1489; Prüss, 1511) and the *Agenda siue Exequiale sacramentorum* (Strasbourg: Prüss, 1505; Beck, 1508; Beck 1513). The *Agenda* contained a German translation of the Creed, the Ten Commandments, and the General Confession. Several other missals and a collection of Latin psalms had been printed in 1520 (see M. Vogeleis, *Quellen und Bausteine zu einer Geschichte der Musik und des Theaters im Elsass, 500–1800* (Strasbourg: Le Roux, 1911; repr. Geneva: Minkoff, 1979), p. 205).

[136] That is, both the bread and the wine were distributed (see *Fragments des anciennes chroniques d'Alsace*, III (1892), no. 3024). Contemporary practice was for only the bread to be taken by the people, but for both to be taken by the celebrant.

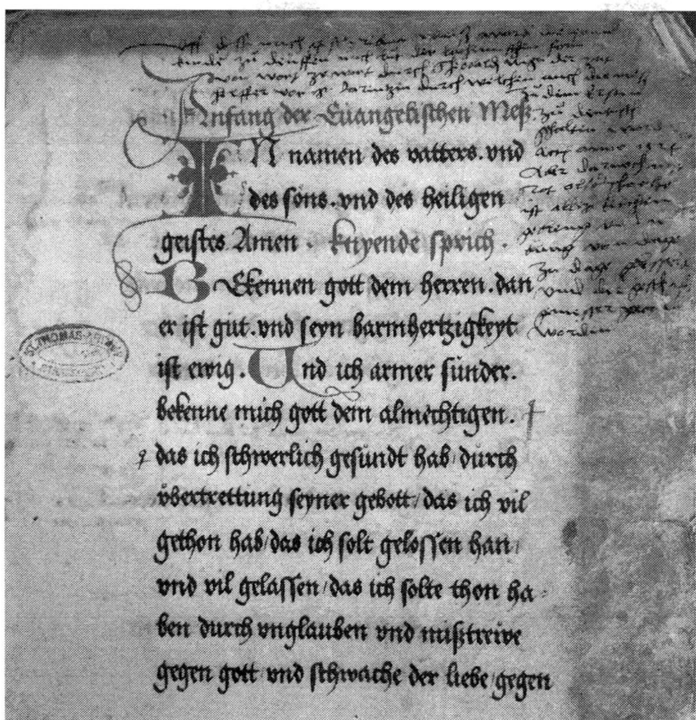

Anfang der Euangelischen Meß.
In namen des vatters. vnd
des sons. vnd des heiligen
geistes Amen. Beyende sprich.
Bekennen gott dem herren. dan
er ist gut. vnd seyn barmhertzigkeyt
ist ewig. Und ich armer sünder.
bekenne mich gott dem almechtigen.
das ich schwerlich gesündt hab durch
übertrettung seyner gebott. das ich vil
gethon hab das ich solt gelossen han
vnd vil gelassen das ich solte thon haben durch vnglauben vnd mißtrüwe
gegen gott vnd schwache der liebe gegen

Figure 1.2 The first page of the manuscript of Diobald Schwarz's German translation of the Mass (AVS, 1 AST 80, 2, fol. 5v). Reproduced by permission of the Archives de la Ville et de la Communauté urbaine de Strasbourg

of the earliest printed liturgical orders.[137] The Mass included one of Luther's folk hymn adaptations,[138] 'Gott sey gelobet', to be sung at Communion, and the order for Vespers contained five hymns by Luther (including his setting of

[137] *Ordenung vnd yn[n]halt Teütscher Mess vn[nd] Vesper* (Strasbourg: Köpfel, 1524). Germany did not align the beginning of its historical year and civil year until 1544, and this poses a problem for dating early Reformation sources. Until 1544, although 1 January was considered the beginning of the historical year, the number of the year did not change until 25 March each year. The sources from Strasbourg do not tend to provide overlapping dates (e.g. 1523/24, as some English sources do, for example) and so the ambiguity remains. Despite this, there can be no doubt that the first German Mass in Strasbourg was celebrated *before* liturgical orders began to be published there. In other words, the year 1524 given in the document (1 AST 80, 2) *must* refer to February in the historical year rather than in the civil year, because it is inconceivable that at least eight liturgical publications printed in 1524 (see Appendix A) either appeared before Schwarz's celebration of the Mass had occurred, or within the five weeks between 16 February and 24 March.

[138] Luther's hymns featured in Strasbourg hymnals throughout the early Reformation period.

Psalm 130: 'Aus tieffer not schrey ich zu dir'[139]) and a German setting of the *Magnificat*[140] by the Strasbourg reformer, Symphorianus Pollio. The musical reformation had begun.

Although disappointingly little is known about the relationship between Strasbourg's Protestant musicians and its preachers, we know from their writings that the reformers were relatively united on the subject of music in church. Although none was a musician of any repute, they saw clearly the problems with the late medieval music of the Church and the need for its reform. It has been said that Bucer, at least, 'valued the hymn in its high spiritual worth and praised its harmonious measure as a divine gift'.[141] Bucer's library at Sélestat included books by four of the Church Fathers, including a short tract by St Athanasius concerning the use of the Psalms in devotion.[142] While comments on music and its role in the liturgy occur in his writings throughout his career as a reformer, some of the most important can be found in his 1524 publication, *Grund und Ursach*,[143] which outlined the proposed reforms to the Church in Strasbourg. With reference to 1 Corinthians 14: 26, he wrote,

> The Apostle [Paul] … informs us that when the congregation of God assembles there are teaching[s], songs of praise, and prayer. And for this reason we have established that instruction, namely concerning both Law and Gospel, should be given in our assembly, and admonitions added thereto; and along with it psalms and songs of praise should be sung to the praise of God and for the strengthening of faith.[144]

It is worth emphasising the extent to which the reformers (not just in Strasbourg, but across Europe) made use of chapter 14 of St Paul's First Letter to the Corinthians. To them, it provided the biblical key to congregational singing in the vernacular and to the importance of preaching. The Strasbourg reformers, like Luther, equated St Paul's references in 1 Corinthians 14: 1–11 to 'speaking in

[139] See Leaver, *Luther's Liturgical Music*, pp. 145–6 about this hymn.

[140] Luke 1: 46–55; the canticle sung at the office of Vespers.

[141] G. J. van de Poll, *Martin Bucer's Liturgical Ideas: The Strasburg Reformer and his Connection with the Liturgies of the Sixteenth Century* (Assen, Netherlands: Van Gorcum, 1954), p. 30; referring to Bucer's *Epistola D. Pauli ad Ephesios* (Strasbourg: Herwagen, 1527), pp. 5, 18–20.

[142] Hughes Oliphant Old believes that this work by Athanasius may have contributed to the positive approach to psalmody in the reforms of Strasbourg and elsewhere. See H. O. Old, *The Patristic Roots of Reformed Worship* (Zurich: Theologischer Verlag, 1975), pp. 120–21 and 267–8.

[143] Bucer, *Grund und Ursach*. Text reproduced in *BDS*, 1, pp. 194–278.

[144] 'das diser Apostel den Corinthiern in gemeltem ca. zuschreibet, werden wir bericht, das, so die gemein gottes zusamenkomet, das seien lere, lobgesang und gepett, und darumb ordnen wirs, das in unsern samlungen lere, das ist gesatz und Evangelion, beide gelerет und mit ermanungen getriben werden und dabey psalmen und lobgesang zu preyß gottes und sterckung des glaubens gesungen'. *BDS*, 1, p. 247. Translated in O. F. Cypris, 'Basic Principles: Translation and Commentary of Martin Bucer's *Grund und Ursach*, 1524' (PhD diss., Union Theological Seminary, New York, 1971), pp. 151–2.

tongues' with singing in Latin or Greek, and to 'prophesying' with preaching.[145] To all Protestants, it appeared that Paul's instructions had been ignored over centuries by successive popes, cardinals, bishops, and priests. It was now vital that the clergy show leadership and address their people, who should also be given their own voice in church.

Bucer believed that music should have a role in disseminating both ethical and doctrinal messages to the faithful. Bucer's position on the issue could not be doubted following his statement that

> those who discard singing in the congregation of God know little, either about the contents of Scripture, or the custom of the first apostolic churches and congregations, who always praised God with singing.[146]

This would appear to be a direct attack not only on the Roman Church, but also on any Protestant groups who were erring on the side of abolishing congregational singing (as Zwingli did in Zurich, in 1525). Those who rejected such a custom were therefore untrue to the practices of the early Church. In support of his argument, Bucer cited St Paul and pagan writers such as Pliny the Younger.[147] In a much later document, he also made reference to practices discussed in writings of St Ignatius, St Augustine, St Basil, and others.[148] The Mass had been added to over the centuries and he and the reformers believed that it was now adorned by

---

145 'Follow the way of love and eagerly desire gifts of the Spirit, especially prophecy. For anyone who speaks in a tongue does not speak to people but to God. Indeed, no one understands them; they utter mysteries by the Spirit. But the one who prophesies speaks to people for their strengthening, encouraging and comfort. Anyone who speaks in a tongue edifies themselves, but the one who prophesies edifies the church. I would like every one of you to speak in tongues, but I would rather have you prophesy. The one who prophesies is greater than the one who speaks in tongues, unless someone interprets, so that the church may be edified. Now, brothers and sisters, if I come to you and speak in tongues, what good will I be to you, unless I bring you some revelation or knowledge or prophecy or word of instruction? Even in the case of lifeless things that make sounds such as the pipe or harp, how will anyone know what tune is being played unless there is a distinction in the notes? Again, if the trumpet does not sound a clear call, who will get ready for battle? So it is with you. Unless you speak intelligible words with your tongue, how will anyone know what you are saying? You will just be speaking into the air. Undoubtedly there are all sorts of languages in the world, yet none of them is without meaning. If then I do not grasp the meaning of what someone is saying, I am a foreigner to the speaker, and the speaker is a foreigner to me'. 1 Cor. 14: 1–11. See also M. Weyer, 'L'*Apologie chrétienne* du réformateur strasbourgeois Matthieu Zell ("*Christeliche Verantwortung*", 1523)', 3 vols (Doctor ès Sciences Religieuses thesis, Université des Sciences Humaines de Strasbourg, 1981), vol. 1, p. 232, n. 3; and *WA*, 8, pp. 621–2.

146 'Deshalb wissen die, so das gesang in der gemein gottes verwerffen, wenig weder umb der schrifft inhalt noch den brauch der ersten und Apostolischen kirchen und gemeinden, die alweg got auch mit gesang gelobet haben'. *BDS*, 1, p. 276. Translated in Cypris, 'Basic Principles', p. 211.

147 *BDS*, 1, p. 276. Translated in Cypris, 'Basic Principles', p. 211. See Pliny's letter to Trajan, X, 96/97, in J. B. Lightfoot, ed., *The Apostolic Fathers*, 5 vols (London: Macmillan, 1889), part 2, vol. 1, pp. 50–54.

148 CCCC, ms. 418, pp. 138–40; Bucer and Parker, *Florilegium Patristicum*, pp. 56–7.

allegorical ceremonies and opulent rites. They wanted to rediscover the original meaning of worship, as handed down by the Apostles.[149]

Ideas of emotion were also crucial to the reformers' thinking on music. For Bucer, song was to be used because it could help the Word of God penetrate the heart (that is, the human conscience) more deeply.[150] Bucer's most mature and complete comments on hymns and singing arrived in the form of the preface to the Strasbourg *Gesangbuch* of 1541.[151] Here he stated that music, namely 'all singing and playing (which above all things are capable of moving our spirits powerfully and ardently), should be used in no other way except for sacred praise, prayer, teaching, and admonition'.[152] He reiterated that no singing or playing of instruments should take place 'except by and for Christian spiritual activities'.[153] In an echo of Savonarola's concerns at the end of the fifteenth century, Bucer complained of the devil's grasp on music, resulting in the misuse of 'this wonderful art and gift of God' (*dise herrliche kunst vnd gabe Gottes*). And, voicing similar concerns to those of Wimpheling in his preface to *Hymni de tempore & de sanctis* with regard to the education of the young, Bucer expressed his horror at contemplating 'what unpleasantness is stirred up ... by devilish, seductive songs, so that whatever without song is too charming and lies in the senses, is insinuated by song more charmingly and deeper into the senses and the heart'.[154] Music was a sensual art that had to be used with care.[155] The publication of the *Gesangbuch*, which Bucer describes as a 'faithful and useful service', was to 'be received gratefully by the congregations and all those

---

149 Old, *The Patristic Roots of Reformed Worship*, pp. 37–8.

150 Bornert, *Réforme protestante du culte*, p. 470. See also Bucer's 'Rathschlag' (1 AST 38, 3, fols. 88r–88v; *BDS*, 2, pp. 470–71). The heart, since ancient times, had been considered the physical centre of emotion. Susan Karant-Nunn writes that '[w]hile preachers invoke it metaphorically, they simultaneously mean it physically, as the seat of sincerity, conviction, and emotion' (see S. C. Karant-Nunn, *The Reformation of Feeling – Shaping the Religious Emotions in Early Modern Germany* (Oxford: Oxford University Press, 2010), pp. 83 and 248).

151 *Gesangbuch darinn begriffen sind / die aller fuͤrnemisten vnd besten Psalmen / Geistliche Lieder / vnd Chorgeseng / aus dem Wittembergischen / Strasburgischen / vnd anderer Kirchen Gesangbuͤchlin zu̇samen bracht / vnd mit besonderem fleis corrigiert vnd gedrucket* (Strasbourg: Messerschmidt & Köpfel, 1541). Bucer's preface, on fol. A3 of the book, is reproduced in Appendix H. It can also be found in *BDS*, 7, pp. 577–82, and a translation is available in *Garside*, pp. 29–31.

152 'So solte die Music / alles gesang vnd seitenspil (welche vor anderen dingen / das gemuͤt zu̇bewegen / hefftig vnd hitzig zu̇machen / mechtig sind) nirgend anders / dann zu̇ goͤtlichem lob / gebet / lehre vnd ermanung gebrauchet werden' (see Appendix H, p. 343). *Gesangbuch* (1541), fol. A3^r; *BDS*, 7, p. 578.

153 'das kein Lieduͤberal / kein seitenspil / anders dann von / vnd zu̇ christlichen geistlichen hendelen gesungen vnd gebrauchet wuͤrde' (see Appendix H, p. 343). *Gesangbuch* (1541), fol. A3^r; *BDS*, 7, p. 579.

154 'Daher es auch erschroͤklich ist zu̇ gedencken / was ergernis / bei der juget vnd anderen / durch die teufelischen bu̇llieder / angestifftet wuͤrt / so das / welches ondas zu̇ fil anmuͤtig vnd im sinne ligt / erst durchs gesang noch anmuͤtiger / vnd tieffer in sinne vnd hertz gestecket wuͤrt' (see Appendix H, p. 344). *Gesangbuch* (1541), fol. A3^r; *BDS*, 7, p. 579.

155 See *Garside*.

who are Christians, inasmuch as by means of it the general improvement of the kingdom of Christ is sought'.[156] But although the reformers attempted to limit popular repertoire to those songs which they deemed suitable for use – whether inside or outside church – they were forced to tolerate another (unsuitable) sort of popular song which was very close to their cause (indeed, one which might even have been crucial to its success): the polemical song. Especially during the first decade or so of the Reformation, song was a vital tool in disseminating news of the religious reforms occurring across Europe.[157] The appearance in Strasbourg of various illicit, polemical songs during the 1520s illustrates that music functioned not only as a means of reform in its own right but also as a promoter of the religious changes occurring.

In summary, music, and congregational singing in particular, was important in Strasbourg for several reasons. Its use in worship had scriptural origins, as well as a precedent in the practice of the early Church, but it also had emotional qualities that edified those who listened to and participated in it. For the correct sort of emotions to be brought forth, the music had to serve the text;[158] it could not be distracting for the listener or performer. Song also played an important part in the polemic of the Reformation, spreading news and opinions via print and performance media.

The fact that the city was, in the earliest days of reform, theologically very close to the Swiss Protestants makes Strasbourg's positive approach to music all the more remarkable. Huldrych Zwingli, who began implementing reforms in Zurich at the beginning of the 1520s, differed from Luther in his theology on several points, most significantly in his understanding of the Eucharist. Zwingli rejected the notion that Christ was corporeally present in the bread and wine, and saw it merely as a signifier of Christ's body. The Strasbourg reformers, for the most part, followed this view.[159] As Thomas Brady writes, 'Strasbourg appeared in early 1524 to be the major free city sailing most nearly in Zurich's wake'.[160] But, crucially, the reformers did not follow Zwingli's lead in abolishing all music from the liturgy. In the words of Hughes Oliphant Old, bearing in mind the constant presence of Luther's own hymns in Strasbourg's subsequent orders of service,[161] 'to claim that the [early Reformation] Strasbourg liturgy is the result of Swiss influence is rather difficult'.[162] Strasbourg's mixture of influences led

---

156 'Disen getrewen vnd nutzlichen dienst wo̊llen die Gemeinden / vnd alle die Christen sind / danckbarlich auffnemen / wie dann hiemit gemeine besserung des reichs Christi gesuchet ist' (see Appendix H, pp. 346–7). *Gesangbuch* (1541), fol. A3v; *BDS*, 7, p. 581.

157 See Chapter 4.

158 Bornert, *Réforme protestante du culte*, p. 472.

159 Steinmetz, *Reformers in the Wings*, p. 88; Chrisman, *Lay Culture, Learned Culture*, p. 145; J. M. Kittelson, *Wolfgang Capito, From Humanist to Reformer* (Leiden: Brill, 1975), pp. 146–8.

160 Brady, *Turning Swiss*, p. 162.

161 'Gott sei gelobt' was particularly common.

162 See Old, *The Patristic Roots of Reformed Worship*, p. 41.

to it developing a very particular and independent liturgy[163] and therefore also a very particular and independent approach to church music. Throughout the next four decades this influence spread both throughout Germany and abroad.[164]

It was ultimately in sharing Luther's intention to disseminate the Word of God through music that Martin Bucer and his colleagues embraced their commitment to congregational singing. The need for 'improvement' (*besserung*)[165] or making things 'noticeably better' (*mercklich besserten*)[166] in the Church of God was paramount from the beginning of the reforms, and one such way of achieving this, as Bucer made clear in his writings, was through music. Singing, however, had to be performed in a correct, artful manner,[167] and texts had to be chosen carefully (only very few non-scriptural texts were allowed into the Strasbourg hymn canon[168]). It was clear to Bucer that lascivious, devilish, and ruinous songs would be 'cast out and destroyed' (*abgethan vnd verspuͤlget*),[169] yet those who sang from their hearts would please God, and promote 'joy and happiness' (*rechte freud vnd lust*).[170] Singing, then, was important to the reformers not just because of its historical status, but because it was a vital way of cultivating certain emotions in Christians, and ultimately a more effective way of praising God.

As shall be demonstrated in the following chapters, although the preachers spoke out against singers, they were opposed only to a very particular type of singing. Much in the same way as the reformers made generalisations about priests, monks, and nuns, but were in fact only opposed to those within these categories who refused to reform, they did not believe that all singers were bad. The reformers took it upon themselves, however, to return church music to the people. This task was undertaken without hesitation, and without any significant lead from Wittenberg.

---

[163] Pettegree, *Reformation and the Culture of Persuasion*, p. 47.

[164] See Chapter 5.

[165] Appendix H, p. 347. *Gesangbuch* (1541), fol. A3^{v}; *BDS*, 7, p. 581.

[166] Appendix H, p. 343. *Gesangbuch* (1541), fol. A3^{r}; *BDS*, 7, p. 579.

[167] 'artliche Musicgesang' (see Appendix H, p. 342). *Gesangbuch* (1541), fol. A3^{r}; *BDS*, 7, p. 578.

[168] 'Gott sey gelobet' being one such example.

[169] Appendix H, p. 345. *Gesangbuch* (1541), fol. A3^{v}; *BDS*, 7, pp. 579–80.

[170] Appendix H, p. 343. *Gesangbuch* (1541), fol. A3^{r}; *BDS*, 7, p. 579.

CHAPTER 2

Abolishing the Mass[1]

The liturgical priority of Strasbourg's reformers was to establish a vernacular service with vernacular music, even before the Roman Mass had been formally abolished and before a new evangelical service had been finalised. This meant that, during the first few years of the Reformation, new liturgical publications were constantly coming off the press, as more songs were introduced into the church and the liturgy underwent further revisions. In musical terms, the model of worship was not, initially, very close to that of Wittenberg, where a choir was usually retained alongside congregational singing. In other words, choral music did not play a part in Strasbourg's new liturgy.

After a quick glance at Strasbourg's first hymn books, the modern lay observer may be tempted to assume, without considering the books' historical context, that the Strasbourg lay folk simply picked up new hymns and sang them. The first few German liturgical orders did not contain music; the next few, on the other hand, did. The naïveté of the modern reader might be exacerbated by the fact that, in our own time printed hymns have no function other than to be sung. That is, they have not been produced by an enthusiastic printer with the hope of enticing congregations to sing them for the first time, as was the case in Strasbourg (or, if they have been, then printers most likely already have a guaranteed market before going to press – something which was almost certainly not the case during the Reformation). The importance of these early hymn books must not be underestimated. First and foremost, they obviously contain some of the earliest congregational hymns known, and from a time when most people could read neither text nor music. Second, they enable us to trace a chronology of the development of the vernacular liturgy and also the hymn book, two types of publication still important in church life today. Third, the prefaces of the Strasbourg orders reveal a great deal about the intentions of the printers, regardless of whether or not they corresponded with the intentions of the reformers. Some of Strasbourg's publications were obviously unofficial, published without the approval or perhaps even the prior knowledge of the reformers.

It is vital, therefore, that the hymn books and liturgical orders be looked at within the context of other contemporary material. The existence of early liturgical orders would suggest that congregations began singing German hymns

[1] Some parts of this chapter are reproduced from D. Trocmé-Latter, 'Thieves, Drunkards, and Womanisers? Perceptions of Church Musicians in Early Reformation Strasbourg', in R. G. Hobbs and A. Noblesse-Rocher, eds, *Bible, histoire et société – Mélanges offerts à Bernard Roussel* (Turnhout: Brepols, 2013), pp. 383–99.

within a matter of months of Diobald Schwarz's German Mass being celebrated.[2] However, although not exactly refuting this, Strasbourg's extant text documents from the period paint a more complex, albeit probably a more accurate, picture. Often, singing is only mentioned in passing, as something either to be avoided or encouraged (depending on the type of singing in question). But by simultaneously considering manuscript sources alongside hymns, it is possible to gain a sense of the way music was perceived by the reformers, how they saw it as a necessary part of religious and social ritual, and how they felt that their own use of music was superior to that of the Roman Church. This chapter (along with Chapter 3) will therefore piece together evidence from religious songbooks and manuscript sources in order to provide the most accurate and complete description to date of music in Reformation Strasbourg.[3]

The Early Vernacular Mass

The remarkable changes that occurred in the Strasbourg liturgy between 1524 and 1530 help to demonstrate the city's independent approach to the Reformation. The sudden appearance of a German Mass in manuscript, in 1524,[4] translated by Diobald Schwarz, took many in Germany by surprise, including, one presumes,

[2] Appendix A lists all of Strasbourg's liturgical orders and sacred music books between 1524 and 1541.

[3] There is a wide range of sources relating to the primary material, dating back to the first half of the nineteenth century, a large proportion of which is still relevant to current scholarship. Most notable are K. E. P. Wackernagel, *Das deutsche Kirchenlied von der altesten Zeit bis zu Anfang des XVII. Jahrhunderts*, 5 vols (Leipzig: Teubner, 1864–1877; repr. Hildesheim: Olms, 1964) (hereafter: *Wackernagel DKL*) and J. Zahn, *Die Melodien der deutschen evangelischen Kirchenlieder* (Reinheim: Lokay, 1889–93; repr. Hildesheim: Olms, 1963; 1997; 2006). In 1900, *Hubert* relied on both Wackernagel and Zahn for a lot of his information about hymns. A decade later, M. Vogeleis published *Quellen und Bausteine zu einer Geschichte der Musik und des Theaters im Elsass, 500–1800* (Strasbourg: Le Roux, 1911; repr. Geneva: Minkoff, 1979), which refers to several publications from the Reformation period not listed in *Hubert*. More recently, in 1975, the *Répertoire International des Sources Musicales* produced a bibliography of German-language hymn books printed between 1481 and 1800 (*RISM DKL*), which supersedes a large deal of this earlier work. Within the *DKL* series, *Abteilung II* lists songs contained in manuscript sources until 1530 (M. Lütolf, ed., *Geistliche Gesänge des deutschen Mittelalters: Melodien und Texte handschriftlicher überlieferung bis um 1530* (Kassel and New York: Bärenreiter, 2003–)), and *Abteilung III* lists songs from printed sources until 1680 (J. Stalmann et al., eds, *Die Melodien aus gedruckten Quellen bis 1680* (Kassel: Bärenreiter, 1993–) (hereafter: *DKL* III)). A limitation, as Rebecca Wagner Oettinger points out, is that *RISM DKL* does not include songs relating to church politics, even though church politics 'were the driving force behind hymn composition in the sixteenth century, and it is difficult to draw the line between political songs that are religious and religious songs that are also political' (*MPGR*, p. 2).

[4] This was Diobald Schwarz's translation, with a few modifications, of the Low Mass. See R. Bornert, *Réforme protestante du culte à Strasbourg au XVI*[e] *siècle (1523–1598)* (Leiden: Brill, 1981), p. 113. Some chronicles even suggest that Schwarz *sang* the German Mass in 1524. See, for example, *Fragments des anciennes chroniques d'Alsace*, III (1892), no. 3024.

Luther himself, who had not yet published his own *Deutsche Messe*.[5] René Bornert is of the opinion that the conservatism shown by Luther in his Latin *Formula missae* of 1523 is due in part to the fact that the reformer attached only secondary importance to matters of liturgy.[6] By this argument, Luther was more interested in adapting faith gradually, rather than making hasty and sweeping liturgical changes that might not be understood. Furthermore, there was little room for error: liturgy, and music's role therein, was something that required the exercising of caution during the planning stage, the intention being that once it was finalised there would be no further need to make changes. In *Wider die himelischen Propheten* (1525), the reformer wrote:

> I would like very much to have a German Mass, and I am preoccupied with the idea. But I want it to have a real German quality. If the Latin text is translated and the Latin tones or notes are preserved, I do not object, but it sounds neither agreeable nor correct. Text and notes, accent, melody, and movement must come out of the correct mother tongue and voice. Otherwise everything is a monkey-like imitation.[7]

Without explicitly referring to him, Luther was criticising Thomas Müntzer, whose *Deutsch Euangelisch Messze* (Allstedt: Müntzer, 1524)[8] contained original plainchant melodies superimposed onto the German text (see Figure 2.1).[9] Melismas and long syllables must have sounded bizarre to those accustomed to hearing German sung only in a syllabic style. Luther clearly objected to such a practice, and fear of its gaining popularity must have galvanised him into action. In a sermon in Wittenberg in 1525, Luther announced:

> You have often heard that one should not teach unless one is sure that what is taught is God's Word … Also for this reason I have resisted to make an effort concerning the German Mass for so long, so that I did not become a cause for the gangs of spirits

[5] The *Deutsche Messe* was not actually published until 1526.

[6] Bornert, *Réforme protestante du culte*, p. 5.

[7] 'Jch wolt heute gerne eyne deutsche Messe haben, Jch gehe auch damit umbe, Aber ich wolt ja gerne das sie eyne rechte deutsche art hette, Denn das man den latinischen text verdolmetscht und latinischen don odder noten behellt, las ich geschehen, Aber es laut nicht ertig noch rechtschaffen. Es mus beyde text und notten, accent, weyse und geperde aus rechter mutter sprach und stymme komen, sonst ists alles eyn nachomen, wie die affen thun'. M. Luther, *Wider die himelischen Propheten. Vo[n] den bildern und Sacrament Marti. Luth.* (Wittenberg: Schirlentz, 1525), in *WA*, 18, p. 123. Quoted in F. Blume, trans. F. Ellsworth Peterson, 'The Period of the Reformation', in Blume, ed., *Protestant Church Music – A History* (London: Gollancz, 1975), p. 60.

[8] See P. Matheson, ed., *The Collected Works of Thomas Müntzer* (Edinburgh: Clark, 1988), pp. 180–82.

[9] R. A. Leaver, *Luther's Liturgical Music: Principles and Implications* (Grand Rapids and Cambridge: Eerdmans, 2007), p. 62.

who put their foot in it thoughtlessly; they do not pay attention to whether God wants it so.[10]

We cannot know whether Luther considered the Strasbourg reformers to be one of those thoughtless 'gangs of spirits', but it is clear from this quotation that Luther considered himself to have the talent to produce a German Mass which was pleasing to God – something that, to his mind at least, not every reformer

Figure 2.1 The end of the *Kyrie* and beginning of the *Gloria* from Müntzer's *Deutsch Euangelisch Messze* (Allstedt: Müntzer, 1524), fol. B[v]. The German text of the Mass (except the *Kyrie*, which remained in Greek) was set to plainchant. D HAu – Pon Vg 646, QK. Reproduced by permission of Universitäts- und Landesbibliothek Sachsen-Anhalt, Halle

[10] 'Jhr habt offt gehort, das man nicht leren solle, man wis denn, das es Gottis wort sey … Darumb hab ich mich auch so lang gewert mit der deutsche Messe, das ich nicht ursach gebe den rotten geystern, die hyneyn plumpen unbesunnen, achten nicht, ob es Gott haben wolle'. Quoted and translated in N. H. Petersen, 'Lutheran Tradition and the Medieval Mass', in E. Østrem et al., eds, *The Arts and the Cultural Heritage of Martin Luther* (Copenhagen: Museum Tusculanum Press, 2003), pp. 41–2; *WA*, 17[I], p. 459.

may have possessed. Nevertheless, he did not expect all churches to adopt his model, so long as they had an acceptable Mass order of their own: 'For I do not propose that all of Germany should uniformly follow our Wittenberg order. Even heretofore the chapters, monasteries, and parishes were not alike in every rite'.[11]

As noted in Chapter 1, complaints about music in the pre-Reformation years, although they did feature, were not a priority for Strasbourgeois figures such as Geiler von Kaysersberg, Sebastian Brant, and Jakob Wimpheling. This makes it all the more fascinating that the Protestant reformers found it to be such a vital topic of discussion, a fact that is in no small part due to the writings and sermons of Martin Luther. However, the stance taken by the reformers in Strasbourg (as well as in Nuremberg, Augsburg, and Allstedt, all of which had produced their own vernacular versions of the Mass by the end of 1525[12]) differed from Luther's, inasmuch as they did not seem to be deterred by the Wittenberg reformer's hesitation in formulating his own German Mass. Certainly, the printers in Strasbourg, if not the reformers, were not so concerned with creating the perfect service with a view to retaining the majesty of the Latin of which Luther spoke.[13] They also seemed unconcerned with finding the 'correct' German translation before proceeding. Instead, the priority for Strasbourg in 1524 was to enable laypeople to understand the liturgy and participate in it through song. Song therefore became one of the principal means by which congregations were educated in Scripture and the fundamentals of the Christian religion.

Evidence for such concerns about the 'true' understanding of Christianity began appearing in Strasbourg at the beginning of the 1520s. The *Christeliche verantwortung*[14] was written in 1523 by the reformer Matthias Zell in response to a piece published by the bishop of Strasbourg. In the work, Zell accused clerical singing of being nothing more than 'a cold murmuring without devotion, done out of habit', with an 'ignorance of the Psalms'.[15] This sort of activity helped

---

[11] 'Denn es nicht meynunge ist, das gantze deutsche land so eben müste unser Wittembergische ordnung an nemen. Ists doch auch bis her nie geschehen, das die stiffte, klöster und pfarhen ynn allen stucken gleych weren gewesen'. *WA*, 19, p. 73; translated in *LW*, 53, p. 62. See also Petersen, 'Lutheran Tradition and the Medieval Mass', pp. 36–7.

[12] Leaver, *Luther's Liturgical Music*, p. 292.

[13] In fact, a stable Strasbourg church liturgy did not really occur until the Ecclesiastical Ordinance of 1598 (see Bornert, *Réforme protestante du culte*, pp. 1–3), after almost 75 years of Swiss- and Lutheran-style reforms, Catholic counter-reforms, and, in the second part of the century, orthodox Lutheran reforms.

[14] Zell, *Christeliche verantwortung* (Strasbourg: Köpfel, 1523). The text is also available, with a commentary, in M. Weyer, 'L'*Apologie chrétienne* du réformateur strasbourgeois Matthieu Zell ("*Christeliche Verantwortung*", 1523)', 3 vols (Doctor ès Sciences Religieuses thesis, Université des Sciences Humaines de Strasbourg, 1981), vol. 1.

[15] 'So ist das yetzig betten, singen und lesen nit vil anders dann ein kalt gemürmel, on andacht, gleich uß einer gewonheit, wie ein ander handtůbung, die bŏse lüst und gedåncken nit allezeit ußschleißt, wie auch dises kalt, lewe gemürmel, vorab in den unverstendigen der psalmen, nit allzeit on ist'. Zell, *Christeliche verantwortung*, fol. n2v; Weyer, , 'Apologie chrétienne', vol. 1, p. 103.

'to waste the fruit of the earth', he stated,[16] and was often directed more towards payment than towards God. As evidence, Zell pointed to Ephesians 5:18–20, in which Paul admonishes the people to 'be full of the spirit and speak among each other in psalms and spiritual songs'.[17] Zell placed a great emphasis on the (lack of) training and behaviour of the clergy, complaining that there were too many priests singing and reading, and not enough preaching and carrying out pastoral duties.[18]

> Have you trained [in ministry] so that you can stand there and sing, in order that you are given the *Präsenz*-penny, as any travelling student could do?! Doctors [of religion] exist to be useful to Christianity; they give their jurament and oaths and are awarded their doctorate for this; not so that they stand there like idols.[19]

Zell's condemnation also extended to the Roman Church's interpretation of Scriptures and their treatment of the Gospel. He provided a challenge to his opponents to correct him if he had misspoken in his claim that the Gospel had not been preached correctly for several hundred years: 'It has been preached, but how? It has also been sung, kissed, and held in silver and gold: but how has this helped the poor, hungry souls?'[20] He also parodied Mark 16:15,[21] reminding his readers that 'the Lord did not declare: "Go out into the world and sing so that

[16] 'Desszhalb auch wie nutzlich soliche diener seien anders, weder das sye die frůcht des erdtrichs helffen verzeren, mag ein yeder wol ermessen'. Zell, *Christeliche verantwortung*, fol. F2v; Weyer, 'Apologie chrétienne', vol. 1, p. 232.

[17] Zell, *Christeliche verantwortung*, fol. F3v; Weyer, 'Apologie chrétienne', vol. 1, p. 234.

[18] Weyer, 'Apologie chrétienne', vol. 1, p. 103. This point was also made by Erasmus: 'They chant nowadays in our churches in what is an unknown tongue and nothing else, while you will not hear a sermon once in six months telling people to amend their lives' (*At nunc in nonnullis regionibus totos dies psallitur spiritu, nec modus, nec finis cantionum: quum vix intra sex menses audiatur concio salubris adhortans ad veram pietatem*). See D. Erasmus, *Desiderii Erasmi Roterodami Opera Omnia*, 10 vols (Leiden: Vander, 1703–6), vol. 6, col. 731. Translated and quoted in J. A. Froude, *Life and Letters of Erasmus* (London: Longmans, Green, 1894), p. 116 (new edn p. 130). N.B.: Two editions of Froude's book appeared in this year, with different pagination. The later one claims to be a 'New Edition'.

[19] 'Hastu darumb gestudiert daß du da standest und singest, bitz man dir den presentz-pfennig gibt, das ein yeder bachant wol kůndt ?! Man macht *Doctores*, das sye nütz seient der Christenheit; also lauten jre *iurament* und eyde, so man sye promoviert; nit darumb, das sye da standen, wie die gőtzen'. Zell, *Christeliche verantwortung*, fol. S3r; Weyer, 'Apologie chrétienne', vol. 1, p. 236.

[20] 'Nůn sag hăr, meynstu, ob ich unrecht geredt hette, das Evangelium were in etlich hundert jaren nit recht geprediget worden? Es ist prediget worden, aber wie? Es ist auch gesungen worden, geküsset und in silber und gold gefasset worden : was hat es aber die arme, hungerige seel gehelffen?' Zell, *Christeliche verantwortung*, fol. T1v; Weyer, 'Apologie chrétienne', vol. 1, p. 330. See also Erasmus's observation below, on p. 93.

[21] 'He said to them, "Go into all the world and preach the gospel to all creation"'.

no one may understand and no one might be improved by it", but: "preach the Gospel to all creatures"'.[22]

One early manuscript (written in Bucer's hand), listed 12 points of agreement between the Strasbourg reformers and Martin Luther – points that differed from the conventional Roman theology of the time. In *Dass D. Luthers und seiner nachfolger leer ... christlich und gerecht ist* the Strasbourg reformers concluded that Luther's writings were in accordance with Holy Scripture. The 12 points of agreement concerned the principle of *sola scriptura*, the principle of *sola fide*, dietary laws, the priesthood of all believers, the sacraments, monastic vows, adoration of the saints, purgatory, singing, secular authority, the power of councils, and the abolition of the Mass.[23]

Article 10 is devoted entirely to singing. It reads as follows:

> The tenth [article] is about song, and about how Scripture and everything which Christ has done for us should be accorded with, and that the songs and prayers of the seven offices[24] and others are not Christian.[25] In 1 Corinthians 14:[1–14] it is clearly taught that foreign tongues should not be used in the Christian Church, unless there is someone present who can interpret for the church, so that everyone is edified through it and is able to say 'Amen'. That which one person does should improve their neighbour. And this does not happen now, because even those who read and sing do not know for the most part what they are saying. Furthermore, one sells the precious Word of God for money and uses the people, and this happens for the [redemption from] sin that Christ alone has already accomplished. In addition, much has been sung and read which is not the Divine Word, and instead is therefore detrimental and pernicious. While everything which Scripture teaches is good,[26] that which it doesn't teach is bad, and therefore much is sung and read in the church that is not in accordance with Holy Scripture.[27] Namely, as they pray for God's mercy through the merit of the saints, none of which is deserved; but Christ alone has merited it for us all, and much more.[28]

[22] 'das der herr nit hat gesprochen "Gend hyn in die welt und singen, das niemant verstot, niemant darab gebessert würt", sonder: Predigen das Evangelium allen creaturen'. Zell, *Christeliche verantwortung*, fol. S4v; Weyer, 'Apologie chrétienne', vol. 1, p. 329. Also quoted in Vogeleis, *Quellen und Bausteine*, p. 210.

[23] 1 AST 174, 6, fols 17r–48v, printed in *BDS*, 1, pp. 304–44. See also E. Rummel, ed., with M. Kooistra, *The Correspondence of Wolfgang Capito*, 2 vols (Toronto: University of Toronto Press, 2005–) (hereafter: *CorrCapito*), vol. 2, pp. 53–4. This manuscript has been dated October/November 1523 by *BDS*, but mid-October 1524 by *CorrCapito*.

[24] The seven canonical hours.

[25] This is based on Luther's pronouncements in *An den Christlichen Adel deutscher Nation* (Wittenberg: Lotther, 1520) and *Ad Librum Eximii Magistri* (Wittenberg: Lotther, 1521). See *WA*, 6, pp. 444–5; and *WA*, 7, p. 765.

[26] See 2 Tim. 3:16.

[27] See *WA*, 6, pp. 444–5; and *WA*, 7, p. 765.

[28] 'Zum zehenden folget vom gesang, seiten mal man by der schrifft bleiben soll vnd Christus fur vnss genů gethon hatt, das das gesang vnd gepet der siben zeyt vnd anders nit christlich sein. Dan I. Cor. 14 [1–14] wurdt clerlich gelert, das in frembder sprach in christlicher gemein nyt gelesen soll

Although this text was almost certainly not intended for public consumption, being an unpublished manuscript,[29] many of these concerns were reiterated in Martin Bucer's *Grund und Ursach*, published in 1524, and therefore available to the general populace. In this work, Bucer wrote:

> It has been customary, and continues to be so, that many prescribed songs and prayers are used in the Masses and at the Divine Offices for payment of money, and this is done by those who do not yet know Christ, and is done in many places contrary to the Scriptures, and drawn out of fables, such as: collects and prayers of St. Barbara, St. Catherine, St. Christopher, St. Margaret, St. George and many more.[30]

The opposition to 'fables' did not originate with Bucer, having been appearing in polemical writings for several years, if not decades. Luther had previously complained of the 'unchristian fables and lies' used in church in 'legends, songs, and sermons'.[31] Criticism of fables also occurred in songs, such as 'Merckt jr herren myner sag' (1520).[32] Even seven years before this, however, the craft guilds of Cologne decreed that preachers should 'preach nothing but the true word of God and to utter no lies or fables, rather to be silent altogether and say nothing'.[33]

---

werden, es sy dan alss bald einer do, der es der gemein vssleg, das sy sich alle drab [daran] bessern vnd mögen sprechen amen. Dan was man do thůt, solle zu besserung geschehen der nechsten. Das geschicht nun nit, das auch sy selb, die singen vnd lesen, den meren theil nit wissen, was sy sagen. Darzu verkaufft man die theuren wort gotes vmbs gelt vnd verwent die leut, es geschehe do mit genůg für die sund, das doch Christus allein volbracht hat. Zů dem allen wurdt fil gesungen vnd gelesen, das nit das gotlich wort ist vnd darumb schedlich vnd verterblich. Dan so die schrifft alles gůts hat, můss das böss sein, das sy nit lert, des fil in der kirchen nun gesungen vnd gelesen würdt, das sich mit gotlicher schrifft gar nit vertreyt. Alss nemlich, so sy bitten vmb gotes gnad durch verdienst der heiligen, so sy alle nyt verdient haben, sonder allein Christus fur vnss alle vnd der gleichen fil mer'. 1 AST 174, 6, fol. 44r; *BDS*, 1, pp. 339–40.

29 The editors of *BDS* suggest that it may have been written for Matthäus Zell, in whose house Bucer was living at the time, or else for some members of the city council. See *BDS*, 1, p. 308.

30 'Man hat vil geordnet geseng und gepet in den Messen und siben zeiten umbs gelts willen, bißher getriben und treibents noch, die Christum noch nit kennen. Woͤlchs in vilen orten wider die schrifft und auß fabeln herzogen als collecten und gepet von sant Barbaren, Katherinen, Christofferen, Margareten, Goͤrgen und vilen andern mer'. *BDS*, 1, p. 274; translated in O. F. Cypris, 'Basic Principles: Translation and Commentary of Martin Bucer's *Grund und Ursach*, 1524' (PhD diss., Union Theological Seminary, New York, 1971)', p. 208.

31 'da Gottis wort geschwygen gewesen ist, sind neben eyn komen so viel unchristlicher fabeln und lugen, beyde ynn legenden, gesange und predigen, das greulich ist tzu sehen'. Luther, *Von ordenung gottis dienst yn[n] der gemeyne* (Wittenberg: Cranach & Döring, 1523), printed in *WA*, 12, p. 35. See also J. Herl, *Worship Wars in Early Lutheranism: Choir, Congregation, and Three Centuries of Conflict* (Oxford: Oxford University Press, 2004), p. 193.

32 See Chapter 4.

33 'Grievances and Demands of the Craft Guilds of Cologne' (1513), in G. Strauss, *Manifestations of Discontent in Germany on the Eve of the Reformation* (Bloomington and London: Indiana University Press, 1971), p. 143. The original document is, according to Strauss, in the Cologne city archives: 'Verfassung und Verwaltung', V61, fols 224r–232v.

On the use of foreign languages without an interpreter, and the edification of the whole congregation, Bucer stated that

> they [the Papists] sing and read such prayers and songs in Latin, which the ordinary man cannot understand at all, and they themselves often hardly understand ... And since all the actions of the congregation of God should serve for the edification of every man, we pray and sing nothing except in the common German language, so that the lay people are able to say Amen together as it is taught by the Spirit of God, I Corinthians 14:16.[34]

It was Erasmus who preceded the Protestant reformers in claiming – or perhaps demonstrating – that those who sang the offices and Mass in church often did not understand what they were singing. He perceived that the ordinary listener was unable to distinguish individual voices in church polyphony. No one, either listening or singing, understood what was being sung, and 'what little delight that has been gained soon perishes'. He prophesied that this would continue so long as the congregation agreed with the clergy that singing in this fashion constituted the 'highest form of piety'.[35]

The essential point, however, was that these complaints were in relation to the nature and the language of the texts being sung, rather than the action of singing itself. The problem was that such singing, in some sense, was seen by the Strasbourg reformers as a superstitious ritual or a way of making money,[36] rather than an act of worship and thanksgiving.[37] Around the same time, Wolfgang

---

[34] 'singen und lessen sye solichs zů latein, das der gemein man gar nit und sye offt selb auch wenig verston ... dieweyl, was in der gemein gottes gehandelt würt, jederman in gemein besserlich sein soll, betten noch singen wir nichs, dann in gemeiner teütscher sprach, das der ley gemeincklich möge amen sprechen, wie das der geist gottes lernet, 1. Corinth. 14 [16]'. *BDS*, 1, pp. 274–5; translated in Cypris, 'Basic Principles', pp. 208–9.

[35] 'Ut omittam interim hujusmodi musices genus inductum esse in cultum divinum, ut ne liceat quidem ullam vocem liquido percipere. Nec iis qui cantillant otium est attendendi quid canant. Tantum vocum tinnitus aures ferit, & mox peritura delectatiuncula mulcet. Ferendum & hoc, nisi vulgus Sacerdotum ac Monachorum in hujusmodi rebus summam constitueret pietatem'. Erasmus, *Opera Omnia* (1703–6), vol. 6, col. 731. Translated and quoted in Froude, *Life and Letters of Erasmus*, p. 116 (new edn p. 130). Compare with Luther's estimation of polyphony from 1538: 'Here it is most remarkable that one single voice continues to sing the tenor, while at the same time many other voices play around it, exulting and adorning it in exuberant strains and, as it were, leading it forth in a divine roundelay, so that those who are the least bit moved know nothing more amazing in this world' ('in quo genere hoc excellit, quod vna et eadem voce canitur suo tenore pergente, pluribus interim vocibus circum circa mirabiliter ludentibus, exultantibus et iucundissimis gestibus eandem ornantibus, et velut iuxta eam diuinam quandam choream ducentibus, vt iis, qui saltem modice afficiuntur, nihil mirabilius hoc seculo extare videatur'). *WA*, 50, pp. 372–3; translated in *LW*, 53, p. 324.

[36] The pre-Reformation clerical benefice system comprised multiple sources of income. See F. Rapp, *Réformes et Réformation à Strasbourg : Église et société dans le diocèse de Strasbourg (1450–1525)* (Paris: Ophrys, 1974), pp. 265–79.

[37] See pp. 72–3.

Capito had criticised the medieval Church's 'service and ordinances, such as the Mass, vigils, [and] the singing, reading, and piping of the hours'.[38] Rather than abolishing music altogether, he proposed that the use of singing needed urgent reform.[39]

Later in *Dass D. Luthers*, however, during a criticism of Roman priests' giving of the last rites,[40] the Strasbourg reformers made a radical suggestion. Although oil was to be used in the rite, recovery to good health did not occur because of the oil itself, but rather because of prayer and the grace of the Lord. 'From this shall come the forgiveness of sins', and it was therefore these aspects of the ritual that ought to have been considered sacramental.[41]

By extension, therefore, sung prayer was also to be considered sacramental in certain circumstances. The singing of God's praises could be considered of equivalent value to actions such as the anointing of the sick, and through this suggestion the reformers invited a broader examination of the Roman Church's designation of a sacrament.[42] Indeed, in the *Apology of the Tetrapolitan Confession* of 1531,[43] Bucer conceded that the seven ancient sacraments of the Roman Church might be called 'sacraments', provided that they are celebrated along with sermons and prayers, and that it is understood that human actions do not affect the glory of Christ. On the other hand, he continued, conferring the Holy Spirit by the laying on of hands and prayer was a benefit that had not continued after the time of the Apostles, much like the healing of the sick through the anointing of oil.[44]

It would, of course, be naïve to assume that everyone who favoured reform in Strasbourg at this time was in agreement about how exactly that should come about and what the new church order might entail. At the beginning of the 1520s,

38 'gottes dinst und ordnungen, als Meß, Vigilien, horas singen, lesen, pfeiffen'. W. Capito, *Was man halten unnd antwurten soll von der spaltung zwischen Martin Luther und Andreas Carolstadt* (Strasbourg: Köpfel, 1524). Text available on the website of the Electronic Capito Project, ed. Rummel: http://cf.itergateway.org/capito/Letter224.pdf, p. 73, paragraph 2 (accessed 22 December 2014).

39 Capito was himself an author of three Strasbourg hymn texts, published after 1530. See J. M. Kittelson, *Wolfgang Capito: From Humanist to Reformer* (Leiden: Brill, 1975), p. 142.

40 This was done by Luther himself in *Da captivitate Babylonica ecclesiae* (Wittenberg: Lotthier, 1520). See *WA*, 6, pp. 568–70.

41 'Die gesundtheit aber gibt er nit dem öle, sonder dem gleubigen gepet zů, der gnad des Herrn, do her dan auch kumbt verzyhung der sund. Solt aber dorumb die ölung ein sacrament sein, wie der tauff, so müst das betten vnd psalmen singen auch eins sein'. *BDS*, 1, p. 334.

42 Compare also with Luther's discussion of the use of water in baptism in his Small and Large Catechisms.

43 *Schriftliche Beschirmung vnd verthe- | digung der selbigen Bekantnusz / gegen der Confuta- | tion vnd Widerlegung / so den gesandten der vier | Stätten / vff bemeldtem Reichstage / offen | lich fürgelesen / vnnd hie getrewlich | einbracht ist* (Strasbourg: Schweintzer, 1531).

44 'Mit dem hånd ufflegen und betten den heyligen geyst geben, was eyn gab, die mit der zeit der Apostel hat uffgehört, Wie dann auch die krankken durch das salben mit dem öle gesundt machen und andre sölche wunder gaben mer'. *BDS*, 3, p. 272. See also M. Lienhard, 'Bucer et la Tétrapolitaine', *Bulletin de la Société de l'histoire du protestantisme français*, 126 (1980), pp. 281–2.

the Reformation was still in its embryonic stages, and many sympathisers, whether in Strasbourg or beyond, had not sworn allegiance to any particular side. Desiderius Erasmus, for example, although a very vocal critic of several aspects of the Roman Church, remained steadfast in his belief that the Church needed to be reformed from within. Simultaneously with Luther, Huldrych Zwingli was forming his own opposition to the Roman Church, which was generally more radical than that of other reformers.[45] As scholars and theologians moved from city to city, different ideas were circulated and developed.

Consequently, one Strasbourg manuscript, although in favour of reform, seems remarkably conservative compared to the others. The document, a single page, entitled 'Conclusiones Jacobj', is not listed in Jean Adam's inventory of the Archives du Chapitre Saint-Thomas,[46] and carries no date other than that estimated by the archivists: 'début des années 1520'.[47] Thomas Brady suggests that this document could be by Jakob Sturm, a noble of the city (and the only city councillor to have studied theology),[48] although he acknowledges that equally it could have another origin.[49] In 10 points on a variety of matters, this text defends several things which would not have been acceptable in Strasbourg once the Reformation had been formally established, several years later.

The first and fourth points defend the use of the vernacular in church, while at the same time stressing the need to retain foreign languages. The second criticises the notion of the Mass as a sacrifice. The eighth point concerns images, and the ninth is a defence of clerical marriage. Crucially, in the fifth and sixth points we read that:

> 5. Choir singing, in all churches where it has happened until now, on Sundays, not for the sake of profit but for the sake of the honour of God, is not blasphemy but praise to God.
>
> 6. The introit, *Kyrie eleison*, *Gloria in excelsis*, Epistle, Gospel, Gradual, Alleluia, etc.: Apart from the sacrifice and canon, everything else conceived in the Sunday

---

45 For Zwingli, see U. Gäbler, trans. R. C. L. Gritsch, *Huldrych Zwingli: His Life and Work* (Philadelphia: Fortress Press, 1986); and W. P. Stephens, *The Theology of Huldrych Zwingli* (Oxford: Clarendon Press, 1986).

46 J. Adam, et al., *Inventaire des Archives du Chapitre Saint-Thomas de Strasbourg* (Strasbourg: Imprimerie Alsacienne, 1937).

47 'Beginning of the 1520s'. Annotated in pencil on the document.

48 T. A. Brady, *Ruling Class, Regime and Reformation at Strasbourg, 1520–1555* (Leiden: Brill, 1978), p. 189. On Sturm, see also Brady, *Protestant Politics: Jacob Sturm (1489–1553) and the German Reformation* (Boston: Humanities Press, 1995).

49 Brady, '"Sind also zu beiden theilen christen, des Gott erbarm" : Le mémoire de Jacques Sturm sur le culte publique à Strasbourg (août 1525)', in M. Kroon and M. Lienhard, eds, *Horizons européens de la Réforme en Alsace : Mélanges offerts à Jean Rott pour son 65e anniversaire* (Strasbourg: Istra, 1980), p. 71, n. 21.

> Mass is not an insult to the honour of Christ but a proclamation and a dissemination of his honour.[50]

This was therefore a defence of the Mass in its current form, with the use of a choir – so long as the singing of the choir was carried out as a spiritual, rather than profit-making, exercise. It cannot be said for certain whether these two points were written in response to accusations of choirs blaspheming merely by singing in Latin, but clergymen and choirmen were verbally attacked on multiple occasions on moral and behavioural grounds by the reformers, as shall be seen below.

The Printing Trade[51]

The Roman Mass, however, provided no exciting opportunities for printers, and the prospects for printing liturgical polyphony and plainchant at this time were non-existent. The printing trade was, though, of vital importance to the success of the Reformation and its music (and vice-versa). Religious books were being printed in Strasbourg as early as 1466, when the first German bible was published by Johannes Mentelin. Other printers in the city followed suit.[52] From around 1508, the printing industry began a period of acceleration. During the 1520s, Reformation writings, especially those by Luther, dominated the market.[53] Several printers began competing to publish liturgical orders containing music, in an output unseen elsewhere in Germany at the time. This has no doubt something to do with the sense of progression of Strasbourg's reforms, and suggests that very early on there was an awareness that music would become an increasingly important part of any new liturgy. Many, but not

---

50 '5 Daß korgsang byßher sonder am sontag in allen kÿrchen wo es nit vmß gwÿns wÿllen sonder vm der ehre Gottes wÿllen geschehen ist, ist nit ein Gotts lesterung sonder Gotts lob

6 Jntroit Kyrieleÿson, gloria in excelsis, Epistel Eua[n]geliu[m] gradual all[elui]a. &c Vßgeno[m]en die oppfren vn[nd] Canon sonst alles begriffen jn der sontag meß jst nit ein schmelerung der ehre Christj sonder ein vßrüeffen vn[nd] vßbreÿtten seiner ehre'. 1 AST 75, 3.

51 Jean Rott has published a 'family tree' of Strasbourg printers. See J. Rott, 'Note sur l'imprimerie alsacienne aux XVe et XVIe siècles', *Revue d'Alsace*, 95 (1956), between pp. 72 and 73.

52 Bornert, *Réforme protestante du culte*, p. 610. L. J. Abray, *The People's Reformation: Magistrates, Clergy, and Commons in Strasbourg, 1500–1598* (Oxford: Blackwell, 1985), pp. 22–3, also refers to early Strasbourg editions of the Bible, but mistakenly states that the Mentelin Bible was in Latin.

53 M. U. Chrisman, 'Printing and the Evolution of Lay Culture in Strasbourg 1480–1599', in R. P. Hsia, ed., *The German People and the Reformation* (Ithaca and London: Cornell University Press, 1988), p. 84. See Pope Adrian VI's plea that the Strasbourg authorities stay true to the old faith, and not allow Luther's works to be printed (H. Virck, *Politische Correspondenz der Stadt Strassburg im Zeitalter der Reformation*, 2 vols (Strasbourg: Trübner, 1882–87), vol. 1, p. 77. Luther's translation of the Psalms appeared in 1524 (Luther, *Der Psalter Teutsch* (Strasbourg: Köpfel, 1524)).

all, were sympathetic to the new faith, but all of them had realised that printing such material could be a profitable exercise.

Johann Schwan ran his business on a small scale, producing 23 editions in his name.[54] Four of these were books containing music, all published in 1525, including the important *Ordnung des Herren Nachtmal*.[55] In addition, he produced some publications associated with the Anabaptist movement.[56] When Johann Knobloch I, another early printer, died in 1528, his son, Johann Knobloch II, took over the shop.[57] Calvin's 1539 publication of metrical psalms, *Aulcuns pseaulmes et cantiques mys en chant*, was advertised as having been produced 'en l'imprimerie de Jean Knobloch jun'.[58] Another small business was that of Jakob Frölich, who specialised in printing vernacular literature. During the 1530s he was responsible for the printing of Katharina Schütz Zell's four volumes of hymns by the Bohemian Brethren, and he also published popular songs in later years. Peter Schöffer first began printing music in Mainz in 1512, later working in Worms, Strasbourg, Basel, and Venice.[59] In Strasbourg he undertook the publication of a great number of Protestant (including Anabaptist) texts.[60] In 1534 Schöffer began a partnership with the younger printer Matthias Biener, or Apiarius. Far from being of any obvious financial benefit to the older printer, Apiarius instead provided him with specialised musical knowledge and contacts in the music world. This lasted until 1537, when Apiarius ended the alliance.[61]

By far the most productive printer of liturgical books in the first years of the Reformation was Wolfgang Köpfel. He began his trade in Strasbourg in 1522, when he printed four works by Luther, followed by five more the following year. His two editions of the *Teutsch Kirchenampt* were published in 1524 along with further works by Luther and by the Strasbourg reformers. This fruitful career continued until his death in about 1554.[62] Köpfel, whose workshop in Strasbourg was financially supported by Wolfgang Capito, who was also a relative of the printer,[63] enjoyed close associations with the reforming movement, a link which probably provided him with some protection in the early years of his career, and enabled him to became the 'semi-official' printer of the Reformation

---

[54] Chrisman, *Lay Culture, Learned Culture*, p. 3.

[55] See below, pp. 79–81.

[56] Chrisman, *Lay Culture, Learned Culture*, p. 34.

[57] Ibid., p. 17.

[58] Ibid., p. 17, n. 63.

[59] Catalogue of the exhibition 'Musik in Bern zwischen Spätmittelalter und Reformation', Universitätsbibliothek, Bern, 29 June to 13 October 2007, p. 31. His father, of the same name, had been an employee of Johannes Gutenberg.

[60] Chrisman, *Lay Culture, Learned Culture*, pp. 35, 157.

[61] Catalogue of the exhibition 'Musik in Bern zwischen Spätmittelalter und Reformation', p. 31.

[62] Rott, 'Koepf(f)el, Wolfgang', in C. Baechler et al., eds, *Nouveau dictionnaire de biographie alsacienne*, 49 vols (Strasbourg: Fédération des sociétés d'histoire et d'archéologie d'Alsace, 1982–2007), vol. 22, pp. 2069–71.

[63] Rott, 'Note sur l'imprimerie alsacienne', p. 71.

in Strasbourg.[64] Most of the treatises written by Bucer and Capito were published in Köpfel's workshop. He also printed several propaganda pamphlets in English (presumably on behalf of English reformists who would have endangered themselves if they had printed such material at home),[65] as well as a Greek version of the Psalms in 1524.[66]

The modern printing press had been a German invention, and was therefore intrinsically linked with a growing nationalist sentiment, which was being exploited by Luther and the reformers. Such a sentiment also surrounded the idea of a German Mass, in which singing should occur in the mother tongue, for the people of the nation.[67]

The Dawn of Congregational Singing

During November 1524, the preachers produced a proposal for the Lord's Supper in which the whole congregation was to sing some psalms, the *Kyrie eleison*, and *Gloria in excelsis*,[68] as well as a setting of the Ten Commandments. After the sermon, the people were to 'take up' the confession of faith: *Credo in unum Deum*. The priest (*prespyter*) would then proceed to the Preface, and then the *Sanctus*. He was to remind the people that Communion was observed 'in memory of the death of Christ'. The general prayers were followed by the Lord's Prayer and *Agnus Dei*, and then 'Gott sey gelobet' was sung.[69]

---

[64] Chrisman, *Lay Culture, Learned Culture*, p. 31.

[65] See A. F. Johnson, 'English books printed abroad', *The Library*, 5th series, 4 (1950), pp. 273–6. Sixteen English books had been printed in Strasbourg by 1556, according to A. Wolff-Hoffmann, 'L'Influence de l'hymnodie strasbourgeoise sur l'Eglise d'Angleterre à ses débuts, par l'intégration de mélodies dans des recueils de cantiques publiés entre 1535 et 1610', 2 vols (Master's diss., Université de Paris X Nanterre, 2006), vol. 1, p. 22.

[66] See J. B. Riederer, *Nachrichten zur Kirchen- Gelehrten- und Bücher-Geschichte; aus gedruckten und ungedruckten Schriften*, 4 vols (Altdorf: Schüpfel, 1764–68), vol. 4, pp. 382–3.

[67] It is intriguing that Luther claims that people from many countries have asked him to undertake such a task (see above).

[68] 'Mox canit ecclesia psalmu[m] alique[m], Kyrieleison, Gloria in ex[celsis]'. 1 AST 40, 1, p. 7; *BDS*, 3, p. 408.

[69] 'Cuius ubi finem fecit, canit rursu[s] Ecclesia, uel X. praecepta, uel ps[almum] alique[m], postea prespyter Suggestu[m] conscendit, ex Euangelicis hystorijs populo p[rae]dicaturus, iusta concione, qua[m] plebs confessione fidei 'Credo in vnu[m] Deum', suscipit. Rursu[s] p[re]sbyter versus plebem, hortatur, vt se ipsos d[omin]o offerant et vitulos labroru[m] suoru[m], Et mox ad p[rae]fatione[m] p[er]git, adiungit 'sanctus' et precationem, pro magistratu[m] et tota ecclesia, quam finit, in verbis Eua[n]gelistaru[m] de coena d[omi]nica. Narrans aut[em] verba Christi, ut antea solit[us] fuit, panem et calice[m] eleuans pop[u]lo ostendit. Mox precatur rurs[us] paucis, et simul explicat, ad quid habenda sit memoria mortis Christi, cuj preci subiungit oratione[m] d[omi]nicam, Agnus dei, postea com[m]unicat, cu[m] aliquib[us]. Ilico canit Ecclesia Got sy gelobet'. 1 AST 40, 1, p. 7; *BDS*, 3, p. 408.

At exactly the same time, the preachers wrote to both Luther[70] and Zwingli,[71] outlining their version of the same service.[72] Both letters explained the format of the Strasbourg service in equal detail, and very similarly to the proposal above. In their letter to Zwingli, Bucer and Capito expressed their desire for conformity on ceremonies such as baptism and the celebration of the Lord's Supper, and explained the format that had been adopted in Strasbourg. They complained that since the beginning of the reforms in Strasbourg, people had been publishing their own, unauthorised liturgies for the Eucharist, for the sole purpose of making money.[73] Because of this, there was confusion in the churches. Some items, such as German psalms, and the *Kyrie* and *Gloria*, had been printed in these books, again without permission.[74] Thus, it becomes clear that the very first printed Protestant liturgies in Strasbourg were not commissioned by the reformers, but were more likely to have been attempts by opportunistic publishers to profit from the uncertain situation and lack of any official decree on the matter. The printer Wolfgang Köpfel himself admitted this in his preface to the *Straszburger Kirchenampt* (1525), when he stated that he 'and others have often printed the church order as it was first carried out by our preachers and priests, against their will'.[75] He defended his actions, however, by arguing that 'the congregation was so impatient to read'.[76]

René Bornert has noticed that the descriptions of the liturgy in these letters do not match up completely with the format found in the printed service books.[77] Fascinatingly, the letters specified that 'the whole church' (*ecclesia tota*) was

70 Zentralbibliothek, Weimar: Q 16 (Spalatiniana II), fols 648v–660v. Printed in Rott et al., eds., *Correspondance de Martin Bucer*, 5 vols (Leiden: Brill, 1979–) (hereafter: *CorrBucer*), vol. 1, pp. 288–97.

71 Staatsarchiv, Zurich: E II 347, no. 10, pp. 5–12. Printed in *CorrBucer*, 1, pp. 281–7.

72 The correspondence also provided an explanation of the positions taken with regard to Andreas Bodenstein von Karlstadt's symbolic view of the Eucharist and rejection of infant baptism. Karlstadt, a former ally of Luther, had been banished from Saxony after becoming more extreme in his views and, in the opinion of Luther and his allies, for undermining Luther's authority. Although Bucer had begun his Protestant life agreeing with Luther's view of the Eucharist, continued exposure to the interpretation that Christ was only symbolically present in the Eucharist led to his accepting this version of events.

73 'nam ab initio vnusquisque dere suum morem habebat. Hinc est varietas in libellis, quos, de caenae dominicae ritu nostro, nobis ignorantibus, typographi, dum suo student lucro, excuderunt'. Staatsarchiv, Zurich: E II 347, no. 10, p. 6; *CorrBucer*, 1, p. 282.

74 'Ilico ecclesia tota canit aliquem psalmum germanice, postea Kyrie et Gloria, omnia germanice, vt forte in libellis hic absque nostro iussu editis legistis'. Staatsarchiv, Zurich: E II 347, no. 10, p. 9; *CorrBucer*, 1, p. 285.

75 'Jch vnd andere / haben das kirchen ampt wie es von vnsern predicanten vnd pfarherrn erstlich fürgenomen / offt getruckt / wider iren willen vn[nd] gehelle'. *Strasz- | burger kirchen | ampt / nemlich von Jnse- | gu[n]g d[er] Eeleüt / vom Tauf | vnd vo[n] des herre[n] nacht | mal / mit etlicher Psal | men / die am end des | bůchlins / orden- | lich verzeych- | net sein* (Strasbourg: Köpfel, 1525), fol. Aij^r; *Hubert*, p. 140.

76 'die gemein begirig was sollichs zů lesen'. *Straszburger Kirchenampt*, fol. Aij^r; *Hubert*, p. 141.

77 Bornert, *Réforme protestante du culte*, p. 111.

to sing not only the psalms but also the *Kyrie*, the *Gloria*, and the *Credo*.[78] The congregational singing of the *Kyrie* and the *Credo*, at least, were confirmed by a letter written by Gérard Roussel (who had taken refuge in Strasbourg along with Jacques Lefèvre d'Étaples) to an acquaintance in Meaux, describing worship in Strasbourg in December 1525. In the letter, Roussel explained that 'the Creed is sung by everyone … During Communion, and while everyone receives their part of the supper, everyone sings the *Kyrie eleison* as a hymn of thanksgiving for the benefit received'.[79] That the *Kyrie* was sung during Communion contradicts the reformers' own description in the letters, but it is possible that it was sung once at the beginning of the service and again during the distribution of the bread and wine, or indeed that singing it during Communion was a practice peculiar to certain churches (in any case, Roussel's letter was an entire year later; a great deal could have changed in that time). The fact that the whole church sang the *Credo* is curious, as liturgical orders from this time, despite directing the congregation to sing, did not provide music for this part of the service.

In a reply to the Strasbourg preachers dated 16 December 1524, Zwingli revealed that he and his colleagues approved of the singing of psalms in the vernacular, if indeed it was pleasing for the whole church (*toti ecclesię*) to do so.[80] Although it cannot exactly be called an unconditional approval of church music, this quotation nevertheless stands in opposition to the traditional view of Zwingli as a man vehemently opposed to any sort of music in church. According to Ulrich Gäbler, the reformer's reputation for being anti-music began in the early 1520s, when he made negative comments aimed mainly at the choral chanting of priests and monks. This was done in the context of a criticism of other traditional practices including the use of images and vestments, which could distract people from the true spirit of their religion. However, the content of this letter certainly refutes Gäbler's claims that 'what Zwingli thought about the early Protestant church musical practices … is not known', and that 'Zwingli made no effort to encourage congregational singing, for instance,

[78] Staatsarchiv, Zurich: E II 347, no. 10, pp. 9–10; *CorrBucer*, 1, pp. 285–6. The letter to Luther also mentions the *Sanctus* and the *Agnus Dei*, but does not specify by whom these texts are sung. See Zentralbibliothek, Weimar, ms. Q 16, fol. 656r; *CorrBucer*, p. 293. Bornert notes that the *Sanctus* had disappeared from the Strasbourg liturgy by 1526 (Bornert, *Réforme protestante du culte*, p. 543). The form of the liturgy set out in these letters is very similar to that given in *Grund und Ursach* (1524) (see Cypris, 'Basic Principles', pp. 149–51).

[79] 'canitur symbolum ab omnibus … Dum fit communio et suam quisque cœnæ portionem accipit, canitur ab omnibus *kyrie eleeson*, hoc veluti hymno agentibus gratias pro accepto beneficio'. Letter from Gérard Roussel to Nicolas Le Sueur (December 1525), printed in A.-L. Herminjard, ed., *Correspondance des réformateurs dans les pays de langue française*, 9 vols (Geneva: Georg; Paris: Levy, 1866–97), vol. 1, p. 413. See also below, p. 64.

[80] 'Quę de cantionibus Germanicis ac psalmis scribitis, fratribus omnibus placent, quę vero de missa, non vndequaque probantur ; nam hoc sacramentum aliud non est quam cęlebris gratulatio et confędcratio [consideratio]. Quam igitur toti ecclesię ipsam cęlebrare placebit, cęlebretur, ac interim detur opera, vt, quod Paulo inconsultius ędificatum est, maiore consilio melioreque soluatur'. Zurich Staatsarchiv: E I 3.1, no. 10, fol. 6v; *CorrBucer*, 1, p. 313.

singing Psalms'.[81] Clearly, Zwingli was supportive of the Strasbourg reformers' attempts to introduce congregational singing, and perhaps even saw it as a way in which the Church could be built up according to Paul's commandments.[82] Some evidence for Zwingli's more moderate approach to music is available in two other letters from 1530 and 1531,[83] in which Capito asked Zwingli to send him songs written by the latter – 'even those composed for the lute'.[84]

Strasbourg's liturgy printing industry took off almost immediately following the celebration of Diobald Schwarz's German Mass in the cathedral on 16 February 1524.[85] Surprisingly, in that year alone there were at least eight publications for use in the new Protestant liturgy.[86] With one exception (a liturgy for baptism), these publications appeared under one of three titles (with various deviations in spelling): *Teutsche Mess*,[87] *Teutsch Kirchenampt*, and *Ordenung vnd inhalt Teutscher Mess*. All of these are presumed to have been printed without the approval of the reformers. Of these eight early liturgies, six appear not to have contained any printed music. Of the two that did contain music (both editions of the *Teutsch Kirchenampt*), one was at some time held in the collection of the Bibliothèque nationale et universitaire in Strasbourg,[88] but is now lost.[89] Therefore, the only remaining example of an original 1524 Strasbourg publication with music is the first edition of the *Teutsch Kirchenampt*.[90]

---

[81] Gäbler, *Huldrych Zwingli*, pp. 107–8.

[82] Zwingli repeated his comments about singing church songs in the vernacular in 1525 (M. Jenny, *Luther, Zwingli, Calvin in ihren Liedern* (Zurich: Theologischer Verlag, 1983), p. 175. See also Jenny, 'Kirchenlied, Gesangbuch und Kirchenmusik', in G. Bott, ed., *Martin Luther und die Reformation in Deutschland* (Frankfurt am Main: Insel, 1983), p. 302).

[83] Staatsarchiv, Zurich: E II 349, fol. 204v (27 September 1530) (E. Egli et al., eds., *Zwinglis Briefwechsel*, 5 vols (Zurich, 1911–1935) (hereafter: *ZwBw*), vol. 5, pp. 161–3); and E II 349, fols 195–197 (22 January 1531) (*ZwBw*, 5, pp. 312–316). See also *CorrCapito* 2, pp. 435–6, 449.

[84] 'Mitte cantiones, sed compositas etiam ad testudinem, si tibi est, qui talibus curis distringendus. Nam vides, opinor, quam seria mediter sub tanto incendio. Sed amo tua, mi frater ac domine'. Staatsarchiv, Zurich: E II 349, fol. 204v; *ZwBw*, 5, p. 163. As the editors of *ZwBw* observe, nothing further is known about these songs. It is not even clear whether 'lute songs' literally meant social songs with lute accompaniment, or else serious songs such as hymns, especially if Capito's request relates in any way to Strasbourg's liturgical aspirations (see *ZwBw*, 5, p. 163, n. 12).

[85] See p. 36.

[86] *Hubert*, pp. XI–XIII.

[87] See description in T. W. Röhrich, *Geschichte der Reformation im Elsass und besonders in Strassburg: nach gleichzeitigen Quellen bearbeitet*, 3 vols (Strasbourg: Heitz, 1830–32), vol. 1, pp. 208–9 (including n. 18).

[88] Hereafter: BNUS.

[89] However, in 1848 this book was reprinted by Karl Reinthaler in the second half of a volume also containing a copy of the Erfurt *Enchiridion* of 1525 (see p. 84, n. 230 for full title). Copies of this facsimile can be found in the British Library and the BNUS.

[90] *Teütsch | Kirchen ampt / | mit lobgesengen / vn[nd] gőtlich | en psalmen / wie es die ge | mein zu Strasbourg | singt vn[nd] halt / gantz | Christlich* (Strasbourg: Köpfel, 1524), Bayerische Staatsbibliothek, Munich, classmark: Rar. 1085. This volume is not lost, as stated in *RISM DKL* and in Hobbs, 'Connaissances bibliques, religion populaire: les premiers psaumes versifiés de la Réforme à Strasbourg 1524–1527', *Revue d'histoire et de philosophie religieuses*, 78 (1998), p. 421.

These publications were catalogued in various ways during the nineteeth and twentieth centuries. Friedrich Hubert, in his 1900 volume on Strasbourg's liturgical orders of the Reformation,[91] provided basic bibliographical information on each of the publications that were known to him. Martin Vogeleis's 1911 publication did likewise.[92] As these two books provide details of orders both with and without music – unlike publications such as *RISM DKL*, which only lists volumes containing printed music – it is possible to compare them so as to see how music was integrated into the process of adapting and modifying the liturgy.

It is curious that publishers should have gone to the trouble of printing books both with and without musical notation, especially at the dawn of congregational singing in the city.[93] It may have been that, because of the costs involved in printing music, printers would often choose not to print a song with music if it had already been printed in another recent book, saving themselves time, space, and money.[94] Reformation publications, as Kyle Sessions has observed, combined musical memory with a print medium.[95] Leaving aside issues of music and textual literacy for now,[96] it is important to remember that these initial liturgical orders were published a matter of months after the introduction of the vernacular language in church. A variety of factors therefore makes the lack of music in some editions less surprising. First, owing to the technology involved, books with music would have been considerably more expensive to produce, which in turn made them more expensive to buy.[97] If sales of the editions with music had not been as high as the printers had hoped, the decision may have

However, Vogeleis (*Quellen und Bausteine*, p. 213) suggests that there were in fact two 1524 editions with this exact title. No further evidence of this second book was found, so it is considered here not to have existed. It is nevertheless acknowledged that the ordering of the two verified 1524 editions of *Teutsch Kirchenampt* (see Appendix A) is open to some debate. See G. Birkner, 'Zur Chronologie und Abhängigkeit der ältesten Quellen des deutschen evangelischen Kirchenlieds', in *Jahrbuch für Liturgik und Hymnologie*, 12 (1967), p. 135; and K. Ameln, 'Zur Frage der Datierung des "Teutsch Kirchenampt"', in *Jahrbuch für Liturgik und Hymnologie*, 12 (1967), p. 148. For the purposes of clarity, the ordering adopted by *RISM DKL* will be used in this book.

[91] See p. 36, n. 134.

[92] See p. 44, n. 3.

[93] Hubert writes of the first edition (*RISM DKL* no. 1524[15]) that it contains, apart from a few interjections, only songs, consistently printed with music. *Hubert*, p. XIII.

[94] See, for example, the direction given on fol. Bvi^v of the 1525 *Ordnung des Herren Nachtmal*: 'Darnach singt man dz lobgsang / Gott sey gelobet' ('Then the song of praise "Gott sey gelobet" is sung'), after which neither the words nor the music for this hymn are given (see Figure 2.2).

[95] K. C. Sessions, 'Song Pamphlets: Media Changeover in Sixteenth-Century Publicization', in G. P. Tyson and S. S. Wagonheim, eds, *Print and Culture in the Renaissance* (Newark: University of Delaware Press; London: Associated University Presses, 1986), p. 116.

[96] This will be discussed in Chapter 4.

[97] On the varying techniques used to print early music, see S. Boorman et al., 'Printing and publishing of music, §I: Printing', in D. Root, ed., *Grove Music Online* (www.oxfordmusiconline.com) (accessed 10 June 2014). In Strasbourg, both staff lines and notes were usually printed together in one woodblock imprint.

been taken to remove just the music in subsequent editions (and therefore reduce costs), rather than to withdraw the book altogether. Second, since many of the earliest liturgies were not published with the consent of the clergy, they would have been aimed at a market of individuals, rather than churches.[98] Third, and perhaps most significantly, any singing by the whole congregation would have been a new and probably unsettling experience, and the melodies used would not all have been familiar. Leaver observes that at the introduction of Luther's hymns into the Strasbourg liturgy in 1524, many were set to Strasbourg tunes instead of those to which they were sung in Wittenberg.[99] However, as tunes were mostly being learnt from scratch, it would have made very little difference to the musically illiterate majority whether or not the printed notes were on the page in front of them. For cantors and for those who could read music, as long as editions of the book with music existed, these could be referred to when needed. If, as Bucer had wished, the tunes were first taught to the congregations by cantors leading the singing[100] (the method adopted by Geneva in the 1540s[101]), the learning of melodies would in any case principally have been an issue of aural, rather than visual, transmission.

Hubert correctly observes that the first edition of the *Teutsch Kirchenampt* consists almost entirely of musical notation (with very little actual liturgy), but also suggests that it was designed as 'a little musical handbook for use in worship or for the education of children by their teachers'.[102] This implies that there was some special role for children in liturgical singing. However, there is no evidence to suggest that children were being taught to lead singing in church in Strasbourg until the 1530s.[103] There can be no doubt, however, that the book

[98] Blume suggests that in Germany, on account of 'the high cost of printing and the limited editions that were brought out … not every member of the congregation had a songbook in his hand during the service' (Blume, 'The Period of the Reformation', p. 46). Although not refuting this statement, Chrisman nevertheless observes that hymn books feature among the publications most likely to be owned by common people (Chrisman, *Lay Culture, Learned Culture*, pp. 154–5), while Markus Jenny claims that in some areas of Germany hymn books were used as prayer manuals in a domestic environment, being more affordable than bibles (Jenny, 'Kirchenlied, Gesangbuch, und Kirchenmusik', p. 311). Blume's opinion is contradicted by the situation at the French refugee church in Strasbourg some years later. The account of one refugee from the early 1540s states that 'everyone has a music book in his hand' (*chascun a vng libvre de musicque en sa main / tant ho[m]me que fe[m]me*). 1 AST 41, II, fol. 5v. Also quoted in A. Erichson, *L'Église française de Strasbourg au seizième siècle d'après des documents inédits* (Paris: Fischbacher, 1886), p. 21.

[99] Leaver, *'Goostly psalmes and spirituall songes': English and Dutch Metrical Psalms from Coverdale to Utenhove 1535–1566* (Oxford: Clarendon Press, 1991), pp. 29–30.

[100] Bucer, 'Rathschlag' (1526) (1 AST 38, 3, fols 88r–88v; *BDS*, 2, pp. 470–71).

[101] See Trocmé-Latter, 'The Psalms as a Mark of Protestantism: the Introduction of Liturgical Psalm-Singing in Geneva', *Plainsong & Medieval Music*, 20 (2011), pp. 145–63.

[102] 'Die erste Ausgabe … besteht fast nur aus Gesängen mit Noten und scheint so ein musikalisches Handbüchlein zur Benutzung beim Gottesdienst oder auch beim Unterricht der Kinder durch die Lehrmeister und Lehrfrauen gewesen zu sein', *Hubert*, p. LXVIII.

[103] See Chapter 3, pp. 150–54.

was intended to be used during the service. Joseph Herl has noted the significant mention of the congregation (*wie es die gemein zu Straßburg*) in the title of the *Teutsch Kirchenampt*.[104]

The introit (an extract from Psalm 119) as well as the subsequent *Kyrie eleison* and *Gloria in excelsis Deo* were all sung, as they were in liturgical orders of subsequent years. The first printed instruction occurs only after the announcement of the sermon: 'Here, the preacher gives a sermon, and after the sermon the *Credo* is sung'.[105] The music for the Apostles' Creed is given, and in the second and third editions this is followed by that of the Nicene Creed (intended to be sung as an alternative). Hubert shows that in the book's third edition (1525), a paragraph of alternative text is inserted, informing us that the priest[106] was to speak the *Nunc dimittis* or else the congregation was to sing. All three versions, after Communion, contain Luther's adaptation of the hymn 'Gott sey gelobet'.[107] Hubert also traces the development of this liturgy from an earlier version of the Mass in 1524, *Ordenung vnd ynhalt Teutscher Mess*, published anonymously by Köpfel.[108] The contents of the *Teutsch Kirchenampt* are a reduced form of the *Ordenung*, although some elements were clearly adopted from it, including the Apostles' Creed, the Alleluia, the Song of Thanksgiving, and the introit.[109]

It is worth considering whether liturgical orders were always printed with the intention of being sung, or whether some services were still intended to be wholly spoken. The chance of the latter option becomes less likely as the 1520s progress, as communal singing became an increasingly vital aspect of the evangelical service. Earlier, though, this would have been theoretically possible. As far as we know, the *Sanctus*, *Benedictus*, and *Agnus Dei* were never sung congregationally in the early evangelical liturgy, as there are never any melodies alongside their vernacular translations. However, the final 1524 edition of the *Ordenung vnd ynhalt Teutscher Mess* contains different liturgical prefaces for the seasons of Christmas, Easter, Ascension, and Pentecost. In the general liturgy, the preface ends with the words: 'bitten wir mit vndertheniger bekantnüß

[104] Herl, *Worship Wars*, p. 97.

[105] 'Hie prediget der pfarrher / vnd nach der predig singt man das Credo. Patrem'. *Teutsch Kirchenampt* (*RISM DKL* no. 1524[15]), fol. Av[r]. The subsequent two editions of this book instead read 'Folget die predig; darnach der glaub', and 'Darnach volgt der glaub', respectively. See *Hubert*, p. 79.

[106] The term 'priester' is still being used, rather than 'diener', which appears in later liturgies.

[107] *Hubert*, p. 81. See Appendix D for the text to this hymn.

[108] This appeared in three editions (see Appendix A), the enlarged third version of which was entitled: *Ordenung vnd | yn[n]halt Teütscher Mess vn[nd] | Vesper / So yetzund im ge | brauch haben Euangeli- | sten vnd Christlichen Pfarr | herren zů Straßburg. | Mit etlichen Neüwen ge- | schrifftlichen Jntroit / Ge- | bet / Vorred oder Prefation | vnd Canon / vor vnd nach | vffhebu[n]g des Sacrame[n]ts / | auch andren ordenunge[n] / in | vorigem bůchlin nit | begriffen* (Strasbourg: Köpfel, 1524). The copy consulted, and indeed the only surviving example, is in the Bibliothèque Wilhelmitana, Médiathèque protestante, Strasbourg.

[109] *Hubert*, p. LXVIII.

/ vn[nd] sagen. ¶ Sanctus. Heyliger / heyliger / heyliger herr'[110] (that is, the direction given is that the *Sanctus* should be spoken). In the prefaces for all the other seasons except Pentecost, the direction is also given to speak this part of the service,[111] but in that for Pentecost, the preface follows these words: 'Des halb mit außtringenden frewden / in alle[m] erdtrych / die welt sich frewet / auch die Engel deyn lob *syngen vnd sprechen*. Sanctus (das ist) Heyliger / heyliger / heyliger. &c'. (my emphasis on 'syngen vnd sprechen').[112] Although this may not have had any bearing on practice, it is interesting to note the inclusion of the word 'syngen' in this particular phrase.

Furthermore, Hubert comments that in the Eucharistic liturgy of the 1524 *Ordenung*, Luther's hymn 'Gott sey gelobet' is perhaps the first church song to be spoken rather than sung.[113] However, this appears unlikely; 'Gott sey gelobet' was almost certainly sung, whether or not a tune was printed alongside. First, the order of Mass in this publication is relatively free from instructions of any sort, consisting mostly of continuous sections of prose. Therefore, a distinction would not necessarily have been made between those parts of the service that were sung and those that were said. Second, Luther's hymn is likely to have already been well known in Strasbourg, having previously been published in the *Enchiridions* of Erfurt.[114] These volumes were compiled from individual broadsheets and therefore 'Gott sey gelobet' as a printed hymn is likely to have first appeared in broadsheet form (albeit probably without music).[115] Both its tune and its text are also known to have existed during the fifteenth century.[116] It seems highly unlikely that the congregations would have spoken the words to a hymn when there was a tune available, even if that tune had not yet been printed in a Strasbourg liturgical book. The same can be said of the six hymns printed, again without music, in the order for Vespers in the *Ordenung*. There would have been little point printing these songs in verse, had the intention been to speak them rather than sing them. Therefore, a lack of written direction to sing cannot, at least in the early liturgies, be taken as a sure sign that singing did *not* take place.[117]

---

110 *Ordenung vnd yn[n]halt Teütscher Mess vn[nd] Vesper* (1524), fol. Aviij^v.

111 'Deßhalb wir mit den Engeln vnnd allen hym[m]elischen hårscharen / dir syngen on vnderlaß / den breyß deyner ere / vn[nd] sagent. Sanctus (dz ist) Heyliger heyliger &c'. *Ordenung vnd yn[n]halt Teütscher Mess vn[nd] Vesper* (1524), fols Cij^v–Ciij^r, emulated in the following prefaces on fols Ciij^r and Ciij^v.

112 L. Büchsenschütz, *Histoire des liturgies en langue allemande dans l'église de Strasbourg au XVIe siècle* (Cahors: Coueslant, 1900), pp. 59–60.

113 *Hubert*, p. LXVII.

114 See below, p. 84.

115 Leaver, *Luther's Liturgical Music*, p. 19, n. 69.

116 Ameln, *The Roots of German Hymnody of the Reformation Era* (St Louis: Concordia, 1964), p. 9.

117 Within the wider discussion of the words *singen* and *sagen*, it should be remembered that the Latin word *dicere* was often used not only to mean 'to say', but also 'to sing'. However, there is

Gérard Roussel spoke fondly of the singing of congregations in his correspondence from the end of 1525. He described the practice of assembling twice a day to sing psalms, and spoke of the delightful sound made by the singing of the women mixing with that of the men.[118] Admittedly, however, it is highly implausible that congregational singing was introduced into the service overnight, with hymn texts spoken one day and sung the next. The introduction of singing was gradually implemented, and the lack of instruction in this order of service suggests only that churches had some choice in the matter at this stage.[119]

The Books and their Prefaces

Hymn books and liturgical orders of this time often included one or more forewords to the reader.[120] These were by no means an invention of the Reformation, although they became a useful tool at a time when the printing press was undergoing considerable growth. Prefaces were the principal means by which printers – or theologians or other scholars who had endorsed a particular book – would communicate with their readers by providing a message of introduction or explaining the necessity for a particular publication. They were especially useful in the case of the Reformation, for polemical reasons, to explain and justify changes to the liturgy. At first, prefaces to these liturgical books made little or no reference to singing or music; gradually, as music became a more

no indication that this practice spread into the German language. The J. and W. Grimm *Deutsches Wörterbuch* (Leipzig: Hirzel, 1854–1965) entries for *singen* and *sagen* both mention the increasing frequency of the phrase 'singen und sagen', around this time, but *sagen* is never defined as meaning 'to sing'.

118 Letters from Gérard Roussel to the Bishop of Meaux and to Nicolas Le Sueur (December 1525), printed in Herminjard, *Correspondance des réformateurs*, vol. 1, pp. 406–7, 411–12. In a 1991 paper, Christian Meyer asserted that there is no evidence for congregational singing, apart from these accounts by Roussel, during this period (later published as C. Meyer, 'Gesangbuch, darin begriffen sind ... Martin Bucer et le chant liturgique', in C. Krieger and Lienhard, eds, *Martin Bucer and Sixteenth Century Europe: Actes du colloque de Strasbourg (28–31 août 1991)*, 2 vols (Leiden: Brill, 1993), vol. 2, pp. 214–25). Gerald Hobbs, however, has shown convincingly that congregations were in fact singing this early in the Reformation (see Hobbs, '"Quam Apposita Religioni Sit Musica": Martin Bucer and Music in the Liturgy', *Reformation and Renaissance Review*, 6 (2004), pp. 155–78).

119 Hobbs has observed that in Bucer's *Psalter wol verteutscht* (Basel: Petrus, 1526), fol. CXCVI^v, the reformer comments: 'die glaubigen nach der lere Pauli habe[n] angefangen in gemeyner sprach zů singen / wan[n] sy zů h$\overset{e}{o}$ren das heilig g$\overset{e}{o}$ttlich wort zů samen komen sind' ('The faithful have now begun, following St Paul's admonition, to sing psalms in their own language each time they gather to hear God's holy word'). Translated in Hobbs, '"Quam Apposita Religioni Sit Musica"', p. 162. N.B.: *BDS*, 2 does not contain a full transcription of *Psalter wol verteutscht*.

120 A selection, including some of the Strasbourg songbooks, can be found in K. E. P. Wackernagel, *Bibliographie zur Geschichte des deutschen Kirchenliedes im XVI. Jahrundert* (Frankfurt am Main: Hender & Zimmer, 1855), pp. 545–711.

important element in the service, the prefaces stressed the importance of singing God's praises. Also, as shall be demonstrated later on, biblical references were very often used as evidence for the need to reform.

The earliest Protestant liturgies printed in Strasbourg contain a short preface. This first appeared in the *Ordenung* of 1524, and was reprinted in several subsequent editions. Perhaps for reasons of space and cost, the first edition of the *Teutsch Kirchenampt* does not include this preface; it is only found in the second and third editions. The text, only 77 words in length, is modified in the *Teutsch Kirchenampt* to include the mention of singing. The original text noted that the celebration of 'the order of the Mass [is] carried out in a Christian way'.[121] The revised text built on this idea, and reiterated the use and importance of singing in the service: 'The servants of the Word ... now follow the order of *singing* of the Mass and Vespers, etc., carried out in a Christian way',[122] and it confirmed that such advances had led to an increase in the number of the faithful in the community.[123] Written as such, the preface presented the new service as a continuation, adaptation, and improvement of the old, rather than a new beginning, the latter perspective being one that Luther, too, was keen to avoid. This preface also confirmed the integral role of singing in the new liturgy.

As Hubert's study shows, a repertoire of several prefaces gradually emerged over the years, combinations of which were printed in various Strasbourg service books (including those in which no music is printed, and which are simply liturgical orders).[124] As time went on, not only did the number of psalms or hymns increase, but the number and length of the prefaces also multiplied.

Liturgical Reforms: The Abolition of the Mass in 1525

At the beginning of April 1525, the town council abolished the singing or saying of the Latin Mass, except in the cathedral and four collegiate churches, which were permitted to read or sing the Mass just once daily.[125] This was not a

121 'Es habe[n] die diener des worts zů Straßburg / dem alten gebrauch (so vil müglich ist) nachgegeben / vnd also nachgeende ordenu[n]g d[er] Mess Christlicher weyß fürgenum[m]en'. *Ordenung vnd yn[n]halt Teütscher Mess vn[nd] Vesper* (1524), fol. Aj^{v}.

122 'Es haben die diener des worts zů Straßburg / dem alte[n] gebrauch / so vil müglich ist / nachgeben / vnd also nachgeende ordnung des gesangs der Meß / vnnd vesper &c. Christlicher weyß fürgenommen'. *Teutsch Kirche[n] ampt mit lobgsangen* (1524), fol. Aj^{v}. My emphasis in translation.

123 'darin[n] wir von der gemein taglich befunden grossen fürgang vnd merung des glaubens'. *Teutsch Kirche[n] ampt* (1524), fol. Aj^{v}. See Appendix B.

124 Some of the prefaces appearing in Strasbourg books are transcribed in *Hubert*, pp. 139–51.

125 L. P. Wandel, *Voracious Idols and Violent Hands: Iconoclasm in Reformation Zurich, Strasbourg, and Basel* (Cambridge: Cambridge University Press, 1994), p. 140 (including n. 106), suggests the Mass was to be spoken, but Chrisman (*Strasbourg and the Reform: A Study in the Process of Change* (New Haven and London: Yale University Press, 1967), p. 155), suggests that

rejection of the sacrament of the Eucharist, but rather of a Latin rite (the Mass) which the Strasbourg reformers believed had nothing to do with the ceremony instituted by Christ.[126] The story of how this small victory for the reformers was achieved is not so much told by hymn books or liturgical orders as by archival documents, which paint a picture of strife and conflict both within and without the city's churches.

René Bornert has named the period 1524–30 the time of 'deconstruction and reconstruction' of liturgy in Strasbourg.[127] This is reflected in the great number of writings about the liturgy from this time, particularly in 1524 and 1525. There was, as part of this, a dramatic rise in discussions of music. On 24 June 1524 the reformers stopped celebrating Masses for the dead, and the city banned such services in April the following year. Priests were ordered not to celebrate the cycle of Masses for Holy Week in 1525. Then, on 7 May, the Mass was abolished everywhere except the cathedral and the collegiate churches of St Thomas, St Peter the Young, St Peter the Old, and All Saints. During the same year, feast days in the liturgical calendar were abolished.[128] Given the persistent lobbying by the reformers for the suppression of the Mass, as well as the council's underlying fear of a civilian uprising, such moves were inevitable.[129]

Indeed, there was also desire for reform among at least some of Strasbourg's wider populace. In 1524, the parishioners of five churches[130] wrote to the authorities asking them to appoint pastors who were sympathetic to the reforms in all parishes of the town.[131] In their third point, relating to church services, the parishioners complained of the 'disorder of church splendour and futile singing of the choir' (*myßordnung des kirchen geprengs / vnd vergeblichem chorgesengs*) on feast days, destroying the peace which they desired, and asked that the 'temple singers' be stripped of their responsibility and replaced by 'preachers and godly Christian officials'. The parishioners desired 'only *freedom, unity, civil peace, silent obedience*, and the honour of God'.[132] Such a striking appeal reveals a fair amount about the values of the new urban culture

these chapters actually sang the Mass, See also the letter from Peter Butz to All Saints' Church (1525), classmark: II 22a, 20, and the petition of six citizens (March 1525), classmark: 1 AST 87, 29.

126 See, for example, the anonymous pamphlet of 1525 attacking the Mass, described on pp. 76–7.

127 'Déstructuration et Restructuration (1524–1530)', title of chapter 3 of Bornert, *Réforme protestante du culte*, p. 84.

128 Bornert, *Réforme protestante du culte*, pp. 134–5, lists various sources in support of these changes.

129 See Brady, *Ruling Class*, p. 204.

130 St Laurence, St Peter the Young, St Martin, St Aurelia, and St Stephen.

131 1 AST 87, 13. The petition put to the emperor by the peasants of Germany in 1524 included an article calling for the right for parishes to appoint their own ministers. This, and the 11 other articles, were ignored by the emperor, a decision which helped lead to the so-called Peasants' War in southern Germany.

132 'vnß zuuollendung der predigen vnd göttlichen Christlichen ämpteren / von tempel singern gewichen werde / dan[n] wir sonst jrs gutts oder arbeit nit begeren / sonder allein / frid / einigkeyt /

emerging at this time.[133] Citizens did not want to hear music if it was not orderly and did not serve its purpose.[134] They did not require people to sing loudly, but wished to create a community in which spiritual and civil values were cherished. Here, then, is an example of music being used as part of an attempt to create an ideal sort of culture and community.[135]

One of the most important documents of its time is a work penned by Bucer on behalf of all the reformers, following a complaint to the Imperial Government at the end of 1524 by the canons who had fled Strasbourg in response to the growing momentum in the reforming camp.[136] The canons also petitioned the Strasbourg municipal authorities, calling for them to take action against the 'innovations' (*neuerungen*) taking place. Bucer and the other preachers responded by submitting an apology in February 1525, entitled *Der predicanten verantwortten vff die verclagung der vßgedreiten pfaffen an keyserlich Regiment* (*The preachers respond to the accusation sent by the priests who have resigned to the Imperial Government*).[137] In the document, they sought to answer 15 points, the eleventh point of which concerned church song, repeating several familiar complaints about the singing practices of the Roman Church. In addition it attempted to prove that the singing and reading of the Papists was anti-Christian, whereas the Strasbourg preachers were using song for the improvement of the community. The distinction was intentionally made here between the music of

burgerliche rug [*sic*] / stille gehorsame / vnd gottliche Ere suchen'. 1 AST 87, 13, pp. 1–2. My own emphasis in translation. See also Chrisman, *Strasbourg and the Reform*, p. 115.

133 See also Brady, *Turning Swiss: Cities and Empire, 1450–1550* (Cambridge: Cambridge University Press, 1985), pp. 23, 27.

134 A decade later, Katharina Schütz Zell may well have felt that the songs in her Bohemian Brethren songbooks would encourage good civil behaviour, as well as promoting spiritual values. See pp. 124–31.

135 This is connected to the notions of freedom of which Luther spoke in *Von der Freyheyt eyniss Christen menschen* (Wittenberg: Rhau, 1520) (printed as *Von der freyhayt aines christen menschen* (Strasbourg: Beck, 1520)). In it, Luther writes that Christians should willingly and freely serve God and those around them in order to promote and maintain civil peace (while Murner, on the other hand, interpreted this 'freedom' as a sort of licence for rebellion). Other letters to the Strasbourg authorities demonstrate the extent to which its reforms were partly led by the populace. The parishioners of St Aurelia's Church had a reputation for being particularly rebellious. It was they who, with the help of the gardeners' guild, had forced the hand of the council into making Bucer their pastor in 1523, a responsibility which did not officially lie with the council at this point (see Chrisman, *Strasbourg and the Reform*, pp. 113–14). A letter from 3 January 1525 (1 AST 111, 8) relays the tense situation with the gardeners at the Church of St Peter the Young. Strasbourg's authorities were well aware of the outbreaks of rebellion in other parts of Germany, and were no doubt wary of ignoring the ever-growing voice of the common people (see also Brady, *Ruling Class*, pp. 199–201 and Bornert, *Réforme protestante du culte*, p. 138).

136 The complainants were Sixt Hermann, Diebold Balthener and Jakob Schultheiss, all former canons of St Thomas's Church.

137 1 AST 170, 4. Text printed in *BDS*, 2, pp. 434–60. Also mentioned in *Fragments des anciennes chroniques d'Alsace*, III (1892), no. 3030. See also *BDS*, 2, pp. 432–3; *CorrCapito*, 2, pp. 109–10; *CorrBucer*, 2, pp. 14–16; and Eells, *Martin Bucer*, pp. 45–6.

the Roman Church and the music of the Protestants. Apparently, Bucer saw the chance to turn the situation back around on the canons when he wrote:

> All singing and reading which is not done for the edification of the congregation of God does not come from the Spirit of God. May then everything be carried out for the honour of God and for the building up of one's neighbour.[138] Furthermore, singing and reading which is not from the heart is but a mockery to God. Therefore it must certainly be devilish.[139]

The ancient notion of singing from the heart was prominent in the writings of the reformers. The use of words such as 'mockery' (*verspottung*) and 'devilish' (*tuffelich*) leaves no doubt as to the opinion in which the preachers (or at least Bucer) held singing which was not heartfelt. To their mind, the Latin singing of a select few was not only inexcusable and insincere, but also evil, whereas hymn singing was carried out for the good of the Church.[140] The document continued by drawing attention to the hypocrisy of the singers, who sang such passages as 'I will not neglect your word' (Psalm 119:16). If these words had been sung sincerely, from the heart (*mit hertzen*), then their integrity would have been revealed.[141] A damning conclusion followed: 'Yea, in one hundred of them there is not one who understands a tenth of their song'.[142] Instead, an interpreter was needed if a foreign language was to be used in church, as commanded by Scripture, in 1 Corinthians 14:27, so that the congregation could understand and be edified.[143]

The reformers, then, claimed to have been genuinely dismayed when church song did not come 'from the heart'. However, the irony is that none of the principal reformers appears to have been qualified to specify exactly how those singing were expected to demonstrate their sincerity. Although, therefore, there were plenty of points of criticism, there were no technical suggestions for improvement. Whether they were expected to sing loudly, or with mouths wide open, was not indicated. Instead, we read that what should have taken a week

---

138 See 1 Cor. 14:3–5, 12, 26.

139 'alles singen vnd lesen, So nit zuor besserung der gemeinde gottes beschicht, kompt nit vom geist gottes, der dan alle ding zur eer gottes vnd vffbuwung der nechsten anstelt; mer [noch], by welchem singen vnd lesen das hertz nit ist, Wurt dadurch got nur verspottet; deßhalb solichs gewißlich tuffelich sin muß'. 1 AST 170, 4, fols 33r–33v; *BDS*, 2, p. 450.

140 See also Adam, *Evangelische Kirchengeschichte der Stadt Strassburg* (Strasbourg: Heitz, 1922), pp. 85–6.

141 See Matt. 7:16. Susan Karant-Nunn observes that 'For Luther and Calvin … References to the corporal heart nevertheless direct attention toward that organ as the generator and repository of feeling and persuasion … Meaning something equates to *heartfelt* sincerity. Indeed, no sincerity can be other than heartfelt'. See S. C. Karant-Nunn, *The Reformation of Feeling: Shaping the Religious Emotions in Early Modern Germany* (Oxford: Oxford University Press, 2010), p. 249.

142 'Ja, vnder hundertten ist nit einer, der den zehenden theil irs gesangs verstande'. 1 AST 170, 4, fol. 33v; *BDS*, 2, p. 450.

143 1 AST 170, 4, fol. 33v; *BDS*, 2, p. 450.

to recite or sing, the choir singers preferred to 'babble' (*schlappern*) in a day, or even as little as five hours. This was, the reformers stated, clearly contrary to Christ's own commandment: 'And when you pray, do not keep on babbling like pagans, for they think they will be heard because of their many words'.[144] In other words, quality of prayer – and not quantity – would assure the faithful of their salvation. Those who prayed by 'wailing and mumbling' (*geplerre vnd gemůrmel*) would not be saved. The singing of psalms was an activity that featured in the humble life led by Jesus; it was therefore a divine tradition, and one which deserved to be continued by all – not just by priests and the religious in the privacy of their cloisters.

The reformers' final criticism was of the behaviour of the singers. None of the choirmen, the reformers claimed, wanted to translate the Latin being sung, and instead the words were sung hurriedly so that they could collect their payment and join the maid behind the stove![145] They led a wanton life to please their stomachs,[146] and instead of honouring God they shamed him while thinking of worldly things.[147] The document also referred to the *Decretum* of Canon Law, which commanded that deacons should not sing as part of their office. The citing of such a serious authority of the Church could not have failed to add weight to the argument being set out by Bucer and his colleagues:[148]

> Whence there are many elected to the sacred mystery, while a sweet voice bewails seductive things, the appropriate life is neglected, and the cantor – minister of God – incites morality, while he delights the people with his voice. On which present topic I am inclined to this decision: that they who are in the position of this sacred ministry at the altar ought not to sing … They who have not been ordained to do so by the

144 Matt. 6:7. Bucer seems to contradict himself by using this citation, which refers to the number of words recited, rather than the speed at which they are recited. It is therefore not clear at this point whether Bucer was happy with the number of psalms texts being recited, or whether he felt that they should be fewer in number.

145 'zů dem allem begerts nyemants vßzulegen, das doch ieman ein besserung dauon prechte, sonder nur vffs ylendtsts vbereinander geworffen, Vnd mit der presentz vß der kirchen zur magt hinder den offen'. 1 AST 170, 4, fols 33v–34r; *BDS*, 2, p. 451.

146 This may be a reference to Rom. 16:18 ('For such people are not serving our Lord Christ, but their own appetites. By smooth talk and flattery they deceive the minds of naïve people'). See also the accusation under point eight, that their opponents' singing and services give pleasure to nothing but their own bellies (*Darumb irs gesangs vnd gotsdiensts niemants erfrewet wurt, dan ire Beuch, Bauchdiener vnd dienerin*). 1 AST 170, 4, fol. 32r; *BDS*, 2, p. 448.

147 'Vnd so ir gesang widder das hell wort gottes ist, als ob bewert vnd am tag leit, Haben wir solichs dem heiligen geist nit mogen zuschriben. vnnd so alles ir ding dahin zihet, dassie vil feußter pfrunden hetten, ein feig, gemachsam leben zufuren, můsen wir ye veriehen, das er got der bauch ist, vnnd ir eer zu schaden wurt, Dwil sie vffs irdisch gesandt sint, philip. 3 [19]'. 1 AST 170, 4, fol. 34r; *BDS*, 2, p. 452.

148 For an account of Bucer's position on canon law, see R. Stupperich, 'Martin Bucers Gebrauch des kanonischen Rechts', in Kroon and Lienhard, eds, *Horizons européens de la Réforme en Alsace*, pp. 241–52.

> bishop shall not sing psalms in the pulpit or read. Singing psalms or reading in the pulpit is not allowed, except by those who are ordained readers by the bishop.[149]

Although it is not used as part of the reformers' argument, the first part of the same section of the *Decretum* expands on St Jerome's opinion on singing:

> If people come to church, let them remember that they must sing to God as much with their hearts as with their voices ... Let the young people hear this, let them hear, whose duty it is to sing the Psalms: God must be praised not with the voice, but in your hearts, not in the tragic style where the throat and jaws are smeared with potions, so that instead they hear in church theatrical chants and songs.[150]

To summarise, the 'wailing' of those who sing in church (and who have not been ordained to do so) was, according to the preachers, blasphemous, done for money, and not understood by those who do it. It was contrary to the commandments of God, as confirmed in the commandments of canon law. On the other hand, the singing of the reformed congregations was commendable, because it was done in the vernacular in order that the people would understand, so that it could build up the Church and improve God's people, and it came from the heart, as is commanded in Scripture.

Further complaints about singers and about the use of Latin can be found in an open letter written by Capito in August 1525. *Von drey Straßburger Pfaffen, und den geüsserten Kirchen güttern* (*Concerning three Strasbourg priests and the removal of the church goods*)[151] was written in response to an attack on Capito

---

149 'Unde fit plerumque ut in sacro ministerio, dum blanda uox queritur, congrua uita negligatur, et cantor, minister Deum moribus stimulet, cum populum uocibus delectet. Qua de re presenti decreto constituo, ut in sede hac sacri altaris ministri cantare non debeant ... Qui ab episcopo non ordinantur, in pupito non psallant uel legant. Non liceat in pupito psallere aut legere, nisi qui ab episcopo ordinati sunt lectores'. Distinctio XCII, *Decretum*, in A. L. Richter and E. Friedberg, eds, *Corpus Iuris Canonici*, 2 vols (Graz: Akademische Druck, 1959), vol. 1, cols 317–18. A translation also exists in J. Gilchrist, *The Collection in Seventy-Four Titles: A Canon Law Manual of the Gregorian Reform* (Toronto: Pontifical Institute of Mediaeval Studies, 1980), pp. 203–4.

150 'Cum autem ad ecclesiam uenerint, corde magis quam uoce Deo cantandum meminerint ... Audiant hec adolescentuli, audiant hi, quibus in ecclesia est psallendi offitium: Deo non uoce, sed corde cantandum, nec in tragediarum modum guttur et fauces medicamine liniendae sunt, ut in ecclesia teatrales moduli audiantur et cantica'. Distinctio XCII, *Decretum*, in Richter and Friedberg, *Corpus Iuris Canonici*, vol. 1, col. 317. See also 1 AST 80, 26, fols 108r–108v; *BDS*, 2, p. 543. This is also, incidentally, a fact that Erasmus had picked up on in his *Apologia adversus rhapsodias Alberti Pii* (Basel: Froben, 1528): 'Why does Gregory, in the *Decretum*, express anger that priests, whose duty is to expound the Gospel, are singing in the churches?'. Erasmus, 'Apology against the patchworks of Alberto Pio', in N. H. Minnich, ed., and D. Sheerin, trans., *Collected works of Erasmus: Controversies* (Toronto: University of Toronto Press, 2005), p. 218. See also Distinctio XCII, *Decretum*, in Richter and Friedberg, *Corpus Iuris Canonici*, vol. 1, col. 318.

151 (Strasbourg: Köpfel, 1525). Appendix G is an excerpt of the letter in German and in English. The German text is available on the website of the Electronic Capito Project (http://cf.itergateway.org/capito/Letter246a.pdf) (accessed 20 November 2010), and in Rummel and

in the form of a Catholic broadsheet[152] posted in Strasbourg in August. This was compiled by the same canons who had complained about the Strasbourg reforms to the Imperial Government.[153] Capito's response was centred on the removal by the canons opposed to the Reformation of items from the Church of St Peter the Young. He claimed that on Monday 7 March 1524 the items had been removed, but that 'much later, on a Sunday', an uprising had occurred

> when the choir at St Peter began to sing [the office of] Prime[154] during the Lord's Supper, which appeared to go against the people's inclination. Several of the congregation went into the choir and told the priests to be silent, whereupon a part of them left. The others, however, remained in their seats, keeping silent until the service had ended. No one desired to harm them, nor were any of them driven out of the choir by force. They were told to be silent, not to leave the choir. The images, which were the object of ungodly adoration and attention, were removed only after the canons left. This was done in an orderly fashion on the direction of the government of Strasbourg. The images were not, as they write, torn down in a lawless fashion by the common people.[155]

If we are to take Capito at his word, this account is useful for several reasons. First, it suggests that the choir was acting in defiance by singing an office in Latin while a German service was taking place, sabotaging an act of worship which the people considered to be of value.[156] Second, it demonstrates the divisions that were present in churches and their congregations, the level of tension that existed in Strasbourg at this time, and that (as in all conflicts) accounts of events were prone to exaggeration.

Furthermore, this letter contained possibly the most comprehensive attack on the singing of the Roman Church in Strasbourg at this time. Although most of the arguments are similar, if not identical, to those found in *Der predicanten*

Kooistra, eds, *Reformation Sources: The Letters of Wolfgang Capito and his Fellow Reformers in Alsace and Switzerland* (Toronto: Centre for Reformation and Renaissance Studies, 2007), pp. 207–39. An English translation by Erika Rummel is given in *CorrCapito*, 2, pp. 123–53. Capito's relationship with the canons of St Thomas was complicated. Some of the canons were in favour of the reforms, while others were not. See Rummel and Kooistra, *Reformation Sources*, pp. 201–6.

152 *Warhafftige verantwurt dreyer Summissarien zu Sant Thoman auf doctor Wolfgang Capito jüngst unwarhafftige, nichtige ußgangene protestation* (*True response of three summissaries of St Thomas to Dr. Wolfgang Capito's recently published false and groundless protestation*). When Capito asked for permission to post his response in Freiburg, where the broadsheet had also been distributed, the authorities refused, and saw to it that his response was burned. See *CorrCapito*, 2, pp. 124 and 187–98.

153 See *CorrCapito*, 2, pp. 123–4. For a detailed version of events, see Rummel and Kooistra, *Reformation Sources*, pp. 201–6.

154 The translation in *CorrCapito* reads at this point: 'when the choir at St Peter began to sing primes during the Lord's Supper'.

155 Appendix G, p. 332; http://cf.itergateway.org/capito/Letter246a.pdf, p. 5; Rummel and Kooistra, *Reformation Sources*, p. 216. Translated in *CorrCapito*, 2, p. 132.

156 Compare this with the case of the friar interrupting Bucer's sermon (see p. 144).

verantwortten,[157] Capito went into much more detail on most points. Another crucial difference is that Capito's response did not acknowledge the singing of the Protestants. It was simply a detailed criticism of Latin choir singing. His main points, once again, were that such singing was not Christian, that the Word of God was being used for profit and for nourishment of the singers' stomachs, that Latin was of no use to the laity, that the singers did not understand what they were singing, and that they sang too quickly.

Capito argued that the singing and reading of the Papists was not Christian, 'for it is not praying or honouring God. The Christian practice is an internal one. Those who pray truly to the Father pray in the spirit and in truth'.[158] He questioned the value of 'our so-called clergy's singing and piping' (*unnsers gepffess singen und pfeyffen*) and abuse of holy words. Furthermore, Latin was of no use to the congregation.

> For they cannot understand it, just as an Italian [*ein welscher*][159] would make no progress and have no effect presenting his case to a German judge ... In their debt calculations and their trading in benefices, they do not understand what they are singing ... Thus, it is a dull and confounded noise.[160]

Capito, surely exaggerating for effect, wrote that 'it would take a month for a person experienced in spiritual exegesis to study in depth the meaning of the psalms and scriptural passages they burble out in a day'.[161]

Another point was that singers accepted generous payment for their work, 'like a merchant for his goods and merchandise' (*wie ein kauffman umb sein war und kauffmans gutter*). This in itself was an abuse.[162] Capito lamented that singers were

> much more eager to hear sad requiems and songs for the dead than the joyful *Gaudeamus*. For although the organ pipes sound good in both cases, the fee and the

157 I AST 170, 4.

158 Appendix G, pp. 333–4; http://cf.itergateway.org/capito/Letter246a.pdf, p. 11; Rummel and Kooistra, *Reformation Sources*, p. 227. Translated in *CorrCapito*, 2, p. 142.

159 The term *welsch* is a colloquial term for a speaker of Romance languages, primarily used to describe Italians. See H. Puff, *Sodomy in Reformation Germany and Switzerland, 1400–1600* (Chicago and London: University of Chicago Press, 2003), p. 81.

160 Appendix G, pp. 336–7; http://cf.itergateway.org/capito/Letter246a.pdf, p. 12; Rummel and Kooistra, *Reformation Sources*, pp. 229–30. Translated in *CorrCapito*, 2, pp. 143–4. The language of such phrases is remarkably similar in places to the complaints made by Savonarola at the end of the fifteenth century. See P. Macey, *Bonfire Songs: Savonarola's Musical Legacy* (Oxford: Clarendon Press, 1998), esp. pp. 93–8.

161 Appendix G, p. 337; http://cf.itergateway.org/capito/Letter246a.pdf, p. 12; Rummel and Kooistra, *Reformation Sources*, p. 229. Translated in *CorrCapito*, 2, p. 144.

162 Appendix G, p. 335; http://cf.itergateway.org/capito/Letter246a.pdf, p. 11; Rummel and Kooistra, *Reformation Sources*, p. 228. Translated in *CorrCapito*, 2, p. 143.

> holy penny make the sad song for the dead a happy occasion for the servant of the belly, whose devotion evaporates when the holy penny declines.[163]

The price of having a Requiem Mass celebrated for a dead relative was one of the grievances that had been raised at the Imperial Diet of Worms in 1521. Accusations were made of priests in some places shaming the poor 'into paying a few pennies to have a Mass sung, *or at least to have one read*'.[164] The implication, then, was that a sung Mass had a higher spiritual value, and therefore also a higher monetary value, than one which was merely spoken. A typical (spoken) Mass foundation around the year 1500 would have cost around 2 shillings. This was within the grasp of a worker on a generous salary, but for the lower classes this would often have been an unaffordable luxury. For them, a sung Mass was not even worth considering.[165]

Capito concluded his tract by adding a familiar observation – one also made in *Der predicanten verantwortten* – that once they had received their payment, the choirmen 'hurry out of the church, toss their choir robe behind the door and join the maid behind the stove'.[166] The reformers thereby brought another dimension to the attack by making such accusations against the singers: not only did these people blaspheme in their church singing, but they also led immoral, unchristian lives outside of church. It was a demonstration that they were unfit to serve in the House of God.[167]

As well as the Mass, the seven monastic offices were also eradicated from Strasbourg's churches.[168] Special celebrations on Palm Sunday, during Holy Week and at Easter were banned in all churches and convents.[169] Until the end

---

163 Appendix G, p. 338; http://cf.itergateway.org/capito/Letter246a.pdf, pp. 12–13; Rummel and Kooistra, *Reformation Sources*, p. 230. Translated in *CorrCapito*, 2, pp. 144–5. For another reference to the *Gaudeamus*, see S. Brant, *Das Narrenschiff* (Basel: Olpe, 1494), chapter 108.

164 'von ainer singenden mess vier albus und von ainer lesenden mess drei albus reder munz zu geben' (my emphasis in translation). *Deutsche Reichstagsakten: jüngere Reihe*, 19 vols (Gotha: Perthes; Göttingen: Vandenhoeck & Ruprecht; Munich: Oldenbourg, 1893–), vol. 2, p. 690. Translated in Strauss, *Manifestations of Discontent*, p. 60.

165 C. A. Stanford, *Commemorating the Dead in Late Medieval Strasbourg: The Cathedral's Book of Donors and its Use (1320–1521)* (Farnham: Ashgate, 2013), p. 68, incl. n. 96.

166 Appendix G, p. 338; http://cf.itergateway.org/capito/Letter246a.pdf, p. 13; Rummel and Kooistra, *Reformation Sources*, p. 230. Translated in *CorrCapito*, 2, p. 145. See above, p. 69. This language is no doubt inspired by Sebastian Brant's estimation of the choir in *Das Narrenschiff* (see Chapter 1, p. 26).

167 For more on the perceived morality of church musicians, see Trocmé-Latter, 'Thieves, Drunkards, and Womanisers?'.

168 *Fragments des anciennes chroniques d'Alsace*, I (1887), no. 76. See also P. Fritsch, ed., *Die Strassburger Chronik des Johannes Stedel* (Strasbourg: Sebastian Brant-Verlag, 1934), pp. 97–8.

169 *Fragments des anciennes chroniques d'Alsace*, III (1892), no. 3030. Despite the ruling, the Mass was celebrated in Latin in various churches on All Saints' Day in both 1526 and 1527 (see Bornert, *Réforme protestante du culte*, p. 135; R. Reuss, ed., 'Strassburg im sechszehnten Jahrhundert, 1500–1591: Auszug aus der Imlin'schen Familienchronik', *Alsatia*, 10 (1873–74), p. 407; *Fragments des anciennes chroniques d'Alsace*, III (1892), no. 3036).

of 1525, the unwillingness of either party to make way for the other meant that, in each of the chapters, the Roman clergy would sing Mass in the choir while the Protestant preachers were celebrating the Eucharist elsewhere in the church. This simultaneous arrangement was abolished by the council in December 1525, and from this point onward the two services were celebrated successively.[170]

On 1 May 1525 a committee was established with the role of reorganising worship in those churches which were no longer celebrating the Mass. It was to consider liturgy and song, as well as the provision of schooling.[171] It is in this year, therefore, that we begin to find manuscript proposals for alternative orders for the Mass and the offices, a huge number of which have been preserved. Many are similar in design, and some are based on Luther's model for the pre-Reformation offices. Joseph Herl observes that Lutheran Vespers was much like its medieval predecessor, although usually with fewer psalms.[172] In his 1523 essay, *Von ordenung gottis diensts ynn der gemeyne*,[173] Martin Luther had written that during the time of the apostles, Christians assembled in the morning and in the evening for a service of devotion to God. The two services shown here are based on Luther's suggestions. A typical service of Matins in Lutheran areas of the Holy Roman Empire may have looked like this:[174]

Domine, labia mea aperies or *Deus in adiutorium meum intende*;[175]
Invitatory and Psalm 95 (*Venite, exultemus*);
Three or four psalms with one or more antiphon;
Three lessons with several responsories;
Sermon (optional);
Benedictus[176] with antiphon;
Benedicamus or a German psalm.

A typical order for Vespers in Lutheran Germany may have looked like this:[177]

Deus in adiutorium meum intende;
Antiphon, one to five psalms, doxology, antiphon;
Lesson(s) or chapter;

[170] See *Fragments des anciennes chroniques d'Alsace*, IV (1901), no. 4648; Bornert, *Réforme protestante du culte*, p. 136.

[171] Brady, '"Sind also zu beiden theilen christen"', pp. 71–2; *Fragments des anciennes chroniques d'Alsace*, III (1892), no. 4610.

[172] Herl, *Worship Wars*, p. 63.

[173] Printed in *WA*, 12, pp. 35–7; translated in Herl, *Worship Wars*, pp. 193–5.

[174] Adapted from the order for East Frisia (1535), given in Herl, *Worship Wars*, p. 65.

[175] Herl notes that the versicle and responsory are not always mentioned in orders, either because they were not performed or because their inclusion was taken for granted and therefore not worth mentioning. See ibid., p. 62, n. 25.

[176] Luke 1: 68–79, borrowed from the Roman office of Lauds.

[177] Taken from Herl, *Worship Wars*, pp. 62–3.

Responsory or hymn;
Sermon (optional);
Magnificat with antiphon, *or* Litany;
Kyrie (optional);
Collect (optional);
Benedicamus;
Hymn (optional).

As will be seen, service proposals in Strasbourg differed in their suggestion of how many psalms should be sung, with some suggesting two or three,[178] and others three or four.[179]

During May 1525, the Strasbourg preachers[180] submitted a proposal to the council, which sought to advise the city 'on how a godly service should be carried out and held'.[181] The letter, written during a tense and volatile period in Strasbourg's history, called on the council to act on these proposals in order to achieve peace in the city, and 'to seek and encourage God's honour'.[182] The reformers called for a complete ban on singing and reading in a foreign tongue, and the holding of vigils, the Mass, and other services in the chapters and cloisters, and they proposed that the seven offices be replaced with the following order: At eight o'clock in the morning and at three o'clock in the afternoon, the prebendaries (*verpfründten*) were to assemble in each chapter. The Prime bell was rung, and afterwards a confession and a 'Christian absolution' (*christl[ich] absolution*) spoken. Three or four psalms should then be sung, with an antiphon, and the prebendaries were then to read a chapter or half a chapter from the Bible. They were to begin at Genesis, and then read through the books of the Bible in order at subsequent services. The Lord's Prayer was then recited, 'for mercy' (*vmb gnad*), presumably instead of the Hail Mary, and then a canticle (the *Benedictus* in the morning or the *Magnificat* in the afternoon), with an antiphon, and finally a collect. The service was to finish with a blessing.[183]

---

178 For example, 1 AST 80, 4.

179 For example, 1 AST 166, 5.13. Later proposals are more precise, suggesting that three psalms be sung. For example, see 1 AST 80, 19, fol. 84r.

180 The proposal is signed by Wolfgang Capito, Caspar Hedio, Matthäus Zell, Martin Bucer, Symphorian Altbiesser, Joannes Latomus and Diobald Schwarz.

181 'Der Predicanten Rahtslag [*sic*] wie man gottgevellig[en] dienst thun und halten soll'. 1 AST 166, 5.13 (fols 104v–106r); *CorrBucer*, 2, pp. 25–8. This document is a copy of 1 AST 84, 7, which does not carry this title.

182 'das man vffs ernstlichst gottes Ehr zeuor suche vnd furdere'. 1 AST 166, 5.13, fol. 105r; 1 AST 84, 7, fol. 16r; *CorrBucer*, 2, p. 25.

183 See also Martin Bucer's letter to Jakob Otter (17 September 1525): 'Pridem et iam christiana psallendi ratio per senatum canonicis, postquam nullae horae (quas vocant) canuntur, oblata fuit, sed quia illis, quae Christi sunt [Phil. 2, 21], nondum probari coeperunt, et alia multa negocia senatum distinent, adhuc in templis propter missas illas siletur'. 1 AST 40, 1, p. 31; printed in J. V. Pollet, *Martin Bucer – Études sur la correspondance*, 2 vols (Paris: Presses Universitaires de France, 1958–62), vol. 2, p. 72.

Although not mentioned by name, these were obviously the revised services of Matins and Vespers respectively. It is made clear that the services were 'not to be spoken or sung with tongues or in a foreign language, where there is no interpreter present'.[184] For there to be an interpreter present implies that there would have been people in attendance in need of edification and who needed to understand what was being said or sung in a foreign language.[185] The order of service outlined by the preachers roughly corresponds with the order for Vespers set out in the *Straszburger Kirchenampt* of 1525 (see below), with the exception of some variations in the ordering, and the omission of the initial Confession and Absolution.

The preachers continued by addressing the need to abolish the Mass in the chapters. Holding the Mass was not necessary, they said, because every Sunday the new service of the Lord's Supper was celebrated before the whole community (*vor der ganzen gemein*). The preachers then attacked the Mass as anti-scriptural:[186] the Eucharist was to be held not only amongst the clergy, but in front of many people.[187] 'Our praise', they continued, 'should not consist of church pomp, but of the enlightened Word of God'. The former was built on the sand,[188] and was 'a great hypocrisy'.[189] The preachers sought to reassure the council about the innovations (*nuwerung*), announcing that they were in accordance with the Word of God. In places such as Nuremberg, the preachers continued, such innovations had already been put in place, and very successfully, which was to be taken as an indication of their effectiveness.[190]

The lack of any mention of congregational singing in this document is perplexing. On the other hand, it specified that the use of any Latin must be accompanied by a translation or interpretation (which would be for the sake of the whole assembly) and psalm singing was an important part of this service. It is possible that the writer took for granted that its intended recipients would have understood the need for the congregation to be included in this service.

---

184 'nichts soll mit zungen od[er] in fremden sprach geredt od[er] gesungen werden, wo nit ein vßleger zugegen ist'. 1 AST 166, 5.13, fol. 105r; 1 AST 84, 7, fol. 16r; *CorrBucer*, 2, p. 25.

185 See also Bornert, *Réforme protestante du culte*, pp. 150–51.

186 This in spite of the fact that the canon had already been omitted from Diobald Schwarz's first German Mass (see above, p. 36), one of the few liturgical changes he had made. The reason for its deletion was that the reformers objected to the notion of the Mass as a sacrifice, which the canon implied.

187 'Man weißt, das ir messen wider die Schrift sind und obschon der canon geendert, so soll doch das nachtmal vnder vylen gehalten werden, vnd nit also zwüschen inn selbs allein'. 1 AST 166, 5.13, fol. 105r; 1 AST 84, 7, fols 16r–16v; *CorrBucer*, 2, p. 26. As part of the canon, the priest could pray silently for anyone he wanted. See A. Fortescue, 'Canon of the Mass', *The Catholic Encyclopedia (Online)* (www.newadvent.org/cathen/03255c.htm) (accessed 22 August 2011)

188 Matt. 7:26.

189 'Ouch soll vnser andacht nit stan vff kirchengepreng, sonder vff dem hellen wort Gottes, sunst were sie uff ein sandt gebuwen, vnd ein lauter glychßnerey'. 1 AST 166, 5.13, fol. 105r; 1 AST 84, 7, fol. 16v; *CorrBucer*, 2, p. 26.

190 1 AST 166, 5.13, fol. 105r; 1 AST 84, 7, fol. 16v; *CorrBucer*, 2, p. 26.

Whether the congregations were themselves interested in singing German hymns is another matter entirely. One contemporary pamphlet suggested that it was not a priority. The document in question,[191] from around 1525, called for the abolition of the Mass in the strongest terms possible, by listing individual elements of the liturgy and explaining that they had not originated with Jesus or the Apostles. Even the introit, it stated, 'which originates from the customs of the first churches, has now been turned into a song, and helps to make the Mass idolatrous, even though it was first useful when the Church began'.[192] Other parts of the service, the pamphlet claimed, had originated with various popes throughout the ages.[193] 'In short, from the Lord's Supper a blasphemy has occurred [i.e. the Mass]. What then should we do?'[194] Abolish the Mass, is the conclusion. Song is depicted in this pamphlet as a waste of time, rather than something that deserved reform.

The Revised Printed Liturgy

Following the adaptation of the Latin Mass into the simpler vernacular service of the Lord's Supper, the printed books begin a transformation from service books, in which people could read the liturgy and sing the printed psalms at specified points, into what we might be more used to calling hymnals (that is, collections of hymns that could be sung), albeit still with a section containing the liturgy.[195] In 1525, six sacred music books and liturgical orders were printed – fewer than in 1524, but still under a diverse range of titles. These included the *Theütsch kirchenampt*, a collection of three volumes (whose contents are discussed below), now lost, that would have been of huge historical and musicological interest. Each volume appeared under a different title, and contained various settings of songs of praise.[196]

---

191 *Das die papistische[n] | opffermessen abzuthun: | vnd dagegen das nachtmal | Christi: Christlicher weisz | vffzurichten sey. || Sampt eim kurtzen bericht: | wie das zů der Apostelzeyten gehalten / | vnd durch welche es zů solchem | mißbrauch des opfferns | kommen sey* (Strasbourg: Prüss/Schwan, c. 1525).

192 'Zům fierdten so kompt der Jntroit auch her vo[m] gewonheit der erste[n] kirchen / der yetz zů eim gesang worden ist / vnd hilfft auch wol zůr abgo̊tterey d[er] messen / wiewol er erstlich zů nutz der kirchen angefange[n] ward'. *Das die papistischen opffermessen abzuthun*, fol. B[v].

193 *Das die papistischen opffermessen abzuthun*, fols B[v]–Biij[r].

194 'Kurtzlich / vß dem nachtmal Christi ist ein gotßlesterung worden. Was sollen wir dan[n] darzůthůn?' *Das die papistischen opffermessen abzuthun*, fol. Bij[r].

195 Not until 1538 did the printing of *Gesangbücher*, which contained music, but no actual liturgy begin. See Bornert, *Réforme protestante du culte*, p. 180.

196 As given in *RISM DKL* (all published by Köpfel, 1525):

I: *Theütsch | kirche[n] ampt mit lob | gsenge[n] vī gottlich- | en Psalmen, wie es die ge- | meyn zu Straßburger singt | vnnd halt, mit meer gantz | Christlichen gebette[n], dan[n] | vor getruckt.* | ... |

The year 1525 was also marked by three other musical publications that were not liturgical books as such, but nevertheless contained sacred music potentially suitable for singing in the service. They are not included in Hubert's volume, either because they were not known to him, or because of their lack of liturgical content. The first of these is a metrical setting of the German Creed (*Der Glaube Deütsch*),[197] versified into seven verses by Paul Speratus.[198] The music, which includes a text underlay of the first verse, was printed on the *recto* and *verso* of the same sheet, and so not designed in an entirely practical way for singing the remaining verses. The publication contains no preface or explanation of any sort. Another book of this kind, entitled *Ein schoner kurtzer begriff*, contains the Lord's Prayer, the *Ave Maria* (set to music), the Creed, and the Ten Commandments.[199] The inclusion of the *Ave Maria* betrays the fact that it was not an officially sanctioned document of the Church in Strasbourg. The reformers would have strongly disputed the claim in the title that such a text was 'useful to sing and to consider' (*Nützlich zů singen vnnd zů betrachten*), given their feelings about other devotions to the saints. Intriguingly, this was the only of the four texts to be both versified and set to music, suggesting that the tune, if not the text, was not familiar. The Creed was directly translated without any attempt at versification. The Lord's Prayer and the Ten Commandments, although in verse, neither were accompanied by nor named a tune.[200] A setting of Psalm 51, *Miserere mei*, was also published by Johann Schwan this year.[201] Publishers were making the most of the fact that no liturgy had been fixed for the new faith at this time. The idea behind such small collections of sung prayers, psalms, or canticles was probably to encourage devotional practices in the home

II: *Das an- | der theyl. | Straßburger kirchengesang. | Das vatter vnser. Der glaub. | Die zehn gepott. | Das Miserere. Psal. Der dorecht* [*sic*] *spricht. | Psal. Wer gott nicht mit. | Die acht ersten psalmen, | vff die melody, Ach gott | von himel.*

III: *Das dritt | theyl Straßbur | ger kirchen | ampt.*

197 *Der Glaube | Deütsch zů singen | in einer schönen me- | lodey* (Strasbourg: Knobloch, 1524/1525). This dating is that of *RISM DKL*, although as it is ordered under 1525 rather than 1524, for the purposes of this study it is assumed to be from that later date. One copy remains in the Bibliothèque Wilhelmitana, in Strasbourg's Médiathèque protestante. See also Wackernagel, *Bibliographie*, p. 52.

198 The text is reproduced in *Wackernagel DKL*, vol. 3, no. 57, pp. 35–6.

199 *Ein schoner kurtzer be- | griff des vatter vnsers | Vn[nd] Aue Maria / | Glauben / | Zehe[n] gebotte[n] / | Nützlich zů singen vnnd | zů betrachten* (Strasbourg: Schwan, 1525). This publication is held by the Koninklijke Bibliotheek in the Hague. See Appendix D for the texts to the first two songs.

200 The Hague copy contains a handwritten note directing the reader to sing the Lord's Prayer 'to the melody of *Christ ist erstanden*' ('vff die melody christ ist e[r]sta[n]d[en]'), fol. Aij^{r}. This version of the Ten Commandments also appeared in other Strasbourg publications. In the *Straszburger Kirchenampt* (1525), fol. xxxx^{v}–xxxxj^{r}, for example, a melody is provided.

201 *Der .li. | Psalm Dauids | Miserere mei deus hoch | zů singe[n] da der Prophet | Nathan zů im kam / | als er war zů Bath | Saba ein | gange[n]* (Strasbourg: Schwan, 1525). One copy is held in the Staatsbibliothek, Berlin, and is available to view online: http://digital.staatsbibliothek-berlin.de/werkansicht/?PPN=PPN732086000&PHYSID=PHYS_0005 (accessed 30 December 2014).

and other private settings. Shorter volumes would have been more transportable than books containing the whole liturgy, and as can be seen in the case of *Ein Schoner kurtzer begriff* and Speratus's *Glaube Deütsch*, the fact that they were often given simple and enticing titles suggests that they were aimed at a lay audience who would sing, perhaps not only in acts of private devotion, but also simply to pass the time together. Singing religious songs at home, of course, was a common pastime throughout Renaissance Europe.[202]

Of the liturgical orders, let us turn first to the *Ordnung des Herren Nachtmal* (see Figure 2.2).[203] Two editions of this book appeared within the first few weeks of 1525, following the liturgical recommendations set out in Bucer's *Grund und Ursach*, published the previous year.[204] The book contained a preface: the first significant hymn book preface of the Reformation in Strasbourg, and written by Schwan himself. It referred to the 'many errors in our conventions' and, in a reference not only to the new Protestant reformers but possibly also echoing calls of the pre-Reformation preachers such as Geiler von Kaysersberg, noted that the ministers had 'heartily complained of [these errors] in their sermons, and would like to change them'.[205] Schwan then proceeded to explain the changes, namely the abolition of 'gestures, vestments, and other ceremonies' (*geberde[n] kleydungen vnd andern ceremonien*). Perhaps repeating Thomas Müntzer's call for all churches to have their own liturgical peculiarities,[206] and pre-empting Luther's later acknowledgement that parishes should not be tied to any set programme of hymn singing,[207] Schwan referred to Christian freedom

---

[202] See, for example, the case of sixteenth-century printing in Venice, in M. S. Lewis, *Antonio Gardano, Venetian Music Printer – 1538–1569*, 3 vols (New York and London: Garland [vols 1–2]; Routledge [vol. 3], 1988–2005); and J. A. Bernstein, *Music Printing in Renaissance Venice – The Scotto Press (1539–1572)* (New York and Oxford: Oxford University Press, 1998), esp. pp. 933–50 (this is appendix C, which lists domestic bindings of various publications, including music books).

[203] The first edition, *Ordnu[n]g des | Herren Nachtmal: so | man die messz nennet, sampt der | Tauff vn[nd] Jnsegu[n]g der Ee* … (Strasbourg: Schwan, 1525), is in the Bayerische Staatsbibliothek, Munich, and also available to see online, at: http://daten.digitale-sammlungen.de/0002/bsb00029012/images. The second edition, *Ordnu[n]g des herren | Nachtmal: so man die Messz nennet / sampt der Tauff vn[nd] Jnsegung | der Ee* … (Strasbourg: Schwan, 1525), is in the BNUS and again also available online at the website of St John's University, Minnesota: http://cdm.csbsju.edu/cdm4/document.php?CISOROOT=/SJRareBooks&CISOPTR=2218&REC=1 (accessed 22 December 2014).

[204] *Grund und Ursach* is analysed and translated in Cypris, 'Basic Principles'.

[205] 'die dyener des wort gottes / bey vns langzeyt vil yrrung so ym brauch gewesen / mit grossem schmertzen getragen vnd doch nitt haben on grosse ergernüs stimpfflingen mogen endern / des syc sich offt hertzlich in ire[n] predigen beklagt'. *Ordnung des Herren Nachtmal* (1525), fol. Aj^{r}.

[206] See Matheson, *Works of Müntzer*, p. 177.

[207] 'Doch ist nicht dis unser meinung, das diese Noten so eben musten in allen Kirchen gesungen werden. Ein igliche Kirche halte jre Noten nach jrem Buch und Brauch. Denn ichs selbs auch nicht gerne hore, wo in einem Responsorio oder Gesang die Noten verruckt, anders gesungen werden bey uns, weder ich der in meiner Jugent gewonet bin. Es ist umb verenderung des Textes und nicht der Noten zuthun'. Luther, *Dem Christlichen Leser* (1542); *WA*, 35, pp. 479–80; translated in *LW*, 53, pp. 327–8.

Darnach spricht der die
ner zů dem volck.

¶ So kument nůn här die ir wöl
lent mitt mir des herren nacht mal
halten / vñ entpfahen / er wöl vch da
zů geschickt machen / vñ verleyhen
sein todt mit rechtem glauben zů be
dencken / vnd mit warer danckbar
keit verkünden.

Vnd in dargebung des
brots vnd des kelchs des herren /
Spricht er also.

Gedenckent / glaubēt verkündēt
das Christus für vch gestorben ist.

Darnach singt man dz
lobgsang / Gott sey gelobet.
oder ein Psalmen.

¶ Ach herr wie sind meiner
sünd so vil.

Mein stim zům herrē rüffen sol /
vō berg würt er mich hören. Ich lag
vnd schlieff erwachet wol / mein find
mocht mich nit stören. Wañ got der
herr mich selb enthelt / ob hūdert tau
sēt wirt gezelt / die sich wid mich legē.
Stand vff o herr zů helffen mir /
dañ du schlegst all myn fynde. vff dē
kinbackē mit begyr / vñ dē gotlosen
gsinde / Brichstu ir zeen herr mit ge
walt / die hilff sich herr by dir erhalt /
über dein volck der segen.

Nach disem gesang
Spricht der diener.

¶ Der herr gesegne vch ō herr be
hüt vch / der herr erleücht sein ange
sycht über vch vñ sy vch gnedig / der
herr heb sein angesycht über vch / vñ
sy vch gnedig / der herr heb sein ange
sycht über vch vñ geb vch dē friden.
Gont hyn ō geist des herrē / gebeüt

Figure 2.2 *Ordnu[n]g des Herren Nachtmal: so man die messz nennet, sampt der Tauff vn[nd] Jnsegu[n]g der Ee* (Strasbourg: Schwan, 1525), fols Bvi^{v}–Bvii^{v}. D Mbs – Rar. 4114 Beibd.4 (http://daten.digitale-sammlungen.de/0002/bsb00029012/images). Reproduced by permission of the Bayerische Staatsbibliothek, Munich

(*Christlich freyheyt*) and free prayer, 'which the spirit of God supplies' (*was der geist gottes yngibt*). The preface concluded with a declaration of assurance that in Strasbourg everything was based on truth and reason:

> in Strasbourg nothing will be done without being based on Scripture and truth. Pray that all who may read this will know that the Word of God is the truth, and is not to be despised. May the grace of God be with us all. Amen.[208]

Schwan's rhetorical strategy was to assure his readers that the Strasbourg Protestants, unlike the Papists, had no reason to conceal the content of Scripture from the people. It was therefore presented to them in his book, translated into German and published for the good of all who read it. There was nothing odious about it: it was the Word of God, and it was pleasing to God that his truth be known.[209]

There is a comparatively small amount of music in the book. However, unlike the order of the Lord's Supper in the *Teutsch Kirchenampt* of 1524, which only contained printed music for the texts of the Mass as well as 'Gott sey gelobet', the *Ordnung des Herren Nachtmal* version of the Lord's Supper contained the music for four songs, but not for any of the Mass texts. However, it was still intended that at least the Creed be sung (*Nach der predig singt ma[n] de[n] glaube[n]*). No instruction is given for the *Kyrie* and *Gloria* (either to sing or to speak). Could it have been that, as the Mass was already being banned in the churches, it was therefore no longer considered suitable for these texts to be sung, or indeed used at all? The Creed would have been exempt from this rule, being the Christian declaration of faith, indispensable to anyone who considered themselves a follower of Christ. As in *Ein schoner kurtzer begriff*, the Creed was presented as an unmetrical, direct translation into German.[210] In the *Ordnung des Herren Nachtmal*, as in previous liturgies, the *Sanctus* was to be spoken (*wie wir mitt demutiger veriehung spreche[n]. Heylig heylig / heylig ...*). The song 'Gott sey gelobet', or its alternative, 'Ach herr wie sind meiner sünd so vil' (Psalm 3),[211] appeared to function as a replacement for the *Agnus Dei*, a text which did not feature in this volume. In 1525, then, the assumption was being made by those who prepared the liturgical books that people would either already have memorised the tunes for the Mass texts, or would be reading them from elsewhere (for example, Speratus's *Glaube Deütsch*), or else would not be using them at all.

---

208 'bey vns zu Straßburg nichts on geschrifft vn[nd] grundt der warheit gehandelt wirt. Bitt hye bey alle so das lesen / die weyl es das wort gottes ist / nit zu verachten. Die gnad gottes sey mit vns allen / Amen'. *Ordnung des Herren Nachtmal* (1525), fol. Aij^{r}.

209 Bucer had also employed the words 'truth and reason' in the title of his treatise of 1524, *Grund und Ursach*.

210 In letters to Zwingli and Luther in 1524, the Strasbourg reformers report that the Creed was sung by the whole congregation (see pp. 57–8).

211 See Figure 2.2.

By far the largest number of hymns reproduced in one collection up to that point appeared under the title *Straszburger Kirchenampt*.[212] A copy of this volume, previously thought to be lost,[213] is held by the Regensburg Staatliche Bibliothek.[214] The book contains 24 songs,[215] including Luther's 'Gott sey gelobet', Symphorianus Pollio's[216] German setting of the *Magnificat*, settings of the Lord's Prayer and the Ten Commandments, two settings of Psalm 14, as well as Psalms 1 to 8 which the reader is directed to sing to the tune of 'Ach gott von hymel' (Psalm 12, also contained in this volume). In addition, settings of the *Kyrie*, *Gloria*, *Alleluia*, and *Credo* are to be found within its pages, all set to music. The layout is such that the book might be viewed as an intermediary stage between those publications in which hymns were integrated into the liturgy and those in which hymns were separated from the liturgy and printed as an appendix.[217] Some hymns, as well as the *Kyrie*, *Gloria*, and the two settings of the *Credo*, were contained within the liturgy of the Lord's Supper or Mass[218] (fols viij^{r}–xxj^{v}), and the remainder were included in the liturgy for Vespers (fols xxj^{v}–xxxxiiij^{v}).[219] However, the liturgy for Vespers provided multiple options for the psalm to be sung at the beginning of the service,[220] and Kōpfel printed 19 of them (taking up 38 pages of a total 92!). It is perhaps while printing this volume that Köpfel realised the sense in separating hymns from the liturgy.

The book contained two prefaces, both by Köpfel. The first explained that the *kirchenampt* was based on the 'three little books' (that is, the 1525 *Theütsch kirchenampt* trilogy), but that it had undergone a few corrections.[221] Köpfel also

212 *Strasz- | burger kirchen | ampt / nemlich von Jnse- | gu[n]g d[er] Eeleüt / vom Tauf | vnd vo[n] des herre[n] nacht | mal / mit etlichen Psal | men / die am end des | bůchlins / orden- | lich verzeych- | net sein* (Strasbourg: Köpfel, 1525). This title appears in *RISM DKL* (1525[21]) with slight orthographical differences..

213 *Hubert*, p. XVI; Bornert, *Réforme protestante du culte*, p. 120.

214 The last two pages of this copy are missing.

215 The 1525 *Theütsch Kirchenampt* trilogy may exceed this number (the hymn count for the second and third books together is 19), but as the contents of the first cannot be determined, a total number cannot be established.

216 Symphorianus Pollio and Wolfgang Musculus were perhaps the only Strasbourg reformers with any notable talent in music. Symphorianus's father had been a city musician in Strasbourg, and Symphorianus himself also took an interest in theology and literature. On both these men, see T. Gérold, *Les plus anciennes mélodies de l'Eglise protestante de Strasbourg et leurs auteurs* (Paris: Alcan, 1928), pp. 32–8.

217 See pp. 96–102 regarding *Psalmen gebett*.

218 'Von des herrn nachtmal / oder Mess'. *Straszburger Kirchenampt* (1525), fol. viij^{v}.

219 Except the *Alleluia*, which is printed at the very end of the book, after the table of contents. It may well have been a late addition.

220 'Zum ersten singt man ein psalmen / welche[n] man will / auß dem andern theyl der wie hienach volget'. *Straszburger kirchenampt* (1525), fol. xxj^{v}. The 'andern theyl' referred to is presumed to be the second volume of the 1525 *Theütsch kirchenampt*.

221 'DEr Straßburger kirchen handlu[n]g / mit gepreüchlichem gesång der gemein / hab ich inn dreyen bůchlin getrucket … Welche ich nůn vnder dem tittel / trucke mitt vast weniger verendrungen

sought to reassure readers that those who had bought this latest edition had not bought his earlier church orders in vain – every book had a role to play.[222] In the second preface, he implied that the orders of service contained in the book were in line with the wishes of the preachers, whereas before they had been printed without the preachers' permission (*gehelle*) and against their will.[223] Apparently for the first time, Bucer's name appears, and the recent changes in the liturgy are attributed to him: 'the servant of Christ, Martin Bucer, announced all innovations in *Grund und Ursach*, which I printed'.[224]

Perhaps the most perplexing and intriguing songbook of the early Reformation in Strasbourg is the *Enchiridion* of 1525.[225] Earlier sources, for reasons that will become clear, completely overlook this publication. The title page reads as follows:

> *Enchiridion geist | licher gesenge / so man yetzt | (Gott zů lob) yn der kirchen | syngt. Getzogen auß der hey | ligen geschrift des ware[n] vnd | heyligen Euangelions / wel | ches jetzt von gottes gnaden | wider auffgange[n] ist / vnd mit | etzlichen gesenge[n] Gemehrt / Gebessert / vn[nd] mit fleyß Cor | rigyert / mit einer Vorrede Docto. Martini Luther. Wittemberg. | M. D. XXV.*

Despite the title's claim that the book had emerged from the Wittenberg presses, the publication details given by *RISM DKL* are: 'Strasbourg: Schürer Erben, 1525'.[226] As the book actually originated with a Strasbourg printer, there must have been a good motive for having printed 'Wittemberg' on the cover. The reason is straightforward: the mention on a book's cover of Wittenberg

/ wie wol etwz correcter'. *Straszburger Kirchenampt* (1525), fol. Ajv. Reproduced in *Hubert*, p. 140.

222 'Des ich den leser verwarnet haben will / auff das er nit vergeblich kauffe / das er zů vor bezalet hat / Dan ich niemant beger zů beschweren'. *Straszburger Kirchenampt* (1525), fol. Ajv. Reproduced in *Hubert*, p. 140.

223 'Jch vnd andere / haben das kirchen ampt wie es von vnsern predicanten vnd pfarherrn erstlich fürgenomen / offt getruckt / wider iren willen vn[nd] gehelle … Nun haben die diener des worts / der gemein weitern v[er]stand angesehe[n] / vn[nd] jüngst als weyt ichs verstǒ / vffs aller nechst zur geschrifft getretten / vnd Christlich endrung fürgenommen … Welche ich aller gestalt / wie sys jetzund halte[n] / bedacht hab / an tag zů bringen'. *Straszburger Kirchenampt* (1525), fol. Aij. Reproduced in *Hubert*, p. 141.

224 'Wie der diener Christi Martin Butzer grund vnd vrsach aller newerung angezeygt, vnd ich getruckt habe'. *Straszburger Kirchenampt* (1525), fol. Aijr. Reproduced in *Hubert*, p. 141.

225 Influenced by the Erfurt *Enchiridion* (see p. 84).

226 The idea of a 'Schürer Erben' printing company originates with Joseph Benzing, who in 1960 identified a printer who, after Matthias Schürer's death in 1520, had published using Schürer's typescript (J. Benzing, 'Die Druckerei der Matthias Schürer Erben zu Strassburg (1520–1525)', *Archiv für Geschichte des Buchwesens*, 2 (1969), pp. 173–4). Benzing disagrees with Charles Schmidt's conclusion that the press came to a stop after Schürer's death, instead asserting that his widow or other heirs continued the trade (ibid., p. 170, referring to C. G. A. Schmidt, ed., *Répertoire bibliographique strasbourgeois*, 8 vols (Strasbourg: Heitz und Mündel, 1896), vol. 8: *Matthias Schürer – 1508–1520*).

suggested to the reader that Luther himself had endorsed the book, and thus dramatically increased sales potential. The inclusion of a preface by Luther, as in this volume, furthered that potential. In this time before copyright, piracy in printing was a common occurrence. There is no evidence whatsoever that Luther played any part in the publication of the Strasbourg *Enchiridion*, and it can be said that in all probability he knew nothing of it until its appearance. In fact, Luther was involved in the publication of only a few liturgical songbooks throughout Germany, most of which were produced in Wittenberg.[227] The earliest was probably Johann Walter's set of partbooks, *Geystliche gesangk Buchleyn*, commonly known as the *Chorgesangbuch*,[228] which Luther authorised, and to which he wrote the preface. Walter's book was produced partly in response to the appearance of publications such as the *Achtliederbuch*[229] (also claiming to be from Wittenberg, but actually published in Nuremberg) and the various editions of the Erfurt *Enchiridion*,[230] reproduced from broadsheets, and which included some of Luther's hymns.[231] The Strasbourg *Enchiridion* is similar in content to that of the Erfurt versions.

Luther's preface to Walter's *Geystliche gesangk Buchleyn* was subsequently published in several other hymn books,[232] including the Strasbourg *Enchiridion* (1525). Because the Strasbourg *Enchiridion* contained only unison melodies, its version of the preface did not include the final paragraph referring to Walter's polyphonic arrangements of the hymns, and instead retained only the sections that refer to hymn singing in a more general sense. Luther began by giving hymn singing historical precedent, referring to 'the example of the prophets and kings in the Old Testament who praised God with song and sound, with poetry and psaltery', and to 'the common and ancient custom of the Christian church to

---

227 See *LW*, 53, pp. 191–4.

228 *Geystliche gesangk | Buchleyn* (Wittenberg: Klug, 1524).

229 *Etlich Cristlich lider | Lobegesang / vn[nd] Psalm / dem rai- | nen wort Gottes gemeß / auß der | heylige[n] schrifft / durch mancher- | ley hochgelerter gemacht / in der | Kirchen zu singen / wie es dann | [z]um tayl berayt zu Wittenberg | in ubung ist* (Nuremberg: Gutknecht, 1524). Three editions of this book appeared in Nuremberg during 1524. Two of these mistakenly carry the date *M. D. Xiiij*. A facsimile of the last edition (held in the Niedersächsische Staats- und Universitätsbibliothek, Göttingen) appears as an insert to *Jahrbuch für Liturgie und Hymnologie*, 2 (1956).

230 *Eyn Enchiridion oder | Handbuchleyn. eynem ytz- | lichen Christen fast nutzlich bey sich | zuhaben / zur stetter vbung vnd | trachtung geystlicher gesenge | vnd Psalmen / Recht- | schaffen vnd kunst- | lich verteutscht* (Erfurt: Loersfeld, 1524).

Loersfeld made a second edition of this title in the same year: *Eyn Enchiridion oder | Handbuchleyn. eynem ytz- | lichen Christen / fast nutzlich bey sych zuha- | ben / zur stetter vbung vnnd trachtung | Geystlicher gesenge vnd Psalmen | Rechtschaffen vnnd Kunstlich | verteutscht / vnd mit grosserm | fleyß (dan vor) vebersehe[n] / gecorrigiert vn[nd] | Gedruckt.*

The third version, published by Maler, is entitled: *Enchiridion | Oder eyn Handbuchlein / | eynem yetzlichen Christen fast nutzlich | bey sich zuhaben / zur stetter vbung vnnd trachtung geystlicher ge- | senge / vnd Psalmen / Recht- | schaffen vnnd kunstlich | vertheutscht* (Erfurt: Maler, 1524).

231 Leaver, *Luther's Liturgical Music*, p. 19, n. 69; Blume, 'The Period of the Reformation', p. 46.

232 Leupold, *LW*, 53, p. 315.

sing Psalms'.[233] He then gave several scriptural references as further examples of how important it is to praise God through music, 'so that God's Word and Christian teaching might be instilled and implanted in many ways'.[234]

The idea that music could instil and implant God's Word 'in many ways' is a crucial point. Early Reformation thought made much of the necessity of the Word of God in the existence of the true Church, and it was sometimes asserted that simply by hearing the Word, the hearts of the faithful would be made gracious. For Luther, this was part of his effort to allow the Gospel message to be received as an act of hearing, rather than as an act of seeing.[235] As Ulinka Rublack has pointed out, it is therefore not difficult to see why early Reformation sermons attracted such crowds, if one considers that they were told that the Word of God would literally 'fall' into their hearts if they were listening.[236] These ideas, also adopted by the Strasbourg reformers, were largely based on the Augustinian thinking that placed the sense of hearing above that of seeing, a view shared by the humanists of the sixteenth century.[237] Music, for Luther as well as for Bucer, was an essential element in the process of disseminating the Word of God, because singing enabled the Word to be more easily internalised, and enhanced the meaning of the text in question. The reformers may have been familiar with the works of the German mystic Meister Eckhart (c. 1260–1327), who wrote, 'Hearing brings things to me'.[238] By using congregational singing, though, in which all the people participated, the reformers were able to turn this into a multi-directional process: not only was the Word *heard*, but it was also *produced*. In a space where people were hearing words, internalising them, and then reproducing them, it could be suggested that the reformers were quite literally putting words in the mouths of the laity, in the expectation that such

233 'dieweyl man yederman nit allein das exempel der Propheten vnd Konige ym alten Testament (die mit tichte[n] vnd allerley seytten spiel Gott gelobet haben) sondern auch solcher brauch sonderlich mit Psalmen gemeyner Christenheit vo[n] anfang / kundt ist'. *Enchiridion geistlicher gesange* (1525), fol. Aj[v]; *WA*, 35, p. 474; translated in *LW*, 53, pp. 315–16.

234 'Auff das dadurch Gottes wort vnd Christliche leere / auff allerley weyse getryben vnd geubt werden'. *Enchiridion geistlicher gesange* (1525), fol. Aij[r]; *WA*, 35, p. 474; translated in *LW*, 53, p. 316.

235 Em Griffin argues that the rise of print culture installed 'sight at the head of the hierarchy of senses' (E. Griffin, *A First Look at Communication Theory*, 5th edn (New York: McGraw-Hill, 2003) p. 346), and Robert Jütte has written that 'the invention of printing decisively assisted the breakthrough of visual culture' (R. Jütte, trans. J. Lynn, *A History of the Senses: From Antiquity to Cyberspace* (Cambridge: Polity, 2005), p. 66). True as that may be, experiencing vision in terms of printed material was nevertheless a different sort of sight – not the same as experiencing the visual aspects of religious ceremonies before the Reformation, for example – and, given the fact that texts tended to be read out loud at this time, this sort of sight was surely closer in nature to the act of hearing. The issue of overlap between sight and hearing is discussed in 'Classification: The Hierarchy of the Senses', the third chapter of Jütte's *A History of the Senses*, pp. 54–71. See also U. C. Rublack, *Reformation Europe* (Cambridge: Cambridge University Press, 2005), p. 158.

236 Rublack, *Reformation Europe*, p. 48.

237 Jütte, *A History of the Senses*, pp. 55, 61, 64; Rublack, *Reformation Europe*, p. 48.

238 Cited in Jütte, *A History of the Senses*, p. 67.

words would enter and remain in their hearts and minds.[239] Furthermore, because of the nature of a collective setting and oral culture of this kind, the reformers would have anticipated that the Word of God would also be spread outwardly, from person to person.[240]

The Ongoing Liturgical Battle

Around the middle of 1525 Capito and his colleagues wrote to Klaus Kniebis, *Ammeister* of Strasbourg,[241] asking that the Mass, 'clerical singing' (*pfaffen gesang*), and 'Pagan usages' (*heidnysche gewonheiten*) be abolished.[242] This, they argued, was for the honour of God, and for the good of weak-willed people. Such people ought to abstain from the Lord's Supper until they have been strengthened by the Word of God.

The committee appointed to oversee changes in the service[243] submitted a report in July 1525, entitled *Vnser herren Meister und Rats Bedacht*,[244] proposing that the canons and vicars, instead of celebrating the traditional offices, sing a service of psalms and readings in German, and explain to the people present the meaning and background to the readings. They should start by singing *Deus in adiutorium* and *Domine ad adiuvandum*, and these should be followed by two or three psalms with a scriptural antiphon. These would be sung 'with devotion and unhurried voice' (*mit andacht und gemacher stim*).[245] Following this, there should be a reading from either the Old or the New Testament. This was to be followed by a sermon lasting a quarter of an hour, after which the people were to recite the Lord's Prayer together. This service should replace the medieval

---

[239] See Deut. 11:18: 'Fix these words of mine in your hearts and minds; tie them as symbols on your hands and bind them on your foreheads'.

[240] The belief in such a strong and direct connection between the body and the mind was also apparent in cures for those thought to be possessed by demons. Priests in Liège in 1374, for example, performed exorcism rituals by forcing open the mouths of the afflicted and shouting into them, 'Get thee hence, thou damned and foredoomed spirit!' Quoted in E. L. Backman, trans. E. Classen, *Religious Dances in the Christian Church and in Popular Medicine* (London: Allen & Unwin, 1952), p. 199; and J. Waller, *A Time to Dance, a Time to Die: The Extraordinary Story of the Dancing Plague of 1518* (Royston, Herts.: Icon Books, 2008), p. 155.

[241] 1 AST 80, 3; *BDS*, 2, pp. 462–5. Kniebis was a councillor in Strasbourg from 1512, and was a member of the Council of the XIII (responsible for dealing with political and military matters) from 1519. In addition, he was a staunch supporter of the preachers and the evangelical reforms (see *CorrCapito*, 2, p. 5; *BDS*, 2, p. 462), and it was likely that the Mass was abolished in most of the city's churches in 1525 with his help.

[242] 1 AST 80, 3, fols 1v–2r; *BDS*, 2, pp. 464–5.

[243] See p. 74.

[244] 1 AST 80, 4; 1 AST 166, 5.17 (fols 107v–108r).

[245] The reformers believed that with slower singing (and therefore slower breathing), the words being sung would 'fall' into the heart, thus making the process not just a mental, but also a physical one. I am grateful to Ulinka Rublack for this observation.

offices of Prime, Terce, Sext, and None. Vespers, however, should be retained, but should take the following form: Beginning again with *Deus in adiutorium*, the canons and vicars would also then sing two or three psalms with a scriptural antiphon, with unhurried and devotional voice. Again, a biblical passage was to be read, and the service was then ended with the *Magnificat* and the blessing.

As for the Mass, however, the committee at this stage wished to keep it in its current form, 'as before', except that the Epistle and Gospel readings should 'be read out loud in clear German', and that the canon also be omitted, since it was considered contrary to Scripture.[246] The service was to end with a song of praise such as the Song of Zechariah (the *Benedictus*, perhaps in the form later published in the 1530 edition of *Psalmen gebett*),[247] a sung scriptural antiphon, and a blessing.

Similar proposals, up until the citywide ban of the Mass was achieved in 1529, exist in abundance. Jakob Sturm,[248] councillor in Strasbourg and a member of the reforming committee,[249] wrote about a multitude of matters in a document from August 1525,[250] including Latin, the use of Scripture, payments for singing, the Mass, and services for the deceased. This report was written in light of other recent proposals, including *Vnser herren Meister und Rats Bedacht* mentioned above, and another[251] which stated that church song needed to be changed in order to be compatible with the Word and commandment of Christ.[252] One of the document's most important aspects is the position it takes regarding the Mass. Sturm was in favour of reform, but urged caution over the abolition of this ancient form of worship, warning that 'such change or rejection of the Mass would bring a great deal of unwillingness not only from those who live outside, but also inside, the city'. The matter needed further consideration, and no hasty decision was to be made.[253]

---

[246] 'und sonst wie bitzher, doch das die Epistel und das Evangelium im Lectorio, den man den Lettener nent, in tutscher heller sproch gelesen werd, ouch das der Canon in den stucken, do er wider [die] schriffte, geendert oder gar vnderlossen'. 1 AST 80, 4, fol. 32v; 1 AST 166, 5.17, fol. 108r; *BDS*, 2, p. 467.

[247] The manuscript sources refer to the 'Benedictus', which has been identified in this case as the Song of Zechariah. See *BDS*, 2, p. 467, n. 10.

[248] Thomas Brady's suggestion that this latter document was penned by Sturm is convincing (Brady, '"Sind also zu beiden theilen christen"', p. 71, n. 21); that assumption has therefore been made here.

[249] Brady, '"Sind also zu beiden theilen christen"', p. 71.

[250] 1 AST 166, 8.5 (fols 128v–129v). Printed in Brady, '"Sind also zu beiden theilen christen"', pp. 73–6. N.B.: Brady has taken liberties with some of the original spellings, but unless they are considered drastic misreadings, Brady's spellings have been retained here.

[251] Brady, '"Sind also zu beiden theilen christen"', p. 71.

[252] 1 AST 37, 4, fols 49r–49v; *BDS*, 2, p. 468.

[253] 'Der mess halben, dweyl solliche enderung oder abthun der mess ein grossen voratt widerwillen nit allein bey denen, so usserhalb, sonder auch in der statt wonen, bringen wurt, zu dem ein sach, die wol weithers und meres bedenkes und rots erheischt, mocht man noch zur zeit besorgen

Significantly, the first major aspect to be discussed in the report was song. He perceived three problems with the songs of the Roman Church: first, that they were too lengthy and too numerous; second, that many were unscriptural; and third, that they were performed by ignorant, unscholarly people.[254] Lengthy songs and prayers could lead to annoyance. For that reason, the service of Matins (which was rushed and 'held without devotion') could be dropped. Christ himself, said Sturm, was critical of length and idle talk.[255] Likewise, he continued,

> instead of the services of Prime, Terce, Sext, and None: one might hold in their place Prime (wherein the Athanasian Creed is sung as a confession of faith), to be sung before Mass with gentle voice, in order to be accounted for what one sings, and instead of the appointed reading a whole or half chapter is thereafter read from the New Testament in a slow and steady manner.[256]

Furthermore, one was to 'refrain from the sort of antiphon, collect, or responsory which is not taken from Scripture or comparable to it'. The Scriptures already contained an abundance of material, without the need to create more.[257] He repeated the request that foreign languages should not be used unless an interpreter was present.[258] However, the Latin language in itself could not be considered blasphemous or false, as Scripture stated that God may be praised in all languages.[259] Songs for the deceased should not be used, as they were intended for the benefit of the living rather than for the dead. 'Instead, though, at someone's departing, whosoever desires may pray silently to God, and ask for his merciful judgement'.[260] Discussions of music at funerals and burials are

---

und die fronmess in den stifften halten lassen'. 1 AST 166, 8.5, fols 129r–129v; Brady, '"Sind also zu beiden theilen christen"', p. 75.

[254] 'nemlich die lenge und vile des gesangs und dannoch, das ettlich gesang nit schrifftlich sonder wider schrifft durch unverstendig, ungelert leut ussgericht, mochten die selben gebessert werden'. 1 AST 166, 8.5, fol. 128v; Brady, '"Sind also zu beiden theilen christen"', p. 74.

[255] 'Der erst: dweil in langem gesang und gebett nit wol moglich, das nit verdruss infell, des halben man darnoch on andacht zum end eilet, auch sollich lenge und vil geschwetz in Evangelio von Christo verworffen wirt, mocht man die metten am morgen underlossen'. 1 AST 166, 8.5, fol. 128v; Brady, '"Sind also zu beiden theilen christen"', p. 74.

[256] 'desglichen an statt prim, tertz, sextum, non, derselbigen zeit ein, nemlich die prim, dorin das symbolum Athanasii als ein bekanntnuss des glaubens gesungen wird, vor der mess singen mit gemacher stimm, domit betracht werden mocht, was man singe; und an statt des capittel ein gantz oder halb, ie darnoch es lang wert, capittel uss dem neuen testament lessen'. 1 AST 166, 8.5, fol. 128v; Brady, '"Sind also zu beiden theilen christen"', p. 74.

[257] 'Zum andern: was fur antiphon, collecten, responsoria, himni &c., so nit uss der schrifft genommen oder derselben sich verglichen, mocht man underlossen, dweyl man der schrifftlichen genug hat, besonders die so alt und de tempore bissher gesungen worden'. 1 AST 166, 8.5, fol. 129r; Brady, '"Sind also zu beiden theilen christen"', p. 74.

[258] 1 AST 166, 8.5, fol. 129r; Brady, '"Sind also zu beiden theilen christen"', p. 74.

[259] 1 AST 166, 8.5, fol. 128v; Brady, '"Sind also zu beiden theilen christen"', p. 74.

[260] 'Vigilien, selmessen, gesang über den grebern und ander dotten gesang, dweyl es für gesichtig und eigennutzug angesehen werden will und den abgestorbenen nit hoch furtreglich,

especially lacking at this time in Strasbourg's Reformation, nor is there any direction about the matter in the printed liturgies until 1537. This comment is therefore one of the few insights into the reformers' thinking on the subject.[261]

In the following paragraph, Sturm addressed the *Präsenz*, the stipend awarded to singers. He acknowledged that in times past, the chapter had dealt with payment as it saw fit, usually by dividing the money between those present at the service. Sturm's proposal was that

> to avoid causing upset, one should not divide [the money] in the church, but rather write down on a board the names of those who are present, and then distribute [the money] weekly or daily in the [chapter] house.[262]

In the section concerning preaching, Sturm criticised the recent quarrels and division of the Church, which had been happening instead of fraternity and Christian unity – the true aims of Christian worship. While arguments about such things as vestments, gestures, and so on were taking place, society was

> losing the goal and the purpose for which the sacrament was institutionalised, which is brotherly love. It is because of external things that we fall into disputes, quarrels, hate, and jealousy. Each despises the other as if his Mass and his form were better that those of the other. Some Christians call themselves evangelical, and call the others Papists and hypocrites, whereas the others say that they themselves are the true, old Christians and that the others are heretics, Hussites, and so on. In fact, both parties are Christian, of God's mercy, etc.[263]

---

mocht man gar underlassen; sonder so yemans abschidt, der des begert mit einem innerlichen gebett gott dem herrn und siner barmhertzigen urteyl bevelhen'. 1 AST 166, 8.5, fol. 129r; Brady, '"Sind also zu beiden theilen christen"', p. 75. N.B.: Brady reads the fourth word as 'üzer'.

[261] *Psalmen vnnd geystliche Lieder* (Strasbourg: Prüss & Köpfel, 1537) makes no mention of psalms or singing more generally in the case of burials and marriages, but recommends only communal and silent prayers. See also Gérold, *Les plus anciennes mélodies*, p. 78.

[262] 'doch das umb verletzung willen ettlicher ungestimmen, sie nit in der kirchen umgetheilet; sonder die, so zugegen weren, durch einen in ein tafel uffgezeigt und als dann all wochen oder tag in den husern ussgeteilt wurden'. 1 AST 166, 8.5, fol. 129r; Brady, '"Sind also zu beiden theilen christen"', p. 75.

[263] 'Dan dodurch volgt, so wie unss zancken, mit was kleidung, mit was geberden, mit was vor oder nochgonden gebett, gesangen, zu was zeiten und was des usserlichen plunderwerks ist, die mess gehalten soll werden, das wir dadurch das furnemen und das end, darumb diss sacrament uffgesetzt ist, verlieren, das ist die brüderliche liebe. Dan durch das usserlich fallen wir in widerwillen, zanck nit und hass gegen einander, veracht ie einer den andern, als ob sin mess, sin manier, besser dan des andern wer; nennen sich etlich christen evangelisch, die andern papistisch und glisner, dargegen die andern nennen sich die rechten, alten christen und die andern ketzerlichen Hussen &c. und derglichen. Sind also zu beiden theilen christen, des gott erbarm &c'. 1 AST 166, 8.5, fol. 129v; Brady, '"Sind also zu beiden theilen christen"', pp. 75–6. N.B.: Brady incorrectly reads 'uffgericht' instead of 'vffgesetzt', towards the end of the first sentence of this quotation. In the second part of the penultimate sentence, Brady reads 'nennen ettlich christen [sich] evangelisch', instead of 'nennen sich etlich christen evangelisch'.

This was an extremely liberal and generous statement, and one that must have been quite rare, even among the reformers of such 'middle-way' places of reform as Strasbourg. Sturm was reminding his readership that Christian unity was still the objective, and that all those who believed – even the Papists – were Christians. He added that 'internal devotion and reverence in song and Masses may not be produced through ordinances, law, and orders from authority, but must be given by God and his Spirit'.[264]

In summary, Sturm showed favour towards the Mass and towards the Latin language, but believed that the chapters should negotiate with the preachers for the establishment of a Christian service.[265] He acknowledged that clerical abuse had occurred in Strasbourg, and that the council should take measures to prevent this happening in the future. Singing also needed to be improved, so that the words were not sung too quickly, but the practice was not to be abolished. From a musical perspective, the tone of the document is similar to the 'Conclusiones Jacobi' discussed earlier, and broadly in line with Luther's views.

Choral Experiments

Bucer, however, was less convinced about the value of the Mass. In his 'Rathschlag' from 6 May 1526,[266] he called the Mass the 'greatest form of entertainment of the anti-Christian empire',[267] criticising it in particular for its lack of admonition and teaching. The council was reminded that only by listening to sermons would the people encounter Scripture in any meaningful way. In addition, any new service had to be compatible with Scripture, and the reformers expressed disappointment that one proposed order sent to the council, which included singing and reading, had been dismissed.[268]

However, on this occasion, Bucer did not rule out the use of Latin – even in music. He instead suggested using an interpreter who 'would interpret

[264] 'Die innerlich andacht und uffmercknus im gesang und messen mag durch ordnungen gesetz vnd gebott der oberkeit oder ander nit geben werden, sonder die muss durch gott und seinen geist geben werden'. 1 AST 166, 8.5, fol. 129v; Brady, '"Sind also zu beiden theilen christen"', p. 76. N.B.: Brady incorrectly reads 'gestz' instead of 'gesetz'.

[265] 1 AST 166, 8.5, fol. 129v; Brady, '"Sind also zu beiden theilen christen"', p. 76.

[266] 'Rathschlag M. butzers vom singen, lesen, vßlegen vnd tisch des herren: das ist gantzer kirchen ybung, wie die dem wort gottes nach zu Straßbůrg möchte angericht vnd gehalten werden' ('Martin Bucer's advice on singing, reading, interpreting, and the table of the Lord: as is the practice of the whole church, and how it is prepared and carried out in Strasbourg according to the Word of God'). 1 AST 38, 3, fols 87r–96v; printed in *BDS*, 2, pp. 470–82. Several other versions also exist, including 1 AST 38, 3a; and 1 AST 166, 9.6 (fols 130r–134v). See also *CorrBucer*, 2, pp. 109–10.

[267] 'Die meß, wie sy bißher gehalten ist, nun ein lange zyt, ist die gröste vnderhaltung des wider christlichen rychs gewesen'. 1 AST 38, 3, fol. 89r; *BDS*, 2, p. 472.

[268] 1 AST 38, 3, fol. 90v–91r; *BDS*, 2, p. 474.

something every time from song for the laypeople'.[269] In light of some of his earlier comments on Latin, this appears to be somewhat of a U-turn. In *Grund und Ursach* (1524), Bucer had written that the language 'does not contain anything that is good or useful which could not be said more artistically and better in the Hebrew and Greek languages'. It was a language 'used by the old Romans and even more so by the new Papists to blind other nations and to bring them into subservience'.[270] But Latin continued to be taught in the schools of Strasbourg.[271] Later evidence suggests that there was a somewhat schizophrenic approach to Latin among the city's scholars, not least in Bucer himself. Brady has suggested that Jakob Sturm's defence of the use of Latin in August 1525[272] was in response to Bucer's attack on it in *Grund und Ursach*, and he implies that Sturm may have helped change Bucer's mind over the matter.[273] But in a letter to Zwingli dated 25 May 1530, Bucer expressed his horror that the Church in Saxony had reintroduced Latin singing and vestments, adding that he would rather undergo torture than become a Christian of that sort![274] Many years later, Johann Sturm, rector of the Gymnasium established in 1538, considered it necessary to defend the language when writing to a teacher:

> I know that you would like to teach a more advanced class but now we need you as a fighter in the arena against the barbarous gladiators who destroy the party of Latin. But eventually the Latin language will spread and bear great fruit in public and judicial life, in the Magistracies and the Councils, in the churches, everywhere in the Christian Republic.[275]

The use of Latin in Wittenberg should also be borne in mind. Luther's *Formula Missae* (1523) enabled the choir to sing the Mass in Latin. As time

---

[269] 'Wyter, die wyl mit frembder sprach in der gemein on ein yßleger nit gesungen oder gepettet werden soll, so wurdt man ouch in ieden stifften miessen haben, die zu ieder zit, vom gsang ettwas für die leyen vßlegen'. 1 AST 38, 3, p. 98; *BDS*, 2, p. 471.

[270] Bucer, *Grund und Ursach*, p. 209.

[271] 1 AST 174, 16, fol. 180v mentions two schools that taught Latin and Greek. Printed in *BDS*, 2, p. 556.

[272] See above, p. 88.

[273] Brady, '"Sind also zu beiden theilen christen"', pp. 72–3.

[274] Zurich Staatsarchiv, E. II. 339, fol. 327r; Zentralbibliothek Zürich, ms. S 25, 138. Printed in *CorrBucer*, 4, pp. 112–13.

[275] 'Fateor sanè in superioribus te curiis utilem & idoneum esse posse: & aliquando ex illis tibi aliqua committetur: breui fortassis: sed nunc in hac arena te pugile habemus opus contra barbaros gladiatores: qui latini sermonis puritatem propter negligentiam corrumpunt: & propter in uidiam non patiuntur efflorescere. Efflorescit autem in hac ætate cui tu præpositus es: & maturescit in superioribus gradibus: & fructus edit uberrimos in foro & iudicio: in magistratu et curia: in templis & Ecclesiis Christi: in omnibus locis Reipublicæ Christianæ'. 'Ioannes Sturmius Abrahamo Feisio Praefecto decimæ curiæ', fol. 5v, in J. Sturm, *Classicarum epistolarum Lib. III. Siue Scholae argentinenses restitutæ* (Strasbourg: Rihel, 1565). See also the modern edition by Rott (Paris, Droz, 1938), p. 31. Translated in Chrisman, *Lay Culture, Learned Culture*, p. 196.

went on, however, and especially after 1525 (following the publication of Johann Walter's *Chorgesangbuch*), the singing of a section of Latin Mass text would sometimes be followed by a congregational German translation in the form of a hymn.[276] Perhaps this acted as a signal to the reformers in Strasbourg that the use of Latin in church was acceptable, so long as the congregation was able to understand the text through an interpreter or a vernacular reiteration.

As in Sturm's document from August 1525,[277] singing was discussed first in Bucer's *Rathschlag*, surely emphasising the importance of music in the eyes of the Strasbourg reformers. The Word of God had been corrupted, said Bucer, by people who spoke or sang it without understanding its meaning. All praises should be Christian, and all other songs and prayers, according to Scripture, were a disgrace to God. Singers and interpreters should be Christian, and should already receive a salary from elsewhere and therefore not receive payment for their extra duties.[278]

> It befits authority to appoint, just as David did, the most holy and pious to oversee such singing [in church], and on no grounds to appoint lechers, the miserly, idol worshippers, slanderers, drunkards, thieves, or those with other disorderly lives … Therefore it will be necessary specifically to appoint some Christian God-fearing men over Christian song and practice, such as the ones that can, God willing, be found in the chapters, in order that the praise of God might not be a blasphemy of God.[279]

As becomes clear from later Strasbourg documents, the suggestion here was that existing church singers be put to use under the new regime. Bucer provided scriptural evidence that those who sang in church should be good people. He strongly recommended that the churches of Strasbourg should emulate the practice exemplified by David[280] of appointing devout individuals to lead the service of singing. He suggested that the singers would 'become distinctly better' if the Psalter was 'sung from the beginning to the end, and also that books

276 Blume, 'The Period of the Reformation', p. 58.

277 1 AST 166, 8.5.

278 1 AST 38, 3, p. 98; *BDS*, 2, p. 471.

279 'so gepürt doch der oberkeit, das sy wie Daůid die geistlichsten vnd frumbsten yber sollch gesang verordne, vnd vmb keiner vrsach willen buler, geytzige, götzendiener, schelter, trunckenböltz, reuber, vnd die sunst ouch vnordelich leben … Darumb wirt von nöten sin, das die oberkeit yber solch christlich gesang vnd ybung sunderlich verordne vnd sötze etlich Christliche gotzförchtige menner, wie man die noch wol vff den stifften, ob gott will, fünden würdt, domit nit vß dem lob gottes ein lösterung gottes werde'. 1 AST 38, 3, p. 97; *BDS*, 2, p. 471. This is possibly a reference to the passage in 1 Corinthians in which Paul lists those who will not be let through the gates of Heaven (1 Cor. 6: 9–10). Other reformers compiled similar lists of immoral traits. See, for example, Calvin's sermon on Matt. 28:1–10, in J. I. McCord and E. Mülhaupt, eds, *Supplementa Calviniana – Sermons inédits*, 12 vols (Neukirchen-Vluyn: Neukirchener Verlag, 1961–), vol. 7, p. 98.

280 See 1 Chr. 6:31.

of the Bible be read in order'.[281] All this, he stated, was based on the teachings of St Paul.

Several years into the Reformation, the notion of a group of singers appointed to sing in church also seems to have found favour in the eyes of Erasmus. In a discussion of the development of church music throughout history, he wrote,

> In early times the entire congregation sang and responded 'Amen' to the priest. The consequent thunderous noise and ridiculous confusion of voices produced a spectacle unworthy of divine worship. In our day those who are appointed sing fittingly and the rest sing to the Lord in their hearts.[282]

In other words, the current arrangement, whereby the congregation remained silent while the choir sang on their behalf, had been instituted for a reason – namely to avoid 'thunderous noise and ridiculous confusion'. He was also complimentary about the quality of music-making in contemporary church practice. However, in a later text, Erasmus made less favourable comparisons. Professional singers, whom he called

> the dregs of humanity, the vile and unreliable (as a great many are drunken revelers), are kept on a salary, and because of this pernicious custom the church is burdened with heavy expenses. I ask you to consider, how many paupers, dying in want, could be supported on the salaries of singers?[283]

Bucer, on the other hand, avoided bringing the standard of singing into the discussion on that occasion, believing the morals of the singers to be of greater significance.

However, it is not clear whether Bucer intended the congregation to sing along with the 'God-fearing men' of which he spoke. The implication was indeed that these men were to be put in place to teach the singing to the people, but as this was not specifically said, it is difficult to make a definitive statement about their intended function. Robin Leaver has suggested that during the first few years

---

[281] 'Mer, das die senger firnemlich gebössert werden vnd nit wie dis här on verstandt psallieren vnd lesen, würdt nutzlich sin, das der psalter von anfang biß zu end gesungen werd, vnd also ouch die biblischen biecher noch ordenung werden gelesen'. 1 AST 38, 3, p. 99; *BDS*, 2, p. 472.

[282] 'Olim totus populus canebat et sacerdoti respondebat: amen. Ibi strepitus tonitruo non absimilis et ridicula vocum confusio spectaculum exhibebat indignum cultu diuino; nunc designati sunt qui canant decenter, caeteri psallunt in cordibus suis Domino'. Erasmus, 'Contra Pseudevangelicos' (1530), in K. Kumaniecki et al., eds, *Opera Omnia Desiderii Erasmi Roterodami*, 9 parts (Amsterdam: North-Holland, 1969–), part 9, vol. 1, p. 306. Translated and quoted in C. E. Miller, 'Erasmus on Music', *The Musical Quarterly*, 56 (1966), p. 334.

[283] 'Alitur sordidorum ac levium, ut plerique sunt Dionysiaci, hominum colluvies, ac tantis sumptibus oneratur Ecclesia ob rem pestiferam etiam. Quæso te ut rationem ineas, quot pauperes de vita periclitantes poterant ali cantorum salariis?' Erasmus, *Opera Omnia* (1703–6), vol. 6, cols 731–2. Translated and quoted in Miller, 'Erasmus on Music', p. 339.

of reform in Lutheran parts of Germany, the choir acted 'as the representative of the congregation', so that the choir could teach the congregation the new hymns.[284] There is evidence to suggest that a trial along similar lines was attempted in Strasbourg (although in the hope that the choir would eventually become obsolete as the congregation learnt the tunes), although it seems to have failed quite remarkably.

One document from the late 1520s[285] states the reasons for the decline in church song over the centuries and outlines a plan for its renewal. It explains that in the days of the Church Fathers, 'the laity was taught and admonished … through interpretation and homilies'. However, because of the increasing number of endowments and payments for sung Masses, the frequency of such events had multiplied over time in such a way that it was no longer possible for them to be 'performed with correct devotion and with the fruit of improvement, nor kindheartedly or spiritually'.[286] As a possible solution, it is explained that during the mid-1520s the canons were asked to lead the singing of the German hymns in church (rather than sing by themselves in Latin), so that once again the people could be led to devotion in song, and that the canons themselves might receive salvation. Unfortunately, the canons had no desire 'to be reasonable' on this point, and essentially refused the council's request. Therefore, 'both for reasons of conscience and of civil peace', hired singers and readers were thereafter no longer to be used in worship.[287]

Even if the canons as a group were not willing to be a part of the new liturgical setup, some individuals employed as cantors and organists were a little more adaptable. They were, unsurprisingly, keen on maintaining a regular source

284 Leaver, 'The Lutheran Reformation', in I. Fenlon, ed., *The Renaissance* (Macmillan: Basingstoke, 1989), p. 270.

285 AA 420, Fassung A (fols 14r–30r) and Fassung B (fols 31r–41r). Printed in *BDS*, 3, pp. 342–92.

286 'Zeÿgten an / wie das von den heÿligen allten vätternn dermassen vffkhom[m]en / das dadurch / neben den heilig[e]n psalmen vnnd gebett / durch die lectionen vnnd Capitelen / erstlich die solchs yebeten gepessert / vnnd zue geÿstlichen empternn geschickt / Demnach auch durch vßlegung vnnd Omelÿen / die leÿen geleeret vnnd ermanet wurden. Nun aber were es dahyn geratten / das erstlich von wegen der Stifftungen vnnd presentzen / die täglich zůegeno[m]men / solich gesang also gemeeret vnnd gehaufet / das nit wol möglich / das es mit rechter andacht vnnd frucht der Besserung / auch vonn den guethertizgen vnd rechtgeÿstlichen volbracht werden möchte'. AA 420, fol. 35r; *BDS*, 3, p. 373.

287 'Vnnd Alß aber solche vergleÿchung nach vÿlfälltigem[m] ansuechen / beÿ den Stiffts vnnd Closter personen nit statt haben wöllen / damit dan[n] nit geachtet wůrde eins Raths meinung zusein / khein kirchen gesang oder vebung fur die geÿstlichen zugedulden / haben sÿe durch etlich gelerte ein gesang vnnd üebung / so erstlich göttlicher geschrifft / dem nach dem brauch der elltern kirchen / vnnd leere der heÿligen / vätter gemeß / vß dem die singer vnnd zuehörer frucht / vnnd furderung zue gotseligheÿt erlangen möchten / Anstellen / vnnd jnen furhallt[e]n lassenn. Aber es hatt beÿ den Stiffts personen auch nit annemlich wöllen sein / Deshalb[e]n dann einen E. Rath / beÿde der gewissen vnnd auch Burgerlichs frides halb nit meer möglich / das angestellt singen vnnd lesen wider in ÿebung zukhom[m]en lassenn'. AA 420, fol. 35v; *BDS*, 3, p. 375. See also 1 AST 37, 6, fol. 77v.

of income. In 1528, a group of musicians, including the cathedral organist Maternus Kreiss,[288] while acknowledging in a letter to the council (in a rather desperate tone) that the Mass was indeed an abomination to God, requested permission to continue collecting the *Präsenz* for as long as the Mass was celebrated, and asked that once it was abolished other work might be provided.[289] An assurance of job security was a reasonable thing to seek, given not just the religious instability across Europe but also the disappearance of ecclesiastical music in several cities.

The role of the cantor in late medieval times was to lead the choir in its singing, and to begin the singing of plainchant. In addition to this, he was often responsible for the singers in the choir. During the Reformation in those Protestant areas still employing music in the liturgy, Strasbourg being no exception, the cantor maintained a very important role.[290] In 1522, Matthias Greiter, described in the chronicles as 'a good musician' (*ein guter musicus*), was appointed *Vorsänger*, or cantor, at the cathedral. He continued to work at the cathedral as Strasbourg's first Protestant cantor. Like his colleague Wolfgang Dachstein, his role was now to compose new melodies for the congregation to sing, and the fruits of their labour are to be found in the liturgical orders and hymn books.[291] After the city's failed attempt at getting the canons to lead the congregational singing in Strasbourg, it would no doubt also have been Greiter's job to teach the new songs to the cathedral congregation. Clearly, his contributions to the Strasbourg reforms were enough to keep him in place for many years. He held benefices from various churches,[292] including St Thomas,[293] but his role as cathedral cantor was financed by the city council rather than out of the medieval benefice system.[294] With the return of Catholicism to Strasbourg

---

288 On Kreiss, see II 47a, 2, fols 106v–107r (also 90 Z 13, pp. 38–40), and 1 AST 87, 20 (also 90 Z 16, pp. Ntr 2–Ntr 3).

289 1 AST 87, 32; 90 Z 16, pp. Ntr 4–Ntr 6. See also A. Baum, *Magistrat und Reformation in Strassburg bis 1529* (Strasbourg: Heitz & Mündel, 1887), pp. 204–5; and *Fragments des anciennes chroniques d'Alsace*, IV (1901), no. 4721.

290 On the position of cantor during the Reformation, see H. Robinson-Hammerstein, 'The Lutheran Reformation and its Music', in Robinson-Hammerstein, ed., *The Transmission of Ideas in the Lutheran Reformation* (Dublin: Irish Academic Press, 1989), pp. 159–60.

291 *Fragments des anciennes chroniques d'Alsace*, III (1892), nos 2657 and 3027; *Fragments des anciennes chroniques d'Alsace*, II (1889), no. 2245. Cantors are also known to have been appointed before and during the Reformation at St Thomas's Church, one of the bigger chapters in Strasbourg. Laurentius Schenkbecher was cantor there from 1521 to 1524. See 90 Z 13, p. 4.

292 See M. H. Schmid, *Mathias Greiter: Das Schicksal eines Deutschen Musikers zur Reformationszeit* (Aichach: Mayer & Söhne, 1976), pp. 63–73. More details about Greiter and Dachstein are given on pp. 30–32.

293 See II 70b, 26 (19 August 1534) (also 90 Z 13, pp. 295–9).

294 B. A. Föllmi, 'Calvin und das Psalmsingen. Die Vorgeschichte des Genfer Psalters', *Zwingliana*, 36 (2009), pp. 81–3. See also 1 AST 23, 2, fol. 24r; 1 AST 23, 3, fol. 29r; and 1 AST 23, 1, pp. 23–4.

in 1549, he swore allegiance to Rome once more, and by doing so managed to retain his job at the cathedral.[295]

Hymn Books and Scriptural Familiarity

As noted by Gerald Hobbs, Bucer's 1526 German translation of the Book of Psalms, *Psalter wol verteutscht*, confirmed that the congregations were at least beginning to sing at this time. Bucer noted that 'the faithful have now begun, following St Paul's admonition, to sing psalms in their own language each time they gather to hear God's holy word'.[296] The same year also, ironically, saw a sudden decline in the production of hymn books and liturgies in Strasbourg. However, bucking the trend, Köpfel published yet another title, *Psalmen gebett vnd Kirchenübung*, which appeared in four different editions during the year.[297] Two further editions of the title were eventually published, in 1530 and 1533, each with enlarged contents.[298] Crucially, in contrast to the earlier printed songbooks of 1524 and 1525, this book was not an order of the liturgy in which the hymns were integrated into the order of service, but was instead divided into two sections, with the liturgy printed at the beginning, and the hymns and psalms (with their melodies) printed afterwards.[299] This innovative design became the norm for subsequent liturgical publications in Strasbourg. The title page of the *Psalmen gebett* of 1526 includes various woodcut illustrations of, among others, God in Heaven, the Last Supper, and Jesus victorious over death (see Figure 2.3). These were no doubt intended to provide a visual link to the salvation that would be achieved through true Christian worship and the singing of psalms.

Curiously, despite the abolition in Strasbourg of the Mass in 1525, the book began with the orders of service for weddings, baptisms, Vespers, and 'the Lord's Supper *or the Mass* and sermon',[300] much in the same way as the 'Mass'

---

295 See Schmid, *Mathias Greiter*, pp. 175–9.

296 Bucer, *Psalter wol verteutscht*, fol. CXCVIv; translated and quoted by Hobbs, '"Quam Apposita Religioni Sit Musica"', p. 162.

297 See Appendix A. Copies of each edition exist in Zurich's Zentralbibliothek, Göttingen's Niedersächsische Staats- und Universitätsbibliothek, the library of Nuremberg's Germanisches National-Museum, and Wittenberg's Bibliothek des Evangelischen Predigerseminars, respectively. The Nuremberg copy does not appear in the museum's online catalogue. The Wittenberg copy was discovered after the publication of *RISM DKL*, and appears as an addendum in *DKL* III, vol. 1 (Register, p. 9), numbered 1526[27]. Reference is made hereafter to the Göttingen copy of 1526 (*Psalme[n] | gebett / vnd Kir | chen ůbu[n]g wie sie zů Straß | burg gehalten werden* (Strasbourg: Köpfel, 1526), and to the BNUS copy of 1530 (*Psalmen | gebett / vnd kirch- | en ůbung / wie sie zů Straß | burg gehalten werden* (Strasbourg: Köpfel, 1530)).

298 Vogeleis mentions a fourth edition in 1536, but no further reference to this could be found. See Vogeleis, *Quellen und Bausteine*, p. 237.

299 *Hubert*, pp. XVI–XVII.

300 'Von des herren nachtmal / *oder meß* vnd predigen', from the contents page of *Psalme[n] gebett / vnd kirchen ůbu[n]g wie sie zů Straßburg gehalten werden* (Strasbourg: Köpfel, 1526), fol.

Psalme
gebett vnd Kir
chen übūg wie sie zů Straß
burg gehalten werden.
Bey Wolff Köpphel. 1526

Figure 2.3 Title page of *Psalmen gebett vnd Kirchenübung*, 2nd edition (Strasbourg: Köpfel, 1526). D Gs – 8 TH POLEM 514/51 RARA. By permission of the Niedersächsische Staats- und Universitätsbibliothek, Göttingen

had been introduced in the *Straszburger Kirchenampt* of 1525. This explicit reference to the 'Mass', rather than simply the 'Lord's Supper', as well as the fact that the first pieces in the book are settings of the *Kyrie*, the *Gloria*, the *Alleluia*, and the *Credo*,[301] may indicate that Köpfel was proceeding with some caution in relation to the 1525 ruling, and keeping his market open to ensure that, should the Mass be reintroduced, his publication would, at least in theory, remain commercially viable. Furthermore, the cathedral and remaining four chapters that were still permitted to celebrate the Mass after this time would therefore have had the option, should they wish, to use the vernacular settings printed in Köpfel's book. This, however, is extremely unlikely to have been

A ijr. My emphasis.

[301] Just as in the second edition of the *Teutsch Kirchenampt* of 1524.

the case. Even in the 1530 edition of *Psalmen gebett*, 'Meß' was still being offered as an alternative, suggesting either that Köpfel had omitted to update his printing type, or else had again kept it intentionally, lest some form of the Mass be reintroduced in Strasbourg. The final edition having been lost, it is not known how Köpfel referred to this service in 1533. However, some of the Mass Ordinary texts were reauthorised after 1536,[302] which explains their appearance in later Strasbourg publications, most notably in the *Gesangbuch* of 1541.[303] There is also the possibility that, by including these Mass texts in *Psalmen gebett*, Köpfel was allowing for the book being adopted by other towns in German-speaking areas in which the Mass was still being celebrated, but where there was a movement towards the use of the vernacular.

The 1526 edition contains 24 psalms, although not apparently in any logical order, and there are multiple settings of Psalms 119 and 124. Three of the melodies were by Wolfgang Dachstein, and several others were by Matthias Greiter. At least two of the three settings of Psalm 119 (two of which are by Greiter) had previously appeared in the last of the three-volume *Theütsch kirchenampt* of 1525.[304] Luther's version of Psalm 124 had first appeared in Strasbourg in the second of the same three volumes, and the other version, by Justus Jonas, was first published in Strasbourg in the *Straszburger Kirchenampt* of 1525.

In the book's first preface, Wolfgang Köpfel wrote 'zu dem leser' (to the reader) that, although the book is small, it was intended to reflect God's Word in a most precise (*fleissigst*) way.[305] It essentially acted as a copyright declaration, not altogether a familiar thing in a time when, as we have already seen, piracy in the printing trade was so common. The third preface had previously appeared in the *Straszburger Kirchenampt* (1525).[306] The second was a collection of scriptural paraphrases, demonstrating how to praise God, entitled 'Etliche sprüch vsz der gschrifft / von gotlichen lobgesange[n]' ('Some words of Scripture about divine songs of praise'). The author (unnamed, but probably Köpfel) paraphrases four biblical passages (in a similar way to Luther's use of Scripture in the preface to the Strasbourg *Enchiridion*), each with limited explanation. Curiously, despite the title of the preface, neither the first of these quotations (from 1 Chronicles 16), nor the last (from 2 Peter 1), makes any mention of music. This is in spite of

[302] G. J. van de Poll, *Martin Bucer's Liturgical Ideas: The Strasburg Reformer and his Connection with the Liturgies of the Sixteenth Century* (Assen, Netherlands: Van Gorcum, 1954), p. 29.

[303] *Gesangbuch / darinn begriffen sind / die aller fu̍rnemisten vnd besten Psalmen / Geistliche Lieder / vnd Chorgeseng / aus dem Wittembergischen / Strasburgischen / vnd anderer Kirchen Gesangbu̍chlin zůsamen bracht / vnd mit besonderem fleis corrigiert vnd gedrucket. Fu̍r Stett vnd Dorff Kirchen / Lateinische vnd Deudsche Schůlen* (Strasbourg: Messerschmidt & Köpfel, 1541).

[304] See p. 77, n. 196; and see Zahn, *Die Melodien der deutschen evangelischen Kirchenlieder*, vol. 6, no. 24. See also melody nos 8303 and 8304.

[305] 'wiewol dis buchlin kleyn ist / dan[n] daran gelegen sein wil / das nur auffs fleissigst / was das gotswort belangt / außgehe'. Reproduced in *Hubert*, p. 141.

[306] The text of the preface is reproduced in *Hubert*, pp. 140–41. See p. 83 for a discussion of this preface.

the fact that chapter 16 of 1 Chronicles is teeming with musical references, and surely can only be summed up as the story of David's appointment of various people, whose role it was to sing praises to the Lord:

> And David appointed certain Levites to serve before the Ark of the LORD to praise and laud the God of Israel. They were Asaph, Zechariah, and also Heman and Jedutlun, and others, there to thank the Lord that his mercy is eternal.[307]

Why, then, especially considering that other biblical references in this preface do explicitly mention music-making, would the author not make mention of the central aspect of this story, namely music? A quick glance over the full chapter reveals that the author's paraphrase jumps from halfway through verse 5 to verse 41, missing all references to musical instruments, and completely skipping over David's Song of Thanks, given in the middle of the chapter.

The author's paraphrase therefore appears to have two functions. First, it acts as an introduction to the other scriptural passages given in this preface, by speaking more generally about the importance of praising God. Second, it allows anyone who wishes to, and who has access to a copy of the Bible, to look up the passage in question; in doing so, the reader would discover all the details relating to how such praise is to be given, through singing and the playing of instruments.[308]

The second passage is from Ephesians 5, verses 15 to 20 (although the verse numbers are never specified in this preface, nor in most texts from this time).[309] This passage, which instructs the reader to beware of the time, 'because it is an evil time',[310] makes allusion to the ongoing struggle between the Roman Church

[307] 'Vnd Dauid stellet vor die laden des herren / etlich leuiten zu dienern / dz sy preyseten / vnd lobten den Gott Israhel. Nemlich Assaph / zacharias / auch Heman / vnd Jeduthun [*sic*] / vnd andere erwelet / zu danken dem Herren / das seine barmhertzigkeit weret ewigklich'. *Psalmen gebett* (1526), fol. A iij^{v}.

[308] There is also a third (but more unlikely) possibility, namely, that the author was concerned that a literal interpretation of this passage, if printed more fully, which mentions the playing of harps, lyres, cymbals, and trumpets, might have resulted in rather more instrumental music than the reformers deemed necessary for a service of orderly praise and worship.

[309] Bucer would write about the final three verses of this in his commentary on Ephesians, published one year later (*Epistola D. Pauli ad Ephesios* ... (Strasbourg: Herwagen, 1527)).

[310] 'vnd loset die zeyt / denn es ist bose zeyt'. *Psalmen gebett* (1526), fol. A iij^{v}.

and the reformers. People, therefore, must be orderly and sober,[311] and full of the Spirit.[312] Then comes the first overt reference to music:

> And speak to each other with psalms and songs of praise and spiritual songs, sing and play to the Lord in your hearts, and always give thanks to God the Father for everything, in the name of our Lord Jesus Christ, and be subject to one another in the fear of God.[313]

The implication is clear: the performance of music had the ability to fill those who partake in it with the Spirit of God.[314] The mention of 'each other' is also significant, presenting the acts of praising God and of making music to praise God as communal activities, in which one could engage with friends. This approach also stood in stark contrast to the Zwinglian call for silent worship.[315]

The subsequent reference, from Colossians 3, verses 16 to 17, was a natural progression from the previous one. Indeed, this passage had been used by Zwingli to argue his point about silent worship, the Zurich reformer having taken a rather literal interpretation of the instruction to sing 'in your hearts' (i.e. not out loud), from verse 16. Placed here, it led the reader on from the notion of praising God with one another to engaging actively with the Word of God through teaching and admonition delivered by songs of praise. The phrase was again addressed to a group (*euch selbs*):

> Let the Word of God dwell abundantly among you in all its richness. Teach and admonish yourselves in all wisdom with psalms and songs of praise and spiritual

[311] Drunkenness and gluttony had apparently already been German-wide problems during the late fifteenth century. Geiler von Kaysersberg, who had had a pulpit built for him in the nave of the cathedral, called upon the Strasbourgeois to give up drinking and gambling, a generation before the beginning of the Reformation (see '"Gluttony and Drunkenness": A Sermon by Johann Geiler von Kaisersberg on Sebastian Brant's *Ship of Fools (1498)*', in Strauss, *Manifestations of Discontent*, pp. 211–15. Jakob Wimpheling, too, complained about those who brought beer into the cathedral chapels on the feast day of St Adelphe (see R. Oberlé, *La vie quotidienne en Alsace au temps de la Renaissance* (Strasbourg: Oberlin, 1983), p. 127). In 1527, the authorities were still trying to bring the problems of drinking and gambling, and general disorder, under control (see Chrisman, *Strasbourg and the Reform*, pp. 68–71, 160). During the Reformation, drinking was also frequently portrayed as one of the many monastic abuses that needed to be done away with (see R. W. Scribner, *For the Sake of Simple Folk* (Oxford: Oxford University Press, 1981), p. 177).

[312] 'Darumb werdent nit vnuerstendig / sonnder verstendig / was da sey des Herren wille / vnnd saufft cüch nitt voll weyns / daruß eyn vnordenlich wesen folget [*sic*] / sonder werden vol geysts'. *Psalmen gebett* (1526), fol. A iij[v].

[313] 'Vnd redt miteynander von Psalmen vnd lobgesengen vnnd geystlichen liedern / singend vnd spielend dem Herrn in ewern hertzen / vnd sagen danct allzeit vor iederma[n] Gott dem vatter / im[m] namen vnsers herrn Jesu Christi / vn[nd] sind eynander vnderrhan in der forcht Gottes'. *Psalmen gebett* (1530), fols A iiij[r]–A iiij[v].

[314] Whether a similar spiritual fulfilment might occur among those who only listen to music is not made clear.

[315] Jenny, *Zwinglis Stellung zur Musik im Gottesdienst* (Zurich: Zwingli Verlag, 1966), pp. 36–9. Compare also with Col. 3:16.

> songs, and with thankfulness sing to the Lord in your hearts. All that you do with words or with works, do it all in the name of the Lord Jesus, and thank God the Father through him.[316]

As in Luther's preface which appeared in the Strasbourg *Enchiridion*, the writer here admonished the reader to let the Word of God be embodied, or 'implanted', within himself or herself, in such a way that the Word would bestow wisdom and grace upon its recipient.

The final biblical reference, to 2 Peter 1, verses 19 to 21, confirmed to the reader the sureness of the prophetic Word; that is, the Scriptures. Everything already mentioned in this preface is therefore confirmed and summarised by this final quotation. This prophetic Word is like 'a light that shines in a dark place' (*ein liecht / das da scheynet inn eynem duncklen ort*[317]): it should be held onto in this darkness and during these evil times, 'until the day breaks and the morning star rises into your hearts' (*bis der tag anbreche / vnnd der morgen stern auffgee in eüwerm hertzen*[318]). Such writing also revealed the rather typical eschatological views of the time. A great deal was made of the importance of the soul, and of its final judgement, constant reminders being issued of human frailty and mortality.[319] Luther subscribed to the popular belief that the end of the world was imminent.[320] Robert Scribner has spoken of the 'apocalyptic fervour' created by the evangelical movement at this time.[321]

Perhaps to subdue the reader's fears of imminent disaster, the *Psalmen gebett* preface continued with a reminder that prophecy is not a matter for human interpretation, but that God spoke to the prophets through the Holy Spirit.[322] This was almost certainly another allusion to the ways of the Roman Church – a mildly disguised accusation of human interpretation overriding the

316 'Laßt das wort Gottes in eüch wonen reyhlich / in aller weyßheyt / lernent vn[nd] vermanent eüch selbs / mit Psalmen vnd lobgsengen vn[nd] geystlichen liedern / in d[er] gnad vnd singet dem herren in eüwern hertzen / vn[nd] alles was ir thut mit worten / oder mit wercken / das thund alles in dem namen des herren Jesu / vnnd danckt Gott dem vatter durch jn'. *Psalmen gebett* (1526), fol. A iiij^r These two scriptural passages, from Corinthians and Ephesians, were also used by Bucer in his *Ein Summarischer vergriff der Christlichen lehre vnd Religion* ... (Strasbourg: Rihel, 1548) (see D. F. Wright, *Common Places of Martin Bucer* (Appleford, Abingdon: Sutton Courtenay Press, 1972), p. 83).

317 *Psalmen gebett* (1526), fol. A iiij^r.

318 Ibid.

319 Scribner, *Simple Folk*, pp. 115–16.

320 See Rublack, *Reformation Europe*, p. 27.

321 Scribner, *Simple Folk*, pp. 116–17. See also W.-E. Peuckert, *Die grosse Wende: Das Apokalyptische Saeculum und Luther. Geistesgeschichte und Volkskunde* (Hamburg: Claassen & Goverts, 1948).

322 'vnd das soltir für das erst wissen / das kein weissagu[n]g in der geschrifft geschicht auß eygner außlegung / den[n] es ist noch nie keyn weyssagung auß menschlichem willen fürgebracht / sonder die heylgen menschen gottes / haben geret getriben von dem heilgen geyst'. *Psalmen gebett* (1526), fol. A iiij^r.

truths of Holy Scripture, and the Church having become a human, rather than divine, institution.

Further Proposals

In 1527 or 1528, Bucer and Capito reignited their efforts at citywide liturgical reform by producing a seven-page document suggesting how the Mass might be replaced.[323] The document outlined an alternative form of worship, similar to those orders of Matins shown above. The Mass, wrote the reformers, was not to be tolerated by Christians because it attempted to recreate the 'greatest and highest work' carried out by Christ on the cross for the sin of the world, and when celebrated it dishonoured that sacrifice.[324] It was the reformers' wish, however, to abolish only those services that were offensive.[325] The first half hour of the new service should involve singing three or four psalms and a scriptural antiphon or responsory, followed by a reading from the Bible. The other half hour should be taken up with the reading, translation (*vßlegung*), and explanation of a psalm, 'so that everyone understands the Latin, if done in Latin. But where there are people – or amongst the singers there are those – who are acquainted with German more than with Latin, one would translate into German'.[326] This was to be followed by a silent, scriptural prayer, and a Christian collect.[327] Vespers in the cathedral was to take a similar form.[328] The use of bells was not prohibited, but specific bells were to be rung at specific times.[329] Bucer and Capito also

323 1 AST 80, 7 (original); 1 AST 75, 1; 1 AST 80, 8; printed in *BDS*, 2, pp. 519–23. See also *CorrBucer*, 3, pp. 96–7. This document is dated 1527 by the AVS, but 1528 by *BDS*. According to the AVS, one of the copies of the original, 1 AST 75, 1, is written in the hand of Klaus Kniebis, to whom the reformers had written two years earlier regarding the Mass. See *BDS*, 2, p. 519.

324 'Die weyl die Meß, by criste[n] gar nit mag geduldet werde[n] / daru[m]b das durch sy / das grost vnd höchst gut werck / das alleyn den vater versünen hat / vnd die selgikeyt bringt / namlich das opfer cristi / vnsers herre[n] am creutz geschehen / grewlich geschmehet wurdt / dan[n] yr zu geben wurdt / sy syge ein newe vffopfferu[n]g christi fur die su[n]d der welt / domit das recht opfer verneuet wurdt'. 1 AST 80, 7, fol. 49r; 1 AST 75, 1, p. 1; *BDS*, 2, p. 519.

325 1 AST 80, 7, fol. 49r; 1 AST 75, 1, p. 1; *BDS*, 2, p. 520.

326 'das man morgens / winter zeyt zu neune[n] / somer zeyt zu achte[n] / vff den stiffte[n] zusame[n] keme Singe mit ernst / vnd dapferer weyl / eyn psalm[en] dry oder fier nach dem sy kurtz oder lang weren vnd druff eyn schrifftliche[n] A[n]tiphon / oder responsori / Dan[n] eyn lection aus seym biblische[n] buch / das sichs vff ein follige halbe stund verzöge / dem nach were do / der die ander halbe stund / e[n]tweders die gelesene Lection / oder eyn psalme[n] auslegte vnd erklerete / were[n] do die alle das Lateyn verstu[n]den / mochte mans zu Latyn thun'. 1 AST 80, 7, fol. 49v; 1 AST 75, 1, pp. 2–3; *BDS*, 2, pp. 520–21.

327 1 AST 80, 7, fol. 49v; 1 AST 75, 1, p. 3; *BDS*, 2, p. 521.

328 1 AST 80, 7, fol. 50v; 1 AST 75, 1, pp. 4–5; *BDS*, 2, p. 522.

329 1 AST 80, 7, fol. 50v; 1 AST 75, 1, p. 4; *BDS*, 2, p. 522. At the beginning of the Reformation, the cathedral had more than 18 different bells, each with a particular function. See Föllmi, 'Création et reconfiguration de l'espace sonore : les activités musicales à Strasbourg avant et pendant la Réforme protestante', in L. Gauthier and M. Traversier, eds, *Mélodies urbaines : La musique*

suggested that a 'public Christian reading' (*offenlich christliche Lection*) could occur in Latin in one church, for scholars, and in German in all the other churches for the laypeople. The reading would last less than an hour for both groups.[330] Also, as suggested in Sturm's proposal from August 1525,[331] these activities would earn the priests their stipends, but these were not to be distributed in the church after the service, but at a later time.[332]

According to Bucer and Capito, church practice had been carried out in a similar way during the times of the Apostles, 'to which Eusebius, Tertullian, and other elders refer … One can still take good advice from them'.[333] The reformers' aim was now to emulate contemporary practice in Zurich, Saxony, and Hesse, where the Lord's Supper was held just once, every Sunday, for the whole community.[334] With reference to the various problems with canons outlined above, they commented that some chapters may be too stubborn to adopt such practices, but there were other godly ones that would gladly do so.[335] They stated that documents in the chapters proved that in the earliest days of Christianity donations were given and received only for the teaching and practising of Scripture, rather than for the Mass and for 'trade' (*dem handel*).[336]

Another document by the reformers referred again to the hypocrisy (*gleyßnerey*) and avarice (*geytz*) of the singers of the Mass, and all this, it was said, was apparent from their own saying: 'copper money, copper Requiem' (an alternative to our contemporary saying: 'you get what you pay for'). The writer also added that they were 'no longer [allowed to] practice all their singing and reading, since it costs so much money'.[337] This once again demonstrates the dichotomy: music was a bad thing that the priests used to – albeit no longer – do, but which would be a good thing in the hands of the reformed Church.

---

dans les villes d'Europe (XVIe–XIXe siècles) (Paris: Presses de l'Université Paris-Sorbonne, 2008), pp. 108–10.

330 1 AST 80, 7, fol. 49v; 1 AST 75, 1, p. 3; *BDS*, 2, p. 521.

331 See pp. 160–62.

332 1 AST 80, 7, fol. 50v.

333 'Vff solche weyß / hat man von der Apostel zeyt her kirche[n] vbu[n]g gehabt / wie das Eusebius / Tertullianus / vnd andere alte[n] / die ouch glych nach / … bezeuge[n] / Man hett auch des noch gut anzeyg'. 1 AST 80, 7, fol. 50r; 1 AST 75, 1, p. 3; *BDS*, 2, p. 521.

334 1 AST 80, 7, fols 51v–51r; 1 AST 75, 1, pp. 5–6; *BDS*, 2, pp. 522–3.

335 'Vnd wie wol zu besorge[n] etliche vff den stiffte[n] / werde[n] so verstocket syn / das sy zu solcher vbo[n]g nit komen werde[n] / doch wurde man auch etliche gottselige[n] finden / die gern da by seyn wurde[n]'. 1 AST 80, 7, fol. 50v; 1 AST 75, 1, p. 5; *BDS*, 2, p. 522.

336 'Es ist auch kundtlich / auß den historie[n] / vnd der stifft fundation briefe[n] / auch alte[n] ordnunge[n] / das sy anfenglich / nur zur leer vnd vbu[n]g göttlicher schrifft / vnd gar nit zun Messe[n] / vnd dem handel / den sy jn[n]erthalb ij^{c} jore[n] angefang[en] habe[n] / gestyfftet sind'. 1 AST 80, 7, fol. 51r; 1 AST 75, 1, p. 6; *BDS*, 2, p. 523.

337 'das sy zum geytz alleyn braucht werden, zeugtt yr eygen sprich wort: kupferen gelt, kupferen seelmeß; vnd zwar all yr singen vnd lesen wirdt nicht weyter von ynen gevbet, dann so fil es gelt tregt'. 1 AST 80, 12, fol. 2r; 1 AST 166, 9.8, fols 140r–140v; *BDS*, 2, p. 535.

In 1528, the council produced a proposal of its own on how to regulate the new service. Although it is not clear what form this proposal took, there are many extant – and lukewarm – responses to it by the reformers. One of the most liturgically detailed of these extant documents consists of a text specifically calling for the use of congregational singing, and, in addition, an appendix listing the Psalms, responsories, and collects to be used over a period of five weeks. The proposal[338] was read by the council on 16 May 1528:

> It is now undeniable that in church song much honour, to which only God is entitled, has been given to [earthly] creatures ... In addition, song itself has been mistaken as a commendable deed, through which one earns forgiveness and other blessings.[339]

It was clear that song had been misused in several ways, the document stated: first, by giving praises to earthly beings (namely the saints) that did not deserve to be praised – at least not in the same way as God; and second, by singing in the hope of securing salvation, mistakenly believing it to be a good work which would help secure them eternal life. Both of these, of course, were repetitions of concerns about 'fables' and superstition expressed by Bucer in *Grund und Ursach*. It was recommended that such unacceptable practices be stamped out immediately. Whereas Luther was very willing to continue using extra-biblical texts in church, Bucer, following Zwingli's example, was less so. Therefore, all elements of this proposed liturgy were scriptural: antiphons, responsories, collects, and so on.

One claim about the new order of service was that 'nothing in opposition to God will be practised, and [that] these [things] will come from God himself, religiously, with spirit and improvement'.[340] Once again, the intention was made to provide an interpreter in each of the chapters, to instruct the laypeople.[341] The

338 1 AST 80, 24. A later copy, bearing the description 'Der Predicanten Ordnung eins Gotgevälligen Gesangs' (The preachers' order of singing which is pleasing to God), can be found in 1 AST 166, 5.16, fols 106v–107v. The later copy contains the whole text, and some of the five-week order, but ends abruptly with 'etc. etc. etc.'. This copy has been transcribed in *BDS*, 2, pp. 528–31, but the folios are incorrectly numbered 166v–167v, rather than 106v–107v. The original, with the complete five-week order, is printed in *CorrBucer*, 3, pp. 145–57.

339 'Nun ists unleügbar / das im Kirchen gesang / vil ist / Das die Ere so allein gott zu steht / den Creaturen zugibt / alß hilff von sünden und andern übel / den abgestorbenn heiligen / ouch andern Creaturen / und menschl[iche] wercken / zu geben würdt / dazu ist das gesang selbs / auch fur ein verdienstl[ich] werck / dadurch man verzihung der sund / under ander gnad verdiene / gehalten worden'. 1 AST 80, 24, fol. 99r; 1 AST 166, fol. 106v; *CorrBucer*, 3, p. 145; *BDS*, 2, p. 528. See also 1 AST 80, 23, fol. 97r.

340 'under dem Namen / gottsdienst / nichts wider gott / und das jene so von im selbs gottlich / ouch gottseligklich / mit geist und besserung / geübet werde'. 1 AST 80, 24, fol. 99r; 1 AST 166, fol. 107r; *CorrBucer*, 3, p. 146; *BDS*, 2, p. 529.

341 'einer uß inen der stifftverwanten / uff die Cantzel gon das volck so zu gegen uff ein halb od[er] ein furtel stund zu underwisen'. 1 AST 80, 24, fol. 99v; 1 AST 166, fol. 107r; *CorrBucer*, 3, p. 147; *BDS*, 2, p. 529.

orders for Matins and Vespers are identical to those mentioned above,[342] except for the starting times. Also, rather than the usual 'two or three' or 'three or four', the reformers specified that exactly three psalms should be sung, 'to the familiar melody, but with good spirit' (*in gewonl[icher] Melodey / und aber gutter weil und uffmercken*) (that is, without hurrying, and with concentration).[343] Just as the readings were to remain in the same sequence in which they appeared in the Bible, starting with Genesis, the Book of Psalms was also to be worked through in order from the beginning.[344] However, this does not seem to be reflected in practice in the orders themselves.

The order for the festival of Pentecost, for example, was presented as follows:

> At the festival of Pentecost in the morning assembly, after the usual beginning:[345] We sing Psalms: *Omnes gentes* [Ps. 47], *Magnus Dominus* [Ps. 48], *Exurgat Deus* [Ps. 68]. The antiphon: *Factus est repente* [Acts 2: 2, 4].[346] The reading is the second chapter of Acts. The responsory. These things having been completed, [we sing] the *Benedictus* [Luke 1: 68–79]. The antiphon: *Accipite spiritum sanctum* [John 20: 22–3]. The collect: *Deus qui corda fidelium*.[347] *Benedicamus Domino*.[348]
>
> In the afternoon assembly: The Psalms: *Dixit Dominus* [Ps. 110], *Confitebor* [Ps. 9], *Beatus vir* [Ps. 1]. Antiphon: *Loquebantur varijs* [Acts 2: 4]. The reading is Isaiah, chapter 44. Responsory: *Repleti sunt omnes spiritu* [Acts 2: 4]. *Magnificat* [Luke 1: 46–55]. The antiphon: *Non vos relinquam* [John 14: 18]. The collect: *Deus Innocentie restitutor*.[349] *Benedicamus Domino*.[350]

---

342 See pp. 75–6.

343 *BDS*, 2, p. 529, n. 8. This phrase is actually crossed through in 1 AST 80, 24.

344 1 AST 80, 24, fol. 99v; 1 AST 166, fol. 107r; *CorrBucer*, 3, p. 146; *BDS*, 2, p. 529.

345 *Deus in adiutorium meum intende* and *Domine ad adiuvandum me festina*.

346 See C. Marbach, *Carmina Scripturarum* (Strasbourg: Le Roux, 1907), p. 490.

347 Prayer for Pentecost Sunday. See A. Schott and P. Bihlmeyer, eds, *Das vollständige Römische Meßbuch* (Freiburg im Breisgau: Herder, 1927), p. 556.

348 This text originated from the canon of the Mass. See A. Pflieger, *Liturgicae orationis concordantia verbalia, pars prima* (Freiburg: Herder, 1963), p. 50.

349 Traditionally the final prayer for Wednesday after the Second Sunday of Lent. See Pflieger, *Liturgicae orationis concordantia verbalia, pars prima*, p. 317; and Schott and Bihlmeyer, *Das vollständige Römische Meßbuch*, p. 184.

350 'In festo Penthecostes in Conventu promeridiano post solitum initium Cantentus psalmi / Omnes gentes / Magnus Dominus / Exurgat Deus Antiphon / factus est repente. Lectio / Caput secundum in actis. Responsiorum / Dein complerentur / Benedictus / Antiph[on] Accipite spiritum sanctum / Collect. Deus qui corda fidelium. Benedicam[us] Domino. In Conventu pomeridiano Psalmi / dixit Dominus / Confitebor. Beatus vir / Antiphon. Loquebantur varijs. Lect. Caput 44. Iesaia. Respons. Repleti sunt omnes spiritu. Magnificat / Antiphon / Non vos relinquam. Collect. Deus Innocentie restitutor / Benedicamus Domino'. 1 AST 80, 24, fols 99v–100r; 1 AST 166, fol. 107v; *BDS*, 2, p. 530. The biblical sources suggested here are from *BDS* and *CorrBucer*.

Capito's own response to the proposal of the Strasbourg authorities came two weeks later, on 29 May.[351] It is of particular value, because although it is written in response to a proposal for a new liturgical structure, it is quite revealing of current practices of the time. In it, Capito commented that the council was indeed proposing 'a divine service that greatly serves the improvement of the community', but that on the other hand, no mention of the Mass was made. His fear was that the council was willing to let the Mass coexist with the new reformed service, and on behalf of the canons of St Thomas, he urged the council not to let this happen.[352] If it were to have happened, then the reformers would have had to endorse the singing of the clergy in Latin, 'which would be quite awkward and ungodly'.[353] He reminded the council 'to think of the opportunity given to the public church of Strasbourg'.[354] Twice a day, Capito's proposal suggested, the people could assemble in the churches to 'sing something specific' and to listen to a brief sermon for half an hour or a quarter of an hour:

> Furthermore, we give consideration to the fact that our people have more need of exegesis and less of singing, for we are not much practised in the Scripture. That is why, in consideration of Your Graces' intent, we gather in the morning for about a quarter of an hour and sing a psalm in Latin, as is done in German by the congregation everywhere in conjunction with the German sermon, and to use the remainder of the time for a Latin sermon and exegesis. Thus the Word of God is not shortchanged, nor does one sermon get in the way of the other.[355]

In light of this statement, there can remain no doubt that by 1528 the congregations were singing in German. It is also clear that Latin had not been suppressed. This suggests that at least some of the reformers, Capito among them, had been keen to retain Latin in some capacity. What seems to be important is that where both Latin and German were used, the congregation be preached to in such a way as to enable them to gain an understanding of the Latin text. In other

---

351 1 AST 16, 23, which is a draft of a manuscript in the Basel Universitätsbibliothek: Ki.Ar.25a, 158. A translation of the Basel version is printed in *CorrCapito*, 2, pp. 330–33.

352 See pp. 73–4.

353 'sy ein gotts dinst furgebt der zur besserong d[er] gemein hoch dinstlich ist. Aber es wurt nit angezeigt / wie es mit d[er] messs solle gehalt[en] w[er]d[en] … Wir haben vnß der meß jed[er] sym v[er]standt noch lang nit angenom[en]. Vnd fürter müsten wir die neben dem gesang bestetig[en] / das gantz vngeschickt vnd vngotselig syn würde'. 1 AST 16, 23, pp. 1–2 (including margin); *CorrCapito*, 2, p. 331.

354 1 AST 16, 23, p. 2; *CorrCapito*, 2, p. 332.

355 'Da zu bedenk[en] wir auch / das vnsern p[er]son[en] / noter ist vil vßlegens vnd wenigs syngens / dan[n] wir gar wenig jn d[er] geschrifft geubet syn. Drümb wie vff E. G. v[er]besserong vnd wolgefell[en] bedecht haben am morgens ein viertel vber ein stunt vngeüerlich zusam[m]en zukommen / vnd wie jm teutsche[n] p[re]dig all[en]thalb von d[er] gemein zu tutsch beschiecht / ein psalm zu latin zusing[en] / Vnd druff die uberig zyt mit latinischer p[ro]phetij vnd vsslegong zuv[er] zeren / domit das gotts wort nit in v[er]kleinerong keme / vnd ein p[re]dig der and[er] v[er]hinde[n]'. 1 AST 16, 23, pp. 2–3; *CorrCapito*, 2, p. 332.

words, intelligibility was what made the Word of God useful. This was why, Capito explained, it had been requested that readings be added to the sermon.

Capito's comment that the people had less need for singing should not be considered indicative of his general approach to church song. In all likelihood he was making the point that German singing, although a good thing, was a lower priority than exegesis and the reading of Scripture, and that there was no need for any increase in the amount of Latin singing taking place. As he concluded, 'singing a great deal in Latin would only embitter the common people, and German sermons would displace the other necessary sermons, as we said. But Latin exegesis would yield much benefit without hindering anyone'.[356] Benefit without hindrance, then, was Capito's aim, and he believed that readings were the key to creating a community that understood God.[357]

Another response, this time from the Provost and Administrator of the Dean and Chapter of St Thomas (*Probst / verweser des decanats vnd Capitel der stifft zu sanct Thoman zu Straßburg*) to the council[358] proposed the replacement of the midday Mass – or *Fronmesse*,[359] the one Mass that the chapters in the city had been allowed to continue celebrating after the 1525 abolition – 'in order to maintain peace and goodwill among citizens'.[360] Now, he opined, the time had come to replace even this service. The proposal is much like those described above, except that no specific songs or psalms are mentioned, and that the timings given are less specific. Furthermore, the proposal is written in the first person plural. 'We want to come together twice every day' (*wir alle tag zwey mal wolten zusammen komen*), in the morning and in the evening. In the morning, after the introit, the General Confession and the Absolution were to be spoken – in Latin – and then three or four psalms sung. 'A chapter from a book of the Bible' was read, 'which should thereafter be interpreted in German, as Paul commands in 1 Corinthians 14'.[361] The Lord's Prayer was followed by the *Benedictus*,[362] which here was specified as being 'sung with an antiphon and collect' (*mit eim Antiphon vnd Collect gesungen*). This was to be followed by

---

356 1 AST 16, 23, p. 3; *CorrCapito*, 2, p. 333.

357 Capito was to return to the importance of readings in April the following year. In this document, he stated his wish that the 'reader' (*leser*) would sing or speak a collect and a psalm, to which the choir and 'listeners' (*zuhoren*) answer 'Amen'. 1 AST 16, 27, p. 1.

358 1 AST 16, 24. The document is undated, but is with regard to the same proposal.

359 *Fronmesse* was the term used in this part of Germany and in some Swiss areas for the high Mass.

360 'vmb friden vnd gutten willen gemeiner burgerschafft zuerhalten'. 1 AST 16, 24, p. 1.

361 'nach dem jntrat / wir vns versamleten / anfangs ein christlich confiteor vnd absolution zu latin mit gebognen vnÿen sprechen / vff das glich sungen dry oder vier psalmen vngeuarlich / mit eim schrifflichen antiphon, demnach vßs eim biblischen buch ein capitel verlesen / welches einer darnach zu teutsch'. 1 AST 16, 24, p. 1.

362 '*Benedictus*' is likely to refer to the Song of Zechariah (Luke 1:68–79), as it does in the case of 'Vnser herren Meister und Rats Bedacht' (see p. 87) and 'Der Predicanten Ordnung eins Gotgevälligen Gesangs' (see p. 105).

the blessing. The afternoon service was similar, but the canticle used should be the *Magnificat*, sung with an antiphon.[363]

Coming from inside St Thomas's Church itself, this was an intriguing proposition. It seems that at this stage, those clergy at St Thomas's Church who were keen on reform outweighed those opposed to it. It is possible that the provost hoped to make the most of a bad situation by pre-empting any council decision. This, at least, would explain the lack of detail and apparent lack of familiarity with specific Protestant songs, as well as his desire to speak the Confession and Absolution in Latin. Other than this, however, the proposed form of the service is not unlike those being put forward by the reformers.

Further lobbying occurred during the summer of 1528. The preachers wrote to the Strasbourg authorities to remind them that the new evangelical teaching was founded on the Bible.[364] The topic of singing was approached at the end of the letter. The preachers acknowledged the need to speak 'against church song' through which people were promised the remission of sins, since only Christ was able to do this. However, when Christian singers were used (who were not mean, or drunks, or fornicators), the Psalms and other parts of the Scriptures *could* be sung in Latin, so long as there was an interpreter present. Unfortunately, though, a great number of church singers were like asses with a lute (*esel die lauten geben*)[365] who did not know what they were doing, and had nothing to do with Christ.[366]

Proposals for services to replace the Mass continued to flood in.[367] Two such documents[368] also made further reference to the habit of singing to Mary and the saints (*vnser frawen vnd den heyligen*), and of their 'superstitiously fantastic legends' (*abergloublischen fabulosischen legenden*). Such 'kitchen

---

[363] 1 AST 16, 24, pp. 1–2. The council responded by stating that such a service would need to begin with *Deus in adjutorium* and the doxology (*Gloria patri*) (*Fragments des anciennes chroniques d'Alsace*, IV (1901), no. 4741).

[364] VI 701a, 15, fols 24r–25r (modern fols 402r–403r). Printed in *CorrBucer*, 3, pp. 185–7.

[365] That is to say they are uncultured people, unable to do their work properly. See *CorrBucer*, 3, p. 187, n. 1. As observed by Herl (*Worship Wars*, p. 95), the preface to the Erfurt *Enchiridion* also makes reference to the lazy lifestyle of the clergy and to choristers braying like asses. See *Eyn Enchiridion oder Handbuͤchlein ... kunstlich verteutscht* (Erfurt: Loersfeld, 1524), fol. A^v.

[366] 'Wo die senger aber christen weren, vnd begereten Gottes, weren nicht geytzyg oder truncken böltz, hurer vnd der gleychen, möchte man wol auch in latinischer sprach auch etlich psalmen vnd ander gschrift in der kirchen singen oder leßen, Sover doch daß auch zvm volk ein vßlegung beschehe, wie Paulus leret, vnd daß solchs mit ernst beschehe vnd besserung, deßhalb dan wenig vff einmol vnd mit verstandt müste gehandlet werden. Doch vor allem müste man nicht dem esel die lauten geben, daß ist zw göttlichem gesang ordenen die nicht mechten mit Gott zw schaffen haben, als leyder ein großer teyl der kirchen senger sich erzeygen'. VI 701a, 15, fol. 25r (modern fol. 403r); *CorrBucer*, 3, p. 187.

[367] See, among others: 1 AST 80, 20; 1 AST 80, 21; and VI 701a, 15, fols 19r–23r (all from 1528).

[368] 1 AST 80, 19.

songs (*kuchen gesangs*)[369] should no longer be used,[370] and for this reason, the evangelical service should be imposed upon all churches of the city.[371] There was also some concern among the reformers that everyone should be able to take Communion. It was offered in both kinds in Schwarz's first German Mass in 1524, and at evangelical services thereafter. One document, very similar in liturgical design to those mentioned above, states that any 'old and weak people, or pregnant women' (*alte vnd schwache leut sÿndt / oder schwanger frawen*), wishing to partake of the sacrament, or anyone who cannot stay to the end of the service, should come forward to receive it between the prayer and the singing of the psalm.[372]

Strasbourg Abolishes the Mass

Finally, following years of intense petitioning on the part of the reformers, on 20 February 1529 the city council agreed to abolish the Mass in all of the city's churches.[373] As has been demonstrated, this was the result of numerous and repeated appeals to the authorities. Variations on the same arguments had been put forward time and time again. Certain figures, not least Jakob Sturm (as we have seen) had been reluctant to move too quickly, and the council no doubt took heed of his and others' advice before eventually bowing to the pressure of the reformers. This decision took its toll on some of the city's musicians. The cathedral choir was officially dismissed in 1529. A declaration from the cathedral chapter from that year simply stated that 'neither the singers nor the choir students' were to process between the cathedral and the Brüderhof (a collection of buildings situated next to the cathedral), since they were no longer required.[374]

Although the reformers stopped writing against the Mass at the time of its abolition, the archives contain a great number of manuscripts dated 1529 in

369 So-called because of connotations with the mundane, unspiritual elements of life, possibly also connected to notions of femininity. I am grateful to Ulinka Rublack for this observation. The expression perhaps equates to our modern English expression: 'old wives tales'.

370 1 AST 80, 19, fol. 84v–85r.

371 In a last-ditch attempt for concord, Balthasar Merklin, Bishop of Hildesheim, outlined a treatise of agreement on 21 January 1529 between the former canons of the chapters and the city of Strasbourg. Its first point was that the council should allow 'singing and reading to continue everywhere in an amicable, Christian, and correct way'. See *Fragments des anciennes chroniques d'Alsace*, III (1892), no. 3040. The call for the chapters to establish an agreement with the preachers had also been made in May 1525. See 1 AST 166, 5.15, fol. 106v; *BDS*, 2, p. 461.

372 1 AST 16, 25, pp. 2–3; 1 AST 176, 93, fol. 231r–231v.

373 C. Wilsdorf et al., *La Musique en Alsace, hier et aujourd'hui* (Strasbourg: Istra, 1970), p. 52; Brady, *Ruling Class*, p. 167.

374 'A[nn]o 1529 Das Capittel beschleußt, es soll hinführ[en] weder den Sängern, noch den Chorschülern ihr gefäll auß dem Bruderhoff gelüffert werden, weile man ihrer nit mehr bedarff'. AA 2479, fol. 3v.

which plans for the new service were drawn up in an attempt to finalise them as soon as possible. Following the ruling, the senatorial commission immediately asked the preachers to replace the Mass with something conforming to the Bible. One problem was to consider what should be done with the old choir and clergy. The reformers informed the commission that the prebendaries could be asked to provide Bible study in Latin before the morning and evening sermons, and so earn their income in this way, but they insisted that psalms be sung before and after each sermon.[375] Citizens who up to that point had attended Mass would just have to get used to the fact that the Mass had been suppressed and be won over to the evangelical cause.[376] Only Christian singing was to take place.[377] 'We allow', they explained, 'the singing of a psalm before and after the sermon so that we know how to console ourselves in the great congregation. A number of people do this with their hearts so that others may also be awoken [through it]'.[378] Singing was therefore explained as something that happened at the heart of the community, and which edified and galvanised others (especially the young[379]) in their spiritual experience. They reminded the council that 'the Psalms and many other songs were taken from Scripture'.[380] Latin, on the other hand, was considered to be an irritating clerical practice.[381] At the end, the reformers noted with a hint of regret that in Zurich and some other places church singing had been left to 'pass by'.[382]

On 10 April, the commission informed the chapter of St Thomas of its decision. The new morning service[383] was to take the following form:[384]

Bell-ringing for half an hour;
Seven o'clock in summer and eight o'clock in winter: service begins;

---

375 1 AST 80, 26, fol. 106v; *BDS*, 2, pp. 539–40. The report makes no specific mention of congregational singing, but this is implied.

376 *CorrBucer*, 3, pp. 252–3.

377 'Dann der zweck in diesem, vff den vor allem zusehen ist, das S. paulus lernet, 1. Cor. 14, das nichts gesungen oder gelesen werde, das nit verstanden vnd demnach zu gemeiner besserung eigentlich dienet. Nun wißt jr, das die personen also sind, das jnen viel geschriefft vßlegen vnd nit viel gesang dienen mag. Dazu ist das gesang dann allein christlich, so es zu erwecken die gemuter furgenommen oder so es vß inbrunst, der sich jm hertzenn vß gehortem wort gottes oder sunst ernstlicher betrachtung der werck vnd hendel gottes quillet. Gesang on hertzlich begirde vnd anmut ist ein gespötte vor gott, dorumb syn als wenig als des gebets, besonder meß zyl, Stett oder personen geordnet werden mag'. 1 AST 80, 26, fols 107v–108r; *BDS*, 2, p. 542.

378 'Das wir vor vnd nach der predig ein psalmen singen lassen, thun wir, das wir jn so grosser gemein vns gentzlich wissen zuuertrösten, etlich seyen, die das mit hertzen thun, da durch dann die anderern auch erwecket werden mogen'. 1 AST 80, 26, fol. 108r; *BDS*, 2, p. 542.

379 AA 420, fol. 40r; *BDS*, 3, p. 389.

380 'Es soll E. g. nit yrren, das die psalmen vnd viel ander gesang vß der geschriefft genommen sind'. 1 AST 80, 26, fol. 108r; *BDS*, 2, p. 543.

381 *CorrBucer*, 3, p. 253; 1 AST 80, 26, fol. 108v; *BDS*, 2, p. 544.

382 'Ewer g. sehen Zurich vnd andere ort an, do mit grosser frucht gelesen vnd das singen vnderwegen gelassen wirt'. 1 AST 80, 26, fol. 109v; *BDS*, 2, p. 545.

383 Taken from 1 AST 80, 27. See also 1 AST 166, 10, fol. 154v.

384 Compare with the 'typical' Lutheran form, shown on p. 74.

The canons and vicars assemble in the choir and sing (with doxology):

Domine, labia mea aperies, Deus in adiutorium meum intende, Dominum ad adiuvandum me festina;

A psalm;

A chapter from the Bible (Old or New Testament), read in Latin, but interpreted for the people;

Benedictus;[385]

Psalm 102 (*Domine exaudi orationem meam*);

A collect;

The blessing (*Benedicamus domino*).

The form of the evening service[386] was as follows:

Bell-ringing for one hour;

Three o'clock in summer and two o'clock in winter: service begins;

Domine, labia mea aperies, Deus in adiutorium meum intende;

A psalm;

A chapter from the Bible;

Magnificat;

Psalm 102 (*Domine exaudi orationem meam*);

A collect;

The blessing (*Benedicamus domino*).

For whatever reason, this order for worship contained fewer psalms than the 'three or four' that had been proposed in 1525.[387] The commission also accepted that a reading and exegesis was necessary, and so these were introduced. Significantly, Latin was still a prominent feature of the service; it was not dropped in favour of German, except on Sunday mornings, when no Latin was to be used, and the singing was to take place in German. It was primarily on these occasions, then, that the printed psalm books must have been employed.[388]

* * *

This chapter has emphasised several points. First and foremost, it has demonstrated Bucer's belief that the use of the vernacular combined with congregational song was crucial to the dissemination of the Gospel message. The year 1524 saw the almost simultaneous introduction of both, and the following years witnessed a

385 Luke 1: 68–79.

386 Taken from 1 AST 80, 27. See also 1 AST 166, 10, fol. 154v.

387 See above, p. 75.

388 See also 1 AST 174, 16, which is a defence of the modifications undergone during the period 1522–1529. Printed in *BDS*, 2, pp. 546–58. See also *CorrBucer*, 3, pp. 386–405.

concerted effort to develop a form of worship in which the laity could participate through song. Chrisman writes,

> Through congregational singing the laymen learned the psalms in German, and the words of the Scriptures became an intimate part of their own thoughts and prayers. Music thus played an important role in opening up the Scriptures to the laity. Through singing they became familiar with the Word.[389]

The transformation undergone between the beginning of 1524 (when the Mass was sung in Latin by the choir and clergy) and 1529 (when much that was sung was done so in German by the congregation, from printed books containing a wide choice of musical material) is truly remarkable. The old rite, described as 'contrary to the Word and commandment of Christ'[390] had been suppressed, and replaced with a new service of scriptural readings and prayers. Furthermore, song, at least in the views of the reformers, had been returned to the people: the opportunity was now there for the people to sing from their mouths and from their hearts, as it had been in the early Church.

Second, this chapter has shown that, unevenly, and over the course of just a few years, the Strasbourg liturgy and hymn book underwent several changes in function and composition. There was no black-and-white approach to reform. The liturgy began in its most primitive state as a manuscript translation of the Latin Low Mass, with minor changes that opened the way for more rigorous reforms. As soon as several churches in the city had opted to take this path, printers seized the opportunity to publish the liturgy in German, and points were introduced at which the congregation could actively participate in singing. Melodies and texts were taken from a variety of sources, some being composed by Strasbourg's own musicians including Wolfgang Dachstein and Matthias Greiter. The legislation introduced in 1525 by the city authorities limiting the celebration of the Mass to the chapters once again produced a need for new liturgies. As the new service of the Lord's Supper was developed, psalms and spiritual songs played an increasingly crucial role. Over time, the traditional texts of the Mass were replaced with new texts.[391] Soon, the number of songs in circulation led to them being printed as an appendix to the liturgy, rather than being integrated into it. Publishers used prefaces in their books to explain the reforms and their necessity, including the need for singing. Alongside the developing liturgy, separate books of psalms and canticles appeared on the market, not necessarily intended for use in the liturgy.

---

389 Chrisman, *Lay Culture, Learned Culture*, p. 166.

390 'Der Meßhalb diweil solche glat wider das wortt vnd den beuelch Christj'. 1 AST 37, 4, fols 49r–49v; *BDS*, 2, p. 468.

391 For example, the introit was replaced by the singing of a psalm.

It needs to be noted that neither the printing boom nor its general decline, which occurred from 1529 to 1544, were limited to music.[392] The decline in music printing, however, did not quite follow the general trend, having already begun in 1527. Looking at the printing statistics alone, though, can be very misleading. A good example of this is the large number of liturgical orders with music that were printed in the year 1525. No doubt this number was in part due to popular demand for such songs, which were already being sung in other reformed parts of Germany. In light of the writings of the reformers, however, it might also be suggested that these publications were in fact a form of encouragement from the printing industry for the city to adopt the reforms. By showing the variety of songs and musical text settings available, the printing press was making the most of the uncertain and volatile situation in the city. Some churches were probably already following the printed liturgies, but others had yet to begin, and as no set order for the evangelical service had been imposed at this time, the printing presses were doing their utmost to create a market for their wares. This explains musical peculiarities such as Speratus's *Der Glaube Deütsch* (Strasbourg: Knobloch, 1524/1525), or *Ein schoner kurtzer begriff* (Strasbourg: Schwan, 1525) which contains the Lord's Prayer, the *Ave Maria*, the Creed, and the Ten Commandments.[393]

The third point demonstrated concerns the importance of scrutinising archival manuscripts alongside printed sources. For example, the song publications fail to inform us that Latin singing continued to take place in some churches after the start of the Reformation. As can be seen above, there are numerous examples of the reformers advocating the use of Latin, both in song and in exegesis, so long as an interpreter is present. Often it is not clear whether a text is a proposal or a reflection of current practice. Bucer's *Grund und Ursach* (1524), however, is unambiguous:

> When the congregation assembles on Sundays … the whole congregation sings some short psalms or a song of praise. After that the minister prays a short prayer and reads to the congregation some sections of the writings of the Apostles and gives a very brief explanation of the same. Following this the congregation again sings the ten commandments or something else; after this the priest reads the Gospel and preaches the sermon proper; then the congregation sings the articles of our faith … the priest distributes the bread and the cup of the Lord among them and partakes of it himself. Then the congregation once more sings a song of praise; after that the minister concludes the Lord's Supper with a short prayer, blesses the people and lets them depart in the peace of the Lord. *This is the manner and the custom according to which we now observe the Lord's Supper only on Sundays.*[394]

392 Chrisman, *Lay Culture, Learned Culture*, p. 3.

393 See Appendix A.

394 'So am Sonnetag die gemein zůsamenkompt … singt die gantz gemein etlich kurtz psalmen oder lobgesang. Dem nach thůt der diener ein kurtz gebett und liset der gemein etwas von Apostel schrifften und verclert dasselbig auffs kürtzest. Daruff singt die gemein wider die zehen gebott oder

What is not clear, however, is how the congregations went about learning the music. Some documents suggest that the reformers wanted this done by a cantor, or else by a group of pious singers, who were not to be paid in the same way that choirs had been under the old regime. As the following chapter will reveal, other documents from the 1530s suggest that the singing was led by schoolchildren from the front of the church by the pulpit, as was the case in Geneva from the 1540s onwards. In all likelihood, all these methods – and others – were used.

Following the complete abolition of the Mass in 1529, the scaling back of the sacred music-printing industry continued, until a revival occurred in the middle of the next decade. The market had been exhausted and such books were probably not selling as well as they had done during the 1520s. The Mass had been successfully abolished, and the book men would have to find alternative products in order to make a living. For the reformers, on the other hand, the fight was far from over. The Strasbourg preachers now had to defend their decision to abolish the Mass at the 1530 Diet of Augsburg. This, along with other developments of the 1530s, will be explored in the following chapter.

etwas anders, alsdann so verkündt der priester das Evangelion und thůt die recht predig, auff die singt die gemein die artickel unsers glaubens … Darauff teilet der priester das brot und den kelch des herren under sye und neüsset es auch selb. Also bald singet die gemein wider ein lobgesang, demnach beschleüst der diener das nachtmal mit eim kurtzen gebett, segnet das volck und lasset es im friden des herren hingon. Diß ist die weiß und der brauch, mit dem wir nun me das nachtmal Christi auff die Sonnentag allein halten'. *BDS*, 1, pp. 246–7; translated in Cypris, 'Basic Principles', pp. 149–51. My emphasis on last sentence.

CHAPTER 3

The Move Towards Conformity

If the 1520s were Strasbourg's chance to deconstruct and reconstruct the liturgy,[1] embrace reform, and establish a reputation as a city of evangelism, the 1530s were a decade of broken and re-established allegiances. Like the previous chapter, this chapter uses the innovative and fruitful method of applying music as a historical filter through which to assess the reforms.

No sooner had the city council decreed that the Roman Mass be abolished throughout Strasbourg's churches did the need arise to solidify and strengthen allegiances, both locally and further afield. Unsurprisingly, the majority of the reformers' writings in the 1520s had been theological in nature, many concerned with the nature of the Eucharist: in other words, debating the degree to which one could say that Christ was present – or not – in Communion. This, together with the fact that Strasbourg had sought to *replace* the Mass, whereas Wittenberg had *reformed* it, resulted in Bucer and his colleagues falling out of favour with Luther and his supporters. Crucial to the decision taken by the Lutherans to retain the Mass in a modified form was their belief in the real bodily presence of Christ in the Eucharist. At the 1530 session of the Diet of Augsburg, Emperor Charles V attempted to gain control over the perceived heresies occurring in the Holy Roman Empire. By way of a defence, the Lutherans produced the Augsburg Confession, while four cities – Strasbourg, Constance, Memmingen, and Lindau – signed what became known as the Tetrapolitan Confession (eucharistically a more 'Zwinglian' counterpart to the Augsburg Confession). Among the many other points made, it was in this way that the reformers of Strasbourg officially set out their opposition to the Latin songs of the Roman Church, and depicted them as unholy and unhistorical.[2] The 21st article of the Confession discussed the use of song in liturgical worship, and is entitled 'Von gemeinem gesanng vnd gepett der gaistlichen', or 'Of congregational song and prayer of the holy people'.[3] It set out the principal reasons for Protestant opposition to the use of song in the Roman Church.

---

[1] 'Déstructuration et Restructuration (1524–1530)', title of chapter 3 of R. Bornert, *La Réforme protestante du culte à Strasbourg au XVIe siècle (1523–1598)* (Leiden: Brill, 1981), p. 84.

[2] 'Wellches gesang dann gar groblich von dem ersten prauch der hailligen vätter abkomen ist, wie das nyemanndt laugnen mag'. *BDS*, 3, p. 147. In contrast, the Augsburg Confession contains nothing specific pertaining to music. See 'Confessio Fidei exhibita inuictiss. Imp. Carolo V', in K. G. Bretschneider and H. E. Bindseil, eds, *Philippi Melanthonis Opera quae supersunt omnia*, 28 vols (Halle [Saxony-Anhalt] and Brunswick: Schwetschke, 1834–60), vol. 26, cols 263–336.

[3] *BDS*, 3, pp. 146–51.

First, the Confession stated that the ministers had condemned any additions to the sung Word of God that were not based in Scripture (in other words, praying to the saints for deliverance from sins, and other prayers that should be directed only towards Christ).[4] In addition, these songs were so great in number that, even with the removal of the superstitious parts of the text, they could not be sung with full attention and devotion.[5] Opposition was also demonstrated to the fact that choral singing had previously been presented to the people as a work through which salvation could be bought and sold for a high price.[6] Finally, the authors cited St Paul, who in 1 Corinthians 14 stated that such praise, in tongues that the people cannot understand, is contrary to the commandment of God.[7] Fascinatingly, the Confession tried to cover a broad spectrum of liturgical practice, so as to be acceptable to all four cities, by deliberately neither insisting upon nor rejecting the singing of psalms and prayers in church.[8] Instead, it simply advocated (in the event that singing should take place) the use of the vernacular, and the removal of 'superstitious' elements. Nothing was said of the necessity for congregations to participate in that singing.

A confutation to the Tetrapolitan Confession was subsequently produced and read at the Diet.[9] The four cities were forced to write a defence, which was then published along with the Confession itself in 1531.[10] In the apology of the 21st article of the Confession, the contentious abolition of the seven offices of the Church was discussed. The confuters had accused the followers of the

[4] Gerald Hobbs has suggested that this first point also refers to Latin antiphons and responsories (R. G. Hobbs, '"Quam Apposita Religioni Sit Musica": Martin Bucer and Music in the Liturgy', *Reformation and Renaissance Review*, 6 (2004), p. 163). However, as will be demonstrated below, the opposition mounted was not to antiphons and responsories themselves, but rather to the non-scriptural variety. Medieval antiphons would not necessarily have been scriptural, some being texts about Mary and other saints. The 1528 proposal by the reformers (1 AST 80, 24) provided a table for readings, psalms, antiphons, collects, and responsories, the vast majority of which are biblical in origin. See *CorrBucer*, 3, pp. 145–58; and *BDS*, 2, pp. 528–31.

[5] Christian Meyer observes that this is typical of the 'minimalisation' of reformed liturgies in south-west Germany at this time (C. Meyer, 'Gesangbuch, darin begriffen sind … Martin Bucer et le chant liturgique', in C. Krieger and M. Lienhard, eds, *Martin Bucer and Sixteenth Century Europe: Actes du colloque de Strasbourg (28–31 août 1991)*, 2 vols (Leiden: Brill, 1993), vol. 2, p. 219).

[6] The book of donations in the cathedral provides evidence of payments for votive Masses and endowments for remembrance Masses and other services. Ibid.

[7] *BDS*, 3, pp. 146–51.

[8] The Tetrapolitan Confession, despite being limited to the needs of only four cities, aimed to encompass different practices that had emerged in these places. Similarly, the writers made sure to word very carefully the sections on the Eucharist, despite differences in the cities' interpretation of the sacrament, so that the Confession would be acceptable to all.

[9] See *BDS*, 3, pp. 15–24; and H. Eells, *Martin Bucer* (New Haven: Yale University Press; London: Oxford University Press, 1931), pp. 101–2.

[10] *Schriftliche Beschirmung vnd verthe- | digung der selbigen Bekantnusz / gegen der Confuta- | tion vnd Widerlegung / so den gesandten der vier | Stätten / vff bemeldtem Reichstage / offen | lich fürgelesen / vnnd hie getrewlich | einbracht ist* (Strasbourg: Schweintzer, 1531). Published in the same volume as the Tetrapolitan Confession (see p. 376). Printed in *BDS*, 3, pp. 194–318.

Tetrapolitan Confession of abolishing the prayer and song of the Church[11] – something the four cities denied. The confuters had claimed that the ancient prophets had prayed at certain times during the day, that the Church had followed this model of worship, and that it would therefore be 'a shame … if the Church were silent and the Synagogue were to sing'.[12] The Tetrapolitan reformers dismissed these allegations, saying that

> We would like nothing more than for the clerics simply to pray and sing much, but [they should have songs and prayers] to the Lord from the heart and for the improvement of the Church. But we know only too well how these same [clerics] really sing and read. Therefore … we have arranged that the church community may also have their song and prayer at particular times, but with understanding and devotion.[13]

They went on to emphasise, 'we have not suppressed prayer and song [themselves], but abuse and inversion of prayer and song'.[14] The number seven, they argued, was not to be taken literally as the number of times prayer and praise should occur, but the meaning was rather that God may be praised 'many' times a day.[15] They then re-emphasised their belief that much prayer and song was 'not prayed or sung, but more murmured and clamoured', and done without understanding or faith, but only for the sake of payment.[16]

The confutation had claimed that the Tetrapolitan approach to music was not based in Scripture. The apologists also denied this strongly, for several reasons. First, the Bible stated that only God – and not the saints – should be praised for

---

[11] *Schriftliche Beschirmung vnd verthedigung*, fol. Q3r; *BDS*, 3, p. 292.

[12] 'und were eyn schand (sagen sie), das die Kirche schweigen und Synagog singen solte'. *Schriftliche Beschirmung vnd verthedigung*, fols Q3r–Q3v; *BDS*, 3, p. 293.

[13] 'Unß were nichts liebers gewesen, dann das die geystlichen nur vil gepettet und gesungen hetten, aber dem Herren von hertzen und mit besserung der Kirchen. Wir aber derselbigen singen und lesen sey, weyß man nur zu wol. Derhalb … haben wir angerichtet, das die gemeyne Kirche ir gesang und gebett auch zu bestimpten zeitten, aber mit verstand und andacht habe'. *Schriftliche Beschirmung vnd verthedigung*, fol. Q3v; *BDS*, 3, p. 293.

[14] 'Mißbreuch und verkerung deß gepets und gesangs, nicht das gepett und gesang, ist bey unß abgestellet'. *Schriftliche Beschirmung vnd verthedigung*, fol. Q3v; *BDS*, 3, p. 293.

[15] This progresses into an argument about the biblical significance of the number seven.

[16] *Schriftliche Beschirmung vnd verthedigung*, fol. Q4r; *BDS*, 3, p. 294. Such vocabulary as 'murmuring', 'grumbling', and 'clamouring' was a favourite of reformers across the continent when referring to the music of the Roman Church. See H.-A. Kim, 'Erasmus on Sacred Music', *Reformation and Renaissance Review*, 8 (2006), p. 289. Indeed, so unpopular was the habit of clerical mumbling that the tale of a mumble-catching demon was in existence in English folklore since at least the thirteenth century. This fiend would collect in a bag syllables and words skipped over by priests and monks in worship, as evidence to be presented at their days of judgement. See C. Mazzio, *The Inarticulate Renaissance: Language Trouble in an Age of Eloquence* (Philadelphia: University of Pennsylvania Press, 2008), p. 28.

such things as justice, protection from the devil, and redemption from sins.[17] Secondly, it stated that prayer and song should occur with 'true devotion' (*warer andacht*).[18] 'Every external thing is an abhorrence to God if it does not come from the faithful heart'.[19] Thirdly, song and prayer were being sold as merchandise, as if God needed to be compensated (*abverdienet*).[20] Fourthly, it was not carried out in the common language of the people:[21]

> But now, these our clerics behave yet more oddly, shout loudly, turn to the people and speak peculiarly to them, climb up to the highest place, in order that they might be heard far and wide, and stand all over the place, as they would want this thing likewise to give understanding to and educate the whole congregation, and then do this in language which the congregation cannot understand at all and which they themselves often do not either.[22]

All these arguments are familiar, having been made multiple times during the run-up to the abolition of the Mass in 1529.

The Tetrapolitan reformers also noted that endowments in times past had been made not for singing and reading, but rather to provide for the poor and for the furtherment of Christian teaching. It should therefore not be considered wrong, they said, to reassign those endowments that have been left for the singing of remembrance Masses (something done contrary to God's commandments).[23]

Although impossible to tell for sure, it is unlikely that Constance, Lindau, and Memmingen had embraced congregational singing with the enthusiasm that Strasbourg had. For a start, Lindau seems not to have had a working press until 1585. Constance printed its first book of hymns in 1545 (albeit without musical notation), and Memmingen's presses disappeared in 1519, before the

---

17 No biblical citations are given, however.

18 John 4:23–4; 1 Cor. 12:7; 1 Cor. 14:26; Matt. 6:7. *Schriftliche Beschirmung vnd verthedigung*, fol. Q4r; *BDS*, 3, p. 295.

19 'Dann ye alles eusserlichs Gott eyn greuwel ist, wo das selbig nicht auß gleubigem hertzen qwillet'. *Schriftliche Beschirmung vnd verthedigung*, fol. Q4v; *BDS*, 3, p. 296.

20 This, they say, is contrary to Phil. 2:13.

21 Vogeleis (*Quellen und Bausteine zu einer Geschichte der Musik und des Theaters im Elsass, 500–1800* (Strasbourg: Le Roux, 1911; repr. Geneva: Minkoff, 1979), p. 227), after Philippe-André Grandidier (*Essais historiques et topographiques sur l'église cathédrale de Strasbourg* (Strasbourg and Paris: Levrault, 1782), p. 95), claims that the Passion text was sung in German in Strasbourg for the first time in 1531. No further details are given, however.

22 'Nun sind aber dise unsere geystlichen noch seltazamer, schreyen uberlaut, keren sich zum volck und sprechens besonders an, steigen uff erhöchte ort, damit sie weit und breyt gehört werden, und stellen sich in alle weg, alß wolten sie die sach gantzer gemeyn gleich wol zu verstohn geben und einbilden und thun denn solchs in der sprachen dar, wölche die gmeyn gar nicht verstohn kan und offt sie selb auch nicht'. *Schriftliche Beschirmung vnd verthedigung*, fol. Q4v; *BDS*, 3, pp. 296–7.

23 *Schriftliche Beschirmung vnd verthedigung*, fols Rr–Rv; *BDS*, 3, p. 298.

Reformation had taken off.[24] In contrast, and despite the general decline in music publications at the time, Strasbourg was still printing hymns.

Köpfel's Psalters

In 1530, Wolfgang Köpfel was again the only publisher to print a liturgical order or hymn book,[25] namely a new edition of his successful 1526 title, *Psalmen gebett*.[26] The next hymnal to appear was yet another edition of the same book, three years later.[27] The 1530 *Psalmen gebett* contains 27 psalms, as well as a selection of biblical canticles, the Lord's Prayer, the Ten Commandments, and some of the Mass Ordinary texts (but the *Sanctus*, *Benedictus*, and *Agnus Dei* once again are notably absent). In addition, it features Luther's folk hymn adaptation, 'Nun bitten wir den heyligen geyst';[28] Speratus's hymn 'Es ist das heyl vns kommen her' (first published in the 1524 Erfurt *Enchiridion*[29]); the Song of Zechariah, or *Benedictus* (Luke 1:68–79); the Song of Simeon, or *Nunc dimittis*; and the Song of Ambrose and Augustine, or *Te Deum*. As in the 1526 versions, the liturgies are printed at the beginning of the book, with the hymns, psalms, and canticles printed separately. The woodcut illustrations on the front are also identical. The 1530 edition contains three prefaces, the first two having also appeared in the 1526 edition (the first being his copyright message, the second being a selection of scriptural passages from 1 Chronicles 16, Ephesians 5, Colossians 3, and 2 Peter 1),[30] and the third preface being a completely new piece by Köpfel which replaces the preface that had previously appeared in the *Straszburger Kirchenampt* and the 1526 *Psalmen gebett*. In addition, the 1530 edition contains a 'Closing remark on the liturgical orders'.[31]

This new third preface is of greater musicological interest than the others, as the role of singing in worship is mentioned within it. Köpfel used it to relate the introduction of psalm singing in the Lord's Supper and other ceremonies, with the ability of the congregations to understand the services in question, performed in the vernacular. He added that such comprehension would avoid people

24 Data from the Universal Short Title Catalogue (www.ustc.ac.uk) (accessed 12 June 2014).

25 Vogeleis refers to a book by Sebald Heyden, *Der Passion oder das Leiden Jhesu Christi, inn gesangsweiss gestalt, inn der melody des Psalms Es sind doch selig alle die* (Strasbourg: Frölich, 1530). However, apart from a pamphlet published in Nuremberg and Augsburg with the same name (published by Georg Wachter and Narziß Ramminger respectively), no trace of it is to be found. It is therefore assumed to have been an error by Vogeleis (see Vogeleis, *Quellen und Bausteine*, p. 225).

26 *Psalmen gebett / vnd kirchen ůbung / wie sie zů Straßburg* (Strasbourg: Köpfel, 1530).

27 The book, with the same title as the 1530 version, was actually dated 1534 (see *RISM DKL*). Unfortunately it is no longer extant.

28 See p. 274.

29 *MPGR*, p. 265 (no. 71).

30 See pp. 98–102.

31 'Schlußbemerkung zu den liturgischen Ordnungen', printed in *Hubert*, p. 143.

having a 'thirst for personal glory' in church.[32] The newly produced psalms had 'refreshed the practice and diligence of the congregations and spurred them to further knowledge of Christ'.[33] This had produced improvement especially in simple-minded (*enfeltigen*) parishes.[34] Köpfel did not specify what exactly had been improved, but one can presume that he was referring to devotion, and methods thereof, if not also the quality of singing. He was not concerned that the parishes might become overwhelmed and confused (*uberschüttet vnd verwūrret*) with singing. And in an elaboration of the Ephesians and Colossians references in the second preface, Köpfel reiterated that singing the Psalms was something that not only benefitted God, but also those who sang them: 'that which anyone takes from a Psalm cannot be without fruit if it is treated with reverence and God gives it his grace'.[35] The unique living Word of Christ (*einig lebendig wort Christus Jesus*), therefore, in a sort of musical epistemology, bore spiritual fruit in its readers through the singing of psalms and songs of praise to God. Köpfel thereby managed to link psalm singing to a notion of eternal grace.

These references to the diligence of the congregations and the useful and fruitful nature of singing the texts of the Psalms are thought-provoking, and they appear here for the first time in a Strasbourg hymn book. They are, however, ideas that are taken up in later writings, not least in Bucer's preface to the 1541 *Gesangbuch*. In this, Bucer acknowledged that people had 'from the beginning' (*von anfang*) used song as a means of prayer, and that 'in their actions they have poured forth absolutely truly, earnestly and reverently their lamentation, prayer … and admonition'.[36] Bucer also noted that sacred songs made people 'noticeably better'.[37] An ancestral lineage was thereby created between the Church Fathers and the reformers, and singing was demonstrated to be a means of internalising the Word. Those who sang sincerely and with diligence (*fleiß*) would reap the benefits.

Such notions also became relevant in Geneva's reforms during the 1540s and 1550s. The Genevan cantors often wrote prefaces to their psalters, and in these sometimes made reference to the need to improve the quality of the congregational singing in parishes. Louis Bourgeois, for example, asked that 'the ignorant in music always lend their ear to those who know [what they are doing], that is to say, in singing, that they do not push and raise their voice

[32] 'Das leichtlich verstanden von allen / so nit mit rumsuchtigem zanct die sach erwegen vnd richten'. *Psalmen gebett* (1530), fol. B^{r}.

[33] 'Vnd daneben durch newe erfurbrachte Psalmen / der gemeynd ubung vnd fleiß erfrischt / vnd nach weiter erkantnuß Christi zebekommen gereytzt vnd getriben werde'. *Psalmen gebett* (1530), fol. B^{r}.

[34] 'nit on nutz vnd besserung vilen enfeltigen gemeynden'. *Psalmen gebett* (1530), fol. B^{r}.

[35] 'Dann was ieder fur eynen Psalmen furnimpt / der kan nit on frucht / so andacht deß gemuts vnd gnad Gottes dabei ist / gehandelt werden'. *Psalmen gebett* (1530), fol. B^{r}.

[36] 'Dann sie in jrem thun gantz warhafftig / ernsthafftig / vnd andechtig / jre klag / gebet … vnd ermanung'. *Gesangbuch* (1541). See Appendix H, pp. 341–2.

[37] 'zu dem das sie vns mercklich besserten'. *Gesangbuch* (1541). See Appendix H, p. 343.

as loud as they would like … in order that everything be well-ordered in the Church of God'.[38] Later editions also included hints about the quality of congregational singing, and various methods to aid the reading of music were introduced.[39] However, Calvin himself was not concerned with the quality of musical performances. Music was secondary to the text, and it was instead the action of singing that moved people's hearts. For Calvin, as for Bucer, through this action came improvement. In this way it can be seen that this aspect of reform was embedded in the cultural practice of music-making.

Let us return now to Köpfel's preface. A large proportion of the text was devoted to the notion of the Church as a divine institution. In an expansion of the quotation from 2 Peter 1 given in the preceding preface, Köpfel stressed the need for the Church not ever again to be 'led by men and moved by men's inventions', which explained the decision to include in his book only song texts pertaining to the Word of God (namely the Psalms, for the most part). Furthermore, he had not printed many songs written by famous and intellectual people, 'for simple people are likely to be blinded by great names'.[40] Köpfel concludes the preface by announcing:

> We must not allow entry to any new deviations from God which surely exist where [people] believe something which diverts them from Christ Jesus to some human, especially since we humans are easily misled towards human [earthly] consolation … May God help us to stay in the school of the Holy Spirit and use every help for edification in God … so that … through him [we] may constantly grow in the knowledge of his fatherly grace to his praise and glory.[41]

---

[38] 'Parquoy, que chacun en soit aduerti, & que les ignorans de la musique en tout temps prestent l'aureille à ceus qui s'y entendent : c'est à dire, qu'en chanta[n]t ils ne presument de pousser & eleuer leurs voix si haut qu'ils voudroye[n]t bien … à fin que tout aille de bon ordre en l'eglise de Dieu'. L. Bourgeois, preface to *Pseaumes Octantetrois de | Dauid, mis en rime Francoise. A sauoir, qua- | ra[n]teneuf par Clement Marot, auec le Canti- | que de Simeon & les dix Commandemens. | Et trentequatre par Theodore de Besze, de Vezelay en Bourgongne. || Auec priuilege pour les Pseaumes dudict de Besze* (Geneva: Crespin, 1551). This quote is reminiscent of St Paul's advice in 1 Cor. 14:29–33.

[39] Pierre Davantès introduced a new numbering system for reading music, described by Frank Dobbins as a 'simple mnemonic aid' (F. Dobbins, 'Davantes, Pierre', in D. Root, ed., *Grove Music Online* (www.oxfordmusiconline.com) (accessed 14 November 2014)). However, it was probably in fact rather baffling, and there is little to suggest that it was a success (see D. Trocmé-Latter, 'The Psalms as a Mark of Protestantism: the Introduction of Liturgical Psalm-Singing in Geneva', *Plainsong & Medieval Music*, 20 (2011), pp. 158–9).

[40] 'Wiewol aber sunst geystliche lieder / von achtbaren vnd geystreichen gmacht / hab ich der selbigen nit vil mitgetruckt / vff das die gmein Gottes nit wider vff die menschen gefurt / vnd zu menschen gedicht bewegt werde / Dann ie die eyn- | falt an hohen namen sich gern vergafft'. *Psalmen gebett* (1530), fols B^{r}–B^{v}.

[41] 'Wir sollen zwar vermeiden allen inngang neuwer abfurung von Gott / so gwislich furhanden / wo etwas glauben von Christo Jesu auff einigen menschen gekeret wirt / seitemal wir alß menschen / zu menschlicher vertrostung bald seind abzefuren … Gott helf vnß das wir in der schul deß heiligen geysts bleiben / vnd zur vff bawung an Gott iedermans hulf gebrauchen … Vff das wir Christum nit

In this paragraph there may also be a subtle reference to the message found in 1 Peter 2 of the faithful as living stones, being built into a spiritual house. The congregation's increased knowledge of God's grace, and the subsequent edification of the Church becomes possible through the singing of psalms.

The importance of the second preface, containing scriptural passages, also became more apparent in light of the new third preface. The technique of giving scriptural quotations or paraphrases at the outset of a text enabled the writer (be he preacher or printer) to progress to more freely written prose, and relate the quotations more specifically to the situation in question – in this case, the Europe-wide church reforms taking place. By doing so in a book that doubled as an order of liturgy and hymnal, Köpfel was therefore able to demonstrate the importance of music and communal singing as part of the liturgy, but also to advertise it more widely as a commendable activity that should be carried out at all times, as long as it was specifically for the praise of God. As we have already seen,[42] such was the format adopted by Luther in the preface to Walter's *Chorgesangbuch*. It was also adopted by Bucer in the Strasbourg *Gesangbuch* of 1541 – a book that begins with several scriptural references before proceeding to Bucer's crucial preface.[43]

The book's 'closing remarks' were apparently printed simply to defend the abundance of recent changes to the church service. He noted that there had been increases and decreases in the number of words, and 'changes of statements and of substance' (an allusion to the Eucharistic debate). This is because such modifications always led to improvement.[44] There was no need now for a service of the letter (*bůchstabendienst*), but rather a service of the spirit (*dienst deß geysts*).[45]

After this, there is no record of any hymn book or religious musical pamphlet being published in Strasbourg until 1533, when Köpfel's third edition of *Psalmen gebett* was printed.[46] Although the book was already lost at the time of publication of *Die Straßburger liturgischen Ordnungen* (1900), Hubert specifies that it contained Köpfel's prefaces, and three extra songs: 'Kum heyliger Geyst', 'Mitten wir im leben sind' (both by Luther, and originally published in the 1524 Erfurt *Enchiridion*), and a new song attributed to Wolfgang Capito, 'Gib frid zu

blieren / sunder imm erkantnuß der vatterlichen gnaden / durch jn / furderlich erwachsen / zu seinem pryß vn[nd] herrligkeyt'. *Psalmen gebett* (1530), fol. B^v.

42 See pp. 84–5.

43 See Appendix H. The preface is reproduced in full in *BDS*, 7, pp. 576–82, and translated in *Garside*, pp. 29–31.

44 'Bißher die ordnung Straßburger kirchen, welche vngeuerlich eyn muster vnd vorbild ist aller jrer kirchenůbung, danach sich die diener ettwas richten, mit mehr vnd minder worten, auch mit endrung der sententz vnd des inhalts, wie es ieder zeit ieden zur besserung fůr dienstlichen anst[e]het'. *Psalmen gebett* (1530), fol. XVII^v. Printed in *Hubert*, p. 143.

45 *Psalmen gebett* (1530), fol. XVII^v.

46 *Psalmen* | *gebett, vnd kirch-* | *en ůbung, wie sie zů Straß* | *burg gehalten werden* (Strasbourg: Köpfel, 1533).

vnser zeit o Herr'.[47] The success of the *Psalmen gebett* series is not altogether surprising, given Köpfel's family connections to Capito.[48]

Lutheran Alliances and Bohemian Imports

In much the same way as printed psalm and hymn books notably reduce in number after the year 1530, the correspondence and official documents of the following decade do not yield anywhere near as many references to music as those of the 1520s. The reason for this is that progress was being made: the council had been convinced to abolish the Mass, and the people had begun to sing regularly in German. There was less need to press the case for the reform of music.[49] The death of Zwingli in 1531 lessened the importance in Strasbourg of a religious alliance with the Swiss, and throughout the decade more efforts were gradually put into improving relations with German cities, especially those aligned with Luther's reforms.[50]

The first major stage in this process was the formation of a synod in June 1533 in order to revise the city's confession of faith and align the churches more closely with the Lutheran camp.[51] The synod resulted in the publication of the *Ordnung und Kirchengebreuch* of 1534.[52] Somewhat surprisingly, very little direct reference was made to church singing in this document,[53] although the reformers did specify that 'it should always be forbidden to drum, play instruments, or to use or practise some worldly luxuriance' at wedding ceremonies.[54] Almost three years after the synod had met, the Strasbourg Church was brought into an alliance with the Lutherans on 21 May 1536, when Bucer and

---

47 *Hubert*, p. XX; *Wackernagel DKL*, vol. 3, no. 841, pp. 731–2.

48 See pp. 55–6.

49 The one exception is 1 AST 75, 9, from 1533, which discusses lost property, the need to preach and sing without disruption, and the need to admonish people to prayer and song for the correct reasons.

50 T. A. Brady, *Turning Swiss: Cities and Empire, 1450–1550* (Cambridge: Cambridge University Press, 1985), pp. 206–7.

51 For the 16 articles see 1 AST 75, 18.

52 *Ordnung vnd Kirchenge- | breuch | für die Pfarrern vnnd Kirchen- | dienern | zů Straßburg vnd der selbigen angehörigen | vff gehabtem Synodo fürgenommen* (Strasbourg: Prüss, 1534). Reproduced in *BDS*, 5, pp. 22–41.

53 One mention appears in relation to the minister admonishing the people to prayer and song. See *BDS*, 5, p. 36.

54 'Und solle in alweg hiemit verbotten sein, zů solichen kirchgang paucken, seytenspyl oder etwas weltlicher üpigkeyt zů gebreuchen oder ůben'. *BDS*, 5, p. 38. See also T. W. Röhrich, *Mittheilungen aus der Geschichte der evangelischen Kirche des Elsasses*, 3 vols (Paris and Strasbourg: Treuttel und Würtz, 1855), vol. 1, p. 239. Wedding-related behavioural problems were apparently an ongoing problem. In 1537 a decree was issued warning people not to travel outside the city for lavish celebrations with dancing, eating, and drinking in the 'popish' (*Bapstlicher*) tradition, with fines for those who disobeyed (1 MR 3, fol. 258r).

Luther signed the Concord of Wittenberg.[55] There were no immediate changes required of the Strasbourg reformers in terms of their musical practice, but in the years following there was a noticeable increase in the number of songs from more Lutheran parts of Germany being printed in Strasbourg publications.[56]

Nevertheless, one might have expected more Lutheran songs to begin appearing in the city in the run-up to the signing of the Concord of Wittenberg, reflecting the increasing influence that Luther was gaining over Strasbourg. Although the years 1534 to 1536 were indeed remarkable in the history of the Strasbourg hymn book, they can in fact only be fully understood in the context of events of a few years earlier, not in Wittenberg, but in Bohemia. In 1531, a former monk named Michael Weisse translated the hymn book of the Bohemian Brethren (a sect founded in the mid-fifteenth century out of the Hussite movement, which adopted Lutheran sympathies at the beginning of the German Reformation)[57] from Czech into German. The book was entitled *Ein New Geseng buchlen.*[58] At some point, 'out of special love and friendship', a copy of this book was given to Katharina Schütz Zell,[59] wife of the Strasbourg preacher Matthäus Zell. She was deeply impressed by it, and decided to have it republished in Strasbourg. In 1534, the first volume of her four-volume edition appeared, containing Weisse's hymn translations, but with her own preface and commentary.[60] She, or possibly an assistant, also selected the music for

---

55 The Latin text is reproduced in Bretschneider and Bindseil, *Melanthonis Opera omnia*, vol. 3, cols 75–6. The German text is reproduced in E. Bizer, *Studien zur Geschichte des Abendmahlsstreits im 16. Jahrhundert* (Gütersloh: Bertelsmann, 1940), p. 117–19. See also J. V. Pollet, *Martin Bucer – Études sur la correspondance*, 2 vols (Paris: Presses Universitaires de France, 1958–62), vol. 2, pp. 161–74.

56 See Chapter 5.

57 For background information about the music of the Bohemian Brethren, see W. Blankenburg, trans. H. Heinsheimer, 'The Music of the Bohemian Brethren', in F. Blume, *Protestant Church Music* (London: Gollancz, 1975), pp. 591–607.

58 (Bohemia: Buntzel & Wylmschwerer, 1531). A facsimile also exists, published as K. Ameln, ed., *Gesangbuch der Böhmischen Brüder, 1531* (Kassel and Basel: Bärenreiter, 1957).

59 'Mir ist ein Gsangbuoch auß sunder lieb und freundtschafft gegeben worden'. K. Schütz Zell, preface to *Von Christo Jesu vnserem sa̋ligmacher*, fol. A1v. Reproduced in E. A. McKee, *Katharina Schütz Zell*, 2 vols (Leiden: Brill, 1999), vol. 2, p. 58 (hereafter: *KSZ*); translated in McKee, ed., *Katharina Schütz Zell. Church Mother: The Writings of a Protestant Reformer in Sixteenth-Century Germany* (Chicago: University of Chicago Press, 2006), p. 92 (hereafter: *Church Mother*).

60 Elsie McKee has written extensively about Schütz Zell and the preface to this book. See *KSZ* (vol. 2 of which contains the preface in German on pp. 58–64); *Reforming Popular Piety in Sixteenth-Century Strasbourg: Katharina Schütz Zell and Her Hymnbook*, Studies in Reformed Theology and History, vol. 2, no. 4 (Princeton: Princeton Theological Seminary, 1994) (containing a translation of the preface and a copy of the hymn book annotations); and *Church Mother* (also containing a translation of the preface on pp. 92–6). All English citations of the preface are taken from *Church Mother*.

the hymns.[61] This first volume was entitled *Von Christo Jesu vnserem såligmacher seiner Menschwerdung, Geburt, Beschneidung, &c.*[62]

In the preface to his 1531 Bohemian publication, Michael Weisse wrote that after requests from the elders and ministers of the Bohemian Brethren, he had worked diligently to provide the German speakers of the Brethren with songs in German rhyme, adopting the principle of one syllable (or as few as possible) per note.[63] Schütz Zell's own preface was highly complimentary of Weisse's work. She explained that although she did not personally know Weisse, she deemed him to be 'a God-fearing man, indeed, a man who knows God', and believed that he had 'the whole Bible wide open in his heart'.[64] Her edition, she continued, had been prepared in such a way that all might understand the book and its contents, and for that reason it perhaps ought to be called 'a teaching, prayer, and praise book rather than a songbook'.[65] She littered her preface with biblical references, providing evidence of the goodness of singing to God, especially from the Old Testament. From these examples, she reasoned, 'have also come all the songs of the church, where they [were] kept in the right way

---

61 *Church Mother*, pp. 89–90.

62 The full title is *Von Christo Jesu vnserem såligmacher seiner Menschwerdung / Geburt / Beschneidung / &c. etlich Christliche vnd trostliche Lobgsång / auß einem vast herrlichen Gsangbůch gezogen / Von welchem inn der Vorred weiter anzeygt würdt* (Strasbourg: Frölich, 1534). This translates as: *Of the incarnation, birth, circumcision, etc. of Christ Jesus our Saviour, some Christian and consoling songs of praise, taken from a very magnificent songbook, about which more is to be said in the preface*. It currently resides in the collection of the Rossiyskaya Gosudarstvennaja Biblioteka, Moscow, having been removed from the Berlin Staatsbibliothek after the Second World War. A microfilm was made by Ernest Muller in the 1930s, a photocopy of which is said to exist in the Bibliothèque Wilhelmitana, Médiathèque protestante, Strasbourg. See Lienhard, 'Catherine Zell, nee Schütz', in A. Séguenny, ed., *Bibliotheca Dissidentium : Répertoire des non-conformistes religieux des seizième et dix-septième siècles*, Tome 1: *Johannes Campanus, Christian Entfelder, Justus Velsius, Catherine Zell-Schütz* (Baden-Baden: Valentin Koerner, 1980), pp. 111–15.

63 'NAch dem yhr ewer Eltisten vnd seelsorger offtmal mit beth ersucht / vn[nd] sie da durch / auch euch deutsche[n] (wie die behmischen brůd[er]) mit geistliche[n] gesengen zu versorgen / verursacht habt / Vnnd nu solche arbeit mihr aufgelegt hab jch auch nach vermůgen all meynen fleis angewandt / ewer alt sampt d[er] behmischen brůd[er] Cancional vor mich genommen / vnd den selben sihn / nach gewisser heiligenn schriefft / jnn deutsche reym bracht / die sillaben wort vn[nd] gesetz also gestellt / dz sich ein jeglichs vnder seine[m] zugeschriebene[n] thon sein singe[n] lest'. M. Weisse, preface to *Ein New Geseng buchlen* (Bohemia: Buntzel & Wylmschwerer, 1531), fol. Aij^{r}.

64 'einem gottsförchtigen: ja gottsbekanten mann … diser mann die gantz Bibel offen inn seim hertzen habe'. Schütz Zell, preface, fol. A1^{v}. Printed in *KSZ*, vol. 2, pp. 58–9; translated in *Church Mother*, pp. 92–3.

65 'Ja ich muoß es vil mehr ein Leer: Gebett und danckbuoch (dann ein gsangbuoch) heyssen'. Schütz Zell, preface, fol. A1^{v}. Printed in *KSZ*, vol. 2, p. 59; translated in *Church Mother*, p. 93. The title of the fourth book in the collection is especially revealing about how Schütz Zell wished this collection of songs to be regarded: 'The fourth little book of spiritual songs, of songs of praise, prayer songs, teaching songs, songs for [different] times of day, songs for children, funeral songs for the dead, for the Day of Judgement, of the true saints, and of the testament of the Lord' (see p. 129, n. 83 for the original German title). In later writings Schütz Zell also referred to the book as a 'teaching book' (see *Church Mother*, pp. 122–3, incl. n. 105).

and with the right heart, as they were by the first singers'.[66] Elsie McKee points out that this last comment is crucial to the argument presented in the preface, and also that it is compatible with the standpoint of the Strasbourg reformers at large on church song. In other words, only singing which conforms with the Bible and with the Christian faith is acceptable. Humanism and Protestantism were portrayed as having a common history, linking back to the correct understanding of Scripture as found in the early Church.[67] To emphasise the point, Schütz Zell complained of the 'many scandalous songs [being] sung by men and women and also children throughout the world – songs in which all slander, coquetry, and other scandalous things are spread through the world by young and old'.[68] The problem, then, was that people sang songs that were either badly suited to the praise of God, or that were blasphemous. Weisse's songs, on the contrary, were deemed by Schütz Zell to be good examples of the type of material that should instead be sung. Despite this, the subject matter of the songs in *Von Christo Jesu vnserem saͤligmacher* was rather different from what had been customarily printed in Strasbourg since the imposition of Protestantism. She explained that

> here there are to be found many attractive songs about the feast days: the coming and the work of Christ, such as the angels' salutation, Christmas, Easter, Ascension, Pentecost, and so on and about the true dear saints – so that many good people may not complain, 'The holy remembrances themselves will all be forgotten, if no one ever celebrates the feasts of Christ and the saints'.[69]

The implication, namely that there had been complaints from the laypeople about the suppression of feast days in Strasbourg, perhaps led Schütz Zell to try to demonstrate to the preachers that both the feasts mentioned and the songs about them were biblical in nature, even if not always in content.[70] The melodies originate from a variety of sources, including late-medieval liturgical or popular

---

66 'dahar auch alle gsang der Kirchen kommen seind: wo sye mit rechter weiß und hertzen gehalten werent worden: wie von den ersten sengernn'. Schütz Zell, preface, fols A1^{v}–A2^{r}. Printed in *KSZ*, vol. 2, pp. 59–60; translated in *Church Mother*, p. 93.

67 *Church Mother*, p. 93, n. 59.

68 'Dieweil dann nun so vil schandtlicher Lieder: von mann und frawen: auch den kinden gesungen werden: inn der gantzen welt: inn welchen alle laster: buolerey und anderer schandtlicher ding: den alten und jungen fürtragen wirt'. Schütz Zell, preface, fol. A2^{r}. Printed in *KSZ*, vol. 2, p. 60; *Church Mother*, pp. 93–4.

69 'Dann seer vil hibscher gsang von den Festen: der zukunfft unnd handlung Christi: Als vom Engelischenn gruoß: Weinachttag: Ostertag: Hymmelfart: Pfingstag: &c. Und den rechten lieben heyligen hie funden werden: Damit sich auch vil gutter leut nit beklagen mögen: die selben heyligen gedechtnissen: werden all vergessen: so man die tag der Fest Christi und der heyligen nymmen feyre'. Schütz Zell, preface, fol. A2^{v}. Printed in *KSZ*, vol. 2, p. 61; translated in *Church Mother*, pp. 94–5.

70 *Church Mother*, p. 95, n. 62. For a table of the songs and their provenance, see A. Wolff, 'Le recueil de cantiques de Catherine Zell, 1534–1536', 2 vols (Master's diss., Université des Sciences Humaines de Strasbourg [Institut d'Études Allemandes], 1986), vol. 1, pp. 44–9.

religious songs and the Bohemian Brethren's tradition. The origins of some others cannot be traced at all.[71]

Anne Wolff-Hoffmann comments that *Von Christo Jesu vnserem s̊äligmacher* may well have been a marginal publication, but points out that it was not published in Strasbourg with a marginal audience in mind, the effects of the church synod of 1533[72] having just begun to make survival more difficult for separatist religious groups.[73] McKee claims that at the beginning of the Strasbourg Reformation 'there was not a great deal of appropriate Protestant song, and what existed was primarily intended for public worship, and not everyone found this equally suitable for private prayer ... there was relatively little material available which was appropriate for followers of the Gospel to sing or pray in their homes'.[74] However, she does not qualify the term 'appropriate', and so we are left with two impressions by her last comment: first, that the new metrical psalms and other songs being printed in Strasbourg hymn books and liturgical orders were emerging in a slow trickle, and were being published only with the intention of being used in church; and second, that the public did not appreciate them. Although there seems to be some truth in the latter point, judging in particular by the comments made by Schütz Zell in her preface, there is certainly nothing to suggest that the laypeople were being discouraged from singing these songs outside of church.[75] Indeed, Christopher Boyd Brown asserts that the hymn printing industry across Germany at this time 'was directed primarily to a domestic market'.[76] However, in the case of Strasbourg at the beginning of the Reformation, it seems that neither McKee nor Brown is right. Hymns were indeed being printed in great quantity, but publishers took care to be ambiguous about their purposes: it is not stated in any early preface that they were either for private or public use. Despite this, we know that hymn-singing in church was taking place at this time,[77] despite our uncertainty over whether they were also being used in private devotion. There is no reason, however, why people might not have sung psalms in their homes.

---

71 *KSZ*, vol. 1, p. 100.

72 See above, p. 123.

73 Wolff-Hoffmann, 'L'Influence de l'hymnodie strasbourgeoise sur l'Eglise d'Angleterre à ses débuts, par l'intégration de mélodies dans des recueils de cantiques publiés entre 1535 et 1610', 2 vols (Master's diss., Université de Paris X Nanterre, 2006)', vol. 1, pp. 20 and 41.

74 *KSZ*, vol. 1, p. 98.

75 See, for example, Köpfel's preface to the 1530 *Psalmen gebett*, which quotes Ephes. 5:19: 'And speak to each other with psalms and songs of praise and spiritual songs, sing and play to the Lord in your hearts, and always give thanks to God the Father for everything', and Col. 3:17: 'All that you do with words or with works, do it all in the name of the Lord Jesus'. This may not be motivating people explicitly to use these songs outside of church, but the sentiment is implied.

76 C. B. Brown, *Singing the Gospel: Lutheran Hymns and the Success of the Reformation* (Cambridge, MA, and London: Harvard University Press, 2005), p. 11.

77 See Hobbs, '"Quam Apposita Religioni Sit Musica"', pp. 155–62.

Schütz Zell's writing contained a great deal of concern for the spiritual wellbeing of the common people (and especially of women). She referred to 'the artisan at his work, the maidservant at her dishwashing, the farmer and vine dresser on the farm, and the mother with the wailing child in the cradle',[78] and explained how women can use song to turn to God as they 'keep house, obey, cook, wash dishes, wipe up and tend children'. In this way,

> they please God much better than any priest, monk, or nun in their incomprehensible choir song, as they lifted up some foolish devotion of useless lullaby to the organ. A poor mother would so gladly sleep, but at midnight she must rock the wailing baby and sing it a song about godly things. That is called, and it is, the right lullaby (provided it is done in the faith) – that pleases God. Not the organ or the organist – He is no child, and you may not silence Him with piping and singing! But silence yourself: He requires something else.[79]

Schütz Zell's words to the laypeople were intended to encourage them not only that their work was necessary for the well-being of themselves and their families, but that it was pleasing to God. Moreover, God commended it much more than he commended any efforts by the clergy to charm or soothe him. The laity's efforts were worth more.

She also makes explicit her target audience in her comments about the pricing of the songbooks. She apparently considered there to be too much material to fit into a single volume, as this would have made the collection too expensive for people to buy. 'So I took the book in hand, for the use and service of children and the poor, and divided it into several small booklets costing two, three, and

---

[78] 'Der handtwercks gsell ob seiner arbeyt: Die dienstmagt ob jrem schisselweschen: Der acker und rebmann uff seinem acker: und die muoter dem weinenden kind inn der wiegen'. Schütz Zell, preface, fol. A3r. Printed in *KSZ*, vol. 2, p. 63; translated in *Church Mother*, p. 96. Schütz Zell's comments here are remarkably similar to those of Miles Coverdale in his preface to the early English psalter, *Goostly Psalmes*: 'wolde God that oure mynstrels had none other thynge to playe vpo[n], nether oure carters & plow men other thynge to whistle vpon, saue Psalmes, hymnes, and soch godly songes as Dauid is occupied with all. And yf women syttynge at theyr rockes, or spynnynge at the wheles, had none other songes to passe theyr tyme withal, tha[n] soch as Moses sister, Elchanas wife, Debora, and Mary the mother of Christ haue song before the[m], they shulde be better occupied, then with hey nony nony, hey troly loly, & soch lyke fantasies', M. Coverdale, *Goostly psalmes and spirituall songes | drawen out of the holy Scripture, for the co[m]for- | te and consolacyon of soch as loue | to reioyse in God and | his worde* (London: Rastell & Gough, *c.* 1535), fol. iiv. See the discussion of this publication on pp. 237–9.

[79] 'Das sye darinnen vil baß Gott gfallen: dann keyn Pfaff: Münch: oder Closterfraw inn jrem unverstendigen Chorgsang: wie man auch etwan thorechte andacht gehebt hat: des unnützen kindelwagens auff der orgel: Ein arme muoter so gern schlieff: unnd aber zu mitternacht muoß das weynent kindel wagen: jm also ein Lied von götlichen dingen singt: Das heysset und ist das recht kindel wagen (so es geschicht im glauben) das gfellt Gott: und nicht die orgel oder der orgler: er ist keyn kindt: darffest jn nicht geschweygen mit pfeiffen und singen: sonder dich selbs: er erfordert ein anders'. Schütz Zell, preface, fol. A3r. Printed in *KSZ*, vol. 2, pp. 62–3; translated in *Church Mother*, p. 95.

four pennies'.[80] Four books were published in total, containing a total of 167 songs:[81] the first, mentioned above (containing 24 songs), the second appeared a year later (containing 21 songs),[82] and the remaining two came off the press in 1536 (containing 20 and 102 songs respectively).[83] An index to the contents of all four volumes was put into the first booklet.

McKee suggests that Schütz Zell's wish to distinguish her book from a songbook (*gsangbuoch*)[84] 'reflects a certain critique of the popular songs that circulated both orally and in print'.[85] This seems improbable, however. Given the number of religious songbooks that had been in circulation during the past decade, as well as the implications of the title of her collection,[86] it seems unlikely that there may have been any misapprehension on the part of the laypeople that this set of books might contain anything other than spiritual songs. Furthermore, the term 'Gesangbuch' was gaining a religious connotation,[87] and she had in fact herself used this term to describe Weiss's original songbook. In any case, popular songs did not usually appear in printed collections, being more often printed in small pamphlets or on broadsheets. Her wish that each volume be referred to as a 'teaching, prayer, and praise book' was in fact in all likelihood aimed at convincing the preachers that these songs were suitable alternatives to the Psalms, and that the people should be allowed to sing them, rather than anything to do with distancing her publication from popular song publications.

As will be demonstrated in the following chapter, the reformers, both in Strasbourg and elsewhere, had certainly been keen to weed out profane songs from society and replace them with sacred songs of praise and thanksgiving.[88] René Bornert has suggested that the reformers used religious song not only as a means of propaganda for the new religious thinking, but also as a form

80 'Darumb hab ich mich (zu dienst und nutz den kinden und armen) gewalts inn disem Buoch gebraucht: und das zertheylt inn etlich kleyne Büechlin umb ij. iij. und iiij. pfennig'. Schütz Zell, preface, fol. A2v. Printed in *KSZ*, vol. 2, p. 61; translated in *Church Mother*, p. 94.

81 J. Zahn, *Die Melodien der deutschen evangelischen Kirchenlieder* (Reinheim: Lokay, 1889–93; repr. Hildesheim: Olms, 1968), vol. 6, pp. 13–14.

82 *Das ander Byechlin der Geystlichen gsång / Von der Erscheinung / Wandel vnd Leiden Christi vnsers heylandts* (Strasbourg: Frölich, 1535).

83 *Das dritt Byechlin der Geystlichen gsång / Von der Aufferstehung / Hym[m]elfart Christi vnsers Herren / vnd von dem Heyligen Geyst* (Strasbourg: Frölich, 1536); *Das vierde Byechlin d[er] Geystlichen gsång / Von Lobgsången / Bettgsången / Leergsången / Gsang auff die tag zeytten / Gsang für die Kinder / Gsang für die Gefallenen / Gsang zům begrebnüß der todten / Vom Jüngsten tag / Von den rechten Heyligen / Vnd vom Testament des Herren* (Strasbourg: Frölich, 1536).

84 *Church Mother*, p. 93; *KSZ*, vol. 2, p. 59.

85 *Church Mother*, p. 93, n. 58.

86 See p. 125, n. 62.

87 See P. Veit, 'Piété, chant et lecture: les pratiques religieuses dans l'Allemagne protestante à l'époque moderne', *Revue d'histoire moderne et contemporaine*, 37 (1990), pp. 624–41.

88 Bucer, preface to the *Gesangbuch* (1541). See also Röhrich, *Geschichte der Reformation im Elsass und besonders in Strassburg: nach gleichzeitigen Quellen bearbeitet*, 3 vols (Strasbourg: Heitz, 1830–32), vol. 1, pp. 210–11.

of competition for popular songs of the time.[89] The accessibility of different forms of popular culture was increasing with developments in the printing press, and even before the 1520s there had been efforts by the authorities to suppress inappropriate songs.[90] Bucer believed strongly that the young should be weaned away from such songs and poems, which throughout the course of the 1541 *Gesangbuch* preface he describes as devilish, seductive, injurious, lascivious, ruinous, frivolous, worldly, and wanton.[91] The reformers placed such songs in direct opposition to sacred (and in particular biblical) songs.[92] Thus, it should not be surprising to observe that the publication of popular song pamphlets declined significantly during Bucer's time as leader of the Strasbourg Church. Most were pamphlets containing single songs.[93] After Bucer's departure, during the so-called Imperial Interim or Augsburg Interim of the 1550s,[94] popular music once more became a publishable genre. The printer Theobald Berger made a living from printing popular music in the second half of the century.[95] Roughly 65 secular popular song publications carry his name.[96]

Thus, it is demonstrated how the Reformation had an effect not only on the music of the church, but on music in society as a whole. In light of this, one function of hymn publications becomes clear. It is possible that the reformers actively sought to cut off the supply of profane music, which they saw as damaging and unholy, and publishers were therefore obliged to replace it with a supply of sacred music (to be sung both in and out of church), in order to fill the vacuum and stay in business.

Evidence for such a popular song purge in Strasbourg is visible in Schütz Zell's preface. People had complained, she implies, that the preachers had taken away all the songs they were used to singing, and replaced them with new and presumably unfamiliar songs. She emphasises that people should still be allowed to sing, but that they must sing songs that are pleasing to God. Interestingly, for Schütz Zell this includes songs about the 'true dear saints',

89 Bornert, *Réforme protestante du culte*, p. 179.

90 See Chapter 4.

91 See Appendix H.

92 Mary Douglas has studied notions of dirt and defilement in opposition to 'sacred things and places' (M. Douglas, *Purity and Danger* (London and New York: Routledge, 1966; repr. 2002), p. 9).

93 Data from M. U. Chrisman, *Bibliography of Strasbourg Imprints, 1480–1599* (New Haven: Yale University Press, 1982), pp. 189–95. See also Chapter 4, Table 4.1. Chrisman's method of songbook classification is not always logical. She counts *Fünff und sechzig teütscher Lieder* (Strasbourg: Schöffer & Apiarius, before 1537) in the 'Popular songs' category, whereas other publications such as *Viginti Cantiunculae gallicae quatuor vocum* (Strasbourg: Schöffer, 1530) are grouped under 'Collections for group singing'. See Chrisman, *Bibliography of Strasbourg Imprints*, pp. 191, 195. Deciding on song book categories, though, is never easy (see McKee, *Reforming Popular Piety*, p. 9).

94 See Chapter 5, p. 233.

95 Chrisman, *Lay Culture, Learned Culture: Books and Social Change in Strasbourg, 1480–1599* (New Haven and London: Yale University Press, 1982), p. 10.

96 Data from Universal Short Title Catalogue (www.ustc.ac.uk) (accessed 1 July 2014).

implying, therefore, that the laity should be able to sing non-scriptural texts, which up to this point had not appeared in the Strasbourg canon of hymns, apart from a handful by Luther and others. She is careful, however, to ensure that this approach remains compatible with Bucer's opposition to the collects and prayers of the Roman Church which were based on 'fables' of figures such as St Barbara, St Catherine, St Christopher, St Margaret, and St George.[97] In other words, the songs must be about those who really lived and died for God, and whose example we can follow, rather than pagan legends of doubtful historicity. In the opinion of McKee, Schütz Zell had helped to fulfil a real need, and her opinions had perhaps also encouraged the clergy to provide the laity with songs to 'fill the gaps' in their private devotion.[98]

For all her enthusiasm and determination, Schütz Zell never apparently saw a reprint of her books. McKee suggests three reasons for this. One is that 'more hymnbooks were beginning to be published'.[99] This was not the case, however, as we know that Schütz Zell's four books were published at a time of relatively low production in hymn books in the city.[100] McKee's other two reasons are far more likely: that the book's editor was a woman; and that the publication was associated with the circles of Caspar Schwenckfeld, a Protestant with Anabaptist leanings,[101] who refused to join a parish congregation in Strasbourg. He was eventually asked to leave Strasbourg in 1533.[102] Despite this, Katharina Schütz Zell maintained contact with Schwenckfeld, and he is likely to have been the one who, 'out of special love and friendship', originally presented her with a copy of Weisse's book.[103] Such a connection to the Anabaptists would not have been well received among the Strasbourg reformers, and perhaps neither with some of the populace. We must also be open to a further (and less complicated) possibility, namely that the books just might not have been as popular and therefore did not sell as well as Schütz Zell had hoped.

---

97 *BDS*, 1, p. 274, translated in O. F. Cypris, 'Basic Principles: Translation and Commentary of Martin Bucer's *Grund und Ursach*, 1524' (PhD diss., Union Theological Seminary, New York, 1971), p. 208. See below, p. 00.

98 *KSZ*, vol. 1, p. 101.

99 Ibid.

100 See Appendix A.

101 The Anabaptist situation in Strasbourg was complicated. For a time, the city and its reformers had provided a safe haven for Anabaptists who had been expelled from other areas. In 1531, their leader in Strasbourg, Pilgram Marpeck, wrote to the reformers asking them to demonstrate the reason for which infant baptism had not been banned. Marpeck saw no reason not to do this, since the reformers had abolished the Mass, feast days, singing, prayers, and many other extremities of the Church of Rome (1 AST 75, 50, pp. 746–7; *BDS*, 14, p. 39). Bucer became increasingly frustrated with Marpeck, and he was eventually expelled from the city in 1532. However, there were still those such as Katharina Schütz Zell who had connections with Anabaptist figures.

102 D. Steinmetz, *Reformers in the Wings: From Geiler von Kaysersberg to Theodore Beza*, 2nd edn (Oxford: Oxford University Press, 2001), pp. 136–7.

103 *Church Mother*, p. 89.

Polyphony in Strasbourg

The 1530s also saw an increase in the printing of another sort of music genre about which the Strasbourg reformers would have been uneasy. There was no place in Strasbourg's churches for Latin polyphony, which to the reformers' ears would have reeked of popery. German polyphony may have been acceptable in theory, but without a trained choir there would have been no point attempting to integrate it into worship. Secular songs were problematic in their own way, whether polyphonic or not. Nevertheless, sources show that during the 1530s there was an increasing market in the city for all these genres.

Two polyphonic publications appeared in Strasbourg in the year 1534. One was a collection of pieces by the composer Sixt Dietrich, entitled *Epicedion Thomae Sporeri Musicorum Principis*,[104] the first musical work published jointly by the Schöffer and Apiarius partnership.[105] As the title suggests, this was a work of homage to the composer Thomas Sporer, who had died earlier that year.[106] It was edited by the humanist Johannes Rudolphinger and illustrated with woodcuts by Hans Baldung (including a self-portrait). The book's preface, written by the Sélestat humanist Johannes Sapidus on behalf of Rudolphinger,[107] sang the praises of the deceased musician. Sporer was admired, Sapidus wrote, not only because of his musical gift but also because of other outstanding talents. He also added that Sporer had no need for external recommendation; his achievements alone would enable him to be remembered. The second part of the preface gave thanks to those involved in the publication.[108] The book would not have received the approval of the Church authorities in Strasbourg, as Sapidus and others were considered epicureans by Bucer.[109]

The second anomaly in 1534 in the history of the Strasbourg religious songbook was the appearance of *Wittenbergische Gsangbüchli*: a reprint by Peter Schöffer and Matthias Apiarius of Johann Walter's *Geystliche gesangk Buchleyn*, originally printed in Wittenberg 10 years earlier; as far as we know

104 *Epicedion | Thomae Sporeri Musicorum | Principis, Modulis musicis à | Sixto Dittricho | illustratum* (Strasbourg: Schöffer & Apiarius, 1534). Copies of the alto, tenor 1, and tenor 2 partbooks are held in the Augsburg Staats- und Stadtbibliothek.

105 See Chapter 2, p. 55.

106 For more information about this publication, see S. Söll-Tauchert, *Hans Baldung Grien (1484/85–1545): Selbstbildnis und Selbstinszenierung* (Cologne: Böhlau, 2010), pp. 66–99. Passing references can also be found in Meyer, 'Introduction', in S. Dietrich, ed. M. Honegger and Meyer, *Magnificat Octo Tonorum, Strasbourg, 1535* (Strasbourg: Convivium musicum; Stuttgart: Carus-Verlag, 1992), pp. VII–VIII; and W. Young, 'Music Printing in Sixteenth-Century Strasbourg', *Renaissance Quarterly*, 24 (1971), p. 492.

107 Söll-Tauchert, *Hans Baldung Grien*, p. 67.

108 Ibid., pp. 67–8.

109 Ibid., p. 92.

this was the first time it was printed in Strasbourg.[110] A second edition appeared in 1537.[111] Walter's preface stated that many things risked being destroyed along with the 'Papist Mass', including music, which was 'currently despised and scorned', and that he had published those pieces 'in defiance of the devil and his disdain', 'so that this beautiful art does not get completely destroyed'.[112] Luther's preface was printed in full, unlike in the Strasbourg *Enchiridion* of 1525, whose editors were forced to remove the final paragraph about multiple-voice singing.[113] In this final paragraph, he wrote that the songs were written for multiple voice parts 'to give the young … something to wean them away from love ballads and carnal songs[114] and to teach them something of value in their place, thus combining the good with the pleasing, as is proper for youth'.[115]

This renewed warning against popular songs apparently had not been heeded, especially not by the book's Strasbourg publishers, Schöffer and Apiarius. This pair was also responsible for the publication of *Fünff vnd sechzig teütscher Lieder*, an important collection of, as the title suggests, 65 songs in German.[116] Nor was this warning taken on board by the Strasbourg composer,

---

110 *Wittenber- | gische Gsangbüchli | durch Johan. Walthern / | Churfürstlichen von | Sachsen senger mey- | stern vff ein newes | corrigiert / gebes | sert vnd ge- | meret* (Strasbourg: Schöffer & Apiarius, 1534). Various copies of the five partbooks are scattered across Europe, a copy of the tenor and alto partbooks, for example, being available in the British Library.

111 *Wittenber- | gisch Gsangbiichli* [*sic*] | *durch Johan. Waltern / | Churfürstlichen von | Sachsen senger mey- | ster / vff ein newes corrigiert / gebes | sert / vnd ge- | meret* (Strasbourg: Schöffer & Apiarius, 1537). Various sources suggest that Schöffer had already published an edition of Walter's book in 1525, although it is not agreed where. See B. J. Blackburn, 'Josquin's Chansons: Ignored and Lost Sources', *Journal of the American Musicological Society*, 29 (1976), pp. 61–2; Blume, trans. F. Ellsworth Peterson, 'The Period of the Reformation' in Blume, *Protestant Church Music*, p. 47.

112 'ES ist nicht wunder / das die Musica ietzt zurzeit so gar veracht vnd verschmet wirt / seitemal das andere künste / die ma[n] doch haben soll vnd můß / so jemerlich von iederman schier fürnichts gehalten werden. Aber der Teufel thůt / wie sein art ist / die weyl man jm von Gots genade[n] / die Papistiche Meß mit allem anhang vmgestosen / stőst er / so viel an jm gelegen / alles was Gott gfelt / widderumb zůboden. Auff das aber die schone kunst nicht also gar vertilget werde / hab ich / Gott zů lob / dem Tufel vnd seiner verachtung nur zů trotz / die geischliche[n] [*sic*] lieder / so ma[n] zůuor zů Wittemberg gedruckt / das mehrenteil / so vil mir Gott verlihen / aufs new / gesetzt / die andernn mit fleis corrigirt vnd gebessert / auch mit etlichen sechstim[m]ige[n] vnd fünfstimmige[n] stucklein / gemehret / vnd jm druck ausgehn lassen'. J. Walter, preface to *Wittenbergische Gsangbüchli* (Strasbourg: Schöffer & Apiarius, 1534), tenor partbook, fol. A iij[r]. All quotations are taken from the British Library copy.

113 See p. 84.

114 See Wimpheling's comments about the songs of 'gentile poets' in Chapter 1, pp. 23–4.

115 'Und sind dazu auch inn vier stimme bracht / nit auß anderer vrsach denn das ich gern wolte / die jugent … etwas hette / damit sie der bul lieder vnd fleyschichen gesenge loß würde / vnd an der selben[n] stat / etwas heylsames lernete / vnd also das gut emit lust / wie den junge[n] gepürt / ingienge', *Wittenbergische Gsangbüchli* (Strasbourg: Schöffer & Apiarius, 1534), tenor partbook, fol. Aij[v]. Also printed in *WA*, 35, pp. 474–5; translated in *LW*, 53, p. 316.

116 *Fünff vnd | sechzig teütscher | Lieder / vormals | im[m] truck nie vß | gangen* (Strasbourg: Schöffer & Apiarius, before 1537). See Chapter 4, pp. 188–9 and 192.

Matthias Greiter, who composed five songs in this collection. The majority of composers in this collection were German or active in Germany, including Sixt Dietrich, Thomas Sporer, and Ludwig Senfl. The music is mostly in four-part polyphony,[117] although several pieces are written for five voices (and five partbooks were published). Most are relatively short in length and are not particularly demanding. The presence of this title in *RISM DKL* is erroneous, and probably due to a comment made by Wackernagel in his 1855 *Bibliographie*. Wackernagel comments that the twelfth song, the *Judaslied* or *Judasstrophe*, is 'the only spiritual poem in the book' (*das einzige geistliche Gedicht in dem Buch*).[118] The word 'geistliche' seems to have been misinterpreted by the *RISM* editors as having a liturgical connotation in this case, when in fact the song did not have an official liturgical role (Wackernagel meant only that it had a religious theme). As explained in Chapter 4, the *Judaslied* (also known as 'O du armer Judas') was a popular devotional song, lamenting Judas's betrayal of Jesus and often used in a ceremonial evicting of Judas in Holy Week. The song was adapted for polemical uses during the Reformation,[119] and was arranged by various composers.[120] It is clear from the titles of some of the other songs that *Fünff vnd sechzig teütscher Lieder* included many of the types of songs about which religious leaders like Luther and Bucer were concerned.[121] Indeed, some of the songs contained religious references, as might be expected at a time in which the Church was so central to people's lives – such as 'Auff diß faßnacht' ('On this Shrove Tuesday')[122] – but their content cannot exactly be said to be pious.

In 1535, Sixt Dietrich composed yet another collection of polyphonic music. The *Magnificat Octo Tonorum*[123] comprised eight settings of the Magnificat for the office of Vespers, although their polyphonic nature of course made them most unlikely to have been used in a public liturgical setting in Strasbourg. The collection was reprinted in 1537 in Strasbourg as well as Nuremberg, but Christian Meyer believes that the original edition was intended to be the first in

[117] Only Hulrich Brätel's 'Ein läppisch man' and, to some extent, Matthias Greiter's 'Ein seltzam newe abentheür' are written in a homophonic note-against-note style.

[118] K. E. P. Wackernagel, *Bibliographie zur Geschichte des deutschen Kirchenliedes im XVI. Jahrundert* (Frankfurt am Main: Hender & Zimmer, 1855), p. 45.

[119] R. W. Scribner, 'Ritual and Reformation', in R. P. Hsia, *The German People and the Reformation* (Ithaca and London: Cornell University Press, 1988), p. 139.

[120] The most famous setting is probably Ludwig Senfl's five-part motet.

[121] See Chapter 4. This publication is erroneously included in *RISM DKL*.

[122] This song references another popular and lascivious song of the time, 'Der Pfarrer von St. Veit'.

[123] *Magnificat Octo Tonorum* (Strasbourg: Schöffer & Apiarius, 1535; repr. 1537). A complete set is held by the Ratsschulbibliothek, Zwickau (1535) and in the Bayerische Staatsbibliothek, Munich (1537). A critical edition was produced by Honegger and Meyer.

a series that never materialised.[124] There may also have been printed a book of 53 motets by various composers, [125] although its existence cannot be verified.[126]

One final polyphonic book of interest that ought to be mentioned is the *Cantiones quinque uocum selectissimæ*, published by Peter Schöffer in 1539.[127] This was a set of 28 motets in five voices, with a privilege issued by Ferdinand I, King of Bohemia and Hungary (but addressed in the preface also as King of Rome, Germany, and many other places). The motets are by composers including Jacques Arcadelt, Pierre Cadéac, Jacquet de Berchem, Philippe Verdelot and Adrian Willaert.[128] Once again, the motets are all in Latin, and the subject matter of some of them would have made them very unsuitable for certain types of Protestant devotion at this time. Although a great deal of the material is biblical in origin, much of it is also not, and references to the Virgin Mary appear several times.[129] The preface explains that Schöffer published them in Germany for the first time, having collected the songs from Italy for German people to use. Quite why this collection came to be printed in Strasbourg in the midst of such suppression of choral music is unknown.

This sudden increase in the publication of polyphonic music in Strasbourg is curious. The reason may in part have been Schütz Zell's call for a greater variety of songs to be available in Strasbourg. Even if none of the reformers picked up on her hints, it seems that the publishers saw a sales opportunity. Although there is no documentation to support such a view, there would almost certainly have been demand from those choirmen who had lost their jobs as singers of the Roman Mass and offices, as well as from others who simply enjoyed the sound of multiple-voice singing and did not wish for it to disappear completely. It is certain, though, that many such songs would not have been performable by commoners at an inn or indeed by churchgoers at a service. All the polyphonic collections mentioned above contained art music of a sort. The pieces in the *Wittenbergische Gsangbüchli* may not be grand-scale works, but they would

---

124 Meyer, 'Introduction', in Dietrich, *Magnificat Octo Tonorum, Strasbourg*, p. VIII.

125 *Motetarum quatuor vocum a diversis musicis liber primus* (Strasbourg: Schöffer, 1535).

126 First mentioned by François Joseph Fétis in his *Biographie universelle des musiciens*, 10 vols (Paris: Didot, 1860–80), vol. 7, p. 499. See also Young, 'Music Printing in Sixteenth-Century Strasbourg', p. 492.

127 *Cantiones quinque uocum selectissimæ, a primarijs (Germnaiæ* [*sic*] *inferioris,* | *Galliæ, & Italiæ) musices magistris editæ. Ante hac typis* | *nondum diuulgatæ. Numero uigintiocto.* || *Mutetarum liber primus* (Strasbourg: Schöffer, 1539). Chrisman suggests that this was in fact a reprint of a work originally published in 1529 in Strasbourg, although no trace of this earlier edition could be found. See Chrisman, *Bibliography of Strasbourg Imprints*, p. 195; Young, 'Music Printing in Sixteenth-Century Strasbourg', p. 492; and F. Ritter, *Répertoire bibliographique des livres imprimés en Alsace au XVIe siècle de la Bibliothèque nationale et universitaire de Strasbourg*, 4 vols (Strasbourg: Heitz, 1937–60), no. 1276.

128 William Young mistakenly refers to this book as a collection of secular music (Young, 'Music Printing in Sixteenth-Century Strasbourg', p. 492).

129 Texts include 'Ave Maria', 'Inviolata, integra et casta es Maria', 'Ave et gaude gloriosa virgo Maria', 'Letare sancta mater ecclesia', and 'Et beata viscera Marie uirginis'.

have perhaps been performed as devotional songs in the home by those with a basic training in music.[130] Likewise, even the secular pieces in *Fünff vnd sechzig teütscher Lieder* could not have been performed by anyone without prior musical training. The quality of music in Dietrich's two polyphonic books is such that it was most definitely intended for performance by professional musicians.

Further Expansions

As Bornert notes, from around 1537 the published format of the liturgy began to stabilise. In printed liturgies, the orders for marriage, baptism, the Lord's Supper, the visitation of the sick, and burial were placed at the front of the book, and these were followed by a selection of psalms and an increasing number of spiritual songs.[131] This new approach coincided with the partial reintroduction in Strasbourg of liturgical feasts such as Christmas, Easter, and Ascension. The first example of such a publication is *Psalmen vnd geystliche Lieder*, which Prüss and Köpfel printed in 1537.[132] The only known example of this edition is kept in the Bibliothèque nationale et universitaire, Strasbourg and has several pages (including the front cover) missing. The book is divided into several sections. At the beginning, the liturgical orders were printed, with directions as to when psalms or hymns should be sung. The first section of hymns contained 'spiritual songs', such as 'Kum heyliger geyst', but also liturgical texts such as the *Kyrie*, *Gloria*, and settings of the Lord's Prayer. Following this section were the canticles from the New Testament, as well as 'Gott sei gelobet' and Luther's German *Sanctus*. About 20 assorted songs follow, including 'Media Vita in morte sumus' and the *Te Deum*. Then, a series of songs relating to Christmas and Easter were given, followed by a large selection of psalms. Most of the time a melody was provided; when it was not, the name of a melody was given in its place. This book contained several melodies that had not previously appeared in Strasbourg.[133]

---

130 However, the role that polyphonic music would have played in domestic circles in Strasbourg at this time is unclear.

131 Bornert, *Réforme protestante du culte*, p. 613.

132 *Psalme[n] vnd geystliche Lieder / die man zu Straßburg, und auch / die man inn anderen Kirchen pflegt / zu singen. Form und gebett zum eynsegen der Ee / den heiligen Tauff Abendmal / besuchung der Kranken, und begrebnůss / der abgestorbenen. / Alles gemert und gebessert / auch mit seinem Register* (Strasbourg: Prüss & Köpfel, 1537). A damaged copy exists in the BNUS. A similar (but not identical) version was published by Köpfel in 1537. *RISM DKL* lists this edition as being held in the BNUS, but this could not be located. It is possible that the editors were confusing the incomplete copy by Prüss and Köpfel (1537^{05}) with this other edition by Köpfel (1537^{03}). See also *Hubert*, pp. XXII–XXIII.

133 T. Gérold, *Les plus anciennes mélodies de l'Eglise protestante de Strasbourg et leurs auteurs* (Paris: Alcan, 1928), pp. 63–4.

Köpfel joined forces with Messerschmidt in 1538 to produce a second edition.[134] The same team produced a further edition in 1541,[135] and Köpfel produced yet another by himself in 1543.[136] The success of this book was no doubt partly down to the separation of liturgy and song, a format that had been tested in *Psalmen gebett*, but without the order for visitation of the sick and for the burial of the dead. There was, as well, an ever-increasing repertoire of songs. One remarkable aspect about this series is that composers' or poets' names are given with great frequency. In most cases, the name given is that of Luther, thus showing an increasing willingness to embrace the direction and music of Wittenbergian reform.[137] More generally, this readiness to print names demonstrates a changing attitude towards music-making in this religious community. Singing and music were gaining a new meaning and value, and concerns such as Köpfel's from several years earlier that people would be 'blinded by great names'[138] apparently ceased to be relevant. It is not known whether the 1537 and 1538 editions contained prefaces, but the 1541 version used the preface by Köpfel which had also appeared two years earlier in *Psalter mit aller Kirchenübung* (see below).

In 1538, Köpfel also produced a new title: *Psalter. Das seindt alle Psalmen Dauids*,[139] a book that is something of an enigma. Like Katharina Schütz Zell's collection, this book contains no liturgical instruction or order (despite the mention of 'Kyrchen ůbungen' in the title!); it is a religious songbook in the purest sense. The majority of the texts are not accompanied by a melody, although in such cases there is instead an instruction indicating to which tune the words should be sung. As was now the norm in Strasbourg, the Hebrew numbering of the Psalms was used. But despite the fact that the title claims that the book contains 'all the Psalms of David', 32 of them are missing, including ones commonly included elsewhere, such as Psalms 1 and 137.[140] The reason for this is not immediately clear, but a note at the very end of the book provided a clue: 'The second part of the Psalms and Christian songs follows'.[141]

134 Once held by the university library of the Uniwersytet Wrocławski, Wrocław, but now lost.

135 Held in the BNUS. The 1541 edition contained five more songs, three of which were printed without melodies (*Hubert*, p. XXVII).

136 Held by the Bayerische Staatsbibliothek, Munich.

137 See Chapter 5.

138 See pp. 121 and 214.

139 *Psalter. | Das seindt alle | Psalmen Dauids / mit | jren Melodeie[n] / sampt | vil Schönen Christli- | chen liedern / vnnd | Kyrche[n] ůbunge[n] / | mitt seynem | Register* (Strasbourg: Köpfel, 1538). Examples exist in the BNUS and the Bayerische Staatsbibliothek, Munich.

140 Neither René Bornert nor Théodore Gérold make any mention of these omissions. Psalms 1–10 first appeared (without melodies) in the second volume of the 1525 *Theütsch kirchenampt* trilogy. Psalm 1 was not printed with a tune until 1530, in *Psalmen gebett*. Psalm 137 was first printed in the third volume of the *Theütsch kirchenampt*. See *Hubert*, pp. XV and XX.

141 'Folgt das andertheyl / der Psalmen vnd Christlichen liedern'. *Psalter. Das seindt alle Psalmen Dauids*, fol. CLI^r. The book also contains a number of hymns translated from the Latin, as well as other devotional texts, all without printed melodies, but many with the instruction to sing

But there is neither an indication as to where this second part might be, nor what form it might take. The fact that Psalm 1 is missing is made stranger by the fact that many of the texts printed without a melody advise the reader to sing them to the melody of the Psalm 1! It does seem, therefore, that by this stage people were expected either to know certain melodies from memory or to find the tune from an alternative existing source. The most likely explanation for these omissions is that this book was intended as a supplement to *Psalmen vnd Geistliche/Geystliche lieder*, the first edition of which appeared in 1537, and of which later editions claim on the title page to be 'Das Erst Teyl' ('the first part') of an unspecified collection.[142] Between them, *Psalter. Das seindt alle Psalmen Dauids* and *Psalmen vnd Geistliche lieder* cover all the Psalms, with the exception of Psalm 53, which is mysteriously absent from both books. In a short preface to the reader, Köpfel writes that this new accomplishment (the compiling of the 'whole Psalter') has dictated that the Psalms be printed separately from the liturgy. This is in contrast to the previous method, whereby the Psalms would be printed in the order in which they were to be sung, 'piece by piece'.[143]

In addition, 20 'Geystliche Gesang' (spiritual songs) were included at the end of the book. The texts were largely biblical, but it is interesting to see that translations of a number of ancient Latin hymns were also included, such as 'Kum heiliger geist Gott schöpffer' ('Veni, Creator Spiritus'), 'Laßt vns nun all fůrsichtig sein' (the early Ambrosian hymn, 'Ad cenam Agni providi'), and 'Das liecht vnd tag ist vns Christus' ('Christe qui lux es et dies'). The inclusion of such ancient hymns may again have been a result of Schütz Zell's appeal to give the people, who had been accustomed to songs about the saints, something other than metrical psalms to sing. It is likely that they recognised the texts of the ancient hymns of the Church, even if they were in a language which they could not understand. If this was the reasoning behind the (re)introduction of such songs, then the texts were now considered acceptable (at least by the printers, if not by the preachers). The last song in the book is Hans Sachs's adaptation of the popular devotional song to Mary, 'Maria zart von edler Art', 'modified and Christianly corrected' (*verendert vnd Christlich corrigiert*)[144] to form a contrafactum entitled 'O Jesu zart, Götlicher art'. This song was first printed

them 'to their own tune' ('Jn seiner eygnen weiß'), suggesting a degree of familiarity on the part of the congregations.

[142] See Appendix A. Reference to these collections is also made in Meyer, *Les mélodies des églises protestantes de langue allemande – Catalogue descriptif des sources et édition critique des mélodies : I. Les mélodies publiées à Strasbourg (1524–1547)* (Baden-Baden and Bouxwiller: Koerner, 1987), pp. 11–12, and M. Jenny, *Geschichte des deutschschweizerischen evangelischen Gesangbuches im 16. Jahrhundert* (Basel: Bärenreiter, 1962), p. 109.

[143] 'LJeber leser / Bitzhichar hab ich die Psalmen / vnd Geistlichen Lieder wie man die in[n] den Christlichen gemeinden hien vnd wider pflegt zů singen stucks weyß / Wie ich die selben zů yeder zeyt hab mögen bekum[m]en / getruckt'. *Psalter. Das seindt alle Psalmen Dauids* (1538), fol. ii^r.

[144] *Psalter. Das seindt alle Psalmen Dauids* (1538), fol. CXLIX^v.

in the *Enchiridion oder handbůchleyn geystlicher gesenge vn[nd] Psalmen* (Nuremberg: Herrgot, 1525).[145] Like many of the others, however, this song carries the direction to sing it 'to its own tune' (*Jn seyner eignen weyß*). One wonders if the fact that so many songs were intended to be sung to their own tunes, but that these tunes were missing from this book, is a sign of realisation on the part of Köpfel that to include in his book the melodies of all the texts he had borrowed would be a huge undertaking, considerably increasing the size and cost of his volume. He must nevertheless have felt that his book would be profitable, even without including the melodies.

Köpfel's preface to the *Psalter mit aller Kirchenübung*[146] of 1539 is slightly more informative (see Figure 3.1). It is actually a rewriting of a previous preface; namely that which first appeared in the 1530 edition of *Psalmen gebett*. The first half of the original preface was retained, but the second half was rewritten (albeit with a very similar message), the reason being that new, unscriptural songs had been included in the book. He defended the inclusion of these songs by claiming that St Paul advocated the use not only of the Psalms but of other spiritual songs,[147] and also that Tertullian's writings made reference to the use of such songs in the early Church.[148] For that reason, Köpfel had decided to print here not only songs that were purely scriptural, 'but also those that powerfully prove the manner and power of the Holy Spirit'.[149] He warned against the use of songs which might not only 'lack the correct [spiritual] manner and courteousness, but would also introduce teaching which would trouble and contaminate the purity of the

145 See *Wackernagel DKL*, vol. 3, no. 80, pp. 55–6. A similar contrafactum entitled 'O Jesu zart in newer Art' had originated with the Bohemian Brethren, and featured in Katharina Schütz Zell's fourth hymn book, *Das vierde Byechlin der Geystlichen gsång* (1536), fol. Riiij^{v}. Schütz Zell's annotation reads: 'Ein lobgsang zuo Christo, und wie wir alleyn durch yn müssen selig werden, Im thon, Maria zart von edler art' ('A song of praise to Christ, and how we must only be blessed through him. To the tune of "Maria zart von edler art"'). Quoted in McKee, *Reforming Popular Piety*, p. 75.

146 *Psal- | ter mit al- | ler Kirchenůbu[n]g | die man bey der | Christlichen Gemein zů Straß- | burg vnd anders | wa pflågt zů | singen* (Strasbourg: Köpfel, 1539). A copy exists in the Bibliothèque Wilhelmitana, Médiathèque protestante, Strasbourg.

147 1 Col. 3:16 ('teach and admonish one another with all wisdom through psalms, hymns, and songs from the Spirit'); Ephes. 5:18–19 ('be filled with the Spirit, speaking to one another with psalms, hymns, and songs from the Spirit').

148 'each, from what he knows of the Holy Scriptures, or from his own heart, is called before the rest to sing to God' ('ut quisque de scripturis sanctis vel de proprio ingenio potest, provocatur in medium deo canere'). Q. S. F. Tertullianus, trans. T. R. Glover, *Apology* (London: Heinemann; Cambridge, MA: Harvard University Press, 1966), pp. 180–81.

149 'Und will der heilig Paulus nicht allein zů den Psalmen / sonder auch zů anderen geistliche[n] Liedern ermanet / wellichen brauch der Kirchen / auch der heilig marterer Tertulians meldet / Habe ich solicher geistlicher Lieder / auch etliche / alte vnnd neüwe / inn dis Gsangbůchlin trucken wőllen / doch nur die bewereten / vn[nd] die nit allein den reinen schrifftlichen sinn inn sich halten / sonder auch die art vn[nd] krafft des heyligen Geists etwas gewaltiger beweisen'. *Psalter mit aller Kirchenübung* (1539), fol. Aii^{v}; *Hubert*, p. 142.

Psal-
ter mit al-
ler Kirchenübūg
die man bey der
Christlichen Ge-
mein zů Straß-
burg vnd anders
wa pflägt zů
singen.
*
Mit seinem orden
lichen Register.
Straßburg bey
Wolff Köphl.

Figure 3.1 Title page of *Psalter mit aller Kirchenuͤbu[n]g* (Strasbourg: Köpfel, 1539) F Ssp – 16. 293. Reproduced by permission of the Médiathèque protestante, Strasbourg

Holy Gospel', and would therefore 'burden the congregation of Christ'.[150] This point is much the same as that made in the 1530 version of the preface: 'We also wanted to guard against the presumption of anyone thinking he could burden the congregation with his songs and ditties, for people are likely not to judge [their own] poems critically'.[151] In other words, although the approach –

[150] 'Dann ich nit gern vrsach geben wolte / das ein yeder mit seinen gedichten die gemeind / Christi beschweren solte / darauß auch entston moͤchte / das etwan[n] Lieder in[n] den brauch der Kirchen kemen / die nit allein die rechte art vnd lieblicheit nit hetten / sonder auch leren einfuͤreten / welche die leutere des H. Euangeli betruͤben würde[n]'. *Psalter mit aller Kirchenübung* (1539), fols Aij^{v}–Aiij^{r}; *Hubert*, pp. 142–3.

[151] 'Wir haben auch hiemit dem furwitz wollen weren / vff das nit eyn ieder mit seinen gediechten vn[nd] liedlin eyn gantze gemeynd beschwere / Dann niemandts mag sein gedicht bald mißfallen'. *Psalmen gebett* (1530), fol. B^{v}.

that non-scriptural songs were acceptable, as long as they were truly spiritual in content and would not lead people astray – had not changed, the definition of 'spiritual' had been somewhat loosened.

Interestingly, this volume contains liturgical orders (the *Kirchenübung*) as well as all the songs contained in *Psalter. Das seindt alle Psalmen Dauids* and *Psalmen vnd geystliche Lieder*.[152] Köpfel seemed to have lost his concern about the cost and work involved in producing a book of this size, and reverted to the previous design in which the liturgical orders and songs were printed within the same cover. The volume's preface was reused in many subsequent publications until 1561,[153] including the 1541 edition of *Psalmen vnd geystliche Lieder*.

A study of these hymn books alone gives the impression of a thriving community with a willingness to attend church and sing psalms and spiritual songs. Once again, though, the view of the contemporary archival documents reveals a drastically insecure series of moves by the reformers in the latter years of the 1530s. Practical matters, such as the issue of what to do with priests' benefices,[154] needed to be resolved, and the Strasbourg reformers began to feel increasingly vulnerable with regard to a number of other issues. Over the course of 1538, the Strasbourg preachers wrote three letters to the (exiled) Bishop Wilhelm von Hohnstein, outlining their doubt that the city's reforms had been successful. This had been their first correspondence with the episcopal office in 14 years. The preachers now felt that they had lost control over their Church, and were no longer finding the city council co-operative. Chrisman suggests that the reformers 'felt that the bishop would provide the weight and authority that they themselves did not possess. They may also have wished to extend their efforts to reestablish the unity of the Church'.[155] In their first letter, the preachers repeated the points made in the Tetrapolitan Confession:

> We use the prayer and song of the Church in the common language, so that everyone understands and knows better the Spirit of God as shown in 1 Corinthians 14, and this was recognised to be necessary by all the ancient Holy Fathers and Canons … That we should sing in Latin, which the common people do not understand, was never ordained in any council, nor used by the Holy Fathers.[156]

152 See *Hubert*, p. XXVI.

153 See ibid., pp. 119, 141–3.

154 1 AST 23, 5e, fols 9r–52v; *BDS*, 16, pp. 369–425.

155 Chrisman, *Strasbourg and the Reform: A Study in the Process of Change* (New Haven and London: Yale University Press, 1967), pp. 250–51.

156 'Wir prauchenn jn den gemeinen gebetten vnnd gesengen der kirchen die gemeine sprach / die jederman verstohn vnnd sich des besseren mage / wie das der geyst gottes gepeütet .1. Corinth 14. vnnd das alle .h. alte vätter vnnd Canones notwendig sein erkennen … gepottenn würt. Das wir latin solten singen / so das gemein volck das selbig nit verstöht ist jn keinen Concilio nie geordnet / oder von heÿligenn Vatteren gebrauchet worden'. 1 AST 47, III, 1, fol. 106v.

The evidence for this, they once again claim, is to be found in the *Decretum* of Canon Law.[157] The bishop, however, did not acknowledge the first letter, nor the second, and his eventual reply to the third offered no hope to the reformers.[158]

Having failed to reopen dialogue with the bishop, the reformers began to formulate plans aimed at reuniting the Churches of Germany. Bucer was instrumental in this operation, the idea for which had been aired in Strasbourg as early as 1534.[159] The first stage involved another synod of the Strasbourg church leaders in the year 1539,[160] and this was followed by negotiations with the Catholics. The aim was not to realign the Protestant Churches with Rome, but rather for the major denominations to form a united front within the Holy Roman Empire, thereby also making the Empire a stronger political and military force.[161] Music was incidental to the plans, but in one copy of the attempted reconciliation between the 'Papists and Lutherans' (*papstlich vnd Lutherisch*),[162] mention is made of the need for the 'faithful' (*gleubigen*), having assembled in church, to pray and sing songs of praise.[163] Unsurprisingly, the Protestants insisted upon the need for understanding, and referred to the customs of the Apostolic Church[164] and the Church Fathers, which led to 'real improvement of the people'.[165] The Mass should 'heartily incite the correct faithful remembrance of the death of Christ … so that the Holy Mass is saved from a lack of correct healthy teaching'.[166]

According to D. F. Wright, the production of the so-called Regensburg Book, formed as a result of the dialogue between several parties, was the 'high-water mark of reconciliation between Catholic and Protestant, not only in the Reformation period, but perhaps in the whole pre-Vatican II era'. The Holy Roman Emperor

---

157 Distinctio XCII, *Decretum*, in A. L. Richter and E. Friedberg, eds, *Corpus Iuris Canonici*, 2 vols (Graz: Akademische Druck, 1959), vol. 1, col. 318. See also above, pp. 69–70.

158 Chrisman, *Strasbourg and the Reform*, p. 255.

159 See 1 AST 42, 5, written by Caspar Hedio and Ulrich Chelius, concerning a possible concord with the Papists. See also Eells, *Martin Bucer*, p. 160.

160 Church songs were discussed at this synod. See Bornert, *Réforme protestante du culte*, pp. 8–9; 1 AST 38, 20, fol. 4v.

161 D. F. Wright, *Common Places of Martin Bucer* (Appleford, Abingdon: Sutton Courtenay Press, 1972), pp. 41–2.

162 1 AST 39, 1.

163 'Mann die gleubigen in der kirchen versamlet / vnd die heiligen lectionen / aus dem gesetz vnd Euangelio / jr gepet vnd lobgesang gehalten / auch die opffer dem Herren fur die armen gebracht'. 1 AST 39, 1, p. 11.

164 1 AST 39, 1, pp. 17–18.

165 'so fil sie zu warer besserung des volcks jiner dienen köndten'. 1 AST 39, 1, p. 13.

166 'Dann sie es darfur achten / wa man die Messen täglich halte / doch allein die offentlichen gemeinen gesungnen empter / das man die leute damit bas zur kirchen bringen / vnd auch zu recht glaubiger gedächtnüs des tods Christi / hertzlicher anreitzen möge / vnd doch dabei durch die lere / das falsche vertrawen vff das eusser werck / vnd allen anderen aberglauben vnd misbrauch abtreiben vnd verhieten / so bei den h. Messen / aus mangel recht gesunder lere eingerissen ist'. 1 AST 39, 1, p. 15.

approved of it, as did Calvin, but the problem seems to have lain with Luther at one end, and with Rome at the other, and so the deal was never sealed.[167]

* * *

There are three other aspects of the Reformation in Strasbourg that deserve special mention. One is the city's monastic reforms, another is the use of the organ during the Reformation, and the last is the education of the young and the role this had in learning and singing of church songs.

Reforming the Monastic Life

Because of their semi-autonomous nature, the attempted reform of the monasteries and convents was in many ways a separate operation from that of the city's churches.[168] Having previously been a friar himself, Bucer was an early critic of the monastic life after his conversion, and published polemical writings early in his Protestant career. In 1523, Bucer complained that monks and nuns

> claimed their singing and muttering, which they did not even understand, to be work; sleeping half the day was a vigil, and filling themselves up with fish was to fast … A Christian must make his vigil not as a monk says Matins, getting up in the middle of the night and howling away for an hour or two … but the Christian must really break his sleep and spend the time in prayer or other useful exertion.[169]

More harsh words followed: righteous people should have nothing to do with unjust priests or those whom Bucer accused of defiling wives and daughters;[170] treating others how you would yourself like to be treated did not include

---

167 Wright, *Common Places of Martin Bucer*, p. 44.

168 The cloistered religious are often treated separately in literature on the Reformation. They were, in some cases, the last strongholds of the Catholic faith in Strasbourg, a considerable time after the establishment of the Reformation and the abolition of the Mass. This is true of the knightly orders such as the Knights of St John (see Chrisman, *Strasbourg and the Reform*, p. 238). Regarding the nuns of Strasbourg, see A. Leonard, *Nails in the Wall: Catholic Nuns in Reformation Germany* (Chicago and London: University of Chicago Press, 2005).

169 Bucer, *An ein christlichen Rath vn[nd] Gemeyn der statt Weissenburg Summary seiner Predig daselbst gethon* (Strasbourg: Schott, 1523), reproduced in *BDS*, 1, pp. 97–8; and quoted in Chrisman, *Strasbourg and the Reform*, p. 125. David Steinmetz comments that *An ein christlichen Rath* makes it clear both that Bucer was Luther's disciple and that from the very first he was independent of him' (Steinmetz, *Reformers in the Wings*, p. 86). See also Bucer's similar comments made in Wissembourg (see M. Greschat, trans. S. E. Buckwalter, *Martin Bucer – A Reformer and His Times* (Louisville and London: Westminster John Knox Press, 2004), p. 43).

170 Bucer, *An ein christlichen Rath*, fol. Bii^{v}; *BDS*, 1, p. 87.

celebrating services and singing in the middle of the night at a time when God has decreed that there shall be quiet;[171] the lives of monks and nuns were of no help to anyone but themselves; and so-on. Bucer must have felt that his point had been demonstrated when, during a sermon he was giving at the cathedral on 13 February 1524, a monk began chanting Mass. It is said that no one else joined in with the singing, but a riot was caused.[172] The annals of Brant and the Imlin family chronicle give an account of another event, just eight days later, on 21 February, in which two men entered the Dominican church during the monks' singing of the office of Compline and disrupted the service. One of the men began to whistle like a nightingale (*zu pfiffen wie ein nachtigall*),[173] whereupon the men were asked to leave the church. They did so, but not before one of the monks had been knocked to the ground and the pulpit had sustained damage.[174] The monks claim that the two men, both said to be carpenters, asked the monks what they were murmuring, questioning whether they thought 'that it is pleasing or agreeable to God?'[175] One monk answered that it should not matter to the two men what the monks sang or read in their church, and that they should leave if they did not approve. The carpenters claimed that they were told by the monks to go to the cathedral 'to Master Matthäus [Zell] the heretic'. One of the carpenters responded by quoting the Scriptures: 'What my heavenly Father has not planted will be uprooted' (Matthew 15:13).[176] The verbal exchange continued until one of the men grabbed hold of the pulpit, apparently tearing it – or a piece thereof – from the wall, struck one of the monks with it, and reached for his sword. The monks then wrestled the men and threw them out of the church. Later, 300 or more citizens gathered outside the cathedral, demanding to know why the monks (and not the carpenters) had caused this disruption.[177]

---

171 Ibid., fol. Dii^r; *BDS*, 1, p. 98.

172 J. Smend, *Der erste evangelische Gottesdienst in Straßburg* (Strasbourg: Heitz, 1897), p. 15; A. Straub, *Geschichtskalender des Hochstiftes und des Münsters von Strassburg* (Rixheim: Sutter, 1891), p. 36.

173 The *Imlin'schen Familienchronik* suggests instead that the man imitated a quail (*zu schlagen wie eine wachtel*). R. Reuss, ed., 'Strassburg im sechszehnten Jahrhundert, 1500–1591: Auszug aus der Imlin'schen Familienchronik', *Alsatia*, 10 (1873–74), p. 395.

174 *Fragments des anciennes chroniques d'Alsace*, IV (1901), no. 4504; Reuss, 'Strassburg im sechszehnten Jahrhundert, 1500–1591', pp. 395–6.

175 'daß euch botz marter aller münch schneidt, waß murmeln ir da, meint ir daß gott ein wollgefallen oder angenem sey?' Reuss, 'Strassburg im sechszehnten Jahrhundert, 1500–1591', p. 395.

176 *Fragments des anciennes chroniques d'Alsace*, IV (1901), no. 4504.

177 Reuss, 'Strassburg im sechszehnten Jahrhundert, 1500–1591', p. 395. The chronicles of both Specklin and Wencker seems to confound the two events, claiming that while Bucer was preaching, the monks came into the choir and began to sing, after which the carpenter asked them to be quiet (although Specklin's chronicle seems to make reference to two events involving monks and carpenters). See *Fragments des anciennes chroniques d'Alsace*, II (1890), nos 2240 and 2247; *Fragments des anciennes chroniques d'Alsace*, III (1892), no. 3022; Eells, *Martin Bucer*, p. 32; and Röhrich, *Geschichte der Reformation im Elsass*, vol. 1, p. 215. It is worth noting that the instance of

Although violent acts by monks may not have been so frequent, the ordinary people of Strasbourg were no doubt already used to hearing verbal criticisms of the religious. These had been plentiful even in pre-Reformation times.[178] The 54th point of the 1521 Diet of Worms noted that the poor were 'sorely oppressed' by mendicant monks, and in particular friars who begged for alms, despite receiving support from their orders. According to the Diet, bishops favoured this arrangement in return for a percentage of the takings.[179] Scribner observes that it is unsurprising that the supporters of the new faith made use of such forms of mockery relating to the reputations of priests, monks, and nuns. 'They provided ready-made forms of irreverence towards a faith now held to be useless'.[180]

Luther similarly directed much of his writing against the monastic life. Scribner notes the irony in the fact that towards the beginning of the Reformation the most popular image of Luther was of him in monastic vestments.[181] In Luther's case, the monastic habit seems to have been a symbol of piety, in contrast to the traditionally popular view of the monk as described above. Traditional images of Luther also depict him in a doctoral beret, and holding a copy of the Bible, signifying his academic status and his faith in the Scriptures and authority on scriptural matters.[182] Bucer, on the other hand, seems normally to have been depicted in his doctoral outfit, an image focusing more on academic, rather than spiritual, standing.

Restrictions against monks and nuns appeared early on in the Reformation. In 1525 the council made provisions for monks and nuns to be able to leave their convents, marry, and wear 'worldly clothes' (*weltliche Kleider anzulegen*). The Wencker chronicle reports that a significant number did so.[183] The Brant annals claim that the nuns of St Clara auf dem Wörth requested help from the city council as early as 1524 to help them leave their convent. Their request was apparently to get married, or to attain an otherwise 'honest' standing in life.[184] It is difficult to tell from the other evidence about nuns and convents whether

---

the carpenters disrupting the singing of the Latin office is comparable (and opposite) to the case of the canons disrupting the celebration of the Lord's Supper, as described by Capito (see pp. 71 and 332).

178 See Chapter 1.

179 See *Deutsche Reichstagsakten: jüngere Reihe*, 19 vols (Gotha: Perthes; Göttingen: Vandenhoeck & Ruprecht; Munich: Oldenbourg, 1893–), vol. 2, pp. 670–704. Translated in G. Strauss, *Manifestations of Discontent in Germany on the Eve of the Reformation* (Bloomington and London: Indiana University Press, 1971), pp. 59–60.

180 Scribner, *For the Sake of Simple Folk* (Oxford: Oxford University Press, 1981), p. 68.

181 Ibid., p. 37.

182 See Scribner, *Simple Folk*, pp. 17–19; M. U. Edwards, Jr, *Printing, Propaganda, and Martin Luther* (Berkeley and Los Angeles: University of California Press, 1994), pp. 83–4; and L. Roper, 'Martin Luther's Body', *American Historical Review*, 115 (2010), pp. 351–84.

183 *Fragments des anciennes chroniques d'Alsace*, III (1892), nos 3030 and 3031.

184 'Der Frauen zu S. Clara uff dem Wördt supplication inen zu verhelffen üß dem closter in die ee oder sonst in ein erlichen standt, dann sie nim im closter bliben wollen, und daß man inen ein ziemlich narung geben soll'. *Fragments des anciennes chroniques d'Alsace*, IV (1901), no. 4523.

this was propagandistic wishful thinking on the part of the reformers, or whether it actually occurred.

In a document from May 1525,[185] the reformers asked the Strasbourg authorities to close certain drinking establishments, to reinforce the policing of inns, to introduce sermons in the female convents and allowing the preaching of the Gospel in such sermons, and to ban the singing of monks and nuns. They were to remain silent (*irem singe[n] still zu ston*) to avoid a revolt in the city (*witt[er]s vffrür zü verhütte[n]*). As a separate point it is written that the *Salve Regina* chants should no longer be sung, although the use of the *Salve* bell may continue.[186]

Those who chose to remain in their convents were banned from administering the sacraments.[187] A call was made for monasteries and convents to be inspected, and, of course, for the singing and reading of the Mass to be suppressed.[188] The town council replied that the Mass would be abolished in the convents and chapels of Strasbourg, and in some of the parishes, as it was confirmed in Scripture that their singing and their reading of the Mass was an abomination to God.[189] The suppression of this singing and reading, however, was far from immediate. Records show that in 1527, the Mass was still being sung or read, and money was still available for this to happen.[190] In 1529 it was once again decreed that the singing and reading by the nuns of the city was to stop.[191] The Augustinian and Franciscan monasteries were closed in 1530 and 1532 respectively,[192] but some convents and monasteries continued to resist long after the establishment of Protestantism.[193]

Amy Leonard writes that in convent education there was 'a special emphasis on studying music, because so much of the nuns' world revolved around singing

[185] IV 98, C, 'f. 2', printed in *CorrBucer*, 2, pp. 21–2. According to *CorrBucer*, 2, p. 21, this document is from 6 May 1525 or shortly before. The folio number appears in the top right-hand corner of the first page, but does not help in locating the document, which is stored in the AVS amongst an assorted and unnumbered collection of other documents.

[186] IV 98, C, 'f. 2'; *CorrBucer*, 2, p. 22.

[187] *Fragments des anciennes chroniques d'Alsace*, III (1892), no. 3030.

[188] Bibliothèque municipale de Strasbourg (hereafter: BMS) ms. 745, fol. 39r; *CorrBucer*, 2, p. 23. This document includes both the original letter from the preachers and the council's reply.

[189] 'diwil man uß der geschrift befindt, daß ir singen und meßlesen Gott ein abschü ist'. BMS, ms. 745, fol. 39r; *CorrBucer*, 2, p. 24.

[190] 1 AST 35, 9, fols 13v–14r, concerning the nuns of St Marguerite (1527); 1 AST 35, 5, fol. 8r, concerning the Order of St John: 'Herr Johann von hattstadt Sant Johanns ordens Meister Jmm Teutscen landen / schreibt dem Couenthur zu Sant Johanns bey altem geprauch des singens vnnd lesens ouch der Ceremonien pleibn zelassen / jt[em] der Burgerlichen beschwerden zuentladen / von den nuwerungn abzestan / ouch die furgenomenen pensionen den abtrinngen zegebn dem Couenthur nit zebringen'.

[191] *Fragments des anciennes chroniques d'Alsace*, I (1887), no. 243; P. Fritsch, ed., *Die Strassburger Chronik des Johannes Stedel* (Strasbourg: Sebastian Brant-Verlag, 1934), p. 100.

[192] *Fragments des anciennes chroniques d'Alsace*, I (1887), nos 107 and 108.

[193] See Leonard, *Nails in the Wall*, p. 99, incl. n. 82 for sources.

the Divine Office, and nuns were some of the earliest composers'.[194] In 1537, the nuns of St Mary Magdalene[195] were accused of singing a setting of *Haec dies, quam fecit Dominus* (Ps. 118:24) and the other psalms in Latin at Vespers, and claimed to have done so because that is how they had learned to sing them. They complained that they were too old to learn to sing in German, and had not taken on any younger recruits since the early years of the Reformation.[196] However, they claimed not to have used the organ at Vespers, nor for the *Salve Regina*.[197] Leonard comments that this case is a good illustration of how the nuns manipulated the situation – especially at a time when the relationship between reformers and the city authorities were not at their best – in order to promote a 'crypto-Catholicism'.[198]

The Organ

The Reformation's relationship with the organ was an unstable one. Those areas which maintained a choir also had need for an organ, but several cities, most notably Zurich and Geneva, had theirs removed.[199] The organ was seen partly as representative of Roman ritual, and partly as a distraction from, rather than an aid to, worship. References to church organs in writings from this period of Strasbourg's history are rather sparse, although we know that organs were in use in Strasbourg from the early Middle Ages until the Reformation. The historical fragments of Daniel Specklin's chronicle refer to an organ first being used in Strasbourg in the year 640 AD, 'in order to improve the devotion of the people' by encouraging them to sing.[200] Another chronicle refers to the cathedral organ being renewed in 1489.[201] We know that Wolfgang Dachstein was employed as organist of St Thomas from 1521, and as organist of the cathedral from 1541 following the death of Maternus Kreiss in that year.[202] The cathedral organ had

---

194 Ibid., p. 33.

195 The Penitents of St Mary Magdalene were known as the 'Reuerinnen', or 'ruwern'. See Gérold, *Les plus anciennes mélodies*, p. 36, n. 4.

196 'Zu dem hab jr predicant / am ostertag gepredigt es sey nit vnrecht / so sie singn haec dies qua[m] fecit d[omi]nus vnd psalmen / so haben sie es zu latein leren singen / seyen nun zu alt jn teutsch zusingn zu lernen / daruf sie jnen gesagt / sie solten lugen vnds nit mehr thun man / Wurde sie sonst stroffen / die sagtn sie wollen sich des beuehls halt[en] vnnd haben kheine jungen angenomen'. 1 AST 35, 10, fols 21r–21v. See Bornert, *Réforme protestante du culte*, p. 152.

197 'aber erst nach der predig vnnd doch weder zur Vesper noch zum Salve georgelt'. 1 AST 35, 10, fol. 21r.

198 Leonard, *Nails in the Wall*, p. 85.

199 D. E. Bush and R. Kassel, *The Organ: An Encyclopedia* (Routledge: New York, 2006), p. 550.

200 'domit das volck besser ahndechtige wehre'. *Fragments des anciennes chroniques d'Alsace*, II (1890), no. 639.

201 Reuss, ed., 'La Chronique strasbourgeoise de Jean-Jacques Meyer', *Bulletin de la Société pour la conservation des monuments historiques d'Alsace*, 2nd series, vol. 8 (1872), p. 135.

202 See Gérold, *Les plus anciennes mélodies*, pp. 24–5; and 90 Z 13, pp. 3, 35–43.

been installed in 1489, consisting of 2136 pipes,[203] and had been rebuilt during the period 1507–1511.[204] St Thomas had only recently had a new organ installed, and in 1515 the chapter had written to the Bishop of Strasbourg regarding the payment of the new organist.[205] Although such posts continued to exist in many Strasbourg churches throughout the Reformation, Théodore Gérold points out that the work of organists during this period appears to have been rather intermittent.[206] The Strasbourg chronicles contain no fewer than five references to the city council declaring that organs were indeed still to be used, but there are also others that state the opposite.

In 1525, a group of ministers desired to know whether certain practices should be continued during Lent, such as removing pictures and displaying the Lenten veil. They also enquired as to whether the *Salve Regina* should be sung at the end of Lent with the use of the organ and with holy water. The council decided that the *Salve* was to be sung, but not with the organ.[207] Beat Föllmi reports that soon after, however, the council decided that the organ was to be silenced altogether. He suggests that this was probably not for any theological reason, but rather for a political purpose, in order to show unity with the Swiss reformers, for whom the organ had papist connotations.[208] In 1529, however, a statement was issued that the cathedral organ 'should be played, and so not remain idle'.[209] Just two years later, the council again decreed that the cathedral organ should be played during the day, before the psalms.[210] Föllmi suggests that the organ was once again considered acceptable for liturgical use because the Mass had been abolished.[211]

In 1540 the cathedral administrators were asked to see that the organ be 'repaired and improved' (*gemacht und gebessert*), and that at every Sunday

203 *Fragments des anciennes chroniques d'Alsace*, III (1892), no. 2987.

204 Hobbs, '"Quam Apposita Religioni Sit Musica"', p. 170.

205 See Chapter 1, p. 30.

206 Gérold, *Les plus anciennes mélodies*, p. 25. The cathedral organist, at least, would have continued to receive his prebend, which was paid by the city council. See B. A. Föllmi, 'Création et reconfiguration de l'espace sonore : les activités musicales à Strasbourg avant, pendant et après la Réforme protestante', in L. Gauthier, and M. Traversier, eds, *Mélodies urbaines : la musique dans les villes d'Europe (XVIe–XIXe siècles)* (Paris: Presses de l'Université Paris-Sorbonne, 2008), p. 116.

207 *Fragments des anciennes chroniques d'Alsace*, III (1892), no. 3494; *Fragments des anciennes chroniques d'Alsace*, IV (1901), 4589.

208 Föllmi, 'Création et reconfiguration de l'espace sonore', pp. 115–16. Unfortunately, Föllmi does not cite evidence for the council's initial opposition to the use of the organ.

209 'Item dass man die orgel im Münster slagen und nit also müssig ston solt lassen'. *Fragments des anciennes chroniques d'Alsace*, III (1892), no. 3523. See also *Fragments des anciennes chroniques d'Alsace*, IV (1901), no. 4770.

210 *Fragments des anciennes chroniques d'Alsace*, III (1892), no. 3565. See also *Fragments des anciennes chroniques d'Alsace*, IV (1901), no. 4910.

211 Föllmi, 'Création et reconfiguration de l'espace sonore', p. 116.

sermon the instrument be used between the verses of the psalms.[212] Once again, in 1541, the *Ammeister*, having acknowledged that work on the organ had been carried out, questioned why one would not now want it to be played.[213] It was ordered that the organ be played on all subsequent Sundays, 'as previously decreed' (*wie vor auch erkant*).[214]

It is difficult therefore to determine how much the organ was used, either in general or at any one time. There seems at least not to have been any dismantling of organs, as there was in Geneva during the 1530s,[215] but there is evidence of some reluctance among the reformers to make use of the instrument.[216] Bucer himself, however, appears to have been relatively accepting, at least in principle, of the organ's role in church, although critical of the way it had been used recently. In his 1529 commentary on the Psalms, he wrote that 'a short time ago, the Church introduced not only sacred hymns, but different musical instruments'.[217] This, he explained, was not done with the intention to charm people, but to ignite religious feeling among them, just as David had done in his time with his harp. However, David's criteria were not observed, and sections of hymns were omitted so that more time could be devoted to organ playing.[218]

---

212 'Und sol man auch alle sontag zu den predigen daruff psalmen ein vers und den andern schlagen lassen'. *Fragments des anciennes chroniques d'Alsace*, III (1892), no. 3602. It is important to note that this would not have involved accompanying the psalms in the sense of playing along with the congregation. The common practice until the seventeenth century was that the organist would play interludes between verses of a hymn, rather than play along with the congregation. See G. Webber, *North German Church Music in the Age of Buxtehude* (Oxford: Clarendon Press, 1996), p. 38; and R. A. Leaver, *The Liturgy and Music: A Study of the Use of the Hymn in Two Liturgical Traditions* (Bramcote, Notts.: Grove Books, 1976), p. 20.

213 'Der herr ammeister ... vermeint ob man sie [die orgel] nit wolte schlagen lassen'. *Fragments des anciennes chroniques d'Alsace*, III (1892), no. 3606.

214 *Fragments des anciennes chroniques d'Alsace*, III (1892), no. 3606.

215 The organs of Geneva had mostly been demolished in 1535, although that of the cathedral of St Pierre survived until 1562, when the council decided to melt its metal pipes, giving one portion to the hospital and selling the remainder. See R. Weeda, *Le Psautier de Calvin* (Turnhout: Brepols, 2002), pp. 25–6, referring to the Registres du Conseil in the Archives d'État de Genève, 57, fol. 101r (17 August 1562).

216 Katharina Schütz Zell, for example, wrote that the songs of mothers to their children 'please God much better than any priest, monk, or nun in their incomprehensible choir song, as they lifted up some foolish devotion of useless lullaby to the organ' (*Das sye darinnen vil baß Gott gfallen: dann keyn Pfaff: Münch: oder Closterfraw inn jrem unverstendigen Chorgsang: wie man auch etwan thorechte andacht gehebt hat: das unnützen kindelwagens auff der orgel*). Schütz Zell, preface to *Von Christo Jesu vnserem sảligmacher*, fol. A3r. Reproduced in *KSZ*, vol. 2, pp. 62–3; translated in *Church Mother*, p. 95.

217 'Recepit ante paucos annos et Ecclesia, ad sacros hymnos uaria Musices organa'. Bucer, *S. psalmorum libri quinque: ad Ebraicam veritatem genuine versione in latinum traducti; primum appensis bona fide sententijs, deinde pari diligentai adnumeratis verbis, tum familiari explanatione elucidate* (Basel: Heruagium, 1547), p. 246. However, we are not aware of any other instruments being used in services in Strasbourg during the Reformation.

218 Bucer, *S. psalmorum libri quinque* (1547), p. 246. See also Hobbs, '"Quam Apposita Religioni Sit Musica"', pp. 169–71. Hobbs notes that in the 1529 edition the word 'cantiones' had

During this interlude, the people should have been able to meditate on the words that had been preached, but the organist had played more for general amusement than to encourage prayer among the congregation. This was an insult to the memory of Christ's sacrifice.[219] It is not clear whether Bucer was here referring to specific organists in Strasbourg,[220] or to a more general trend in churches of the day.

The Youth and Singing

Concern for the youth of Strasbourg had long been on the reforming agenda. The reformers had desired the further development of the school system in Strasbourg from the very beginning of the Reformation, and had lobbied for the appointment of learned men to provide the youth of the city with an education,[221] and for the foundation of schools.[222] Two scholars, Lucas Hackfurt and Otto Brunfels, opened private schools during the 1520s, and in 1526 the council established a body responsible for policy and administration in schools. Soon there were 13 separate schools operating in the city, which led to duplication and rivalry in places. In 1527 it was decided that the institutions should be amalgamated.[223] This occurred in 1538, with the founding of the Strasbourg Gymnasium by Johann Sturm. This led to a greater percentage of the population being educated, as the children of aristocrats and master guildsmen, rather than only those of professionals such as clerics and lawyers, were now able to receive a classical education.[224]

Several documents from the first part of the 1530s relating to the education and conduct of the Strasbourg youth mention music. Three reports relating to

been printed as 'conciones' (sermons), leading René Bornert to mistakenly interpret that sermons were cut short in order to make way for organ playing (see Bornert, *Réforme protestante du culte*, pp. 471–2, 483; Bucer, *S. psalmorum libri quinque* (Strasbourg: Andlanus, 1529), fol. 170r.

219 Bucer, *S. psalmorum libri quinque* (1547), pp. 246–7. A similar view was taken in the Roman Church by those at the 1528 Council of Sens (see Veit, *Das Kirchenlied in der Reformation Martin Luthers* (Stuttgart: Steiner, 1986), p. 13).

220 Hobbs suggests that this complaint might be directed at Bucer's colleague at St Thomas's Church, Wolfgang Dachstein.

221 E. W. Kohls, *Die Schule bei Martin Bucer in ihrem Verhältnis zu Kirche und Obrigkeit* (Heidelberg: Quelle & Meyer, 1963), pp. 50–51. Luther, too, had called on Germany to improve its schools (see L. C. Green, 'The Bible in Sixteenth-Century Humanist Education', *Studies in the Renaissance*, 19 (1972), pp. 115–16).

222 BMS, ms. 745, fols 38v–39v (6 and 8 May 1525).

223 Chrisman, *Lay Culture, Learned Culture*, p. 193.

224 For a brief summary of the school situation in Strasbourg around this time, see M. Fournier and C. Engel, eds, 'Gymnase, académie, université de Strasbourg, 1525–1621', in *Les Statuts et privilèges des universités françaises depuis leur fondation jusqu'en 1789*, 4 vols (Paris: Larose & Forcel, 1890–1894), vol. 4, p. 6, n. 2.

the synod of 1533[225] are particularly insightful. The concerns set forth in one document from 29 November 1532, a proposal for improving the organisation of the Church, appear to be twofold. The pupils had to attend church, both so that they could be cultivated in the correct way, and so that church singing would be fruitful. In a section subtitled 'How to draw the children to the Word of God' (*Wie die kinder zum wort gottes zu ziehen[n]*), it was stated that the children were to be led by their teachers each Sunday morning to their special place by the pulpit in the church, where they were to remain throughout the service to lead the singing.[226] They were then to stay for the sermon. Several children were to be present at each sermon (day and evening), in order that Christian song be performed more magnificently (*statlicher*), which in turn would improve both citizens and foreigners.[227] 'Such encouragement of the young towards the Word of God and holy song is not only done henceforth, but was also used by the ancient Holy Fathers'.[228] The implication is, then, that children were being trained to lead the singing in worship, and were therefore also made to 'preach' through their singing.[229] Proposals along similar lines are to be found in the church order of 1534.[230] This is significant, as this was exactly the setup adopted by Calvin in Geneva after his stay in Strasbourg from 1538 to 1541. The influence of Strasbourg on Geneva in terms of the development of psalm singing in the latter city has long been acknowledged,[231] but this extends further – to the use of children to lead the congregational singing of psalms.

The 16 articles in Bucer's hand from the synod itself also included a similar proposal: the teachers (*schul- vnd leermeistern*) were to assemble all the boys whom they taught every Sunday morning before the service in their school or reading house, 'and no one without honest reason is permitted to be absent' (*kheinen on ridlich vrsach vßzubleyben gestatten*). They were to go to their parish churches, to the special place where they are to sing. They were to remain there until the end of the service.[232]

---

225 Regarding the Strasbourg synod, see Eells, *Martin Bucer*, pp. 146–59.

226 'Vnnd die selbig dan[n] mit feiner ordnu[n]g zum ampt by rechter zeÿt jeder schul oder leermeister in seine pfarkirche zu fieren / an[n] jr besonder ort bÿ dem pulpito ordenlich zum gesang zu stellen / vnnd biß zum end des ampts zu halten'. 1 AST 75, 10, p. 152.

227 'das zu jedem predigen obents vnnd morgens etliche kinder da weren / damit das christlich gesang auch desto statlicher gehalt[en] würde / zu besserung bede[r] frembd[er] vnnd heymischen'. 1 AST 75, 10, p. 153.

228 'Solich anhaltung der Jung[en] zum wort gottes vnnd geystlichem gesang ist nit allen hievor / sonder[n] auch by den alt[en] heiligen vätteren im[m] brauch gewesen'. 1 AST 75, 10, p. 152.

229 It should be noted that boys seem to have been involved in plainchant singing before the Reformation, as suggested by 1 AST 192, 1523, fol. 6v (see Chapter 1, Figure 1.1).

230 Röhrich, *Mittheilungen*, vol. 1, pp. 235–6.

231 For example, O. E. Douen, *Clément Marot et le psautier huguenot*, 2 vols (Paris: Imprimerie Nationale, 1878–79); F. Bovet, *Histoire du psautier des églises réformées* (Neuchâtel: Sandoz; Paris: Grassard, 1872); and P. Pidoux, *Le Psautier huguenot du XVIe siècle*, 2 vols (Basel: Bärenreiter, 1962), in addition to some more modern studies.

232 1 AST 75, 11, pp. 165–6.

A further document from October 1533 also mentions song in this context. The third point stated that the young were to be taught the ways of the 'correct Christian life' (*zu recht[em] christlichen leben gelert*), demonstrating the importance that the Protestants of Strasbourg, and indeed elsewhere, attributed to the 'correct' education of children.[233] Reference is made to an ordinance concerning the young boys who were taught in schools and educational houses, who were to be taken to the sermons 'to *lead the singing*, and it should be considered how this can be achieved in the Church here and there, and indeed everywhere throughout the German nation where the Gospel is preached and the Psalms are sung in church'.[234] We see in these examples a strong desire for German unity and homogeneity, in the hope that the whole nation will conform to the reforms.[235]

The church order of 1534[236] contained nothing specific in relation to children and music, but it did reiterate that children should attend the Sunday sermon.[237] In the same year, however, Bucer formed a proposal recommending that a music teacher be appointed for the young.[238] This tuition is likely to have started in a humanistic, theoretical vein,[239] but the opportunity to teach psalms to the children was soon taken.[240] Little is known of the early methods by which the German psalm texts were taught. The Lord's Prayer and the Ten Commandments were to be learnt as part of Bucer's catechism of 1534.[241] It may well be that children were taught the sung versions of these texts so that they might be memorised with greater ease. The Latin schools of the city, which had existed since before the

233 It should also be noted that the convents that managed to survive the Reformation were eventually permitted by the Strasbourg authorities to take in girls and provide them with a 'fitting Christian upbringing'. See Leonard, *Nails in the Wall*, p. 91; as well as II 57, 13, fol. 1r (1547); and 1 AST 87, 44, fol. 5r (1555).

234 'das vor bedacht ordnung / mit den Jungen knaben / die man jn[n] schulen / vnnd leerheüseren leret / die selbigen zum predigen / vnnd gesang zu fieren / vnnd halten / für gen[n] omen / vnnd jns werck bedacht werde wie das jn[n] der kirchen je vnnd je / vnnd noch allenthalb / wo ma[n] in[n] gantzer teütscher nation / das Euangelj prediget / vnnd psalme[n] in[n] der kirchen singet / gehalten würdt'. 1 AST 75, 9, p. 134. My emphasis in translation. A copy of this document can be found at 1 AST 166, 20.5, although much of this version is illegible owing to its condition.

235 Schoolchildren had been leading church singing in Wittenberg since at least 1524. Bucer also recommended the teaching of psalms and spiritual songs to children in and around the city of Ulm. See *Ordnung, die ain Ersamer Rath der Statt Ulm* (Ulm: Varnier, 1531), fol. C3r; *BDS*, 4, p. 240. See also Chapter 5.

236 *Ordnung und Kirchengebreuch* (1534).

237 *BDS*, 5, pp. 34–5.

238 As observed by Hobbs, '"Quam Apposita Religioni Sit Musica"', p. 173. See 1 AST 21.13, fol. 296v; *BDS*, 7, p. 532.

239 In medieval times, music was taught as one of the seven liberal arts, divided into the trivium (grammar, logic, rhetoric) and quadrivium (arithmetic, geometry, music, and astronomy).

240 Föllmi, 'Le "Psautier de Calvin" : Théologie, pratique, usage', *Revue d'histoire et de philosophie religieuses*, 89.4 (2009), pp. 484–5.

241 Bucer, *Kurtze schrifftliche erklårung für die kinder vnd angohnden* (Strasbourg: Apiarius, 1534).

Reformation, devoted time to singing.[242] At Otto Brunfels's school, for example, an hour of music tuition was given each day between noon and one o'clock.[243] This was a common time for music instruction in other German schools.[244] The Latin school of St Peter the Young, established in 1537, scheduled music classes several times per week.[245] There are even mentions from 1539 of a *Singschul*, the council apparently having found it necessary to stipulate that its pupils' repertoire be limited only to spiritual songs.[246] From 1542, both Matthias Greiter and Wolfgang Dachstein were employed as music teachers at the Gymnasium, founded in 1538. The school's statutes stipulated only that music tuition should occur on Saturday afternoons,[247] and that psalms in Latin and German were to be sung at midday and in the evening, presumably on other days of the week.[248] The reformers recognised the sense in teaching the psalm texts and melodies to the students in order to disseminate them to the wider population of the city. Johann Sturm wrote a letter to one of the teachers decades later, reminding him that his job was to ensure that the choir sang without making unpleasant or contorted sounds, and that his duty was to ensure that the students did 'not sing the Psalms by random chance but especially in church and in class by the rules of art'.[249] Bucer's 1543 catechism[250] also specified the importance of music in

---

242 C. W. Young, 'School Music in Sixteenth-Century Strasbourg', *Journal of Research in Music Education*, 10.2 (1962), p. 129. See also 1 AST 324, 21.13, fol. 296r (also 90 Z 18, p. Ntr 1351) about the importance of music in education.

243 'Musicæ donamus quotidie horam unam, eam, quæ est a duodecima ad primam'. Otto Brunfels, *CATECHE | SIS PVERORVM, IN FIDE, IN LI- | teris, et in moribus* ... (Strasbourg: Egenolff, 1529), fol. 93v, cited in Fournier and Engel, 'Gymnase, académie, université de Strasbourg', p. 9. See also 90 Z 18, p. Ntr 1343.

244 See Green, 'The Bible in Humanist Education', p. 120.

245 Fournier and Engel, 'Gymnase, académie, université de Strasbourg', p. 16. See also 90 Z 18, p. Ntr 1368.

246 *Fragments des anciennes chroniques d'Alsace*, III (1892), no. 3597.

247 L. W. Spitz and B. S. Tinsley, *Johann Sturm on Education* (St Louis: Concordia, 1995), p. 104; Fournier and Engel, 'Gymnase, académie, université de Strasbourg', pp. 31–2. See also 90 Z, p. Ntr 1378.

248 See Vogeleis, *Quellen und Bausteine*, p. 250.

249 'Es ist diene Pflicht zu lehren, dass die Psalmen in Kirche und Schule nicht aufs Geratewohl, sondern kunstgemäss gesungen werden'. Letter from Sturm to M. Stiffelreuter (March 1565), quoted in Vogeleis, *Quellen und Bausteine*, p. 250; translated in Spitz and Tinsley, *Johann Sturm on Education*, p. 305. The chronicle of the sixteenth-century humanist and schoolteacher Hieronymus Gebwiler makes reference to the singing of schoolchildren in 1520. It therefore seems that the reformers revived the tradition of having the schoolchildren lead singing in worship rather than having invented it themselves. See K. Stenzel, *Die Straßburger Chronik des Hieronymus Gebwiler* (Berlin and Leipzig: Grunter, 1926), p. 23.

250 *Der Kürtzer Catechismus. Das ist / Christliche vnderweisung von den Articklen vnsers Glaubens [/] Vatter vnser / Zehen gebotten / H. Sacramenten / Vnd anderen Christlichen Kirchenzucht vnd uͤbungen. Für die Schůler vnd andere kinder zů Strasburg* (Strasbourg: Rihel, 1543). Reproduced in *BDS*, 6, 3, pp. 225–65.

worship, describing church singing as 'the third commual church practice' (*die dritte allgemeine Kirchenuͤbung*).[251]

* * *

This chapter has again revealed the importance of dealing with multiple types of source in historical investigations. In a history of singing, it would be easy to think of songbooks and liturgical orders as definitive resources, first because they contain the songs themselves, designed to be sung, and second because they are in print, which allows them to present themselves with a (sometimes false) sense of authority. It is therefore crucial to balance out information gained from songbooks with that found in manuscript sources. This is precisely because manuscript sources are not usually the 'final version'. They contain ideas that were exchanged among city council, Protestant preachers, Catholic priests, monks, and nuns, and the public. These documents therefore balance out what at first appears to be a 'final' form in print with what was more likely to have been actually occurring. One example is the fact that the children of the city led the singing in church. No hymn book ever makes mention of this, yet the description of this in the archival manuscripts goes a long way towards explaining how congregations learnt the ever-increasing number of melodies during the 1530s.

The reformers of Strasbourg were pioneers in this respect. They had chosen to retain music in church, but had dispensed with the choir. Whereas the Lutherans had a choir to provide music and to bolster the singing of the congregation, the Strasbourgeois chose to employ either a group of singers or a collection of schoolchildren.[252] It is likely that the adult singing groups comprised some of the former church singers who had suffered verbal attacks for most of the 1520s, and who had perhaps converted to Protestantism.[253] The Brant *Annals* mention that on Wednesday after the fifth Sunday of Lent, 1530, a request was submitted for compensation for some of the Latin choir singers who were not surrendering their civil rights and were therefore planning to remain in Strasbourg.[254] Some of them may well have helped run music in the city's schools and churches. A brief note in the Imlin chronicle declares that 'in the year 1532 the choir of the

[251] The others are coming together in holy assembly, communal prayer in the assembly, fasting, and communal works. See *BDS*, 6, 3, p. 255. The paragraph relating to church singing can be found on p. 257.

[252] The problems with such a system are discussed in Trocmé-Latter, 'The Psalms as a Mark of Protestantism'.

[253] See also Théodore Gérold's comments about congregational singing and the need for pastors and readers to contribute to the singing when they were not otherwise occupied (Gérold, *Les plus anciennes mélodies*, pp. 54–5).

[254] *Fragments des anciennes chroniques d'Alsace*, IV (1901), no. 4859.

Franciscans was stopped and then began [again]', but no further clues are given as to what exactly that entailed.[255]

One particularly remarkable aspect of the manuscript writings is that Bucer and the preachers did not ever give specific descriptions of the music of the Roman Church to which they were opposed. Figures such as Savonarola, Erasmus, and even Calvin all explained, in musical terms of varying proficiency, why such music was of so little value to Christians or even to God.[256] But Strasbourg's reformers never expressed, for example, the opinion that polyphony obscured the text, nor did they give even a vaguely analytical description of the music. Neither in Strasbourg did there seem to be any Catholic defence of plainchant or polyphony with regard to the music itself. None of the canons are recorded as having expressed distaste at the fact that their art was threatened with elimination. This could have been due to a lack of polyphonic music being performed in Strasbourg prior to the Reformation, and is also no doubt down to the fact that any advanced musical training was lacking among the Protestant preachers.[257] The debate, then, was instead centred on participating, understanding, sincerity, and the Word of God. Song was to be used for no other reason than it was advocated in the Bible and had taken place in the services of the early Church. It is almost as if the reformers believed it to be too obvious to mention that Latin polyphony, being (at least in their belief) so far removed from these early practices, was intrinsically unsuited to worship.

Nor must it be forgotten that the words of popular and sometimes 'inappropriate' songs also remained a part of people's thoughts. The reformers certainly wished for spiritual songs to replace profane songs throughout society, but the very fact that Bucer was still speaking in such strong language about popular songs in 1541 – despite the reduction in popular music publication in the city – suggests that this was an ongoing problem. As we shall see in the following chapter, people often clung to popular music in a way the clergy found deeply worrying.

As a final point, it must be noted that such criticisms of church music were by no means new to the sixteenth century.[258] The Strasbourg preachers, like many

---

255 'Jn dem iar [1532] hatt man daß chor zu den Barfüssern abgebrochen und angefangen'. Reuss, 'Strassburg im sechszehnten Jahrhundert, 1500–1591', p. 422.

256 For Erasmus, see pp. 51. For Savonarola, see P. Macey, *Bonfire Songs: Savonarola's Musical Legacy* (Oxford: Clarendon Press, 1998), pp. 93–8. For Calvin, see Pidoux, *Psautier huguenot*, vol. 1, 'Introduction', esp. pp. XIV–XV.

257 Although it seems that there was not an abundance of polyphony in pre-Reformation Strasbourg, Christian Meyer's assumption ('Gesangbuch, darin begriffen sind …', p. 217) that polyphonic music was more or less non-existent at this time is put into doubt by the vast range of complaints about church musicians found in the writings presented in this chapter. Nor does it explain the polyphonic music editions being printed in Strasbourg in the 1530s.

258 The sixth-century *Regula Benedicti* (Rule of St Benedict), for example, contains quite striking similarities to the Strasbourg preachers' ordinances on the practice of the divine worship (see The Monks of Glenstal Abbey, trans., *The Rule of Benedict* (Dublin: Four Courts, 1994), esp.

of their clerical predecessors, were trying to reform the definition of singing. They wanted 'singing God's praises' to mean a heartfelt, devoted, and edifying experience, rather than a routine, meaningless performance which was insulting to God. However, it was due to the efforts of the sixteenth-century reformers, both of Strasbourg and of other reforming Churches, that congregational singing across the world is today an accepted practice. In the shorter term, Strasbourg's model of sung worship influenced Calvin in Geneva, as well as the reformers of cities such as Ulm and Cassel.

chapters 9 and 17–19). The visitation records of the Benedictine reforms of the fifteenth century also make mention of the poor state of singing in monasteries (see J. Angerer, *Die liturgisch-musikalische Erneuerung der Melker Reform. Studien zur Erforschung der Musikpraxis in den Benediktinerklöstern des 15. Jahrhunderts* (Vienna: Verlag der Österreichischen Akademie der Wissenschaften, 1974). I am grateful to Susan Rankin and Barbara Eichner for alerting me to these similarities.

CHAPTER 4

Song Texts and their Messages

In 1528, a group of Strasbourg orphans found themselves being reprimanded (for the third time) for singing devotional songs to Mary and the saints. The two offending songs, 'Stüren, das üch Gott vergelt' and 'Unsere liebe Frau' were no doubt deemed to be unnecessarily and unhealthily complimentary towards their subjects, possibly to superstitious levels, and the orphans were warned in future instead to show 'true veneration' (*ein recht verehrung, die recht vererung*) towards Mary and the saints.[1] This stands in apparent contrast to a ruling from 1523, which had stated that 100 poor children were permitted to go singing devotional songs around the houses to collect money.[2] That, however, was before the Reformation, and stricter rules had since been put in place about what should be sung, by whom, and when.

In 1533 the Strasbourg populace were warned about their behaviour on Sundays. They were reminded that dancing in the street was not allowed, and that although round-dancing was permitted, singing 'shameful' songs with the dance was not.[3] The authorities also tried to crack down on dancing and drinking on feast days (*Meßtagen*) and in the period 'approximately up to Christmas' (i.e. Advent?). Young people were reminded to behave in a modest and measured way with their friends and in their pastimes.[4]

---

1 *Fragments des anciennes chroniques d'Alsace*, III (1892), no. 3513; *Fragments des anciennes chroniques d'Alsace*, IV (1901), no. 4716.

2 T. W. Röhrich, *Mittheilungen aus der Geschichte der evangelischen Kirche des Elsasses*, 3 vols (Paris and Strasbourg: Treuttel und Würtz, 1855), vol. 1, pp. 157–8; F. J. Mone, 'Ueber die Armenpflege v. 13. bis 16. Jahrhundert in Konstanz, Günthersthal, Straßburg, Bretten, Baden, Bruchsal', *Zeitschrift für die Geschichte des Oberrheins*, 1 (1850), p. 151.

3 'Der tanz ist erkannt, wie es vormals mit dem spiel nicht zu tantzen auf der gassen verbotten; und die rundtänze (doch nicht schändliche lieder daran zu singen) zugelassen'. *Fragments des anciennes chroniques d'Alsace*, IV (1901), no. 5002.

4 'Den 4 punkten Tanzens und Zechens halben auf den Kirchweihen, Meßtagen und andern zeiten auch nach gebürlicher zeit – etwa bis um Weihnachten – samt der H. H. Präsidenten bedacht auch gelesen. Erk[annt]: also wie herbracht zu verordnen, damit die Jugent dennoch nicht gar in sack gestoßen, und aber zucht und maaß bei ihrer freud und kutzweil gehalten werden'. *Fragments des anciennes chroniques d'Alsace*, IV (1901), no. 5059. See also no. 5099 regarding dancing and shameful songs. The law on dancing lasted well into the next decade. See Bucer's reminder from 1546 that dancing on Sundays has been banned by a Council decree 'for many years' (*ante multos an[n]os*) (1 AST 39, 13, p. 299). The same rules were imposed upon the country parishes around Strasbourg (see Röhrich, *Mittheilungen*, vol. 1, p. 242). Other cities enforced similar laws. Augsburg, for example, had in 1526 announced that 'all piping, drumming, and other hitting and playing of instruments, as well as all blaring and the unseemly clamouring of ridiculous and

These examples demonstrate the authorities' fear of certain songs. On the one hand, people should not have been singing songs to the saints; on the other hand, people should not have been singing secular songs with immoral subject matter. Both sorts of songs could be replaced by godly hymns and psalms of the type that were being printed in the liturgical orders.

So far in this book, the vast majority of songs examined have been religious. At times, however, the boundary between sacred hymns and religious polemical songs is blurred; many of the songs discussed in this chapter could fall into both categories. Although divisions between popular and religious songs can be useful, they can also end up seeming artificial. Religious songs and popular song genres both played parts in people's lives, and studying them in parallel is the only way to approach a fuller understanding of how religious upheaval affected music, and in turn how music affected religious upheaval.

The songs that appeared in print in Strasbourg during the first two decades of the sixteenth century were very often devotional, either to the Virgin Mary (such as 'Maria zart, von edler Art'[5]) or to other saints such as St Katherine.[6] The texts often also discussed such subject matter as the Eucharist[7] or the seven words spoken by Jesus on the cross[8] – songs that promoted some level of understanding of Christianity among the laity. In addition, there was a variety of popular songs on secular and political subjects,[9] including songs of love and heroism.[10]

The records show that this began to change during the 1520s. Not only were the subjects of religious devotional songs modified to become less orientated around Mary and the communion of saints, but members of the public were now also exposed to an array of liturgical songs, which they were expected to sing on a regular basis. This is not to say that the genre of the popular song disappeared; indeed, many of the songs actually being heard and learnt by the Strasbourg public in the 1520s did not belong to the canon of devotional religious music. Secular songs continued to be printed in considerable quantity until the middle of the decade; the decline of secular songs in print coincided with the beginning of the rise of the hymn book, though secular songs continued to be printed, albeit less regularly, after this time. In fact, the vast majority of printed songs of all types, until at least the time when hymn books began expanding considerably in

shameful songs in the streets' were outlawed, both during the day and at night ('Deßgleichen alles pfeiffen / Trum[m]en / vnd annder Saitenspil schlahen vnnd vben / auch alles plerren / vnzimlichen geschrayes / spotlichen vn[nd] schmachlichen lieder vnd gesangs / auff der gassen / tags vnd nachts in allweg můssig steen so̊lle'. 1 MR 4, fol. 83r). See also 1 MR 3, fols 232v–233r.

5 *VD16* (www.vd16.de, accessed 23 May 2011) ZV 277 (from 1505). See also nos D 173, D 150, S 3519, and M 7061.

6 *VD16* H 5741.

7 *VD16* V 2488.

8 *VD16* B 6362.

9 *VD16* D 174, ZV 10048, G 1175.

10 M. U. Chrisman, *Lay Culture, Learned Culture: Books and Social Change in Strasbourg, 1480–1599* (New Haven and London: Yale University Press, 1982), p. 268.

size, would have been popular songs published on broadsheets or in pamphlets. Songs were also spread by word of mouth. Given the historical period in question, it should not be a surprise that many of these were polemical or propagandistic in nature, on the subject of Luther and the unfolding Reformation, designed to sway public opinion in one direction or another, and to establish or increase popular support for a religious group, matter, or point of view. Indeed, Jean-François Gilmont believes that during the Reformation,

> the vital link between printed text and oral culture is best demonstrated by the many songs produced. The pedlar himself might advertise his wares by singing the versified title or the text of the song itself ... Songs were a vehicle for imparting news of the latest developments, for pouring scorn on the Catholic clergy, for poking fun at church music and the liturgy, and for professing the new faith.[11]

The Reformation and Song Censorship

Pro-Reformation songwriters and their Catholic opponents spent a great deal of energy on passionate exchanges, sometimes ridiculing each other with songs designed for comic effect, although the messages conveyed were often of a more serious nature, and, on the Protestant side in particular, designed to frighten the faithful into following their conscience for the sake of their souls. However, the reformers and city authorities were not so supportive of such underhand tactics – at least not publicly. There was the added complication that the Strasbourg reformers did not want people to associate the text of any pre-existing secular song with a newly written church text of the Reformation.[12] To some extent, therefore, the choice of music had to be controlled.

As the dissemination of Luther's writings continued across Europe, the issue of censorship had become an increasingly urgent matter for the papacy and for national and local governments. Different areas reacted in different ways, some falling in line with papal requests, others forbidding all religious polemic. This extended to the treatment of polemical songs. In 1523, as a result of pressure from a complaint from Pope Adrian VI to Emperor Charles V, the Nuremberg authorities forbade the selling of satirical songs, insulting texts, and

[11] J.-F. Gilmont, ed., trans. K. Maag, *The Reformation and the Book* (Ashgate: Aldershot, 1988), p. 83. On the Lutheran thinking behind liturgical songs, see P. Veit, *Das Kirchenlied in der Reformation Martin Luthers* (Stuttgart: Steiner, 1986), pp. 70–72. Sometimes song genres overlapped or combined. For example, 'Ein Ziegler zu Bar, ein burger wars', a song about the Peasants' War which was to be sung to the tune of 'Aus tieffer not' or 'Ach got von himel', both Lutheran psalms (listed in M. Vogeleis, *Quellen und Bausteine zu einer Geschichte der Musik und des Theaters im Elsass, 500–1800* (Strasbourg: Le Roux, 1911; repr. Geneva: Minkoff, 1979), p. 217).

[12] This differs from the approach in Nuremberg, for example, where secular songs and Catholic folk hymns were often used as a basis for the new Protestant hymns. Folk melodies were also used for this purpose to a limited extent in Wittenberg.

broadsheets featuring Luther and the pope.[13] Similar steps to suppress polemical and propagandistic material were taken in Strasbourg.[14] The authorities were closely observing the material being sold and distributed, and in 1524 passed a mandate banning the publication, promotion, and transmission of all scandalous writings which were likely to 'provoke, mock, or cause annoyance' to one's neighbour.[15] One such song, described as part of a collection of 'Libelli famosi', featured in the so-called 'placard affair' of 1529. The magistrates accused the Anabaptists of inciting tensions by posting particular songs in public areas, and as a result forced several of their members to produce handwriting examples in an attempt to find the culprit(s).[16] Figure 4.1 shows one of the songs, a piece of satirical literature against the Roman Church, beginning 'Wir armen papisten' ('We poor papists'), copied out by the city scribe, Peter Butz.[17]

Polemical Songs in Strasbourg

The complexity of undertaking a survey of polemical and propagandistic songs, and the effect that they had on a populace, is that it is often extremely difficult to establish the origin both of the song texts themselves and of the publications in which they occur. For example, one can almost never say that a layperson in Strasbourg in the early 1520s definitely either would or would not have known a particular song, or whether they would have sung it with family or comrades on social occasions. Furthermore, it is extremely likely that songs from Swiss and other German cities, especially those in relative proximity,[18] would have found their way to Strasbourg, often without necessarily ever being recorded in printed or written form. Nevertheless, it *is* possible to gain a sense of impact by studying those songs which are likely to have been, or definitely were, printed in Strasbourg. Concentrating on this period – the time at which Luther's reforms were gaining momentum across Germany – is essential if we are to get close to understanding the mindset of the urban population of Strasbourg.

Appendix E lists Strasbourg's polemical song publications of the 1520s and 1530s. Despite the likelihood of a number of other such texts having also been

[13] R. W. Scribner, *For the Sake of Simple Folk* (Oxford: Oxford University Press, 1981), pp. 73–4. See also Gilmont, *The Reformation and the Book*, pp. 93 and 95.

[14] Johann Grüninger's press was ruined in 1523 after action by the Strasbourg city council, following Grüninger's printing of Thomas Murner's anti-Protestant *Von dem grossen Lutherischen Narren* of the previous year. See Gilmont, *The Reformation and the Book*, p. 95.

[15] 'dadurch der gemein Christenmensch gegen seinen neben menschen zu anreitzung, gespött vnd Ergernus bewegt wurdt'. Quoted in P. Fritsch, ed., *Die Strassburger Chronik des Johannes Stedel* (Strasbourg: Sebastian Brant-Verlag, 1934), p. 96.

[16] 1 AST 166, 5.4

[17] 1 AST 138, 30. This document is dated 1524/1525 by the AVS, although this seems unlikely, given that the placard affair happened in 1529.

[18] Such as Nuremberg, Augsburg, Frankfurt, and Basel.

printed in the city, this list contains the only ones whose names have survived.[19] Although the songs cover a range of topics, they are very diverse in terms of style, length, and approach taken. The shortest is just one verse in length (37 words), while the longest has 21 verses (1011 words). Some take up a number of issues, such as 'Welt ir hören gesanges schall', which discusses food, objects, money, and idolatry. Others, in contrast, focus on one element of current church practice; for example, 'Ir brüder in Christo Jesu' devotes all nine of its verses to the best way to console the dying and the sick. Abuses of the clergy feature often and strongly. Although the Eucharist is sometimes mentioned in passing, only one song ('Es ist die warheyt') is devoted entirely to this topic. Use of evidence from Scripture to support the authors' claims is frequent, as are pleas to the emperor to resist the calls of the priests and papacy (for example, verse 12 of 'Gott Vatter in trifalde'). Not all of these songs were founded on attacks on Catholic faith or practice. Sometimes the aim seemed genuinely just to be to educate people in God's Word (for example, verse 2 of 'Meyn hertz'). Crucially, none of them were Catholic propaganda songs. This suggests that in Strasbourg, at least, very little effort was being made on the Catholic side to counteract these songs, although there was a flow of non-musical polemical material being printed in opposition to Luther's writings.[20]

Rebecca Wagner Oettinger's detailed research into the polemical songs of the Reformation has left us in a stronger position to collect and analyse data regarding this repertory.[21] Following on from work undertaken by Philipp Wackernagel and Friedrich Leonard von Soltau in the nineteenth century,[22] Oettinger began the process of analysing the effect of the texts on those who heard them, sang them, and were portrayed by them. The appendix to her book lists details for songs from across Germany, as well as the full texts of only a few, including some from Strasbourg; the texts of the Strasbourgeois songs have been reproduced here in Appendix F along with those of a variety of other popular songs and non-scriptural religious songs.

According to *VD16*, the date of the pamphlet containing 'Merckt jr herren myner sag' is 1520, although Oettinger estimates it as having appeared 'after 1520'.[23] In any case, it cannot have been printed after 1525, as this is the year in which the workshop of Martin Flach, its printer, was shut.[24] This song was overlooked by Wackernagel, but appears in Soltau's *Hundert deutsche*

---

19 Based on the work undertaken by Rebecca Wagner Oettinger (*MPGR*) and on *VD16*.

20 See M. U. Edwards, Jr, *Printing, Propaganda, and Martin Luther* (Berkeley and Los Angeles: University of California Press, 1994), pp. 57–63.

21 *MPGR*.

22 *Wackernagel DKL*; F. L. von Soltau, *Ein Hundert deutsche historische Volkslieder* (Leipzig: Weber, 1836; repr. Schrey, 1845; repr. Mayer, 1856).

23 *MPGR*, p. 315.

24 F. Ritter, *Histoire de l'imprimerie alsacienne aux XV*[e] *et XVI*[e] *siècles* (Strasbourg: Le Roux, 1955), p. 192.

(a) Recto

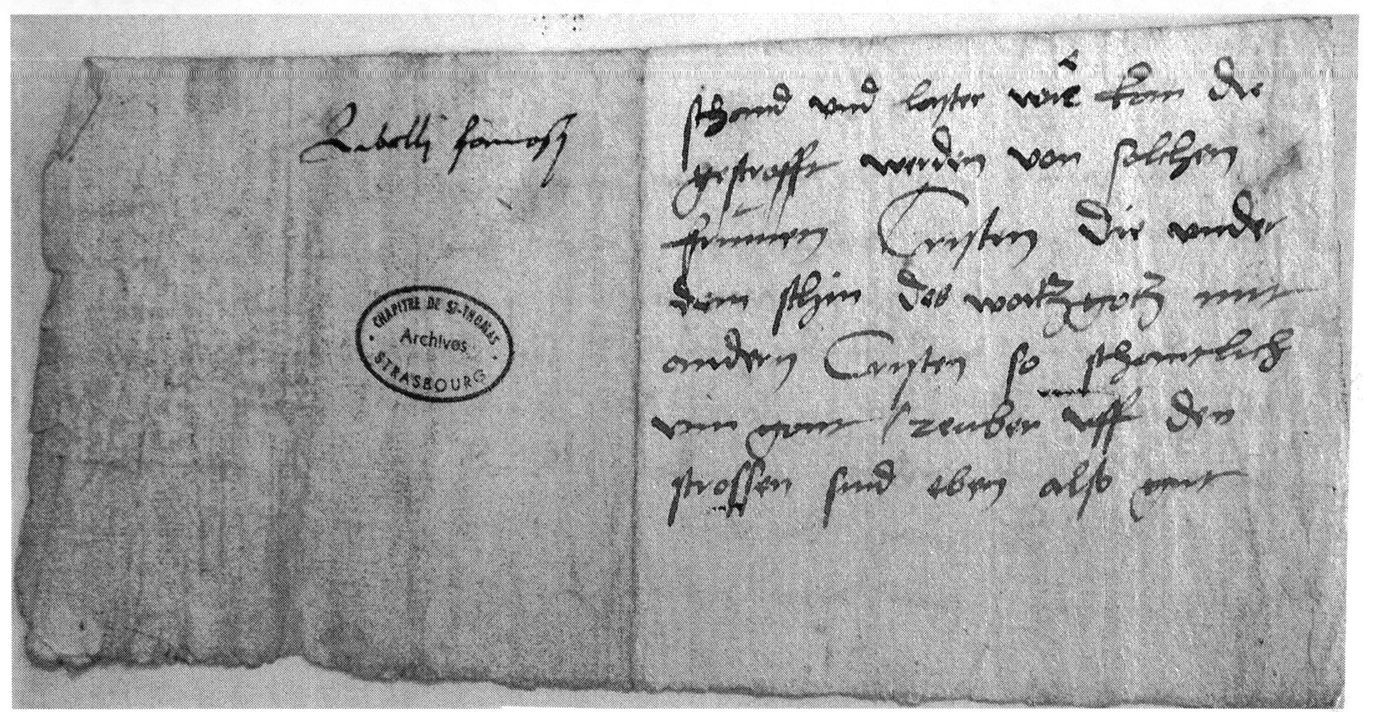

(b) Verso

Figure 4.1 'Wir armen papisten', in the hand of Peter Butz. Strasbourg, AVS, 1 AST 138, 30. Reproduced by permission of the Archives de la Ville et de la Communauté urbaine de Strasbourg

historische Volkslieder.[25] The song criticises certain Catholic practices, and attacks monastic orders and false preachers. In verse 14, Thomas Murner[26] is specifically mentioned, and is compared to one of the fools that Sebastian Brant had depicted in his *Ship of Fools*.[27] Devotion to the saints is particularly criticised in this piece. Verse 2 attacks pilgrimages, and argues that people have been blinded by the ways of the medieval Church. Verse 4 opposes fables and made-up stories (*fabel ding vnd klappery*) against the truth of God, anticipating Luther's complaint against fables made in 1523,[28] as well as Bucer's in 1524.[29] Two verses later, the practice of making offerings of clothes and candles to the saints as if they were grocers or merchants (*als ob sy krämer vnd kaufleüt syen*) is condemned. Verse 7 affirms that eternal life is an honour that God alone can give us, and therefore no amount of praying to the saints will help us. The final verse, longer than the others, sums up the complaints of the song. The author writes that 'they have recited the Rosary, and highly praised the Psalter', so that these two things are now 'broken'.[30] It is interesting to note that, of these two abused aspects of medieval piety, the former was considered superstitious and therefore abolished by the reformers, while the latter turned out to be one of the most central characteristics of Protestantism. The theme of fools is then briefly revisited, with mention made of the long ears with which fools were caricatured at this time:[31] 'dem from[m]en gemeinen volck die oren, | vnnd sy gemacht zů grossen thoren'.

During the early 1520s, a dispute broke out between Thomas Murner and Michael Stiefel, a former Augustinian monk. Stiefel had composed one of the earliest popular German psalm settings, 'Dein armer Hauf', and was also known both as a theologian, devoting himself to Luther's Reformation, and as an important mathematician.[32] The debate took on an intriguing form, as both Murner and Stiefel made use of musical means to put across their arguments. In 1522, Stiefel left his monastic order, having convinced himself that Luther was the angel described in Revelation 14:6. He wrote the song 'Joannes thüt uns schreiben', which was printed several times in various cities, including Strasbourg. The song was originally written in three sections, although two

[25] Soltau, *Ein Hundert deutsche historische Volkslieder*.

[26] For more information about Thomas Murner's Strasbourg publications during the 1520s, see Edwards, *Printing, Propaganda, and Martin Luther*, pp. 57–76.

[27] Murner features in several polemical songs in Strasbourg, being Luther's principal rival in the city at the time.

[28] *WA*, 12, p. 35. See p. 50.

[29] M. Bucer, *Grund vn[nd] vrsach ausz gotlicher schrifft d[er] neüwerungen* (Strasbourg: Köpfel, 1524). See pp. 50 and 104.

[30] 'sy habe[n] gemacht de[n] roßen krantz, | auch den Psalter hoch gelobt, | da mit sy haben zu gestopt'.

[31] See, for example, S. Brant, *Das Narrenschiff* (Basel: Olpe, 1494).

[32] W. Meretz, 'Die Melodie "in Bruder Veiten Ton" zu Stiefels erstem Lied', in *AKS Bericht* (journal of the Altkönigschule, Kronberg) (1975–76), p. 18.

additional sections were added later. The longer version of the song was published in the Strasbourg edition, which intersperses each verse with prose polemic, and an interpretation (*vßlegung*) is placed alongside each verse.[33] The first part of the song speaks of Luther, his teachings, and his writings. The fourth line of verse 1, 'quite loudly and openly' (*gantz luter offenbar*), is a pun on Luther's name.[34] As Oettinger has pointed out, eschatological imagery plays a prominent part in this song. Stiefel refers to the pope as 'the wolf in God's stable' (*die wölff in gottes stal*). Oettinger argues that Stiefel intended the listener or singer to draw parallels between the imagery of Revelation 14:6, which is paraphrased in verse 1, and Revelation 14:8.[35] Verse 7 claims that 'many pious people suffer pains' for 'crossing over' to Wittenberg. This presumably means that those who choose the faith of Luther put themselves in great (and sometimes mortal) danger. Much of the first section is a highly dramatised, almost excessive description of Luther's powers, leaving the listener in little doubt as to Stiefel's sincere belief that Luther was an angel in human form.

The second part of the song is subtitled 'about God's Ten Commandments' (*von den Zehen gebotten gottes*). It is not a paraphrase of the Commandments, but a complaint about how people are inclined to sin. Stiefel often uses the first person in this section, making it clear that he, too, is but a mortal sinner (as opposed to Luther, who is superhuman). Luther's name is not explicitly mentioned in the song until the very end of the second part, which describes the uselessness of meritorious works, and proclaims that many doctors of the Church would still be wondering about this, if it were not for Luther.[36] In the third part, which acts as a concluding section, Luther's name is mentioned twice in verse 22 and then not again until the fourth part. Stiefel makes it clear that Luther is not power-hungry, and does not wish to be a ruler himself.[37] This section is once again very personal; Stiefel talks about his own experience as a Christian, and as someone who has been converted and seen the light: the real solution to sin. The last two verses of section three are a prayer to God, asking for grace and goodness, and protection from the devil.

In the fourth and fifth sections, Stiefel intensifies his attack on the papacy. In verses 35 and 36 he urges people to 'flee this wolf's lair' (*fliecht dißer wölffen hyl*), as the pope is not looking after his sheep as commanded by Christ. Stiefel

33 M. Stiefel, *Von der Christfoͤrmigen / rechtgegründten leer Doctoris Martini Luthers / ein überuß schoͤn kunstlich Lyed / sampt seiner neben vßlegung* (Strasbourg: Schott, 1522; repr. 1525?).

34 This has also been noted by Edwards, *Printing, Propaganda, and Martin Luther*, p. 88; and R. W. Oettinger, 'Thomas Murner, Stifel, and Songs as Polemic in the Early Reformation', *Journal of Musicological Research*, 22 (2003), p. 54.

35 'A second angel followed and said, "Fallen! Fallen is Babylon the Great, which made all the nations drink the maddening wine of her adulteries"'. See Oettinger, 'Murner, Stifel, and Songs as Polemic', pp. 54–5.

36 'Die sach vil Doctor wundert, die diser kunst sind lår, einr wisszts nit vnder hundert, wenn Luther noch nit waͤr' (verse 20).

37 'Er mag sich selbs nit regen, doch ist die hilff nit fer' (verse 22).

also adheres to the propagandistic image of the pope as Antichrist,[38] claiming that he calls himself a god on earth (*Ein gott vff erd*)[39] but in fact allows evil to take place, robbing people, seducing women, living in splendour, and abusing his power.[40] The longer version of the song also ends with a prayer to God, in the first person, asking him for preservation from the Antichrist and the 'devil's army' (*teüffels list*), and for help and comfort at the time of death.[41]

At around the same time as 'Joannes thüt uns schreiben' was published, Thomas Murner was already emerging as an opponent to Luther's reforms. In 1520 he published an appeal to the Wittenberg reformer to abandon his agenda,[42] and he wrote several others in subsequent years. Murner also published a song lamenting the downfall of the Church, 'Nun hört ich wil euch singen', in part a response to 'Joannes thüt uns schreiben', and set to the same tune, the 'Bruder Veiten Ton' (a tune used for many of the popular songs of the time).[43] It appeared in an Augsburg pamphlet entitled *Ain new lied von dem vndergang des Christlichen glaubens Doct. Murner*. As a counter-response to this song, Stiefel published a pamphlet in Strasbourg soon after, entitled *Wider Doctor Murnars falsche erdycht Lyed: von dem vndergang Christlichs glaubens*, which contained the short song, 'Ach du armer Murnar'. Following this, Murner himself published an apology of his original writing in Strasbourg in 1522, entitled *Antwurt vnd klag mit entschuldigung*.[44] Stiefel also wrote a longer song set to the 'Bruder Veiten Ton', as part of the ongoing debate. Oettinger comments that 'by consistently reusing the same melody, Stifel and Murner attempted literally to rewrite the songs of their opponent, each putting new words into the mouths of their singers and trying to erase the erroneous views of the other'.[45]

The technique of using a pre-existing popular tune in these songs was commonplace. This aided the listener to memorise the words, and also enabled the listener to 'hear between the lines'.[46] 'Ach du armer Murnar' is, as Oettinger has observed, one of several sixteenth-century contrafacta of the popular devotional song 'O du armer Judas',[47] which in late medieval Germany was extremely well

38 Verses 43, 45, and 51.

39 Verse 46.

40 Verses 46–8.

41 Verses 51–2.

42 T. Murner, *Ein christliche vnd briederliche ermanung zů dem hochgelerten doctor Martino luter Augustiner orde[n] zů Wittemburg* (Strasbourg: Grüninger, 1520).

43 For more information about the history of the 'Bruder Veiten Ton' and Stiefel's connection to it, see Meretz, 'Die Melodie "in Bruder Veiten Ton"', pp. 18–20; and Oettinger, 'Murner, Stifel, and Songs as Polemic', pp. 50–62.

44 Murner, *Antwurt vnd klag mit entschuldigung doctor Murners wider bruder Michel stifel weyt von eßlingen da heim, vff das stüfelbuch so er wider meyn lied gemachet hat, daruß er des lieds den rechten thon erlernen mag* (Strasbourg: Grüninger, 1522).

45 Oettinger, 'Murner, Stifel, and Songs as Polemic', p. 47.

46 *MPGR*, p. 112. Oettinger devotes a chapter of her book to the contrafactum: see pp. 89–136.

47 See Appendix F.

known. Commonly referred to as the *Judaslied* or *Judasstrophe*, the song was in turn modelled on the sequence, 'Laus tibi, Christe', a Latin meditation on the cross, which had been sung as a part of the Good Friday liturgy before the Reformation.[48] The *Judaslied* itself was sung at the expulsion of Judas, a popular ceremony that took place in Holy Week, usually on Maundy Thursday.[49]

Although no direction is given to the effect that this song should be sung to the melody of the famous *Judaslied*, the format, title, and design of this one-stanza song should have made this point clear to a sixteenth-century person. The one-verse 'Murner-song' (see Example 4.1) was a simple ditty designed to do what Murner's much longer song probably would not: enter the memories of simple folk. By doing so, the song would relay the message that Murner and his theology were incorrect. As is common in propagandistic material at this time, Murner's name is here spelt 'Murnar', translating as 'grumbling fool', something that would not be lost, even on simpler folk. *Wider Doctor Murnars* makes this particularly clear, as Stiefel ends the song 'Ach du armer Murnar' by stating that Murner is considered nothing but a grumbling fool (*MURR, NARR*). In propagandist images from 1520 (including that on the front of *Wider Doctor Murnars falsch erdycht Lyed*[50]), he is often also depicted as a cat, because his name sounded like a cat's meow.[51]

The information provided about this pamphlet in Oettinger's work is confusing, to say the least. Oettinger states that *Wider Doctor Murnars*, which as far as we know appeared in a single edition, originated in Johann Prüss's printing shop around 1523. She also claims, however, that Murner's pamphlet, *Antwurt vnd klag mit entschuldigung* (written in **response** to *Wider Doctor Murnars*), is usually estimated as dating from 1522 (at the earliest).[52] Obviously, *Wider Doctor Murnars* must have appeared before *Antwurt vnd klag*. Indeed, the handwritten note on the Munich example of *Wider Doctor Murnars* (which was consulted by Oettinger[53]) in fact reads: 'Straßburg: J. Prüß d. J. um 1522'.[54] *VD16* and Hans-Joachim Köhler's *Bibliographie der Flugschriften des 16. Jahrhunderts*[55] back up this view by also estimating that this pamphlet was

48 *MPGR*, pp. 113–18; Oettinger, 'Ludwig Senfl and the Judas Trope: Composition and Religious Toleration at the Bavarian Court', *Early Music History*, 20 (2001), p. 200. Several other contrafacta of this song were already in existence by the beginning of the Reformation period.

49 Scribner, 'Ritual and Reformation', in R. P. Hsia, ed., *The German People and the Reformation* (Ithaca and London: Cornell University Press, 1988), pp. 138–9.

50 See http://daten.digitale-sammlungen.de/bsb00052091/image_3 (accessed 27 December 2014).

51 Scribner, *Simple Folk*, p. 74.

52 Stiefel did not become a Protestant until 1522. See *MPGR*, p. 221.

53 The title page of the Munich (Bayerische Staatsbibliothek) example appears as Figure 2 in Oettinger, 'Senfl and the Judas Trope', p. 206.

54 See http://daten.digitale-sammlungen.de/bsb00052091/image_2 (accessed 27 December 2014).

55 (Tübingen: Bibliotheca Academica, 1991–), part 1 (1501–1530).

Example 4.1 The *Judaslied* tune to the text of 'Ach du armer Murnar'. Melody adapted from F. M. Böhme, *Altdeutsches Liederbuch* (Leipzig: Breitkopf & Härtel, 1877), pp. 645–6. The version used here differs slightly from that found in *DKL* III, vol. 1, no. 2 (melodies), p. 170

printed in 1522.[56] Oettinger's dating of the song 'Ach du armer Murnar', then, must be revised to the year 1522. The identity of the pamphlet's publisher, however, may still apparently be open for debate.[57]

[56] Both also believe the printer to have been Reinhard Beck.

[57] There is one other mystery surrounding this pamphlet. Oettinger states that another song, 'Ich ka[n] nit gnügsam seine', appears in the publication, alongside 'Ach du armer Murnar' (*MPGR*, p. 221). 'Ich ka[n] nit gnügsam seine' was indeed also by Stiefel, and also written in response to Murner's 'Nun hört ich wil euch singen' and set to the same melody as Murner's song (the 'Bruder Veiten Ton'). But it did not appear in *Wider Doctor Murnars* (as specified in *MPGR*, p. 221), but was instead printed in *Ain new lied* (Augsburg: Steiner, 1523), alongside Murner's 'Nun hört ich'. However, Stiefel's rebuttal to Murner's song is dated 1522, whereas Murner's song has been dated 1523 (both datings are by the Bayerische Staatsbibiliothek). So either the two pamphlets have been wrongly dated, or, more likely, *Ain new lied* was in fact a reprint of Murner's 'Nun hört ich' and possibly also of Stiefel's 'Ich ka[n] nit', grouped together for the sake of comparison. Otherwise it would be impossible for one song to have been a response to the other, unless the two men had swapped notes privately beforehand! Certainly, Oettinger's assertion that *Ain new lied* 'contains Stifel's point by point rebuttal' of Murner's song (*MPGR*, p. 290) is not true; this rebuttal happens in *Wider Doctor Murnars*. Oettinger seems therefore to have confused the two pamphlets. Information concerning these three songs should therefore be treated with the utmost caution. See *MPGR*, pp. 116, 118, 221, 290, 318–19. Oettinger unfortunately repeats this latter claim in her more recent

The 'Murner-song' appears on the front cover on the pamphlet, a simple but familiar ditty designed to attract attention and spark interest in the pamphlet's contents.[58] After a brief introduction, Stiefel begins a detailed rebuttal of Murner's song, 'Nun hört ich wil euch singen'. Murner is referred to as a 'grumbling fool', or even 'the grumbling fool' (*Der Murnar*) throughout the pamphlet, and Stiefel starts off by accusing him of speaking so much that he has become like a cat and a dragon.[59] He then opens his rebuttal, commenting sometimes on as little as two lines and as many as three verses of Murner's song. The pamphlet ends with the remainder (*vollendung*) of Murner's song, without any further comment.[60]

Jörg Graff was a poet, born in the duchy of Württemberg, who began his career as a mercenary in the army of Emperor Maximilian I (1459–1519). After losing his sight in battle, he lived in Strasbourg and Augsburg before settling in Nuremberg, where he died in 1542.[61] His songs are described by the *Allgemeine Deutsche Biographie* as possessing a 'double character', suited to both folksinging and meistersinging.[62]

'Gott Vatter in trifalde' is one of three songs published in a collection by Graff in around 1523, entitled *In disem tractetlin sind drey hübsche lieder new gemacht in Christus namen vo[n] Bapst Cardinal Bischoff prelate[n] Pfaffe[n] vnd Münch*. Oettinger suggests that Graff's songs may have appeared through Prüss's printing press in Strasbourg,[63] and many library catalogues (and *VD16*) are in agreement. For this reason, Graff's three songs are considered here. Unsurprisingly, given his condition, Graff alludes to the human senses a fair amount in these songs. 'Gott Vatter in trifalde' bemoans the abuses of the clergy, claiming that they pervert the Word of God, collect as many benefices as they can in order to achieve great standing,[64] and are unfamiliar with the Scriptures themselves.[65] The second song, 'Herr Jesu Christ in himels tron' claims that the clergy 'have made us blind' (*hand vns gemachet blind*) through their abuses.

---

article 'Murner, Stifel, and Songs as Polemic', pp. 70–71, incorrectly stating that *Ain new lied* 'reproduced Stifel's entire argument against Murner's *Lied*'.

58 Oettinger has since stated that Stiefel was not in fact aware that this version of the *Judaslied* would be included in the pamphlet, implying he was not in fact the composer. She attributes the discovery of this fact to Tilman Matthias Schröder, but unfortunately does not provide a more precise reference than 'Schröder, 59'. See Oettinger, 'Murner, Stifel, and Songs as Polemic', p. 69, incl. n. 54.

59 'Der Murnar hat ein zeitlang gesproche[n] bitz er darob worden ist zů einer katzen / vnd zů einem drachen'. M. Stiefel, *Wider Doctor Murnars falsch erdycht Lyed* (Strasbourg: Beck, 1522), fol. Aj^{r}.

60 'Die vollendung des lyeds Murnari'. *Wider Doctor Murnars falsch erdycht Lyed*, fols Giij^{v}–Giiij^{r}.

61 See also K. Bartsch, 'Graff: Jörg', in *Allgemeine Deutsche Biographie*, vol. 9 (Leipzig: Duncker & Humblot, 1879), pp. 570–71.

62 Ibid., p. 571.

63 *MPGR*, p. 272.

64 Verses 3 and 4.

65 Verse 9.

The final song in the trilogy, 'Welt ir hören gesanges schall', calls in its first line for the world to 'hear the sound of song'.

A note above 'Gott Vatter in trifalde' reads: 'To the tune that one sings, "First we want to praise Mary, the pure maiden"'.[66] The song refers to several different characters throughout, sometimes addressing them directly. It begins in verse 1 with a plea to God to instruct and teach. In verse 6, Graff explains that the pope must turn the Church around, to get rid of abuses and to punish those priests responsible, rather than employing simony. Verse 12 seeks the attention of the emperor, who is advised to ignore the priests.[67] Significant frustration is shown not only towards the clergy in this song, but also towards the scholars, who have inverted God's Word.[68] Verse 10 speaks of the devil's hog (*teüfels mastschweyn*).

'Herr Jesu Christ in himels tron' is presented in much longer stanzas than 'Gott Vatter in trifalde'. However, like 'Gott Vatter', it addresses various figures at different points in the song. This song alternates between addressing God and the people of Germany, beginning in verse 1 with a prayer to Jesus to 'hold us in your charge … [and] teach us also to hold ourselves in good measure'.[69] John 14:6 is quoted, although Graff mistakenly cites it as the tenth chapter of the Gospel in question.[70] The prayer to Jesus continues with acknowledgement of his painful and miserable time on Earth, and mention is made of the 'thirty-fourth year' (the year of Jesus's life in which it was believed that he died).[71]

Verse 2 portrays Jesus as a 'faithful shepherd' (*ein trewer hirt*), showing mercy to his flock, in direct contrast to the pope, who has 'unfaithfully herded his creatures', shearing and ridiculing us.[72] Attention is then once again directed to the clergy, who have 'turned around God's Word',[73] celebrating anniversaries (of saints), vigils, and Compline. The point is made at the end of verse 3 and the beginning of verse 4 that one must serve God oneself, and not rely on anyone else (and especially not priests) to do it on one's behalf. Verse 5 complains that the clergy have swindled land for money, and show no mercy. Graff also names a certain 'Roterdamus', which in this context must be a reference to Erasmus. It has been revealed to us, Graff writes, that Jesus Christ is a 'shepherd saint', who grazes his sheep.[74] A paraphrase of Jesus's words in Matthew 24:35, Mark 13:31,

---

[66] 'Jm thon als man singt, Zům ersten woln wir loben Maria die reine maid'.

[67] 'Löblicher Keyser frumme, | glaub nit der pfaffenn list'.

[68] See verses 2 and 3.

[69] 'halt vns in deiner pflicht, | Du aller hốchste gottheit fron, | gib vns auch vnterricht | Dz wir vns halte[n] der rechte moß'.

[70] 'wie das zehe[n]d capitel seyt | "ich bin der weg vn[nd] thir, | dar durch jr geht die rechten stroß"'.

[71] 'Macht vns den glauben offenbar | in wunderwerck vnd pein, | bey vns fierthalb vnd dreyssig jar | spreyt aus den [dein] some[n] sein: | Dein ellend war so gros vff erd …'.

[72] 'der vntreülich geweydet hot | sein schaff, begert er wol | von vns, geschoren frů vnd spot'.

[73] 'gots wort haben sie verkert'.

[74] 'Jetz ist es kummen an den tag, | Jesu Christ vns ein hirten sant, | den glerten zů einer stroff, | der ist Roterdamus genant, | weydet Christus sein schaff, | die warheit brinngt er an den tag'.

and Luke 21:33 is then given: ‘My word will not melt away before Heaven and Earth have passed away; the sun and also the moon’.[75]

The following two verses come to the defence of Martin Luther, who Graff says has been accused (*verklagt*) by pope and bishop (that is, with charges of heresy and with excommunication), but has not been forsaken by God, having been given an escort by Elector Friedrich III of Saxony. Luther is depicted as a clever and learned man who knows the tricks of the Roman Church, and who can reveal the ‘Evangelical freedom’ (*euangeli frey*) to the world because he speaks Greek and Hebrew. Praise is then poured upon Elector Friedrich, who Graff says ‘rules powerfully’, and whom ‘God has in his charge’. The shameful scholars, he continues, will no longer be so powerful, as the duke has a number of *reformed* scholars to whom he can turn.[76] The final two verses are addressed both to Christ and to the people. The listener is told to ‘call to Christ with a loud voice’, and to ‘thank him all together’.[77] This is a reference to communal singing, not just *about* God, but *to* God, in his praise. The narrative position then changes, as Graff calls to Christ in a personal prayer (in the first person singular). By drawing in his audience, Graff encourages others to do the same:

> Christ, show me the great sins
> Of my soul, heart and mind,
> That I might praise you now and always,
> Your creature I am.
> Lord, may your will come to me,
> Christ, enlighten me to love
> My neighbour as I should … [78]

Song endings such as this one shift the listener’s attention to the interiorisation of God’s relationship with the individual.

The last of Graff’s three songs in this collection, ‘Welt ir hören gesanges schall’ addresses key figures in the kingdom: emperor, king, knight, and nobleman, and asks them to resurrect love, hope, and faith (the three qualities mentioned in 1 Corinthians 13:13), and to assure that God’s Word is not kept concealed in the kingdom. They have ‘fallen asleep’ and forgotten God by venerating the saints instead. Instead, they should wake up to God’s Word, which the clergy

---

75 ‘Ehe meine wort solte[n] zergon, | ehe mu̇̊st himel vnd erd | zůbreche[n], son[n] vnd auch der mon’.

76 ‘regiert gewaltiglich, | got der halt jn in seiner pflicht: | Der gelerten bu̇̊berei vnd schand | nit mer so gewaltig wirt, | der hertzog hat in seine[m] land | die gelerten reformiert’.

77 ‘Růfft zů Christo mit lauter stim | vnd neyget ewere kny, | lot vns allsamen dancken jm’.

78 ‘Christus, erleücht mir sünnder grob | meinn seel, herz vnde sinn, | Das ich dich ye vnd ymmer lob, | dein creatur ich bin. | Herr, dein will der geschech an mir, | Christu, erleucht mich, dz ich lieb | mein nechsten als ich soll …’.

have inverted with their idolatry.[79] Criticisms are directed towards prohibitions against certain foods, and the sacralising of things like candles, palms, and fire. Verse 4 attacks the money that is exchanged between priests and bishops for a priest's 'waitress' (*kellerin* – a euphemism for concubine). 'If a priest has a waitress', Graff writes, 'who is young and can still have children, he must give three gulden to the bishop. If she is old, he gives him one gulden'.[80]

The final verse speaks of driving out the plump hogs (*die feyste[n] mastschweyn*), who are not Evangelical. Jörg Graff then signs off, as he does in both other songs. As a ballad singer, he would have made a living by singing and selling his songs. Signing off was one way in which he could maintain recognition as writer and performer, and at the same time claim to be singing for the sake of all people, to please God and to save people from the priests. For example, he concludes his second song, 'Herr Jesu Christ', with the words: 'I, Jörg Graff, have sung to Christ in honour, | So that in the hall of Heaven | He may help me and all of you'.[81]

All three of these songs by Graff were reprinted in the *Weimarisches Jahrbuch* of 1855. This volume provides the names of the tunes as given in the songs' original publications. 'Gott vater in trifalde' is to be sung 'Im ton als man singt Zům ersten woln wir loben Maria die reine meid',[82] and 'Herr Jesu Christ' is to be sung 'In nachtigals senstem ton'.[83] 'Welt ir hören' is to be sung 'Im Speten ton'.[84] All these would certainly have been established tunes in use in South Germany. The latter may have been a melody by Heinrich von Meissen (d. 1318), a medieval mastersinger who also called himself Heinrich Frauenlob.[85] References to it also exist in printed songs from several decades before the Reformation. For example, Mathias Hupfuff's 1514 pamphlet, 'Der bundt schuch', also directed its readers to sing this tune to the song contained in the book.[86] A broadsheet song from 1500, printed in Strasbourg, also informs the reader that the song is to be sung 'im speten Ton. das got von vnsz wend' (see Figure 4.2). However, if 'das got von vnsz wend' is indeed a more famous song which makes use of this tune, we are none the wiser for knowing its title.

[79] 'Lat euch lieb, hoffnung vnd gelaub erwecken | vnd das Gotswort nit also nider decken, | das Bapst, Cardinal, Bischoff, münch vnd pfaffen | habe[n] ein lange zeyt verkert | vnd vns abgötterey gelert, dz wir haben die helgen geert, | vergassen Gott: wir waren hart entschlaffen'.

[80] 'wenn ein pfaff hat ein kellerin, | ist sie jung vn[nd] tregt noch kindt, | dem bischoff mus ers jor drey gulden geben, | Jst sy alt, gibt er ein guldein: | solch gelt nemen die bischoff ein'.

[81] 'Jch, Jörg graff, sang Christus zů eer, | dort in des hymels sal | helff er mir vnd euch allen dar'.

[82] H. von Fallersleben and O. Schade, eds, *Weimarisches Jahrbuch für deutsche Sprache, Litteratur und Kunst*, 4 (1855), p. 441.

[83] Ibid., p. 445.

[84] Ibid., p. 450.

[85] See H. Martens, 'Die Lieder der Hutterer und ihre Verbindung zum Meistersang im 16. Jahrhundert', *Jahrbuch für Volksliedforschung*, 26 (1981), p. 33, n. 9.

[86] *Der bundt schuch | Diß büchlein sagt v[o]n dem bösen | fürneme[n] der Bundtschůcher ...* (Strasbourg: Hupfuff, 1514).

Figure 4.2 A broadsheet containing 'Ein hüpsches lied von allen geschichten von disem jar' (Strasbourg: Grüneck, 1500). One of two examples in D Mbs, classmark: L-170. Reproduced by permission of Bayerische Staatsbibliothek, Munich

Oettinger has rightly noted that Heinrich Müller's song 'Meyn hertz das mag nit rüwe han' ('My heart that may not have anguish'), does not mention Catholicism specifically,[87] but rather alludes to Catholic practices in its stanzas. It focuses on the sacrament of the Eucharist; not on its nature, but rather on how one should be ready and worthy to take it. It appeared in 1524,[88] in a pamphlet entitled 'A beautiful new song of belief and testament, and also of preparing of God's table, of use to the unedified, sung and written by an admirer of the divine truth from Strasbourg'.[89] Müller also specifies two melodies to which this piece can be sung: the tune of the 'flam[m] weyß' (white flame), or the melody to which the popular poem, *Herzog Ernst*,[90] was sung at this time.[91]

The song opens with a prayer to the Holy Spirit to give its author, Müller, force, reason, artfulness, wit, mastery, and instruction, so that he might versify in God's honour.[92] The subject of the song is then presented, with a reminder that worth does not come through 'confession, praying, or other practices'.[93] Rather, one should believe only Jesus's promise, which is then presented in the form of a paraphrase of Matthew 11:28 ('Come to me, all you who are weary and burdened, and I will give you rest'). More scriptural passages are given as proof of God's love and mercy, including John 3:16, John 1:29, and John 14:6. In verse 7, Müller says that faith is more important than outward works, as shown in John 7.[94] The song concludes with a prayer to God to give eternal happiness (*ewig frewd*) to those who say 'Amen', who call his name, and who believe in him. Müller leaves it up to the listener to imagine what the opposite scenario might entail. That the form of this song should be in large part prayers and scriptural passages is also interesting, revealing the hopes of the songwriter that the reforms be founded on prayer and Scripture. Coupled with the reference to the 'artfulness' of Müller, it appears that this song is attempting to be three things at once: pious material, polemical message, and artistic song.

---

87 *MPGR*, p. 316.

88 The existence of this pamphlet is recorded in *Wackernagel DKL*, vol. 3, p. 81, and in *MPGR* (p. 315) as possibly originating in Strasbourg from the press of Ulrich Morhardt, with Oettinger estimating the date as 'c. 1522'. The details used here, however, are taken from the *VD16* online catalogue.

89 'Eyn schőn neüw Lied vom glauben vnnd Testament, auch von der bereyttung zů dem tysch Gottes, zů nutz den vnerbauwenen, von eynem liebhaber Göttlicher warheit zů Straßburg gesungen vnd gedicht'.

90 The story of Herzog Ernst was a popular Rhineland epic poem from the late twelfth century. See B. Sowinski, ed., *Herzog Ernst: ein mittelalterliches Abenteuerbuch* (Stuttgart: Reclam, 1970).

91 It is unclear what melody this may have been, or whether a record of the music has been taken. Such polemical songs do not always indicate a tune to which the song might have been sung.

92 'darumb so will ich hebe[n] an | in gottes er zu dichte[n]. | Heiliger geyst, verlich mir krafft, | vernu[n]fft, kunst, witz vnd meysterschafft | vnd thů mich vndericchten'.

93 'Nit durch beich, bett, ander ůbung'.

94 The heavy reliance on the Gospel of John in this song is intriguing, but there is no encouragement for listeners to familiarise themselves with this Gospel in particular, as not all of these citations list their source.

'In brüder in Christo Jesu' was published in a pamphlet by Heinrich von Zütphen (a pseudonym for Heinrich Müller), in the year the Reformation reached Strasbourg. The title of the pamphlet explains, in verse, that

> In this song will you understand
> How the religious [priests, monks, and nuns] have always
> Led the sick in their last distress
> So far from God,
> So that many become fearful.
> But now, to this end
> You will find the correct method of consolation
> In this poem. So take note
> How one should console the sick,
> O Christian men, consider this well,
> That you may yet console the sick,
> And this [poem] is sung to the 'Speten' tune.[95]

Consoling the sick and the dying was to become a major part of the role of the Protestant clergyman, and so this song unknowingly anticipates this development.[96] Such songs promoted the idea that the new clergy were able to offer something of use to the people, and so had a practical role in society. This stood in contrast to the view, which had been maintained since late medieval times, of the clergy and religious being lazy, drunk, and immoral.[97]

The song begins by requesting the attention of the 'brothers in Christ Jesus', so that they might listen to the reasons that the sick should be consoled and told of God's mercy, rather than scolded for their sins and for the good works which they did not manage to do in their lifetime. In verse 1, the singer laments that while in their deathbed, the devil visits the sick and tells them that it is too late for them to make their peace with God. Because of this, many people begin to say, 'If only I could live for one more month; I first want to deserve the Kingdom of Heaven'.[98]

Verse 2 begins by once again addressing the 'dear brothers', and instructing them not to be scared or to despair in the face of the evil one. The singer requests

---

95 H. von Zütphen (H. Müller), *In disem lied wirstu verston | wie allweg die geystlichen hon | Die krancken in der letsten not | gefuͤret all so ferr von Gott | Mit erschröcklichen worten vil: | aber yetz nün zů disem zil | Finstu die rechte troͤstung gar | in disem dicht: so nym du war | Wie man die krancken troͤsten sol, | o Cristen mensch, betracht das wol, | Das du die krancken troͤstest schon, | und syngt man es ins Speten thon* (Strasbourg: Morhardt, c. 1522). As 'Welt ir hören gesanges schall', this song is also to be sung to the 'Speten ton'.

96 See, for example, C. Koslofsky, *The Reformation of the Dead: Death and Ritual in Early Modern Germany, 1450–1700* (Basingstoke: Palgrave, 2000).

97 See pp. 25–8.

98 'solt ich doch | nur eyne[n] monat lebe[n] noch,| das hym[m]elrych dz wolt ich erst verdiene[n]'.

that the dying specifically stop wishing for more time alive in order to earn blessedness and do more good on Earth, so that they might receive the reward of Heaven. Instead, one should place one's trust in God's judgement and in his mercy. The third and fourth verses then turn to scriptural evidence for the above. As in all biblical references of this time, verse numbers are not given, and citations are often paraphrased quite liberally. Titus 3:4–5 and 1 Timothy 1:15–16 are used here, followed by Psalm 5:11–12 and Romans 8:24. At the end of verse 4, the listener, after hearing these citations, is invited to say, 'I know indeed that I may not earn blessedness until the Day of Judgement'.[99]

The singer then repeats the argument, but this time rather than referring to the devil, lays the blame on monks, nuns, priests, and Beguines (semi-monastic communities founded in the thirteenth century).[100] They come with their tricks, says the singer, asking the sick to remember their sins, their judge, their past life, and the strict judgement of God, and telling them that eternal life is possible, depending on these things. The singer chastises the clergy for doing this, and in verses 7 and 8 offers them an alternative means with which they might remind the sick that Christ, before his death, offered his body and blood for the forgiveness of sins, confirmed his covenant through the epistles and the Scriptures, and through death revitalised this covenant and gave us his mercy. Verse 8 explains how in this way, the sick will depart this life believing Christ's promise, and will, through faith, overcome the devil. To conclude, 1 Peter 5:8–9 is paraphrased: 'You should bravely resist your enemy', followed by Ephesians 2:5: 'You were saved entirely through grace'. Verse 9 finishes by commanding that 'All of you who want to be recognised as Christian, ask God to send us his divine mercy which eternally comforts us'.

Again, there is little direct anti-clerical sentiment in this song. Although the comparison is subtly made between the devil and the clergy, the clergy are asked to reconsider their position, and to console the sick rather than discourage them. Considering the date of this publication, the somewhat reserved position

[99] 'ich waiß gentzlich fürware, | das ich die seligkeit nit mag | verdiene[n] biß an jüngsten tag'.

[100] Strasbourg had a large number of Beguine communities in medieval times. The authorities had taken action against them in 1317, and by 1400 they had lost any remaining popular sympathy (see D. Phillips, *Beguines in Medieval Strasburg: A Study of the Social Aspect of Beguine Life* (Stanford: Edward Brothers, 1941), pp. 11–12; and F. Rapp, *Réformes et Réformation à Strasbourg : Église et société dans le diocèse de Strasbourg (1450–1525)* (Paris: Ophrys, 1974), p. 444). A community apparently still existed at the beginning of the Reformation, as it is mentioned in the Wencker chronicle (*Fragments des anciennes chroniques d'Alsace*, III (1892), no. 3040), as well as in 1 AST 176, 91. See also C. G. A. Schmidt, 'Die Strassburger Beginenhäuser im Mittelalter', in *Alsatia*, 7 (1858–61), pp. 149–248. Beguines had also become increasingly unpopular in other cities. The craft guilds of Cologne, for example, had as recently as 1513 decreed that the Beguines be 'gathered into a few houses where they may occupy themselves with spinning and sewing until they die' (see G. Strauss, *Manifestations of Discontent in Germany on the Eve of the Reformation* (Bloomington and London: Indiana University Press, 1971), p. 140). The original document is, according to Strauss, in the Cologne city archives: 'Verfassung und Verwaltung', V61, fols 224r–232v.

of the author is not surprising. The Reformation had not yet been established in Strasbourg; indeed there was no guarantee of safety for anyone who published anti-Catholic material.

Also in 1524, a pamphlet by Niklaus Manuel appeared in Strasbourg entitled *Eyn schön reygenlied im thon / Rusticus ambilem, Neüwlich geschmidet durch Meyster Hemerlin jm berg Ethna* (translated as *A beautiful roundel*[101] *song to the tune of* Rusticus ambilem, *newly devised by Master Hemmerlin in Mount Etna*). 'Master Hemmerlin' might refer to Felix Hemmerlin, a reformist priest who died in the mid-fifteenth century, but this is unlikely, given that the tune is said to be 'newly devised'. In addition, it is unclear what Hemmerlin might have been doing in Mount Etna![102] It is also not clear to what the tune of *Rusticus ambilem* might refer, although it is was probably a peasants' dancing song.[103]

The song in the pamphlet is 'Der Babst rüfft Küng vnd Keyser an', which consists largely of a monologue by the pope, who is worried that Luther will expose his shame and corruption.[104] The pope is presented as ridiculous, now that Luther does not care about the medallions, wax seals, bulls, or the interdict at the pope's disposal – all material objects that are presented here by Manuel as having little significance in the eyes of God. The pope reminisces about how he was 'elevated far above God', but is now 'a mockery'. In verse 7, a reference is made to annates and the pallium keeping the pope's coffers full. Oettinger explains that the *Annatengeld* were the taxes paid to the papal treasury. The mention of the pallium (a band worn by the pope and metropolitan archbishops, and previously by some other bishops) is in reference to the selling of indulgences by the Archbishop of Mainz in 1517 to repay a loan made by the Fugger Bank.[105] The pope explains in the following verse that although many people had attacked him, they had done so secretly. In other words, Luther has denounced the pope publicly, and so now everyone does.[106] This was true to some extent: the issue of Rome's control over Germany had been a problem since the mid fifteenth century, and had become further politicised during the 1521 Diet of Worms, in which the emperor was urged to take steps against

101 This poem does not meet our modern criteria for a roundel, which has nine lines with a shorter refrain after the third and last lines.

102 The mention of a historical reforming figure, however, would remind audiences that church reformers were not a new phenomenon. Historical precedent would thereby help legitimise current reforms.

103 F. M. Böhme, *Altdeutsches Liederbuch* (Leipzig: Breitkopf & Härtel, 1877), p. 817.

104 A translation can be found in Appendix F, based on that found in *MPGR*, pp. 251–2. The following description and analysis uses that translation and her accompanying comments as a foundation.

105 I am grateful to Ulinka Rublack for this observation. Oettinger, however, interprets it in a wider sense as a reference to the selling of bishoprics (*MPGR*, p. 251, n. 70).

106 *MPGR*, p. 252, p. 71.

the 'oppressive burdens and abuses imposed on and committed against the Empire by the Holy See in Rome'.[107]

The pope refers to his 'flea market' (*grempelmarckt*) having come to an end. The analogy is clear: by presenting the Church as a flea market, the pope is seen to admit to trickery, illusions, and extortion being at the centre of the institution. Furthermore, such an admission of guilt apparently originating from the pope might lead the common people to consider him a less formidable enemy than they otherwise may have done – propaganda at its most effective. The song continues: death awaits, but the pope must go and beg (verse 10, line 4).[108] In a hint at German nationalism, the pope cries that he is a 'mockery' (*spott*) to the Germans, and that no one should be angry that he is 'French'. Oettinger suggests that this is a reference to Pope Adrian VI, who was born in Utrecht, and the only pope of the first half of the sixteenth century not to have been a native Italian.[109] The last two verses are told from Manuel's point of view rather than the pope's, although nationalist sentiments continue to be emphasised. The German people have been foolish, he writes, but now the papal empire and regiment (and not just the pope) have been put to shame in German lands, because God has enlightened his people, allowing them to recognise the Antichrist. Interestingly, Manuel does not call the pope the Antichrist explicitly. It is implied, of course, but he found room here for a more obscure approach.

Manuel was also well known as a writer of *Fastnachtspiele* (popular plays performed by the common people traditionally on Shrove Tuesday) and, before the Reformation, as an artist. He was also a high-ranking civil servant, and was appointed governor of Erlach in 1523.[110]

Some polemical songs were deliberately disguised as hymns or spiritual songs, including 'Lob sei dir, jesu Christe', by Heinrich Vogtherr, a painter by trade,[111] which appeared in a 1526 pamphlet entitled 'A new evangelical song in every cross, very comforting for every Christian. Taken from divine Scripture'.[112] Scriptural references in these sorts of songs would have helped

---

[107] See 'The Statement of Grievances Presented to the Diet of Worms in 1521', in Strauss, *Manifestations of Discontent*, 19 vols (Gotha: Perthes; Göttingen: Vandenhoeck & Ruprecht; Munich: Oldenbourg, 1893–), pp. 52–63. The original text can be read in *Deutsche Reichstagsakten: jüngere Reihe*, vol. 2, pp. 670–704.

[108] Wackernagel has observed that this line is a pun: 'gen betlen gan' ('to go and beg') as opposed to 'gen Bethlem gan' ('to go to Bethlehem') (*Wackernagel DKL*, vol. 3, p. 394; see also *MPGR*, p. 252, n. 73).

[109] *MPGR*, p. 252, n. 74.

[110] For more about Manuel's life, see P. Pfrunder, *Pfaffen Ketzer Totenfresser. Fastnachtskultur der Reformationszeit: Die Berner Spiele von Niklaus Manuel* (Zurich: Chronos, 1989), pp. 35–7.

[111] Röhrich, *Mittheilungen*, vol. 1, p. 211. See also 90 Z 17, p. Ntr 763.

[112] H. Vogtherr, *Ein neuwes Euangelisch | Lied in allem creütz | Jedem Christenn gantz tröstlich | Auß göttlicher schrifft ge- | zogen* (Strasbourg: Kornmann, 1526). It should be noted that the publisher, Peter Kornmann, was based in Augsburg, and that the pamphlet claims to originate in Augsburg. However, *VD16* has corrected the place of origin to Strasbourg, and the song is considered here on the strength of that decision.

to 'legitimise' them, and their aim would be to convince the public that they were by people who were educated and familiar with the Bible. By mentioning a song's scriptural origins in its title, a composer would have hoped to achieve this to an even greater extent.

The first few lines of the song could well be mistaken for a hymn: 'Praise be to you, Jesus Christ | In your heavenly throne'.[113] However, by the end of the first verse allusions begin to appear to standard Reformation complaints. Vogtherr writes that God's Word, having previously been kept a secret, now shines in all places. By the end of verse 2 it is clear that this is a propagandistic song, with the mention of the 'false papists' and their 'merchants'.[114] The following two verses make familiar criticisms: the papists have used false laws, and tried to frighten us with letters and swords.[115] Verse 5 advises the pious Christian to take comfort in God. Verse 7 advises that Christ must be known through death and martyrdom. The rest of the song prepares its listeners for a struggle, encouraging them to take up their cross. It is one of the more serious polemical songs, not poking fun at the hierarchy of the Church, but rather preparing the faithful for the possibility of martyrdom.

The Eucharist in Polemical Song

The final polemical song to have been published in Strasbourg in the 1520s was 'Es ist die warheyt pracht an tag', in the pamphlet *Warer verstand / von des herren Nachtmal* (1527).[116] At this point, the Reformation was well under way in Strasbourg, the Mass had already been abolished in most of the city's churches, and pressure was being put on the monasteries and convents to disband.[117] Close ties were being maintained with the reformers in Zurich, which meant a Zwinglian, symbolic understanding of the Eucharist was being adopted in Strasbourg's churches.

'Es ist die warheyt' reflects that stance. It is a contrafactum of Speratus's song 'Es ist das heyl vns kommen her', which had been published in Strasbourg for the first time that same year. The first verse sums up the argument: the truth has already been revealed, and the Antichrist has blinded the world by falsely teaching that during the Sacrament, actual bodily flesh is eaten.[118] This custom,

---

113 'Lob sei dir, jesu Christe, in dinem himels tron'.

114 'von den falschenn Papistenn mit Jrer kauffmans war'.

115 Verses 4–5.

116 See the discussion of *Warer verstand des herren Nachtmal* on pp. 181–3; see Appendix F for a translation.

117 See, in particular, A. Leonard, *Nails in the Wall: Catholic Nuns in Reformation Germany* (Chicago and London: University of Chicago Press, 2005).

118 'Damit er hatt die welt verplent / | vnd valsch gelert vom Sacrament / | das leyblich fleisch werd gessenn'.

the writer says, is erroneous (*falscher*). Then, in verse 4, Luther is criticised for insisting on a similar argument. Jesus said, 'This is my body', but the 'breaking' refers not to the body but to the bread. The author explains: 'The bread did not suffer on the holy cross for us'.[119] If we follow Luther's understanding, then we must be actually breaking Jesus's body in the Eucharist. 'It follows that we would have to kill the Lord unceasingly'.[120] Instead, we break the bread in the assembly in order to remember the death of the Lord, who was 'broken' (*zerbrochen*) on the cross. From verse 11, the author begins describing the Last Supper as 'a Passover' (*ein phaße*), and comparing Jesus to a sacrificial lamb. The lamb, he explains, was a sign of remembrance.

The final two verses, 16 and 17, discuss idolatry. Honour should be bestowed on the subject of this event (namely Jesus Christ), and nothing or no one else. He continues, 'The creator is keen that honour not be given to just any creation'.[121] The author concludes verse 17 by stating that Luther and the pope, 'although they are not allied, have become united' through their belief that Christ is truly and actually present in the Eucharist.

The strength of the anti-Lutheran stance comes as somewhat as a shock to the modern reader. Although it is known and acknowledged that Strasbourg's churches believed in the Eucharist only as a sign of remembrance at this time, there was nevertheless dialogue and co-operation between the Strasbourg reformers and Martin Luther. Was this song an attempt to stir up trouble? The publisher, Johann Prüss, certainly did not seem to have any particular alliances. His firm had already reproduced many writings by Luther, as well some by other writers as varied as Erasmus of Rotterdam, Martin Bucer, Thomas Murner, and Andreas Karlstadt. Indeed, Prüss is known to have carried on printing Karlstadt's work even after the latter had lost all popularity with the Strasbourg reformers.[122] Of course, it was probably a question of surviving at any costs in a newly expanding industry. Interestingly, the author of the song chose to keep his anonymity, possibly for fear of an unfavourable reaction from the city authorities.

'Es ist die warheyt pracht an tag', was not included in Oettinger's appendix of polemical songs,[123] the reason for which is initially unclear, its contents evidently being a polemical discussion of the nature of the Eucharist. Part of the reason may be that in previous studies this song has repeatedly been labelled a spiritual song. It in fact exists in two versions. The second of these had an added verse, and was classified as a 'spiritual song' in Wackernagel's *Bibliographie*.[124] Since then, the song has maintained its unchallenged position in the canon of

119 'Dann brott für vns kein rodes not / | gelitten am kreytz frone'.

120 'So volgt dz wir on vnderlaß / | den herren muͤsten toͤdten'.

121 'Der schoͤpffer ist ein eyferer / | last keiner geschoͤpfft die ere'.

122 Chrisman, *Lay Culture, Learned Culture*, p. 30.

123 *MPGR*, pp. 213–402.

124 K. E. P. Wackernagel, *Bibliographie zur Geschichte des deutschen Kirchenliedes im XVI. Jahrundert* (Frankfurt am Main: Hender & Zimmer, 1855), p. 45.

sixteenth-century church texts, emerging in other studies of liturgical material, such as Hubert's *Die Straßburger liturgischen Ordnungen* of 1900. It is omitted from some more modern studies, such as Chrisman's survey of the Strasbourg printing press, but crucially the original pamphlet of 17 verses is listed in *RISM DKL*, a volume which claims specifically to exclude 'songs pertaining more to church politics than of a spiritual nature'.[125] Nor does the original version of 'Es ist die warheyt' fit *RISM*'s own definition of a hymn, which includes the prerequisite of being a sacred text.[126] It must be acknowledged that the text refers to one of the most spiritual of all aspects of Reformation dispute, and indeed of Christianity – the Eucharist. Furthermore, it is to be sung to the tune of the 1524 Lutheran hymn by Paul Speratus, 'Es ist das heyl vns kommen her',[127] as indicated on the pamphlet title page (see Figure 4.3). However, the original text of the contrafactum, 'Es ist die warheyt', contains a comparison of Luther to the pope which is blatantly political, and its pro-Swiss, anti-Lutheran stance is unlikely to have been wholly representative of the Strasbourg preachers at this time (1527).

Suggesting that the 1527 pamphlet contains a spiritual song, then, is ultimately a mistake. However, such an error is nevertheless understandable, when one considers the context in which this pamphlet was produced. As far as we know, no liturgical orders were printed in Strasbourg between 1527 and 1529. We do know, however, of several pamphlets that were printed during the same period. One was *Warer verstand von des herren Nachtmal* (*True understanding of the Lord's Supper*), containing 'Es ist die warheyt pracht an tag'.[128] Wolfgang Köpfel produced two editions of another pamphlet in 1527, containing various songs suitable for the liturgy.[129] Another publication, *Der siben vnd dreyssigst psalm Dauids* came off Köpfel's press in the same year, containing a version of Psalm 37, the Song of Zechariah, and the *Nunc Dimittis*, all suitable for the liturgy and all from scriptural sources. In 1529, the same printer produced *Das Te Deum laudamus verteütscht*, again, suitable for liturgical use. In addition to this material, which could have been used in a liturgical setting, the mention of the Lord's Supper in the title of *Warer verstand* may have led to the assumption that this was a song designed to be sung at the Eucharist. (Many of the early vernacular liturgies published in Strasbourg include the words 'Herrn Nachtmal' in their title.) Therefore, during the period 1527 to 1529, amidst a flurry of pamphlets with songs suitable for worship, it is understandable why

125 *RISM DKL*, vol. 2, p. 20*, also noted in *MPGR*, p. 2.

126 *RISM DKL*, vol. 2, p. 20*.

127 See C. B. Brown, *Singing the Gospel: Lutheran Hymns and the Success of the Reformation* (Cambridge, MA, and London: Harvard University Press, 2005), pp. 94–6.

128 *Warer verstand / von des herren Nachtmal. Vff die weyß zů singen / Es ist das hayl vns komen her. &c.* (Strasbourg: Prüss, 1527).

129 *Die zween Psalmen* and *Die zwen Psalmen*. Included was the song 'Es ist das heyl vns kommen her', on which 'Es ist die warheyt pracht an tag' is based.

Figure 4.3 The title page (left) of *Warer verstand* (Strasbourg: Prüss, 1527) and the first verse of 'Es ist die warheyt', set to music (right). The text is to be sung to Speratus's 1523 hymn 'Es ist das heyl vns kommen her', CH Zz – Res 1041. Reproduced by permission of Zentralbibliothek, Zurich

a publication entitled *Warer verstand von des herren Nachtmal* could also be assumed to contain material suitable for liturgical use.

Hubert has observed that the song also appears in the Augsburg *Form vnd Ordnung gaystlicher Gesang vnd Psalmen* of 1533[130] and it also can be found in several subsequent editions of this book.[131] Interestingly, in the Augsburg version, the references to Luther have been removed,[132] and an extra verse has been put in place of the single line at the end of the Strasbourg version. The additional verse reads as follows:

So offt mans Herren brot nun yßt /	As often as one eats the Lord's bread
Vnnd seinen kelch will trincken /	And drinks from his chalice,
Wie man klerlich in Paulo ließt /	As one clearly reads in Paul,
Sol man seins tod gedenken /	One should think of his death,
Mit glauben preysen Got den Herrn /	Praise God the Lord with faith,
Dem nåchsten dienen auch so gern /	And serve one's neighbour gladly:
Dann werd wir ewig leben.[133]	Then we will live eternally.

In short, the song has been deliberately appropriated and 'Lutheranised', to fit with the rest of the book's contents, which included some song texts by Luther himself. These cunning changes ensure only the pope and the anonymous 'some people' (*der Bapst vnd etlich klug*) are mentioned in verse 17, and the extra verse ends on a slightly more peaceful note than the original version does. Rather than concluding with a bitter image of the pope, the listener is instead drawn back to the righteous Christian way of life, through the example of St Paul, and so the spiritual aspect of the song is played up. It is no doubt this factor that led to the inclusion of the original (polemical) version in *RISM DKL*. However, the song also continued to be printed in its original form, without the extra verse. The Universitätsbibliothek in Bern, for example, contains a copy of the anti-Lutheran version in a book dated between 1537 and 1565.[134]

Many references to the Eucharist can be found in other Strasbourg polemical songs of the time. Jörg Graff, however, is much less concerned with the issue than is Heinrich Müller. Graff alludes to it only in passing in verse 2 of 'Herr Jesu Christ',[135] whereas Müller refers to it multiple times in each of his songs.

130 J. Dachser, *Form vnd Ordnung gaystlicher Gesang vnd Psalmen: mit sonderm Fleiß corrigiert auch zu rechtem Verstand punctirt und virguliert, welche Got dem Herren zu Lob und Eer gesungen werden* (Augsburg: Ulhart, 1533).

131 See J. B. Riederer, *Nachrichten zur Kirchen- Gelerten- und Bůcher-Geschichte; aus gedruckten und ungedruckten Schriften*, 4 vols (Altdorf: Schüpfel, 1764–68), vol. 1, pp. 460–64.

132 In the Augsburg version, verse 4, line 1 reads: 'Es bochend etlich …', and verse 17, line 5 reads: '… etlich klug'.

133 Source: Riederer, *Nachrichten zur Kirchen- Gelerten und Bůcher-Geschichte*, vol. 1, pp. 462–4.

134 Classmark ZB Rar alt 605 : 67. See http://www.e-rara.ch/bes_1/content/titleinfo/245725 (accessed 28 December 2014).

135 'dein leib du für vns hie | Hast geben willig in den todt'.

Müller's 'Meyn hertz', while concentrating on the attainment of justification, does so with reference to the Eucharist. The end of verse 1 states that only through faith and belief does one become worthy of the Holy Sacrament.[136] In verse 2, Müller states that one should consider Christ's words in Matthew 11:28, 'Come to me, those who are weary and heavily burdened, I will give you comfort'[137] when one approaches the Lord's table (*tisch gotts*). More is made of the Sacrament in verse 5 of the same song, as well as in verses 8, 11, and 13. A reference to 'bread' is also to be found in the final line of verse 10. Müller's second song, 'Ir brüder', makes reference in verse 7 to the body and blood of Jesus, through which Christ has confirmed his covenant.[138]

Of course, during the early 1520s, the debate on the Eucharist was still in its infancy. There was very little on the subject that could be communicated to the laypeople in song. Especially in Strasbourg before 1524, when the Latin Mass was still commonplace, there was no particular reason to advertise an alternative world view – at least not to the laity. In 1527, however, change was taking place rapidly, and the Protestant camps were moving towards a schism over their different interpretations of the nature of the Sacrament.[139]

Anger Directed towards the Clergy

Since at least the fourteenth century, the clergy and religious had been viewed with a certain amount of suspicion and resentment by a large proportion of the laity.[140] Owing to disagreements with civil authorities, the residence of the bishop had been located in Saverne since the final years of the fourteenth century, and relations had not improved between Strasbourg and the office of bishop since that time. The bishop was represented in Strasbourg by the cathedral chapter. The outrage at ongoing abuses by the priests, monks, and nuns, as described by commentators such as Sebastian Brant, Geiler von Kaysersberg, and Erasmus of Rotterdam, was gaining momentum in the run-up to the Reformation.[141] During the Reformation years, those members of the clergy who had not converted to Protestantism suffered at the hands of polemical songwriters such as Graff and Müller. No allowances were made for lowly priests and monks who may have

136 '... durch welchen glauben er erkent, | das er wirt wirdig vnd geschickt | zu dem heyligen sacrament'.

137 'kumpt all zů mir, die arbeyten | vnnd schwer belade[n] synde, | ich will eüch selb ergetze[n] thon'.

138 'Hat auch seyn testament durch das | sacrament seynes leybs fürbaß | vnd seynes blůts zů glycher maß | bestetiget mit brieff vn[nd] sigels krafftc'.

139 L. P. Wandel, *The Eucharist in the Reformation: Incarnation and Liturgy* (Cambridge: Cambridge University Press, 2006).

140 Rapp, *Réformes et Réformation à Strasbourg*, p. 106.

141 See Chapter 1.

wanted to do good deeds while remaining within the established Church. The songwriters showed no mercy towards them.

As can be seen above, one man who featured often in such songs in Strasbourg was Thomas Murner. Many of Murner's satires of the previous years had been directed against 'fools' of various sorts. In 'Merckt jr herren myner sag', he is himself satirised as a fool, compared to the fools in Sebastian Brant's *Narrenschiff* (1494), and therefore also to the fools in his own satires, *Die Narrenbeschwörung* (1512) and *Die Schelmenzunft* (1512).[142]

'Merckt jr herren myner sag' is also critical of clergy more widely. 'There are already many preachers in the world', the author writes in verse 11, 'who are better suited to fighting wars in the field than to preaching God's favour and Word'.[143] In verse 17, preachers are told to follow the example of St Paul. The last three verses of this song criticise certain monastic orders, namely the Franciscans, Carmelites, and Augustinians. 'Saint Francis was a pious man',[144] verse 18 explains, but the Franciscans have become barefooted beggars.[145] The other orders beg too, and the final verse complains that 'their begging sack will never be full, for as it gets filled up it remains empty'.[146]

Graff's 'Gott Vatter in trifalde' makes the point that preachers do not want to preach God's Word, in case their benefices are taken away, and their sin and shame is revealed (verse 4). In many places, Graff accuses the clergy of inverting God's Word (see, for example, the second part of verse 2 of 'Herr Jesu Christ in himels tron'). Perhaps the most vicious attack on a clergyman that can be seen in these songs is Manuel's 'Der Bapst rüfft Küng vnd Keyser an', which, while not naming the pope personally, ridicules his office in a way that would surely make any defender of the papacy seethe. The pope's fear is again that his shame will be made public (verse 1), unless Luther is stopped. Even some melodies themselves had anti-clerical associations, including the 'Bruder Veit' tune, which had originated as a popular song complaining about clerical abuses.[147]

142 *Die Narrenbeschwörung* and *Die Schelmenzunft* were similar in subject matter to Sebastian Brant's *Narrenschiff*. These were followed by *Die Gäuchmatt* (Basel: Gengenbach, 1519) and *Die Mühle von Schwindelsheim und Gretmüllerin Jahrzeit* (Strasbourg: Hupfuff, 1515), in which Murner criticises 'fools of love'.

143 'Es synd noch vil prediger in d[er] welt | die gebent besser krieger in das feldt, | den[n] prediger gottes gonst vn[nd] wort'.

144 'sant Franciscus was ein from[m]er man'.

145 'Darnach kompt der barfůsser, | der ist ein rechten betler'.

146 'jr bettel sack wirt nym[m]er vol, | wie man fůllt so bleybt er hol'.

147 Oettinger, 'Murner, Stifel, and Songs as Polemic', p. 53.

The Cross-Border Influence of Songs

So far, this study has been concerned only with the relationship between music and the Reformation from inside Strasbourg. There were, of course, also songs about Strasbourg written elsewhere, and songs published in Strasbourg about other cities. One such example is 'Strasbourg, cite dempire', a song which expresses negative sentiments about Strasbourg's rejection of Catholicism. It exists in two manuscripts in the AST in Strasbourg. The song was originally written in French, but also appears in German in a 1529 manuscript, described as 'A new song of new prospective things that the city of Strasbourg should encounter' (*Eyn Nuw lied nuwer zükunfftiger ding so der Stat Straßburg begegnen soll*).[148] It is a polemical song that, over eight verses, condemns Strasbourg to eternal damnation for having abandoned the Christian faith and having listened to heretical preachers. From the last line of the song we learn that its author is called Joannes Dulcis.[149] A later manuscript of this song provides a little more information about Dulcis. In the eighteenth-century *Varia ecclesiastica* of Jacques Wencker, in which the song is given in both French and German,[150] we learn that this song was often sold in the small Lorrainese village of Saint-Quirin, situated between Strasbourg and Nancy. The song, in its French version, is to be sung to the tune of 'Regrets, soucis, et peine'.[151] It is clear from the German version, which does not rhyme or have any regular metre, that this was merely a translation for reference only.[152] Wencker explains that Dulcis was also responsible for another song opposing Lutheran and Evangelical teaching, and provides a version of it in Latin. He explains that this song was also often found for sale in Saint-Quirin.[153]

The song begins by lamenting 'Strasbourg, city of Empire', which having once flourished is now 'going from bad to worse'.[154] The devil and Hell make regular appearances in the song, beginning in verse 2, when Satan is accused of governing the city and driving it into Hell. The only sixteenth-century figure mentioned by name is the 'accursed heretic' (*heretique mauldict*) François Lambert (c.1486–1530), a French reformer who lived briefly in Strasbourg, and preached to the refugee community from 1524 to 1526. He gained no favour with the humanists of the city and in 1526 acquired an appointment

148 1 AST 138, 3.

149 This is possibly a pseudonym for Nicolas Pantallion, whose name is given next to that of Dulcis at the end of the song. See 1 AST 166, 5.2, fol. 86r.

150 1 AST 166, 5.2, fols 85v–87r.

151 'Schmachlidlin von Str[aßburg] im hertzogthumb Lothring[en] zu S. Kurin offentlich feyl gehabt. Chanson nouvelle augurative de Strasbourg sur le chant. Regrets soucy et peine'. 1 AST 166, 5.2, fol. 85v.

152 See Appendix C.

153 'Das Schmachlidlin von Str[aßburg] hat man im hertzogthumb Lothringen zu St. Kurin offentlich feyl gehabt'. 1 AST 166, 5.2, fol. 87r.

154 'Strasbourg cite dempire | Qui as jadis flory | Tu vas de pis en pire'. 1 AST 166, 5.2, fol. 85v.

in Hesse.[155] This fact makes the mention of Lambert in this song (dated 1529) rather surprising, as he had not been the most popular figure during his time in Strasbourg, and in any case had not been in the city for three years. It is therefore very likely that the song itself dates from the period in which Lambert was resident in Strasbourg, but that the manuscript on which it appears[156] was not produced until 1529. Verse 4 makes reference to figures of classical mythology, warning the Strasbourgeois that 'the Furies of Hell, with Rhadamanthus, judge of damnable affairs, Charon and Cerberus, are ready to hear your case', and that Atropos (one of the Fates) 'wants to cut your thread'. Verse 6 makes reference to the 'good Duke of Lorraine' who 'reddened his two hands in the blood of your confederate brothers'. This may refer to the defeat by Duke Antoine of the Alsatian peasants who had invaded Lorraine in 1525.[157] The final two verses bring a ray of hope to the situation, as Dulcis advises Strasbourg in verse 7 to 'abandon your false heresies, [and] guide your ship well'. The final verse calls on Strasbourg to 'hear the trumpet, [and] the singing of the song' of Dulcis, who is 'a cleric, departed from Chartres'.[158] Judging by its presence in the Archives du Chapitre St-Thomas, Dulcis's song was heard loud and clear in Strasbourg – and his message ignored by the majority.

Likewise, songs relating to foreign political and religious topics also found their way to Strasbourg. One such example is a song about the Swiss forest canton of Unterwalden, published in Strasbourg in 1536. The song, 'Wie es jn disen tagen zu Bern ergangen ist', appeared in a pamphlet entitled *Ein nüw Lied von der vffrůr der landtlüten zů Jnderlappenn in der herschafft Bern in ůͤchtlandt*.[159] It supports the peasants' revolt in Interlaken, situated in the dominion of Bern, and mocks the Catholic faith. It was written by the composer Cosmas Alder, and was to be sung either to the tune of 'Ich stund an einem morgen' or 'Das frewlein von Britanyen'. Alder provided Apiarius with the song, which the latter then published in Strasbourg. In 1538, the book dealer Hans Hippocras offered the song for sale at a book fair, where some citizens of Unterwalden obtained it. This resulted in the Unterwalden authorities, along with those of five other Catholic cantons, writing to Bern to demand that the author, printer, and distributor of the

155 See the *Neue Deutsche Biographie, dreizehnter Band* (Berlin: Duncker & Humblot, 1982), pp. 435–7.

156 1 AST 138, 3.

157 See R. Briggs, *The Witches of Lorraine* (Oxford: Oxford University Press, 2007), p. 14. This is also further evidence of an earlier dating for this song: c. 1526.

158 At this point, the German translation departs from the French. Whereas the French version reads: 'Sa fait ung clerc, des chartraines partis', the German reads: 'Es hats gemacht ein Clerc von den Carmeliten gescheyden'. See Appendix C.

159 A facsimile of the title page is available in the *Neues Berner Taschenbuch*, 9 (1904 [published 1903]), p. 260.

song be punished. Alder was fined, and the first Bernese censorship order was put in place in 1539. Apiarius, however, was dealt no punishment.[160]

The Fall of the Popular Song and the Rise of the Liturgical Song

As the Reformation gained momentum, the need for polemical and propagandistic songs in places such as Strasbourg dwindled. For many years there was no perception of any immediate threat to the reforms.

The beginning of the Reformation in Strasbourg coincided with a considerable reduction in the number of popular songs being printed.[161] A glance through Chrisman's *Bibliography of Strasbourg Imprints* would suggest that popular music almost died out during the first two or three decades of the Reformation,[162] but there are in fact several titles that escaped Chrisman's attention, as can be seen in Table 4.1. The sparseness of popular song publication in Strasbourg is nevertheless discernible. Such songs (if we accept that this sample is an accurate representation of frequency of printing) appear to have been published in 'pockets' lasting no more than a couple of years each. Furthermore, if one considers the number of printers who chose to publish liturgical orders and hymns, it is remarkable that the publication of 'popular' material was undertaken by only a very small number of printers. The Schürer Erben press dominated this section of the market in the 1520s, but stopped printing such songs in 1521, before wholeheartedly reappearing from 1524 to 1526. The market then seems to have been non-existent until the turn of the decade, when Schöffer may have published a book of chansons. Then there was nothing, once again, until Schöffer and Apiarius jointly published the monumental *Fünff vnd sechzig teütscher Lieder*.

As mentioned in Chapter 3, *Fünff vnd sechzig teütscher Lieder* is a collection of polyphonic songs in German.[163] The songs are a mixture of folksongs and ballads, usually relatively short and simple in style, with religious content usually only occurring in passing. Eighteen composers contributed to the collection, including Matthias Greiter, who composed five of the songs, as well as Sixt Dietrich, Thomas Sporer, Ludwig Senfl, and Cosmas Alder, who arranged the

[160] A. Fluri, 'Mathias Apiarius, der erste Buchdrucker Berns (1537–1554): Das Interlachnerlied und die erste bernische Censurordnung', *Neues Berner Taschenbuch*, 2 (1897 [published 1896]), pp. 209–30; H. Türler, 'Drei Lieder aus dem 16. Jahrhundert', *Neues Berner Taschenbuch*, 9 (1904 [published 1903]), pp. 259–65; Catalogue of the exhibition 'Musik in Bern zwischen Spätmittelalter und Reformation', Univerversitätsbibliothek, Bern, 29 June to 13 October 2007, p. 32.

[161] See Chapter 2.

[162] Chrisman, *Bibliography of Strasbourg Imprints*, p. 191.

[163] *Fünff vnd | sechzig teütscher | Lieder / vormals | im[m] truck nie vß | gangen* (Strasbourg: Schöffer & Apiarius, before 1537). The contents are listed in Vogeleis, *Quellen und Bausteine*, pp. 234–5. For the names of similar collections printed in other German cities, see Gilmont, *The Reformation and the Book*, p. 76.

Judaslied, mentioned above, also known as 'O du armer Judas'. Although five partbooks were published, the majority of pieces are for four voices only. Some of the songs may have been found objectionable by the Strasbourg preachers, such as 'Die welt die hat einen thumben mut', 'Frawe, libste frawe', and 'Lieb ist subtil'. It was the only set of popular partsongs published in Strasbourg during this time,[164] and therefore does not truly deserve to be grouped with these other publications, many of which would have been published without music, and were designed to be sung in unison or simplistic harmony, in taverns and on an otherwise *ad hoc* basis.

One typical example of the type of song included in this collection is 'Frawe, libste frawe', set to music by Balthasar Arthopius. The text consists solely of two sentences: '"Woman, lovely woman, where is your husband?" "He is in the church praying to the saints"'.[165] The implications are multiple: first that her husband is a papist, who still insists on saintly devotion; and second that whoever is asking the question is intent on seducing the woman. By extension, the message may be that remaining faithful to the old papacy may render one a cuckold. The reformers are unlikely to have objected to the first (and perhaps not the third) implication, but they may well have objected to the second on moral grounds. Indeed, further verses were added in the seventeenth century, along the lines of the story told in 'Die welt die hat einen thumben mut', discussed below.[166] These added verses tell the story of a farmer who goes into the wood, unwittingly leaving his wife to be seduced by a passing scribe. The scribe asks the wife where her husband is, and she answers that he is in church. The farmer returns, striking the scribe with a stick, after which the scribe protests, blaming the woman for daring to ask to have the lute played to her.[167] This addition softens the song's anti-Catholic implications.

'Lieb ist subtil', by Thomas Sporer, is a rather less optimistic love song. It highlights the hazards of love, which, through dangerous play, can lead to unfortunate accidents. The narrator speaks of his dismay that, having gone to great lengths to secure the favour of one particular young woman, the result was a sad end. He then warns that suspicion leads to great despising, that pain can lead to remorse, hatred, disloyalty, and that it overturns all grace and favour. The narrator expresses the loyalty of his heart to the woman.[168] 'Die welt die hat einen thumben mut', by Thomas Stoltzer, on the contrary, is an arrangement of a

164 Apart from the possible existence of the *Viginti Cantiunculae gallicae quatuor vocum* (1530).

165 'Frawe, libste frawe, vnd wo ist ewer maw maw man? Er ist wol in der kirchen vnd bet't die heilgen aw aw an'.

166 H. J. Moser, ed., *65 Deutsche Lieder für vier- bis fünfstimmigen gemischten Chor a cappella nach dem Liederbuch von Peter Schöffer und Mathias Apiarus (Biener) (Straßburg spätestens 1536)* (Wiesbaden: Breitkopf & Härtel, 1967), p. 179.

167 These additional verses are printed ibid.

168 In this song we encounter, once again, familiar language relating to the heart as the organ of emotion.

Table 4.1 Publications containing non-religious popular songs in Strasbourg, 1520–1540. The majority are individual anonymous songs that were published on broadsheets or in pamphlets, but nos 16 and 17 are collections in which the songs are provided with attributions of authorship. Data taken from the Universal Short Title Catalogue and *VD16*, with reference to Chrisman, *Bibliography of Strasbourg Imprints, 1480–1599* (New Haven: Yale University Press, 1982), p. 191

Publication title	Publication details
1. *Ein new Lied von eym | Schneyder vnnd Schůmacher wie sie rechten vmb | die Geyß*[a]	Schürer Erben, 1520 (reprinted as no. 21)
2. *Alexander von metz | in gesanges weiß*	Flach, 1520
3. Ludwig Binder, *Dieß lied sagt von Lucretia, wie sie vmb ir ere kam, vnnd sich selbst ertödtet. Vn[nd] ist im Späten thon*	Schürer Erben, 1520; and Morhart, 1520
4. *Ein hüpsch lied neüw | gemacht. Jn dem thon Mit | lust so wil ich singen. | Ein knab wolt spacieren gon*	Schürer Erben, 1520
5. *Ein hüpst schimpflichs | lied von eim reichen Baur | wie er den orden an sich nam*	Schürer Erben, 1520
6. *Ein hübsches Lied von einer Königin von Aivnon | Diß lied saget vo[n] einer kron | Welch die künigin von Afion | Wol zwölff küngen het machen lon*[a]	Schürer Erben, 1521
7. *Ein hübsch lied: | Von | dem Hammen Reystett / | wie jn der Peter von Zey- | tenen gefangen hat*[a]	Schürer Erben, 1521
8. *Ein hüpsch news lied, von den roß teütschern vnd iren kluge[n] hendeln so sie treiben biß sie den bawren die augen vercleibe[n] oder noch etwan einem der nit gern für einen bawren geacht wölt werden, vndndoch jr lob dar bey vnverschwigen, so herren und fürsten jnen nit wol ablegen mögen*	Morhart, 1522
9. *Ein Lied von einer faulen Dieren Jm thon, Von vppigklichen dingen, so wil ichs heben an, etc.*	Schürer Erben, 1524
10. B. Jobin, *Ein hüpsches lied von allen geschichten von disem jar von krieg und von widerwertikeit die sich verloufenn*	Kistler, 1525
11. *Ein hübsch new Lied, genant Zucht und Unzucht der Jungen*	Schürer Erben, 1525
12. *Eyn hübsch neüw Lied | von der statt Waltzhůt*	Schürer Erben, 1525

Publication title	Publication details
13. *Ein schon lied newlich | gemacht / im gulden kron thon*	Schürer Erben, 1525
14. *Eyn new lied von den | Baure / wie sye Weispeg gestürmbt | hand*	Schürer Erben, 1525
15. *Zwey schöne Lieder: | von d[er] Küngin von Hungern, Fraw | Maria, vnd jre[n] gemahel Künig Lud- | wig, als er von jr inn streyt zoch, wider | den Türcken*	Schürer Erben, 1526
16. *Viginti Cantiunculae gallicae quatuor vocum*[b]	Schöffer, 1530
17. *Fünff vnd | sechzig teütscher | Lieder*[a]	Schöffer & Apiarius, before 1537[c]
18. *Das Narren Giessen*	Frölich, 1538[d]
19. *Diß Lied sagt von eim | Kauffman / der seine gůte werck | wolt sparen an des todes beth*	Frölich, 1540
20. *Diß Lied sagt von einem | alten Schüsselkorb / wie es jm | gieng auff der Hochzeit*	Frölich, 1540
21. *Ein hüpsch new | Kurtzweilig Lied / von eim | Schneider vnnd Schůmacher / wie | sie rechten vmb die Geyß*	Prüss, 1540 (reprint of no. 1)
22. *Ein schoͤn new Lied / wie | ein fraw jren man strafft / vnd weret | jm er sol nit zů dem wein gehn*	Frölich, 1540
23. *O reicher Gott, in deinem Saal ... | Das Lied von dem Ritter | auß Steürmarckt / wie er ein Künig in | Dennmarck ward / auch wie es jhm | gieng mit einer Künigin in Fran- | ckreich*	Frölich, 1540
24. M. Maier, *Das Lied von dem Ritter | auß Steürmarckt / wie er ein Künig in | Dennmarck ward / auch wie es jhm | gieng mit einer Künigin in Fran- | ckreich*	Frölich, 1540

a. Nos 1, 6, 7 and 17 are listed in Chrisman, *Bibliography of Strasbourg Imprints*, p. 191.

b. Listed in Chrisman, *Bibliography*, p. 195. No examples are known to exist. See also Blackburn, 'Josquin's Chansons', p. 61; Fétis, *Biographie universelle des musiciens*, vol. 7, p. 499; and Vogeleis, *Quellen und Bausteine*, pp. 225–6.

c. This dating is based on the information given in the modern edition of this book, Moser, ed., *65 Deutsche Lieder*, p. XIX. *VD16* suggests the earlier date of 1535.

d. This song was also published in several other German-speaking cities. See *VD16*.

folk song which tells of a farmer going into the forest, bringing back a cartload of wood to his lord with his proud horse. Some of the songs in the collection also make reference to religion or devotion, although they are often about what the reformers would have considered to be the 'wrong' sort of devotion. 'Auff diß faßnacht' ('On this Shrove Tuesday'),[169] another song by Thomas Sporer, for example, discusses a procession and the cheerful singing to St Vitus.[170] The song also makes reference to the *Mumschanz* – a term for carnival amusements.

It is clear from Table 4.1 that there was nevertheless a dramatic reduction in the number of printed popular songs during the early Reformation period. This reduction is most likely to have been the result of an intentional wave of suppression. Although there is no known documentary evidence to support the claim that there was a deliberate censoring process, Bucer is known to have been opposed to the singing of profane unholy songs from an early date,[171] and the city magistrates may well have supported him on this matter. Suppression of popular music printing would surely have been part of an effort to combat the culture of lascivious and immoral singing.

Such publications were, of course, ephemeral, and it is likely that many more popular songs were printed than have survived. Nevertheless, if we are to assume that the extant publications represent an accurate sample of printing numbers, the theory that popular song numbers reduced still holds.[172]

Prayerful Pastimes

Songs in the vernacular were also, of course, of great value in professing the new faith.[173] One important distinction between popular songs and the new congregational songs of the Church is that the former, more often than not, were printed without melodies. Instead, a pre-existing tune was designated, and it was assumed that people would know that tune by heart and be able to fit the words to it. For this reason, popular songs were successful as a form of communication in early modern Europe. It can therefore be deduced, quite sensibly, that the

[169] This song references another popular and lascivious song of the time, 'Der Pfarrer von St. Veit'.

[170] It is not known when this song was written, but if it was composed after 1518 then this mention of St Vitus could be in reference to the dancing plague of 1518. See Chapter 1, pp. 32–3.

[171] See Veit, 'Piété, chant et lecture: les pratiques religieuses dans l'Allemagne protestante à l'époque moderne', *Revue d'histoire moderne et contemporaine*, 37 (1990), pp. 624–41; R. Bornert, *La Réforme protestante du culte à Strasbourg au XVIe siècle (1523–1598)* (Leiden: Brill, 1981), p. 179.

[172] This situation is comparable to the case of the Company of Stationers of London, whose sixteenth-century records include many broadsheet publications of which there are no known extant copies.

[173] Bornert (*Réforme protestante du culte*, p. 179) calls them 'means of propaganda' in their own right.

average common man or woman did not read music.[174] Why then, were congregational hymns and psalms so often printed with music? Although we do not know exactly who bought hymn books in the early Reformation, the fact that they were produced time and time again with music indicates that they were popular purchases. Any printer would have realised that the cost of printing a book with music would only have been worthwhile if a profit could be made on it. Apart from those who may have collected hymn books as objects of prestige, there would also have been people who bought them for their intended purpose. This suggests that there were educated, but essentially musically 'illiterate', people who were willing to learn to read music, or at least to match the tune which they heard to the assortment of black lines and dots on the page in front of them. We must assume, then, that of those who had not received formal training in music, a considerable number were nonetheless able to develop a basic understanding of the semantics involved so as to be able to judge the pitch contours of a tune with enough accuracy to be able to sing in a group, under the natural leadership of a more confident music reader.

The reformers would have preferred that people sang only songs based on Holy Scripture.[175] Bucer wrote in the Tetrapolitan Confession that songs that are not based on Scripture are 'disobliging to God, and horrible'.[176] Accordingly, the songs printed in the liturgical orders and hymn books of Strasbourg are, in the vast majority of cases, biblical canticles or the Psalms.[177] However, some were more loosely based on Scripture (such as paraphrases of biblical passages), others were translations of Latin liturgical hymns (especially in the later years of reform), and some were completely new poetic creations.[178] In all cases, however, these songs were considered primarily to be prayers, and for that reason alone they were deemed more suitable than the popular songs normally sung by the common people.[179] As observed by Patrice Veit, Luther believed that

174 Rebecca Wagner Oettinger writes: 'If at best 30 per cent of an urban audience could read the text, certainly even fewer could read music … Except for professional musicians, then, musical literacy appears to have been limited to those with a basic education, and depending on the schools they attended, many of these probably never learned to read musical notation'. *MPGR*, pp. 27–8.

175 Bornert confirms that the reformers sometimes used spiritual songs as 'instruments of competition' in the fight against popular songs. Bornert, *Réforme protestante du culte*, p. 179.

176 'Zum dritten, das man auch aus sollichem gesanng vnnd gepett, wie vnschrifftlich es vnnd desshalben Gott vngefölig, ja abscheichlich ist'. Bucer et al., *Confessio Tetrapolitana*, in *BDS*, 3, p. 149. See Chapter 3, pp. 117–18.

177 See S. J. Lenselink's convincing attempt to trace the origin of some of the early Strasbourg psalm texts from Luther's *Psalter teutsch* (Strasbourg: Knobloch, 1524) (S. J. Lenselink, *De Nederlandse psalmberijmingen in de 16e eeuw van de Souterliedekens tot Datheen met hun voorgangers in Duitsland en Frankrijk* (Assen: Van Gorcum, 1959), pp. 108–12).

178 Bornert, *Réforme protestante du culte*, p. 473.

179 Veit, *Kirchenlied in der Reformation*, p. 62.

Table 4.2 German songs of a religious nature in Strasbourg not directly from the Bible and not from the Mass Ordinary* (1524–1540). Most of the texts of these songs are given in Appendix D

Author and song title	First published in Strasbourg	First published elsewhere (if earlier)
M. Luther, 'Gott sey gelobet vnd gebenedeiet'	*Ordenung vnd yn[n]halt Teütscher Mess vn[nd] Vesper* (3rd edn) (Köpfel, 1524) Later published with music in:	–
S. Pollio (?), 'Jesus der hat vns zugeseit'[a]	*Teutsch Kirche[n] ampt mit lobgsengen / vn[nd] gotlichen psalmen* (Köpfel, 1524)	–
M. Luther, 'Nu bitten wir den heiligen Geist'	*Teutsch Kirche[n] ampt mit lobgsengen / vn[nd] goͤtlichen psalmen* (Köpfel, 1524)	*Geystliche gesangk Buchleyn* (Wittenberg, 1524)
Anon., 'Vatter vnser der du bist / im himel zů ewiger frist'	*Ein schoner kurtzer begriff des vatter vnsers Vn[nd] Aue Maria / Glauben / Zehe[n] gebotte[n]* (Schwan, 1525)	[Unknown][b]
Anon., 'Du meinsch d[omi]ne vnd auch Aue Maria bist genennet'	*Ein schoner kurtzer begriff des vatter vnsers Vn[nd] Aue Maria / Glauben / Zehe[n] gebotte[n]* (Schwan, 1525)	[Unknown][b]
S. Pollio, 'Vatter vnser, wir bitten dich'	*Das ander theyl. Straßburger kirchengesang* (Köpfel, 1525)	–
S. Heyden, 'Salue Jesu Christe'	*Das der | eynig Christus vnser mitler vn[nd] für | sprech sy by dem vatter / nitt sin | muter / noch die heyligen. Da- | rumb nun Christo / vnd nit siner | můter / das in dem gsang so SAL | VE REGINA anfacht / gesungen soll werden* (Knobloch, 1525)	–[b]
P. Speratus: 'Es ist das heyl vns kommen her'	*Die zween Psalmen* (Köpfel, 1527)	*Etlich Christlich lider* (Nuremberg, 1523)
Anon., 'Das Te Deum laudamus verteütscht'	*Das Te Deum laudamus verteütscht* (Köpfel, 1529)	[Unknown][c]
J. Brenz, 'Te Deum'	*Psalmen gebett / vnd kirchen ůbung* (Köpfel, 1530)	*Deůtzsch kirche[n] ampt* (Alstedt, 1524)[d]

Author and song title	First published in Strasbourg	First published elsewhere (if earlier)
W. Gernoldt, 'Das Aue Maria außgeleyt'	*Das Aue Maria außgeleyt* (Frölich, 1540)	–[e]
H. Sachs, 'Jm Richter bůch das sechzehend sagt'	*Drey Schőne Meyster Lieder* (Frölich, 1540)	–[f]
H. Sachs, 'Lucas im ersten Capitel sagt'	*Drey Schőne Meyster Lieder* (Frölich, 1540)	–[f]
H. Sachs, 'Das sibend im andern Machabeorum sagt'	*Drey Schőne Meyster Lieder* (Frölich, 1540)	–[f]

* For a discussion of the early musical settings of the Ordinary of the Mass in Strasbourg's Reformation, see Bornert, *Réforme protestante du culte*, pp. 477–9.

a. Wackernagel implies that this hymn was by Pollio (despite the fact that it is often attributed to Luther), by placing it among other hymns ascribed to Pollio. See *Wackernagel DKL*, vol. 3, no. 564, p. 681. I am grateful to Robin Leaver for this observation.

b. Not listed in *DKL* III, vol. 1, or in *Wackernagel DKL*.

c. Not listed in *DKL* III, vol. 1. As this publication is now lost, we cannot be certain which text was used, and so locating it in *Wackernagel DKL* has proven impossible. The publication also contained a versified translation of Psalm 46 by Johannes Frolsch, which *is* reproduced in *Wackernagel DKL*, vol. 3, no. 802, pp. 695–6.

d. According to *DKL* III, vol. 1, part 2 (text), p. 50.

e. Not listed in *DKL* III, vol. 1, or in *Wackernagel DKL*. Dated 1540 on USTC (www.ustc.ac.uk) (accessed 16 March 2014).

f. Not listed in *DKL* III, vol. 1, or in *Wackernagel DKL*. The boundary between popular devotional songs and liturgical songs can sometimes be difficult to draw. Sachs's three songs would almost certainly never have been sung in church. They are listed here as interesting examples of the extent to which some popular songwriters drew on Scripture. See also Appendix E.

the sung word influenced the affect rather than the intellect of a person, and this view was shared by the Strasbourg reformers.[180]

Several of these songs were printed many times over the years, alongside the psalm tunes. The most successful of these, both then and now, was probably

180 Ibid., p. 28. See *WA*, 4, p. 140. The importance of the religious song texts of the German Reformation is discussed in detail in Veit, *Kirchenlied in der Reformation*. The subject also receives some treatment in Veit 'Le chant, la Réforme et la Bible', in G. Bedouelle and B. Roussel, eds, *Le temps des Réformes et la Bible* (Paris: Beauchesne, 1989), pp. 659–81, and in S. C. Karant-Nunn, *The Reformation of Feeling: Shaping the Religious Emotions in Early Modern Germany* (Oxford: Oxford University Press, 2010), pp. 81–2.

Luther's 'Gott sey gelobet'. Table 4.2 shows that it was printed in one of the first German orders of service in the city, *Ordenung vnd yn[n]halt Teütscher Mess vn[nd] Vesper*, a book that contained the texts of songs without music. 'Gott sey gelobet' is the only song provided within the order of service for the Mass. In the order of Vespers, six songs are printed ('Jesus der hat vns zugeseit', four psalms, and the *Magnificat*). The presence of Luther's texts in the book is overwhelming, all songs being by the reformer except the setting of the *Magnificat*, which is by Symphorianus Pollio. Interestingly, the lack of musical notation suggests that users of this book were already expected to know the songs and their melodies; this book just served as a visual aid for the words.

According to Wackernagel,[181] 'Gott sey gelobet' was first published in the Erfurt *Enchiridion* of 1524. However, as the *Enchiridion* was compiled from songs circulating on broadsheets at the time,[182] the song must already have been travelling around Germany by the time it was bound in book form. As mentioned in the previous chapter, Hubert suggests that in the 1524 *Ordenung*, 'Gott sey gelobet' was spoken rather than sung.[183] However, being a liturgical book of hymns and psalms, the likelihood that any of these were spoken rather than sung seems far-fetched. There would be no reason for a congregation to speak the words to a hymn when there was an existing tune in common usage.[184]

Another of Luther's folk song adaptations was published in Strasbourg in 1524, as part of the *Teutsch kirche[n] ampt mit lobgsengen*: 'Nu bitten wir den heiligen Geist'. This song appeared alongside the same songs by Luther and Pollio that had been printed in the 1524 *Ordenung*, with the exception of 'Gott sey gelobet', but with an extra setting of Psalm 12 by Matthias Greiter.[185] It was originally printed in Walter's *Chorgesangbuch* of 1524. Johann Brenz's setting of the *Te Deum* at the end of the 1530 *Psalmen gebett* may well have been the version published three years earlier in *Das Te Deum laudamus verteütscht*. However, the 1527 version is lost, so there is now no way of being sure.

Paulus Speratus's 'Es ist das heyl' (on which the contrafactum 'Es ist die warheyt' was based[186]) first appeared in 1523 in a Nuremberg publication, but was not sung in Strasbourg until 1527, when it was published alongside 'Nu bitten wir' and three psalms in *Die zween Psalmen*. The last two verses of 'Es ist das heyl' incorporate the Lord's Prayer (the version found in Luke 11:2–4). Indeed, it was not uncommon to find the Lord's Prayer in song, even

[181] Wackernagel, *Das deutsche Kirchenlied von Martin Luther bis auf Nicolaus Herman und Ambrosius Plaurer* (Stuttgart: Liesching, 1841), p. 134.

[182] R. A. Leaver, *Luther's Liturgical Music*, p. 19, n. 69.

[183] *Hubert*, p. LXVII.

[184] The hymn was also an adaptation of a pre-existing popular devotional song, and so provides an interesting link between popular and religious music.

[185] This was Greiter's first published Protestant psalm setting, according to the data in *Hubert*, p. XIII.

[186] See pp. 180–83.

if not in a directly translated form. Pollio's 'Vatter vnser', for example, is an expansion of the Lord's Prayer, closely based on the original, but set over three verses. It appeared for the first time in the second volume of the 1525 *Theutsch kirchenampt*.

The anonymous setting of the Lord's Prayer that was published in *Ein schoner kurtzer begriff* is similarly an expansion of the version in Luke's Gospel.[187] In this case, the author uses a line of the original text as the first line of each of the song's eight verses. A refrain, 'Lobt den herren', features at the end of each verse. The only time the pattern is disrupted is in verse 6, where 'Lord, forgive us our faults' is followed by the non-scriptural 'Grant us your favour', which then reverts to the next line of the prayer, 'So that we might forgive (and forget) that which has been done against us'.[188] The final verse asks God to keep us 'from evil in the Valley of Death' (*Yamertal*), which is probably the closest the author was able to get to the word '*Jammertag*', meaning the Day of Judgement. Settings such as these are of interest because they expound upon one of the most fundamental Christian texts. Indeed, songs based on the Lord's Prayer remained popular choices for printers throughout the next decade.[189] Verse and rhyme enabled the reader, singer, or listener to remember the text more clearly than they otherwise might. They also provided a small expansion on the meaning of the text.

The second song in *Ein schoner kurtzer begriff*, however, is evidence that this pamphlet was not officially sanctioned. It is presented as a German setting of the *Ave Maria*, but much like the Lord's Prayer it is in fact a modified version of the text which was, and still is, used in the Roman Catholic Church to recite the Rosary.[190] Two of the phrases used in the *Ave Maria* also originate in Luke's Gospel: the opening five lines are based on Luke 1:28 and Luke 1:42. This version, however, is a three-verse song bearing very little resemblance to the

187 The copy kept in the Koninklijke Bibliotheek in the Hague contains a handwritten note directing the reader to sing this setting 'to the melody of *Christ ist erstanden*' (*vff die melody christ ist e[r]sta[n]d[en]*). *Ein schoner kurtzer begriff* (1525), fol. Aij^r^.

188 'Herr vergib vnns vnser schuld / verleych vns dein goͤttliche huld / das wir verzeihe[n] vn[n]d ablon / was wider vns der nechst hat thon / Lob den herren'. *Ein schoner kurtzer begriff* (1525), fol. Aii^r^.

189 *Psalme[n] vnnd geystliche Lieder* (Köpfel, 1537), for example, contained four settings of the Lord's Prayer (nos 562, 949, 592, and 670 in *Wackernagel DKL*, vol. 3).

190 The English version in use today reads as follows: 'Hail Mary, Full of Grace, The Lord is with thee. Blessed art thou among women, and blessed is the fruit of thy womb, Jesus. Holy Mary, Mother of God, pray for us sinners now, and at the hour of death. Amen'.

Ave Maria.[191] It is not as structured as the expanded Lord's Prayer, instead seeming to be a more-or-less original composition.[192]

What is it about these songs that meant those compiling the early Strasbourg liturgies were willing to print some of them alongside the Psalms and scriptural canticles? In other words, why were they deemed acceptable? The 1541 *Gesangbuch* did not contain all these songs, but by this stage other songs had been added instead. 'Jesus der hat vns zugeseit' did not make it into this volume, nor did Pollio's 'Vatter unser', which was replaced by two (more faithful to the original) settings of the Lord's Prayer. Despite the fact that the *Te Deum* was printed in the *Gesangbuch*, the version used in 1541 is that by Luther. Although the decision to include these texts in the early liturgies would often have been taken by printers rather than by theologians, the reformers would nevertheless have deemed them suitable for Christian reformed worship. 'Gott sey gelobet' appeared early on and was reprinted in many hymn books and liturgical orders in Strasbourg. It is a hymn of thanksgiving and praise to God, who 'has fed us with his body and with his blood'.[193] It reminds the listener or singer of the sacrifice made by Jesus, and asks God for his blessing and mercy. In the last verse it also calls for the peace and unity of the Church. It is essentially a post-Communion prayer, with similarities to those used in many churches today. Rather surprisingly, the reference to being fed with Christ's body and blood, hinting at the notion of real presence, does not seem to have presented a problem for the Strasbourg reformers, who continued to use this hymn throughout the 1520s and 1530s.

'Jesus der hat vns zugeseit' appears not to have been printed in Strasbourg after 1525, having appeared in the order for Vespers in the 1524 *Ordenung* and in the three editions of the *Teutsch Kirchenampt*, under the title 'Antiphona'. The layout of the piece does not make it clear how antiphonal singing was to be employed, but in any case, antiphony is unlikely to have taken place in the Strasbourg Protestant service as early as 1524 or 1525. 'Nu bitten wir' asks God for faith, light, grace, and comfort. It may simply have been incorporated into the service because it was useful for reminding the community of the virtues of God and of the virtues of praying.

It is remarkable that the reformers chose not to set the Lord's Prayer to music earlier on. Although the Lord's Prayer was obviously being spoken in the early German services in Strasbourg, there may have been the deliberate intention to introduce Pollio's 'Vatter unser' as a sung alternative (albeit significantly more

---

[191] Another versified version of the *Ave Maria* was published by Frölich around 1540: W. Gernoldt, *Das Aue Maria außgeleyt* (see Table 4.2). It is a miniature book containing eight folios, clearly designed to be carried in one's pocket. But it contains neither music, nor any indication to which tune it might be sung. Each verse is an expounding of one word from the Latin angelic salutation: *Ave* ... *Gratia* ... *Plena* ... *Dominus* ... *Tecum* ... *Benedicta* ... *Tua* ... *In mulieribus* ... *Et benedictus* ... *O fructus* ... *Ventris* ... *Tui*. See Appendix D.

[192] It has, however, been omitted from *DKL* III, vol. 1.

[193] 'der vns selber hat gespeiset | Mit seinem fleische vnd mit seinem blute'.

lengthy). Speratus's hymn, 'Es ist das hayl', at 14 verses, is relatively long for a liturgical song. It doesn't openly criticise the Roman Church, of course, but it carries the message of the Reformation unashamedly, reminding us in the opening lines that 'Salvation has come to us from grace and sheer kindness. Works never help – they cannot protect us'.[194] The hymn's theology is Lutheran, with justification by faith alone being emphasised time and time again. It also tells of the wrath and distress that arose because of people's inability to keep God's commandments, and of temptations of the flesh. The final verse is a paraphrase of the Lord's Prayer (the version found in Luke 11:2–4). Finally, the *Te Deum*, although not a scriptural canticle, was nevertheless based on the Apostles' Creed, a text traditionally said to have been written by Saints Ambrose and Augustine in the year 387, and so of particular importance.

Most of these songs would not have been deemed unsuitable by Bucer, especially as time went on. During the 1530s, as demonstrated in Chapter 3, the repertory of Strasbourg hymns expanded considerably, as closer alliances were made with the Lutheran reformers. The number of non-scriptural texts employed in church songs underwent a dramatic increase, although the singing of the Psalms remained an important aspect of the Strasbourg church service. In Bucer's preface to the 1541 *Gesangbuch*, the Strasbourg reformer pours praise over Luther for the great work he has achieved in writing songs for the Church. Bucer believed that the songs in the *Gesangbuch* were inspired by the Holy Spirit, and so were completely acceptable for singing in church. Moreover, for Bucer, church songs were not meant to be limited to liturgical use. They were designed to be memorised easily, so that even the illiterate could sing them at home. The Psalmist sang praises to God in many different places, and this was something that the reformers wanted to emulate in Strasbourg.

* * *

Although the reformers would have deemed certain popular songs a hindrance to the progress of the Reformation, propagandistic songs would have been for many people, particularly the illiterate, the principal means by which they learnt about church reform. But, however officially opposed to slanderous songs the Strasbourg reformers tried to be, there must have been some comfort among them that part of their work was being done for them by zealous printers all over Europe.

The Strasbourg reformers (and in particular Martin Bucer), however, made different uses of the print medium, namely to continue their diplomatic efforts at reform. The following chapter explores the influence on Strasbourg from elsewhere, as well as the influence it had on other parts of Europe.

194 'Es ist das hayl vns kummen her | von gnad vnnd lauter gůten; | die werck helffen nymmer mer, sie můgen nicht behůten'.

CHAPTER 5

The 1541 *Gesangbuch* and Strasbourg's External Influence

The year 1541 is widely considered to have been Strasbourg's peak in terms of a formulation of a coherent approach to music in relation to reform. This chapter seeks to chart the development of this policy and the way in which it was expressed in the 1541 *Gesangbuch*, and will explore the influence Strasbourg had on church music in other parts of Europe, including England and Geneva.

The *Gesangbuch*

In 1541, Wolfgang Köpfel, in collaboration with Paul Messerschmidt, produced a 196-page music book in 2°, with red and black lettering. This was the first edition of the monumental Strasbourg *Gesangbuch*. The title page translates as follows:

> Songbook, containing all the noblest and best psalms, spiritual songs, and choral songs, brought together from the little songbooks of Wittenberg, Strasbourg, and other churches, and corrected and printed with particular care. For municipal and rural churches, and Latin and German schools.[1]

There are several striking aspects to this title. The most remarkable is perhaps the reference to 'psalms, spiritual songs, and choir singing' (*Chorgeseng*). What reason did the Strasbourg reformers now have, after so many years of rejecting liturgical choir singing, to publish a book apparently containing choir pieces? In this case, in fact, 'Chorgeseng' does not refer to performances by professional singers, but simply songs sung by a group of people, possibly in an antiphonal style (see Example 5.1). Indeed, apart from the occasional florid 'Hallelujah',

1 *Gesangbuch / darinn | begriffen sind / die aller | fuͤrnemisten vnd besten | Psalmen / Geistliche Lieder / vnd | Chorgeseng / aus dem Wittem- | bergischen / Strasburgischen / vnd anderer | Kirchen Gesangbuͦchlin zuͦsamen | bracht / vnd mit besonderem | fleis corrigiert vnd gedrucket. | Fuͤr Stett vnd Dorff Kirchen / | Lateinische vnd Deudsche | Schuͦlen* (Strasbourg: Köpfel & Messerschmidt, 1541). Two original examples are known, one in the Bibliothek der evangelischen Stadtkirche in Isny, Württemberg, and the other in the Erzbischöfliche Akademische Bibliothek, Paderborn. Two further editions appeared in 1560 and in 1572. A facsimile of the 1541 edition was produced in Stuttgart in 1953. A free PDF download is available on Google Books.

Example 5.1 'Veni sancte Spiritus' as it appeared in the *Gesangbuch* (1541), transcribed into modern notation

'Amen', or other melismatic final word of a phrase,[2] the songs in this volume are generally written in a one-note-per-syllable fashion, as would be expected from a vernacular congregational songbook. The most notable exceptions to this rule include Luther's translation of the *Te Deum laudamus*,[3] a setting by Luther of the hymn *Veni sancte Spiritus*, a German version of the Nicene Creed (or 'Das Deutsche Patrem', as it is called here),[4] and an 'improved' version by Luther of 'Jesus Christus vnser Heiland',[5] a song said to be originally by 'S[anct]' Jan Hus (a medieval Czech priest whose scholarship and example influenced many of the reformers, including the Bohemian Brethren; the designation of 'Saint' here is honorific (from a Protestant perspective); Hus was burned at the stake by the Church for heresy in 1415[6]). This is in reference to a Latin hymn, 'Jesus Christus nostra salus', attributed to Hus. In all cases, the text is in German, and in the case of the *Te Deum*, the music is closely based on plainchant (see Example 5.2). Also, the music of the Creed is based on a metrical German version dating from the turn of the fifteenth and sixteenth centuries, and Konrad Ameln has commented upon its descent from plainchant.[7]

The second interesting aspect about the title is that it claims to be a compilation of the best music from the churches of Wittenberg, Strasbourg, and elsewhere. The fact that Wittenberg is mentioned first is significant; it is a nod towards the authority of Luther and towards the fact that Strasbourg had fallen in line with the Lutheran reforms over the previous decade. However, as far as can be told, Luther had no direct involvement with the preparation of this edition. Also significant is the lack of any mention whatsoever of the Swiss or South German churches, such as Memmingen, Lindau, and Constance, which had been allied with Strasbourg just a decade earlier at the time of the Tetrapolitan Confession.

Third is the fact that the songs have been collected and printed 'with particular care' (*mit besonderem fleis*). This was not an especially unusual turn of phrase

---

2 Théodore Gérold commented that it was popular in Strasbourg to end a piece or phrase with a 'little vocalise'. See T. Gérold, *Les plus anciennes mélodies de l'Eglise protestante de Strasbourg et leurs auteurs* (Paris: Alcan, 1928), p. 73. All the Strasbourg melodies printed between 1524 and 1547 can be found in C. Meyer, *Les mélodies des églises protestantes de langue allemande – Catalogue descriptif des sources et édition critique des mélodies : I. Les mélodies publiées à Strasbourg (1524–1547)* (Baden-Baden and Bouxwiller: Koerner, 1987).

3 See Example 5.2.

4 This was first published in Johann Walter's *Geystliche gesangk Buchleyn* (Wittenberg: Klug, 1524) (see K. Ameln, ed., *Handbuch der deutschen evangelischen Kirchenmusik* (Göttingen: Vandenhoeck & Ruprecht, 1933–38), vol. 1: *Der Altargesang*, part 1, p. 50).

5 'JEsus Christus vnser Heiland / der von vns den Gottes zorn wand / Durch das bitter leiden sein / half er vns aus der hellen pein …'. *Gesangbuch*, pp. XXVI–XXVII. The song first appeared in this form in 1524, in at least three different publications. See *LW*, 53, pp. 249–51; and A. B. Mullinax, 'Martin Bucer and the "Strasbourg Song Book", 1541' (Master of Church Music diss., Southern Baptist Theological Seminary, 1985), p. 103.

6 See M. Spinka, *John Hus: A Biography* (Princeton: Princeton University Press, 1968).

7 Ameln, *The Roots of German Hymnody of the Reformation Era* (St Louis: Concordia, 1964), p. 7.

Example 5.2 Luther's 'Te Deum' from the *Gesangbuch* (1541), fols. A[r]–E[r], in modern notation. Taken from Ameln, *Handbuch der deutschen evangelischen Kirchenmusik*, vol. 1: *Der Altargesang*, part 1, pp. 407–8. Note: The antiphonal singing of this piece is an editorial suggestion by Ameln, a practice that probably would not have occurred in Strasbourg at this time

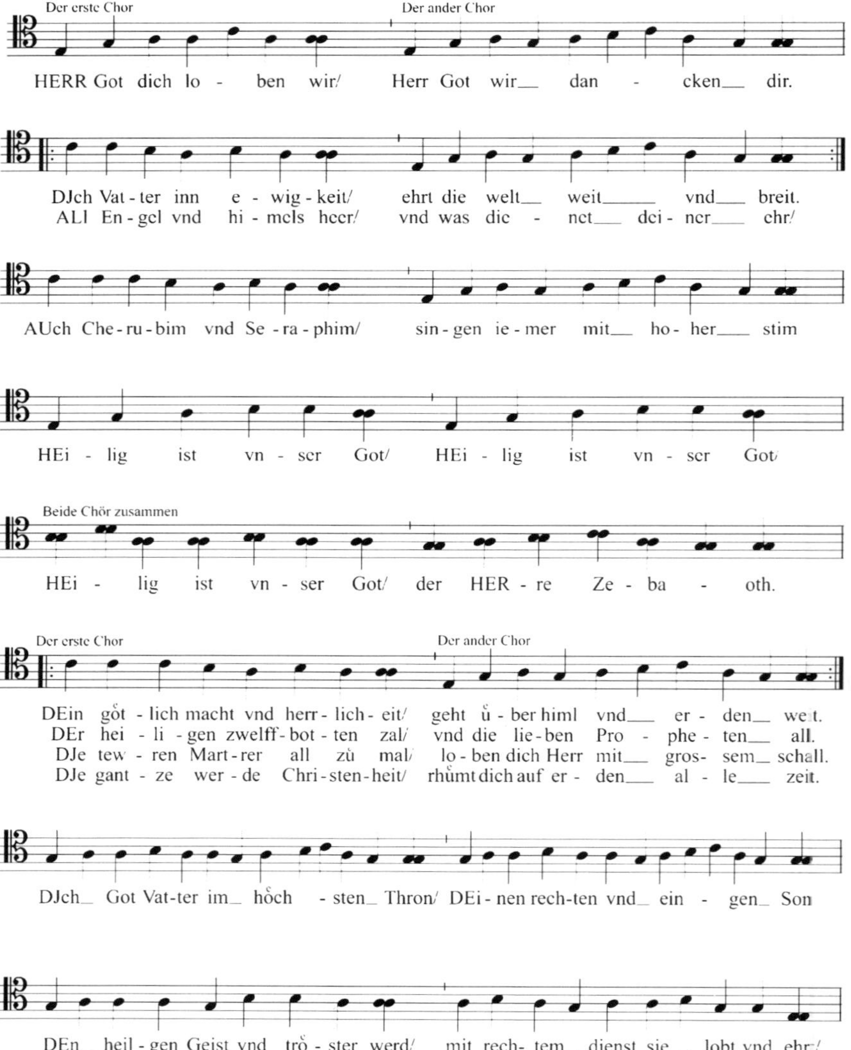

DU Kő̈ng der eh - ren Je - su Christ/ Got Vat - ters Ew - ger Son du bist/
DEr iung - frawn leib nicht hast ver - schmecht/ zur - lő - sen das mensch - lich ge - schlecht/
DU hast dem tod zer - stőrt sein macht/ vnd all Chri - sten zum hi - mel bracht
DU sitzst zur rech - ten Got - tes gleich/ mit al - ler ehr ins Vat - ters reich/
EJn rich - ter du zů kűnf tig bist/ al - les das tod vnd le - bend ist/
Be☐le Chör zusammen
NL N hilff vns Herr den die - nern dein/ die mit deim tewrn blůt er - lő - set seind/
Der erste Chor
Der ander Chor
LA☐ss vns im hi - mel ha - ben teil/ mit den Heil - gen inn ew - gem heil/
H☐ff dei - nem volck Herr Je - su Christ/ vnd seg - ne das dein erb - teil ist/
WArt vnd pfleg ihr zů al - ler zeit/ vnd heb sie hoch inn e - wig - keit/
T☐g - lich Herr Got wir lo - ben dich/ vnd ehrn dein na - men ste - tig - lich/
BE - hűt vns heut o trew - er Got/ fűr al - ler sűnd vnd mis - se - that/
SEi vns gne - dig o Her - re Got/ sei vns gne - dig inn al - ler not/
ZEig vns dei - ne barm - hert - zig - keit/ wie vn - ser hof - fen zů dir steht/
Beide Chör zusammen
A☐f dich hof - fen wir lie - ber Herr/
n schan - den lass vns ni - mer - mehr/ A - men.

used to describe hymn books:[8] in his preface to that of the Bohemian Brethren (1531), Michael Weisse described the book as having been produced 'with great care' (*mit allem fleiß*);[9] in his preface to the *Chorgesangbuch*, a version of which appeared in Strasbourg in 1534, Walter wrote that his songs had been 'diligently corrected and improved' (*mit fleis corrigirt vnd gebessert*);[10] in 1538 Kōpfel referred to the way in which the psalms and hymns had been compiled 'with the highest diligence' (*mit hochstem fleiß*);[11] and in 1545 Luther commented in his preface to Valentin Babst's songbook[12] that the printers 'print good songs diligently, and with various decorations' (*sie gute lieder vleissig drucken / vnd mit allerley zierde*).[13] Indeed, on seeing the Strasbourg *Gesangbuch*, one is particularly inclined to agree with the statement here. It was larger than any other book of its kind to be published in Strasbourg since the beginning of the Reformation. It contains 196 pages, and its dimensions are 33cm × 48.5cm (2°). The text is unusually large, as are the musical systems. Both red and black ink is used: red for page numbers, the titles of songs, names of composers, verse numbers, decorated first letters of verses, and staves; and black for other text, note heads, clefs, barlines, woodcuts, and other decorations. The main woodcut, which is repeated at the beginning of each section of the book, contains the Father, Son, and Holy Spirit (as a dove) in the middle, surrounded by choirs of angels to both sides. One choir is holding a sheet containing the music for the *Gloria in excelsis Deo*, and the other has the music of Luther's German *Te Deum*, 'Her Got dich lobe[n] wir'. Both these scores appear upside down to the reader, being held from above by the angels. On the left of the image stands King David, playing the harp (standing above the Hebrew text of Psalm 146:1–2[14]), and on the right St Paul carrying a sword and a book (standing above the Greek text of an extract from Ephesians 5:18–19[15]). In the centre of the woodcut is a blank space in which the song title appears.[16]

Finally, it should be observed that the makers of this book were trying their best to reach as wide an audience as possible, not only by advertising its contents

---

8 This kind of phrase was also extremely common in other European printed material at this time, and is likely to have been used as marketing ploy by printers, especially when it appeared in title pages or in dedications. I am grateful to Iain Fenlon for this observation.

9 *Ein New Geseng buchlen* (Bohemia: Buntzel & Wylmschwerer, 1531), fol. N XI^{v}. Quoted in A. Wolff, 'Le recueil de cantiques de Catherine Zell 1534–1536', 2 vols (Master's diss., Université des Sciences Humaines de Strasbourg, 1986), vol. 1, p. 12.

10 *Wittenbergische Gsangbüchli* (Strasbourg: Schöffer & Apiarius, 1534), tenor partbook, fol. A iij^{r}.

11 *Psalter. Das seindt alle Psalmen Dauids* (1538), fol. ii^{r}; *Hubert*, p. 144.

12 *Geystliche Lieder. Mit einer newen vorrhede / D. Mart. Luth* (Leipzig: Bapst, 1545).

13 *Geystliche Lieder*, fol. A3^{v}. *WA*, 35, p. 304.

14 'Praise the Lord. Praise the Lord, my soul. I will praise the Lord all my life; I will sing praise to my God as long as I live'.

15 'Be filled with the Spirit, speaking to one another with psalms, hymns, and songs from the Spirit'.

16 A detailed bibliographical description of the *Gesangbuch* can be found in F. Hubert, 'Martin Butzers Großes Gesangbuch', *Monatschrift für Gottesdienst und kirchliche Kunst*, 3 (1898), p. 54.

as coming from a variety of sources (Wittenberg, Strasbourg, and elsewhere), but also by promoting the fact that the songs therein were suitable not only for urban churches, but also for rural parishes, as well as for musical training at both Latin schools and German schools.[17] The scriptural passages within the woodcut in Hebrew and Greek were part of this appeal to the educated. In other words there is no one, they claimed, who would not benefit from this book. However, the prospect of rural parishes singing some of the songs contained in the *Gesangbuch* is unlikely; they would not have had the vocal resources to sing anything other than the simplest and most familiar hymns and psalms, and no doubt in many cases would not have had the financial means to pay for such a grand and ornate book.

After the title page there is a two-sided folio of scriptural references to singing. Here, there are no surprises: 1 Corinthians 14 (vv. 12, 15, 26), Colossians 3 (vv. 15–17), and Ephesians 5 (vv. 19–20). The excerpts from Corinthians and Ephesians contain '&c'. symbols, indicating to the reader the incompleteness of these excerpts, and encouraging them to seek out and read the remainder of the chapters in question. This is the same technique that had been used in Köpfel's first preface in *Psalmen gebett* (1526, 1530, and 1533).[18] The three scriptural passages are preceded by this introduction:

> To sing psalms, songs of praise, and spiritual songs in the congregation of God is good, edifying, and pleasant to God; Alongside the examples of the dear prophets and kings in the Old Testament, St Paul also used and cultivated these in the New Testament, namely … [19]

The *Gesangbuch* is widely thought to have been an official publication, owing to the presence of Bucer's endorsement of the book in the form of a lengthy preface – his most important writing on music. In it, Bucer referred to music as 'this wonderful art and gift of God'.[20] Much of the preface acted as an expansion of the points made on the title page, but Bucer also made more fundamental points about the use and purpose of such songs.

His first step was to link the modern-day practice of psalm singing to the singing of praise to God 'from the beginning' (*von anfang*) of time, and the effect that this activity had on singers and listeners. He also discussed the

---

[17] Allen Bruce Mullinax believes that the large format of the book suggests that several people, perhaps children, sang from the score at the same time. See Mullinax, 'Bucer and the "Strasbourg Song Book"', p. 6. The large-scale choir book was a medieval practice which was emulated by some Lutheran parishes.

[18] See Chapters 2 and 3.

[19] 'Psalmen / Lobsenge / vnd Geistliche lieder in der Gemein Gotes singen / ist gut / auf bewlich / vnd Got angenem / Welches / neben den Exempelen der lieben Propheten vnd Ko̊nigen / im alten Testament / auch der heilig Paulus / im newen Testament einsetzet vnd gebeut / namlich …'.

[20] 'dise herrliche kunst vnd gabe Gottes' (Appendix H, p. 344). *Gesangbuch* (1541), fol. A3r; *BDS*, 7, p. 579. This and subsequent translations of Bucer's 1541 preface are from *Garside*, pp. 29–31.

power of music, which was followed by his criticism of secular songs and a strong warning to parents to educate their children in sacred song. After this admonition followed a commendation of the contents of the book, and Bucer acknowledged Luther's contribution[21] and thanked the printer, Messerschmidt, for his role in printing the book, which was produced

> with no little cost and trouble. He bent every effort, as the work itself shows, with the result that the Psalms and spiritual songs included herein might be published as clearly as possible and corrected to the best of knowledge.[22]

Bucer then explained the importance of singing these 'beautiful Christian songs' (*schöne christliche Geseng*) in church, explaining that the practice of congregational singing had been adopted in Strasbourg and in many other places, with songs published 'in little books which each Christian uses individually in [c]hurches and elsewhere'.[23] Here is confirmation that members of the congregation were expected to have their own hymn books – for use both inside and outside church. Bucer wrote that such books are particularly suitable 'for the young, so that they might better ... keep the measured and unison song in the sacred congregations',[24] affirming the continued use of children to lead the singing in Strasbourg worship.[25]

The notion of 'improvement' was a frequent feature of this preface. The first two paragraphs do not mention it specifically, but the point was made that pious and faithful singers had 'always desired right earnestly to bring their godly attitude into the hearts of others'.[26] Further on, he reiterated his commitment to education of the young, by stating that song, as well as instrumental music (*seitenspil*), should only be used for 'sacred praise, prayer, teaching, and admonition'.[27] Such 'holy, sacred songs', he continued, made us 'noticeably

---

[21] There are more songs by Luther in this volume than by anyone else.

[22] 'nicht mit geringem kosten vn[nd] mu̇h … auch allen fleis an zů wenden / wie es das werck selb zeuget / das die Psalmen vnd geistliche Lieder / so hierin begriffen / auffs seuberlichest / vnd zům besten corrigieret ausgiengen' (Appendix H, p. 346). *Gesangbuch* (1541), fol. A3v; *BDS*, 7, p. 580.

[23] 'inn handbu̇chlin / welche die Christen / jeder fu̇r sich selb inn den Kirchen versamlungen vnd sunst gebrauchen' (Appendix H, p. 345). *Gesangbuch* (1541), fol. A3v; *BDS*, 7, p. 580.

[24] 'fu̇r Juget / sie desto bas zů gleichfȯrmigem mensurischem gesang zů gewehnen vnd anzůhalten / inn den heiligen Versamlungen' (Appendix H, p. 345). *Gesangbuch* (1541), fol. A3v; *BDS*, 7, p. 580.

[25] See Chapter 3, pp. 150–54.

[26] 'auch allemal recht ernstlich begeret / jr gȯtlichs fu̇rhaben / anderen zů hertzen zů fu̇ren' (Appendix H, p. 342). *Gesangbuch* (1541), fol. A3r; *BDS*, 7, p. 578.

[27] 'So solte die Music / alles gesang vnd seitenspil … nirgend anders / dann zů gȯtlichem lob / gebet / lehre vnd ermanung gebrauchet werden' (Appendix H, p. 343). *Gesangbuch* (1541), fol. A3r; *BDS*, 7, p. 578.

better', whereas lascivious, devilish songs stirred up all sorts of unpleasantness, especially in the young.[28] This was followed by a stark and merciless warning:

> And woe to all who see and hear in this description their children, household, and whomsoever they must protect. But here one sees, sadly, what sort of Christians these people are, and (as the proverb has it) every bird will be known by his song, and the word of the Lord will be fulfilled: with whatever the heart is full, the mouth comes forth.[29]

At the end of the preface, Bucer reminded his readers:

> Woe to us if we do not wake up, if we do not look more deeply into ourselves, and become more zealous in Christian action.
>
> Therefore fathers and mothers should remember to whom they have given and offered their children in baptism … And since this age has a preference for singing, and wishes to be led to the good in joyful ways, they should turn their efforts toward teaching the children such holy, sacred songs faithfully, and accustoming them to sing the same.[30]

The language here is strong, and reminiscent of some of Bucer's comments in the 1520s about insincere singing of the Mass, most notably those of *Der predicanten verantwortten*,[31] in which he argued that singing is devilish, and a mockery of God, unless it was done 'for the improvement of the community of God', and came 'from the Spirit of God'.[32] It was also surely influenced by Luther's preface to Walter's *Chorgesangbuch*, in which the reformer expressed

28 'heiligen / goͤtlichen Liedern … sie vns mercklich besserten … Daher es auch erschroͤcklich ist zů gedencken / was ergernis / bei der juget vnd anderen / durch die teufelischen bůllieder / angestifftet wuͤrt' (Appendix H, pp. 343–4). *Gesangbuch* (1541), fol. A3r; *BDS*, 7, p. 579.

29 'Vnd weh allen / die jren kindern / gesinde / vnd wem sie es zů wehren haben / hierinn zůsehen vnd losen. Aber hie bei sihet man / leider / was die leuͤt fuͤr Christen sind / vnd wuͤrt (wie das sprichwort lautet) ein jeder vogel bei seinem gesang erkennet / auch das wort des Herren erfuͤllet / Wes das hertz vol ist / gehet der mund uͤber' (Appendix H, pp. 344–5). *Gesangbuch* (1541), fol. A3r; *BDS*, 7, p. 579.

30 'wee vns / wa wir nicht auffwachen / nicht zů vns selb bas lugen / vnd in Christlichem thůn eiferiger werden. Darumb woͤlle Vatter vnd mutter sich erinnern / wem sie jre kinder im Tauff ergeben vnd geopffert haben … Vnd so dis alter ondas zům gesang geneigt / vnd mit lustlichen mitlen zům gůten gefuͤrt sein wil / fleis ankeren / das sie die kinder solich heilige goͤtliche Lieder getrewlich leren / auch die selbigen zů singen anhalten' (Appendix H, p. 348). *Gesangbuch* (1541), fol. A3r; *BDS*, 7, p. 582.

31 1 AST 170, 4.

32 'die worheit halt sich also, vnd nit anders wurt sichs finden mogen: alles singen vnd lesen, So nit zuor besserung der gemeinde gottes beschicht, kompt nit vom geist gottes … mer, by welchem singen vnd lesen das hertz nit ist, Wurt dadurch got nur verspottet; deßhalb solichs gewißlich tuffelich sin muß'. 1 AST 170, 4, fols 33r–33v; *BDS*, 2, p. 450. See Chapter 2.

that the young should be given 'something to wean them away from love ballads and carnal songs and teach them something of value in their place',[33] as well as Erasmus's fear that girls' dancing endangers their morals.[34]

Gerrit Jan van de Poll agrees with Hubert's view that the Strasbourg *Gesangbuch* was principally designed as a book to instruct the youth.[35] However, this is explicit neither in the book's title, nor in Bucer's preface, and although children had a leading role in congregational singing in Strasbourg,[36] it seems highly unlikely that Bucer and Messerschmidt would have gone to the trouble of producing such an elaborate and expensive book with the primary aim of selling it to schools and teaching houses. Indeed, Bucer's warning to the parents of the young suggests that the songs contained in the book were for the benefit of both young and old, and perhaps even a resource that more affluent parents could use to teach their children.

Another notion that features commonly in the preface is that of a tangible physical change in those who partake in the activity of singing. Thus, we encounter once more the idea that the Word of God would literally be absorbed by those who sang it, and would improve them. For example, Bucer explained that singing was useful because the words that were sung by the congregation would 'be brought into the hearts of the people all the more thoroughly'.[37] He continued: 'there is nothing that should penetrate our hearts more deeply ... than the sacred'.[38] However, the effects of music work in both directions. Lascivious texts could equally be 'insinuated by song more charmingly and deeper into the

[33] 'Und sind dazu auch ynn vier stymme bracht, nicht aus anderer ursach, denn das ich gerne wollte, die iugent ... ettwas hette, damit sie der bul lieder und fleyschlichen gesenge los werde und an derselben stat ettwas heylsames lernete'. *WA*, 35, pp. 474–5; translated in *LW*, 53, p. 316.

[34] 'Ad hanc Musicam saltant virgines, huic adsuescunt, nec putamus ullum esse periculum moribus'. D. Erasmus, *Institutio Christiani Matrimonii*, in *Opera Omnia* (1703–1706), vol. 5, col. 718; translated in J. W. O'Malley and L. A. Perraud, *Collected Works of Erasmus*, 86 vols (Toronto: University of Toronto Press, 1974–), vol. 69, pp. 426–7. As Hyun-Ah Kim has observed, this idea is itself reminiscent of St Jerome's advice on the moral and spiritual lives of women. See H.-A. Kim, 'Erasmus on Sacred Music', *Reformation and Renaissance Review*, 8 (2006), p. 286; and H. M. Schueller, *The Idea of Music: An Introduction to Musical Aesthetics in Antiquity and the Middle Ages* (Kalamazoo, MI: Medieval Institute Publications, Western Michigan University, 1988), pp. 234–5.

[35] G. J. van de Poll, *Martin Bucer's Liturgical Ideas: The Strasburg Reformer and his Connection with the Liturgies of the Sixteenth Century* (Assen: Van Gorcum, 1954), p. 30; Hubert, 'Martin Butzers Großes Gesangbuch', p. 55.

[36] See Chapter 4.

[37] 'auf das dauon / nicht allein gesagt / sonder auch gesungen / vnd dadurch den leuten alles desto gründtlicher zů hertzen gebracht vnd eingelassen werde' (Appendix H, p. 342). *Gesangbuch* (1541), fol. A3r; *BDS*, 7, p. 578.

[38] 'ja nichts anders überal zů hertzen gehn / vnd angelegen sein solle / dann das gőtliche' (Appendix H, pp. 342–3). *Gesangbuch* (1541), fol. A3r; *BDS*, 7, p. 578.

senses and the heart'.[39] This sort of singing ensnares the heart and mind.[40] But by using the songs contained in the *Gesangbuch*,

> our souls will be drawn towards, instructed in, and educated to God our Creator and Christ our Saviour, and to all other discipline, edification, Christian love, and friendship, and will be led on to cast out and destroy the lascivious, injurious, alluring, and other worldly songs, including the poison leading to all vices and evil which they leave behind.[41]

These final few words make it clear that 'worldly' songs had a lasting effect, and a person could only be cleansed through the casting out of such thoughts, which was achievable only through the singing of psalms and spiritual songs.

Bucer also emphasised the notion of understanding and intelligibility: unless people enjoy singing holy songs, 'no good understanding, and therefore more gall than honey (as someone says) is found, where otherwise there is a God and understanding'. But if there is no understanding, God is not present, and 'there is literally eternal Hell, even if one does not now perceive it as such, and one goes on living in a storm, singing and dancing and behaving absurdly'.[42] For the people of Strasbourg, these words were perhaps a haunting reminder of the dancing frenzy of 1518.[43] Although Bucer was not in Strasbourg at the time of the plague, he would have been well aware of the event, and he could be fairly certain that images of the erratic and distressing behaviour of the afflicted would not have left the minds of those who had witnessed it. Bucer, in the simplest terms possible, also aligned God's presence with understanding, joy, and happiness, things which can be achieved through the singing of holy songs. On the other hand, God's absence was analogous with 'literally eternal Hell' (*eigentlich die ewige helle*), but Bucer warned his readers that this would be the case even if things did not currently seem so bad.

---

39 'welches ondas zů fil anmůtig vnd im sinne ligt / erst durchs gesang noch anmůtiger / vnd tieffer in sinne vnd hertz gestecket würt' (Appendix H, p. 344). *Gesangbuch* (1541), fol. A3r; *BDS*, 7, p. 579.

40 'jr hertz vnd gedancken durchs gesang / můtwilliglich verhefften' (Appendix H, p. 344). *Gesangbuch* (1541), fol. A3v; *BDS*, 7, p. 579.

41 'durch welche dann vnsere gemůter zů Got vnserem Schöpffer / vnd Christo vnserem Heiland / vnd also zů aller zucht / erbarkeit / christlicher liebe vn[nd] freuntschafft durcheinander / gelert / vnderwisen / gereitzet vnd gezogen / die üpige / schandliche bůl vnd andere weltlieder / sampt dem gifft / das sie zů allen lasteren vnd bösen sitten / hinder jnen lassen / abgetriben / vnd verspulget werden' (Appendix H, pp. 347–8). *Gesangbuch* (1541), fol. A3v; *BDS*, 7, p. 581.

42 'ja in solchem mag man allein rechte freud vnd lust haben / Dann sunst kein gůt gewissen / vnd deshalb jmer mer gallen dan honigs (wie jhener sagt) befunden würt / wa anders auch ein Got vnd gewissen ist / Wa dann kein Got vnd gewissen ist / da ist eigentlich die ewige helle / ob mans gleich ietzt nicht befindet / vnd jmer hin im sause lebet / singet vnd springet vnd ist gar vnsinnig' (Appendix H, pp. 343–4). *Gesangbuch* (1541), fol. A3r; *BDS*, 7, p. 579.

43 See Chapter 1.

Finally, we see in this text various suggestions that Bucer was, for the first time, concerned with the *quality* of music used for the praising of God. He wrote that

> [t]he nature and temperament of man is so formed that nothing moves it so powerfully to all sorts of moods … than artful musical singing and playing directed with skill at such moods and affections.[44]

People 'gladly direct their efforts' towards the performance of pleasant thoughts. These should, he continues, be sacred thoughts.

Furthermore, in his praise of Luther's songs, Bucer made sure to mention that Luther was 'highly gifted' (*zům hoͤchsten begabet ist*) in such matters,[45] and later re-emphasises that point by stating that 'some Psalms and spiritual songs are definitely better in art and spiritual nature than others (among them are all those which Dr. Martin Luther has composed)'.[46] Anne Wolff-Hoffmann reaches a similar conclusion about Bucer's attitude to the aesthetic value of song, based on a statement made at the end of the reformer's preface to the *Gesangbuch*.[47]

Although these were just passing references, they were nevertheless significant, as they demonstrated that Bucer was not interested in singing hymns merely because it was a custom of the ancient Church, but also because, when performed artfully and skilfully, the notes accentuated or enhanced the words being sung. St Augustine, in his *Confessions*, observed a similar effect:

> I feel that by those holy words my mind is kindled more religiously and fervently to a flame of piety because I hear them sung than if they were not sung: and I observe that all the varying emotions of my spirit have modes proper to them in voice and song, whereby, by some secret affinity, they are made more alive.[48]

---

[44] 'Demnach des menschen art vnd natur so gestaltet ist / das jn zů allerlei anmuͤtigkeit … nichs so gewaltig beweget / als artliche Musicgesang / vn[nd] seitenspil / aus warer kunst / auf solche anmuͤtigkeiten vnd affection gerichtet' (Appendix H, p. 342). *Gesangbuch* (1541), fol. A3r; *BDS*, 7, p. 578.

[45] Appendix H, p. 345. *Gesangbuch* (1541), fol. A3r; *BDS*, 7, p. 580.

[46] 'Vnd ob wol etliche Psalmen vnd geistliche Lieder / die anderen (als dann alle sind / die D. Mart. Luther gesetzet hat) in kunst vnd geistlicher art / mercklich fuͤrtreffen' (Appendix H, p. 347).

[47] Wolff[-Hoffman], 'Le recueil de cantiques de Catherine Zell', vol. 1, p. 148; and Gérold, *Les plus anciennes mélodies*, p. 78. See Appendix H, p. 347. N.B. These authors cite the preface in the 1545 edition of the *Gesangbuch*, which is similar, but not identical, to the versions in the 1541 and 1560 editions (see K. E. P. Wackernagel, *Bibliographie zur Geschichte des deutschen Kirchenliedes im XVI. Jahrundert* (Frankfurt am Main: Hender & Zimmer, 1855), pp. 584–5).

[48] 'dum ipsis sanctis dictis religiosius et ardentius sentio moveri animos nostros in flammam pietatis, cum ita cantantur, quam si non ita cantarentur, et omnes affectus spiritus nostri pro sui diversitate habere proprios modos in voce atque cantu, quorum nescio qua occulta familiaritate excitentur'. M. Skutella, ed., *S. Aureli Augustini Confessionum* (Leipzig: Teubner, 1934; repr. Stuttgart: Teubner, 1981), p. 246. Translated in F. J. Sheed, trans., *The Confessions of Saint Augustine* (New York: Sheed & Ward, 1942), book X, chap. 33, p. 197.

St Augustine's views on music were highly influential for many of the Protestant reformers. Bucer would have been familiar with his writings, which had been in print in Strasbourg since 1466.[49] Zwingli seems to have headed towards what Augustine considered 'the direction of over-severity'[50] in his decision to ban liturgical music. Calvin's preface to the Genevan Psalter[51] is heavily reliant on Augustine as a historical source, and his name is cited five times within the text. Bucer, however, seems less concerned with using the authority of Augustine's name in this matter, possibly because Augustine's slightly reserved endorsement of liturgical music is not decisive enough for Bucer's argument that congregational singing is not only a desirable but a necessary aspect of God's praise.

Strikingly, the *Gesangbuch* contains only about 70 pieces. Considering that it was a compilation of different musical traditions, and that the majority of the Psalms had been translated in Strasbourg by this time, it is clear that the book was intended to comprise only a selection of the best material available.[52] Bornert counts 26 songs by Luther or his close associates, against just 16 songs originally from Strasbourg.[53] The book is systematically arranged according to song type. After the 'Register uͤber dis gesangbůch', which lists the contents of the book alphabetically, with page references, seven versions of the lesser doxology are given under the title 'Die Gloria patri / oder beschluͤsse der Psalmen / so in etlichen Kirchen gesungen werden sind dise' ('The *Gloria patri*, or ending of the Psalms; as is sung in some churches').[54] Thus, at least some Strasbourg congregations were in the habit of concluding psalm singing with the doxology at this time (a tradition reaching back to ancient Jewish rites,[55] but also in use throughout the Middle Ages). The reason for the seven different forms is that each would have to fit with the metre of a particular psalm.[56] Points of reference, in the form of

49 The Universal Short Title Catalogue counts 15 editions of St Augustine's writings in Strasbourg between 1466 and 1508 (www.ustc.ac.uk) (accessed 6 February 2012). However, Irena Backus suggests that, at least in the early stages of his life, Bucer's knowledge of patristic writings was minimal. See I. Backus, 'Ulrich Zwingli, Martin Bucer and the Church Fathers', in Backus, ed., *The Reception of the Church Fathers in the West*, 2 vols (Leiden: Brill, 1997), vol. 2, pp. 645–6.

50 Sheed, trans., *The Confessions of Saint Augustine*, p. 198.

51 See below, pp. 223–4.

52 See also Bucer's comment (Appendix H, p. 346).

53 R. Bornert, *Réforme protestante du culte à Strasbourg au XVIe siècle (1523–1598)* (Leiden: Brill, 1981), p. 182.

54 Worthy of note is the fact that the first two versions of the doxology do not end in 'Amen', presumably owing to a lack of space in the metre.

55 E. Foley, 'Doxology', in D. Root, ed., *Grove Music Online* (www.oxfordmusiconline.com) (accessed 18 April 2011).

56 Psalm and doxology are not always well matched, however. For example, Psalm 14, 'Der dorecht spricht', in the metre 8.7.8.7.8.8.7.8.8.7, would need to be fitted to the third doxology, in the metre 8.7.8.7.8.8.7, presumably either missing out three lines of music, or repeating the last three lines of text: 'DAS III. GLORIA. EEr sei dem Vatter vnd dem Son / vnd auch dem heilgen

symbols, are given in the text.[57] Following the doxologies is a section numbered fols A to L. These contain settings of some of the most commonly used texts: the *Te Deum laudamus* (translated by Luther), 'Das Deudsche Sanctus' (based on Isaiah 6:1–4 and translated by Luther),[58] the *Kyrie eleison* and *Gloria in excelsis Deo* by Matthias Greiter, the Apostles' Creed by Greiter, the Lord's Prayer (version from Matthew 6:9–13), and a German translation of *Da pacem Domine* ('Give peace in our time'). Many of these pieces are melismatic, none of them are strophic, and all except *Da pacem Domine* are lengthy, so it is likely that they were intended to be sung with the help of a group of singers to lead the congregation. Whether this would have happened in Strasbourg at this time is another matter; it seems unlikely, considering the stance previously taken by the Strasbourg reformers towards choirs.

It is also interesting that authors' names are given for some (but by no means all) pieces in this volume. This marks a change in stance in such matters from the 1520s and 1530s, when names were not usually given. In 1530, Köpfel had proclaimed his hope that the Church 'might not again be led by men and moved by men's inventions, for simple people are likely to be blinded by great names and to admire in spiritual songs more the poet than the basis of truth and [the impetus] toward improvement'.[59] This was a wholly different approach from the one set out by Bucer, who explained that

> the name of the poet is placed under each Psalm and spiritual song so that one may recognize who has created each poem and work and thereby no one will be accredited with what is not his.[60]

This emerging awareness of intellectual property issues was partly due to a complaint by Luther that 'many unnecessary and unspiritual songs' were mixed up, presumably in songbooks, with the 'appropriately pleasing and spiritual

Geiste ж Als es im anfang was vnd nun / der vns sein gnade leiste. Das wir wandlen inn seinem pfad / das vns die su͂nd der seel nicht schad / Wer das begert / sprech Amen'.

[57] In the case of Psalm 14 and the third doxology, the two points of reference are a red crossed symbol (ж) between the second and third lines of text, and the first word of the fifth line printed in red.

[58] On Luther's paraphrase of Isaiah 6: 1–4, see N. H. Petersen, 'Lutheran Tradition and the Medieval Latin Mass', in E. Østrem, et al., eds, *The Arts and the Cultural Heritage of Martin Luther* (Copenhagen: Museum Tusculanum Press, 2003), p. 45.

[59] 'vff das die gmein Gottes nit wider vff die menschen gefurt / vnd zu menschen gedicht bewegt werde / Dann ie die eynfalt an hohen namen sich gern vergafft / vn[nd] etwa meer in[n] geystlichen liedern den beschreiber / dann den grund der warheit vnd die besserung ansihet'. *Psalmen gebett* (1530), fol. Bv.

[60] 'damit man dann vnderschiedlich erkennete / welches eines jeden gedicht vnd werck seie / ist fu͂r jeden Psalmen vnd geistlich Lied / des dichters namen gesetzet / Damit niemand das jenige zu͂gemessen werde / das nicht sein ist' (Appendix H, p. 346). *Gesangbuch* (1541), fol. A3v; *BDS*, 7, p. 581.

songs by him and others'.[61] Furthermore, as pointed out by Hubert, Lutheran poets hold the majority in this book, with those of Strasbourg appearing only in second place[62] (another two examples of the way in which this *Gesangbuch* seems to have been unofficially influenced by Wittenberg). Perhaps to redress the balance, the names of Strasbourg musicians Matthias Greiter and Wolfgang Dachstein were the only ones to appear in full.[63] Other Strasbourg names included were those of Symphorianus Pollio, Johann Englisch, and Heinrich Vogtherr , all in an abbreviated form.[64]

From here onwards the pages are numbered individually. The songs that appear in the rest of the book are for the most part strophic, the first being 'Kum heiliger geist Herre Got' (*Veni sancte Spiritus*) in three verses. Others in this section include 'Nun bitten wir den Heiligen Geist' and 'Nun frewt euch lieben Christen gmein' (both by Luther), a translation of the responsory *Media vita in morte sumus* ('In the midst of life we are in death'), two versions of the Ten Commandments (two tunes are given for the first version, the explanation being that 'in some churches this first Commandment is sung to another melody',[65] and the second is a shorter version by Luther), the Nicene Creed, and a nine-strophe arrangement by Luther of the Lord's Prayer. After this point, the songs tend to be arranged thematically; for example, songs for the Lord's Supper (*von Abentmal*), songs of prayer (*Betgesänge*), songs of praise (*Lobgesänge*), songs of lamentation (*Claglieder*), songs of acts, faith, works, salvation (*Gesatz, Glauben, Wercken, Erlosung*), as well as canticles such as the *Magnificat*, the *Benedictus*, and the *Nunc dimittis*. Significantly, the book also contains songs to be sung on the high feasts (*auff die hohen Fest zů singen*) of Christmas and Easter,[66] a result of the gradual reintroduction of some festivals during the later 1530s.[67] The hymn 'Von himel hoch da kom ich her' is presented as a Christmas *Kinderlied*, or 'Children's song'. Also included in this section is the hymn 'Jn dulci iubilo', described as 'Another ancient Christmas song, half in Latin and half in German' (*Ein ander alt Weihenacht Lied / halb Latein vnd halb deudsch*). Among the Easter songs printed is Luther's 'Jesus Christus vnser Heiland'.[68]

---

61 'Nach dem aber / wie D. Luther billich klaget / vnder seine vnd andere recht artige vnd geistliche Lieder / fil onnötigs / ongeistlichs vnd onbesserlichs / eingemischet worden' (Appendix H, p. 346). *Gesangbuch* (1541), fol. A3v; *BDS*, 7, p. 581.

62 Hubert, 'Martin Butzers Großes Gesangbuch', p. 55.

63 The observation that these two are the only names to appear in full is that of Hubert, in 'Martin Butzers Großes Gesangbuch', p. 55.

64 Regarding the inclusion of authors' names in this volume, see J. Ficker, 'Das größte Prachtwerk des Straßburger Buchdrucks – Zur Geschichte und Gestaltung des großen Straßburger Gesangbuches 1541', *Archiv für Reformationsgeschichte*, 38 (1941), p. 201.

65 'Jnn etlichen Kirchen / singet man ein andere Melodei ůber dis erst gesetze'. *Gesangbuch* (1541), p. VIII.

66 *Gesangbuch* (1541), pp. LXX–LXXXVIII.

67 *Church Mother*, p. 89.

68 A different text from the 'Jan Hus hymn' of the same name. See above, p. 203.

The remainder of the book[69] contains a selection of psalms.[70] Two melodies each are provided for Psalms 12 and 128. Two versions of Psalm 130 ('Aus tieffer not') are given; the second[71] (to a different melody, with a different text, but with the same metre, and with four rather than five stanzas[72]) is described as being the earlier version.[73] This four-stanza version had appeared in the first *Teütsch Kirchenampt* of 1524, and the five-stanza version had first been published in Strasbourg (without music) in *Psalter. Das seindt alle Psalmen Dauids* (1538). Verses 1 to 32 of Psalm 119 are also set to two melodies (Aleph and Beth [vv. 1–16] to the first,[74] Gimel and Dalech [vv. 17–32] to the second). Both of these had appeared in *Theütsch kirchenampt* (1525) and *Psalmen gebett* (1526).

Unlike the vast majority, if not all, of the other Strasbourg songbooks of this period, the *Gesangbuch* provides absolute clarity regarding the melodies. In the case of more than one melody being appropriate for a particular text, the editors went to great effort, not only to describe the alternative tune, but also to print it in full, with word underlay for the first verse. For example, Psalm 12, the first psalm printed in the *Gesangbuch*, has two melodies assigned to it. At the end of the first there is a note in red ink that reads: 'Jn etlichen Kirchen pfleget man die volgende melodei ůber disen Psalmen zůsingen' ('In some churches the following melody continues to be sung with this Psalm').[75] This is followed by a second melody, which first appeared in the Erfurt *Enchiridion* of 1524 and had also been published in Wittenberg.[76] By printing both tunes, the compilers ensured that any existing variations in 'alternative' tunes were overridden. In addition, there could be no confusion regarding fitting together of text and melody. In other words, everybody was literally reading from the same page.

---

69 *Gesangbuch* (1541), pp. XCI–CLVIII. Note: The 1953 facsimile edition does not include pages LXXXIX and XC, which are presumably blank.

70 These are Pss. 12, 14, 46, 67, 123, 128, two versions of 130 (all Luther), 124 (Justus Jonas), 117 (Johannes Agricola), 51 (Erhardus Hegenwald), 2 (Andreas Knöppen), 127 (Johann Kohlros), 13 (Matthias Greiter), another version of 14 (Wolfgang Dachstein), 15 (Dachstein), another version of 51 (Greiter), 71 (Heinrich Vogtherr), 114 (Greiter), 115 (presumably also by Greiter, as it follows on directly from 114, with no new melody being given), 119 [vv. 1–16 to one melody; vv. 17–32 to another] (Greiter), 125 (Greiter), 137 (Dachstein), and 139 (Vogtherr). No name is given for Ps. 127, but Hubert assigns it to Kohlros (see Hubert, 'Martin Butzers Großes Gesangbuch', pp. 54 and 55).

71 pp. CIX–CXI.

72 See R. A. Leaver, *Luther's Liturgical Music: Principles and Implications* (Grand Rapids and Cambridge: Eerdmans, 2007), pp. 145–6 concerning the two versions of this text. The two melodies can be found in *DKL* III, vol. 1, part 2 (melodies), pp. 99 and 115.

73 'Der vorig Psal. De profundis / wie er zum ersten ist ausgangen'. *Gesangbuch* (1541), p. CIX.

74 Today known as 'Old 113th'.

75 Strasbourg congregations may have been familiar with both tunes. One version was printed in the *Strassburger Kirchenampt* (1525), and the other first appeared in the *Teutsch Kirchenampt* (1524). The first tune was also used in the *Ordnung des Herren Nachtmal* (1525) set to Psalm 3 at the end of Lord's Supper as an alternative hymn to 'Gott sei gelobet' (see Figure 2.2).

76 See J. Zahn, *Die Melodien der deutschen evangelischen Kirchenlieder*, 6 vols (Reinheim: Lokay, 1889–93; repr. Hildesheim: Olms, 1968), vol. 3, p. 71 (no. 4431).

Rather than, as in some other songbooks, being told to sing a text to an alternative tune which then had to be recalled from memory or found in another publication, the readers had all the necessary information in front of them, and the tune was familiar, whether it originated from Strasbourg or Wittenberg.

One final observation about the *Gesangbuch* relates to language and orthography. The local practice in Strasbourg was to refer to the Lord's Supper as the 'Nachtmal' (literally 'night meal').[77] However, the section of the book containing songs for Communion refers to songs for the 'Abentmal' (literally 'evening meal'), which was the word always used by Luther to refer to the same sacrament. Likewise, the south-west German spelling of 'Deutsch' (as used today in modern German) or 'Teutsch' varied from the form used in Wittenberg: 'Deudsch', which was used in the *Gesangbuch*. These changes are peculiar; as previously mentioned, Luther did not have any direct involvement in the production of the Strasbourg *Gesangbuch* of 1541, as far as we know, and the printers of the volume, Messerschmidt and Köpfel, were both from Alsatian families[78] and would have had no reason to modify their spelling other than perhaps to avoid alienating (or even to attract) potential buyers in other areas of Germany.

Thus, it can be seen that, more than 15 years after abolishing choir singing and introducing congregational metrical hymns and psalms, Strasbourg's musical policy became more 'Lutheran' in nature by bowing to pressure from Wittenberg. It reintroduced plainchant, songs for Christmas and Easter, and began printing more songs by Lutheran authors. Thus, in his preface, Bucer demonstrated his by now unquestioning approval of hymn singing. This, however, was not simply a shift in theological beliefs, but a result of the accelerating politicisation of the Reformation. Strasbourg could no longer afford to act alone.

During the 1520s, the situation had been quite different. Strasbourg was then trying to develop in relative isolation, adopting a reformation strategy whose theology is now considered to lie somewhere between the beliefs of Zwingli and of Luther. Bucer's approach to church music, although offering cautious approval, was at this time fluid, uncertain and, on the matter of extra-biblical texts, suspicious. Nevertheless, Strasbourg's moderate approach quickly earned it an international reputation for progress and diplomacy. Throughout the 1540s Strasbourg began to lose its religious upper hand, as pressure from the emperor for religious unity increased. In some senses, therefore, the *Gesangbuch* was Strasbourg's tipping point. The city was still strong enough to produce a book of this magnitude and beauty, but no longer as a way of exerting the type of influence seen during the 1520s and 1530s. Instead, the *Gesangbuch* formed

---

77 See the titles of the earlier liturgical orders in Appendix A.

78 See F. Ritter, *Histoire de l'imprimerie alsacienne aux XVe et XVIe siècles* (Strasbourg: Le Roux, 1955), pp. 213–16, 238–50.

part of a new strategy of reaching out, showing solidarity, and demonstrating a liturgical liberalism unheard of during the earlier days of its reforms.

Strasbourg and the Outside World

People began seeking refuge in Strasbourg from religious persecution in their own lands as early as the mid-1520s. Owing to Strasbourg's location, these were mostly French Protestants, but their numbers included some from other countries including England and Italy. A school was opened for the children of French refugees in 1529,[79] but a French church, known as the 'Ecclesiola Gallicana', was not established until 1533.[80] At the time of Calvin's arrival in the city, the French community met in the Church of St Nicolas-in-Undis. At the end of 1538 they moved to St Mary Magdalene, and then about two years later they were granted permission to use the former Dominican church for their services.[81]

François Lambert, a former Franciscan friar, stayed in Strasbourg before moving on to assist with the Reformation in Hesse. Jacques Lefèvre d'Étaples, despite remaining faithful to the Catholic Church, sought refuge in the city during the winter of 1525–26 after being condemned by the Sorbonne, and the future Genevan reformer Guillaume Farel may have stayed in the city from 1524 to 1526.[82] George Joye, an early Cambridge Protestant, was among other English refugees who fled to Strasbourg at the end of 1527.[83] Jean Calvin had also visited during his escape from France in the middle of the decade,[84] and tried to visit once again in 1536 in order to seek support for Protestants being persecuted in France.[85] Most famously of all, Calvin returned to Strasbourg in 1538, at the invitation of Bucer, having been expelled from Geneva over disagreements with the city council over the nature of the reforms being implemented there. Calvin spent three years as pastor of the French refugee congregation in the Alsatian city, and initially returned to Geneva only as a temporary measure, in order to begin the process of effectively reforming the Church there.[86]

---

[79] S. J. Lenselink, *De Nederlandse psalmberijmingen in de 16e eeuw van de Souterliedekens tot Datheen met hun voorgangers in Duitsland en Frankrijk* (Assen: Van Gorcum, 1959), p. 116.

[80] Poll, *Martin Bucer's Liturgical Ideas*, p. 112.

[81] Bornert, *Réforme protestante du culte*, p. 194.

[82] See L. Junod, *Farel – réformateur de la Suisse romande* (Neuchâtel: Delachaux & Sandoz; Paris: Librairie de la Suisse Romande, 1865), pp. 35–50.

[83] C. Hopf, *Martin Bucer and the English Reformation* (Oxford: Blackwell, 1946), p. 4.

[84] M. Arnold, trans. J. J. Guder, 'Strasbourg', in H. J. Selderhuis, ed., *The Calvin Handbook* (Grand Rapids and Cambridge: Eerdmans, 2009), p. 38.

[85] Poll, *Martin Bucer's Liturgical Ideas*, p. 108. Calvin was instead forced to make a detour to Geneva.

[86] The fact that the Strasbourg authorities expected his imminent return is confirmed by the knowledge that Calvin was still receiving money from several sources a number of years after leaving the city. The benefice system in Strasbourg was such that Calvin was able to hold the titles

These facts might suggest that Strasbourg was an open-armed community, wholeheartedly welcoming those who had travelled to their free city to express their religion in a safe haven.[87] Despite this impression, there is some evidence that the authorities were uncomfortable with the presence of foreigners in the city. An undated fragment by the early historian of the Reformation, Johann Sleidan,[88] reveals a disciplinarian approach towards the French refugees:[89]

> *Et puis que à cause de la Religion vous estes | retirez de vostre pays et transportez en ceste ville / | messieurs vous co[m]mandent / de laisser les autres | en paix / en leurs eglises / oü autrement on | vous fera vuyder hors de la ville. Et quant | aux ministeres de vostre eglise / messieurs veullent | et entendent / quilz ayent a parler auec | discretion / sans no[m]mer ne le pape ne lempereur | ne aütres.*[90]

> And because, for religious reasons, you have withdrawn from your country and travelled to this city, our lords command you to leave others in peace in their churches; otherwise we will expel you from the city. And as for the ministers of your church, our lords desire and expect that they speak with discretion, without naming the pope, nor the emperor, nor others.

The message is clear: behave yourselves while you are in our city, or leave.

However, the importance of the refugees in the dissemination of Strasbourg's form of Protestantism cannot easily be overestimated. According to Jean Rott, the French refugee church in Strasbourg served as the model for Presbyterian churches throughout the world.[91] Gerrit Jan van de Poll writes that the refugee churches

of vicar of St Thomas and of chaplain of the altar of SS Peter and Paul in the cathedral. When he left the city, supposedly temporarily, he was allowed to keep these sources of income, as well as his citizenship of the city, until such time as the authorities realised he was not planning to return. See J. Rott, 'Documents strasbourgeois concernant Calvin', *Revue d'histoire et de philosophie religieuses*, 44 (1964), pp. 312–25.

87 It might be suggested that the Anabaptists took advantage of this situation.

88 See G. Livet and F. Rapp, eds, *Histoire de Strasbourg des origines à nos jours*, 4 vols (Strasbourg: Dernières Nouvelles de Strasbourg, 1980–82), vol. 2, pp. 470–71.

89 The handwriting has been identified as that of Sleidan by the AVS. The manuscript is marked 'Notes sur le séjour de Calvin à Strasbourg, etc.', but as Sleidan probably did not settle in Strasbourg until 1544, this directive is not likely to have referred to the time during which Calvin was in the city. Nevertheless, there is no reason to doubt that similar sentiments existed beforehand. On Sleidan's arrival date in Strasbourg, see A. Kess, *Johann Sleidan and the Protestant Vision of History* (Aldershot: Ashgate, 2008), p. 35, incl. n. 1.

90 1 AST 90, 8.

91 'l'Eglise des réfugiés "française" à Strasbourg a été le modèle de toutes les églises presbytériennes du monde'. Rott, 'L'Eglise des réfugiés de langue française à Strasbourg au XVIe siècle : aperçu de son histoire, en particulier de ses crises à partir de 1541', *Bulletin de la Société de l'histoire du protestantisme français*, 122 (1976), p. 525.

> became the cradles of the later national churches … In this manner the reformed heritage of Strasburg [*sic*] was scattered over an extensive area, so that when, through the Interim of 1549, Strasburg was temporarily eliminated as a centre [of Protestantism], other centres preserved and passed this heritage, viz.: Zürich, Emden, Geneva, Frankfurt, Frankenthal, Heildelberg, and Wesel.[92]

Along with the spread of Strasbourg's theology went its liturgy, and along with its liturgy went its music. Nowhere is this pattern seen more vividly than in Calvin's reorganisation of the Genevan Church in the 1540s and 1550s.

Little is known about the musical habits of the Ecclesiola Gallicana before the arrival of Calvin. It can be said with certainty that Latin polyphony or plainchant would not have featured in services, and there are no records of any French-language hymn books existing at this time. It seems that the 1533 synod, in an attempt to flush out the Anabaptists in the city, had prohibited any group other than the established Church in Strasbourg from devising a liturgy and administering the sacraments. This also applied to the refugees. The French services, then, consisted only of prayers and sermons, and the refugees were reliant upon their hosts for sacraments and ceremonies.[93]

Once Calvin had arrived in 1538, however, changes were implemented at a rapid rate. He requested permission to celebrate Communion in French, and this was granted.[94] He made use of the liturgies in *Psalmen und geystliche Lieder* (1537) and *Psalter mit aller Kirchenübung* (1539), and these formed the basis of the liturgy adopted in Geneva in the 1540s.[95] In 1539, the first French Protestant psalter was published in Strasbourg: *Aulcuns pseaulmes et cantiques mys en chant*,[96] published under Calvin's auspices, contained psalm melodies from several of the German hymn books that were in circulation in Strasbourg at the time.[97] *Aulcuns pseaulmes* set the trend for the publication of over 45 other books of French metrical psalms in various cities across France, as well as in Strasbourg and Geneva. The volume contained 18 psalms, as well as the *Nunc Dimittis*, the Ten Commandments, and the Creed, all of which were versified and set to music. Most of the psalm texts selected for this edition carry a message

---

92 Poll, *Martin Bucer's Liturgical Ideas*, p. 169.

93 Ibid., p. 112.

94 Ibid.

95 Bornert, 'Martin Bucer et la liturgie strasbourgeoise de 1537–1539', *Archives de l'Église d'Alsace*, 19 (nouvelle série) (1971), p. 105. Föllmi suggests he also used the 1530 and 1533 editions of *Psalmen gebett* (see B. A. Föllmi, 'Calvin und das Psalmsingen: Die Vorgeschichte des Genfer Psalters', *Zwingliana*, 36 (2009), p. 76).

96 *AVLCVNS | pseaulmes et cantiques | mys en chant* (Strasbourg: Knobloch, 1539). A facsimile of this psalter can be found in R. R. Terry, ed., *Calvin's First Psalter [1539]* (London: Benn, 1932).

97 Föllmi considers *Psalmen gebet* (1530/1533) and *Psalmen vnd geystliche Lieder* (1537) to have been the sources of melodies in *Aulcuns pseaulmes*. See Föllmi, 'Calvin und das Psalmsingen, pp. 76–7.

of resistance, deliverance, or salvation – all of which were close to the hearts of French Protestants. Some of the translations were by Calvin himself, and others were by the French poet Clément Marot, whom Calvin may have encountered during his travels in France in 1535.[98]

Congregational singing in church had not been a practice that Calvin was initially prepared to adopt, Geneva having initially followed the examples of places such as Bern and Zurich in limiting its use. However, on 16 January 1537, inspired by the congregational singing that they had witnessed in Strasbourg and Basel,[99] Calvin and Guillaume Farel presented the Genevan town council with a proposal for the introduction of sung psalms into the service.[100] Soon afterwards, the two men were expelled from the city,[101] making it impossible to implement their plans for psalm singing. Strasbourg's refugee community, on the other hand, turned out to be the perfect environment in which to establish such a tradition.

Various historians have argued for Bucer's influence on Calvin's changing opinions on music.[102] Charles Garside demonstrates how Calvin's position on music in his *Institutio Christianae religionis*, first published in 1536, differed significantly from that adopted in his later writings, including the *Articles* presented to the town council in 1537 which proposed the adoption of psalm singing in Geneva.[103] In the *Articles*, Calvin first cited the example of congregational singing in the ancient Church, as well as St Paul's confirmation of such occurrences.[104] This, he claimed, must originate from the mouth and from the heart (*de bouche et de cueur*) – a deliberate rebuttal of the Zwinglian position that prayer should occur in the heart only, suggesting it should thereby

98 See M. Jenny, *Luther, Zwingli, Calvin in ihren Liedern* (Zurich: Theologischer Verlag, 1983), pp. 219–21.

99 Ibid., p. 217. By the 1530s, Basel was using some hymns and psalms from Strasbourg. See Föllmi, 'Calvin und das Psalmsingen', pp. 66–7.

100 J. Calvin and G. Farel, 'Articles proposés par les Ministres, particulièrement au sujet de la Sainte-Cène', p. 12 (Archives d'Etat de Genève, Pièces Historiques [hereafter: PH], 1170). For a transcription of the complete excerpt relating to psalm singing, see D. Trocmé-Latter, 'The Psalms as a mark of Protestantism: the Introduction of Liturgical Psalm-Singing in Geneva', *Plainsong & Medieval Music*, 20 (2011)', pp. 162–3. Four issues of particular importance are mentioned in the *Articles*: the celebration of the Lord's Supper, the singing of psalms, the instruction of youth, and marriage laws (W. de Greef, 'Calvin's Writings', in D. McKim, ed., *The Cambridge Companion to John Calvin* (Cambridge: Cambridge University Press, 2004), p. 50).

101 W. G. Naphy, 'Calvin's Geneva', in McKim, *Companion to Calvin*, p. 28. For information on the structure of government in Geneva at this time, see C. Coignet, *La Réforme française avant les guerres civiles, 1512–1559* (Paris: Fischbacher, 1890), pp. 166–7.

102 Lenselink, *De Nederlandse psalmberijmingen*, pp. 158–69; and *Garside*. See p. 13, n. 69 of *Garside* for his own judgement of Lenselink's work. See also Föllmi, 'Calvin und das Psalmsingen, pp. 59–84.

103 *Garside*, p. 13.

104 'com[m]e nous en auons lexe[m]ple en lesglise ancienne et mesme le tesmoignage de S Paul'. Archives d'Etat de Genève, PH 1170, p. 12.

be silent. He also attacked the papist practice of 'murmuring' the Psalms without understanding,[105] implying that such singing should occur in the vernacular.

A further point of influence between Calvin and Bucer is the use of children to lead the singing, a fact overlooked by the vast majority of scholars.[106] Just as Strasbourg manuscripts from the early 1530s make provision for children to lead the psalm singing from the front of the church,[107] Calvin's *Articles* suggest that, during services,

> some children, to whom a modest and ecclesiastical song has already been taught, sing loudly and distinctly, the people listening with full attention and following with the heart what is sung with the mouth, until little by little everyone becomes accustomed to singing together.[108]

Calvin therefore did not wish simply to emulate Strasbourg's theological stance on music, but had also chosen to imitate it on a practical level: using scriptural songs in the church, led by schoolchildren.

As early as October 1538, a matter of weeks – if not days – after he had arrived in Strasbourg, Calvin was making use of the Strasbourg liturgy of the Lord's Supper in the French refugee church.[109] On 9 November, Johannes Zwick wrote to Heinrich Bullinger, explaining that the French refugees in Strasbourg listened to Calvin's sermons four times per week, and celebrated the Lord's Supper and sang psalms in their own tongue.[110] In December, Calvin announced in a letter to Farel that he was preparing a French-language psalter (*Aulcuns pseaulmes*) with German melodies for the use of the French congregation in the city. He explained that they were sympathetic to the singing of the Psalms, because this was the custom of the ancient Church. Calvin also added that he had already versified two psalms himself.[111] In October 1539, Calvin wrote again to Farel, confirming that 100 copies of *Aulcuns pseaulmes* had been sent

---

105 'les pseaulmes … doibuent estre vrays champs [chants] spirituels a murmurer entre eux sa[ns] aulcune intellige[n]ce'. Archives d'Etat de Genève, PH 1170, p. 12.

106 Beat Föllmi, however, has observed this connection. See Föllmi, 'Calvin und das Psalmsingen', pp. 59–84.

107 1 AST 75, 9; 1 AST 75, 10; 1 AST 75, 11; 1 AST 166, 20.5. See Chapter 3.

108 'La maniere de y proceder nous a semble aduis bonne si aulcungs enfans auxquelz on ayt au p[ar]auant recorde vng chant modeste et eccl[es]iastiq[ue] chantent a aulte voyx et distincte le peuple escoutant en toute attention et suyuant de cuer ce qui est chante de bouche iusque a ce que petit a petit vng chascun se accoustumera a chanter [com]muneme[n]t'. Archives d'Etat de Genève, PH 1170, p. 12.

109 Letter from Calvin to Farel, October 1538, in J. W. Baum et al., eds., *Ioannis Calvini opera quae supersunt omnia* (Brunswick: Berolini, 1863–1900) (hereafter: *COO*), 10.2, epist. 149, cols 276–80.

110 'Gallis Argentorati ecclesia data est in qua a *Calvino* quater in septimana conciones audiunt, sed et coenam agunt et psalmos sua lingua canunt'. *COO*, 10.2, epist. 151, col. 288.

111 'Psalmos ideo miseramus, ut prius cantarentur apud vos, quam illuc pervenirent quo intelligis. Statuimus enim brevi publicare. Quia magis arridebat melodia germanica, coactus sum

to Geneva.[112] This shows that Strasbourg's musical and liturgical reforms were having an immediate effect on the practices of other cities. By sending these copies to Geneva, Calvin was preparing for the adoption of this Strasbourg tradition in Geneva. Several Strasbourg melodies were adopted in Calvin's psalter, including the French version of the Creed, set to an adapted version of Matthias Greiter's German Creed.[113]

Calvin reiterated the main points of the *Articles* in the Genevan 'Projet d'ordonnances sur les offices ecclesiastiques' of 1541.[114] When discussing the marriage service, he wrote that 'it would be good to introduce church songs in order to better incite the people to pray to and praise God'. He then added that 'to begin with the little children should be taught, and then in time the whole church will be able to follow'.[115]

During the following year, Calvin wrote a preface to the first edition of what was to become known as the Genevan Psalter: *La Forme des prieres et chantz ecclesiastiques*.[116] This was a brief explanation on the use of prayer and song. In the 1543 edition,[117] Calvin chose to extend the 'Epistre au lecteur', and this was published in its new, complete form in all subsequent editions of the Psalter.[118] A number of points suggest that Calvin was heavily influenced by Bucer's preface to the 1541 *Gesangbuch*. This is evident in the notion that music should be moderated so that nothing corrupt or obscene comes of it, and that its power be captured and put to good use,[119] and in the fact that singing the Psalms was practised by the Church in the time of the Apostles.[120] Calvin had also been influenced by the Strasbourg reformers in his desire to use metrical psalms as replacements for popular songs. In August 1537, the Swiss city of Bern had passed a law banning the singing of lascivious songs during dances.[121] Bucer clearly had similar wishes:

---

experiri quid carmine valerem. Ita Psalmi duo, 46. et 25., prima sunt mea tyrocinia: alios postea attexui'. *COO*, 10.2, epist. 200, col. 438.

112 'Mandaveram ut centum exemplaria Genevam mitterentur'. *COO*, 10.2, epist. 194, col. 426.

113 Lenselink, *De Nederlandse psalmberijmingen*, p. 123.

114 Archives d'Etat de Genève, PH 1384. *COO*, 10.1, cols 15–30.

115 'Jl sera bon dintroduyre les chantz ecclesiastiques pour mieulx jnciter le peuple a pryer et louer dieu. Pour le commencement on apprendra les petiz enfans, puys avec le temps toutte lesglise pourra suyvre'. *COO*, 10.1, col. 26.

116 *La forme des prieres et chantz ecclesiastiques, auec la maniere d'administrer les Sacremens, & consacrer le Mariage: selon la coustume de l'Eglise ancienne* (Geneva: Gérard, 1542).

117 This edition is lost, its name unknown.

118 The 'Epistre' (1543) is reproduced in *COO*, 6, pp. 165–72, as well as in P. Barth and G. Niesel, eds., *Joannis Calvini opera selecta*, 5 vols (Munich: Kaiser, 1926–1936) (hereafter: *COS*), vol. 2, pp. 12–18. A translation is available in *Garside*, pp. 31–3.

119 *Garside*, pp. 21–4, 28–9.

120 Ibid., p. 28.

121 Ibid., p. 24.

> whoever could or would should give counsel and assistance so that such lascivious, devilish, ruinous songs will be cast out and destroyed, and the holy Psalms and sacred songs made pleasing to all Christians, young and old alike, and brought into steady use.[122]

Calvin, too, expressed his wish that such unfavourable songs be abolished,

> in order that you might have respectable songs that teach you the love and fear of God, instead of those which are sung commonly which are nothing but bawdiness and all sorts of vileness.[123]

Finally, there is the notion of singing as a means of edifying one's neighbour, as alluded to in various verses of 1 Corinthians 14 and Ephesians 5. In the brief preface to the Strasbourg French psalter of 1542, Calvin wrote that in the book the reader will find words and music 'with which you will give your neighbour a good example to incite him to read the Holy Scriptures'.[124] Without claiming that Calvin's approach to music was exclusively influenced by Bucer, it is worth noting the similarities in their language and their reasons for using music in their respective reforms of ecclesiastical practice.

Other German Cities

The skills of the Strasbourg reformers, especially Bucer, were in high demand elsewhere in German-speaking areas, with Bucer helping to write the church orders for Ulm, Memmingen, Hesse, Cologne, Constanz,[125] Cassel,[126] and Augsburg,[127] as well as advising many other cities on their courses of reform, and having indirect influences on numerous other places.[128]

---

122 'Darumb wer da kõndte oder mõchte / der solt dazů rahten vnd helffen / das solche ůppige teufelische / verderbliche gesang abgethan vnd verspůlget würden / vnd die heiligen Psalmen / vnd gotselige lieder / allen Christen / jungen vnd alten gemein / lustig gemacht / vnd in stetig ůbung bracht wurden' (Appendix H, p. 345). *Gesangbuch* (1541), fol. A3r; *BDS*, 7, pp. 579–80.

123 'Affin que tu eusse chansons honnestes t'enseignantes l'amour et crainte de dieu, au lieu de celles que communement on chante qui ne sont que de paillardise et toute villenie'. Calvin, 'Au lecteur Crestien', in *LA MANYE | re de faire prieres aux eglises Francoyes. tant deuant la predica- | tion comme apres, ensemble pseaulmes & canticques francoys quon | chante aus dictes eglises, apres sensuyt lordre et facon d'admini- | strer les Sacrementz de Baptesme, & de la saincte Cene de nostre | seigneur Iesu Christ, de espouser & confirmer le mariage deuant | lassemblee des fideles, auecques le sermon tant du baptesme que de | la cene* (Strasbourg: Knobloch, 1542). *COS*, 2, p. 12.

124 'que pour le bon exemple que tu pourras donner a ton prochain, pour l'exciter a lire la saincte escripture'. Calvin, 'Au lecteur Crestien', in *La Manyere de faire prieres* (1542). *COS*, 2, p. 12.

125 Poll, *Martin Bucer's Liturgical Ideas*, p. 27.

126 R. G. Hobbs, '"Quam Apposita Religioni Sit Musica": Martin Bucer and Music in the Liturgy', *Reformation and Renaissance Review*, 6 (2004), pp. 173–4.

127 *BDS*, 16, pp. 209–68.

128 *BDS*, 16, pp. 9–12.

At the beginning of the 1520s, Luther's writings had found their way to Ulm, leading to the development of an evangelical movement there.[129] By 1523, this was considered to be too popular a movement to be able to suppress. The city, however, had no outstanding clergyman who could push through the reforms.[130] In 1529, the reformers in the city of Ulm wrote to their Strasbourg counterparts asking for details about decisions taken during the reforms in Strasbourg.[131] The preachers responded with a 13-point summary of their teachings,[132] the eighth point of which was a short paragraph concerning music. They explained that at all sermons[133] and at Vespers, a prescribed psalm was sung. They also wrote that the songs to be used at the Lord's Supper had been printed (confirming their use in church services). The preachers also explained that they warn against 'irritating singing and little songs' that despised the Word of God.[134]

In November 1530 the guilds of Ulm voted to join the evangelical movement, the city joining the Schmalkaldic League[135] in February 1531. On 14 April the council appointed a committee to enforce the reforms with the help of outside preachers, one of whom would be Martin Bucer. He arrived in the city on 21 May.[136] Bucer was asked by the Ulm authorities to compile a church order,[137] which he achieved by the middle of June 1531.[138] He devoted a small amount of the order to 'gsang und gepett' (*song and prayer*). The section began with Bucer reminding his readers that Christians have, since ancient times, sung their praises to God. In order to emulate this in this best possible way,

> we want the German and Latin schoolmasters in the city and in the countryside, and, in such places as there are no schoolmasters, the ministers and helpers, to teach the

129 *BDS*, 4, pp. 187–8.

130 T. A. Brady, *Turning Swiss: Cities and Empire, 1450–1550* (Cambridge: Cambridge University Press, 1985), pp. 162–3.

131 1 AST 95, 36.

132 1 AST 95, 37.

133 That is, services at which there was preaching.

134 'Zum acht[en] / haben wir auch in allen predig[en] vnnd vesper gepetten / vor vnd nach der predig, ein psalme[n] zusing[en] verordnet / wie sy im truck syn / vßgenome[n] der morg[en] gebett / darin allein ermanet / vnnd hynnach in der still gepettet würt. Die ordnung im gsang des nachtmals ist im truck / vnnd wurt noch gelegenheit veranderet / gemeret vnnd geminderet. Zu solichem gesang / ermanen wir / das iedes vffmercke / vnnd das thür wort gottes nit verachte / dadurch die ergerliche gesang vnnd liedlin abgang[en] sind. Auch pflegen wir zum jar ettlich mal / soliche psalmen vffs kurzest der gemein zu erklere[n] / da mit alles mit verstandt gesung[en] werde'. 1 AST 95, 37, fol. 90v.

135 A religious alliance formed as a defensive league against possible attack from Emperor Charles V. It was established in February 1531. Strasbourg also joined the alliance.

136 M. Greschat, trans. S. E. Buckwalter, *Martin Bucer: A Reformer and his Times* (Louisville and London: Westminster John Knox Press, 2004), p. 107.

137 *Ordnung, die ain Ersamer Rath der Statt Ulm* (Ulm: Varnier, 1531).

138 H. Eells, *Martin Bucer* (New Haven: Yale University Press; London: Oxford University Press, 1931), p. 120.

> children to sing the German psalms and spiritual songs which are in the little church books, so that the elders may also increase their understand from day to day.[139]

This is reminiscent of Strasbourg's plans to use the children to lead the singing of psalms.[140] It is interesting to note that a similar proposal was recommended to Ulm at around the same time. Also, as in Strasbourg, the church order states that: 'we want no songs to be sung in church other than those conforming to Scripture, as recognised by the common examiners of Christian teaching'.[141]

Between 1538 and 1541, the songbook of the Bohemian Brethren, which had been published in Strasbourg some years earlier, was reprinted four times in Ulm in a similar or slightly expanded version.[142] This may well have been due to the influence of Caspar Schwenckfeld, who was known to be living in Ulm after leaving Strasbourg in 1534.[143]

Bucer's influence on the city of Cologne occurred in the early 1540s. The liturgies printed in *Psalmen und geystliche Lieder* (1537) and *Psalter mit aller Kirchenübung* (1539) supplied Bucer with a certain amount of material for the *Einfeltigen Bedenckens*,[144] a church order also known as the *Consultation*,[145] which he compiled in 1543 with help from Philipp Melanchthon and Caspar Hedio, for the Archbishop of Cologne, Hermann von Wied.[146] However, the influence of Melanchthon, a close colleague of Luther, is particularly clear. The document expressed no opposition to the use of a choir; indeed, it encouraged it.

> Thereafter follows the *Sanctus*, which, where there are clerks present, is to be sung by them in Latin and by the people in German, one group after the other, three times each. So when the clerks sing 'Sanctus', the people sing 'Holy', but the 'Dominus deus sabaoth' and the 'Benedictus' which follow should be sung in German by the whole congregation, in this way: '*Sanctus*, Holy, *Sanctus*, Holy, *Sanctus*, Holy is the Lord of Hosts, Heaven and Earth are full of your glory and power. *Hosanna*, Help us,

139 'woͤllen wir, das die teütschen und latinischen schůlmeister in der Stat und uff dem land und, an woͤlchen orten nit schůlmeister sind, die pfarrer und helffer die kinder die teütschen Psalmen und gaistlichen lieder, die man in den kirchenbuͤchlin findt, singen lehren, damit es die alten auch von tag zů tag begreifen'. *BDS*, 4, p. 240.

140 See Chapter 3.

141 'woͤllen wir, das man kein gsang in der kirchen zů singen anneme dann woͤlche, als der schrifft gemåß, durch die gmainen examinatores christlicher lehr erkennt und der gmain zů singen anneme dann woͤlche, als der schrifft gemåß, durch die gmainen examinatores christlicher lehr erkennt'. *BDS*, 4, p. 240.

142 J. T. Müller, *Hymnologisches Handbuch zum Gesangbuch der Brüdergemeine* (Herrnhut: Vereins für Brüdergeschichte, 1916), pp. 12–13.

143 Wolff, 'Le recueil de cantiques de Catherine Zell', vol. 1, p. 36.

144 *VOn GOttes genaden | vnser Hermans Ertzbischoffs zů Coͤln / vnnd Churfürsten &c. einfaltigs bedencken* ... (Bonn: Laurentius von der Mülen, 1543). Printed in *BDS*, 11, 1, pp. 163–429.

145 *A simple, | and religious consultation of vs | Herman by the grace of God Archebishop | of Colone, and prince Electour* (London: Daye, 1547). See below, p. 235 for more details.

146 Bornert, 'Martin Bucer et la liturgie strasbourgeoise', p. 106.

O Lord, you who are on high. Blessed is he who comes in the name of the Lord; Help us, O Lord, you who are on high'.[147]

And then the priest should sing the words of the Holy Supper, as follow: 'Our Lord Jesus Christ, in the night that he was betrayed, took the bread', etc. These words should be sung with particular reverence by the priest, and slowly for good understanding in a way that can be noted by those nearby, and the people, at the end of these words of the Lord, should respond: 'Amen' … As soon as the people have spoken their Amen, the priest should sing back to them: 'Let us pray: Our Father in Heaven', etc.

After the Lord's Prayer the congregation should sing their 'Amen' again.[148]

It is not clear whether Luther's German *Sanctus* of 1525, or the version found in the Strasbourg *Gesangbuch*, or another, was to be used. Regardless, this gives us a fascinating insight into the dynamic between choir and congregation in this part of Germany. The service order was designed to satisfy the clergy in Cologne who were resisting von Wied's reforms.[149] The priest ('Priester' – a term no longer used in Strasbourg at this time) was still given the opportunity to sing a great deal of the service by himself, with the congregation expected to respond in the appropriate places.

A similar exchange occurred during Communion:

The *Agnus Dei* is to be sung, where there are clerks present, in Latin and in German, one after the other, and the German 'Gott sei gelobt' and 'Jesus Christus, unser Heiland' are to be added, if Communion lasts a long time.

---

147 This section is abridged in the 1547 English translation (the *Consultation*), in which this paragraph ends as follows: 'After these thinges, Sanctus shall be songe, where clerkes be, in latine, but of the people in douche [i.e. German], one syde answerynge the other, thryse of bothe partes. As for that, that is wont to be added The Lorde God of hostes, and Benedictus it shal be songe co[m]munely of the whole congregation, and therefore in douche'. *A simple, and religious consultation*, fol. Ff vj[r].

148 'Darauff folge dan das Sanctus, das, wo Cleriken seind, von jnen zu latein vnd vom volck zu teutsch gesungen werde, eins vmb das ander, jedes drei mal, Als so die Clericken singen Sanctus, das volck singe Heilig, aber das folgend Dominus deus sebaoth vnd das Benedictus sol in teutsch von der gantzen gemein gesungen werden vff diese weiß: Sanctus, heilig, Sanctus, heilig, Sanctus, heilig ist der Herr sebaoth, himel vnd erden ist vol deiner gute vnd herligkeit. Osanna, hilff, O Herr, der du bist in der hohe. Gelobet sei, der da kompt jm namen des Herren; hilff, Herr, der du bist in der hohe.

Vnd gleich darauff sollen vom Priester die wort des heiligen abendtmals, wie folgt, gesungen werden: "Vnser Herr Jesus Christus, in der nacht, da er verrathen wardt, nam er das brot" etc. Diese wort soll der Priester mit sonderer dapfferkeit vnd langsam zu guten verstandt singen in der weisen, die hernaher sol verzeichnet werden, vnd soll das volck zu end dieser wort des Herren "Amen" antworten … Wenn dan das volck sein Amen vff dise wort gesprochen, sol der Priester als bald wider singen: Last vns betten: "Vnser Vatter in dem Himel" etc.

Vff das gebet des Herren sol die gemein abermal jr Amen singen'. *Von Gottes genaden*, fols cx[r]/T2[r]–cx[v]/T2[v]; *BDS*, 11, 1, pp. 350–51.

149 The church order is likely to have been popular in England for similar reasons.

> At the end of Communion, the priest should sing to the people: 'The Lord be with you!' People: 'And with your spirit!'[150]

No suggestion was given as to how the people might have known to what melody or chant these responses were to be sung. It is intriguing that congregations were expected to sing even without clerks present, as then explained:

> Where there are no clerks present, such as in villages, everything should be sung and read in German, and the amount of singing should also be lessened, so that it may serve the improvement of the holiness of every person.[151]

A manuscript from 1528 in the Strasbourg archives contains proposals for the liturgy in the very Lutheran city of Nuremberg. It is entitled 'List of abuses and ceremonies that, through the power of the Word of God, have been discontinued and improved in Nuremberg'.[152] It is unclear which city was influencing the other, but given Nuremberg's initial refusal to co-operate with Strasbourg's reformers over the sacramental issue, it is likely that Strasbourg was observing the success of the reforms that had been carried out in Nuremberg.[153] We know from the archives in Strasbourg that the two cities were communicating about the reforms as early as 1525,[154] the year in which Nuremberg became Protestant, and there is other evidence for regular correspondence.[155] Also, it is noteworthy that several hymns from Strasbourg's *Teutsch Kirchenampt* were in use in Nuremberg during the first months and years of the Reformation.[156]

---

150 'Unther der Communion sol man das Agnus dei zu Latein vnd teutsch, eins vmbs ander, singen, wa man Clericken hat, Vnd das deutsch "Got sei gelobet" Vnd "Jesus Christus, vnser Heilandt," wo das Communicieren so lang wehret.

So die Communion geendet, sol der Priester zum volck singen: Der Herr sei mit euch! Volck: Vnd mit deinem Geist!' *Von Gottes genaden*, fol. cxi^r/T3^r; *BDS*, 11, 1, p. 351.

151 'Wo nicht Cleriken seindt, als vff den Dorfferen, da sol alles Teutsch gesungen vnnd gelesen vnnd das singen auch gemeßigt werden, wie es bey iederem volck zur besserung der Gotseligkeit dienen mag'. *Von Gottes genaden*, fol. cxi^v/T3^v; *BDS*, 11, 1, p. 352.

152 'Verzaichnus der geenderten mißpreuch vnnd Ceremonien so jnn Kraft des wort gottes zu Nurmberg abgestelt vnnd gepessert seyen'. 1 AST 95, 32, fol. 60r.

153 Rott, 'La Réforme à Nuremberg et à Strasbourg. Contacts et contrastes', in A. Chastel et al., *Hommage à Dürer. Strasbourg et Nuremberg dans la première moitié du XVIe siècle* (Strasbourg: Istra, 1972), pp. 105–6. Many scholars have reported that it is impossible to determine whether there was any direct influence. See Bornert, *Réforme protestante du culte*, p. 82; J. Smend. *Die evangelischen deutschen Messen bis zu Luthers Deutscher Messe* (Göttingen: Vandenhoeck, 1896), p. 178–83; J. V. Pollet, *Martin Bucer – Études sur la correspondance*, 2 vols (Paris: Presses Universitaires de France, 1958–62), vol. 2, pp. 83–9, 95–8.

154 1 AST 95, 28.

155 1 AST 95, 29 ('Rapport du sénat de Nuremberg sur le colloque récemment tenu', 1525); 1 AST 30 ('Les 12 articles du colloque', 1525); 1 AST 95, 31 ('Nuremberg à Strasbourg – avis sur la réforme', 1526). However, the only article of any relevance to musical activity is 1 AST 95, 32.

156 Leaver, *'Goostly psalmes and spirituall songes': English and Dutch Metrical Psalms from Coverdale to Utenhove 1535–1566* (Oxford: Clarendon Press, 1991), p. 20.

In 1523, the Nuremberg council forbade the sale of polemical songs in print. Scribner comments on the remarkable sensitivity of the city towards attacks on the Roman Church, despite its allegiance to the evangelical reforms.[157] It is likely, however, that such a move was designed to suppress opposition as much to the new evangelical faith as to the old faith. Nevertheless, the earliest Reformation song book appeared in Nuremberg in 1524, in the so-called *Achtliederbuch*,[158] but the printer, Jobst Gutknecht, protected himself by publishing the work anonymously and claiming that it originated in Wittenberg.[159] The first reformed liturgy used in Nuremberg reserved a place for congregational singing.[160]

The 1528 Strasbourg manuscript may have been copied from the original in Nuremberg. As would be expected, the proposals it contained were not identical to those found in Strasbourg, but did at least bear some resemblance. One of the most noticeable differences was the apparent retention of a great deal more sung Latin in the Nuremberg service, as well as many more of the Mass Ordinary texts. Thus, the Mass began with a sung introit (but one which does not mention the saints), followed by a psalm in its entirety. The words of the introit were to be taken from the psalm text that followed it. The *Kyrie* and *Gloria* came next (presumably sung, but it is not specified by whom), and then a 'Christian' collect was used.[161] It is not specified in which language the gradual was to be sung, but the readings were to be in German, 'so that everyone may understand and comprehend' (*das solchs. yederman versteen. vnnd begreyffen mag*). The Apostles' Creed and the beginning of the Preface were then sung (apparently in Latin, by the priest), and then the church elders may have sung from 'Qui, pridie quam pateretur, accepit panem …' ('Who, the day before he suffered, took bread …') up to the end of the text of the Lord's Supper, but omitting the Canon, 'which would disgrace and slander God and his holy Word, and also the

[157] R. W. Scribner, *For the Sake of Simple Folk* (Oxford: Oxford University Press, 1981), p. 74. Jean-François Gilmont suggests that the council's decision was taken for fear of 'external political repercussions' (F. Gilmont, trans. K. Maag, *The Reformation and the Book* (Ashgate: Aldershot, 1988), p. 95).

[158] *Etlich Cristlich lider | Lobgesang / vn[nd] Psalm / dem rai- | nen wort Gottes gemeß / auß der | heylige[n] schrifft / durch mancher- | ley hochgelerter gemacht / in der | Kirchen zů singen / wie es dann | zum tayl berayt zů Wittenberg in ůbung ist* (Nuremberg: Gutknecht, 1524). The eight hymns it contains are: 'Nun frewt euch lieben Christen gmein', 'Ach got von hymel sihe darein', 'Es spricht der vnweysen mundt wol', 'Auß tieffer not' (all by Luther), 'Es ist das hayl vns kum[m] en her', 'Jn Got / gelaub ich das er hat', 'Hilff got / wie ist der me[n]schen not' (all by Paul Speratus), and 'Jn Jesus namen heben wir an' (anonymous).

[159] Leaver, *'Goostly psalmes and spirituall songes'*, pp. 6, 18.

[160] A. Pettegree, *Reformation and the Culture of Persuasion* (Cambridge: Cambridge University Press, 2005), p. 46.

[161] 'Jnn solchem ampt wurdet anfangs der jntroitus allein von der zeyt. vnnd keinem heligen gesungen, vnnd nach dem verß des jntroitus singet man den ganntzen psalm vom anfanng biß zum ennde. auß welchem des jntroitus genomen ist … Vnnd das kirieleison. Gloria jn excelsis deo. Et interra pax. sampt einer Cristenlichen oration. die man collect[en] nennt'. 1 AST 96, 32, fols 63r–63v.

work of our redemption'.[162] Following this, the priest, and apparently no one else, sang 'Oremus: preceptis salutaribus moniti' (literally: 'Let us pray: Having been reminded by the command of our Saviour'), followed by the Lord's Prayer.

Instead of Matins, the Nuremberg reformers suggested holding an office that, like its Strasbourg and Wittenberg counterparts, included the singing of psalms, readings, and a short sermon. The service of Vespers similarly included psalm singing, readings from the Old Testament, and the *Magnificat*. The people were also encouraged to participate in congregational singing on feast days:

> Likewise, on feast days also, in several churches, before and after the sermon, German songs and psalms are sung by all the people, in order to raise their souls and their faith towards God, so that they may be all the more splendidly illuminated and advised.[163]

One aspect of this liturgical proposal that is not found in those of Strasbourg is an apparent concern with musical unanimity. So, the psalm at the beginning of the Mass was to be sung 'in the tone in which the verse of the introit is likewise to be sung'.[164] Likewise, the gradual was to be sung 'in its given tone' (*Jnn seinem darzu gemacht[en] Tone*). Finally, when the elders sang 'Qui, pridie quam pateretur', etc., it was instructed that this also be 'in the tone or melody of the Preface' (*jnn dem Tone oder Melodey der p[re]fation*).[165]

Nuremberg, then, although perhaps not directly either influential for or influenced by Strasbourg's policy towards church music, was very much aware of the developments occurring in the Strasbourg liturgy, and had certain things in common with it: the liturgy apparently has no provision for a polyphonic choir (and the mentions of 'tones' and 'melodies' implies that any Latin singing would be plainchant only), and makes explicit the point that congregational psalm singing in German is to the benefit of the people and God. On the other hand, as in Cologne, the priest (and it is again notable that the term 'Priester' is used) sings a great deal of the service by himself, and there is a requirement to use the appropriate tone for sung texts.

---

162 'Vnnd facht der priester ob dem altes mit hoher stÿm an zusingen. jnn dem Tone oder Melodey der p[re]fation. Qui pridie qua[m] pateretur. biß zum enndc der wort des herrn nachtmals. Vnnterlesst aber alle anndere / vor vnnd nach geende wort. des gotlosen Canons. darjnn got vnnd sein heyligs wort. auch das werck vnnser erlosung. so hoch geschmecht. vnd verlesstert wurdt'. 1 AST 95, 32, fols 63v–64r. The Canon was the first aspect of the Roman Mass which was removed from the Strasbourg liturgy, in Diobald Schwarz's German Mass of 1524.

163 'Deßgleichen werden auch an den feÿertagen. vor vnnd nach den predigen jnn etlichen kirchen Cristennliche teutsche lieder vnnd psalmen durch alles volck gesungen damit es zu erhebung jrs gemuets vnnd glawbens gegen got. dester statlicher angezindet vnd ermanet werd[en]'. 1 AST 95, 32, fol. 65r.

164 'alles jnn dem Tone darjnn derselb verß des jntroit[us] gesungen wurdet'. 1 AST 95, 32, fol. 63r.

165 1 AST 95, 32, fol. 63v.

In 1533, however, a more concrete proposal for Nuremberg was put forward by Johann Brenz and Andreas Osiander, reformers in Württemberg and Nuremberg respectively. It made clear that there was a role for a choir, if there was a nearby school that could provide singers, and that this choir would sing the introit, *Kyrie*, *Gloria*, and other parts of the service in Latin. The order states that, during Communion,

> the scholars shall sing *Agnus Dei*; but where no scholars are available, the congregation may sing that, or something else agreeable to the word of God and the requirement of the time, as the custom is. Where the number of people is so great that it drags on in length, there shall be sung, not only a Communion (also taken from holy Scripture), but also something else until the people have completed everything.[166]

The direction is strikingly similar to that of von Wied's order for Cologne, mentioned above. In addition, Osiander's church order was influential for the orders of Brandenburg (1540), Brandenburg-Lüneburg (1542), Mecklenburg (1540 and 1552), and Cassel (1539).[167]

Strasbourg's may also have influenced Cassel more directly. Much in the same way as the order for Ulm, the Cassel order of 1539[168] also made provisions for the children to lead the singing:

> On Sundays, at the second signal [of the bells], which should always be rung half an hour before the third, the schoolchildren should be led into the church and sing some Latin psalms and songs for a quarter of an hour. Then a boy should read out the Sunday Gospel, after which the whole congregation should sing the Creed and other spiritual songs until the [beginning of the] sermon.[169]

---

166 'Dieweyl das geschicht, sollen die schuler singen: Agnus dei etc. Wo aber nicht schuler vorhanden sein, mag die gemain das oder etwas anders, das dem wort Gottes und gelegenheyt der zeyt gemeß ist, singen, wie man das im brauch hat. Und wo die menig des volcks so groß ist, das es sich in die lenge verzeůcht, soll man nicht allein ein communio (auß der heyligen schrifft genummen) singen, sunder mag und sol auch etwas mer singen, biß das das volck alles verricht ist'. Quoted in G. Müller, G. Seebass et al., eds, *Andrias Osiander d. Ä. Gesamtausgabe*, 10 vols (Gütersloh: Gütersloher Verlagshaus Mohn, 1975–97), vol. 5, pp. 161–2. Translated in G. J. Cuming, *A History of Anglican Liturgy*, 2nd edn (London: Macmillan, 1982), p. 283; and quoted in Leaver, *'Goostly psalmes and spirituall songes'*, p. 21.

167 Leaver, *'Goostly psalmes and spirituall songes'*, p. 21. See also Osiander's letter from 1531 in Pollet, *Martin Bucer – Études sur la correspondance*, vol. 2, p. 130.

168 *Ordenung der Kirchen zu Cassel alles eusserliches diensts vnd götlicher hendel halben, so die gemeyn Gottes auffzuerbawen jm Glauben von nöten* (Kassel: Engell, 1539); reproduced in *BDS*, 7, pp. 279–318.

169 'Auff die Sontage aber so sollen die schůler zu dem andern zeychen, welchs man allwege ein halbe stunde vor dem dritten leutten sol, in die Kirche gefůrt werden und daselbst uff ein viertel einer stunden etwas latinischer Psalmen und gesang singen, und daruff sol ein knabe das Sonntåglich Evangelion verlesen, uff welchs die gantze gemeyn den glauben und andere geystliche lieder biß zur predige singen sollen'. *BDS*, 7, p. 293.

Strasbourg had not been the first place in Germany to employ children to lead the singing during evangelical worship (Wittenberg had done so since the early 1520s), but considering Bucer's involvement in the proposals for Cassel and Ulm, it seems likely that such a practice was introduced in these cities partly as a result of Strasbourg also having adopted it. The order stated that the people should sing at various points during the service, especially around the time of Holy Communion, beginning with 'Gott sei gelobet' and continuing with other songs.[170] It was also the duty of the preacher to warn or remind the people that songs before and after the sermon were to be sung with great and common devotion, and that only songs suitable for the church were to be used. Finally, as in Strasbourg, the children were not to leave the church after they have sung, but were to remain there until the end of the sermon, with the exception of 'the very small ones or those who are too cold' to remain in the church.[171]

The setup being proposed by Bucer here is that the children could be employed both to sing *to* the congregation in Latin, and to sing *with* them in German. Although no mention was made of the German language in relation to the songs, the fact that Latin was specifically mentioned is significant. This, along with the fact that the Creed and 'spiritual songs' would in all likelihood have been in German, implies that the congregation was singing in the vernacular. It seems also that the reading of the Gospel passage for the day by one of the boys meant that (at least in theory) people could reflect on its significance during the singing, before the sermon had begun.

Other indications of influence are to be found in documents relating to many other cities. Many of these make all-too familiar arguments about the Mass and about the true way to praise God. One report by the Strasbourg preachers advising the Frankfurt authorities on the restitution of a church commented on the 'unspeakable blasphemy and insubordination' (*das unaussprechliche gotteslaesterung und tratzung*) of the Mass-priests, and cited scriptural evidence from Matthew, Mark, Luke, and the Pauline epistles for the way to sing and pray in church.[172] The Augsburg church order of 1537,[173] which Bucer helped to write,

[170] 'daruff das heilig Sacrament, durch sich selbst den leib des Herren, Durch den Capellan zu der andern seitten des tischs das blůt des Herren, außspenden, in dem sol die kirch singen Erstlich Gott sei gelobet, Darnach andere gesenge und Psalmen, so lange das Comuniciren wert'. *BDS*, 7, pp. 288–9.

[171] 'Man sol auch in der Predige das volck trewlich vermanen, daß sie die heiligen gesenge vor und nach der predigen samptlichen und mit gemeiner hoher andacht singen wо̊llen.

Man sol auch nichts denn bewerte gesange in den kirchen singen lassen.

Es sollen auch die schůler hinfurt nit also, wie bißher geschehen, nach den gesengen auß der Kirchen gelassen werden, Es weren dann die gar kleiner oder so kalt, daß sie sich in der kirchen nit erhalten mо̊chten'. *BDS*, 7, p. 293. See also Hobbs, '"Quam Apposita Religioni Sit Musica"', pp. 171–2.

[172] 1 AST 167, 11, p. 507; *BDS*, 16, pp. 157–8.

[173] *Forma / wie von dem hai- | ligen Tauff / vnd dem hailigen | Sacrament des leibs vnd blůts Christi / vnd demnach | vom Elichen Stand bey dem Einsegen der Eeleüt / | zureden sey / Gestellt in die Kirch vnd | Gemaind Christi der Statt | Augspurg* (Augsburg: Otmar, 1537). Reproduced in *BDS*, 16, pp. 215–68.

contained plenteous opportunities for singing. The cantor was to stand up and sing psalms when the people were assembling for the sermon on Sundays and feast days.[174] Psalms and spiritual songs were also sung by the people at the end of the Lord's Supper and before and after Sunday evening and weekday sermons.[175] The churches also held a service of evening prayer on Saturdays at which psalms would be sung and the schoolchildren would sing the German Litany (*darauff die schuller lassen die teutsch letenej singen*).[176] Schoolchildren played a significant part in the leading of psalm singing in Augsburg. The document also stated that this activity was 'to be orderly and held with all devotion' (*Das gesanng soll ordennlich vnd mit aller andacht gehalten werden*).[177]

England

At the Diet of Augsburg in 1548, Emperor Charles V, increasingly determined to reunite Germany under one faith, gave a decree ordering Protestants throughout Germany to re-embrace Roman Catholicism, albeit with some small concessions to the Protestant side. This decree was made law on 30 June 1548, and became known as the Augsburg Interim. It was considered to be a temporary measure until a more permanent solution could be achieved.[178] Bucer, however, refused to accept[179] or even consider adopting the Interim in Strasbourg, which strained the relationship between him and Jakob Sturm, and eventually made his position in the city untenable. In March 1549, Sturm was forced to expel Bucer from Strasbourg,[180] and in December of that year, the Interim was finally introduced in the city. Bucer accepted an invitation from Thomas Cranmer, Archbishop of Canterbury, to travel to England[181] and assist with the church reforms there. He took up the position of Regius Professor of Divinity at the University of Cambridge, and assisted in the preparation of the second edition of the *Book of Common Prayer* (1552), renowned today, ironically, for its lack of provision for music. He died in Cambridge in 1551, without ever seeing the second edition.

In *De Regno Christi* (a work completed in 1550, but not published until 1557),[182] Bucer states that some freedom must be allowed to churches 'so that each may define the content and method of presentation of sacred readings,

174 *BDS*, 16, p. 229.

175 Ibid., pp. 231–3.

176 Ibid., p. 233.

177 Ibid., pp. 240–41, 244.

178 A. Leonard, *Nails in the Wall: Catholic Nuns in Reformation Germany* (Chicago and London: University of Chicago Press, 2005), p. 110.

179 Greschat, *Martin Bucer*, p. 221; D. F. Wright, *Common Places of Martin Bucer* (Appleford, Abingdon: Sutton Courtenay Press, 1972), p. 67.

180 Greschat, *Martin Bucer*, p. 225.

181 Bucer had established connections with England in the early years of Strasbourg reform, in the hope that England might one day prove a useful ally to the city.

182 *De Regno Christi* (Basel: Oporinus, 1557).

interpretations of Scriptures, catechizing, administration of the sacraments, prayers and psalms', for the building up of faith.[183] At this late stage in his life, he also believed that music should be used as a source of recreation, as well as devotion, without fear of 'relaxation of morals or delight in wicked idleness and from which there may also be gained a certain strengthening of health as well as some improvement in the cultivation of the mind'.[184] This stance was certainly more liberal than the one taken almost a decade earlier in the *Gesangbuch*, in which he wrote that no singing or playing of instruments should take place 'except by and for Christian spiritual activities'.[185]

Despite the notable lack of mention of music in the second *Book of Common Prayer*, Bucer may have had a certain amount of influence regarding some music-related changes. In the *Censura Martini Buceri super libro sacrorum*, a report on the first *Book of Common Prayer*, Bucer wrote that he was in favour of singing the *Sanctus*, but not as in some churches where the impatient priest calls for a prayer for the state of the Church.[186] He also considered the separation of choir and congregation to be of no function other than 'to get the clergy some respect above the laity, as if they were nearer to God than laymen are'.[187]

Strasbourg's influence on the English Protestant movement began long before Bucer's arrival on English soil. Valerain Poullain, Marten Micron, Paul Fagius, and Peter Martyr were all present in Strasbourg during the 1540s and were subsequently involved in the English reforms.[188] Bucer had initiated correspondence with Thomas Cranmer (at that time Henry VIII's ambassador at the court of Emperor Charles V) in October 1531,[189] a year before Cranmer was appointed Archbishop of Canterbury. Bornert comments that Bucer 'was

[183] 'Qua in re ecclesijs CHRISTI sua est permittenda libertas, quo unaquæque cum prȩfiniat modum, & rationem, sacrarum lectionum, interpretationum Scripturaru[m], Catechismi, administrationis Sacramentorum, precum & psalmorum'. Bucer, *De Regno Christi*, book 1, chapter 13, p. 73; translated by W. Pauck, in *Melanchthon and Bucer* (London: SCM Press, 1969), p. 256.

[184] 'à quibus non solum nulla morum metuenda sit dissolutio, nefarijq[ue] ocij prolectatio: uerùm certa compareetur, sicut ualetudinis corroboratio: ita etia[m] aliqua culturæ mentis accessio … Hi ludi ex arte Musica, & Gymnastica petendi erunt'. Bucer, *De Regno Christi*, book 2, chapter 54, pp. 206–7.

[185] 'kein Lied ůberal / kein seitenspil / anders dann von / vnd zů christlichen geistlichen hendelen gesungen vnd gebrauchet wůrde' (Appendix H, p. 343). *Gesangbuch* (1541), fol. A3r; *BDS*, 7, p. 579.

[186] *Censura Martini Buceri super libro sacrorum*, chapter 8, in Bucer, *Scripta Anglicana Fere Omnia* (Basel: Perna, 1577), p. 467.

[187] 'Chori tanta à reliquo templo seiunctio, cò seruit, vt ministri, qualescunq[ue] fide sint & vita, ipso tamen ordine & loco habeantur quasi Deo propinquiores quam laici'. *Censura Martini Buceri super libro sacrorum*, chapter 1, in Bucer, *Scripta Anglicana*, p. 457; translated by J. Cosin, *The Works of the Right Reverend Father in God, John Cosin, Lord Bishop of Durham*, ed. J. Sansom and J. Barrow, 5 vols (Oxford: Parker, 1843–1855), vol. 5, p. 436.

[188] Leaver, *'Goostly psalmes and spirituall songes'*, p. 32.

[189] D. MacCulloch, *Thomas Cranmer: A Life* (New Haven and London: Yale University Press, 1996), p. 65.

preceded by his reputation, by a few of his works, and in particular by one of his liturgical formulae',[190] namely, the *Consultation*[191] of Hermann von Wied, Archbishop of Cologne, which found its way to England and played a part in the formulation of the first *Book of Common Prayer*. Of course, Bucer had been an adviser to the Cologne reforms, until the papal excommunication of Hermann in 1546, and the *Consultation* was largely the work of the Strasbourg reformer.

Robin Leaver remarks that the *Consultation*

> first appeared in German in 1543; in Latin in 1545, and in English (from the Latin) in 1547 … Cranmer had his own copy of the Latin version[,] and the German original, as well as the Latin, had had some currency in England before the English version was produced. Consequently it became a major source in the compilation of the first Prayer Book … But … none of [its] suggestions regarding congregational hymn-singing found a place within its pages.[192]

Intriguingly, Bucer's influence on English Protestantism can be traced back even to before the English nation had broken with Rome. In 1530, a book entitled *The Psalter of Dauid in Englishe purely a[n]d faithfully tra[n]slated aftir the texte of Feline*[193] appeared. This was an English translation of the Latin version, which had been published one year earlier,[194] and was the first English version of the Psalter to appear. The preface was by a certain 'Johan Aleph':

> Johan Aleph greteth the Englishe nacion. Beglad in [th]e lorde (dere brothern) & geue him thankes: which nowe at [th]e laste / of his merciable goodnes hath sente ye his Psalter in Englishe / faithfully & purely translated: which ye may not mesure and Juge aftir the come[n] texte.[195] For the trowth of [th]e Psalmes muste be fetched more nyghe [th]e Ebrue verite / in the which tonge Dauid / with the other syngers of [th]e Psalmes firste sunge them. Let [th]e gostly lerned in [th]e holy tonge be iuges. Jt is [th]e spirituall man (saith Paule) which hath the spirit of god [tha]t muste de[ce]rne & iuge all thynges. And [th]e men quietly sittynge (if the truth be shewed them) muste iuge and stand up and speke (the firste interpret[er] holdynge his pease) god geue ye true spirituall & quiete sittynge iuges Ame[n].[196]

---

190 Bornert, *Réforme protestante du culte*, p. 205.

191 See p. 226, n. 145.

192 Leaver, *The Liturgy and Music: A Study of the Use of the Hymn in Two Liturgical Traditions* (Bramcote, Notts.: Grove Books, 1976), p. 7.

193 *The | Psalter of Dauid | in Englishe purely a[n]d | faithfully tra[n]slated af | tir the texte of Feline: | euery Psalme hauyn- | ge his argument befo- | re / declarynge brefly | thentente & sub- | stance of the | wholl | Psal | me* (Antwerp: de Keyser, 1530).

194 See Chapter 3, pp. 149–50.

195 That is, the Vulgate.

196 *The Psalter of Dauid*, fol. A.1v.

Johan Aleph was a pseudonym for George Joye, an English priest with reforming tendencies who fled England in 1527 and worked in Antwerp,[197] famous for its printing industry, and an important centre of trade between the European continent and London.[198] But who was Feline? In a letter to Zwingli in July 1529, Bucer explained that

> I am employed … in an exposition of the Psalms, which, at the urgent request of our brethren in France and Lower Germany, I propose to publish under a foreign name, that the work may be bought by their booksellers. For it is a capital crime to import into these countries books which bear our names. I therefore pretend that I am a Frenchman.[199]

The reason for Bucer's pseudonym was to avoid attracting attention from both the Roman Church and the Lutherans, the latter because of complaints from the Lutherans that Bucer was too close theologically to the Swiss camp, especially with respect to the ongoing and developing debate about the nature of the Eucharist. Bucer was indeed right to err on the side of caution. In 1531, two years before Henry VIII proclaimed himself head of the Church in England, 'The Psalter, in English' was listed by John Stokesley, Bishop of London, in a memorandum against the 'buying, selling, or reading'[200] of heretical books[201] (although it would not have been immediately obvious that Bucer was the author). However, those in England keen to see the country embrace the Reformation made use of Bucer's psalms. In 1534, William Marshall produced one of the first primers – or books of hours – in English,[202] which made use of much material that had already been printed (illegally) in England. As demonstrated by Constantin Hopf, the psalms used were those of Bucer, translated by

[197] C. C. Butterworth, *The English Primers (1529–1545) – Their Publication and Connection with the English Bible and the Reformation in England* (Philadelphia: University of Pennsylvania Press, 1953), p. 19.

[198] Leaver, *'Goostly psalmes and spirituall songes'*, p. 57.

[199] 'sed pro mea facultatula in Psalmis, quorum enarrationem, impulsus a fratribus *Galliae* et *inferioris Germaniae*, statui edere sub alieno nomine, quo a Bibliopolis illorum libri emantur. Capitale enim est nostris nominibus praenotatos libros regionibus illis inferre. Simulo itaque me Gallum'. J. M. Schuler and J. Schulthess, *Huldrici Zuinglii Opera*, 8 vols (Zurich: Schulthess, 1829–42), vol. 8, p. 316; translated by T. McCrie *History of the Progress and Suppression of the Reformation in Italy in the Sixteenth Century* (Edinburgh: Blackwood; London: Cadell, 1827), p. 36. Both English and Latin are also quoted in Hopf, *Martin Bucer and the English Reformation*, p. 208 (incl. n. 2).

[200] J. S. Brewer, ed., *Letters and Papers, foreign and domestic, of the reign of Henry VIII*, 21 vols (London: Longman, 1862–1920), vol. 5 (1531–1532), pp. 768–9. Available as an electronic resource at www.tannerritchie.com/memso.php, ed. J. Gairdner (accessed 8 April 2011).

[201] Hopf, *Martin Bucer and the English Reformation*, p. 214, n. 1.

[202] *A Prymer in Englyshe, with | certeyn prayers & godly meditations, very | necessary for all people that vnder- | stonde not the Latyne tongue* (London: Byddell, 1534).

George Joye.[203] Moreover, 60 per cent of the material contained in the book had first been printed in Joye's *Ortulus Animae*,[204] an earlier primer. The remainder of the book drew largely on Luther's writings, without acknowledgement.[205] But Hopf suggests, rather naïvely, that the vernacular translations 'were already sung and read by congregations who used the Primer, and who thus were acquainted with the English translation of Bucer's Latin Psalter ... before [Miles] Coverdale gave the Bible[206] to his nation' in 1535.[207] It can be stated with certainty that the Psalms were not sung in English by congregations at this stage (despite Joye's comments in the 1530 psalter preface that the Psalms were originally written as songs, and sung by David and his fellow singers). Not being metrical translations, they would not have lent themselves well to common melodies, and we are unaware of any such melodies having been written for these initial translations. Even if they had been somehow sung to plainchant, there is no evidence to support this possibility.

However, as research by Robin Leaver and Anne Wolff-Hoffmann has demonstrated,[208] Strasbourg's influence on the music of the English Reformation had an even more direct route than through Bucer's translations. Leaver suggests that during the years 1530 to 1534, Miles Coverdale, whose influence on English psalmody is beyond question, is known to have travelled around northern Europe, where he encountered the practice of singing hymns in various cities.[209] Coverdale then apparently returned to England in 1535, where he printed his psalter.[210] He left England again in 1540, following the execution of his close friend, Robert Barnes, who had fallen out of favour with Henry VIII. Coverdale arrived in Strasbourg during the second half of 1540 and remained until the following year.[211] This constant travel to and from reforming cities on the continent would have exposed Coverdale to a variety of congregational singing practices and styles, which he would then have taken back to England with him.

In total, 14 Strasbourg melodies found their way into English psalters during the sixteenth century.[212] Five Strasbourg tunes appeared in Coverdale's *Goostly*

203 Hopf, *Martin Bucer and the English Reformation*, p. 223.

204 (Antwerp: de Keyser, 1530).

205 Butterworth, *The English Primers*, p. 59. See also Butterworth and A. C. Chester, *George Joye – 1495?–1553* (Philadelphia: University of Pennsylvania Press, 1962), pp. 60–67; and Leaver, *'Goostly psalmes and spirituall songes'*, pp. 58–62.

206 *BIBLIA | The Bible that | is the holy Scripture of the | Olde and New Testament, faith- | fully and truly translated out | of Douche and Latyn | into Englishe* (Cologne or Marburg?: Cervicornus & Soter?, 1535).

207 Hopf, *Martin Bucer and the English Reformation*, pp. 207, 223.

208 Wolff-Hoffmann, 'L'Influence de l'hymnodie strasbourgeoise sur l'Eglise d'Angleterre à ses débuts, par l'intégration de mélodies dans des recueils de cantiques publiés entre 1535 et 1610', 2 vols (Master's diss., Université de Paris X Nanterre, 2006).

209 Leaver, *'Goostly psalmes and spirituall songes'*, p. 62.

210 Ibid., p. 67.

211 Leaver, *'Goostly psalmes and spirituall songes'*, pp. 32–3.

212 Wolff-Hoffmann, 'L'Influence de l'hymnodie strasbourgeoise', vol. 1, p. 136.

psalmes and spirituall songes (c. 1535), including the setting of the *Magnificat*.[213] Other books, either printed in England or for English refugee congregations in places like Geneva, also contained Strasbourg tunes which then found their way to English as well as to Dutch psalters and hymnals.[214] Wolff-Hoffmann believes that many of the Strasbourg tunes were in use by foreign communities in England before they were printed there.[215]

Not only were Strasbourg's melodies in circulation at this time, but also its texts. Joye's translation of the Psalms into English was no doubt a source of influence for later publications such as *Goostly psalmes and spirituall songes*. Hopf writes that 'as Coverdale knew Latin and Greek but not Hebrew sufficiently, a work like that of Bucer would be invaluable, if available'.[216] Robin Leaver has identified more precisely the likely sources of Coverdale's influence, observing that many of the hymns originated in Wittenberg. Some had also come from Strasbourg.[217] Coverdale's 1535 edition of the Bible includes texts that had been used in *Goostly psalmes*, but also some by Symphorianus Pollio which had first appeared in the first edition of *Psalmen gebett* (Strasbourg: Köpfel, 1526). *Goostly psalmes* appeared in London in around 1535,[218] printed anonymously, but with Coverdale's name in the preface title: 'Myles Couerdale Unto the Christen reader'.[219] In the preface, he complains about the corrupt songs being sung by the youth of England:

> Therfor to geue oure youth of Englonde some occasion to chaunge theyr soule & corrupte balettes into swete songes and spirituall Hymnes of Gods honoure, and for theyr owne consolacion in hym, I haue here (good reader) set out certayne comfortable songes grounded on Gods worde, and taken some out of the holy scripture specyally out of the Psalmes of Dauid … As for the comen sort of balettes which now are vsed in [th]e world. I reporte me to euery good mans conscience what wicked frutes they brynge. Corruppe they not the maners of yonge persones? Do they not tangle them in the snares of vnclennesse?[220]

213 'Mein seel erhebt den herren mein' (Zahn, *Die Melodien der deutschen evangelischen Kirchenlieder*, no. 7550).

214 Wolff-Hoffmann, 'L'Influence de l'hymnodie strasbourgeoise', vol. 1, p. 98.

215 Wolff-Hoffmann, 'Which Texts for Travelling Tunes? The Metrical Psalms which Crossed the Channel from 1535 to 1603', paper presented at the Society for Reformation Studies 18th Annual Conference (Westminster College, Cambridge, 13–15 April 2011).

216 Hopf, *Martin Bucer and the English Reformation*, p. 223.

217 Leaver, *'Goostly psalmes and spirituall songes'*, pp. 79–80.

218 See ibid., pp. 65–6. See also Leaver, 'The Date of Coverdale's *Goostly psalmes*', *Internationale Arbeitsgemeinschaft für Hymnologie Bulletin*, 9 (1981), pp. 58–63.

219 Leaver, *'Goostly psalmes and spirituall songes'*, p. 62.

220 Coverdale, *Goostly psalmes and spirituall songes*, fols iii^{r}–iii^{v}. Quoted in Leaver, *'Goostly psalmes and spirituall songes'*, p. 287.

The language is notably similar to that found in the writings of the Strasbourg reformers against popular songs.

* * *

This chapter has shown that Strasbourg's influence on music in Protestantism was not only far reaching, but appeared in a variety of guises, some of them not always obvious. The *Gesangbuch* of 1541 represents the summation of Strasbourg's policy towards music, and was designed to reach as wide an audience as possible. Despite this, the Strasbourg reformers' attitudes towards music were already being disseminated much earlier in the Reformation.

Although these examples have provided a picture of the international significance of Strasbourg's reforms, there is not scope here to undertake a detailed review. A study of the musical policy of the Church of England, for example, would need to take into account not only the influence of Bucer (which one must be careful not to overestimate), but also that of many other continental reformers who had contact with individuals in England. Nevertheless, if reforming ideas differed between countries and even cities, it is clear that music crossed those boundaries. Strasbourg's role was central to this process. The early editions of the *Teutsch Kirchenampt*, for example, in addition to influencing English psalmody, also influenced congregational songs in Rostock and in Scandinavia, and throughout later decades some Strasbourg hymns found their way into songbooks and liturgical orders in Wittenberg, Leipzig, Augsburg, Bonn, Magdeburg, Pfalz-Neuburg, and Spangenberg.[221]

One major distinction between Wittenberg and Strasbourg is that the former was a university city and therefore a place of learning, whereas the latter, although its political situation was more fragile,[222] became a haven for those fleeing persecution. This means, therefore, that Wittenberg's musical influence, although highly significant, was initially disseminated by other centres of Protestantism that had adopted similar musical practices and were exposing them to religious refugees and other visitors. The fact that this influence occurred both as a result of exiles taking or sending German songs back home, and as a result of continental refugees singing them in their host countries or cities, is a fascinating thought. One of the clearest demonstrations of this process was in Strasbourg's reach across Europe.

221 See Wolff-Hoffmann, 'L'Influence de l'hymnodie strasbourgeoise', pp. 43–6.

222 On the political vulnerability of Strasbourg and its relationship with the English reformers, see P. Ha and P. Collinson, *The Reception of Continental Reformation in Britain* (Oxford: Oxford University Press, 2010), p. 3.

Conclusions

> [S]uch singing is done from the heart, not with the mouth alone, but that it should spring forth and come out of the heart; and this is what the Apostle means when he says: 'and sing to the Lord from your hearts'. For his meaning is not that we should sing without a voice, for then it would be impossible for us to encourage and edify the others, or how else could we speak with one another, concerning that which he writes to the Ephesians [chapter 5]?[1]
>
> Martin Bucer, *Grund und Ursach* (1524)

In 1562, the Council of Trent discussed the provision of music in the ceremonies of the Catholic Church. Its proceedings read: 'Let them keep away from the churches compositions in which there is an intermingling of the lascivious or impure, whether by instrument or voice'.[2] This was the only phrase on music actually published in the canons and decrees of the 22nd session of the Council (17 September 1562).[3] Despite this, a great deal of preparation had been necessary to ensure that music even appeared on the agenda.[4] The 24th session, held the following year, went slightly further in its recommendations, calling for those who held offices in the Church to 'be required to perform the divine offices themselves, rather than by means of substitutes … and, in a choir established for the singing of psalms, to praise the name of God reverently, distinctly, and devoutly with hymns and canticles'.[5] Although the Council therefore addressed in part the concerns relating to liturgical music that had been raised by the

[1] 'solich gesang im hertzen gescheh nit allein mit dem mund, sonder das es auß dem hertzen quelle und herkome. Das der Apostel damit meinet, da er spricht: *und singet dem herrn in ewern hertzen*, dann sein meinung nit ist, on stym zů singen, wie künten sust die andern ermanet und besseren werden'. *BDS*, 1, p. 276; translated in O. F. Cypris, 'Basic Principles: Translation and Commentary of Martin Bucer's *Grund und Ursach*, 1524' (PhD diss., Union Theological Seminary, New York, 1971), pp. 209–10.

[2] 'Ab ecclesiis vero musicas eas, ubi sive organo sive cantu lascivum aut impurum aliquid misceatur'. The Görres-Gesellschaft, ed., *Concilium Tridentinum: Diariorum, actorum, epistularum, tractatuum nova collectio*, 13 vols (Freiburg: Herder, 1901–), vol. 8, p. 963. Quoted and translated in C. A. Monson, 'The Council of Trent Revisited', *Journal of the American Musicological Society*, 55 (2002), p. 11.

[3] Monson, 'The Council of Trent Revisited', p. 11.

[4] The preliminary eighth canon of this session, which was not actually approved, has often been quoted as the decree itself. See Monson, 'The Council of Trent Revisited', p. 11, with reference to G. Reese, *Music in the Renaissance* (New York: Norton, 1954), p. 449.

[5] 'Omnes vero divina per se et non per substitutos compellantur obire officia … atque in choro ad psallendum instituto, hymnis et canticis Dei nomen reverenter, distincte devoteque laudare'. *Concilium Tridentinum*, vol. 9, p. 984.

Protestant reformers in the 1520s and 1530s, it also rejected outright changes to some of the other major issues regarding church music over which there had been initial disagreement between Protestants and Catholics. The use of the vernacular, for example, was specifically ruled out,[6] and, crucially, no provisions were made for congregational singing of psalms and hymns.

The numerous other points of discussion at the Council showed no signs of reconciliation with the Protestants. Although addressing many issues of abuse within the Catholic Church, in most doctrinal matters the Council approved the *status quo*. Protestantism therefore maintained an independent identity, and the schism remained permanent. For four centuries (until the Second Vatican Council of the 1960s) congregational participation in music remained almost exclusively under the ownership of the Protestant Churches. Music had been appropriated by the reformers to further their cause. In other words, music was both an area of reform and a means of promoting reforms. Strasbourg's particular skills had included defining hymnody and helping with its dissemination across the Protestant cities of Europe.

The utilisation of rich and varied accounts of Strasbourg's Reformation has painted a picture of the situation in which music evolved during this period under the difficult circumstances of church reform. Liturgical music, a fundamental part of religious devotion since ages past, underwent a sudden and radical change, both in terms of its perception and its practice. No longer were church choirs to sing in Latin on behalf of the laity. Singing had to be understood, actively participated in, and, above all, heartfelt. The unintelligible 'wailing', 'murmuring', and 'mumbling' of clerics was of no use to congregations, and did more harm than good. Whereas in many areas of reforming Germany, choral music complemented congregational music, in Strasbourg the notion of music as a performance was *replaced* by that of music as an experience: something actually felt communally by the laity.

However, the reformers did not limit their influence to sacred music, but made decisions about – and engaged with – all sorts and styles of music.[7] In the secular sphere, the reformers' attempts to suppress bawdy and lascivious songs were met with little enthusiasm. Rebecca Wagner Oettinger's observation that, for the people of the sixteenth century, no particular distinction existed between songs of the sacred and secular spheres[8] explains the reformers' hope that metrical psalms and spiritual songs could replace what they considered inappropriate rhymes. But despite this initial hope, in 1541 Bucer was still

[6] Sessio sexta (XXII), caput octavum (in *Concilium Tridentinum*, vol. 8, p. 961).

[7] A fact observed by Christopher Boyd Brown, among others. See C. B. Brown, *Singing the Gospel: Lutheran Hymns and the Success of the Reformation* (Cambridge, MA, and London: Harvard University Press, 2005), p. 170.

[8] *MPGR*, pp. 1–2. This is of course not to say that the laity expected to be allowed to sing lascivious songs during worship, but rather that, outside of church, a song was a song. Genres of music were a later innovative subtlety.

emphasising the point in his *Gesangbuch* preface, as well as in later writings, that the young must not sing unsuitable songs, and that it was the responsibility of parents to ensure their children were insulated from them: 'And woe to all who see and hear in this description [of unpleasantness] their children … every bird will be known by his song, and the word of the Lord will be fulfilled'.[9]

In other words, society knew what was 'right' to sing and what was 'wrong' to sing, even if individuals chose sometimes to ignore their consciences. Compared to somewhere like Joachimsthal, where secular music was acknowledged and indeed encouraged in a secular environment,[10] Bucer's position may seem drastic. But although publication of popular songs in Strasbourg slowed during the first 30 years of the Reformation, most likely owing to the reformers' opposition to such music, the genre actually seems to have flourished during the second half of the century, at the time when Johann Marbach was implementing a more conservative form of Lutheranism. The printer Thiebold Berger, for example, produced at least 38 secular song publications in his Strasbourg career.[11] Whether a more 'Lutheran' environment or Johann Marbach had anything to do with this proliferation is possible, but this is, in any case, not the place to determine the answer.

Joseph Herl has written that 'sixteenth-century writers did not attempt to define the purpose of music in church. Its purpose was obvious: it carried the liturgical text'.[12] Whether this is generally true is questionable; this was surely not its universal purpose. In Strasbourg, certainly, the situation was not this straightforward, and Herl's argument must be disputed on two points. First, fixed texts belonging to the liturgy were sung fairly infrequently in Strasbourg; there was a reduction, at least in the 1520s, in the number of Mass Proper texts (including the introit) and Mass Ordinary texts (the *Credo* and *Agnus Dei*, for example) being sung in the *Gottesdienst*. Second, it is clear that for Martin Bucer the purpose of music was not simply to 'carry the liturgical text'. Extra-liturgical texts such as the Psalms of David, as well as an increasing number of extra-scriptural texts, found their way into the hymn books. Their inclusion was not done in order to enable the texts to be repeated and relayed as they had been in late medieval times. Rather, they were there to encourage people to sing them, to absorb them, and to reflect on their relationship with their neighbours and with God. They were designed so that all levels of society could engage

---

9 'Vnd weh allen / die jren kindern … hierinn zůsehen vnd losen … ein jeder vogel bei seinem gesang erkennet / auch das wort des Herren erfüllet' (Appendix H, pp. 344–5). *Gesangbuch* (1541), fol. A3r; *BDS*, 7, p. 579.

10 See Brown, *Singing the Gospel*, pp. 43–53.

11 Other, less prolific, printers of popular tunes included P. Hugg and N. Wyriot. See M. U. Chrisman, *Bibliography of Strasbourg Imprints, 1480–1599* (New Haven: Yale University Press, 1982), pp. 189–95.

12 J. Herl, *Worship Wars in Early Lutheranism: Choir, Congregation, and Three Centuries of Conflict* (Oxford: Oxford University Press, 2004), p. 175.

with them. Although the songs were not accepted overnight, it did not take until the eighteenth century, as Herl proposes, for church music to be expected 'to awaken devotion in the listeners and point them to God'.[13] This sentiment was present much earlier on, and numerous Strasbourg documents, as presented in this book, bear witness to this.[14] The singing of the common people not only helped in the dissemination of reforming ideas, but also helped form the identity of the new Church, eventually becoming one of its defining features.

Of course, whether the Strasbourg congregations initially sang with much enthusiasm, or indeed at all, is another matter altogether. But interestingly, there seem to be no recorded complaints about the quality or lack thereof in church singing in Strasbourg. The French priest Gérard Roussel, visiting Strasbourg in 1525, wrote that in cathedral services 'the voices of women mingle agreeably with those of the men in the congregation in the singing of psalms rendered from Hebrew into the popular tongue'.[15] Likewise, although speaking of the French congregation, Hubert de Bapasme wrote in the mid-1540s that

> Some Psalm of David or another prayer from the New Testament is sung, and this is done by everyone together, men as well as women, in a harmonious way … I began to cry, not of sadness, but of joy in hearing them sing with such good heart, rendering grace to the Lord through song.[16]

Bapasme made a similar remark in a letter to another friend in Anvers in 1545:

> When I heard the singing I could not stop myself from crying. You would not hear any one voice rise above the others; everyone has a book of music in their hands, both men and women; everyone praises the Lord.[17]

---

[13] Ibid.

[14] Indeed, the theme is present much earlier in Christianity: the Church Fathers refer to music's spiritual power over and over again in their writings.

[15] 'adjunctis cantionibus in communem linguam ex hebraico psalterio transfusis, ubi mire assonant mulieres viris', and again, 'adjunctis cantionibus è psalterio hebraico in linguam communem transfuses … In cantionibus illis tam assonant mulieres viris'. G. Roussel, quoted in A.-L. Herminjard, *Correspondance des réformateurs dans les pays de langue française*, 9 vols (Geneva: Georg; Paris: Levy, 1866–97), vol. 1, pp. 407, 411–12. Translated by R. G. Hobbs, '"Quam Apposita Religioni Sit Musica": Martin Bucer and Music in the Liturgy', *Reformation and Renaissance Review*, 6 (2004), p. 155.

[16] 'On chante quelque pseaulme de david ou une aultre oroison prinse du nouveau testament / laquelle pseaulme ou oroison se chante touts ensemble tant hom[m]e que feme auecq vng bel acord / laquelle chose est bel a veoir … je [com]menchoie a plourer non point p[ar] trystesse mais de joie en les oia[n]s chanter de sy bo[n] coeur, [com]me jl chante[n]t rendant grace au se[igneu]r'. 1 AST 41, II, fol. 4v. Also quoted in A. Erichson, *L'Église française de Strasbourg au seizième siècle d'après des documents inédits* (Paris: Fischbacher, 1886), pp. 21–2, with variations in spelling.

[17] 'quant je oioie chanter je ne me savoie tenir de pleurer de joye ; vous ny oieriez point une voix desborder l'autre ; chascun a ung libvre de musicque en sa main, tant homme que femme, chascun loue le Seigneur'. Quoted in Erichson, *L'Église française*, p. 15.

This was exactly the sort of emotion the preachers were hoping to incite in the faithful. People who were moved by the experience of singing or by hearing such singing revealed their piety. Nor do the Strasbourg preachers appear to have complained about a lack of enthusiasm for singing, as Luther did, for example, at a sermon during Advent in 1526:

> The songs have been composed and are sung for your sake so that you can sing them here and at home, but you sit here like blocks of wood. Therefore I beg you, learn these songs from your children and sing them yourselves at the same time, as Paul teaches [in Ephesians 5:18–19].[18]

Nor are there any records of Strasbourg cantors or hymnal editors attempting to improve congregational singing, as was the case in Geneva. In 1551, the cantor Louis Bourgeois wrote a preface to the new edition of the Genevan Psalter, in which he explained the meaning of certain musical symbols and encouraged people to listen to those around them.[19] Solmisation was added to the tunes from 1556, and one editor in 1560 went to the effort of introducing a whole new system of musical notation to complement both solmisation and traditional staff notation.[20] Nothing like this appears to have been considered necessary in Strasbourg, at least during the first half of the century.

In short, the initial degree of quality and enthusiasm of the singing of the Strasbourg Protestants cannot be established. What is certain, however, is that there was a market for such psalms and spiritual songs. The initial flood of books containing hymns during the first four years of the Reformation (at least 25 editions were produced between 1524 and 1527) did not last, but by the mid-1530s at least one or two new editions were being produced in most years.[21] The success of the psalms would not have occurred if people had not been willing to buy them. The fact that these hymn books, the vast majority of which contained music, were so successful indicates that some were willing to attempt 'reading' this unfamiliar system of signs.[22] For this, though, they would already

---

18 'Factae cantilenae et canuntur propter vos, ut hic canatis et in domibus, sed sedetis hic ut die klotze. Ideo oro, ut discatis has cantilenas a pueris et simul canatis'. *WA*, 20, p. 546; quoted and translated in Herl, *Worship Wars*, p. 14. Luther made a similar complaint in 1529 (sermon on 24 January 1529, *WA*, 29, p. 44; see Herl, *Worship Wars*, p. 15). As these complaints were made in Latin, it is hard to envisage how the message reached most people.

19 See D. Trocmé-Latter, '"May those who know nothing be content to listen": Loys Bourgeois's *Advertissement* to the Psalms (1551)', *Reformation and Renaissance Review*, 11 (2009), pp. 335–47.

20 See Trocmé-Latter, 'The Psalms as a Mark of Protestantism: the Introduction of Liturgical Psalm-Singing in Geneva', *Plainsong & Medieval Music*, 20 (2011), pp. 158–60.

21 See Appendix A.

22 The system used in churches today, whereby the congregation is often given a text edition of the hymn book and the organist and other musicians read from the music edition, did not exist. In Reformation Strasbourg, any particular publication either contained music or it did not.

have needed to have the literacy skills to enable them to read the text. In any case, musical notation was increasingly visible to them, whether or not they were literate. Whereas most broadsheets expected the reader to have a memory bank of tunes and to fit the words accordingly, vernacular church books contained the notated melody, usually with a first-verse underlay. The novelty to most people must have been astonishing. For the illiterate, just being able to look at this unknown script would have been a novel experience.

The fact that the church songbook genre developed out of the liturgical order, however, demonstrates that Brown's assertion that the sixteenth-century hymn-printing industry was 'directed primarily to a domestic market'[23] does not apply to early Reformation Strasbourg, and in all likelihood does not apply to the situation in other major German cities at this time either.[24] Despite the fact that the vast majority of such books were no larger than 8° format, their primary function would have been for church singing. Liturgical orders may well have been used domestically for their song content, or else to satisfy an enthusiasm for collecting, but these books were not printed with a domestic environment in mind. Strasbourg's Protestants were not a repressed minority, so there would have been no need to recreate the liturgy in private as, say, there would have been for English Catholics in the second half of the sixteenth century. It is still quite possible, however, that many of these books were aimed at individuals rather than parish churches.[25]

In Strasbourg, the phenomenon of congregational hymnody is part of the broader trend of curiosity in the reforms on the part of the laity. Protestantism was of great interest even to rural inhabitants, who, according to the humanist Nikolaus Gerbel, flocked to hear the first services in German.[26] Although this account, like those that speak favourably of the singing of the congregations, is not likely to have been free from propagandistic bias, there is evidence that Strasbourg's Reformation was popular, and indeed encouraged, at the lower end of the societal spectrum. Brady observes that many groups in society 'briefly saw in the Evangelical movement a common vehicle for liberation' from a

---

23 Brown, *Singing the Gospel*, p. 11.

24 However, the term 'domestic', in this context, probably should be taken to refer to the environment outside the church more generally, rather than specifically inside the home.

25 Nevertheless, many books would only have been any use in worship if enough people were using the same edition.

26 'magna multitudine Rustici ad nos veniunt audituri germanicas missas'. Letter to Johann Schwebel, 30 May 1524, quoted in *Centuria epistolarum theologicarum ad Iohannem Schwebelum*, (Biponti: Wittel, 1597), p. 30; also in T. W. Röhrich, *Mittheilungen aus der Geschichte der evangelischen Kirche des Elsasses*, 3 vols (Paris and Strasbourg: Treuttel und Würtz, 1855), vol. 1, p. 396, n. 1. Röhrich suggests that the services were sung, but there is no concrete evidence for this (ibid., pp. 395–6). See the Meyer/Hobbs debate about the dawn of congregational singing in Strasbourg, the details of which are given in Chapter 2, p. 64, n. 118. On the early modern relationship between townspeople and peasants, see T. A. Brady, *Turning Swiss: Cities and Empire, 1450–1550* (Cambridge: Cambridge University Press, 1985), pp. 33–6.

common oppression, namely imperial control.[27] To minimise the chance of a revolt in lower class circles, the Imperial Diet had decreed on 9 February 1523 that preachers should 'shun everything that might stir up the Common Man against the rulers or confuse the ordinary Christian'.[28] Several of the major cities followed suit with their own legislation, with Strasbourg demanding on 1 December that preachers teach only the Gospel, and avoid 'all provocative and insulting comments, including everything which tends to rouse the Common Man to anger or confusion or to a rebellion against his rulers, lay or ecclesiastical'.[29] Whichever way the preachers interpreted such rulings, the Common Man was not deterred. In February 1524, two men disrupted Compline in the Dominican church by whistling over the singing of the monks.[30] Elsewhere, the militancy of the gardeners' guild, for example, led to the exhumation of St Aurelia's grave in November 1524 (a move supported by Martin Bucer) to see whether her relics actually existed. They found only leg bones.[31] In the same year, the parishioners of five churches had written to the council complaining about the 'disorder' (*mißordnung*) of the church's majesty, and the 'futile' (*vergeblichem*) choir singing. They had also asked for permission to take control of the services from the singers.[32] Likewise, in March 1525 a group of citizens requested that the council abolish the Mass and remove idols from the churches.[33] Instances of spontaneous iconoclasm throughout the mid-1520s also point towards the fact that this was, in many ways, a people's Reformation.[34]

One of the preachers' fundamental demands was that the laity should understand the liturgy and what was said and sung in church. Children were taught in the Strasbourg catechism of 1543 that congregational singing was the third of the 'customary church practices' (*die dritte allgemeine Kirchenůbung*).

---

27 Brady, *Turning Swiss*, p. 155.

28 'zu vermeiden, was zu bewegung des gemeinen mans widder die oberkeit oder aber die cristenmenschen in irrung zu furen ursach geben moge'. *Deutsche Reichstagsakten, jüngere Reihe*, 19 vols (Gotha: Perthes; Göttingen: Vandenhoeck & Ruprecht; Munich: Oldenbourg, 1893–), vol. 3, p. 747. Translated in Brady, *Turning Swiss*, pp. 157–8.

29 'Auch alle Reytz vnnd schmähe wort, darzu alles, das den gemeynen man in ergernysz oder zweyfel füren oder zu eyner embörung vnnd vngehorsame gegen seyner oberkeit, sie sey Geystlich oder weltlich, reytzen oder bewegen möcht'. Quoted in B. Moeller, 'L'Édit strasbourgeois sur la prédication du 1er décembre 1523 dans son contexte historique', in G. Livet and F. Rapp, *Strasbourg au cœur religieux du XVIe siècle*, p. 58. Translated in Brady, *Turning Swiss*, p. 157.

30 See above, p. 144. *Fragments des anciennes chroniques d'Alsace*, III (1892), no. 4504; R. Reuss, ed., 'Strassburg im sechszehnten Jahrhundert, 1500–1591: Auszug aus der Imlin'schen Familienchronik', *Alsatia*, 10 (1873–74), pp. 395–6.

31 L. P. Wandel, *Voracious Idols and Violent Hands: Iconoclasm in Reformation Zurich, Strasbourg, and Basel* (Cambridge: Cambridge University Press, 1994), p. 116. See also *Fragments des anciennes chroniques d'Alsace*, I (1887), no. 214; and Reuss, ed., 'Strassburg im sechszehnten Jahrhundert, 1500–1591', p. 401.

32 1 AST 87, 13, p. 1.

33 1 AST 87, 29. See also Wandel, *Voracious Idols and Violent Hands*, p. 121.

34 See Wandel, *Voracious Idols and Violent Hands*.

The three fundamentals of church worship were that songs should be taken from divine Scripture; that all singing should be directed to God; and that singing was to be carried out with heartfelt devotion.[35] None of these could happen unless the singer understood what they were singing.

Strasbourg's relationship with Latin was a complicated one, however. Bucer's stance towards the language in 1524 was that it was of little use to sixteenth-century society, having been used by the Ancient Romans and by the Papists in modern times as a tool of oppression, and containing nothing that could not be better expressed in Hebrew or Greek.[36] This view did not correspond with that of Jakob Sturm, who defended the use of Latin on various occasions.[37] Nor did it correspond with the opinion of other humanists. Latin had of course been the language of scholarship and diplomacy for many centuries, and that was set to continue. Latin was also, though, the language of the elite, whereas the Reformation, by its very nature, was reaching out to all levels of society. By 1525, however, the Strasbourg reformers' view had been adjusted so that they now considered Latin acceptable in church so long as an interpreter was present to translate for the people, as commanded in 1 Corinthians 14:27 ('If anyone speaks in a tongue, two – or at the most three – should speak, one at a time, and someone must interpret'). Furthermore, an increasing number of Latin schools were set up throughout the 1520s and 1530s until their eventual amalgamation and the formation of the Gymnasium in 1538.[38]

In congregational song, however, Latin – or any other foreign language – was not to be used. The few exceptions to this are macaronic[39] songs with isolated phrases of Latin or Greek, such as the setting of the German *Kyrie* and the hymn 'In dulci jubilo'. In the case of the *Kyrie*, the presence of Greek was deemed acceptable because it contained a German translation after each line of Greek in the following format:

> *Kyrie eleyson* / Herr erbarme dich
> *Christe eleyson* / Christe erbarme dich
> *Kyrie eleyson* / Herr erbarm dich über vns.[40]

'In dulci jubilo', on the other hand, contained untranslated Latin phrases:

> *Jn dulci iubilo* /
> nun singent vnd seind fro /

[35] *BDS*, 6, 3, p. 257.

[36] See above, p. 91. Bucer, *Grund und Ursach*, p. 209.

[37] See pp. 53–4 and 88.

[38] Chrisman, *Lay Culture, Learned Culture: Books and Social Change in Strasbourg, 1480–1599* (New Haven and London: Yale University Press, 1982), p. 193.

[39] That is, comprising a mixed-language text.

[40] This version is from *Psalmen gebett* (1526), fols xv^{v}–xvi^{r}.

vnsers herzens wunne /
leit *in praesepio* /
vnd leuchtet als die sonne /
matris in gremio /
Alpha es et o.[41]

However, this hymn did not enter the Strasbourg canon of hymns until the late 1530s, by which time the reformers were warming to the more liberal Lutheran theology of music.

Unsurprisingly, there do not seem to have been any popular or polemical songs written in Latin.[42] This was not a decision made by the reformers, of course, but by the songwriters themselves, who were trying to reach a local but broad audience. Only songs in the vernacular could appeal to all levels of society. Songs spoke to the common people: they spread news, opinions, myths, and facts. As Oettinger has demonstrated, existing songs were effectively modified in this era, especially in songs with polemical material. A tune would keep its association with the original song, which would add to the overall effect of the text.[43] By appropriating music in this way, the preachers were able to penetrate the private sphere of people's lives through an oral culture that extended into the home – whether or not the people wanted this to happen, and sometimes without their realisation. By implanting texts and melodies in the memories of Strasbourg's citizens, they would spread the Gospel message among family, friends, and passers-by.

Our knowledge of the genre of sixteenth-century popular music is still rather limited, as is our understanding of the relationship and crossover between the religious and secular spheres. As demonstrated in Chapters 2 and 3, a more careful evaluation is needed of the genre of the publications listed in *RISM DKL*. For Strasbourg alone, during the period studied here, there are two books erroneously included in this catalogue. One is a pamphlet containing a polemical song, and the other is a set of popular polyphonic songs.[44] There are, no doubt, others which remain overlooked. A survey of popular songs of the period in question would be a helpful beginning to a long-term evaluation of the problem. However, there is no quick solution. Unlike religious songs of the Reformation, popular songs are likely to have been printed on broadsheets or in small pamphlets, and as Oettinger observes, printed works, like any physical

---

41 This version is from the *Gesangbuch* (1541), pp. LXXVIII–LXXIX. Subsequent verses also contain untranslated Latin phrases.

42 *MPGR*, p. 206.

43 See ibid., pp. 89–136.

44 *Warer verstand von des herren Nachtmal* (Strasbourg: Prüss, 1527) (*RISM DKL* 1527[10]); and *Fünff vnd sechzig teütscher Lieder* (Strasbourg: Schöffer & Apiarius, before 1537) (*RISM DKL* 1537[02]).

objects, are subject to loss or destruction.[45] This means that our knowledge of these works is always likely to be significantly inferior to our knowledge of religious hymns and hymn books. However, we must work with the material that survives if we are to improve further our appreciation of the importance of communal singing.

Singing as a communal activity has of course existed for thousands of years, in all cultures and societies. It was this notion of singing as something so deeply fundamental to human existence that prompted the Strasbourg reformers to make use of it in a liturgical context. To them it was clear that people enjoyed singing (as demonstrated by their delight in immoral songs), and that God enjoyed having his praises sung to him by his people (as demonstrated in various passages of Scripture). The reformers' aim was therefore to exploit this love of singing and to put it to what they considered a better, more worthy use. This 'good' sort of singing induced not just joy, but also solidarity (especially in oppressed communities), empathy, humility, piety, wonder, and inspiration. The 1541 *Gesangbuch* contained songs of different seasons and of different emotions. Singing the Easter hymn 'Christ lag in todesbanden' would have inspired triumph. Psalm 130, 'Aus tieffer not', would have reminded people of their saviour in the darkest times. Likewise, the reformers would have hoped that Luther's text for Psalm 46, 'Ein feste burg ist vnser Got', would have united those who sang it to put their trust in God. But increasing 'good' singing also meant suppressing 'bad' singing: both immoral secular songs and immoral sacred choral music – music which did not come from the heart and which was therefore immoral – and which corrupted those who sang it and those who heard it. The popular genre was therefore to be 'cleansed' and adopted by the Church, brought into the churches to undergo treatment by the Reformation machine, and then sent out again, via the people, into the wider world in a modified, moral format: psalms and spiritual songs. Bucer expressed the hope that people would edify one another in this way, though exposure to and interaction with such songs. Music was therefore used as a tool in the development of society in Germany at this time.

Of the Lutheran reforms, Susan Karant-Nunn writes that

> The visual and palpable textures of the adornment of sanctuaries, the wonderments of organ playing and increasingly multipart choral singing, the retention of some tintinnabulation and modest procession, the regionally variable clerical vestments – all these nurtured a sense of the sacrality of the church interior, its accoutrements, and its immediate environment … The very space and people's experiences within it were to focus their moods as well as their thoughts. They were here to sigh (*seufzen*)

[45] *MPGR*, p. 205.

> to God, thank him for his loving goodness, and beseech him for righteousness, for control over their sinful natures.[46]

Of Geneva, and of areas in Germany that followed its example, she writes that

> those in positions of civic and ecclesiastical power strove to compel an even more thoroughgoing tranquillity. Their ministrations sought drastically to curtail the celebratory transactions of traditional culture. Even dancing at weddings was now forbidden … All were asked to renounce their most outwardly obvious and allegedly disruptive, indeed allegedly evil, expressions of feeling.[47]

Strasbourg found a middle way between the German and Swiss methods, adopting certain elements found in both these models. In the Strasbourg community, a specific type of church splendour was desired: not the visual and auditory 'extravagance' that had existed in medieval times, but a simpler type which involved spiritual values, and everyone's participation in the singing of hymns. Polyphony and choirs were no longer needed, and organ playing was less important, as were vestments and processions. Dancing was strictly controlled. Strasbourg began its liturgical reforms ahead and independently of Wittenberg, translating the Mass into German in 1524 (Luther's *Deutsche Messe* was not published until 1526), and going so far as to abolish this ancient service in 1529 (something Wittenberg never did, preferring instead to reinterpret its theology). On the other hand, Strasbourg was not as strictly controlling as Geneva, but instead people were encouraged to manage their own godly devotion, making proper use of their hearts, minds, and voices. Nevertheless, of course, this process involved a great deal of direction and encouragement from the reformers.

Also worthy of note is the early adoption in Strasbourg of Luther's arguments against the medieval format of divine worship, based on passages in 1 Corinthians 14. Matthäus Zell, for example, in 1523, equated speaking in tongues with Latin liturgical chanting, and prophesying with biblical exegesis. This comparison had already been made by Luther in *De votis monasticis Martini Lvtheri iudicium*,[48] and would be used by Bucer and the other Strasbourg preachers at many later points. This chapter of the Bible would also be used in relation to music by almost every reformer who wrote about music, including Jean Calvin.[49]

For these reasons, it is an error to label Bucer's early views on music 'Lutheran' or 'Zwinglian'. Nor, initially, would he have even considered them to be 'Protestant'. To him, they were simply Christian. The earliest Christian communities had sung the Psalms and other hymns, and the Bible advocated the assembling of the faithful to sing together. Bucer could find no justification

---

46 S. C. Karant-Nunn, *The Reformation of Feeling: Shaping the Religious Emotions in Early Modern Germany* (Oxford: Oxford University Press, 2010), pp. 216–17.

47 Ibid., p. 243.

48 (Wittenberg: Lotter, 1521). See *WA*, 8, pp. 621–2.

49 For example, in his *Institutio Christianae religionis* (1543); *COO*, 2, p. 659.

either for the exclusion of ordinary people from such activity (as had occurred in the late medieval Church) or for the exclusion of music from the service completely (as advocated by Zwingli). As observed by Charles Garside, Bucer's views on the subject (during the middle of his life, at least) were closest in shape and purpose to those of Jean Calvin,[50] but as Bucer was a forerunner of Calvin, it does not do Bucer justice to have his ideas put under the umbrella of a thinker who drew heavily on his own work. A re-evaluation of such theological categories is therefore called for. Bucer deserves greater recognition for the part he played in shaping music in many parts of South Germany, Switzerland (and by extension, Protestant France and Scotland), and England.

More must now be done to explore approaches to music in these areas during this crucial period of liturgical history. There is much in the way of archival information that has not yet been used, either because it does not relate directly to music, or because it is deemed insignificant. Letters, theological writings, and council accounts and proposals are among the types of source at our disposal; we should put them to better use. There is also a great deal of scope for further research on music education in the cities and nations of the sixteenth century. Many of these same documents include information that, if explored, would give us a fascinating insight into music pedagogy and those who were employed to undertake the task. Our knowledge of music education in Strasbourg, for example, has been up to now based on two or three journal articles; the biographies of musicians such as Dachstein and Greiter, who are known to have taught music in the city, are also under-explored, not least in secondary English literature. An example of the type of information that has been overlooked up until now is that which discusses the singing of children in Strasbourg's churches as early as the 1530s. The manuscripts found in the Strasbourg Archives de la Ville that relate to this practice have not been published or discussed elsewhere, and so the idea put forth in other works that children may have led the singing in Strasbourg's churches was based solely on an assumption that, since this was the case in other German cities too, it may also have happened in Strasbourg. In fact, Strasbourg might have been one of the first reformed cities to adopt such methods.

Part of the reason Strasbourg's contribution to church music has been overlooked is because the city's influence on the Europe-wide scene of the Reformation has also been under-emphasised. This, no doubt, is because

[50] *Garside*. This is putting aside issues relating to the use of musical instruments in church, about which Calvin was far stricter.

[51] The obverse reads: 'Omnis terra adoret Deum et psallat ei. Lux post tenebras MDXVII' ('Let all the earth adore God and sing Psalms unto him [paraphrase of Psalm 66:4]. Light after darkness, 1517'), and the reverse reads: 'Pro religionis centum ante annos divinitus restitutæ memoria novique seculi felici auspicio S. P. Q. Argentor. F. F. A. MDCXVII Cal. Novemb'. ('For the hundredth year after the restitution of divine religion, the senate and the people of Strasbourg observe a memorial and a new day of public celebration. Minted in silver on 1 November 1617' (N.B.: Argentoratum

Figure C.1 Commemorative centenary coin issued in Strasbourg in 1617. The importance played by music in the Strasbourg Reformation is demonstrated by this coin.[51] Photograph reproduced by permission of Classical Numismatic Group, Lancaster (Pennsylvania) and London

Bucerian-style reforms did not continue in the latter part of the century, during Strasbourg's revival of a more solid and recognisable form of Lutheranism. It has therefore been wrongly assumed that Bucer's reforms had no major legacy. But the effect that Strasbourg's unique path of reform had in the 1520s and 1530s is reflected not in the longevity of Bucer's theology, but in the endurance of the hymns that originated in the city and spread elsewhere. Strasbourg's melodies travelled to Geneva, other areas of Germany, and to England. Whether the success of hymnody in these places was linked to Bucer's role in forming church policy in these same areas is indeterminate. But although different reforms were pursued in all these places, it is certain that if the Strasbourg reformers had not insisted on the introduction of one very specific musical genre and the exclusion of another, church music in these other places would also have followed a very different path.

was also the Latin name for Strasbourg). The coin also shows quite how influenced by Lutheranism the city became in later years. Although the piece was issued to commemorate the centenary of the Reformation, it observes not the year in which Strasbourg began reforming its liturgy (1524), but the year in which Luther wrote his 95 theses (1517). This coin was sold at the Classical Numismatic Group's Triton auction XI, lot 1283 (7 January 2008).

APPENDIX A

List of Liturgical Orders (in German) and Books of Sacred Music (in German and Latin), Strasbourg, 1524–1541

Notes

1. Library details are not exhaustive, but merely provide an indication of where such items can be consulted, in the UK if possible, and elsewhere if not.

2. An asterisk denotes that the volume contains hymns (with or without musical notation).

3. A year with a figure in superscript is the numbering corresponding to the system used in *RISM DKL* and *DKL* III.

4. A capital letter (sometimes followed by a number) in italics is the Strasbourg liturgy classification system (used by Hubert, Gérold, and Bornert, among others).

5. Titles have been transcribed diplomatically from originals where possible.

6. Volumes in black type are traceable, and those in grey type are lost/untraceable.

1524

Teutsche Meß wie sye yetzund zu Straßburgk gehalten würt.
(n.p., 1524)
[Other than a reference by Röhrich, *Geschichte der Reformation*, p. 208 (incl. n. 18), there is no evidence for the existence of this book. Röhrich claims that the expanded edition (below) published by Köpfel appeared eight weeks after this one.]

Teütsche | Meß vnd Tauff | wie sye yetzund zů Straß | burg gehalte[n] werden. | Register bůchlin / über die ge- | schrifft / von disputierlich | en puncten. | Georgij Spalatini Christ- | liche gebett. | Betbůchlin auß den Euange- | lien vnd Episteln / sampt de[n] | glauben / vater vnser / vn[nd] den sibe[n] Bůßpsalmen.
(Köpfel, 1524)
12°
A1
[DK Kk – 89, 149]

Ordenung vn[nd] | ynhalt Teütscher Meß | so yetzund im gebrauch | haben Euangelisten | vnnd Christlichen | Pfarrherren zů Straßburg.
(Köpfel, 1524)
A2
[D GOl – Druck 8° 01132]

Ordenung vnd in- | halt / Teutscher Mess / | so yetzund im gebrauch ha- | ben Ewangelisten vnd | Christlichen Pfarr- | herren zu Straß | burg.
(Köpfel, 1524)
8°
A3
[F Sn – R.100.477]

Deutsche Mess wie sye yetzundt zu Straßburgk gehalten würt. Item Betbüchlein sampt vil andren, so in volgendem blatt verzeichnet ist.
(n.p., 1524)
A4

Das Tauff- | bůchlin / nach rechter | Form vff Teütsch | zů Tauffen.
(n.p., 1524)
12°
A5
[F Ssp – 16. 87, 4 (Wilhelmitana collection)]

* *Ordenung vnd | yn[n]halt Teütscher Mess vn[nd] | Vesper / So yetzund im ge | brauch haben Euangeli- | sten vnd Christlichen Pfarr | herren zů Straßburg. | Mit etlichen Neüwen ge- | schrifftlichen Jntroit / Ge- | bet / Vorred oder Prefation | vnd Canon / vor vnd nach | vffhebu[n]g des Sacrame[n]ts / | auch andren ordenunge[n] / in | vorigem bůchlin nit | begriffen.*
(Köpfel, 1524)
12°
B
[F Ssp – 16. 87, 11 (Wilhelmitana collection)]

* 1524^{15}: *Teütsch | Kirchen ampt / | mit lobgesengen / vn[nd] goͤtlich | en psalmen / wie es die ge | mein zů Straßburg | singt vn[nd] halt / gantz | Christlich.*
(Köpfel, 1524)
8°
C1
[**D Mbs – Rar. 1085** and also online:
http://daten.digitale-sammlungen.de//bsb00069204/image_3]
[**DK Kk – 96, 79** (also microfilm)]

* 1524^{16}: *Teutsch | Kirche[n] ampt mit | lobgsengen / vn[nd] goͤtlichen psal | men / wie es die gemein zu | Straßburg singt vn[nd] halt | mit mer gantz Christ- | liche[n] gebette[n] / dan[n] | vorgetruckt. || Singet dem Herren eyn Neüw lied / | Das er wunder than hatt. Psal. 98. | Singet frolich Gott / der vnser sterck ist / | Iauchzet dem Gott / Iacob. Psal. 81.*
(Köpfel, 1524)
12°
C2
[**GB Lbl – 3456.aaa.64(2)** and **3456.aaa.42(2)** (FACSIMILE REPRINT: Erfurt: Gerhardt und Schreibers, 1848)]
[**F Sn – M.106.352** (FACSIMILE REPRINT: Erfurt: Gerhardt und Schreibers, 1848)]

1525

* 1525^{02}: *Der Glaube | Deütsch zů singen | in einer schoͤnen me- | lodey.*
(Knobloch, 1524/1525)
12°
[**F Ssp – 16. 87, 15** (Wilhelmitana collection)]

* 1525^{03}: *Ein schoner kurtzer be- | griff des vatter vnsers | Vn[nd] Aue Marie / Glauben / | Zehe[n] gebotte[n] / | Nützlich zů singen vnnd | zů betrachten.*
(Schwan, 1525)
8°
[**NL DHk – 228 J 23**]

* 1525^{10}: *Enchiridion geist | licher gesenge / so man yetzt | (Gott zů lob) yn der kirchen | syngt. Getzogen auß der hey | ligen geschrifft des ware[n] vnd | heyligen Euangelions / wel | ches jetzt von gottes gnaden | wider auffgange[n] ist / vnd mit | etzlichen gesenge[n] Gemehrt / | Gebessert / vn[nd] mit fleyß Cor | rigyert / mit einer Vorrede | Docto. Martini Luther.*
(Schürer Erben, 1525)
8°
[**F Ssp – 16. 87, 12** (Wilhelmitana collection)]

* 1525^{14}: *Der .li. | Psalm Dauids | Miserere mei deus hoch | zů singe[n] da der Prophet | Nathan zů im kam / | als er war zu Bath | Saba ein | gange[n].*
(Schwan, 1525)
8°
[**D Bsb – Hymn. 2175** and also online:
http://digital.staatsbibliothek-berlin.de/werkansicht/?PPN=PPN732086000&PHYSID=PHYS_0005]

* 1525^{18}: [I:] *Theütsch | kirche[n] ampt mit lob | gsenge[n] v[nd] göttlich- | en Psalmen, wie es die ge- | meyn zů Straßburg singt | vnnd halt, mit meer gantz | Christlichen gebette[n], dan[n] | vor getruckt.*
[II:] *Das an- | der theyl. | Straßburger kirchengesang. | Das vatter vnser. | Der glaub. | Die zehn gepott. | Das Miserere. | Psal. Der dorecht* [*sic*] *spricht. | Psal. Wer gott nicht mit. | Die acht ersten psalmen, | vff die melody, Ach gott | von himel.*
[III:] *Das dritt | theil Straßbur | ger kirchen | ampt.*
(Köpfel, 1525)
8°
C3

* 1525^{19}: *Ordnu[n]g des | Herren Nachtmal: so | man die messz nennet / sampt der | Tauff vn[nd] Jnsegu[n]g der Ee / Wie | yetzt die diener des wort gots zů | Straßburg / Erneüwert / vnd | nach goͤtlicher gschrifft gebes- | sert habe[n] vß vrsach jn nach- | gender Epistel | gemeldet.*
(Schwan, 1525)
8°
D1
[**D Mbs – Rar. 4114 Beibd.4**, and also online:
http://daten.digitale-sammlungen.de/0002/bsb00029012/images]

* 1525^{20}: *Ordnu[n]g des herren | Nachtmal: so man die Messz | nennet / sampt der Tauff vn[nd] Jnsegung | der Ee / Wie yetzt die diener des wort | gottes zů Strasszburg / Erneü- | wert / vnnd nach goͤttlicher | geschrifft gebessert haben | vß vrsach jn nach- | gender Epistel | gemeldet.*
(Schwan, 1525)
8°
D2
[**F Sn – R.100.640**]
[**College of St Benedict and St John's University, Minnesota – BX9427 .O7 1525**, and also online: http://cdm.csbsju.edu/cdm4/document.php?CISOROOT=/SJRareBooks&CISOPTR=2218&REC=1]

* 1525[21]: *Strasz- | burger kirchen | ampt / nemlich von Jnse- | gu[n]g d[er] Eeleüt / vom Tauf | vnd vo[n] des herre[n] nacht | mal / mit etlichen Psal | men / die an end des | bůchlins / orden- | lich verzeych- | net sein.*
(Köpfel, 1525)
8°
E
[D Rs – 999/Theol.syst.1160(4, and also online:
http://www.mdz-nbn-resolving.de/urn/resolver.pl?urn=urn:nbn:de:bvb:12-bsb11119376-1]

1526

* 1526[08]: *Psalme[n] | gebett. vnd Kir | chen übu[n]g wie sie zů Straß | burg gehalten werden.*
(Köpfel, 1526)
8°
F1

* 1526[09]: *Psalme[n] | gebett / vnd Kir | chen ůbu[n]g wie sie zů Straß | burg gehalten werden.*
(Köpfel, 1526)
8°
F2
[D Gs – 8 TH POLEM 514/51 RARA; or microfilm: **MF 8 TH POLEM 514/51**]

* 1526[10]: *Psalme[n] | gebett. vnd Kir | chen übu[n]g wie sie zu Straß | burg gehalten werden.*
(Köpfel, 1526)
12°

* 1526[27]: *Psalme[n] | gebett: vnd Kir | chen ůbu[n]g wie sie zů Straß- | burg gehalten werden.*
(Köpfel, 1526)
8°
[D WGp – LC510/2]
[This volume does not appear in *RISM DKL*, but is mentioned in *DKL* III, vol. 1, pt. 3, p. 9.]

1527

* 1527[11]: *Der siben | vnd dreyssigst psalm | Dauids. Noli emulari in malignan- | tibus. Von dem vrteyl Gottes | vber der welt tyrannen. Auch | von der zeitlihen [sic] vnd ewi | gen belonung der gottseligen. | Das lobgesang | Zacharie, Benedictus, Luce j. | Das lobgesang Simeonis, Nunc dimittis. | Luce ij.*
(Köpfel, 1527)
8°

* 1527[12]: *Die zwen | Psalmen: Jn exi- | tu Jsrael &c. vnd Domine probasti | me &c. verteütscht, welche in | den vorigen buͤchlin nit | begriffen seynd. | Jtem ein geystlich lied vom | gsetz vnd glauben.*
(Köpfel, 1527)
8°

* 1527[13]: *Die zween | Psalmen: Jn exi- | tu Jsrael &c. vnd D[omi]ne probasti | me &c. verteütscht / woͤlche in | den vorigen buͤchlin nit | begriffen seynd. | Jtem ein geystlich lied vom | gsetz vnd glauben.*
(Köpfel, 1527)
8°
[D Gs – 8 TH POLEM 514/51 RARA; or microfilm: **MF 8 TH POLEM 514/51]**

1529

* 1529[04]: *Das Te deum lau- | damus verteütscht durch | Jo. Brentz. zů schwebische Hall. | Der sechs vnd viertzigst Psalm, Deus nostrum refugium et | virtus, neülich | verteut- | schet. | Gott selbs ist vnser schutz vnd macht.*
(Köpfel, 1529)
8°

1530

* 1530[06]: *Psalmen | gebett / vnd kirch- | en ůbung / wie sie zů Straß | burg gehalten werden.*
(Köpfel, 1530)
8°
G
[F Sn – R.102.241]

Ein schöner kurtzer begriff des vatter unsers und ave Maria glauben zehen gebotten nützlich zu singen unnd zu betrachten.
(Beck, 1530)
8°
[This title appears in the USTC and in *VD16*, but no further references were found.]

1533

* 1533^{01}: *Psalmen | gebett, vnd kirch- | en übung, wie sie zů Straß | burg gehalten werden [This title appears in the USTC and in VD16, but no further references were found.]*
(Köpfel, 1533)
8°
H

1534

* 1534^{02}: [I:] *Von Christo Jesu vnse- | rem säligmacher / seiner Menschwer- | dung / Geburt / Beschneidung / &c. | etlich Christliche vnd trostli- | che Lobgsäng / auß einem | vast herrlichen Gesangbůch gezogen / Von | welchem inn der Vorred weiter | anzeygt würdt.*
(Frölich, 1534)
8°
[Formerly in **D Bsb – El 3210**; now in **RUS Mrg**]

* 1534^{07}: *Wittenber- | gische Gsangbüchli | durch Johan. Walthern / | Churfürstlichen von | Sachsen senger mey- | stern vff ein newes | corrigiert / gebes | sert vnd ge- | meret.*
(Schöffer & Apiarius, 1534)
Oblong 12°
5 partbooks
[GB Lbl – K.1.c.15 (A, T)]

1535

* 1535[05]: [II:] *Das ander Byechlin | der Geystlichen gsång / Von der | Erscheinung / Wandel vnd | Leiden Christi vnsers | heylandts.*
(Frölich, 1535)
8°
[Formerly in **D Bsb – El 3210**; now in **RUS Mrg**]

Magnificat Octo Tonorum
(Schöffer & Apiarius, 1535)
Oblong 4°
4 partbooks
[D Z]

Motetarum quatuor vocum
(Schöffer, 1535)
Several partbooks

1536

* 1536[01]: [III:] *Das dritt Byechlin der | Geystlichen gsång / Von der Auff- | erstehung / Hym[m]elfart Chris- | sti vnsers Herren / | vnd von dem | Heyligen Geyst.*
[IV:] *Das vierde Byechlin d[er] | Geystlichen gsång / Von Lobgsången / | Bettgsången / Leergsången / Gsang auff | die tag zeytten / Gsang für die Kinder / | Gsang für die Gefallenen / Gsang | zům begrebnüß der todten / Vom | Jüngsten tag / Von den re- | chten Heyligen / Vnd | vom Testament | des Herren.*
(Frölich, 1536)
12°
[CH SH]

* 1536[08]: [title unknown; probably similar in content to 1533[01]]
(Köpfel [?], 1536)

1537

Magnificat Octo Tonorum
(Schöffer & Apiarius, 1537)
Oblong 4°
5 partbooks
[**D Mbs – Mus.pr. 39**, and also online: http://stimmbuecher.digitale-sammlungen.de/view?id=bsb00081893]

* 1537^{03}: *Psalmen vnd geystliche Lieder, die man zu Straßburg, vnd auch die man inn anderen Kirchen pflegt zu singen.*
(Prüss & Köpfel, 1537)
12°
[Lost very similar in content to 1537^{05}]

* 1537^{05}: [*Psalme[n] vnnd geystliche Lieder die man zu Straßburg, vnd auch die man inn anderen Kirchen pflegt zu singen. Form vnd gebett zum eynsegen der Ee, den heiligen Tauff Abendmal, besuchung der Kranken, und begrebnuͤss der abgestorbnen. Alles gemert vnd gebessert. Auch mit seinem Register.*]
(Prüss & Köpfel, 1537)
8°
J1
[**F Sn – R 102.405** (incomplete copy – several pages missing, including title page)]

* 1537^{08}: *Wittenber- | gisch Gsangbiichli* [*sic*] | *durch Johan. Waltern / | Churfürstlichen von | Sachsen senger mey- | ster / vff ein newes | corrigiert / gebes | sert / vnd ge- | meret.*
(Schöffer & Apiarius, 1537)
8°
5 partbooks
[**D Mbs – Mus.pr.3**, and also online: http://stimmbuecher.digitale-sammlungen.de/view?id=bsb00081894]
[**D As – Tonk Sch 520–522** (A, T1, T2)]

1538

* 1538[02]: *Psalmen / | vnd Geystliche | lieder / die man zů Straß | burg / vnd auch die man | inn anderen Kirchen | pflågt zů singen. | Form vnd gebet zum einsegen | der Ee / dem heiligen Tauff / | Abentmal / besůchung der | Krancken / vnd begrebnüs | der abgestorbnen. Alles | gemert vnd gebessert. Das Erst Teyl.*
(Messerschmid & Köpfel, 1538)
8°

* 1538[06]: *Psalter. | Das seindt alle | Psalmen Dauids / mit | jren Melodeie[n] / sampt | vil Schönen Christli- | chen liedern / vnnd | Kyrche[n] übunge[n] / | mitt seynem | Register.*
(Köpfel, 1538)
8°
[F Sn – R.102.406,2]
[D Mbs – Res/Liturg. 1128, and also online:
http://daten.digitale-sammlungen.de/bsb00028709/image_5]

1539

* *Psal- | ter mit al- | ler Kirchenübu[n]g | die man bey der | Christlichen Ge- | mein zů Straß- | burg vnd anders | wa pflågt zů | singen. || Mit seinem orden | lichen Register.*
(Köpfel, 1539)
12°
K
[F Ssp – 16. 293 (Wilhelmitana collection)]

Cantiones quinque uocum selectissimæ, a primarijs (Germnaiæ [*sic*] *inferioris, | Galliæ, & Italiæ) musices magistris editæ. Ante hac typis | nondum diuulgatæ. Numero uigintiocto. || Mutetarum liber primus.*
(Schöffer, 1539)
5 partbooks
[D Mbs – Mus.pr. 48, and also online: http://stimmbuecher.digitale-sammlungen.de/view?id=bsb00086381]
[D As – Tonk Schl 420–424]

1541

* *Psalmen / vnd Geystliche | lieder / die man zů Straß | burg / vnd auch die man | inn anderen Kirchen | pflägt zů singen. | Form vnd gebet zum einsegen | der Ee / dem heiligen Tauff / | Abentmal / besůchung der | Krancken / vnd begrebnüs | der abgestorbnen. Alles | gemert vnd bebessert.*[1] | *Das Erst Teyl.*
(Messerschmidt & Köpfel, 1541)
J2

* 1541[05]: *Psalmen / | vnd Geistliche | lieder / die man zů Straß- | burg / vnd auch die man | inn anderen Kirchen | pflägt zů singen. | Form vnd gebet zum einsegen | der Ee / dem heilgen Tauff / | Abentmal / besůchung der | Krancken / vnd begrebnüs | der abgestorbnen. Alles | gemert vn[nd] gebessert. | Das Erst Teyl.*
(Messerschmidt & Köpfel, 1541)
8°
L
[F Sn – R.102.406,1]
[D Mbs – Liturg. 1123-1; and also online: http://daten.digitale-sammlungen.de/~db/0003/bsb00036692/image_1]]

* 1541[06]: *Gesangbuch / darinn | begriffen sind / die aller | fürnemisten vnd besten | Psalmen / Geistliche Lieder / vnd | Chorgeseng / aus dem Wittem- | bergischen / Strasburgischen / vnd anderer | Kirchen Gesangbüchlin zůsamen | bracht / vnd mit besonderem | fleis corrigiert vnd | gedrucket. | Für Stett vnd Dorff Kirchen / | Lateinische vnd Deudsche | Schůlen.*
(Messerschmidt & Köpfel, 1541)
2°
[D Iek]
[D PA]
[GB Cu – MR250.a.95.1 (FACSIMILE REPRINT: Stuttgart: Evangelischen Verlagswerk, 1953)]
[GB Lbl – 3438.p.1 (FACSIMILE REPRINT: Stuttgart: Evangelischen Verlagswerk, 1953)]
A free PDF download is available on Google Books: http://books.google.co.uk/books?id=ZFkJAQAAMAAJ&dq=gesangbuch+1541&source=gbs_navlinks_s

[1] *sic* (as printed in *Hubert*).

APPENDIX B

Wolfgang Köpfel's First Preface to the Strasbourg Liturgical Orders

1. Taken from *Ordenung vnd yn[n]halt Teütscher Mess vn[nd] Vesper* (Strasbourg: Köpfel, 1524), fol. Aj^{v}

Vorrede

ES habe[n] die diener des worts zů Straßburg / dem alten gebrauch (so vil müglich ist) nachgegeben / vnd also nachgeende ordenu[n]g d[er] Mess Christlicher weyß fürgenum[m]en / darin[n] wir von vnser gemeyn tåglich befunden grossen fürgang / vnnd merung des glaubens. Deßhalb hab ich sie wöllen anderen gebette[n] vorsetzen. Alleyn sey verwarnet / das du nit achtest / als ob solch ordnung můste gehalten werden / Dan[n] hyenach fyndestu / welches sey dz hauptstuck der Mess. Gehab dich wol.

Foreword

The servants of the Word in Strasbourg have (as far as possible) adjusted the old uses, and so now follow the order of the Mass, carried out in a Christian way, in which, daily, we find great occurrence and increase in the faithful of our community. Hence I have wanted to put it [the order] before other prayers. Bear in mind, though, that you are not to assume that this order must be maintained. Hereafter you will find the main part of the Mass. Farewell.

2. Taken from *Teutsch Kirche[n] ampt mit lobgsengen* (Strasbourg: Köpfel, 1524), fol. Aj^{v}

Vorred

ES haben die diener des worts zů Straßburg / dem alte[n] gebrauch / so vil müglich ist / nachgeben / vnd also nachgeende ordnung des gesangs der Meß / vnnd vesper &c. Christlicher weyß fürgenommen / darin[n] wir von der gemein taͤglich befunden grossen fürgang vnd merung des glaubens. Deßhalb hab ich sye neben andern gebetten getruckt. Allein sey gewarnet / das du nit achtest / als ob sollich ordnung můste gehalte[n] werden / Dan[n] hyenach findestu / welchs sey das haubtstuck der Mess. | Gehab dich wol.

Foreword

The servants of the Word in Strasbourg have, as far as possible, adjusted the old uses, and so now follow the order of singing of the Mass and Vespers, etc., carried out in a Christian way, in which, daily, we find great occurrence and increase in the faithful of our community. Hence I have printed it [the order] together with other prayers. Be aware, though, that you are not to assume that this order must be maintained. Hereafter you will find the main part of the Mass. Farewell.

APPENDIX C

Joannes Dulcis's 'Strasbourg cite dempire' (c. 1526) in French and German, from manuscript 1 AST 166, 5.2, fols 85^{v}–87^{r}

Schmachlidlin von Str[aßburg] im hertzogthumb Lothring[en] zu S. Kurin[1] offentlich feyl gehabt.

Chanson nouvelle augurative de Strasbourg sur le chant. Regrets soucy et peine.

[1] Strasbourg cite dempire
Qui as jadis flory
Tu vas de pis en pire
Dont ton dieu est marry
Ce font erreurs, heresis et abus
Tu verras ung jour lire
Du hault dieu de lassus.

[2] Je tay veu singuliere
Entre tous les germains
Deffendant la baniere
Du saulveur des humains
Mais maintenant, le diable te regit
Te privant de lumiere
En enfer te conduyt.

Ein Nuw lied nuwer zükunfftiger ding so der Stat Str[aßburg] begegnen soll.

[1] Straßburg Stat des Richs
die do geblüget hast
Göst aber den bösen inn bösers
Des din Got leydig ist
Das thunt jrrthumb Ketzery und abergloub
Du wurst es uff ein tag sehen lesen
Den hohen Got do oben.

[2] Jch hab dich gesehen sunderlich
Vnder aller Germanien
Beschirmende das Bauer
Das seligmachers menschlich geslechts
Aber yetzundt der tüffel dich regiert
Dich beroubend dins gesichts
Jnn die hell wurt er dich geleytten.

---

1 Saint-Quirin, a village between Nancy and Strasbourg.

[3] Ne crains tu point loffence
Que a Jesus tu faicts
Par ta faulce credence
Et sermons contrefaits
Ce faulx Lambert,[2] heretique mauldict
Te fait prendre la dance
De linfernal deduit.

[3] Förchst du nit die beleydigung
So du Jesus thust
Durch die falsch glouben
Vnd ertichte predigen
Der falsch Lamprecht, kätzer verfluct
Wurt dich bringen an den dantze
Zu der hellen zu zefieren.

[4] Les furies infernalles
Auec Radamanthus
Juge des cas damnables
Charon et cerberus
Sont apprestez, pour ton cas exploicter
Attropos funeralle
Veult ia ton fil coupper.

[4] Die tuffel der hellen
Mit sampt Radamanthus
Vrtheylt die verdamlich sach
Charon und cerberus
Sindt bereyt die sach vßzuleigen
Attroffos die lychmacherin
Wil dir die Fadem abhouwen.

[5] Tu souloys en leglise
Triumpher pour ton dieu
Mais mauldicte heresie
Ta faict changer de jeu
Cest lennemy, de nature peruers
Qui te veult en abisme
Faire cheoir a lenvers.

[5] Du byst gewon gewesen in der kirchen
Zu triumphieren vmb din Got
Aber verfluchte ketzerÿ
Hat dich machen wandeln die spil
Das ist der tuffel von böser natur
Wil er inn die tyeffe
Dich machen fallen inn die hell.

[6] Nas tu plus souvenance
Du bon duc des Lorrains
Qui par sa grant vaillance
A rougy ces deux mains
Dedans le sang, de tes freres fedaulx
Se ne prens autre chance
Jl en viendra grans maulx.

[6] Hastu nit in gedechtniß
Vom gutten hertzogen von Lothringen
Der durch sin grosse manlicheit
Hab rot gemacht sin zwo hende
Jnn dem blut, diner brüder und bundsgenossen
Wurstu nit nemen ein ander schantz
Wurd dir groß vbel douon kom[m]en.

[7] Se je vouloys bien dire
Le mal quas a souffrir
Tu ne deuroys pas rire
Mais tes maulx convertir
Et delaisser, tes faulces heresis
Conduys bien ton navire
Et plus je ne ten dits.

[7] Do ich dir wolt sagen
Daß vbel so du lyden wurst
Du solttest sin nit lachen
Aber din vbels verkeren
Vnd lossen von der falschen ketzery
Regier wol din schiff
Nit mer ich dir sag.

[2] François Lambert (c. 1486–1530), who preached in Strasbourg from 1524 to 1526.

[8] Entens bien la trompette
Le chant de la chanson
De celuy qui la faicte
Sen velx scauoir le nom
Sa fait ung clerc, des chartraines partis
Du surnom si te haite
Jl se nom[m]e Dulcis.

[8] Verston wol die trumpt
Vff die wise des lieds
Das der das gemacht hat
So du wilt wissen den nam[m]en
Es hats gemacht ein Clerc von den Carmeliten gescheyden
Ob dich das zunamens verlangt
Jst er genant Dulcis.

Joannes dulcis Nicolas Pantallion

APPENDIX D

A Selection of German Church Songs in Strasbourg not directly from the Bible, 1524–1540

See also Table 4.2, pp. 194–5.

M. Luther, 'Got sey gelobet vn[nd] gebenedeyet'
Text from *Wackernagel DKL*, vol. 3, no. 11.

1. Got sey gelobet vn[nd] gebenedeyet,	God be praised and blessed,
der vns selber hat gespeyset	He who has fed us
Mit seynem fleische vnd mit seynem blute,	With his body and with his blood,
dz gybt vns, herr Gott, zu gutte.	Which gives us benefit.
Kirieleyson.	Lord, have mercy.
Herr, durch deynen heilige[n] leichnam,	Lord, through your holy body,
der von deiner mutter Maria kam,	Which came from your mother Mary,
Vnd das heylige blut,	And your holy blood,
hylff vns, herr, aus aller nott.	Help us, Lord, in all our need.
Kirieleyson.	Lord, have mercy.
2. Der heylig leichnam yst fur uns gegebe[n]	Your holy body was given for us
zum todt, das wir dardurch leben.	In death, that through it we may live;
Nicht grosser gutte kund er vns geschencke[n],	He could not have given us any greater graciousness;
da bey wir sein soln gedencke[n].	Whereof we should remember this.
Kirieleyson.	Lord, have mercy.
Herr, deyn lieb so groß dich zwunge[n] hat,	Lord, your great love did constrain you,
das dein blut an vns gross wunder that	May your blood be of great wonder to us
Vnd bezalt vnser schult,	And pay our debt,
das vns Got ist worden holt.	Our God is kind to us.
Kirieleyson.	Lord, have mercy.
3. Got geb vns allen seyner gnade[n] segen,	May God bestow merciful blessing on us all,
das wir gehen auff seynen wegen	That we may follow his path
Jn rechter lieb vnd bruderlicher trewe,	In love and brotherly faithfulness,
das vns die speys nicht gerewe.	That we may not repent this food.
Kirieleyson.	Lord, have mercy.

Herr, dein heylig geyst vns nymer las,	Lord, may your Holy Ghost never leave us,
der vns geb zu halte[n] rechte mass,	May he make us 'well-measured';
Das dein arm Christenheytt	May your poor Church
leb ynn fryd vnd eynigkeyt.	Live in peace and unity.
Kirieleyson.	Lord, have mercy.

M. Luther, 'Nu bitten wyr den heyligen geyst'
Text from *Wackernagel DKL*, vol. 3, no. 28.

1. NV bitten wyr den heyligen geyst
vmb den rechten glauben aller meyst,
Das er vns behute an vnserm ende,
wenn wir heym farn[1] aus diesem elende.

2. Du werdes liecht, gib vns deynen scheyn,
lern vns Jhesum Christ kennen alleyn,
Das wyr an yhm bleyben, dem trewen Heyland,
der vns bracht hat zum rechten vaterlandt.

3. Du susse lieb, schenck vns deyne gunst,
las vns empfinden der liebe brunst,
Das wyr vns von hertzen eyn ander lieben
vnd ym fride auff eynem synn bleyben.

4. Du hochster troster ynn aller not,
hilff, das wir nicht furchten schand noch tod,
Das ynn vns die synnen nicht verzagen,
wenn der feind wird das leben verklagen.

S. Pollio (?), 'Jesus der hat vns zůgeseit'
Text from *Wackernagel DKL*, vol. 3, no. 564.

JEsus der hat vns zůgeseit	Jesus who has bestowed on us,
den krancken sein barmherzigkeit,	The sick, his mercy,
Zů gůt den sündern komen ist	He has approached sinners with goodness
vnd nit, spricht er, den nüt gebrist.[2]	And not, he says, those unpraised,
Erbarm dich unser, Jesu christ!	Have mercy on us, Jesus Christ!

[1] = heimfahren.

[2] Past participle of *preisen*?

S. Pollio, 'Vatter vnser, wir bitten dich'
Text from *Wackernagel DKL*, vol. 3, no. 562.

1 Vatter vnser, wir bitten dich,
wie vns hat glert herr jesu christ:
Erhoͤr dein kinder gnediglich,
dann du für wor barmhertzig bist.
    Jn himels tron
bistu on won,
als vns dein wort erlernen thůt,
Doch stets din macht
bey tag vnd nacht
vns hie vff erd behalt in hůt.

2. Geheyliget werd dein nam[m] so groß,
der vns allein zum hymel hilfft.
Er ist mechtig, sin gwalt on maß:
erhoͤr dein gmein, die zů dir gilfft,
    Das jn all gleich
zů kum dein reich,
in dem allein sy herschen sind.
Dein will auff erd
vnnd himel werd,
domit mach vns dein ghorsam kind.

3. Verlyh uns heüt das täglich brot
zů seel und leyb, dz bitten wir;
Vergib vns auch die schuld, gib rot,
das wir von gantzes hertzens gir
    Verzeihen schwind
des brůders sind;
in die versůchung fier uns nit.
Nit gib dem find,
o gott, dein kind,
sonder mach uns vom übel quitt!

Anon., 'Vatter vnser der du bist im himel'

Text from *Ein schoner kurtzer begriff* (Strasbourg: Schwan, 1525), fols Aij^{r}–Aij^{v}.

1. Vatter vnser der du bist /
im himel zů ewiger frist /
dein kinder seind wir all gemeyn /
so wir glauben an dich allein /
Lobt den herren.

Our Father, you are
in heaven for eternity,
we are all your communal children,
so we believe in you alone.
Praise the Lord.

2. Geheyliget werd dein heilger nam /
vo[n] frauwen vnd von yederman /
kein nam ist sunst vff erden /
dar durch wir selig werden /
Lobt den herren.

Hallowed is your holy name,
For women and for everyone
There is no other name one earth
Through which we become blessed.
Praise the Lord.

3. Zů kum vns dein ewigs reich /
vns allen mitt einander gleich /
darmit wir vatter loben dich /
in vnserm erblandt ewigklich /
Lobt den herren.

May your eternal kingdom come to us,
To all of us equally.
So that we praise you, Father,
Eternally in our hereditary lands.
Praise the Lord.

4. Dein wil geschech all zeyt geleych /
in himel vnnd vff erdereich /
dann vnser wil der ist nitt gůtt /
es ist sünd alles das er thůt /
Lobt den herren.

May your will occur all the time
In heaven and on earth,
For our will is not good,
Everything it does is sinful.
Praise the Lord.

5. Gib vns vnser taͤglich brot /
das ist dein heylig goͤttlich wort /
das wir in vnsern engsten schnel /
gespeißt werde[n] an vnser seel [/]
Lobt den herren.

Give us our daily bread
Which is your holy divine word,
That we who are so fearful
Will have sustenance for our souls.
Praise the Lord.

6. Herr vergib vnns vnser schuld /
verleych vns dein goͤttliche huld /
das wir verzeihe[n] vn[nd] ablon /
was wider vns der nechst hat thon /
Lobt den herren.

Lord, forgive us our faults,
Grant us your favour,
So that we might forgive and forget
That which has been done against us.
Praise the Lord.

7. Jn anfechtung für [*sic*] vns nitt /
das ist lieber herr vnser bit /
verleich vns die gedult all zeyt /

Lead us not into temptation,
We ask you, dear Lord,
Grant us patience always,

das wir besitze[n] ewig frewd [/]
Lobt den herren.

That we might possess eternal happiness.
Praise the Lord.

8. Loͤß vns lieber vatter all /
vom übel in dem yamertal / [3]
das vns nit schad vff diser erd /
dan[n] vnser seel / dir ist gantz werd [/]
Lobt de[n] herren.

Keep us, dear Father,
From evil in the Valley of Death,
That there may be no peril to us on this earth,
Then our soul will be fully yours.
Praise the Lord.

Anon., 'Aue Maria'
Text from *Ein schoner kurtzer begriff* (Strasbourg: Schwan, 1525), fols Aij^{v}–Aiij^{r}.

1. Du meinsch d[omi]ne vnd auch Aue
Maria bist genennet /
Der herz mit dir nach seiner gyer /
der geist gotts har bekennet /
Gott vatter sůn im hoͤchsten thron /
on alles wider streben /
hat rab gethon sein gliebten sun /
er ist das liecht vnds leben.

2. Selig ist die stund die ward verkund.
Dein grůß mit grossen frewden /
das ewig liecht / da da erleücht /
die Juden Christen Heyde[n] /
Als da Adam vnd Abraham
die altuetter so frumme /
geschreyn hand zů aller stund /
biß er istzů ynkommmen [*sic*].

3. Maria rein hold selig vn[nd] feyn /
Du leüchtest für die sunne /
du bist dz faß darinne[n] was /
der wein / der leben brunne /
Johannes spricht / dz ist das liecht /
da leüchter vnuerborgen /
Jhesus den gast geboren hast /
zů weyhennacht am morgen.

[3] Probably an equivalent for 'Jammertag', the Day of Judgement.

P. Speratus, 'Es ist das heyl vns kommen her'
Text from *Die zween Psalmen* (Strasbourg: Köpfel, 1527), fols v^{v}–vii^{r}.
Another version is available in *Wackernagel DKL*, vol. 3, no. 55.

1. Es ist das heyl vns kommen her /
von gnad vnd lauter gieten /
Die werck die helffen nymmer mer /
sye mögen nit behieten /
Der glaub sicht Jesum Christum an /
der hat gnůg für vns all gethan /
er ist der mitler worden.

2. Was gott im gsetz gebotten hat /
da man es nit kundt halten.
Erhůb sich zorn vnnd grosse not /
vor gott so manigfalte[n] /
Vom fleysch wolt nicht herauß der geyst /
vom gsetz erfordert aller meyst /
Es war mit vns verloren.

3. Es war ein falscher wohn dar bey /
gott hett seyn gsetz drumb geben.
Als ob wir moͤchten selber frey /
nach seynem willen leben /
So ist es nur ein spiegel zart /
der vns zeigt an die suͤndig art,
jnn vnserm fleysch verborgen.

4. Nicht müglich war die selbig art /
auß eygen krefften lassen /
Wie wol es offt versuͤchet ward /
noch mert sich sünd on massen /
wenn gleyßnere werck er hoch verdampt /
vnnd je dem fleysch der sünde schand /
all zeyt war angehoren.

5. Noch müst das gsetz erfüllet seyn /
sonst wer wir all verdorben /
Darum schickt gott seyn sůn hereyn /
der selber mensch ist worden /
Das gantz gesetz hat er erfüllt /
damit seyns vatters zorn gestullt /
der über vns gieng alle.

6. Vnd wen[n] es nu erfüllet ist /
durch den der es kündt halten /
So lerne jetz ein frommer Christ /
des glaubens recht gestalte /
Nicht mehr den[n] lieber herre mein /
dein todt würt mir das leben seyn /
du hast für mich bezalet.

7. Daran ich keynen zweyffel trag /
deyn wort kan nicht betriegen /
Nun sagstu das keyn mensch verzag /
das wirstu nymmer liegen /
Wer glaubt an mich und würt getåufft /
dem selben ist der hyml erkaufft /
dz er nit würt verloren.

8. Er ist gerecht vor gott allein /
der disen glauben fasset.
Der glaub fibt auß von jm den scheyn /
so er die werck nicht lasset /
Mit gott der glaub ist wol daran /
dem nechsten würt die lieb gůts than /
bistu auß gott geboren.

9. Es würt die sünd durchs gsetz erkant /
vn[nd] schlecht dz gewissen nider /
Das Euangeli kompt zů handt /
vnd sterckt den sünder wid[er] /
Er spricht / nur kreüch zum creütz herzů /
im gsetz ist weder rast noch rhů /
mit allen seynen wercken.

10. Die werck die kommen gwißlich her /
aus einem rechten glauben /
Wen[n] das nit rechter glauben wer /
wölst jn der werk berauben /
doch macht allein der glaub gerecht /
die werck die seynd des nechsten knecht /
darbey wirn glauben mercken.

11. Die hoffnung wart der rechten zeyt /
was gottes wort zů sagen /
Wen[n] das geschehen soll zů freyd /

setz gott keyn gewissen tage /
er weyß wol wens am besten ist /
vnnd braucht an vns keyn argen list /
das sol wir jm vertrawen.

12. Ob sichs an ließ als wolt er nit /
laß dich es nit erschrechen /
Den[n] wo er ist am besten mit /
da wil ers nit entdecken /
seyn wort dz laß dir gwisser sein /
vn[nd] ob dein fleysch sprech lauter neyn /
so laß doch dir nit gruwen.

13. Sey lob vn[nd] ehr mit hohem preyß /
vmb diser gůtheit willen /
Gott vatter sůn vnd heyligem geyst /
der woͤll mit gnad erfüllen
was er in vns angfangen hat /
zů eren seyner maiestat /
das heylig werd seyn name.

14. Seyn reich zů kum[m] /
seyn will auff erd /
gschech wie in hymels throne /
Das taͤglich brot noch heüt vns werd /
woͤll vnser schuldt verschonen /
als wir auch vnsern schuldern thůn /
mach vns nit in versůchung ston /
loͤß vns von übel Amen.

J. Brenz, 'Te Deum' (Das lobgsang Ambrosij vnd Augustini / Dich Gott loben wir)

Text from *Psalmen gebett / vnd kirchen uͤbung* (Strasbourg: Köpfel, 1530), fols LXXX^{r}–LXXXIIII^{v}. This was set to the same melody used for Luther's 'Herr Got dich loben wir' in the *Gesangbuch* of 1541.

Herr Gott wir loben dich
wir bekennen dich eynen Herren.
Der ga[n]tz erdbode[n] /
preiset dich ewigen vatter.
Dein lob preisen alle Engel
vn[nd] alle himlische Fuͤrstenthumb.

Die Engel Cherubin vn[nd] Seraphin /
preisen dich ewig on vnderlaß sagende /
Heyliger / Heyliger /
Heyliger Herre Gott Zebaoth.
Himmel vnd erden seind erfuͤllet /
mit dem lob deiner herrligkeyt.

Die loͤblich samlung aller deiner Propheten /
erwirdiget dich eynen waren gott.
Deßgleiche[n] thůt alle zeit /
der früntlich hauff deiner Apostolen.
Die gantz schar der heylgen martyrer loben dich /
mit lieblich enfrewden.
Alle gotsfoͤrchtigen auß er woͤlten /
bekennen dich im[m] gantzen vmbkreyß der erden.
Eynen vatter der aller hoͤchsten herrligkeyt.
Deinen eynigen sun Jesum Christu[m] /
halten sie mit dir eynen waren Gott.
Sampt dem heylgen geyst dem waren troͤster.

O Herr Jesu Christe du bist eyn kuͤnig der eren.
Du bist eyn ewiger sun deines vatters /
Du hast nit gescheüht vo[n] der jung frawen Maria fleysch werden /
zů erloͤsen all außer woͤlte menschen.
Nach dem du den sieg deß bittern todes behalten hast /
in[n] allen glaubigen eroͤffnet das reich der himmel.
Darumb sitzst du zů der rechten /
im[m] preiß deines vatters.
Hernach wirstu zů künfftig sein /
eyn strenger Richter.
O herr wir vermanen dich /
du woͤllest deinen getrewen behuͤlflich sein /
die du erloͤßt hast mit deinem koͤstlichen blůte.
Gib deinen fründen das sie deiner herrligkeyt /
moͤgen teylhafftig werden.

O Herr hilff deine[m] volck /
vnd gesegne dein erb in[n] ewigkeyt.
Vnd weyde sie vnd lere sie
deinen ewigen willen thůn.
Wir loben dich waren gott /
taͤglich zů aller stund.
Vnd deinen namen ruͤmen wir /

immer vnd weiglich.
O Herr erbarm dich vnser vnd sey vnß gnedig /
O Herr erseyg vnß dein barmhertzigkeyt.
Auff dich Herr stet vnser hoffnung
laß vnß nit zů schanden werden.

W. Gernoldt, 'Das Aue Maria außgeleyt'

Text from *Das Aue Maria außgeleyt* (Strasbourg: Frölich, 1540).

AVe)   Gott gruͤß dich reyne Meydt
Groß lob vnd eer sey Gott geseydt
Das du bist von Dauids stammen
Gegruͤsszt seystu von vns allnsammen
Die groͤst / die heyligst in allem land
Dir ward ein Engel von Gott gesandt
Dieweil du fůrtst ein engelisch leben
Ward dir in dein reyn hertz geben
Gott Vatter / Sun vnd heyliger Geyst
Von der rhů bey dir aller meyst
Dein rigel / schlossz nye ward zertrandt
Als vnd Esaias thůt bekandt.

¶ Gratia)   Gnad frid vnd alles heyl
Du hast erwoͤlt den besten theyl
Das woͤll vns Gott geniessen lon
Durch Jesum Christum deinen Son
Ein doͤrnen kron er für vns trůg
Gott der Holofernem schlůg
Vnd Sodoma versincken liessz
Vnd sich das Meer auff halten hiessz
Vnd Jacobs kind darüber fůrt
Die hand die Adams rypp růrt
Die sollen wir all anbetten fast
Der barmhertzigkeyt nye gebrast.

¶ Plena)   Vol der Gottheyt groß
Der sie am Creütz liessz sehen bloß
Denn du Maria hast geborn
Der in Egypten seinen zorn
Mit syben zeychen sehen liessz
Vnd Balaams esel reden hiessz
Vnd Abraham drey Engel sandt

Deß heylige Můter bistu genandt
Keyn groͤssern dienst kan ich dir thůn
Denn das ich glaub in deinen Sůn
Jn vnsern Herrn Jesu Christ
Das er warer Gott vn mensch ist.

¶ Dominus) Der Herr ist mit dir
Gott hat lust vnd gantz begir
Zů wonen in den reynen hertzen
Du hast jn geborn on allen schmertzen
Als Gabriel die bottschafft warb
Der für vns armen sünder starb
Der alleyn die sünd vergibt
Vnd den hymel auch damit
Der dich von anfang hat erwoͤlt
Dein Sůn ist für vns dargestellt
Als ich im Euangelio speür
Er ist der weg / leben vnd thür.

¶ Tecum) Mit dir der seligkeyt ein hort
Ezechiel beschreibt ein beschlosszne port
Ward dir Gott vom hymel gesant
Du bist der busch gar vnuerbrant
Den Mose sach also geheür
Brinnen ins heylgen Geystes feür
Keyn sünd hast du überal
Gott ist der brun[n] vnd auch der qual
Der zů dir geflossen ist
Du hast geborn vnsern Herrn Jesu Christ
O alle menschen nemen war
Hye ist der brun[n] der auch die schar
Von Jsrahel getrencket hat
Geyst / Vatter mit des Sunes rhat.

¶ Benedicta) Du gesegnet bist
Vnd auch dein frucht das billich ist
O Heylige wurtz dein frucht vollbring
Der stern der auff von Jacob gieng
Der bist du Junckfraw vnd Magd reyn
Gott der auch der schaͤcher zwen
Gar so vngeleiches erbe gab
Vnd Lazarum erquicket auß dem grab.

¶ Tua) Du bist gnaden reich
Mein Herr erbarm dich über mich
Der keüsch in einem hertzen lag
Vnd Noe in der Archen pflag
Vnd Jonas in dem fischin hůt
Gott durch Jesum Christum thůt
Was du an jn zů bitten hast
Das du vns Herr geniessen last
Das ich Gott ym[m]er loben will
Mit meiner vernunfft biß auff das zil
Biß das ich nim[m]e leben soll
O Vatter aller gnaden voll

¶ Jn mulieribus) Vnder den weibern außerwoͤlt
Die dreyfeltig sunn ward dargestellt
Das ist die Heylig Dreyfaltigkeyt
Wie Gott durch den Dauid seyt
Mein sun der het gezylet was
Wie die Sonn scheinet durch ein glaß
Also gebar vns Maria dein keüscher leib
Als der Künig Dauid schreibt
Vnd Samuel des Propheten mund
Deß loben wir Gott zů aller stund
Vnd die Engel in Gottes koͤr
Mein Gott vnd schoͤpffer vns erhoͤr
Wir armen sünder ruͤffendt dich an
Du bist der nit versagen kan.

¶ Et benedictus) Du bist gesegnet schon
Du heyligen Tempel Salomon
Vnd das gezelt der Heyligkeyt
Du bist auch wol das Priester kleyt
Das die Heylig Gottheyt an thet
Da er sein Sun geopffert het
Moses vnd Aaron zeygt mir an
Wie ein Prister ein kleyd soll han
Seid vnser lieber Herr Jesus Christ
Du selbs der oͤberst Priester bist
Mit der Gottheyt wol bekleydt
Geborn von einer reynen Meyd.

¶ O fructus) Vber alle frucht
Dein leib gebar in Gottes zucht

Alltissimum den hoͤchsten Gott
Der alle ding gefuͤget hat
Gott hat sich zů vns verbunden
Ein menschen nach seinem willen funden
O Vatter in dem ewigen leben
Wie hast du ein opffer für vnd geben
Der auch die Sunn hiessz stille ston
Da Josue vnd Karebon
Fünff Künig Herr der Heyden erschlůg
Maria dein reyner leib der trůg
Johannes neyft sich in můter leib
Das loben wir Gott in ewigkeyt.

¶ Ventris) Des leibs vnd auch der seel
Du reynes kind von Jsrahel
Du bist geheyliget hie vnd dort
Maria ich find in deinem wort
Ein dienerin des Herren sehent an
Du hast dich nye anbetten lan
Vnd lasst die eer jrem lieben Son
Von jm würt lebendig wasser gon
Kumpt zů mir die seind beladen
Er vergibt vnd heylt den schaden
Vnd fuͤr vns auff die rechten spůr
Die Enoch vnd Elias für.

¶ Tui) Deins leibs frucht helffe mir
Mein Gott ich beger gnad von dir
Ich man dich an die angst vnd nodt
An den schmertzen vnd bittern todt
Den Jesus leyd dein lieber Son
Wir wurden all gesund daruon
Wie in der wůst von einer schlangen
Die ward von Mosen auffgehangen
Wer von Teuffel ist verwundt
Der Herr macht leib vnd seel gesundt
O fell das Egedion trůg
Da er all seine feynd erschlůg
Hilff all vnser feynd überwinden
Das wir den heyligen fryden finden
Bey Jesu Christo Amen
Gegen disem heyligen namen
Sollen alle knye gebogen werden

Es sey im hymel oder auff erden
Den fisch den Tobias fieng
Da der Engel mit jm gieng
Der den Teüffel überwindt
Vnd hilfft seim vatter der was blindt
O me dann ich kann begeren
Will vns Gott all geweren
Sein lieb / sein fryd / sein Goͤttlich hold
Wünscht vns der blind Wolff Gernoldt.

Polemical Songs about Religion, Strasbourg, 1520–1540

Data adapted from the online version of the *Verzeichnis der im deutschen Sprachbereich erschienenen Drucke des 16. Jahrhunderts* (www.vd16.de); The Universal Short Title Catalogue (www.ustc.ac.uk); Wackernagel, *Bibliographie*; and H.-J. Köhler, *Bibliographie der Flugschriften des 16. Jahrhunderts*, part 1; with reference also to *MPGR* and to *Wackernagel DKL*, vol. 3.

Titles in bold are those discussed in Chapter 4.
See also Appendix F.

Author and title of publication	Title of song(s) (if known)	Publication details
Eeyn new lyed von den | falschen Preedigern. | jn des Einzenawers thon *VD16* N 1264 / USTC 642192	**Merckt jr herren myner sag** (*MPGR* no. 147)	**Flach, 1520**[a]
Man lieset in der wahren Gschrift ...| Diß lied sagt von eine[m] | jungen man[n] / der den Schafft rat nit im | haus het... *VD16* ZV 4521 / USTC 640192		Schürer Erben, 1520
E. Alberus, *Ein hüpsch liedlin von | dem Bock von Leyptzig* *VD16* ZV 317 / USTC 644095	Martinus ist nit gschwigen	Schürer Erben, 1521
Ein hübsch New Lied: | Genant zucht / vn[nd] vnzucht/ der junge[n] / | Vnnd auch darbey / ein ermanung der | ältern / das sie die kinder in der forcht | Gottes / ziehen solle[n] / *VD16* H 5752 / USTC 643996		Schürer Erben, 1522

Author and title of publication	Title of song(s) (if known)	Publication details
M. Stiefel, ***Von der Christförmigen / rechtgegründten leer Doctoris | Martini Luthers / ein überuß schön kunstlich | Lyed / sampt seiner neben vßlegung*** *VD16* S 9020 (and S 9021) USTC 617295 (and 617296) Wackernagel, *Bibliographie*, pp. 42–3 Köhler, *Flugschriften* nos 4284 (and 4285)	**Joannes thůt vns schreiben** (Oettinger, *Murner, Stifel*, app. 1 and 2; *Wackernagel DKL*, vol. 3, no. 107)	**Schott, 1522 (repr. 1525?)**
M. Stiefel, ***Wider Doctor Murnars | falsch erdycht Lyed: von | dem vndergang Christlichs | glaubens. | Bruoder Michael Styfels | von Esszlingen vßleg vnnd | Christliche gloß | darüber*** *VD16* S 9025 / USTC 706719 Wackernagel, *Bibliographie*, p. 44 Köhler, *Flugschriften* no. 4286	**Ach du armer Murnar** (*MPGR* no. 5; *Wackernagel DKL*, vol. 3, under no. 109)	**Beck, 1522**[b]
T. Murner, *Antwurt vnd klag mit ent- | schuldigung doctor Murners wider bruder Mich | el Stifel weyt von eßlingen da heim, vff das stüfel | buch so er wider meyn lied gemachet hat, | daruß er des lieds den rechten | thon erlernen mag* *VD16* M 7023 / USTC 612205		Grüninger, 1522
J. Graff, ***In disem tractetlin sind drey | hübsche lieder new gemacht in Christus namen | vo[n] Bapst Cardinal Bischoff prelate[n] / Pfaffe[n] | vnd Münch / darumb ich Jörg Graff be- | gnad bin mit einem priuilegio solchs mir | nit nach zů drucke[n] / wer solchs überfür | wolt ich beklagen nach lautung mei | nes priuilegiums*** *VD16* G 2744 / USTC 668976 Wackernagel, *Bibliographie*, p. 47 Köhler, *Flugschriften* no. 1350	**Gott Vatter in trifalde** (*MPGR* no. 90; *Wackernagel DKL*, vol. 3, no. 448) **Herr Jesu Christ in himels tron** (*MPGR* no. 99; *Wackernagel DKL*, vol. 3, no. 449) **Welt ir hören gesanges schall** (*MPGR* no. 217; *Wackernagel DKL*, vol. 3, no. 450)	**Prüss, 1523**[c]
Von dem heiligen sacra | ment ein hüpsch lied. Jn der brieff | weyß Regenpogen thon. *VD16* V 2490 / USTC 709503		Schürer Erben, 1523

Author and title of publication	Title of song(s) (if known)	Publication details
H. von Zütphen (H. Müller), *Jn disem lied wirstu verston | Wie allweg die geystlichen hon | Die krancken in der letsten not | Gefuͤret hand so ferr von Gott. | Mit erschröcklichen worten vil | Aber yetz nůn zů disem zil | Finstu die rechte troͤstung gar | Jn disem dicht so nym du war | Wie man die krancken trösten sol* *VD16* H 1893 / USTC 668970		
M. Stiefel, *Ein schones künstlichs | lied / vo[n] der recht gegruͤndte[n] Ewan | gelischen leer Doctoris Mar | tini Luthers. | Jn brůder Veiten thon* *VD16* S 9024 / USTC 646686		Schürer Erben, 1524
Eyn neüw Lied vo[n] dem | Ablaß vnd den Stacionierern. | Jn disem Lied verstanden wirt | Wie vns die Geystlichen verfiert | Haben so lang mit falscher ler | Darin[n] gesůcht gůt weltlich eer | Das merckt man yetzund taͤglich wol | Jm Speten thon mans syngen sol. *VD16* N 1248 / USTC 656211		Schürer Erben, 1524
H. von Zütphen (H. Müller), *Eyn schön neüv Lied | vom glauben vnnd Testament / auch | von der bereytung zů dem tysch Got- | tes / zů nutz den vaerbauwenen / von ey- | nem liebhaber Göttlicher warheit zů | Straßburg gesungen vnd gedicht. Jn | der Flam[m] weyß / oder in Hertzog Ern- | sten melody. | Bruͤder Heynrich* *VD16* H 1891 / USTC 656362 Wackernagel, *Bibliographie*, pp. 64–5	**Meyn hertz das mag nit růwe han** (*MPGR* no. 148; *Wackernagel DKL*, vol. 3, no. 110)	**Schürer Erben, 1524**[d]
H. von Zütphen (H. Müller), *Jn disem lied wirstu verston | Wie allweg die geystlichen hon | Die krancken in der letsten not | Gefuͤret hand so ferr von Gott | Mit erschröcklichen worten vil | Aber yetz nůn zů disem zil | Finstu die rechte troͤstung gar | Jn disem dicht so nym du war | Wie man die krancken trösten sol, o Cristen mensch, betracht das wol, Das du die krancken troͤstest schon, und syngt man es ins Speten thon* *VD16* H 1893 / USTC 668970 Wackernagel, *Bibliographie*, p. 65	**Jr bruͤder in Christo Jesu** (*MPGR* no. 127; *Wackernagel DKL*, vol. 3, no. 111)	**Schürer Erben, 1524**[e]

Author and title of publication	Title of song(s) (if known)	Publication details
N. Manuel, *Eyn schön reygenlied im thon / Rusticus ambilem, Neüwlich geschmidet durch Meyster Hemerlin jm berg Ethna* *VD16* M 753 / USTC 65637 Wackernagel, *Bibliographie*, p. 56	**Der Babst rüfft Küng vnd Keyser an** (*MPGR* no. 45; *Wackernagel DKL*, vol. 3, no. 470)	**Schürer Erben, 1524**
Dies ist ein neues Liedlein evangelische Lehre betreffend *VD16* ZV 4515		Prüss, 1525
Ein schon lied newlich | gemacht / im gulden kron thon *VD16* S 3555 / USTC 646563	Ich kam gezogenn vß Sachser la[n]d	Schürer Erben, 1525
Ein hüpsch new lied von | eine[m] Christenlichen man mit name[n] | Caspar Tauber genant wie man | jm das haupt abgeschlage[n] hat | Vnd zu lest verprentt.| Vn[nd] ist jn Brud[er] Vy | tten tho[n] *VD16* H 5770 / USTC 644109		Schürer Erben, 1525
Eyn new Christlich lied | Jnn Tollner melodey / das eins | teyls verantwurtet der gots | lesterer schmehung / so | der Bauren auffrůr | dem Euangelio | fälschlich zů | legendt *VD16* N 1159 / USTC 656222		Schürer Erben, 1525
Ein nützlich vnd hübsch | new lied / oder spruch / von d[er] Eva[n]gelischen leer / Jn brůder | Veiten thon. | Kauffs vnd ließ es wirt | dir gefallen *VD16* ZV 11816 / USTC 645327		Schürer Erben, 1525
Nüw zeitung betreffend die absterbende papistischen Messen zu Straßburg byßhar loblichen von jn gehalten. *VD16* N 728 / USTC 678766 Vogeleis, *Quellen und Bausteine*, p. 224		n.p., 1525
Ad Martinum Lutherum captivum Lamentatio[f] USTC 751786		
U. Eckstein, *EJn hübsch neüw | lied, betreffend doctor | hans faber, Johannes | ecken, wie sye zů Baden | jm Ergaw gtisputiert haben | vff den. xix. tag des | Meyen als man | zalt. M.D | vnd. xxvj. | Jor | Vnd singt man diß lied in dem don | es fert ein frischer summer do her do | werden ir hőren neüwe mer* *VD16* E 497 / USTC 648711 Wackernagel, *Bibliographie*, p. 91		Schwann, 1526

Author and title of publication	Title of song(s) (if known)	Publication details
H. Vogtherr, *Ein neuwes Euangelisch | Lied in allem creütz | Jedem Christenn gantz tröstlich | Auß göttlicher schrifft ge- | zogen. Jm Jar da man | zalt tausent fünff hun- | dert vnd. xxvj. &c.* *VD16* V 2186 / USTC 644826 Wackernagel, *Bibliographie*, p. 89	**Lob sei dir, jesu Christe** (*MPGR* no. 138; *Wackernagel DKL*, vol. 3, no. 559)	**Kornmann, 1526**
Waren verstand / | von des herren | Nachtmal. | Vff die weyß zů singen / | Es ist das hayl vns | komen her. &c. *VD16* W 177 / USTC 704895 Wackernagel, *Bibliographie*, p. 98	**Es ist die warheyt pracht an tag** (*Wackernagel DKL*, vol. 3, no. 521)	**Prüss, 1527**
Ein new Christlich lied | und sagt von fünff verheissungen, die | Gott der Herr Adam, Noe, Abraham, Lott,| und dem Propheten David verhyesz. | Jm thon, Wach auff meins hertzen ein, &c. *VD16* N 1160 / USTC 644891		n.p., 1530
Ein hüpsch nüw | Lied / wie das wort Gotts | in Zürich ist zum ersten ent- | sprungen vnd geprediget. | Jn der wyß wie das Wirtenberger | Lied / Jch lob Gott in dem | hoͤchsten thron. *VD16* H 5776 / USTC 644130		Frölich, 1535
Ein nüw Lied von der | vffrůr der landtlüten zů Jnderlap- | penn in der herschafft Bern in | uͤchtlandt beschehen Jm[m] | M. D. XXVIII. | Jar[g] *VD16* M 747 / USTC 645344	**Wie es jn disen tagen zu Bern ergangen ist**	**Apiarius, 1536**[h]
Drey Schoͤne | Meyster Lieder / das erst / | Jm Richterbůch das sechzehend sagt. | Vnd ist in des Schillers thon / &c. | Das ander / Lucas am ersten Ca- | pittel spricht. Vnd ist im senfften Nachtigals thon. Das drit / | Das sibent im andern Mach | abeorum sagt. Vnd ist im | thon Roͤmers ge- | sang weiß / &c. *VD16* ZV 8519 / USTC 641478		Frölich, 1540[i]
J. Frölich, *Ein new lied vnd erman- | ung / an die Christliche[n] Potentaten | vnnd Staͤnde / ernstliche tapffere gegenweer | wider den Türcken fürzunemen. Vnnd mag | gesungen werden / Jnn brůder Veyten Thon.| Oder in des Bentzenawers weyß / &c.* *VD16* N 1235 / USTC 644989 Wackernagel, *Bibliographie*, pp. 246–7		Frölich, 1540

Author and title of publication	Title of song(s) (if known)	Publication details
N. Vogel, *Ein hübsch new Lied von dem verlornen Sun* USTC 710323		Frölich, 1540

[a] This pamphlet is recorded in *MPGR* as originating in Strasbourg from the press of Martin Flach, with Oettinger estimating the date as 'after 1520'.

[b] This pamphlet is recorded in *MPGR* and *Wackernagel DKL*, vol. 3, as originating in Strasbourg from the press of Johann Prüss, with Oettinger estimating the date as 'c. 1523'. The details used here, however, are taken from the *VD16* online catalogue and the USTC.

[c] This pamphlet is recorded in *MPGR* and *Wackernagel DKL*, vol. 3, as possibly originating in Strasbourg from the press of Johann Prüss, or else in Nuremberg from the press of Kunigunde Hergotin, in approximately 1523. *VD16*, however, confidently asserts that it is from Prüss's press in Strasbourg, having appeared in 1523.

[d] This pamphlet is recorded in *MPGR* and *Wackernagel DKL*, vol. 3, as possibly originating in Strasbourg from the press of Ulrich Morhardt, with Oettinger estimating the date as 'c. 1522'. The details used here, however, are taken from the *VD16* online catalogue.

[e] This pamphlet is recorded in *MPGR* and *Wackernagel DKL*, vol. 3, as originating in Strasbourg from the press of Ulrich Morhardt, with Oettinger estimating the date as 'c. 1522'. The publication details used here, however, are taken from the *VD16* online catalogue.

[f] Either a reprint of the same title of 1521 (unknown place of publication) (see http://idb.ub.uni-tuebingen.de/diglit/KeXVIII4a_fol_20/0001), or else the year in USTC is inaccurate.

[g] The text of this song can be found in A. Fluri, 'Mathias Apiarius, der erste Buchdrucker Berns (1537–1554). Das Interlachnerlied und die erste bernische Censurordnung', *Neues Berner Taschenbuch*, 2 (1897 [published 1896]), pp. 210-16.

[h] The dating used here follows that found in *VD16*.

[i] The Württembergische Landesbibliothek, Stuttgart estimates that this song originates from c. 1530. The publication details used here, however, are taken from the *VD16* online catalogue. It is unclear from the title whether this song contains any polemical material. See also Table 4.2, pp. 194–5.

APPENDIX F

A Selection of Polemical Song Texts from Strasbourg Relating to the Reformation

See also Appendix E.

'Merckt jr herre[n] myner sag', in *Eeyn new lyed von den | falschen Preedigern. | jn des Binzenawers thon* (Strasbourg: Flach, 1520)
German text from Soltau, *Ein Hundert deutsche historische Volkslieder*, no. 43.

1. Merckt jr herre[n] myner sag,
die welt fuͤrt ein grosse klag,
wie auff woͤll stan vyl ketzerey,
jrttum jm glauben auch darbey,
seyt man[n] Cristus leer fuͤr helt,
werde[n] vyl frommer fuͤr ketzr gezelt,
merck wie es gangen ist biß haͤr
mitt maͤrlinn wynckel prediger.

2. Die hetten einen fund erdacht,
zeychen den heilgen vil auffbracht,
groß walfart alenthalb verkint,
wie die geschende synd worden blind,
tob ghoͤrt stum[m] redt lamer gerad,
sy habe[n] gemacht ein seltzams wildtbad,
auch ander wunder vnzall,
dz ist vol worden berg vnd tall.

3. Das man[n] die heilgen růff an,
vnd land Christum die weil still stonn,
so sy mich jn noͤten liessen,
solt ich dißer gůt rhet nit geniessen,
die Christus thet hie vff erden,
das ich jr moͤcht teylhefftig werde[n],
doch gibt vns Christus zůuersto[n]
wz wir sin vatter jm himels thron.

4. Recht bitten synem namen zwar,
dz woͤll er vns gwaͤren gar,
also ist vnsers hergots leer,
vnd so duͤrffent mir keyns anders meer,
als die rechte[n] prediger verkinden,
die sich beym heiligen Eua[n]gelio land finden,
geschwygt ander fabel ding vnd klappery,
vnd sagt was die warheit sey.

5. Das will die gmein nit han vergůt
vff maͤrlin zeichen setz sie jrn můt,
damit die einfeltigen in groß jrrung,
gesind worden in verfuͤrung,
das macht bracht allein des pfenings lieb,
d[er] hat auch sunst gmacht rauber vn[nd] dieb,
d[er] gytz vn[nd] der eigen nutz,
machen ma[n]che seltzame faßnacht butz.

6. Har wachs kleyder kettinn groß,
henckt man fuͤr den heilgen groß,
als ob sy kraͤmer vnd kaufleuͤt syen,
das sy vns vor aller kranckheit fryen,
dem schenckent mir sylber vn[nd] gold,
vnd find auch jn nit anders holdt,
vnnd das sy vns jr hilff beweysen,
grosse zeychen thond sonst land mirs bleyben.

7. Vnnser andacht thůt nit darnach stelle[n],
dz wir waͤre d[er] heilge[n] geselle[n].
doͤrt jn dem ewigen lebenn,
als die eer dem schoͤpffer geben,
der alle wund[er] eynig thůt,
der selber ist dz ewig gůt,
es hatt geredt sein goͤtlich mund,
wan[n] kom[m]en wirt disse stund.

8. Das falsch prediger vff werden sto[n],
die heissent zů den heilgen gon,
da geschehent grosse wu[n]derzeichen,
folg jn nit du wirst geleichen,
nu[n] sicht die welt jetz sonder wol,
das alle land sind walfart vol,

car by mir vil gebrechen ha[n]d
Christus vnser drumb nit schont.

9. Manger spricht er hab hilff von helgen erworben,
ach gott wer er da fuͤr gestorben,
das er die heilgen an liegen thůt,
verfůrt man groß from[m]es blůtt
so man[n] jn sollichs weren wil,
so kom[m]en d[er] Romaniste[n] vil,
mit jrer straff feuͤer vnd fackel an,
vnd wend verbrennenn jederman.

10. Das keiner soll die warheit sagen,
vnd thůnd sy auß d[er] kilchen jagen,
das weißt jetz mencher biderman,
der anderst wenig leesen kan,
noch eins hett ich vergessen schier,
das můß ich heimlich sagen mir,
in still vnd geheim allein
des hertz als niema[n]s als ich mein.

11. Es synd noch vil prediger in d[er] welt
die gebent besser krieger in das feldt,
den[n] prediger gottes gonst vn[nd] wort,
dz sy nie haben gehort,
sy solten and[er] lewt weißen vnd leeren,
so sagent sy vo[m] seltzen maͤren,
vff der kantzel die leuͤwt vßrichten,
daruff thůnd sy studieren vn[nd] dichten.

12. Machen zanck vnd hader in der gemein,
es gefelt nur jr ding allein,
gůtt spyl haben sy darmit,
das man jn darinn darff rede[n] nit,
wie moͤcht sein baß eim gauch,
so man jm erlaubet auch,
das er vnß zů fantasten dar machen
das[1] wirt jeder hinderm win wol lachen.

---

[1] = des.

13. Ein prediger soll fůren ein schlechtes leben,
dem volck ein gůtt exempel geben,
ha[n]d aber jetz ein sollich lebe[n],
die nichs dan[n] gauckelwerck treibe[n],
ich darff fůrwar nit laut sagen,
wie die roß sind also geet der wagen,
es gschehen grosse wunderzeichen,
da mit man die leůwt thůt leichen.

14. Lauffent alle winckel auß,
bauwent altag ein newes gotzßhauß,
la[n]d die alten fallen darnider,
trag knobloch vß vnd bring zwybel wider,
doctor Murnar hat sollich narren erzelt,
jn seyner narren beschwerung erwőlt,
jtem Basti Brant[2] ist auch jm spyl,
hat anzeig der narren vil.

15. Die hie sunst niemandt hat erkent,
das sy narren weren genent,
den[n] sy an tragen syden gewant,
man[n] soll nit verstan jr nerrisch dant,
vermeinen sy jn jrem syn[n]
dennocht wirt man sinn wol jn[n].
schat nit dz einer ein narr wer,
wan[n] er jm behielt sein leer.

16. Vn[nd] ließ predigen vnderwegen
thet sich seiner thorheit allein pflegen
vn[nd] trett nit daher als kőnt er wol,
verfůret nit mit jm ein statt vol,
wan[n] eyner wolt reden nit daruo[n].
dz gotßwort außlegen thon,
so solt jr predigen den rechten grund,
wie dz geredt hat Christus mund.

17. Vnd prediget auch wie Paul[us] thett
der jederman fůr brůder vnd schwester het,
die leůt nit also gescholte[n],
seiner leer hat niemanß ergolten,
als jetz by vnsern predigern geschicht,

2 Sebastian Brant.

mancher ein faßnacht speyl anricht,
dz man vergessen soll darneben,
wie er fuͤrt eynn schantlichs leben.

18. Darnach kompt der barfůsser,
der ist ein rechten betler,
er sagt von dryer gulde[n] franciscus,
dz warlich als erlogen ist,
sant Franciscus was ein from[m]er man,
vnd konth mit solchem nit vmbgon,
aber die nachkom[m]en die habens erdacht,
die fryheit zů Rom zůwegen bracht.

19. Das wil ich jetz lassen sein[n],
nůn drit vnser frawen brůder harein,
wie jnn d[er] nam sy geben worden,
ich hoͤr sy heyße[n] der Carmeliter orden,
die Augustiner bleiben da hinden nit,
sy samlen bettel auch darmit,
prediger muͤnch wer wol ein rechter orden,
der bettel zů eynem erb ist worden.

20. Jm vnd seinen nachkom[m]en,
sy seind die rechten vnd from[m]en,
man heyßt su meister der ketzerey,
merck wie ichs mein darbey,
nit das sy ketzer solle[n] syn,
also ist nit die meinung mein,
sond[er] dz sy die kennen wol,
wie mann sy all verbrennen sol.

21. Aber wie jrs mercken schlachs ich jn die schantz,
sy habe[n] gemacht de[n] roßen krantz,
auch den Psalter hoch gelobt,
da mit sy haben zu gestopt,
dem from[m]en gemeinen volck die oren,
vnnd sy gemacht zů grossen thoren,
jr bettel sack wirt nym[m]er vol,
wie man fuͤllt so bleybt er hol,
also end ich yetz mein gedicht,
Christus sy vnser zůuersicht.

'Joannes thůt vns schreiben', in M. Stiefel, *Von der Christfoͤrmigen / rechtgegründten leer Doctoris | Martini Luthers / ein überuß schoͤn kunstlich | Lyed / sampt seiner neben vßlegung* (Strasbourg: Schott, 1522)

German text from *Wackernagel DKL*, vol. 3, no. 107. The song is in five parts, totalling 52 verses. The first part only is shown here (*Wackernagel DKL*, vol. 3, pp. 74–5). Translation from Oettinger, 'Murner, Stifel, and songs as polemic', pp. 74–6. The full text and translation is available in *ibid.*, pp. 74–85. A digital version can be viewed at: http://daten.digitale-sammlungen.de/~db/0001/bsb00019466/image_3.

Das erst teyl von dem Luther selbs, vnd nochgonds von seiner leer vn[nd] schreiben.	The first part about Luther himself, and following this about his teachings and writings.
1. Joannes thůt vns schreiben von einem Engel klar Der Gottes wort soll treiben gantz luter offenbar: Zů vns thůt sich auch scheiben, es faͤlt nit vmb ein har, daruff wil ich beleiben, das sag ich eüch fürwor.	John writes to us clearly about an angel who shall stir up God's word quite loudly and openly: He also encircles us so that not a hair is lost. On this [truth] I will remain, I tell you truly.
2. Hoch kunst die lasszt er stieben weyt über berg vnd tal, Den mundt will jm verschieben zů Rom des Bischoffs sal. Es schelten jn die trieben, die wölff in gottes stal: huͤt dich vor dißen dieben, wo sye seind überal.	He lets the high arts scatter far over mountain and valley. His voice will displace the bishop's chamber in Rome. It rebukes the [evil] impulse, the wolf in God's stable. Protect yourself from these thieves, wherever they may be.
3. Du magst nun wol erkennen den Engel den ich meyn, Härnoch will ich jn nennen, die sach die ist nit klein. Lasszt dich nit fuͤrn von dannen, das er hatt fleisch vnd bein: das findst von heylgen mannen vnd nit von jm allein.	Now you would like to recognise the angel of whom I speak. Soon I will name him, for this business is important. Do not be led away from him because he is flesh and bone: You see that among all holy men, and not only with him.

4. Es bdeütet vns das flyegen
verschmähen zeytlich gůt.
Ker dich nit an das lyegen
das man vom frommen thůt:
Er thůt sich worlich fyegen
zů Gott in rechtem můt,
gwalt mag jn auch nit byegen,
er geb ee drumb sein blůt.

This is important to us who flee from
[and] despise worldly goods.
Do not turn to the lies
that some tell of the pious one.
He will truly unite [us]
with the correct spirit to God,
and force will not bend him, either.
He gives honour for the sake of His blood.

5. Sein hertz zů Gott er neyget
recht als ein christen man,
Die gschrifft er rein abseyget,
kein wůst lasszt er doran:
Zů Worms er sich erzeyget,
er tratt keck vff den plan,
sein feynd hatt er geschweyget,
keinr dorfft jn wenden an.

He inclines his heart to God
just as a Christian should.
He keeps Scripture pure.
and allows no confusion.
He showed himself at Worms,
solidly following the scheme.
His enemy had silenced him,
and nobody could address him.

6. Er lasszt sich nit erschrecken
die schühen fledermeyß,
Sein leer thůt er vollstrecken
zů Gottes lob vnd preyß:
Die worheit thůt jn stercken,
sye macht vil menschen wyß:
der baur die sach wil mercken,
das mügt Cölln vnd Paryß.

He did not let himself be afraid
of the fearsome bats.
He carries out his teachings
to the honour and glory of God.
Truth strengthens him:
It makes many people wise.
The peasants take note of the events
as well as theologians in Cologne and Paris.

7. Nůn grüssz ich dich von hertzen,
du edels Wittenberg!
Vil frommer littendt schmertzen,
gieng es dir überzwerg.
Erdtfurt thůt gůtlich schertzen
mit dir in Gott bequem,
es halt euch als zwo kertzen
das new Hierusalem.

Now I greet you from my heart,
you precious Wittenberg!
Many pious people suffer pains,
for crossing over to you.
Erfurt treasures you well,
taking comfort in God with you.
We consider you the two candles
of the new Jerusalem.

8. Vermischet ist ein morgen
in Danielis bůch
Dem abent vnuerborgen:
den rechten grund ich sůch.

The book of Daniel tells of
how one morning is mixed up
with the evening of revelation:
I seek the proper foundation.

Das nimpt mir alles sorgen das ich hett vff den flůch, ich darf nit ewig worgen, in hoffnung ich mich růg.	It takes from me all the sorrows that I had while in flight. I may not be tormented forever: In hope I find fault with myself.
9. Das lyecht des tags kumpt wider, es bricht dohär mit macht, Der engel schwingt sein gfider, das yrdisch er veracht, Er leert die christen glider vnd fuͤrt sye von der nacht, er sey hoch oder nider, das selbig er nit acht.	The light of day comes again: Mightily the dawn breaks. The angel brandishes his weapon and condemns the worldly one. He teaches the Christian followers and leads them from the night. Whether they be high-born or lowly, he pays no heed to that.
10. Sein stimm die thůt er stercken on alles tryegen frey: Herr, gib dz ich mög mercken was diser engel schrey. Zům ersten thůt mich schrecken sein leer, was Adam sey: das gsetz thůt er entdecken, groß forcht erwechßt darbey.	His voice strengthens him, free from all deception. Lord, grant that I may not what this angel cries out. At first it frightened me, his teaching, about what Adam was: [Adam] discovered the law and thus great fear grew [in him].

Das Ander teyl von den Zehen gebotten gottes.	The second part, about God's Ten Commandments.
...	
Das Dritt teyl diß buͤchlins.	The third part of this small book.
...	
Der fyerdt teyl.	The fourth part.
...	
Der fünfft teil.	The fifth part.

'Ach du armer Murnar', in *Wider Doctor Murnars | falsch erdycht Lyed: von | dem vndergang Christlichs | glaubens. | Bruoder Michael Styfels | von Esszlingen vßleg vnnd | Christliche gloß | darüber* (Strasbourg: Beck, 1522)

Based on the translation in *MPGR*, pp. 118 and 221.

Ach du armer Murnar	O you poor Murner,
was hastu gethon,	what have you done?
Das du also blind	You have gone blindly
in der heylgen schrifft bist gon:	into holy Scripture.
Des müst du in der kutten	Thus you must suffer
lyden pein	pain in the [monastic] cowl.
Aller glerten MURR, NARR	You must be Grumbling-Fool
müst du sein.	to all learned folk.
O he ho lieber Murnar.	Oh ha ha, dear Murner.

The original *Judaslied* was as follows (German text from Böhme, *Altdeutsches Liederbuch*, no. 539c; translated in *MPGR*, p. 101):

O du armer Judas,	O wretched Judas,
was hastu gethan,	what have you done?
daß du deinen Herren	You have betrayed
also verrathen hast!	your Lord!
Darumb mustu leiden	That is why you must
in der helle pein,	suffer torment in hell,
Lucifers geselle	and you shall be Lucifer's
mustu ewig sein.	companion in eternity.
Kyrie eleison.	Lord have mercy.

‘Gott Vatter in trifalde’, in J. Graff, *In disem tractetlin sind drey | hübsche lieder new gemacht in Christus namen | vo[n] Bapst Cardinal Bischoff prelate[n] / Pfaffe[n] | vnd Münch* (Strasbourg: Prüss, 1523).

German text from *Wackernagel DKL*, vol. 3, no. 448. Also available in Fallersleben and Schade, eds, *Weimarisches Jahrbuch*, 4 (1855), pp. 441–5.

1. Gott Vatter in trifalde,
aus deines himels sall
Durch dein göttlichen gewalde
send mir herab zů tall
    Deiner genad vrsprunge,
das ich erschell mein zunge:
der kunst bin ich noch junge,
hilff mir, heyliger geist,
das ich werd vnderweist.

2. O Herr, durch all dein giette
die du vns teylest mit
Bewegt sich mein gemiette,
das ich mag lassen nit
    Lenngen das mein gesange:
die warheyt leyt gefange,
der christenn glaub gantz zwange
vnd wir zů ser geblent
durch die glerten verwent.

3. Das Gots wort sie verkeren,
schaffen die grossen pfrind:
Was man thůt geren heren,
dar durch werdens verdient,
    Bis sie gros stend erlangen
vnd vil der pfründ empfangen,
dar nach sicht man sie brangen
in marderen baret:
eim pfaffen kap zů stet.

4. Kein prediger will melde
das gots wort, als im birt,
Vnd forcht, er mů̈s entgelde,
das im genommenn wirt
    Sein grosse pfrind vnd stande
vnnd wirt dar bey erkante

ir eigen sünd vnd schande:
dis treyben nacht vnd tag
münch, pfaffen, wie ich euch sag.

5. Noch eins treyben die pfaffen,
ist ir brauch vnnd gewon:
Wenn einer ein weyb thůt straffen,
so lernen sieß dann an,
    Sie sol sich von jm scheide[n]:
official, sidler, beyde
haben darob ein freyde:
'wilt meine[n] willen don,
ich schend dich von deine[m] man'.

6. Der Bapst solt solches wenden,
mit nemen Simeoney,
Sein Cardinal aus sende[n],
Bischoff, Prelaten frey
    Solt mann auch dar zů halte,
vnd straffen mit gewalte
die pfaffen jung vnd alte,
in stedt, merckt, auff de[m] land,
so wirt gewe[n]t sünd, schand.

7. Weyl die bischoff selb treyben
den jren eygnen will,
So lassen sies wol bleyben
vnd schweygen dar zů still,
    Keins boͤsen sie sich schemen,
aller buberey ruͤmen,
můtter vnd tochter nemen,
laden die man zů haus,
die Complet wirt bald auß.

8. 'Wenn es wirt vmb die metten,
so wöln wir fahen an
Den frummen Luther retten',
redt sich der arm man,
    'Den jr wolt gantz vertreyben
vnd niering lassen bleyben,
was er lert vn[nd] thůt schreyben
will er mit recht bestan
oder jns feüer gan.

9. Wenn man es recht corgieret,
so leyt es an dem tag
Das er die warheyt rieret:
jr wolt nit das man es sag.
    Ein ketzer jr in nennet,
habt jm sein bůch verbre[n]net,
die schrifft jr selb nit kennet,
stet vff des richters heyl
'verhor die beyden teyl'.

10. Es thůt euch aber zoren
das er die warheyt seyt,
Habt zů der kirch geschworen,
vnd wölt vch alle zeyt
    Jn weltlich hendel flechte
mit peinlich straff vnd rechte,
künd vil loica vnd spechte:
dz treybt jr al gemeyn,
seyt des teüfels mastschweyn'.

11. Solch pfaffen vnd prelaten
findt man ietz viel zů hoff,
So man jr nit möcht gratten,
sind nit hertzog noch groff,
    Wölle[n] doch sein in rette,
das man vor zeyt nit thette:
keyser, künig bey in hette
groffen, freye, ritter fron
vnd manchen edelman.

12. Löblicher Keyser frumme,
glaub nit der pfaffenn list!
Lon Christus mir her kum[m]e,
sind jr zů dienst gerist,
    Loßt die pfaffe[n] studieren
vnd ir kirchen regieren,
ein gůt exempel fieren
do heim in jrem land
stroffen ir eygne schand.

13. Solten sie vns verdringen,
das muͤst vnns werden leyd:
Wir wöllen sie abbringen
vnd nemen Christus gleyd.
    Der geb vns seinen segen,
der arm man wirt sich rege[n],
Christus wöll vnser pflegen:
das sang zu wol gefall
Jörg Graff den pfaffenn all.

'Herr Jesu Christ in himels tron', in J. Graff, *In disem tractetlin sind drey | hübsche lieder new gemacht in Christus namen | vo[n] Bapst Cardinal Bischoff prelate[n] / Pfaffe[n] | vnd Münch* (Strasbourg: Prüss, 1523)

German text from *Wackernagel DKL*, vol. 3, no. 449. Also available in Fallersleben and Schade, eds, *Weimarisches Jahrbuch*, 4 (1855), pp. 445–9.

1. HErr Jesu Christ in himels tron,
halt vns in deiner pflicht,
Du aller hoͤchste gottheit fron,
gib vns auch vnterricht
    Dz wir vns halte[n] der rechte moß:
wie da[n] vns Christus hat bescheit
durch sant Johans, merckt ir,
wie das zehe[n]d capitel seyt
'ich bin der weg vn[nd] thir,
dar durch jr geht die rechten stroß',
Macht vns den glauben offenbar
In wunderwerck vnd pein,
bey vns fierthalb vnd dreyssig jar
spreyt aus den [dein] some[n] sein:
Dein ellend war so gros vff erd,
dz kein mensch nie beschloß,
wie dir dein menschheit würd versert,
du wölst vns mache[n] gros
nie all noch der prophete[n] sag.

2. O Jesu Christ, ein trewer hirt
bist du gewesen ye,
Der sein schoff gnediglich regirt,
dein leib du für vns hie
    Hast geben willig in den todt:

aller heyligster vatter in got
den Bapst man nennen sol,
der vntreülich geweydet hot
sein schaff, begert er wol
von vns, geschoren frů vnd spot,
Er vns die seinen vnterdon,
ich mein die cardinäl,
bischoff, prelaten, solt verston,
pfaffen vnd münich[3] al:
Das gots wort haben sie verkert
vnd erdacht die tagzeyt,
dar bey sie newer fünd gelert,
von jartagen geseyt,
seelampten, vigilg [*sic*] vnd complet.

3. Sie hand verkaůfft Christus genod
vns geben vmb das geld,
Bapst Siluester den ersten rot
gab dar zů, wie ich meld.
    Weyter wil ich euch wissen lon:
sie hand dz decretall gemacht
aus krichisch in latein,
zů sam in die Concilium bracht,
darnach corgiert für fein:
das must als glauben der arm mann,
Hand erdacht opffer vnd kirwey,
auff der kantzel verkünd,
vergebung aller sünd da sey,
hand vns gemachet blind:
Darmit hon sie jr schätz gemert,
vnns täglich vor geseyt,
sie dienent gott auff dieser erd
für vns zu aller zeit:
das solt jr all gelauben nit.

4. Niemant für mich kan dienen got,
ich můs es selber thůn:
Wenn ein herr ein trabante[n] hot,
neben im můs er gon:
    Es zimpt nit zweien hern ein knecht,
ein yeder bischoff in seim land

[3] = münch.

hat einen schutzpatron,
vil brůͤderschafft vnd solcher dant
darmit gefange[n] an:
was alles wider got vn[nd] recht,
Ich mein, des heylige[n] geyst bottschafft
reyt vff eim hohen pferdt:
die Johanser herrenn mit krafft
sicht ma[n] kummen dort her,
Sant antonis botschafft ich mein,
weycht vns die roten sew,
sant küres botschafft ist die ein,
sunst vil münich do bey,
schwarz, graw, weyß in mancherley art.

5. Sie hand brieff vnnd siegel gemacht,
gnad, aplas ausgesant,
Darmit das gelt zůsammen bracht,
betrogen alle land:
    Jetz ist es kummen an den tag,
Iesus Christ vns ein hirten sant,
den glerten zů einer stroff,
der ist Roterdamus genant,
weydet Christus sein schaff,
die warheit brinngt er an den tag.
Jesus Christ hat vns angezint
dz liecht der christe[n]heit,
das ietz gewaltiglichenn brint,
wie er vns hat geseyt
'Ehe meine wort solte[n] zergon,
ehe můͤst himel vnd erd
zůbreche[n], son[n] vnd auch der mon':
als er vns ietz bewert:
das gots wort dringt gwaltlich erfür.

6. Bapst vnd bischoff haben verklagt
Martinu[m] Lůther, ich sag,
Habe[n] doch schlechte eer erjagt
zů wůrmes auff dem tag:
    Vor im můsten sie scham rot ston,
zů antwurt was er bald bereyt
keyserlich maiestat,
doch das man im geb ein geleyt:
er fürchtet falschen rot,

wie man Johans Hussen hat gethon.
Martinus hebreisch lert,
krichisch, grekisch dar bey,
dardurch er vns klårlich bewert
die euangeli frey:
Jr vil hand sich doctor genent
vnd selb dar mit geirt,
die schrifft haben sie nit erkent,
wie ma[n] sie ietz corgirt [corrigirt],
Martinus vnd die sein genos.

7. Ein christenlicher Fürst vnd herr,
der helt Martinus hand,
Der Bapst thet in verclagen ser,
[fehlt] er het in gern verbrant,
    Aber Gott lest die seinen nicht:
Hertzog Friderich ist ers genant,
gubernator im reich,
Saxen, Meyxen vnd Dyringer land
regiert gewaltiglich,
got der halt jn in seiner pflicht:
Der gelerten bůberei vnd schand
nit mer so gewaltig wirt,
der hertzog hat in seine[m] land
die gelerten reformiert,
Dem wort christi wil er bey ston,
ist sein getrewer rat,
das ein jecklicher pfaf sol thon
gleich andern in der statt
mit burger recht, steuer vnd wach.

8. O Jesu Christ, du hőchstes gůt,
wie hast du vns geliebt,
Erkauffet hie mit din[em] blůt!
dein gnad sich widerumb iebt
    Bey vns vff erd ietz manigfalt,
mir warde[n] gantz an dir verjrrt,
glaubten der menschen bot:
eim iedem christen zů gebirt
allein anbetten gott:
das bedenckt beyde, jung vnd alt,
Růfft zů Christo mit lauter stim
vnd neyget ewere kny,

Lot vns allsamen dancken jm,
das er so gnedig hie
Vns hat wider gebe[n] den tag:
wir waren gantz benacht
vnd thetten nach der glerten sag,
das opffer han mir bracht
den heylgen, vnd vergassen Gott.

9. Christus, erleücht mir sünnder grob
meinn seel, herz vnde sinn,
Das ich dich ye vnd ymmer lob,
dein creatur ich bin.
Herr, dein will der geschech an mir,
Christu, erleucht mich, dz ich lieb
mein nechsten als ich soll,
mit worte[n], werkenn nit betrieb,
so mag mir werde[n] wol
dort ewig vn[nd] ymer bey dir.
Biß gelobt, du ewiger gott
inn deines himels thron,
der alle ding erschaffenn hot
dem mensch zů vnterthon.
Lot vnns nachfolgen Christus leer,
ir brůͤder vnd schwester all.
Ich, Jörg graff, sang Christus zů eer,
dort in des hymels sal
helff er mir vnd euch allen dar.

‘Welt ir hoͤren gesanges schall’, in J. Graff, *In disem tractetlin sind drey | hübsche lieder new gemacht in Christus namen | vo[n] Bapst Cardinal Bischoff prelate[n] / Pfaffe[n] | vnd Münch* (Strasbourg: Prüss, 1523).

German text taken from *Wackernagel DKL*, vol. 3, no. 450. Also available in Fallersleben and Schade, eds, *Weimarisches Jahrbuch*, 4 (1855), pp. 450–52.

1. WElt ir hoͤren gesanges schall,
Keyser, Künig, Hertzog, Grane[n][4] all,
Frey Ritter, Edelma[n] ich zal,
nun haben růg,[5] ir außerwelte geste,

[4] *Weimarisches Jahrbuch* reads ‘grafen’.
[5] *Weimarisches Jahrbuch* reads ‘vůg’.

Jr hoch weysen herren im reych,
frey stett vn[nd] ander des geleych,
in Christus lieb verman ich eich,
das jr wöllet habe[n] nit lenger reste:
Lat euch lieb, hoffnung vnd gelaub erwecken
vnd das Gotswort nit also nider decken,
das Bapst, Cardinal, Bischoff, münch vnd pfaffen
habe[n] ein lange zeyt verkert
vnd vns abgötterey gelert,
dz wir haben die helgen geert,
vergassen Gott: wir waren hart entschlaffen.

2. Das geystlich recht han sy erdacht,
darmit vns gebandt vnd geacht,
darbey vil boͤser ee gemacht,
soliche weyb handt sy zů jn gezogen,
Vnd schetzten sich doch gott geleich,
wie jr einer het siebe[n] weych,
mit de[m] heyltum man vns bestreych,
hoͤrt, wie sie vns mit vil weych hand betroge[n].
Zů kirchwey han sie gnad vnd ablass gebe[n],
die glocken haben sie gedaufft darnebe[n],
saltz, weychbrun, wachs, würtz, palm vnd auch das feüre,
dz fleysch sy vns geweyhet hen,
fladen, eyer vn[nd] auch den kren,
geweychter weyrach schmecket schen,
darumb muͤsten mir sy täglichen steüren.

3. Darum[m] sten sy in volle[m] rot:
achtzehe[n] tausent gulde[n] hat
maniges kloster ein jar, verstot,
zů versere[n], wie kan es sein mit rechte?
Apt, richter vn[nd] pfennigmeister,
schaffer, kuche[n]meister, kelner,
hoffmeister vnd der zehent herr,
sibe[n]zig münch, köch, fichmeid vnd bauknechte
Nert der arm man mit hacken vnd [mit] dreschen,
so essen sie erlitz, grundel vn[nd] esche[n]
forhen öll, hecht, brotfisch, krebs bringt man balde,
manigerley wein vnd weysses brot,
der ein ieder ein pfeffin hat,
sunst wol sechshundert leydenn not,
die möcht man wol von solchem geld enthalde.

4. Noch eins felt mir auch in den sinn:
wenn ein pfaff hat ein kellerin,
ist sie jung vn[nd] tregt noch kindt,
dem bischoff mus ers jor drey gulden geben,
ist sy alt, gibt er ein guldein:
solch gelt nemen die bischoff ein,
wie ein wirt der helt weyber gmein:
nun hoͤrt fürbas, wies fuͤren ir leben:
Von solchem gelt halten sy seltzem bossen
die mörden vnd berawben auff den strossen,
kein bischoff důt den andren hilff verzeyhen,
wie graff Jochim im rieß geschach,
den man so jaͤmerlich erstach:
es ku[m]pt an tag jetzundt solch sach,
man[n] weiß, wers sind, die hilff detten dar leyhen.

5. Wo dan ein solche rott vm[mb] trapt,
haben ein frum[m]en man erschnapt,
so haust sy der vnd jener apt,
also fecht man vnd fiert vns hinn die frummen.
Klein ist mein brauch vnd der versta[n]t,
wo ich umb ker in allem land,
doch dunckt mich, die gelerten hand
die besten ortt bey stet, merckt, schloß ein genummen.
Des bapst monat het teutsch land schier geerbet,
den löbling Adel vnd die stet verderbet:
ist ein bischoff oder důmher gestorben,
es wer ein apt oder pfarrer,
gen rom [gerom] do můst man eylen ser,
vnd mancher mit grosser vneer
zů Rom hat einer hohen standt erworben.

6. Der etwan hat gedient zů Rom
hat ein pfrünt auff dem vn[nd] jem dom,
fil pfar dar bey, als ich vernom,
sunst vil ander miesen in kummer streben,[6]
Jch mein maniger herren kint,
wol geboren vn[nd] edel sint,
jr eltren hand gstifft die pfrünt,
billich solt man die [den] iren erbe[n] geben.
Was pfrünt vnd stifft vom lobling adel keme

6 *Weimarisches Jahrbuch* reads 'sterben'.

solte[n] jre gechlecht wider an[n]eme,
dar vo[n] enthalte[n] jre weyb vn[nd] kinde;
was dan het gehӧrt zů dem reich,
ir loblich stet, nempt auch zů eich,
christus würt euch helffe[n] geleich,
dz ir wendent der prelaten groß sinde.

7. Nun hӧrt weyter: eins mals ich laß,
das zů Bamberg ein Keyser saß,
Wirtzburg auch ein hertzogthum was:
der bistum sindt vil, loß ich durch kürtz bleyben.
Jr fürsten, herren eebenant,
setzt fürsten in der bischoff landt,
fragt nit, das sie zů Regenspurg hand
euch bandt vnd geecht, bits vnd thůt neüne schreibe[n]!
Jn die apten do setzet ritter here,
die befride[n] witwen, wayßen mit ere,
bey im vier prister, die gots wort verbringe[n],
vn[nd] treybt auß die feyste[n] mastschweyn,
die nit went eua[n]gelisch sein!
ich, jörg groff, bitt euch all gemein
in Christus lieb: jr herren, corgiert mein singen.

'Meyn hertz das mag nit růwe han', in H. von Zütphen (A.K.A. H. Müller), *Eyn schön neüv Lied | vom glauben vnnd Testament / auch | von der bereytung zů dem tysch Got- | tes / zů nutz den vnerbauwenen / von ey- | nem liebhaber Göttlicher warheit zů | Straßburg gesungen vnd gedicht. Jn | der Flam[m] weyß / oder in Hertzog Ern- | sten melody* (Strasbourg: Schürer Erben, 1524)

German text from *Wackernagel DKL*, vol. 3, no. 110.

1. Meyn hertz das mag nit růwe han,
darumb so will ich hebe[n] an
in gottes er zu dichte[n].
Heiliger geyst, verlich mir krafft,
vernu[n]fft, kunst, witz vnd meysterschafft
vnd thů mich vnderrichten.
Seyt das ein yeder Christen soll
den rechten glauben haben
der verhayssung Christi, merck wol,
der jn thut ewig laben,

durch welchen glauben er erkent,
das er wirt wirdig vnd geschickt
zu dem heyligen sacrament.

2. Nit durch beich, bett, ander uͤbung:
der mensch glaub nur der zusagu[n]g
vn[nd] de[m] wort fry fürware
Welches Cristus hat selb geret
'mein blůt vergossen wirt, verstet,
für eüwer sünd so gare'.
    Matthei liß an dem eylfften,
wie Christus spricht so lynde
'kumpt all zů mir, die arbeyten
vnnd schwer belade[n] synde,
ich will eüch selb ergetze[n] thon':
mensch, bedenck die köstlichen wort,
so du zu de[m] tisch gotts wilt gon.

3. Vnd setzst in Gott alleyn deyn trow,
augenblicklich kumpt dir der rouw,
der mißfall vmb die sünde,
Das du gedenckst 'hatt vns nun Gott
so lieb gehabt, dz er vns hot
seyn sůn miltigklich linde
    Geschickt her in diß jamertal,
der für vns ist gestorben
vnd vns erlößt von allem qual,
mit seym todt heyl erworben':
thůt das der me[n]sch mit rechter gir,
bkent sich mit dem offnen sünder
vnd spricht 'herr, bis genedig mir',

4. Vnnd glaubt in die barmhertzigkeit
Christi, sie ist jm vnuerseit,
soll er zu Christo fliehen:
Der ist vnser zůflucht allein,
der vns alweg wil gnedig sein,
barmhertzigklich verziehen,
    Wie auch Johan[n]es klaͤrlich melt:
'nempt war das lemeleyne,
das da hyn nimpt die sünd der welt!'
me thůt Johannes scheyne,
vnd spricht 'der sůn des menschen ist

kum[m]en zu sůchen den sünder
selig zů machen alle frist'.

5. Glaubt nu der me[n]sch gantz vestigklich
in die zůsagung Christi rich
vnd in sein grundloß guͤte,
Begert genad von got dem herrn,
der dich kan war erkentnüß lern,
anzünden deyn gemuͤte
Der geystlichen guͤter in dir,
dz du gest sicher frye
zum Sacrament froͤlich, glaub mir,
der recht glaub wont dir bye:
also mag der mensch alle tag
das hochwirdige sacrament
geystlich empfahen, wie ich sag.

6. Geschicht als durch de[n] glaube[n], merck,
vnd nit durch eüsserliche werck,
thůt die schrifft zeügnüß geben:
Der herr spricht 'wer in mich gelaubt
vnd meinem wort gentzlich vertraut,
der hat das ewig leben'.
Liß Johannis am sechsten klar,
theten die Juden fragen
den herren Jesum offenbar,
das er jn solte sagen,
welchs das hoͤchst, groͤst, best gůt werck wer:
der herr gab jnen antwort bald
vnd beschied sie, der war schöpffer:

7. Sprach 'wölt jr Got das groͤst werck thon,
so glaubt in de[m], welche[n] eüch schon
der vatter hat gesente':
Hoͤr, me[n]sch: sind das nit hohe wort,
das wir allein dem hoͤchsten hort
sond ewigklich on ente
Glauben, auff das wir mögen hye
mit den Apostlen geren,
als sye zů Gott auff ruͤffen ye
'thů vns den glauben meren!'
dann der glaub ein gab Gottes ist,

darumb lond vns alle bitten Gott,
das er erfüll, wo vns gebrist.

8. Jst nun der mensch also geschickt
vn[nd] durch den glaube[n] gantz erquickt,
sich ein sünder bekente,
Růͤfft an gottes barmhertzigkeyt,
die allen sündern ist bereyt,
gang er zum sacramente:
    Seyn gewissen wirt yetz gantz růͤwig
durch die köstlich artznye,
erlangt gnad, seligkeit ewig,
welch jm wont allzeyt bye,
förcht weder todt, teüffel noch hell:[7]
yetz hat dir Christus zů geseyt
vnd dich erlößt von aller quell.

9. Wan[n] Christus hat all ding geschlicht,
überwunden, wie Paulus spricht
zů den Corinthern klare
Am fünffzehende[n] vnderscheyt:
so nun der glaub, hoffnu[n]g, rew, leyt
gots gaben synd, nempt ware,
    So volgt drauß, das der mensch durch gott
vn[nd] nit durch sich selb iste
geschickt, noch durch beycht, bett, verstot
ander ůͤbung, das wiste,
dan[n] es spricht ye Christus der herr
 es mag nyemant kum[m]en zů mir,
es ziehe jn dann mein vatter’.

10. Das gschicht durch den glauben, verstant:
so soll ein yeder predicant
den rechten glauben leren:
Vil hand vns aber gwisen dar,
es můͤß der mensch all seyn sünd gar
nach einander erklere[n],
    Damit sie frauwen vnde man
hand schir verzweyflet gmachte
vn[nd] hand allwegen vff die ban
den Paulu[m] fürher brachte,

[7] See also ‘Jr brůͤder in Christo Jesu’, verse 5.

der spricht 'der mensch soll allweg sich
beweren vn[nd] auch machen frum[m],
vnd ess dan[n] von dem brott', merck mich:

11. Der war verstant der wort Pauli
sol recht vermercket werden hie,
wie er es do thet meynen,
Als er die secten straffet do,
eyner sprach 'ich bin[n] Apollo',
der ander thet bescheynen,
    Er wer Paulus, der drit Cephe,
der vierd ein Christ sich nente,
teylten sich in zwytracht, verste,
name[n] doch sacrame[n]te,
welch Paulus strafft der sünden meil,
sprach 'sie neme[n] das sacrament
vnwirdig, jn zů dem vrteil'.

12. Vn[nd] gab den völckern vnderricht,
das sie sich vndernander nicht
solten in zwytracht geben,
Einander nit verdam[m]en thůn:
yeder vrteyl sich selber nun
vnnd lůg, wie er thet lebe[n],
    So möcht ein yeder wirdigklich
auch wol von dem brot essen,
so ein yeder erkent selb sich,
thet jm seyn vrteyl messenn:
yetz hand ir den spruch in der sum[m],
nun land vns bitten Jhesu Christ,
    das vns seyn sterben zů trost kum[m],

13. Vnd das wir all an vnserm endt
das hochwirdige sacrament
in rechter reüw thůnd erben,
Das es werd vnser letste speyß
vns wir mit aller hͤochstem fleyß
nach Gottes hulden werben.
    Das bitt wir dich, herr Jhesu Christ,
wer das begert, sprech amen,
seyt du der eynig mitler bist:
wer anrͤufft deynen namen,

seyn truw, glaub, hoffnung in dich hat,
dem wiltu geben ewig frewd
    gar hoch in deyner mayestat.

'Jr bruͤder in Christo Jesu', in H. von Zütphen (A.K.A. H. Müller), *Jn disem lied wirstu verston | Wie allweg die geystlichen hon | Die krancken in der letsten not | Gefuͤret hand so ferr von Gott | Mit erschröcklichen worten vil | Aber yetz nůn zů disem zil | Finstu die rechte troͤstung gar | Jn disem dicht so nym du war | Wie man die krancken trösten sol, o Cristen mensch, betracht das wol, Das du die krancken troͤstest schon, und syngt man es ins Speten thon* (Strasbourg: Schürer Erben, 1524)

German text in *Wackernagel DKL*, vol. 3, no. 111.

1. JR bruͤder in Christo Jesu,
ich bitt, hoͤrt mir ein kleyn weyl zů,
so wil ich eüch hie syngen thů
vnd wil auch die aller best troͤstung geben
Den krancken in jr letsten not,
so sie umbfange[n] hal der todt,
kumpt der Teüfel mit list und fot
vnd helt dem krancke[n] für seyn sündtlichs lebe[n].
    Vnd spricht zů jm, er mög nit selig werden,
er hab vil sünd verbracht vff diser erden,
vnd gegen Gott mög er sich nym versienen,
das etwan der kranck mit der sproch
herauß felt vnd spricht 'solt ich doch
nur eyne[n] monat lebe[n] noch,
das hym[m]elrych dz wolt ich erst verdiene[n]'.

2. Hoͤr, lieber brůder, nym[m] bericht:
wan[n] dich der boͤß also anficht,
nit würd kleyn můttig, erschrick nicht,
verzag nit, denck nit 'solt ich lenger leben,
ich wolt die seligkeit erst nůn
verdienen vn[nd] mich fleyssen schůn,
vil gůts allhie vff erd zů thůn,
das mir Gott thet den hym[m]el darumb gäbn[n]':
    O lieber brůder, merck was ich dir sage:
warlich, lebstu biß an den jüngsten tage,
so möchtestu mit deym verdienst vnnd wercken
verdienen nüt, sag ich dir recht,

dann Christus auß den wercken, secht,
der grechtigkeit, so man verbrecht,
sunder auß lauter gnaden, soltu mercke[n],

3. Hat er vns selig gmacht, also
Paulus am dritten zů Tito
vnnd weyter zů Timotheo
am ersten capitel stet es so klare
Der ersten Epistel, ich melt:
Christus sey kum[m]en in die welt,
dz er die sünder zů jm zelt
vnd sie selig zů machen alle gare.
    Jetz hastu bricht vnnd kanst es freylich mercken,
das wir nit mit vnserm verdienst vnd wercken
selig werden, sunder auß lauter gnaden
gots, drumb setz deyn hoffnung alleyn
in Gott, den waren schöpffer deyn,
vnnd nit vff deyne werck, ich meyn,
dan[n] Christus mag dich aller sünd entladen.

4. Dauid am fünffte[n] Psalme[n] spricht
'o herr, all die jr zůuersicht
in dich setzen, werden nit gricht,
sie werden frolocken in ewigkeite'.
Vn[nd] Paulus zu den Roͤmern seyt
klaͤrlich am achte[n] vnderscheyt
'durch die hoffnung synd wir gereyt
selig worden nach göttlicher weyßheite'.
    Durch die hoffnung überwinstu den teüffel,
dz er dich bringe[n] mag in keyne[n] zweyffel
vn[nd] das du spricht 'ich waiß gentzlich fürware,
das ich die seligkeit nit mag
verdiene[n] biß an jüngsten tag,
drumb, fynd, laß ab mit deyner sag,
dan[n] Christus, meyn seligmacher, hats gare

5. Für mich vnd all sünder verdient
vnd mich gen seym vatter versient':
wer sich in hoffnung daruff lient,
der wirt in seyner gwissen růwig seyne,
Vnd gantz gefreyt vor aller quel,
darff weder todt, teüffel noch hell
förchten noch jr grausam geschell,

so du in Christu[m] setzst deyn trost alleyne.
    Es kum[m]en etwan zů den frum[m]en Christe[n]
Münch, Nonnen, Pfaffen, Beginen mit listen,
sprechen zům krancken 'biß gedultig gare,
gedenck an dyne sünd so schwer
vn[nd] auch an de[n] strengen richter,
an deyn vergange[n] lebe[n] her
vn[nd] an das streng vrteyl gottes fürware,

6. Denck an die hell vnd an den todt,
streyt ritterlich in diser nodt,
yetz magstu verdienen vmb Gott
in diser frist gar wol dz ewig leben'.
Wen[n] dan[n] der kranck die wort bedenckt,
wirt er kleynmůttig vnd bekrenckt,
etwan seyn hertz in zweyfel senckt:
O jr Münch, Nonnen, Pfaffen, merke[n] eben:
    Jr kündt gar wol die krancken troͤste[n] zware,
jr machents erst forchtsam vn[nd] zweyflig gare,
jr gwissen macht jr vnruͤwig vnnd schwere:
O jr Münch, Nonne[n], Pfaffen, secht:
wölt jr die krancke[n] troͤste[n] recht,
de[n]ckt, dz jr also zů jn sprecht
'lieber sůn, lieb tochter, lieb brůder, hoͤre:

7. Christus Jesus hat vor seym endt
gemacht vnnd vff gericht, verstent,
seyn leyb vnd blůt zům testament,
zů vergebung der sünd vnnd vns verschaffte,
Hat auch seyn testament durch das
sacrament seynes leybs fürbaß
vnd seynes blůts zů glycher maß
bestetiget mit brieff vn[nd] sigels kraffte,
    Vnd durch seyn todt hat er krefftiget gare
sein testament vn[nd] vns versichert zware
vn[nd] vns gantz gwiss gemacht der gnade[n] seyne,
vns zů gseyt ewig belonung:
drumb glaub vest seyner zůsagung,
denck an seyn lieb vnd groß barmung,
vn[nd] denck nit me an die groß schwer sünd deyne.

8. Denck nit an todt noch an die hell,
erschrick auch nit vor dem teüffel,
denck nit an das streng vrteyl schnell,
sunder glaub in Christum Jesum alleyne'.
So der kranck die troͤstliche wort
gantz der zůsagung Christi hort,
wirt er gantz willig ruͤwig fort
vn[nd] gedultig on alle forcht gemeyne,
    Vnd also durch den glauben überwindet
der kranck den teüffel, als man klaͤrlich fyndet
prima Petri am fünfften offenbare,
der spricht 'jr sollend eüweren
anfechtern dapffer widersten',
meynt er 'alleyn durch den glaube[n]
werd wir selig, auß lauter gnaden zware'.

9. Wie Paulus in der Epistel
sagt zů den Ephesiern schnell
an dem anderen capitel
'jr synd auß lauter gnaden selig worden',
Durch den glauben, muͤst jr verston,
vn[nd] nit durch eüch selbs mags zů gon:
thůt der mensch rechten glauben hon,
so helt er wol ein Christe[n]liche[n] orde[n].
    Jr bruͤder in Christo, das solt jr mercke[n],
vn[nd] die krancken im glauben also stercke[n],
vff das der teüffel keyn gewalt mög haben
an keyner seel an vnserm endt.
all, die wend Christen seyn erkent,
die bitten Gott, das er vns sent
seyn götlich gnad, die vns thů ewig laben.
AMEN.

'Der Babst rüfft Küng vnd Keyser an', in N. Manuel, *Eyn schön reygenlied im thon / Rusticus ambilem, Neüwlich geschmidet durch Meyster Hemerlin jm berg Ethna* (Strasbourg: Schürer Erben, 1524)

Based on translation from *MPGR*, pp. 251–2.

1. Der Babst rüfft Küng vnd Keyser an, das sye vertreyben einen man Dört niden in dem Sachßnerland, dann er wolt offnen all sein schand. O we, o we.	The Pope called the king and emperor, Asking them to banish a man Down in Saxony Because he would make public all his [the pope's] shame. Alas, alas.
2. Er sprach 'ich kan im nit erwern, all mein pracht will er umbkern, Vmb bley, wachß, bullen gibt er nicht noch vmb dz grausam Interdict. O we, o we.	He said, 'I cannot defend myself from him. He wants to undo all my splendour. He doesn't care about lead, wax, bulls, or even the terrifying Interdict. Alas, alas.
3. Ich denck, das meine kelberheüt bezwungen stett, land vnd leüt, Mein bullen waren hoch geacht: jetz hats der Münch zu nicht gemacht. Mordio, mordio.	'I think that my proclamations compelled cities, lands, and people. My bulls were held in high esteem, [But] now that monk makes nothing of them. Death, death.
4. Vil höher hielt man mein gebott dann die vns hatt verordnet Gott, Die gwüßne fieng ich seüberlich, erschrackt die hertzen hoffelich mit listen.	'People heeded my commandments much more Than those God had ordained to us. I neatly captured consciences, Genteelly terrified hearts With cunning.
5. All dise welt kußt meine füß, das schmackt mir so wol vnde süß, Ich was erhöcht weyt über Gott, yetz bin ich aller welt ein spott. O we, o we.	'All this world kissed my foot, Which tasted so good and sweet to me. I was elevated far above God, now I am a mockery throughout the world. Alas, alas.

6. Den aplaß hatt ich inn meinem gewalt,
mit silber, gold man mir inn bzalt,
Yetzund so fart es gar dahyn,
vil leüt sagdne 'ich schisß dir dreyn.'
O we, o we.

'I had the indulgence in my power,
With silver, gold, people bought it from me.
Now it has fallen so far down
That many people say, "I shit upon you".
Alas, alas.

7. Der pfründe[n] marckt thet mir auch wol,
macht mir allzeit die küche vol,
Annaten vnd das Pallium,[8]
ach Gott, yetz bin ich kom[m]en drumb.
O we, o we.

'The market for offices [i.e. benefices] also did me well,
always keeping my kitchen full.
Annates and the Pallium,
O God, now I have fallen down.
Alas, alas.

8. Vil hab ich glößt auß diser whar,
vnd mindert sich net vmb ein har,
Was ich außgab, thet mir nit we,
dann vil steckt mir in pectore
Occulte.[9]

'I have glossed much of the truth
and not minded it a bit.
What I said did not hurt me,
For many stabbed me in the chest
Secretly.

9. Semel pro semper thet auch wol,
Regresß vnd wie ichs nennen sol,
Adiutory vnd Resernat[10]
ligt yetzund alß zümal im kat.
O we, o we.

'"Like as always" did well [for me],
I shall name my recourse:
Adiutory and Resernat
now lie principally in slime.
Alas, alas.

10. Mein grempelmarckt hatt gar ein end,
das Gott den Römschen Keyer schend:
Ich wond, er wölt mir gholffen han,
seinthalb müßt ich gen betlen gan.
Mordtio, mordtio.

'My flea market has come to and end,
For God shames the Roman Emperor.
I think he wants to help me,
On his behalf I must go and beg.
Death, death.

11. Darumb soll nyemant zornig sein,
das ich yetzundt Frantzösisch bin:[11]
Den Teütschen bin ich gar ein spott,
sye kennen yetz den waren Gott.
O we, o we.

'Thus nobody should be angry
that I am now French.
I am a mockery to the Germans,
They now know the true God.
Alas, alas.

---

[8] *MPGR*, p. 251, n. 70: 'Half of locally collected religious taxes were paid to the papal treasury on the first of the year; these taxes were the "Annatengeld"'.

[9] *MPGR*, p. 252, n. 71: 'In other words, those before Luther who disagreed with the pope did so privately'.

[10] *MPGR*, p. 252, n. 72: 'Religious courts'.

[11] *MPGR*, p. 252, n. 74: 'This is probably a reference to Adrian VI, born in Utrecht and the only pope in the first half of the sixteenth century who was not a native Italian'.

12. Sye achte[n] nichts auff meine kron, was ich gebeüt, ist in ein trom, Darum[m]b ich sücht ein ander land, da noch vorborgen ist mein schand. O we, o we'.	They do not pay heed to my crown, what I pray is a fantasy to them. Thus I sought another land, where my shame is hidden. Alas, alas.
13. Der vns das liedlein hat gemacht, der hatt sich schier zü todt gelacht, Das Bäbstlich reicht vnd regiment im Teütschen land so gar ist gschend. Jo, jo.	He who wrote this little song, Nearly laughed himself to death. The papal empire and regiment is utterly shamed in German lands. Ho, ho.
14. Die Teütschen seind lang narren gsein, yetz hat sye gott durch seine[n] schein Erleücht, das sye den Antichrist erkennen, wüssen, wer er ist. Jo, jo.	The Germans have long been fools, Now through his appearance, God has enlightened them, so that they can recognise the Antichrist, and know who he is. Ho, ho.

'Lob sei dir, jesu Christe', in H. Vogtherr, *Ein neuwes Euangelisch | Lied in allem creütz | Jedem Christenn gantz tröstlich | Auß göttlicher schrifft ge- | zogen. Jm Jar da man | zalt tausent fünff hun- | dert vnd. xxvj. &c.* (Strasbourg: Kornmann, 1526)

German text from *Wackernagel DKL*, vol. 3, no. 559.

1. Lob sei dir, jesu Christe,
in dinem himels tron,
Der du der menschen liste
zu boden lassest gan,
    Vns cristen fuͤrst zů dinem wort,
welchs lang zit ist verschwygen,
jetz leichtz an allem ort.

2. Du byst das heyll Der armen,
on dich keyn hilff nit ist:
Laß dich, o gott, erbarmenn
denn grossenn mord vnd list
    Darmit wir waren gfangenn gar
von den falschenn Papistenn
mit Jrer kauffmans war.

3. Mitt vnns hanndt sye ghanndthieret,
wie dann Sannt Peter schreibt,
Mit valscher Lör verfyeret,
dyn wort vom erthrich gereyt:
    So dus nun wider bringst vff ban,
so heyßt manns ketzerye,
will vns den tod ann thon.

4. Sye wellen vnns erschreckenn
mit brieffen vnd mit dem schwert,
Gotts geyst seyn zyll versteckenn,
das seyn wortt nitt werd gelert:
    Vnd hieltens noch so hefftig drob,
so würt yedoch gott sygen,
sein feinden lygen ob.

5. Darumb, Jr frommen Cristenn,
habt trost vnnd fürcht euch nitt,
Secht, wye die Baalisten
Cristus zů hauffenn tritt,
    Wye eer vnns wont so krefftig bey,
das allenthalb seyn worte
yedoch wurdt Predigt frey.

6. So wir nun werden gefyeret
zů Cristo dem heyland,
Zůhand dye welt einrůrett,
damitt vnns volg schmach vnd schand,
    Vff das das crůtz nit lang beleyb auß
welchs erstlich můßs anfahenn
wol an dem gottes hauß.

7. Darumb hebt vff Euer stimme,
trett frőlich vff den plan,
Redt frey wie sichs gezime,
setzt leyb vnd leben daran,
    Dann Cristus můß bekennett seyn,
durch thod vnd grosse marter
gen wir jnns lebenn jnn.

8. Nitt sorgtt, was jr wöltt sagenn,
so man euch für grichtt fuͤrt:
Gotts geyst vff dysem tage
euch eüre zungen ruͤrt,
    Nyemann euch wyder sprechen kan,
gebt man ann euch dann gwalte,
so nemenns hertzlich an.

9. Wöll wir mit gott glorieren
vnd herschen jm hymmels tron,
Můß wir vns jm gleych zieren
mitt creütz vnd marterer kron:
    Der knecht nitt übern herren ist,
für vnns ist auch eyngangenn
der heyland Jhesu crist.

10. Wän gott der herr thůt lieben,
den geyselt er frie vnd spatt,
All sün thůt er betryeben
dye eer vff genummen hatt:
    Wir werdenn All durchs creütz probiert,
recht wie das gold im ofenn,
durch hoffnung durch hyn gfuͤrtt.

11. Also die ersten Cristenn
durchs plůt send gangen eyn:
Bitt gott, das er vnns riste,
jr mitgesellen seyn,
    Den leyb der marter geben dar:
sye thoͤdten nur den leybe,
dye seel würdtz nit gewar.

12. Last vns vil mer ann sehen
der leib vnnd seel thoͤdten kann,
Jnn vor der weldt veriehen
vnd sollt wir zů trimmer gan:
Er ists, der vns erhaltenn mag,
verdampt vnnd selig machet,
so kummet jhenner tag.

13. Dem wöll wir frey ergeben
all vnßer leyb vnd gůt,
Zům thod vnd auch zům leben

befelhenn jnn seynn hůtt.
  Der helff vnns můtig strytten mit,
onn Jnn ists ganntz verlorenn,
keyn syg beym menshen [*sic*] nit &c.

‘Es ist die warheyt pracht an tag’, in *Warer verstand / | von des herren | Nachtmal. | Vff die weyß zů singen / | Es ist das hayl vns | komen her. &c.* (Strasbourg: Prüss, 1527).

Song text taken from the original pamphlet (CH Zz – Res 1041). The song text also appears in *Wackernagel DKL*, vol. 3, no. 521; and Riederer, *Nachrichten zur Kirchen-Gelehrten- und Buͤcher-Geschichte*, vol. 1, pp. 462–4. The latter also gives some history of the text.

1. Es ist die warheyt pracht an tag /
vons herren Nachtmal schone /
Den Endchrist nichtz mer hellfen mag /
sein dunckel vnd sein wone /
Damit er hatt die welt verplent /
vnd valsch gelert vom Sacrament /
das leyblich fleisch werd gessenn.

The truth about the Lord’s Supper
Has already been revealed.
The Antichrist might no more help
his darkness and his delight,
So that he has blinded the world,
And falsely taught of the Sacrament
that bodily flesh will be eaten.

2. Was got in seim wort redden thuͤt /
ist alles geyst vnnd leben.
Also ist es auch nütz vnnd gůt /
sunst ist es vnns vergeben /
Der herr ist der das lebenn bringt /
im glauben man nach d[er] speis ringt /
die vnser seel ergetzet.

All that God’s Word says
is spirit and life.
So it is also useful and good
as it is to forgive us,
The Lord is he who brings life,
In faith one strives for flesh
On which our soul feasts.

3. Es was ein falscher won da bey /
dz wir hie můsten glauben.
Dz Christus so groß wie er sey /
laß sich der statt berauben /
Die er bey Gott seim vatter hat /
zur grechte[n] biß die welt vergad /
als die Apostel leren.

What an erroneous custom thereby
that we must here believe.
That Christ, as great as he may be,
lets himself be deprived of the position
That he has by God his Father,
On his right [hand side] until the world perishes,
as the Apostles teach.

4. Es bochet Luther hoch da her [12] /
mit eim einzige[n] worte.
Als ob sunst nichtz geschriben wer /
jn manchem end vnd orte /
Dan[n] als er sagt dz ist mein leib /
merck aber was er nacher schreib /
der für euch würt zerbrochen.[13]

Almighty Luther insists
on a single word.
As if nothing else had ever been written
in many an end and place
Then as he says, ‘This is my body’
but note that afterwards it is written
that ‘for you it will be broken’.

5. Das brechen ziehens vff das brot /
mag nit also bestone.
Dann brott für vns kein rodes not /
gelitten am kreytz frone /
Sonder Christus mit seinem leib /
das menschlich gschlecht vorm teyfel bleyb /
ist für vns gar zerbroche[n].

The ‘breaking’ refers to the bread,
but this cannot be true.
The bread did not
suffer on the holy cross for us,
But Christ, with his body
that keeps the human race from the Devil,
is actually ‘broken’ for us.

6. Deßhalb so man die erstenn wort /
gantz leiblich wil annemen.
So můß man das nachuolgend ort /
auch dermassen bekennen /
So er nun spricht das ist mein leib /
vnd leiblich den verstand da treibt /
müß er leiblich zerbrechen.

For this, if one wants to accept
the first word as completely real,
Then one must also acknowledge
the following:
If he [Luther] now says ‘This is my body’
and the corporal understanding that prevails
is that he [Jesus] must be corporally broken.

7. So volgt dz wir on vnderlaß /
den herren muͤsten toͤdten.
Darum hat es ein a[n]der maß /
die vns die ist vonnoͤtten /
Das wir in gmein breche[n] dz brot /
vnd dencken ann des herren todt /
der am kreytz ist zerbrochen /

It follows that we would have to
kill the Lord unceasingly.
Therefore it has another manner
which is necessary of us:
That we break the bread in the assembly,
and remember the death of the Lord,
who was broken on the cross.

8. Ein gedechtnüß ist nit selber das /
daran man sol gedencken.
Darum so ist es sunst etwas /
dahin wir muͤssen lencken /

A memory is not the actual thing
about which one should think.
Therefore we must steer
towards something else

12 Riederer’s version reads ‘Es bochend etlich hoch daher’.
13 Quoting the liturgy.

Wann zeychen sein / vnd das bezeicht /	When signs to be, and that which they signify
zů vnmüglichen dingen reicht [14] /	reach impossible things
welchs nimmen würt geschehen.[15]	which would never happen.
9. Gott handelt nůr nach seine[n] wort /	God acts only according to his word
vnd lassets darbey bleyben.	and thereby lets it be sufficient.
Wan er anzeigt an manchem ort /	When he indicates a certain place
last sich nit weytter treyben /	he can't be pushed anywhere
Aber die boͤß vneelich gburt /	But the evil illegitimate birth
die stets wider sein christu[m] můrt /	that stands against his Christ-grumbles (?)
zeychen von himel gerett.[16]	saves signs from Heaven.
10. Allein merck hie du rechter Christ /	Take note only, you true Christian,
das du der schrifft solt glaube[n].	that you should believe Scripture.
Wan sy ir selbs nit wider ist /	Where it [Scripture] does not contradict itself
als es pracht würt für augen /	as it is brought before your eyes,
Auß alt vnd neuwem testament /	Old and New Testaments
würt die warheit gentzlich erkendt /	would wholly recognise the truth
wie es hie zu sey gange[n].[17]	as it is shown here.
11. Ein phaße ward vo[n] got zů gricht /	A Passover from God has happened
vnnd moße hart befolhen.	and Moses commanded it strongly.
Das alles hat er gůtten bricht /	All of that, according to reports
von gott jm nit verhole[n] /	God has not been angry at him.
Das es bedeut den vberschrit /	That it signifies the transformation,
ein lemblin ward getoͤdt darmit /	a lamb was killed so that
das man es solt gedencken.	one should think of it.
12. Vnd wann kinder fragen hernach /	And when children ask hereafter
so sie das lemblin assen.	As they eat the lamb
So antwurten die Juden gach /	The Jews answer quickly
bald in sollicher massen /	soon in this way,
Diß ist alhie der vberschrit /	This is indeed the transformation
das ir verstandenn auch damit /	so you understand that
das vnß gott hat erloͤßet.	God has saved us.

[14] Riederer's version reads 'Hie zu ain gaystlichen ding raicht'.

[15] That is to say, signs are one thing, but if they signify impossible things then they must be steered away from.

[16] The meaning in the second half of this verse is unclear.

[17] That is, the truth has been suppressed in our times, but it is clear in the Old and New Testaments.

13. Nun was lam nitt der vberschrit /
sonder ein dechtnüs zeyche[n].
Also Christus hie redet mit /
wie er sich nůn wol reychen /
Beim brot sich selbs bedeuttet hat /
do er das phaße jnen bot /
vn[nd] sprach das ist mein leibe.

Now the lamb was not the transformation
but a sign of remembrance.
So Christ here also speaks
as he now gives
The bread he meant himself
that he offered to you at the Passover
and says 'this is my body'.

14. Lucas vnns dißes zeugknüs gibt /
das Christus ist ein phaße.
Am zwentzig zweyten caput schreibt /
als ich es etwan laße /
wie der her sagt mit grosser gird /
ich ietz dar zů beweget würd /
Phaße mit euch zu essen.

Luke gives us this testimony
that Christ is a Passover.
In the twenty-second chapter is written
As I leave it:
How the Lord says with great anxiety
'I am now moved to
eat "Passover" [the Last Supper] with you'.

15. Daruff er schnell ergreifft dz brot /
danckt seines vatters guͤtte.
Bricht es alhei in dißer thatt /
daraus wol zů vermůte[n] /
Als der text kurtz hernach vermag /
Darum sein kein beschwerdnüs trag /[18]
es ist ein dechtnüß zeychen.

Then he quickly takes the bread,
thanks his Father's mercy.
Breaks it in this action,
hence well to presume,
(As the text shortly hereafter states
therefore not to be carrying any trouble)
it is a sign of remembrance.

16. Deßhalb jm eer beschehe[n] soll /
vmb den so es bedeute.
Darumbs nieman verachten woll /
dar zů auch nit vermeyde /
Aber du solts anbettern nitt /
dan abgoͤttrey die lieff darmit /
so es ist ein geschoͤpffte.

Therefore honour should be bestowed upon him
about whom this was all about.
Therefore no one wants to despise
Nor avoid it
But you should not worship
idolatry that came with it:
it is a creation.

17. Der schoͤpffer ist ein eyferer /
las keiner geschoͤpfft die ere.
Jn exodo sagts got der here /
da magstu es wol leren /

The creator is keen
that honour not be given to just any creation.
In Exodus, God says of the Lord
that you may teach it well,

[18] The meaning here is unclear.

Darum der Bapst vn[nd] Luther klůg /
der sachen haben gantz kein fůg /
wie wol sie eins seind worden.

Gott allein die Eere.[19]

Therefore the pope and Luther cleverly,
although they are not allied,
have become united.

To God alone the honour.

[19] This line does not appear in Riederer's *Nachrichten*, but is replaced with the following verse: '(18) So offt mans Herren brot nun yßt / Vnnd seinen kelch will trincken / Wie man klerlich in Paulo ließt / Sol man seins tod gedenken / Mit glauben preysen Got den Herrn / Dem nächsten dienen auch so gern / Dann werd wir weig leben'. This verse also appears in *Wackernagel DKL*, vol. 3, no. 521, after which the line 'Gott allein die Eere' is printed in isolation.

APPENDIX G

Excerpt from Wolfgang Capito's *Von drey Straßburger Pfaffen* (Strasbourg: Köpfel, 1525)

The German text is taken from the website of the Electronic Capito Project[1] and from Rummel and Kooistra, eds, *Reformation Sources*, pp. 207–39. Translated by Erika Rummel with the assistance of Milton Kooistra, in *CorrCapito*, vol. 2, pp. 124–53. The excerpt shown here can be found on pp. 124–5, 132, 141–5, 152.

Dem frummen christlichen leser, was würden, wesens oder stands der sey, empieten wir Wolffgang Capito Probst, Martin von Baden Vicedecan, Capitel und gemeyne personen Sanct Thomas Stifft zů Straßburg, wie wir in einer protestation, uff den xxv. tag Februa. nechst verschinen, mit namen underschriben sein, unser underthenig willige dienst und früntlichen grůß, mit geflyßner bitt, uff ein hoche schmachschrifft Sixt Hermanns, Diebolt Baltners, unnd Jacob Schulteissen, alle wylandt Summissarien gemelts unsers Stiffs, so sye inn verwantwortungs weyß, uff unser rechtmessig protestation, under irem title und namen haben lassen außgeen, unser verantworten mitt freyem gemüt unnd fleyssigen oren zů hören …

I, Wolfgang Capito, the provost, and Martin von Baden, vice-dean, the chapter and community of St Thomas, collegiate church in Strasbourg, who appeared to make a statement on 25 February and signed their names, offer you, pious Christian reader, whatever your title, position, or estate, our willing and devoted service and friendly greeting. We respectfully request that you listen with an open mind and attentive ears to our reply to a most abusive tract issued in the name and title of Sixt Hermann, Diebold Balthener, and Jakob Schultheiss, all summissaries of our collegiate church at the time, in response to our lawful protest …

Nun ist es war, das uff montag nechst nach dem sontag Letare, den vii tag des mertzen, in nechstvergangnem

The truth is that on Monday after Letare, on 7 March of the past year 1524, the greater part of the goods

xxiiii. jar, der zyt der besser teil unserer stifft güter von Straßburg abgefürt sind, vor und ehe sich etwas forcht einer uffrůr erreget hat. Dann wäs sy anzeigen ist lang hinach beschehen, so vil anders in den selbigen dingen warhafftig beschehen ist. Dann der Probst hat noch nit zům jungen S. Peter angefangen zů predigen, da die güter schon lengst hinweg waren. So hat sich lang hinach zügetragen, das uff ein sontag als der gantz Chor zům jungen sant Peter, under des herren nachtmal, angefangen primzyt zesingen, das ein schein hatte, als ob es dem volck zůwider beschehe. Sind etlich uß dem volck in den chor gangen, die die priester haben schwigen heissen, uff das sy eins teils selb hinauß gegangen. Die übrigen aber sind stillschweigend sitzen pliben, biß die pfarlichen ämpter auß waren. Den hat niemant kein leid begert zethůn, und ist iren keiner ungestümer wyse auß dem Chor ye getriben worden. Man hat sy heissen schwigen, und nicht auß dem chor gan. Die bildnussen, so in einer ererbietung und gotloßen anbettung waren, sind erst nach abweichung der Thůmherren, durch ein öberkeit zů Straßburg, züchtiglich und ordernlich abgethan, und nicht, alß sy schreiben, ungebürlich von der gemein zerrissen worden. Die begräbnuß zů sanct Aurelien ist von der gantzen kirchen daselbst, uß christlicher bewegung hyn gethan,[2] und der wichwasser stein in der kirchen zů S. Thoman, durch etliche ungezogne umbgestossen worden, die ein Ersamer Ratt ernstlich gestrafft

of our collegiate church were moved from Strasbourg, before there was any fear of an uprising. But what they indicate there [i.e. the uprising] happened much later, although much of it happened in truth quite differently. The goods were gone before the provost started to preach in Young St Peter [in April 1524]. It happened much later, on a Sunday, when the choir at St Peter began to sing primes [*sic*] during the Lord's Supper, which appeared to go against the people's inclination. Several of the congregation went into the choir and told the priests to be silent, whereupon a part of them left. The others, however, remained in their seats, keeping silent until the service had ended. No one desired to harm them, nor were any of them driven out of the choir by force. They were told to be silent, not to leave the choir. The images, which were the object of ungodly adoration and attention, were removed only after the canons left. This was done in an orderly fashion on the direction of the government of Strasbourg. The images were not, as they write, torn down in a lawless fashion by the common people. The grave at St Aurelia was removed by the whole church, out of Christian feeling. The holy water stoop in the church of St Thomas was overturned by some ruffians, who were severely punished by the honourable council, but all that happened after the canons and the other members of the collegiate church had already left …

hat, alles nach dem sy die chorhern und ander stiffts verwandten schon abgetretten waren …

… das wir in allen pfarren, das heylig Evangelium und der Aposteller, und nit in den zweyen kirchen allein, unverdunckelt, und on menschen felschung gepredigt haben, und noch predigen, uff nach geenden innhalt: nemlich das wir von natur alle sünder seint, durch Christum Jesum erlöst …

We preached the holy gospel and the words of the apostles clearly and without human falsification in all the parishes, not only in those two [Young St Peter and St Thomas], and we are still preaching as follows: that we are all by nature sinners saved through Christ Jesus …

Dem volget die liebe gegen Gott und dem menschen, die da statt im vleiß yederman auch den feinden gůts zethun und von yederman auch von den besten fründen, args mit langmůt und gedult anzůnemen, welchem anhangt hertzlich gehorsame, als in augen Gottes gegen zytlicher öberkeyt, und ein strenge zucht gegen sich selbs …

Secondly, [we preach] the love of God and men, which obliges everyone to do good to all, enemies or best friends, and to suffer evil patiently and with equanimity; thirdly, there is obedience from the heart, both in the eyes of God and toward secular authority, and strict self-control …

Wir müssen frey mit Paulo veriehen, das welcher durchs gesetz, das ist, durch werck die er einer usserlichen satzung nach thůn mag, rechtvertig werden wil, das er der gnaden, die da ist in Christo Jesu, gefelet hab. Das thůt den buchdienern[3] zorn, und bringt sy uff, das wort zů lesteren, unnd ire feigen werck zůriemen, die jenen ein grösser genieß bißher gewesen sind. Sollichs dann uns zwinget, die warheit freyer weder sunst zů bezeügen, unnd allen iren falsch zů entdecken, mit aller stille und senfftmůtigkeit, doch on einigs underlassen. Also haben wir ires singen und lesen halb auß der geschrifft fürbracht, das es nitt christlich sey, dann es nitt ein

We must assert with Paul that anyone who wants to be justified through works based on external commandments, misses out on the grace that is in Christ Jesus. Paul's testimony once and for all condemns all merit, works, intercession of saints, and all human effort. That angers the servants of the book and causes them to slander the Word and to glory in their doomed works, which have been a great source of pride to them so far. This forces us to attest to the Truth more freely than we would otherwise, to reveal their wrong beliefs to all quietly and meekly, without however suppressing certain things. Thus, we showed them on the basis of scripture that their singing

anbettung und ehrerbietung gegen Gott ist. Sytemal der christen übung innerlich gegen gott ist, dann die waren anbetter betten an den vatter im geyst und in der warheyt. 'Gott ist ein geyst, die in anbetten, die müssen in im geyst und in der warheit anbetten.' Jo. 4. Was thůt das eüsserlich gepreng dazů? Bey den alten, ist durch eüsserliche übung der opffer, unnd tempel geberden, die zůkünfftig erlösung bedeüttet. Welche die gottseligen nitt umb des wercks willen, sonder umb des wort gottes willen getriben haben. Und so bald sy auß solchen kirchen gepreüchen die schon got zůr selbigen zeyt geheyssen het, ein eygen werck gemacht haben, ist es gott ein grewel gewesen. Ja bey dem propheten Hieremia am vii. sagt der herr, das er ire brandopffer, unnd anders nit gebotten hab, sonder das sye des herren stymm hören solten. So hoch begerte Gott, das man in seinen diensten nůr sein wortt ansehe, das im auch mißfellet, wa etwas das er schon zů jeder zeyt gebotten, auß unwarnemung seynes worts, nach aller uffsetzung, auß gewonheyt oder sunst, gethon würt, wie die Juden ire opffer offt on glauben außriechten. Wie mag nůn unnsers gepffess singen unnd pfeyffen, eyn gottsdienst, unnd Gott gefellig werck sein, so sye kein bůchstaben im wort gottes darvon yendert haben?

and reading was not Christian, for it is not praying or honouring God. The Christian practice is an internal one. Those who pray truly to the Father pray in the spirit and in truth. *God is spirit; those who pray to him must pray in spirit and in truth* (John 4 [24]). What can external pomp add to that? In ancient times, the external practices of offering sacrifice and serving in the temple alluded to our future delivery. These things were done by the faithful, not for the sake of works, but for the sake of God's Word. And if they regarded those ceremonies, which God demanded in those times, as works of their own, it was loathsome to God. Indeed, in Jeremiah 7 [22–23] the Lord says that he did not command them to make burnt offering or other sacrifices, but to listen to the Lord's voice. This is how urgently God desired that in his service one should show regard only for his Word. He took no pleasure in the statutory, habitual performance of his long-standing commands if it was done without regard for his Word; these were like the sacrifices offered by the Jews without faith. How, then, can our so-called clergy's singing and piping be a service to God and a work pleasing to him, when they never speak even one letter of the Word of God?

Ja sagen sy, 'Wir geprauchent uns der wortt der geschrifft". Antwurt, "Die zauberynn unnd warsägerin geprauchent sich auch heyliger wort, aber das unrecht ist so vil dester

They say: 'We are using the words of scripture.' I reply: 'The sorcerers and fortune-tellers likewise use holy words, but their wickedness is all the greater because they have abused

grösser, das die heyligen wort von in mißbraucht werden.' Sy müssen gestan das ir singen und lesen nitt sey ein anbettung des vatters, die innerlich im geist und in der warheit, nach dem willen gottes, und nitt nach fürsatz blůts und fleyschs allein beschehen soll. Ro. 8. Es ist aber ir singen vileycht dienstlich denn menschen, denn sye nemmen ir rychlich bezalung darumm wie ein kauffman umb sein war und kauffmans gütter. Dises ist gröber wider das wort dann das von nöten sein möcht weyters zůverlegen, syternal gottseligkeit nit sein mag umb genieß willen. 1. Timo. 6. Die so infurten die beschneydung, allein das sye nit mitt dem creütz Christi vervolget wurden, sindt so hart vonn Apostel gestrafft zun Gal. am 6., dann die gnad Christi ward durch sye verdunckelt, und dise nuwe pharíseer, habent umb ir heydische beschneydung (dann ir übungen von heyden kommen) bißher auch so hoche belonung genommen, das jetzt Fürsten und Herren, land und leüt umb irs gesängs willen, in ir dienstbarkeit komen, und inen verpflicht worden sindt. O des grüwels! Die herrlickeit Gottes hat uns erlößt durch Christum, auß lautern gnaden, der uns alle ding verdient hatt, und diß loß gesindlin gedarff underston andern leüten zů inen verdienen. Das heyßt die ehr gottes mit irem kot und unflat beschmeyssen! Solten wir aber das, den die Ehr gottes anligen soll nit beweynen, solten wir nit dawider cetermordio růffen, die Gott zů vertedingen sin warheit gesandt hat?

the holy words.' They must admit that their singing and reading is not internal worship of the Father in the spirit and in truth, according to the will of God, and not according to flesh and blood (Rom. 8 [1–21]). Their singing may serve human beings, for they accept generous payment for it, like a merchant for his goods and merchandise. This is too crass an abuse of the Word to need further proof, for godliness must not serve profit (1 Tim. 6 [3–10]). Those who introduced circumcision to avoid persecution with the cross of Christ were severely punished by the apostles (Gal. 6 [11–16]), for the grace of Christ was obscured by them, and these new Pharisees have accepted such generous pay so far for their pagan circumcision (for their practices are derived from heathens), that even princes and lords, countries and people enter their service for the sake of their songs, and become bound to them. Oh horror! God in his glory out of sheer mercy delivered us through Christ, who merited all things for us, and this undisciplined rabble has the nerve to oblige other people to serve them. That amounts to casting filth and dirt on God's honour! How can we not bemoan that, when the honour of God must be our concern? How can we not fight against it, crying murder [*cetermordio*]? No, we shall not leave the Word in captivity! We have strength in God, to the salvation of all the faithful. And even if they accept no money – which is not the case, for larger the crown present in the choir, the larger the number of

Nein, wir werden das wort nit lassen gefangen sein! Es ist uns die krafft gottes, zum heyl allen gleübigen. Und ob sey schon kein gelt darumb nemen, das da nit ist, dann je grösser presentz, je mer prelaten im chor stön, so kan doch der teütschen gemein das latinisch geseng nichts besserlich sein, das sye nit verstön mag, wie auch ein welscher[4] redner vor teütschen richtern on frucht und fürstand der sach handelt. Nun sollen je alle ding zůr uffbawung in christlicher gemein bescheen. 1. Cor. 14.

prelates – of what use is their Latin singing to the German congregation? For they cannot understand it, just as an Italian would make no progress and have no effect presenting his case to a German judge. But everything is supposed to be done to edify the Christian congregation (1 Cor. 14 [1–25]).

Also das Paulus nit will, das jemandts mit zungen rede, es sey dann das ers außlege, welches dannocht ein gab gottes was, zum zeychen der ungleübigen. Wie kan dann das gelert zůngen reden, in so ungeschickter wyse, unnd das umbs gelts willen beschicht, gůt sein, da keyn außleger nit ist? Und in welchem die zůngen reder selbs nit gebessert werden, und nit mit gott reden, als jhene zů der zeytt Pauli thäten, dann ir hertz ist ferr von gott? Das sye aber in selbs für ein besserlich übung ir gesäng halten und fürgeben ist auch nit, sye nemen sunst unbillichen das gelt darumb. So verstön sye auch nit, was sye singen, in schuld registern, in pfrunden kremerey. Und so etlich gelert sein wöllen, in rechten der welt, habent sye allein verstandt, des geysts verstandt ist inen verborgen, das doch nit zůverwunderen, sytemal auch die gelerten genant der heyligen geschrifft, nichts wenigers dann geschrifft verstanden haben, und noch versten. Der spruch Esaie hatt müssen erfüllet sein:

Indeed, Paul does not want anyone to speak in tongues unless as a sign to those without faith and for the sake of interpretation (and even then it is a gift of God). How, then, can it be good to speak in the tongue of scholars, in this awkward manner, and for pay, when there is no interpreter? And when those who speak in tongues are not improved themselves and do not communicate with God, as did those in the time of Paul, is not their heart far removed from God? Nor is it the case that they believe their singing improves them, for in that case it would be improper to take money for it. In their debt calculations and their trading in benefices, they do not understand what they are singing. Some of them may be learned in the law of the world; that is the only thing they understand. The meaning of the Spirit is hidden from them, which is not surprising, since those who are called scholars of scripture never understood and still do not understand Holy Writ – far from it! What Isaiah said had to be

'Die weyßheit der weysen will ich verderben und mit starrblindtheit will ich sy schlagen, dieweyl sye mich vergebenlich, durch menschen gebott ehrent, spricht der herr.' Ja ob sye schon mitt erkandtniß gottes und erfarung der genaden begabet weren, ist in dennocht onmüglich joch den worten nachzůtrachten. Ein geübter mensch im geyst, hette ein monat zeschaffen, biß er im grund beschawet, was allein die psalmen und geschrifft vermöchten, die sye in eim tag herauß ploddern, wider das gebot des herren: 'Wann ir betten,' spricht der herr, 'so schwetzen nitt vil,' Matth. 6. Und Paulus begert fünff wortt zů reden in seynem synn, in der gemein, uff das er sye underwyse, vill lieber dann sunst zehen tausent wort mit zungen, unnd heyßt dennocht Paulus mit zungen reden, da es von redenden verstanden würt, im selbs zur besserung dienet, und da er mitt gott redt. Die tempel senger mögent ir geplärr selbs nitt verstön, also ist es ein eylen, und ungestüm getemmer.

fulfilled: *I shall destroy the wisdom of the wise and strike them with blindness, for they honour me in vain with the decrees of men, says the Lord* [Isaiah 29:14]. Even if they were gifted with knowledge of God and had experienced his grace, they nevertheless would be unable to wrestle truly with the Word. It would take a month for a person experienced in spiritual exegesis to study in depth the meaning of the psalms and scriptural passages they burble out in a day. Their practice is contrary to the Lord's commandment: *When you pray*, says the Lord, *do not prattle much* (Matt. 6 [5]). And Paul wishes to speak five words in the spirit to instruct the community rather than ten thousand words in tongues. Paul also commands us to speak in tongues for the purposes of being understood by people who use that language, for one's own improvement, and speaking with God [1 Cor. 14: 18–19]. The singers in church likely do not understand what they are braying. Thus, it is a dull and confounded noise.

Darumb haben wir nit anders kunnen reden, dann das ir unförmig geseng nit sey vom geyst gottes, das dem bevelch des geysts so hoch entgegen ist. Sonder haben die warheit gestanden, sytemal das der so nit mit Christo ist, der ist widder in, müß ir geseng widerchristisch sein, unnd so ferr sye es für ein gůt werck und verdienstlich achten, ein schwere gotslesterung unnd verschmehung der gnaden, durch die unns mitt Christo frey alle ding geschenckt

Therefore we must conclude that their undisciplined singing is not inspired by God and quite contrary to the command of the Spirit. We have spoken the truth, especially since he who is not with Christ is against him [Matt. 12: 30; Luke 11: 23], and their singing is therefore unchristian and, in so far as they regard it as a good work and to their merit, a grave blasphemy and in contempt of grace. For grace was given us together with all things freely through Christ (Rom.

sein, Roma. 8. Sye sind ja fynd des creützs Christi, das sy mit der that verleügnen. Irend, die verderbniß wirt in nit felen, dann der bauch ist in ein got. Phil. 3. Welchem sye ir kirchen gesang zů nutz treyben, das sye sunst fast gern underlassen, wa sy ir zynß und güldt on singen haben möchten, das bewert ir gemein sprichtwort: 'Ich hab mein zynß und güldt frey,' sagent sye, 'ich darff nit ein choresel sein.' Man sicht in allem irem thun, ob sy der pfennig oder gottes ehr in den chor treybe, dann sy sindt alle mal vill geflissener bey dem traurigen Requiem und dem todten gesang, weder by dem frölichen Gaudeamus. Ob schon nach als woll die orgelpfeyffen lautten, also macht die presentz und der heylig pfennig das unholdtselig todtengesang anmütig dissen bauch dienern, dero andacht verloschen ist, wa der andächtig pfennig abnimpt. Wie ire recht selbs gestön, das ir geystlichen ding, on die zytlichen nit bleyben mögen. Ir hertz und synn tracht nach der presentz, wenn die erlangt ist, so lauffent sye zur kirchen hienauß, werffen den chorrock hinder die thür und mit der magt hinder den offen. Heißt das nit irrdisch gesynnet sein, und umbs bauchfůter dienen? Dazů alle pfaffen gesang geordnet ist, das bedenck der christliche leser …

… wie ein anders verkünden alle so durch menschen lere gotsdienst anrichten, die uff underscheid der speyß, uffhaltung der tag, und spaltung der christlichen gemein trybent, die das lateinisch

8 [1–21]). These people are, in fact, enemies of the cross of Christ, which they deny in their deeds. They will not fail to meet ruin, for their belly is their God (Phil. 3 [19]). The common proverb shows for whose benefit they sing their songs in church: 'I have my tithe and money for doing nothing. I don't want to be a choir ass'. They would prefer not to sing if they could have their tithe and money without doing so. Their actions tell whether they are singing in the choir for their money or for the honour of God, for they are much more eager to hear sad requiems and songs for the dead than the joyful Gaudeamus [sung at Christmas (cf. Matt. 26: 39–41)]. For although the organ pipes sound good in both cases, the fee and the holy penny make the sad song for the dead a happy occasion for the servant of the belly, whose devotion evaporates when the holy penny declines. Their regulations declare in themselves that spiritual matters cannot be without temporal things. Their heart and mind are bent on fees, and once they obtain them, they hurry out of the church, toss their choir robe behind the door and join the maid behind the stove. Is that not showing a secular mind? They serve to feed their bellies. Let the Christian reader consider that every song of the clergy is aimed at that …

For those who set up a divine service on the basis of human teaching, who insist on the difference between foods, on the keeping of special days, on splitting up the Christian community, those who sing in

kirchengesang bey den teutschen, Vigilien, meßlesen unnd anders, fur verdiennstliche werck fürgeben, uff anrüffung der heylgen fürbit, und anbetung der bilder, das arm völckin weysent – die im glauben mer ansehent, was Bäpstliche Bullen frevelich gebietendt, dann was die Biblischen bücher zů glauben frundtlich fürgeben.

church, using Latin before Germans, who give out that vigils, masses, and other such things are meritorious works, and direct the poor people to call upon the intercession of the saints and to adore the images, those people who seek faith always in the blasphemous commands of the papal bills rather than believing in the kind precepts of the biblical books, they are the ones preaching a different gospel.

Notes

1. http://cf.itergateway.org/capito/Letter246a.pdf (accessed 10 August 2011). N.B. The Electronic Capito Project gives the title *Der Stifft von sanct Thoman…* (Strasbourg: Köpfel, 1525), which is in fact an earlier tract by Capito, distinct from *Von drey Strassburger Pfaffen*.

2. Capito is referring to an occasion when members of the gardeners' guild broke into the tomb of St Aurelia, finding nothing but bones. See also *Fragments des anciennes chroniques d'Alsace*, I (1887), no. 214; and Reuss, 'Strassburg im sechszehnten Jahrhundert, 1500–1591: Auszug aus der Imlin'schen Familienchronik', *Alsatia*, 10 (1873–74), p. 401.

3. A *Buchdiener* observes the letter rather than the spirit.

4. The translation in *CorrCapito* reads 'Welshman' at this point. The term *welsch* is in fact a colloquial term for a speaker of Romance languages, primarily used to describe Italians. See H. Puff, *Sodomy in Reformation Germany and Switzerland, 1400–1600* (Chicago and London: University of Chicago Press, 2003), p. 81.

APPENDIX H

Martin Bucer's Preface to the *Gesangbuch* (Strasbourg: Köpfel and Messerschmidt, 1541)

The German text is taken from the *Gesangbuch*, fols. A3^{r}–A3^{v} (and is also available in *BDS*, 7, pp. 577–82). The English text is taken from *Garside*, pp. 29–31.

Martinus Bucer / diener des Worts der Kirchen zů Strasburg / wůnschet allen Christgleubigen / Gnad vnd Frid von Got dem Vatter / vnd vnserem Herren Jesu Christo.

Es ist allen / so die Heilige Bibel lesen / kundtlich / das der gotseligen vnd wargleubigen brauch / von anfang gewesen ist / Gottes lob mit singen zů preisen / vnd inn dem selbigen auszůlassen jre grosse lust / wunne / vnd freude / mit welchen jre hertzen / inn / vnd von Got / gantz uͤberschuͤttet / vnd also erfuͤllet waren / das sie solche lust / wun[n]e vnd freude / bei jnen selb nicht mehr halten kundten; Dadurch dann auch jre zůhoͤrer / zů erkantnis vnd danckbarkeit Gottes / vnd seiner guͤte angereitzet / erinnert / vnd lustig gemacht wuͤrden / Der gleichen haben sie das gesang auch zů jrem gotseligen klagen / betten / verkuͤnden / lehren / weissagen vnd ermanen gebraucht / Dann sie in jrem thůn gantz warhafftig / ernsthafftig / vnd andechtig / jre klag / gebet /

Martinus Bucer, servant of the Word of the Churches in Strasb[o]urg, wishes all Christian believers Grace and Peace from God the Father and our Lord Jesus Christ.

It is acknowledged by all who read the Holy Bible that from the beginning the pious and truly believing custom has been to proclaim God's praise with singing, and in doing so, to give voice to the great pleasure, delight, and joy with which their [i.e., the singers] hearts were filled to bursting in and from God, so full, moreover, that they could no longer contain within themselves such pleasure, delight, and joy. Thus their listeners would also be attracted to, reminded of, and made happy by the acknowledgement of, and thankfulness for, God and His goodness. Likewise, they have used song for their pious lamentations, prayers, proclamations, teachings, prophesyings, and admonitions, for in their actions they have poured forth absolutely truly, earnestly, and

verkuͤndung / lehre / weissagung / vnd ermanung / alweg aus vollem vnd aufquellendem hertzen / gegossen haben / auch allemal recht ernstlich begeret / jr goͤtlichs fürhaben / anderen zů hertzen zů fuͤren / vnd zů solchem erhitzigen vnd begirig zů machen.

¶ Zů welchem / bede die Music / vnd das gesang / von Got geordnet / vnd nicht allein gantz lustig vnd anmuͤtig / sonder auch wunder krefftig vnd gewaltig ist / Demnach des menschen art vnd natur so gestaltet ist / das jn zů allerlei anmuͤtigkeit / es seien freude / leid / liebe / zorn / geistlich andacht / leichtfertige wildikeit / vnd was der affect vnd beweglicheiten sind / nichs so gewaltig beweget / als artliche Musicgesang / vn[nd] seitenspil / aus warer kunst / auf solche anmuͤtigkeiten vnd affection gerichtet / Daher dan komet / wa dem menschen etwas besonders angelegen / vnd sie behertziget / dem sie gern fil nachdencken / vnd jmer mit vmbzůgehn / lust haben / vnd daher auch gern zů richten / wie sie koͤndten, das solichs / wie jnen / also auch anderen bekant / angelegen / vnd hertzlich wuͤrde, das sie gleich von solchen hendlen begeren Lieder zůmachen / auf das dauon / nicht allein gesagt / sonder auch gesungen / vnd dadurch den leuten alles desto gruͤndtlicher zů hertzen gebracht vnd eingelassen werde.

¶ Seitemal dann vns / wie den alten lieben freunden Gottes / ja so fil mehr / so fil vns Got der Vatter / seinen Son / vnseren Herren Jesum Christum weiter zů erkennen geben hat / nichts so tieff / ja nichts anders uͤberal zů

reverently their lamentation, prayer, proclamation, teaching, prophesying, and admonition, always from hearts full to overflowing. And they have always desired right earnestly to bring their godly attitude into the hearts of others, and to make them [i.e., others] desirous and eager for the same.

For this purpose the music and song ordained by God is not only completely joyful and charming, but also marvelous and powerful. The nature and temperament of man is so formed that nothing moves it so powerfully to all sorts of moods – be they joy, sorrow, love, anger, spiritual reverence, giddy abandon, and whatever other emotions and affections there are – than artful musical singing and playing directed with skill at such moods and affections. Add to this whatever especially concerns men and gladdens them – whatever they like to think about most, with whatever they wish always to be involved, and to which they therefore gladly direct their efforts so that these things will also be made known and pleasant as much to themselves as others – regarding such actions they wish immediately to make songs. In this way these things will not only be spoken of, but sung, and thereby everything will be brought into the hearts of the people all the more thoroughly.

For we who are the old dear friends of God – even the more dear since God the Father has enabled us to know His son our Lord Jesus Christ so much more – there is nothing which should penetrate our

hertzen gehn / vnd angelegen sein solle / dann das goͤtliche / wie wir jhn / vnsern schoͤpffer vnd Vatter / recht erkennen / lieben / loben vnd preisen / durch Jesum Christum vnsern Herren vnd erloͤser / vnd hiezů meniglich reitzen vnd bewegen / So solte die Music / alles gesang vnd seitenspil (welche vor anderen dingen / das gemuͤt zůbewegen / hefftig vnd hitzig zůmachen / mechtig sind) nirgend anders / dann zů goͤtlichem lob / gebet / lehre vnd ermanung gebrauchet werden.

¶ Wir sollen je Got von gantzem hertzen / gantzer seel / vnd allen krefften lieben. Wa wir nun solch Liebe hetten / wuͤrden wir eigentlich / wie S. Paulus lehret j. Cor. x. vnd Coloss. iij. wir ehssen oder trehncken / oder was wir sunst jmer anfiengen oder fuͤrnemen / in worten oder wercken / alles im namen vnsers Herren Jesu Christi / zum preis Gottes / anfahen / fuͤrnemen / vnd handlen / Got dem Vatter dancksagende / durch jn / vnsern Herren / Vnd also allweg in allen dingen / allen lust / freud / begirde / reitzen vnd ermanen / vnd was hiezů dienstlich / vnd die gemuͤter zů bewegen krefftig / als dan die Music fuͤr andern dingen ist / zů Got vnserm Vater gerichtet vnd gestellet haben / also das kein Lied uͤberal / kein seitenspil / anders dann von / vnd zů christlichen geistlichen hendelen gesungen vnd gebrauchet wuͤrde.

¶ Koͤnde man doch sich in solchen heiligen / goͤtlichen Liederen auch erfrewen vnd belustigen / zů dem das sie vns mercklich besserten / ja in solchem mag man allein rechte freud vnd lust haben / Dann sunst

hearts more deeply, and be the only thing with which we are concerned, than the sacred: how we might properly acknowledge, love, praise, and exalt Him, our Creator and Father, through Jesus Christ our Lord and Redeemer. And for this purpose many things arouse and affect us. Thus music, all singing and playing (which above all things are capable of moving our spirits powerfully and ardently), should be used in no other way except for sacred praise, prayer, teaching, and admonition.

We should love God with all our hearts, all our souls, and all our strength. Now if we had such love, we would really do as Saint Paul teaches, 1 Cor. X [31] and Coloss. III [17]: whether we eat or drink, or whatever we begin and take up in words or works, we would begin, take up, and do everything in the name of our Lord Jesus Christ to the praise of God, saying thanks to God the Father through Him our Lord. And therefore always in all things – all pleasure, joy, desires, affections, and admonitions and whatever is serviceable for this and capable of moving the spirit – music, as in other things, has been placed before and directed to God our Father, so that absolutely no song and no instrumentalizing may be sung and used except by and for Christian spiritual activities.

If one can rejoice and enjoy oneself with such holy, sacred songs – add to which the fact that they make us noticeably better – then in such endeavours one can have only real joy and happiness. For otherwise no good

kein gůt gewissen / vnd deshalb jmer mer gallen dan honigs (wie jhener[1] sagt) befunden wuͤrt / wa anders auch ein Got vnd gewissen ist / Wa dann kein Got vnd gewissen ist / da ist eigentlich die ewige helle / ob mans gleich ietzt nicht befindet / vnd jmer hin im sause lebet / singet vnd springet vnd ist gar vnsinnig.

¶ Nun hat aber (das ja hoch zů erbarmen) der boͤse feind die sach dahin bracht / das dise herrliche kunst vnd gabe Gottes / die Music / schier alleine zur uͤppigkeit misbrauchet wuͤrt / das dan nicht allein so fil ein schwerer suͤnd / so fil die kunst ein herrlicher gabe Gottes ist / sonder auch / so fil sie gewaltiger machet zů hertzen gehn / vn[nd] jns gemuͤt komen das jenige / da zů sie gebrauchet wuͤrt / Daher es auch erschroͤcklich ist zů gedencken / was ergernis / bei der juget vnd anderen / durch die teufelischen bůllieder / angestifftet wuͤrt / so das / welches ondas zů fil anmuͤtig vnd im sinne ligt / erst durchs gesang noch anmuͤtiger / vnd tieffer in sinne vnd hertz gestecket wuͤrt.

[fol. A3^{v}] ¶ Muͤssen wir dann Got rechnung geben von jedem vergebnen wort / als wir gewislich muͤssen / was solle dann denen geschehen / die erst inn so schedlichen gifftigen / gedichten vnd liedern / jr hertz vnd gedancken durchs gesang / můtwilliglich verhefften? Vnd weh allen / die jren kindern / gesinde / vnd wem sie es zů wehren haben / hierinn zůsehen vnd losen. Aber hie bei sihet man / leider / was die leuͤt fuͤr Christen sind / vnd würt (wie das sprichwort lautet) ein jeder vogel bei

understanding, and therefore more gall than honey (as someone says) is found, where otherwise there is a God and understanding. Where, then, there is no God and no understanding, there is literally eternal Hell, even if one does not now perceive it as such, and one goes on living in a storm, singing and dancing and behaving absurdly.

Now, however, the evil one has brought matters to such a pass (which is greatly to be deplored) that music, this wonderful art and gift of God, is misused for lasciviousness. This is therefore not only a grievous sin insofar as the art is a magnificent gift of God, but also insofar as it intensifies more powerfully, penetrating the heart and bringing into the spirit that [lasciviousness] for which it is being used. Accordingly it is horrible to contemplate what unpleasantness is stirred up among the young and others by devilish, seductive songs, so that whatever without song is too charming and lies in the senses, is insinuated by song more charmingly and deeper into the senses and the heart.

If we must give an accounting to God of every thoughtless word, as in all conscience we must, what, then, shall happen to those who in a headstrong manner through song ensnare their heart and thoughts in such injurious poems and songs[?] And woe to all who see and hear in this description their children, household, and whomsoever they must protect. But here one sees, sadly, what sort of Christians these people are, and (as the proverb has it) every bird will be known by

seinem gesang erkennet / auch das wort des Herren erfüllet / Wes das hertz vol ist / gehet der mund uͤber.[2]

¶ Darumb wer da koͤndte oder moͤchte / der solt dazů rahten vnd helffen / das solche uͤppige teufelische / verderbliche gesang abgethan vnd verspuͤlget würden / vnd die heiligen Psalmen / vnd gotselige lieder / allen Christen / jungen vnd alten gemein / lustig gemacht / vnd in stetig uͤbung bracht wurden. Vnd zům fuͤrnemisten die Fuͤrsteher vnd Diener der Kirchen.

¶ Derhalben hat D. Mart. Luther lengist etliche Psalmen vnd geistliche Lieder / von jhm selb gestellet / wie er dann in solchem / als inn allem / das zů erheben die ware erkantnis Christi / vnd zů recht christlicher bestellung vnd haushaltung der Kirchen / dienstlich vnd besserlich sein mage / zům hoͤchsten begabet ist / vnd dann auch von etlichen anderen fuͤrnemen / vnd zů disen sachen besonders begabten Dienern Christi zůgericht / zůsamen drucken / vnd der gemeinden Christi zůkomen lassen / Desgleichen ist hie vnd inn vilen anderen Kirchen auch geschehen / doch allein inn handbuͤchlin / welche die Christen / jeder fuͤr sich selb inn den Kirchen versamlungen vnd sunst gebrauchen.

¶ Als aber nun etliche Gemeinden Christi auch fuͤr Juget / sie desto bas zů gleichfoͤrmigem mensurischem gesang zů gewehnen vnd anzůhalten / inn den heiligen Versamlungen / gemeine grosse Gesangbuͤcher zůbereiten angefangen / vnd das schreiben diser buͤcher etliche hoch bedeuren wille / hat der Ersam buchtrucker Joͤrg Waldmuͤller / genant

his song, and the word of the Lord will be fulfilled: with whatever the heart is full, the mouth comes forth.

Therefore whoever could or would should give counsel and assistance so that such lascivious, devilish, ruinous songs will be cast out and destroyed, and the holy Psalms and sacred songs made pleasing to all Christians, young and old alike, and brought into steady use, particularly among the leaders and servants of the Churches.

Therefore Dr. Martin Luther sometime ago had published some Psalms and spiritual songs composed by himself – as he is in such matters highly gifted, as indeed also in everything that may strengthen the true knowledge of Christ, and be serviceable and ameliorating for true Christian activity and administration of the Churches – with some other highly placed servants of Christ, also particularly gifted in this matter, and brought them before the congregations of Christ. The same has happened here[3] and in many other Churches, but only in little books which each Christian uses individually in Churches and elsewhere.

But now when some congregations of Christians began to prepare common large hymnbooks, particularly for the young, so that they might better win and keep the measured and unison song in the sacred congregations, some people were of a mind to pay highly for the making of these books. The honored printer, Jörg Waldmüller,

Messerschmid / zů gůt den lieben Kirchen / vnd das gotselig gesang inn den Christlichen Versamlungen / Schůlen vnd Lerheusern zů fuͤrderen / nicht mit geringem kosten vn[nd] muͤh sich lassen erbetten vnd bestellen / ein Gesangbůch zůtrucken / auch allen fleis an zů wenden / wie es das werckt selb zeuget / das die Psalmen vnd geistliche Lieder / so hierin begriffen / auffs seuberlichest / vnd zům besten corrigieret ausgiengen. Weil dann nůn dis werck fuͤr vil Kichen [*sic*] / die nicht einerlei gesang im brauch haben / zůgerichtet ist / sind auch mangerlei Psalmen vnd geistliche Lieder hie zůsamen gesetzet / Damit jede Kirch hierinne auch die finde / die sie zů brauchen pfleget. Also findestu hierin erstlich fast alle die D. Mart. Luther in seinem buͤchlein zů Wittenberg hat lassen ausgehn / darnach die besten / die man hiezů Strasburg / vnd in etlichen anderen Kirchen / so vns bekant sein / zů singen im brauch hat.

¶ Nach dem aber / wie D. Luther billich klaget / vnder seine vnd andere recht artige vnd geistliche Lieder / fil onnoͤtigs / ongeistlichs vnd onbesserlichs / eingemischet worden / vnd auch vnder denen / die schon etwas art haben / vnd besserlich sein koͤnden / noch in solchem ein grosser vnderscheid ist / damit man dann vnderschiedlich erkennete / welches eines jeden gedicht vnd werck seie / ist fuͤr jeden Psalmen vnd geistlich Lied / des dichters namen gesetzet / Damit niemand das jenige zůgemessen werde / das nicht sein ist.

¶ Disen getrewen vnd nutzlichen dienst woͤllen die Gemeinden / vnd

called Messerschmid, to further the good in the dear Churches and to promote sacred song in Christian congregations, schools, and places of learning, was requested and commissioned to print a songbook with no little cost and trouble. He bent every effort, as the work itself shows, with the result that the Psalms and spiritual songs included herein might be published as clearly as possible and corrected to the best of knowledge. Now since this work is directed at the many Churches which do not have the same song [i.e. music] in use, many Psalms and spiritual songs are furnished here with music so that each Church may find herein those [songs] which it is accustomed to use. Thus you will find herein first of all nearly all those which Dr. Martin Luther published in his book at Wittenberg; afterwards the best ones which we are accustomed to sing here at Strasb[o]urg and in other Churches known to us.

But since, as Dr. Luther justifiably complains, among the appropriately pleasing and spiritual songs by him and others many unnecessary and unspiritual and unedifying are mixed – and also among those which already have some style and can be edifying, and even in this there is a great difference – the name of the poet is placed under each Psalm and spiritual song so that one may recognize who has created each poem and work and thereby no one will be accredited with what is not his.

This faithful and useful service should be received gratefully by the

alle die Christen sind / danckbarlich auffnemen / wie dann hiemit gemeine besserung des reichs Christi gesuchet ist. Vnd ob wol etliche Psalmen vnd geistliche Lieder / die anderen (als dann alle sind / die D. Mart. Luther gesetzet hat) in kunst vnd geistlicher art / mercklich fuͤrtreffen / so ist doch nichs in dis bůch gedrucket / das nicht goͤtlichem Wort gemes / vnd zů auffbawen die gotseligkeit / dienstlich sein moͤge / Derhalben jhn den Trucker / sein verdinger[4] vnd rahtgeben[5] niemand[6] verdencken solle / das / so sie filen Kirchen zů dienen begeren / auch filer Psalmen vnd geistliche Lieder hie zůsamen verfasset haben.

¶ Der Herr woͤlle geben / das alle verseher vnd Diener der Kirchen / sampt allen Christen / jres besten vermoͤgens dran seien / das bei der jugen / vnd aller gemein Gottes / solch schoͤne christliche Geseng / inn brauch vnd uͤbung komen / damit wa man zůsamen kompt / oder auch die leut fuͤr sich selb singen / das man sich mit solchen Psalmen vnd Liedern / wie hie fürgeben werden / vnd deren gleichen (wie das alle Heiligen alts vnd newes Testaments gepfleget / vnd der Heilige Paulus vermanet) belustige / durch welche dann vnsere gemuͤter zů Got vnserem Schoͤpffer / vnd Christo vnserem Heiland / vnd also zů aller zucht / erbarkeit / christlicher liebe vn[nd] freuntschafft durcheinander / gelert / vnderwisen / gereitzet vnd gezogen / die uͤpige / schandliche bůl vnd andere weltlieder / sampt dem gifft / das sie zů allen lasteren vnd boͤsen

congregations and all those who are Christians, inasmuch as by means of it the general improvement of the kingdom of Christ is sought. And although some Psalms and spiritual songs are definitely better in art and spiritual nature than others (among them are all those which Dr. Martin Luther has composed), there is nothing printed in this book which does not follow sacred Word, and is not serviceable for the enhancement of piety. Accordingly, no one should object that the printer, his publisher, and adviser have gathered together here so many Psalms and spiritual songs in order to serve so many Churches.

The Lord should see to it that all leaders and servants of the Churches, together with all Christians, exert their best efforts to ensure that among the young as well as the whole congregation of Christ such beautiful Christian songs come into use and practice, so that when there is an assembly, or the people sing among themselves, they will be joyful with such Psalms and songs as are published here and there alike (as all the saints of the Old and New Testament were accustomed to do, and as Saint Paul admonishes). By these means, then, our souls will be drawn towards, instructed in, and educated to God our Creator and Christ our Saviour, and to all other discipline, edification, Christian love, and friendship, and will be led on to cast out and destroy the lascivious, injurious, alluring, and other worldly songs, including the

sitten / hinder jnen lassen / abgetriben / vnd verspulget werden.

¶ Es ist je zeit / das / wer sich Gottes annimet / solichs mit ernst thuͤ. Got mag vnser nicht so lohe. Der lang verdienet zorn Gottes dringet seer streng auff vns / auch mehren sich die warnungen Gottes taͤglich / vnd gehen die straffen alda mit an / wee vns / wa wir nicht auffwachen / nicht zů vns selb bas lugen / vnd in Christlichem thůn eiferiger werden.

¶ Darumb woͤlle Vatter vnd mutter sich erinnern / wem sie jre kinder im Tauff ergeben vnd geopffert haben / vnd nicht an den selbigen / jetzund nicht allein jrem eignen blůt vnd fleisch / sonder auch Gottes kinderen / schuldig werden / Vnd die so die kinder leren / gedencken was thewren schatz / jnen vertrawet seie / soͤne vnd toͤchter des aller Obersten / denen die lieben Engel dienen / Vnd so dis alter ondas zům gesang geneigt / vnd mit lustlichen mitlen zům gůten gefuͤrt sein wil / fleis ankeren / das sie die kinder solich heilige goͤtliche Lieder getrewlich leren / auch die selbigen zů singen anhalten / vnd alle leichtfertige / weltliche bůlerische lieder / jhnen weder zůhoͤren noch zůsingen gestatten. Dann wie der H. Paulus leret / solle bei vns nicht allein kein schandpare vnd schnoͤde / sonder auch kein narren vnd schertztaͤding vernomen werden / oder stat haben / als die ding die sich zů vnserem berůffe gar nicht reimen / Sonder eitel dancksagung/[7] lob vnd preis Gottes / das durch vns sein goͤtlicher name jmer je mehr geheiliget / sein reich erweiteret /

poison leading to all vices and evil which they leave behind.

It is even now the time in which whoever embraces God should do so in all seriousness; God does not like us half-hearted. The long deserved anger of God presses strong against us. The warnings of God increase daily, and punishments keep step with them. Woe to us if we do not wake up, if we do not look more deeply into ourselves, and become more zealous in Christian action.

Therefore fathers and mothers should remember to whom they have given and offered their children in baptism, and remember that they are answerable not to these only, and not to their own flesh and blood only, but also to God's children. And those who teach children should remember what a precious treasure is entrusted to them, sons and daughters of the Most High, whom the dear angels serve. And since this age has a preference for singing, and wishes to be led to the good in joyful ways, they should turn their efforts toward teaching the children such holy, sacred songs faithfully, and accustoming them to sing the same, and not allow them either to hear or to sing any frivolous, worldly, and wanton songs. For, as Saint Paul teaches, not only should no injurious and bad, but also no foolish and flippant things be heard or occur among us, such as things which do not pertain to our calling, but count as vain thanksgiving. But rather praise and exalt God, so that through us His holy name may be ever more sanctified, His kingdom widened,

vnd seinem willen trewlicher vnd mit mehr lůst gelebt werde. A M E N

and His will truly and more joyfully lived. Amen.

Notes

1. This 'someone' is the Roman satirist Juvenal, who wrote about an unhappy marriage in his sixth satire. Gall was used as a healing potion, sweetened with honey. See Juvenal, trans. T. Sheridan, *The Satires of Juvenal Translated* (Dublin: Faulkner, 1777), p. 125.

2. Matt. 12:34.

3. i.e. in Strasbourg.

4. Wolfgang Köpfel.

5. Konrad Hubert (see *BDS*, 7, p. 581, n. 19).

6. *sic* (= niemand).

7. Ephes. 5:4.

Bibliography

Note: Modern collected editions of ancient and early modern writings are to be found under their authors' names.

Abray, L. J., *The People's Reformation: Magistrates, Clergy, and Commons in Strasbourg, 1500–1598* (Oxford: Blackwell, 1985).

— 'The Laity's Religion: Lutheranism in Sixteenth-Century Strasbourg', in Hsia, R. P., ed., *The German People and the Reformation* (Ithaca and London: Cornell University Press, 1988), pp. 216–32.

Adam, J., *Evangelische Kirchengeschichte der Stadt Strassburg* (Strasbourg: Heitz, 1922).

Adam, J. et al., *Inventaire des Archives du Chapitre de St-Thomas de Strasbourg* (Strasbourg: Imprimerie Alsacienne, 1937).

Ameln, K., 'Teutsch Kirchen ampt Straßburg 1524 oder 1525?', *Jahrbuch für Liturgik und Hymnologie*, 1 (1955), pp. 96–7.

— *The Roots of German Hymnody of the Reformation Era* (St Louis: Concordia, 1964).

— 'Zur Frage der Datierung des "Teutsch Kirchenampt"', in *Jahrbuch für Liturgik und Hymnologie*, 12 (1967), pp. 140–48.

Ameln, K., ed., *Handbuch der deutschen evangelischen Kirchenmusik*, vol. 1: *Der Altargesang* (Göttingen: Vandenhoeck & Ruprecht, 1933–38).

Ameln, K., Jenny, M., and Lipphardt, W., eds, *Das Deutsche Kirchenlied DKL*, Répertoire International des Sources Musicales, B/VIII/1–2 (Kassel: Bärenreiter, 1975 and 1980).

Anderson, W. et al., 'Hymn', in Root, D., ed., *Grove Music Online* (www.oxfordmusiconline.com) (accessed 23 March 2010).

Angerer, J., *Die liturgisch-musikalische Erneuerung der Melker Reform. Studien zur Erforschung der Musikpraxis in den Benediktinerklöstern des 15. Jahrhunderts* (Vienna: Verlag der Österreichischen Akademie der Wissenschaften, 1974).

Arnold, M., *Quand Strasbourg accueillait Calvin : 1538–1541* (Strasbourg: Presses universitaires de Strasbourg, 2009).

Arnold, M. (Guder, J. J., trans.), 'Strasbourg', in Selderhuis, H. J., ed., *The Calvin Handbook* (Grand Rapids & Cambridge: Eerdmans, 2009), pp. 38–44.

Augustine (Sheed, F. J., trans.), *The Confessions of St. Augustine* (New York: Sheed & Ward, 1942).

Augustine (Skutella, M., ed.), *S. Aureli Augustini Confessionum* (Leipzig: Teubner, 1934; repr. Stuttgart: Teubner, 1981).

Backman, E. L. (Classen, E., trans.), *Religious Dances in the Christian Church and in Popular Medicine* (London: Allen & Unwin, 1952).

Backus, I., 'Martin Bucer and the Patristic Tradition', in Krieger, C. and Lienhard, M., eds, *Martin Bucer and Sixteenth Century Europe – Actes du colloque de Strasbourg (28–31 août 1991)*, 2 vols (Leiden: Brill, 1993), vol. 1, pp. 55–69.

— 'Ulrich Zwingli, Martin Bucer and the Church Fathers', in Backus, I., ed., *The Reception of the Church Fathers in the West – From the Carolingians to the Maurists*, 2 vols (Leiden: Brill, 1997), vol. 2, pp. 627–60.

Bartsch, K., 'Graff: Jörg', in *Allgemeine Deutsche Biographie*, vol. 9 (Leipzig: Duncker & Humblot, 1879), pp. 570–71.

Baum, A., *Magistrat und Reformation in Strassburg bis 1529* (Strasbourg: Heitz & Mündel, 1887).

Baum, J. W., *Capito und Butzer – Straßburgs Reformatoren* (Elberfeld: Friderichs, 1860).

Benzing, J., 'Die Druckerei der Matthias Schürer Erben zu Straßburg (1520–1525)', *Archiv für Geschichte des Buchwesens*, 2 (1960), pp. 170–74.

— *Die Buchdrucker des 16. und 17. Jahrhunderts im deutschen Sprachgebiet* (Wiesbaden: Harrassowitz, 1963).

Benzing, J. and Muller, J., *Bibliographie strasbourgeoise : bibliographie des ouvrages imprimés à Strasbourg (Bas-Rhin) au XVIe siècle*, 3 vols (Baden-Baden: Koerner, 1981–86).

Bernstein, J. A., *Music Printing in Renaissance Venice: The Scotto Press (1539–1572)* (New York and Oxford: Oxford University Press, 1998).

Bezzel, I. et al., eds, *Verzeichnis der im deutschen Sprachbereich erschienenen Drucke des 16. Jahrhunderts* (Stuttgart: Hiersemann, 1983–) (online resource: www.vd16.de).

Birkner, G., 'Zur Chronologie und Abhängigkeit der ältesten Quellen des deutschen evangelischen Kirchenlieds', *Jahrbuch für Liturgik und Hymnologie*, 12 (1967), pp. 118–40.

Bizer, E., *Studien zur Geschichte des Abendmahlsstreits im 16. Jahrhundert* (Gütersloh: Bertelsmann, 1940).

Blackburn, B. J., 'Josquin's Chansons: Ignored and Lost Sources', *Journal of the American Musicological Society*, 29 (1976), pp. 30–76.

Blankenburg, W. (Heinsheimer, H., trans.), 'Church Music in Reformed Europe', in Blume, F., ed., *Protestant Church Music* (London: Gollancz, 1975), pp. 507–90.

— 'The Music of the Bohemian Brethren', in Blume, F., ed., *Protestant Church Music* (London: Gollancz, 1975), pp. 591–607.

Blume, C., 'Hymnody and Hymnology', in *The Catholic Encyclopedia (Online)* (www.newadvent.org/cathen/07596a.htm) (accessed 20 March 2011).

Blume, F. (Ellsworth Peterson, F., trans.), 'The Period of the Reformation', in Blume, F., ed., *Protestant Church Music* (London: Gollancz, 1975), pp. 3–122.

Blume, F., ed., *Protestant Church Music* (London: Gollancz, 1975).

Blumenthal, U.-R., *The Investiture Controversy: Church and Monarchy from the Ninth to the Twelfth Century* (Philadelphia: University of Pennsylvania Press, 1988).

Böhme, F. M., *Altdeutsches Liederbuch* (Leipzig: Breitkopf & Härtel, 1877).

Bond, J. J., *Handy-Book of Rules and Tables for Verifying Dates with the Christian Era* (London: Bell & Sons, 1875).

Boorman, S., 'Early Music Printing: Working for a Specialized Market', in Tyson, G. P. and Wagonheim, S. S., eds, *Print and Culture in the Renaissance* (Newark: University of Delaware Press; London: Associated University Presses, 1986), pp. 222–45.

— et al., 'Printing and Publishing of Music, §I: Printing', in Root, D., ed., *Grove Music Online* (www.oxfordmusiconline.com) (accessed 10 June 2014).

Bornert, R., 'Martin Bucer et la liturgie strasbourgeoise de 1537–1539', *Archives de l'Eglise d'Alsace*, 19 (nouvelle série) (1971), pp. 105–25.

— *La Réforme protestante du culte à Strasbourg au XVI*[e] *siècle (1523–1598)* (Leiden: Brill, 1981).

Bott, G., ed., *Martin Luther und die Reformation in Deutschland* (Frankfurt am Main: Insel, 1983).

Bovet, F., *Histoire du psautier des églises réformées* (Neuchâtel: Sandoz; Paris: Grassard, 1872).

Brady, T. A., *Ruling Class, Regime and Reformation at Strasbourg, 1520–1555* (Leiden: Brill, 1978).

— '"Sind also zu beiden theilen christen, des Gott erbarm" : Le mémoire de Jacques Sturm sur le culte publique à Strasbourg (août 1525)', in Kroon, M. and Lienhard, M., eds, *Horizons européens de la Réforme en Alsace : Mélanges offerts à Jean Rott pour son 65*[e] *anniversaire* (Strasbourg: Istra, 1980), pp. 69–79.

— *Turning Swiss: Cities and Empire, 1450–1550* (Cambridge: Cambridge University Press, 1985).

— *Protestant Politics: Jacob Sturm (1489-1553) and the German Reformation* (Boston: Humanities Press, 1995).

Brant, S. (Gillis, W., trans.), *The Ship of Fools* (London: Folio Society, 1971).

Braun, G., *Civitates Orbis Terrarum*, 6 vols (Cologne: Agrippina, 1572–1617).

Brewer, J. S., ed., *Letters and Papers, foreign and domestic, of the reign of Henry VIII*, 21 vols (London: Longman, 1862–1920). Available as an electronic resource at http://www.tannerritchie.com/memso.php, ed. J. Gairdner.

Briggs, R., *The Witches of Lorraine* (Oxford: Oxford University Press, 2007).

Brodersen, C. and K., eds, *The* Erfurt Enchiridion *– A Hymn Book of 1524* (Speyer: Kartoffeldruck-Verlag, 2008).

Brown, C. B., *Singing the Gospel: Lutheran Hymns and the Success of the Reformation* (Cambridge, MA, and London: Harvard University Press, 2005).

Bucer, M. (Augustijn, C., Fraenkel, P., and Lienhard, M., eds), *Martini Buceri Opera Latina*, 5 vols (Leiden: Brill, 1982–2000).

Bucer, M. (Rott, J. et al., eds), *Correspondance de Martin Bucer*, 5 vols (Leiden: Brill, 1979–).

Bucer, M. (Stupperich, R. and Seebass, G., eds), *Martini Buceri Opera Omnia: Deutsche Schriften*, 17 vols (Gütersloh: Gütersloh Verlagshaus Mohn, 1960–).

Bucer, M. and Parker, M. (Fraenkel, P., ed.) *Florilegium Patristicum* (= *Martini Buceri Opera Latina*, vol. 3 [Leiden: Brill, 1988]).

Büchsenschütz, L., *Histoire des liturgies en langue allemande dans l'église de Strasbourg au XVIe siècle* (Cahors: Coueslant, 1900).

Bush, D. E. and Kassel, R., *The Organ: An Encyclopedia* (Routledge: New York, 2006).

Buszin, W. E., 'Luther on Music', *The Musical Quarterly*, 32 (1946), pp. 80–97.

Butterworth, C. C., *The English Primers (1529–1545) – Their Publication and Connection with the English Bible and the Reformation in England* (Philadelphia: University of Pennsylvania Press, 1953).

Butterworth, C. C. and Chester, A. C., *George Joye – 1495?–1553* (Philadelphia: University of Pennsylvania Press, 1962).

Calvin, J. (Barth, P. and Niesel, G., eds), *Joannis Calvini opera selecta*, 5 vols (Munich: Kaiser, 1926–1936).

Calvin, J. (Baum, J. W. et al., eds), *Ioannis Calvini opera quae supersunt omnia*, 59 vols (Brunswick: Schwetschke, 1863–1900).

Calvin, J. (McCord, J. I. and Mülhaupt, E., eds), *Supplementa Calviniana – Sermons inédits*, 12 vols (Neukirchen-Vluyn: Neukirchener Verlag, 1961–).

Capito, W. (Rummel, E., ed., with Kooistra, M.), *The Correspondence of Wolfgang Capito*, 2 vols (Toronto: University of Toronto Press, 2005–).

Chastel, A. et al., *Hommage à Dürer. Strasbourg et Nuremberg dans la première moitié du XVIe siècle* (Strasbourg: Istra, 1972).

Chrisman, M. U., *Strasbourg and the Reform: A Study in the Process of Change* (New Haven and London: Yale University Press, 1967).

— *Bibliography of Strasbourg Imprints, 1480–1599* (New Haven: Yale University Press, 1982).

— *Lay Culture, Learned Culture: Books and Social Change in Strasbourg, 1480–1599* (New Haven and London: Yale University Press, 1982).

— 'Printing and the Evolution of Lay Culture in Strasbourg 1480–1599', in Hsia, R. P., ed., *The German People and the Reformation* (Ithaca and London: Cornell University Press, 1988), pp. 74–100.

Clerval, A., 'Strasbourg et la Réforme française', *Revue d'histoire de l'Eglise de France*, 7 (1921), pp. 139–60.

Coignet, C., *La Réforme française avant les guerres civiles, 1512–1559* (Paris: Fischbacher, 1890).

Cosin, J. (Sansom, J. and Barrow, J., eds), *The Works of the Right Reverend Father in God, John Cosin, Lord Bishop of Durham*, 5 vols (Oxford: Parker, 1843–55).

Cuming, G. J., *A History of Anglican Liturgy*, 2nd edn (London: Macmillan, 1982).

Cypris, O. F., 'Basic Principles: Translation and Commentary of Martin Bucer's *Grund und Ursach*, 1524' (PhD diss., Union Theological Seminary, New York, 1971).

De Maio, R. et al., eds, *Bellarmino e la controriforma* (Sora: Centro di studi sorani 'Vincenzo Patriarca', 1990).

Dempsey, C. A., '*Geistliche Gesangbuch, Geistreiche Gesangbuch*: The Development of Confessional Unity in the Evangelical Hymnbook 1524–1587' (PhD diss., University of Nebraska, 2003).

Deutsche Reichstagsakten: jüngere Reihe, 19 vols (Gotha: Perthes; Göttingen: Vandenhoeck & Ruprecht; Munich: Oldenbourg, 1893–).

Dietrich, S. (Honegger, M. and Meyer, C., eds), *Magnificat Octo Tonorum, Strasbourg, 1535* (Strasbourg: Convivium musicum; Stuttgart: Carus-Verlag, 1992).

Dobbins, F., 'Davantes, Pierre', in Root, D., ed., *Grove Music Online* (www.oxfordmusiconline.com) (accessed 14 November 2014).

Douen, O. E., *Clément Marot et le psautier huguenot*, 2 vols (Paris: Imprimerie Nationale, 1878–79).

Douglas, M., *Purity and Danger* (London and New York: Routledge, 1966; repr. 2002).

Douglass, E. J. D., *Justification in Late Medieval Preaching: A Study of John Geiler of Keisersberg* (Leiden: Brill, 1966).

Dürr, A. and Killy, W., eds, *Das protestantische Kirchenlied im 16. und 17. Jahrhundert* (Wiesbaden: Harrassowitz, 1986).

Edwards, M. U., Jr, *Printing, Propaganda, and Martin Luther* (Berkeley and Los Angeles: University of California Press, 1994).

Eells, H., *Martin Bucer* (New Haven: Yale University Press; London: Oxford University Press, 1931).

Erasmus, D., *Desiderii Erasmi Roterodami Opera Omnia*, 10 vols (Leiden: Vander, 1703–06).

Erasmus, D. (Allen, P. S. and H. M., eds), *Opus epistolarum Des. Erasmi Roterdami*, 12 vols (Oxford: Clarendon Press, 1906–58; repr. 1992).

Erasmus, D. (Kumaniecki, K. et al., eds), *Opera Omnia Desiderii Erasmi Roterodami*, 9 parts (Amsterdam: North-Holland, 1969–)

Erasmus, D. (O'Malley, J. W. and Perraud, L. A., eds), *Collected Works of Erasmus*, 86 vols (Toronto: University of Toronto Press, 1974–).

Erasmus, D. (Minnich, N. H., ed., and Sheerin, D., trans.), *Collected works of Erasmus: Controversies* (Toronto: University of Toronto Press, 2005).

Erichson, A., *Die Calvinische und die Altstrassburgische Gottesdienstordnung* (Strasbourg: Heitz, 1894).

— *L'Église française de Strasbourg au seizième siècle d'après des documents inédits* (Paris: Fischbacher, 1886).

— *L'Origine de la confession des péchés dite de Calvin* (Dôle: Bernin, 1896).

Everist, M., ed., *The Cambridge Companion to Medieval Music* (Cambridge: Cambridge University Press, 2011).

Faerber, R., 'La communauté anglaise à Strasbourg pendant le règne de Marie', in Livet, G. and Rapp, F., eds, *Strasbourg au cœur religieux du XVI*e *siècle* (Strasbourg: Istra, 1977), pp. 431–41.

— 'Bucer et Jean Sturm', in Krieger, C. and Lienhard, M., eds, *Martin Bucer and Sixteenth Century Europe – Actes du colloque de Strasbourg (28–31 août 1991)*, 2 vols (Leiden: Brill, 1993), vol. 1, pp. 329–41.

Fallersleben, H. von and Schade, O., eds, *Weimarisches Jahrbuch für deutsche Sprache, Litteratur und Kunst*, 4 (1855).

Fellerer, K. G. (Hadas, M., trans.), 'Church Music and the Council of Trent', *The Musical Quarterly*, 39 (1953), pp. 576–94.

Fenlon, I. A., 'Music and Reform in Sixteenth-Century Italy', in De Maio, R. et al., eds, *Bellarmino e la controriforma* (Sora: Centro di studi sorani 'Vincenzo Patriarca', 1990), pp. 851–89.

—, ed., *The Renaissance* (Macmillan: Basingstoke, 1989).

Fétis, F. J., *Biographie universelle des musiciens*, 10 vols (Paris: Didot, 1860–80).

Ficker, J., 'Das größte Prachtwerk des Straßburger Buchdrucks – Zur Geschichte und Gestaltung des großen Straßburger Gesangbuches 1541', *Archiv für Reformationsgeschichte*, 38 (1941), pp. 198–230.

Fisher, A. J., *Music and Religious Identity in Counter-Reformation Augsburg, 1580–1630* (Aldershot: Ashgate, 2004).

Fluri, A., 'Mathias Apiarius, der erste Buchdrucker Berns (1537–1554). Das Interlachnerlied und die erste bernische Censurordnung', *Neues Berner Taschenbuch*, 2 (1897 [published 1896]), pp. 196–253. N.B.: The *Berner Taschenbuch* and the *Neues Berner Taschenbuch* are available as an electronic resource at: http://retro.seals.ch/digbib/browse5_3.

Foley, E., 'Doxology', in Root, D., ed., *Grove Music Online* (www.oxfordmusiconline.com) (accessed 18 April 2011).

Föllmi, B. A., 'Création et reconfiguration de l'espace sonore : les activités musicales à Strasbourg avant, pendant et après la Réforme protestante', in Gauthier, L. and Traversier, M., eds, *Mélodies urbaines : la musique dans les villes d'Europe (XVI*e*–XIX*e *siècles)* (Paris: Presses de l'Université Paris-Sorbonne, 2008), pp. 103–18.

— 'Rupture and Transformation of Collective Musical Memory among Urban Populations at the Time of the Reformation: The Case of Strasbourg', in Marković, T. and Mikić, V., eds, *Musical Culture & Memory* (Belgrade: Belgrade University of Arts Press, 2008), pp. 16–25.

— 'Calvin und das Psalmsingen: Die Vorgeschichte des Genfer Psalters', *Zwingliana*, 36 (2009), pp. 59–84.

— 'Le "Psautier de Calvin" : Théologie, pratique, usage', *Revue d'histoire et de philosophie religieuses*, 89.4 (2009), pp. 473–88.

Fortescue, A., 'Canon of the Mass', *The Catholic Encyclopedia (Online)* (http://www.newadvent.org/cathen/03255c.htm) (accessed 22 August 2011).

Fournier, M. and Engel, C., eds, 'Gymnase, académie, université de Strasbourg, 1525–1621', in *Les Statuts et privilèges des universités françaises depuis leur fondation jusqu'en 1789*, 4 vols (Paris: Larose & Forcel, 1890–1894), vol. 4.

Fragments des anciennes chroniques d'Alsace, 4 vols, in *Bulletin de la Société pour la conservation des monuments historiques d'Alsace*, 2nd series: vol. I (1887) in 13 (1887–88); vol. II (1890) in 13 (1887–88) and 14 (1889); vol. III (1892) in 15 (1892); vol. IV (1901) in 18 (1897) and 19 (1899). All four volumes of the *Fragments* were also published independently, with precisely the same content. See under 'Chronicles' below.

Froude, J. A., *Life and Letters of Erasmus* (London: Longmans, Green, 1894) [two editions].

Gäbler, U. (Gritsch, R. C. L., trans.), *Huldrych Zwingli: His Life and Work* (Philadelphia: Fortress Press, 1986).

Garside, C., Jr, 'The Origins of Calvin's Theology of Music: 1536–1543', *Transactions of the American Philosophical Society*, 69.4 (1979), pp. 1–35.

Gass, J., 'Organistes et orgues à Strasbourg au 16e siècle', *Caecilia*, 34 (1921), pp. 135–6.

Gauthier, L. and Traversier, M., eds, *Mélodies urbaines : la musique dans les villes d'Europe (XVIe–XIXe siècles)* (Paris: Presses de l'Université Paris-Sorbonne, 2008).

'by a German student', 'On Luther's Love for and Knowledge of Music', *The Musical Times and Singing Class Circular*, 1 (1845), pp. 82–3, 87.

Gérold, T., 'Les premiers recueils de mélodies religieuses protestantes à Strasbourg', *Revue de musicologie*, 6 (1925), pp. 49–58.

— *Les plus anciennes mélodies de l'Eglise protestante de Strasbourg et leurs auteurs* (Paris: Alcan, 1928).

— 'La musique à Strasbourg pendant le premier tiers du XVIe siècle', *L'Est musical*, 1 (1939), pp. 6–11.

Gilchrist, J., *The Collection in Seventy-Four Titles: A Canon Law Manual of the Gregorian Reform* (Toronto: Pontifical Institute of Mediaeval Studies, 1980).

Gilmont, F., ed. (Maag, K., trans.), *The Reformation and the Book* (Ashgate: Aldershot, 1988).

Glenstal Abbey, the Monks of, trans., *The Rule of Benedict* (Dublin: Four Courts, 1994).

The Görres-Gesellschaft, ed., *Concilium Tridentinum: Diariorum, actorum, epistularum, tractatuum nova collectio,* 13 vols (Freiburg: Herder, 1901–).

Grandidier, P.-A., *Essais historiques et topographiques sur l'église cathédrale de Strasbourg* (Strasbourg and Paris: Levrault, 1782).

Greef, W. de, 'Calvin's Writings', in McKim, D., ed., *The Cambridge Companion to John Calvin* (Cambridge: Cambridge University Press, 2004), pp. 41–57.

Green, L. C., 'The Bible in Sixteenth-Century Humanist Education', *Studies in the Renaissance*, 19 (1972), pp. 112–34.

Greschat, M. (Buckwalter, S. E., trans.), *Martin Bucer: A Reformer and his Times* (Louisville and London: Westminster John Knox Press, 2004).

Griffin, E., *A First Look at Communication Theory*, 5th edn (New York: McGraw-Hill, 2003).

Grimm, J. and W., *Deutsches Wörterbuch*, 11 vols (Leipzig: Hirzel, 1854–1965).

Guillo, L., 'Quarante-six psautiers antérieurs à 1562', *Psaume : bulletin de la recherche sur le psautier huguenot*, 2 (1988), pp. 27–34.

Ha, P. and Collinson, P., *The Reception of Continental Reformation in Britain* (Oxford: Oxford University Press, 2010).

Haein, E., *De problematiek van de gemeentezang in de Franse Gereformeerde Kerken en de liturgische rijkdom van het Geneefse Psalter* (Baarn: Gooi & Sticht, 1995).

Harper, J., *The Forms and Orders of Western Liturgy from the Tenth to the Eighteenth Century* (Oxford: Clarendon Press, 1991).

Herl, J., *Worship Wars in Early Lutheranism: Choir, Congregation, and Three Centuries of Conflict* (Oxford: Oxford University Press, 2004).

Herminjard, A.-L., *Correspondance des réformateurs dans les pays de langue française*, 9 vols (Geneva: Georg; Paris: Levy, 1866–97).

Hiley, D. and Szendrei, J., 'Notation, §III, 1: History of Western notation: Plainchant', in Root, D., ed., *Grove Music Online* (www.oxfordmusiconline.com) (accessed 20 September 2011).

Hobbs, R. G., 'How Firm a Foundation: Martin Bucer's Historical Exegesis of the Psalms', *Church History*, 53 (1984), pp. 477–91.

— 'Connaissances bibliques, religion populaire : les premiers psaumes versifiés de la Réforme à Strasbourg 1524–1527', *Revue d'histoire et de philosophie religieuses*, 78 (1998), pp. 415–33.

— '"Quam Apposita Religioni Sit Musica": Martin Bucer and Music in the Liturgy', *Reformation and Renaissance Review*, 6 (2004), pp. 155–78.

Hopf, C., *Martin Bucer and the English Reformation* (Oxford: Blackwell, 1946).

Hsia, R. P., ed., *The German People and the Reformation* (Ithaca and London: Cornell University Press, 1988).

Hubert, F., 'Martin Butzers Großes Gesangbuch', *Monatschrift für Gottesdienst und kirchliche Kunst*, 3 (1898), pp. 52–7.

— *Die Straßburger liturgischen Ordnungen im Zeitalter der Reformation* (Göttingen: Vandenhoeck & Ruprecht, 1900).

Irwin, J. L., *Neither Voice nor Heart Alone: German Lutheran theology of music in the age of the Baroque* (New York: Lang, 1993).

Janota, J., *Studien zu Funktion und Typus des deutschen geistlichen Liedes im Mittelalter* (Munich: Beck, 1968).

Jenny, M., *Geschichte des deutschschweizerischen evangelischen Gesangbuches im 16. Jahrhundert* (Basel: Bärenreiter, 1962).

— *Zwinglis Stellung zur Musik im Gottesdienst* (Zurich: Zwingli Verlag, 1966).

— 'Kirchenlied, Gesangbuch und Kirchenmusik', in Bott, G., ed., *Martin Luther und die Reformation in Deutschland* (Frankfurt am Main: Insel, 1983), pp. 293–322.

— *Luther, Zwingli, Calvin in ihren Liedern* (Zurich: Theologischer Verlag, 1983).

Jenny, M., ed., *Luthers geistliche Lieder und Kirchengesänge* (Cologne and Vienna: Böhlau, 1985).

Johnson, A. F., 'English books printed abroad', *The Library*, 5th series, 4 (1950), pp. 273–6.

Jung, A., *Beiträge zu der Geschichte der Reformation*, 2 vols (Strasbourg and Leipzig: Levrault, 1830).

Junod, L., *Farel – réformateur de la Suisse romande* (Neuchâtel: Delachaux & Sandoz; Paris: Librairie de la Suisse Romande, 1865).

Jütte, R. (Lynn, J., trans.), *A History of the Senses: From Antiquity to Cyberspace* (Cambridge: Polity, 2005).

Juvenal (Sheridan, T., trans.), *The Satires of Juvenal Translated* (Dublin: Faulkner, 1777).

Karant-Nunn, S. C., *The Reformation of Feeling: Shaping the Religious Emotions in Early Modern Germany* (Oxford: Oxford University Press, 2010).

Kess, A., *Johann Sleidan and the Protestant Vision of History* (Aldershot: Ashgate, 2008).

Kim, H.-A., 'Erasmus on Sacred Music', *Reformation and Renaissance Review*, 8 (2006), pp. 277–300.

Kisby, F., ed., *Music and Musicians in Renaissance Cities and Towns* (Cambridge: Cambridge University Press, 2001).

Kittelson, J. M., *Wolfgang Capito: From Humanist to Reformer* (Leiden: Brill, 1975).

— 'Successes and Failures in the German Reformation: The Report from Strasbourg', *Archiv für Reformationsgeschichte*, 73 (1982), pp. 153–75.

— 'Visitations and Popular Religious Culture: Further Reports from Strasbourg', in Bebb, P. N. and Sessions, K. C., eds, *Pietas et Societas: New Trends in Reformation Social History* (Kirksville, Missouri: Sixteenth Century Studies Press, 1985), pp. 89–101.

Köhler, H.-J., *Bibliographie der Flugschriften des 16. Jahrhunderts* (Tübingen: Bibliotheca Academica, 1991–).

Kohls, E. W., *Die Schule bei Martin Bucer in ihrem Verhältnis zu Kirche und Obrigkeit* (Heidelberg: Quelle & Meyer, 1963).

Koslofsky, C., *The Reformation of the Dead: Death and Ritual in Early Modern Germany, 1450–1700* (Basingstoke: Palgrave, 2000).

Kraege, J.-D., 'Luther théologien de la musique', *Etudes théologiques et religieuses*, 58 (1983), pp. 449–63.

Krieger, C. and Lienhard, M., eds, *Martin Bucer and Sixteenth Century Europe – Actes du colloque de Strasbourg (28–31 août 1991)*, 2 vols (Leiden: Brill, 1993).

Krummel, D. W. and Sadie, S., *Music Printing and Publishing* (Basingstoke: Macmillan, 1990).

Le Huray, P., *Music and the Reformation in England, 1549–1660* (London: Herbert Jenkins, 1967; repr. Cambridge: Cambridge University Press, 1978).

Leaver, R. A., *The Liturgy and Music: A Study of the Use of the Hymn in Two Liturgical Traditions* (Bramcote, Notts.: Grove Books, 1976).

— 'The Date of Coverdale's *Goostly psalmes*', *Internationale Arbeitsgemeinschaft für Hymnologie Bulletin*, 9 (1981), pp. 58–63.

— 'The Lutheran Reformation', in Fenlon, I. A., ed., *The Renaissance* (Macmillan: Basingstoke, 1989), pp. 263–85.

— *'Goostly psalmes and spirituall songes': English and Dutch Metrical Psalms from Coverdale to Utenhove 1535–1566* (Oxford: Clarendon Press, 1991).

— 'Music and Lutheranism', in Butt, J., ed., *The Cambridge Companion to Bach* (Cambridge: Cambridge University Press, 1997), pp. 35–45.

— *Luther's Liturgical Music: Principles and Implications* (Grand Rapids and Cambridge: Eerdmans, 2007).

Lenselink, S. J., *De Nederlandse psalmberijmingen in de 16e eeuw van de Souterliedekens tot Datheen met hun voorgangers in Duitsland en Frankrijk* (Assen: Van Gorcum, 1959).

Leonard, A., *Nails in the Wall: Catholic Nuns in Reformation Germany* (Chicago and London: University of Chicago Press, 2005).

Lerner, E. R., 'Some Motet Interpolations in the Catholic Mass', *Journal of the American Musicological Society*, 14 (1961), pp. 24–30.

Lewis, M. S., *Antonio Gardano, Venetian Music Printer – 1538–1569*, 3 vols (New York and London: Garland [vols 1–2]; Routledge [vol. 3], 1988–2005).

Lienhard, M., 'La société strasbourgeoise et la Réformation au XVIe siècle', *Etudes théologiques et religieuses*, 54 (1979), pp. 89–97.

— 'Bucer et la Tétrapolitaine', *Bulletin de la Société de l'histoire du protestantisme français*, 126 (1980), pp. 269–86.

— 'Catherine Zell, née Schütz', in Séguenny, A., ed., *Bibliotheca Dissidentium : Répertoire des non-conformistes religieux des seizième et dix-septième siècles*, Tome 1: *Johannes Campanus, Christian Entfelder, Justus Velsius, Catherine Zell-Schütz* (Baden-Baden: Valentin Koerner, 1980), pp. 111–15.

— 'Jakob Sturm', in Greschat, M., ed., *Gestalten der Kirchengeschichte*, Band. 5: *Die Reformationszeit I* (Stuttgart: Kohlhammer-Verlag, 1981), pp. 289–306.

— 'Le combat de Bucer contre la messe : Le Traité *De Caena Dominica* (1524)', in Augustijn, C., Fraenkel, P., and Lienhard, M., eds, *Martini Buceri Opera Latina*, 5 vols (Leiden: Brill, 1982–2000), vol. 1, pp. 3–15.

— 'Prier au XVIe siècle. Regard sur le Biblisch Bettbüchlin du Strasbourgeois Othon Brunfels', *Revue d'histoire et de philosophie religieuses*, 66 (1986), pp. 43–55.

— 'Thomas Murner et la Réformation', in *Thomas Murner: Elsässischer Theologe und Humanist, 1475–1537* (Karlsruhe: Badische Landesbibliothek, 1987), pp. 51–62.

— 'Une Strasbourgeoise du XVIe siècle hors du commun : Catherine Zell', *Saisons d'Alsace*, 97 (1987), pp. 67–70.

Lightfoot, J. B., ed., *The Apostolic Fathers*, 5 vols (London: Macmillan, 1889).

Livet, G. and Rapp, F., eds, *Histoire de Strasbourg des origines à nos jours*, 4 vols (Strasbourg: Editions des Dernières Nouvelles de Strasbourg, 1980–82).

— *Strasbourg au cœur religieux du XVIe siècle* (Strasbourg: Istra, 1977).

Luther, M. (Knaake, J. C. F. et al., eds), *D. Martin Luthers Werke: Kritische Gesamtausgabe*, 73 vols (Weimar: Böhlau, 1883–).

— *D. Martin Luthers Werke: Kritische Gesamtausgabe – Briefwechsel*, 17 vols (Weimar: Böhlau, 1930–83).

Luther, M. (Pelikan, J. and Lehmann, T., eds), *Luther's Works: American Edition*, 55 vols (St Louis: Concordia; Philadelphia: Muehlenberg & Fortress, 1955–86).

Luther, M. (Plochmann, J., G. et al., eds), *Dr. Martin Luther's sämmtliche Werke*, 67 vols (Frankfurt am Main and Erlangen: Heyder & Zimmer, 1826–57).

Lütolf, M., ed., *Das Deutsche Kirchenlied. Kritische Gesamtausgabe der Melodien*, Abteilung II: *Geistliche Gesänge des deutschen Mittelalters: Melodien und Texte handschriftlicher überlieferung bis um 1530* (Kassel and New York: Bärenreiter, 2003–).

Macey, P., *Bonfire Songs: Savonarola's Musical Legacy* (Oxford: Clarendon Press, 1998).

MacCulloch, D., *Thomas Cranmer: A Life* (New Haven and London: Yale University Press, 1996).

McCrie, T., *History of the Progress and Suppression of the Reformation in Italy in the Sixteenth Century* (Edinburgh: Blackwood; London: Cadell, 1827).

McKee, E. A., *Reforming Popular Piety in Sixteenth-Century Strasbourg: Katharina Schütz Zell and Her Hymnbook*, Studies in Reformed Theology and History, vol. 2, no. 4 (Princeton: Princeton Theological Seminary, 1994).

— *Katharina Schütz Zell*, 2 vols (Leiden: Brill, 1999).

—, ed. and trans., *Katharina Schütz Zell. Church Mother: The Writings of a Protestant Reformer in Sixteenth-Century Germany* (Chicago: University of Chicago Press, 2006).

Marbach, C., *Carmina Scripturarum* (Strasbourg: Le Roux, 1907).

Marcus, K. H., 'Hymnody and Hymnals in Basel, 1526–1606', *The Sixteenth Century Journal*, 32 (2001), pp. 723–41.

Maren, J. W. van, *Marquard von Lindau – Die Zehe Gebot (Straßburg 1516 und 1520)* (Amsterdam: Rodophi, 1980).

Mariotte, J.-Y., *Les Sources manuscrites de l'histoire de Strasbourg,* tome 1 : *Des origines à 1790* (Strasbourg: Ville de Strasbourg, 2000).

Martens, H., 'Die Lieder der Hutterer und ihre Verbindung zum Meistersang im 16. Jahrhundert', *Jahrbuch für Volksliedforschung*, 26 (1981), pp. 31–43.

Martin, R. P., 'A Footnote to Pliny's Account of Christian Worship', *Vox Evangelica*, 3 (1964), pp. 51–7.

Matheson, P., ed., *The Collected Works of Thomas Müntzer* (Edinburgh: Clark, 1988), pp. 162–82.

Mazzio, C., *The Inarticulate Renaissance: Language Trouble in an Age of Eloquence* (Philadelphia: University of Pennsylvania Press, 2008).

Melanchthon, P. (Bretschneider, K. G. and Bindseil, H. E., eds), *Philippi Melanthonis Opera quae supersunt omnia*, 28 vols (Halle [Saxony-Anhalt] and Brunswick: Schwetschke, 1834–60).

Meretz, W., 'Die Melodie "in Bruder Veiten Ton" zu Stiefels erstem Lied', in *AKS Bericht* (journal of the Altkönigschule, Kronberg) (1975–76), pp. 18–20.

Meyer, C., *Les mélodies des églises protestantes de langue allemande : Catalogue descriptif des sources et édition critique des mélodies* : I. *Les mélodies publiées à Strasbourg (1524–1547)* (Baden-Baden and Bouxwiller: Koerner, 1987).

— '*Vesperarum precum officia.* L'office des vêpres à l'époque de la Réforme', *Revue d'histoire et de philosophie religieuses*, 70 (1990), pp. 433–48.

— 'Gesangbuch, darin begriffen sind … Martin Bucer et le chant liturgique', in Krieger, C. and Lienhard, M., eds, *Martin Bucer and Sixteenth Century Europe – Actes du colloque de Strasbourg (28–31 août 1991)*, 2 vols (Leiden: Brill, 1993), vol. 2, pp. 214–25.

Midelfort, H. C. E., *A History of Madness in Sixteenth-Century Germany* (Stanford: Stanford University Press, 1999).

Miles, B., 'Wolfgang Capito's *Warning of the ministers of the Word and the brethren at Strasbourg to the brethren of the regions and cities of the [Swiss] Confederation against the blasphemous disputation of Brother Konrad, provincial of the Augustinian Order*', in Rummel E. and Kooistra, M., eds, *Reformation Sources: The Letters of Wolfgang Capito and his Fellow Reformers in Alsace and Switzerland* (Toronto: Centre for Reformation and Renaissance Studies, 2007), pp. 177–200.

Miller, C. A., 'Erasmus on Music', *The Musical Quarterly*, 56 (1966), pp. 332–49.

Moeller, B., 'L'Édit strasbourgeois sur la prédication du 1er décembre 1523 dans son contexte historique', in Livet, G. and Rapp, F., eds, *Strasbourg au cœur religieux du XVIe siècle* (Strasbourg: Istra, 1977).

F. J. Mone, 'Ueber die Armenpflege v. 13. bis 16. Jahrhundert in Konstanz, Günthersthal, Straßburg, Bretten, Baden, Bruchsal', *Zeitschrift für die Geschichte des Oberrheins*, 1 (1850), pp. 129–163.

Monson, C. A., 'The Council of Trent Revisited', *Journal of the American Musicological Society*, 55 (2002), pp. 1–37.

Moser, H. J., ed., *65 Deutsche Lieder für vier- bis fünfstimmigen gemischten Chor a cappella nach dem Liederbuch von Peter Schöffer und Mathias Apiarus (Biener) (Straßburg spätestens 1536)* (Wiesbaden: Breitkopf & Härtel, 1967).

Müller, H.-C. and Davies, S., 'Greiter, Matthias', in Root, D., ed., *Grove Music Online* (www.oxfordmusiconline.com) (accessed 28 January 2011).

Müller, J. T., *Hymnologisches Handbuch zum Gesangbuch der Brüdergemeine* (Herrnhut: Vereins für Brüdergeschichte, 1916).

Mullinax, A. B., 'Martin Bucer and the "Strasbourg Song Book", 1541' (Master of Church Music diss., Southern Baptist Theological Seminary, 1985).

— 'Musical Diversity in Reformation Strasbourg: Martin Bucer's *Strasbourg Song Book* (1541), *The Hymn*, 45 (1994), pp. 9–13.

'Musik in Bern zwischen Spätmittelalter und Reformation', Catalogue of the exhibition at Univerversitätsbibliothek, Bern, 29 June to 13 October 2007.

Naphy, W. G., 'Calvin's Geneva', in McKim, D., ed., *The Cambridge Companion to John Calvin* (Cambridge: Cambridge University Press, 2004), pp. 25–37.

Neue Deutsche Biographie, dreizehnter Band (Berlin: Duncker & Humblot, 1982), pp. 435–7.

Oberlé, R., *La vie quotidienne en Alsace au temps de la Renaissance* (Strasbourg: Oberlin, 1983).

Oettinger, R. W., 'Ludwig Senfl and the Judas Trope: Composition and Religious Toleration at the Bavarian Court', *Early Music History*, 20 (2001), pp. 199–225.

— *Music as Propaganda in the German Reformation* (Aldershot: Ashgate, 2001).

— 'Thomas Murner, Michael Stifel, and Songs as Polemic in the Early Reformation', *Journal of Musicological Research*, 22 (2003), pp. 45–100.

Old, H. O., *The Patristic Roots of Reformed Worship* (Zurich: Theologischer Verlag, 1975).

Olin J. C., ed., *Christian Humanism and the Reformation – Selected Writings of Erasmus*, 2nd edn (New York: Fordham University Press, 1975).

Osiander, A. (Müller, G., Seebass, G., et al., eds), *Andrias Osiander d. Ä. Gesamtausgabe*, 10 vols (Gütersloh: Gütersloher Verlagshaus Mohn, 1975–97).

Østrem, E. et al., eds, *The Arts and the Cultural Heritage of Martin Luther* (Copenhagen: Museum Tusculanum Press, 2003).

Pauck, W., *Melanchthon and Bucer* (Philadelphia: Westminster Press, 1969).

Petersen, N. H., 'Lutheran Tradition and the Medieval Latin Mass', in Østrem, E. et al., eds, *The Arts and the Cultural Heritage of Martin Luther* (Copenhagen: Museum Tusculanum Press, 2003), pp. 35–49.

Pettegree, A., *Reformation and the Culture of Persuasion* (Cambridge: Cambridge University Press, 2005).

—, ed., *The Reformation World* (London and New York: Routledge, 2000).

Peuckert, W.-E., *Die grosse Wende: Das Apokalyptische Saeculum und Luther. Geistesgeschichte und Volkskunde* (Hamburg: Claassen & Goverts, 1948).

Pflieger, A., *Liturgicae orationis concordantia verbalia, pars prima* (Freiburg: Herder, 1963).

Pfrunder, P., *Pfaffen Ketzer Totenfresser. Fastnachtskultur der Reformationszeit: Die Berner Spiele von Niklaus Manuel* (Zurich: Chronos, 1989).

Phillips, D., *Beguines in Medieval Strasburg: A Study of the Social Aspect of Beguine Life* (Stanford: Edward Brothers, 1941).

Pidoux, P., *Le Psautier huguenot du XVI*[e] *siècle*, 2 vols (Basel: Bärenreiter, 1962).

Pils, H., Ruderer, S., and Schaffrodt, P., *Martin Bucer (1491–1551) Bibliographie* (Gütersloh Verlagshaus: Gütersloh, 2005).

Poll, G. J. van de, *Martin Bucer's Liturgical Ideas: The Strasburg Reformer and his Connection with the Liturgies of the Sixteenth Century* (Assen, Netherlands: Van Gorcum, 1954).

Pollet, J. V., *Martin Bucer – Études sur la correspondance*, 2 vols (Paris: Presses Universitaires de France, 1958–62).

Puff, H., *Sodomy in Reformation Germany and Switzerland, 1400–1600* (Chicago and London: University of Chicago Press, 2003).

Ræuber, E., *Inventaire Général des Archives de la Ville de Strasbourg antérieurs à 1790* (Strasbourg: Istra, 1929).

Rapp, F., *Réformes et Réformation à Strasbourg : Église et société dans le diocèse de Strasbourg (1450–1525)* (Paris: Ophrys, 1974).

Reese, G., *Music in the Renaissance* (New York: Norton, 1954).

Rhenanus, B. (Horawitz, A. and Hartfelder, K., eds), *Briefwechsel des Beatus Rhenanus* (Leipzig: Teubner, 1886).

Richter, A. L. and Friedberg, E., eds, *Corpus Iuris Canonici*, 2 vols (Graz: Akademische Druck, 1959).

Riederer, J. B., *Nachrichten zur Kirchen- Gelehrten- und Bücher-Geschichte; aus gedruckten und ungedruckten Schriften*, 4 vols (Altdorf: Schüpfel, 1764–68).

Ritter, F., *Répertoire bibliographique des livres imprimés en Alsace aux XV*[e] *et XVI*[e] *siècles*, 4 vols (Strasbourg: Heitz, 1937–60).

— *Histoire de l'imprimerie alsacienne aux XV*[e] *et XVI*[e] *siècles* (Strasbourg: Le Roux, 1955).

Robinson, H., ed., *The Zurich Letters (second series)* (Cambridge: Cambridge University Press, 1845).

Robinson-Hammerstein, H., 'The Lutheran Reformation and its Music', in Robinson-Hammerstein, H., ed., *The Transmission of Ideas in the Lutheran Reformation* (Dublin: Irish Academic Press, 1989), pp. 141–71.

Röhrich, T. W., *Geschichte der Reformation im Elsass und besonders in Strassburg: nach gleichzeitigen Quellen bearbeitet*, 3 vols (Strasbourg: Heitz, 1830–32).

— *Mittheilungen aus der Geschichte der evangelischen Kirche des Elsasses*, 3 vols (Paris and Strasbourg: Treuttel und Würtz, 1855).

Roper, C. M., 'The Strasbourg French Psalters, 1539–1553' (DMA diss., University of Southern California, 1972).

Roper, L., 'Martin Luther's Body', *American Historical Review*, 115 (2010), pp. 351–84.

Rott, H.-G., 'Probleme der Straßburger Historiographie des 16. Jahrhunderts: Dr. Nikolaus Wurmser, Dekan des St. Thomaskapitels, und sein Protokoll (1513–1524)', in Andermann, K., ed., *Historiographie am Oberrhein im Späten Mittelalter und in der Frühen Neuzeit* (Sigmaringen: Thorbecke, 1988), pp. 193–204.

Rott, J., 'Note sur l'imprimerie alsacienne aux XVe et XVIe siècles', *Revue d'Alsace*, 95 (1956), pp. 63–76.

— 'Documents strasbourgeois concernant Calvin', *Revue d'histoire et de philosophie religieuses*, 44 (1964), pp. 290–335.

— 'La Réforme à Nuremberg et à Strasbourg. Contacts et contrastes', in Chastel, A. et al., *Hommage à Dürer. Strasbourg et Nuremberg dans la première moitié du XVIe siècle* (Strasbourg: Istra, 1972), pp. 91–142.

— 'L'Église des réfugiés de langue française à Strasbourg au XVIe siècle : aperçu de son histoire, en particulier de ses crises à partir de 1541', *Bulletin de la Société de l'histoire du protestantisme français*, 122 (1976), pp. 525–50.

— 'Koepf(f)el, Wolfgang', in Baechler, C. et al., eds, *Nouveau dictionnaire de biographie alsacienne*, 49 vols (Strasbourg: Fédération des sociétés d'histoire et d'archéologie d'Alsace, 1982–2007), vol. 22, pp. 2069–71.

Rublack, H.-C., 'The Song of Contz Anahans: Communication and Revolt in Nördlingen, 1525', in Hsia, R. P., ed., *The German People and the Reformation* (Ithaca and London: Cornell University Press, 1988), pp. 102–20.

Rublack, U. C., *Reformation Europe* (Cambridge: Cambridge University Press, 2005).

Rummel, E., ed., *The Electronic Capito Project* (online resource: http://cf.itergateway.org/capito).

Rummel, E. and Kooistra, M., eds, *Reformation Sources: The Letters of Wolfgang Capito and his Fellow Reformers in Alsace and Switzerland* (Toronto: Centre for Reformation and Renaissance Studies, 2007).

Savonarola, G. (Firpo, L., ed.), *Prediche sopra Aggeo* (Rome: Belardetti, 1965).

— (Ghiglieri, P., ed.), *Prediche sopra Amos e Zaccaria*, 3 vols (Rome: Belardetti, 1971–72).

— (Ridolfi, R., ed.), *Prediche sopra Giobbe*, 2 vols (Rome: Belardetti, 1957).

— (Romano, V., ed.), *Prediche sopra i Salmi*, 2 vols (Rome: Belardetti, 1969–74).

Schalk, C., *Music in Early Lutheranism: Shaping the Tradition (1524–1672)* (St Louis: Concordia, 2001).

Schmid, M. H., *Mathias Greiter: Das Schicksal eines Deutschen Musikers zur Reformationszeit* (Aichach: Mayer & Söhne, 1976).

Schmidt, A., ed., *Aeneas Silvius: Germania, und Jakob Wimpfeling 'Responsa et replicae ad Eneam Silvium'* (Cologne: Böhlau, 1962).

Schmidt, C. G. A., *Histoire littéraire de l'Alsace à la fin du XVe et au commencement du XVIe siècle*, 2 vols (Paris: Sandoz & Fischbacher, 1879).

— 'Die Strassburger Beginenhäuser im Mittelalter', *Alsatia*, 7 (1858–61), pp. 149–248.

Schmidt, C. G. A., ed., *Répertoire bibliographique strasbourgeois*, 8 vols (Strasbourg: Heitz und Mündel, 1896), vol. 8: *Matthias Schürer – 1508–1520*.

Schott, A. and Bihlmeyer, P., eds, *Das vollständige Römische Meßbuch* (Freiburg im Breisgau: Herder, 1927).

Schueller, H. M., *The Idea of Music: An Introduction to Musical Aesthetics in Antiquity and the Middle Ages* (Kalamazoo, MI: Medieval Institute Publications, Western Michigan University, 1988).

Scribner, R. W., 'Flugblatt und Analphabetentum. Wie kam der gemeine Mann zu reformatorischen Ideen?', in Köhler, H. J., ed., *Flugschriften als Massenmedium der Reformationszeit* (Stuttgart: Klett-Cotta, 1981), pp. 65–76.

— *For the Sake of Simple Folk* (Oxford: Oxford University Press, 1981).

— 'Ritual and Reformation', in Hsia, R. P., ed., *The German People and the Reformation* (Ithaca and London: Cornell University Press, 1988), pp. 122–44.

Sehling, E. et al., *Die evangelischen Kirchenordnungen des XVI. Jahrhunderts*, 18 vols (Leipzig: Reisland; Tübingen: Mohr, 1902–).

Sessions, K. C., 'Song Pamphlets: Media Changeover in Sixteenth-Century Publicization', in Tyson, G. P. and Wagonheim, S. S., eds, *Print and Culture in the Renaissance* (Newark: University of Delaware Press; London: Associated University Presses, 1986), pp. 110–19.

Smend, J., *Die evangelischen deutschen Messen bis zu Luthers Deutscher Messe* (Göttingen: Vandenhoeck, 1896).

— *Der erste evangelische Gottesdienst in Straßburg* (Strasbourg: Heitz, 1897).

Söll-Tauchert, S., *Hans Baldung Grien (1484/85–1545): Selbstbildnis und Selbstinszenierung* (Cologne: Böhlau, 2010).

Sohm, W., *Die Schule Johann Sturms und die Kirche Straßburgs in ihrem gegenseitigen Verhältnis 1530–1581* (Munich and Berlin: Oldenbourg, 1912).

Soltau, F. L. von, *Ein Hundert deutsche historische Volkslieder* (Leipzig: Weber, 1836; repr. Schrey, 1845; repr. Mayer, 1856).

Sowinski, B., ed., *Herzog Ernst: ein mittelalterliches Abenteuerbuch* (Stuttgart: Reclam, 1970).

Spinka, M., *John Hus: A Biography* (Princeton: Princeton University Press, 1968).

Spitz, L. W. and Tinsley, B. S., *Johann Sturm on Education* (St Louis: Concordia, 1995).

Stalmann, J. et al., eds, *Das Deutsche Kirchenlied. Kritische Gesamtausgabe der Melodien. Abteilung III: Die Melodien aus gedruckten Quellen bis 1680* (Kassel: Bärenreiter, 1993–).

Stanford, C. A., *Commemorating the Dead in Late Medieval Strasbourg: The Cathedral's Book of Donors and its Use (1320–1521)* (Farnham: Ashgate, 2013).

Steinmetz, D. C., *Reformers in the Wings: From Geiler von Kaysersberg to Theodore Beza*, 2nd edn (Oxford: Oxford University Press, 2001).

Stephens, W. P., *The Theology of Huldrych Zwingli* (Oxford: Clarendon Press, 1986).

Strauss, G., *Manifestations of Discontent in Germany on the Eve of the Reformation* (Bloomington and London: Indiana University Press, 1971).

— 'Success and Failure in the German Reformation', *Past & Present*, 67 (1975), pp. 30–63.

— *Luther's House of Learning: Indoctrination of the Young in the German Reformation* (Baltimore and London: Johns Hopkins University Press, 1978).

Stupperich, R., 'Martin Bucers Gebrauch des kanonischen Rechts', in Kroon, M. and Lienhard, M., eds, *Horizons européens de la Réforme en Alsace : Mélanges offerts à Jean Rott pour son 65e anniversaire* (Strasbourg: Istra, 1980), pp. 241–52.

Sturm, J. (Rott, J., ed. and trans.), *Classicae epistolae. Siue, Scholae argentinenses restitutae* (Paris: Droz, 1938).

Taruskin, R., *The Oxford History of Western Music*, 6 vols (Oxford: Oxford University Press, 2005).

Terry, R. R., ed., *Calvin's First Psalter [1539]* (London: Benn, 1932).

Tertullianus, Q. S. F. (Glover, T. R., trans.), *Apology* (London: Heinemann; Cambridge, MA: Harvard University Press, 1966).

Trocmé-Latter, D., '"May those who know nothing be content to listen": Loys Bourgeois's *Advertissement* to the Psalms (1551)', *Reformation and Renaissance Review*, 11 (2009), pp. 335–47.

— 'The Psalms as a Mark of Protestantism: the Introduction of Liturgical Psalm-Singing in Geneva', *Plainsong & Medieval Music*, 20 (2011), pp. 145–63.

— 'Thieves, Drunkards, and Womanisers? Perceptions of Church Musicians in Early Reformation Strasbourg', in Hobbs, R. G. and Noblesse-Rocher, A., eds, *Bible, histoire et société – Mélanges offerts à Bernard Roussel* (Turnhout: Brepols, 2013), pp. 383–99.

Türler, H., 'Drei Lieder aus dem 16. Jahrhundert', *Neues Berner Taschenbuch*, 9 (1904 [published 1903]), pp. 240–265.

Tyson, G. P. and Wagonheim, S. S., eds, *Print and Culture in the Renaissance* (Newark: University of Delaware Press; London: Associated University Presses, 1986).

Universal Short Title Catalogue (online resource: www.ustc.ac.uk).

Veit, P., 'Gottes Bild und Bild des Menschen in den Liedern Luthers', in Dürr, A. and Killy, W., eds, *Das protestantische Kirchenlied im 16. und 17. Jahrhundert* (Wiesbaden: Harrassowitz, 1986), pp. 9–24.

— *Das Kirchenlied in der Reformation Martin Luthers* (Stuttgart: Steiner, 1986).

— 'Das Gesangbuch als Quelle lutherischer Frömmigkeit', *Archiv für Reformationsgeschichte*, 79 (1988), pp. 206–29.

— 'Le chant, la Réforme et la Bible', in Bedouelle, G. and Roussel, B., eds, *Le temps des Réformes et la Bible*, (Paris: Beauchesne, 1989), pp. 659–81.

— 'Piété, chant et lecture : les pratiques religieuses dans l'Allemagne protestante à l'époque moderne', *Revue d'histoire moderne et contemporaine*, 37 (1990), pp. 624–41.

Virck, H. et al., eds, *Politische Correspondenz der Stadt Strassburg im Zeitalter der Reformation*, 5 vols (Strasbourg: Trübner, 1882–1933).

Vogeleis, M., *Quellen und Bausteine zu einer Geschichte der Musik und des Theaters im Elsass, 500–1800* (Strasbourg: Le Roux, 1911; repr. Geneva: Minkoff, 1979).

Wackernagel, K. E. P., *Das deutsche Kirchenlied von Martin Luther bis auf Nicolaus Herman und Ambrosius Plaurer* (Stuttgart: Liesching, 1841).

— *Bibliographie zur Geschichte des deutschen Kirchenliedes im XVI. Jahrundert* (Frankfurt am Main: Hender & Zimmer, 1855).

— *Das deutsche Kirchenlied von der ältesten Zeit bis zu Anfang des XVII. Jahrhunderts*, 5 vols (Leipzig: Teubner, 1864–77; repr. Hildesheim: Olms, 1964).

Waller, J., *A Time to Dance, a Time to Die: The Extraordinary Story of the Dancing Plague of 1518* (Royston, Herts.: Icon Books, 2008).

Wandel, L. P., *Voracious Idols and Violent Hands: Iconoclasm in Reformation Zurich, Strasbourg, and Basel* (Cambridge: Cambridge University Press, 1994).

— *The Eucharist in the Reformation: Incarnation and Liturgy* (Cambridge: Cambridge University Press, 2006).

Webber, G. A., *North German Church Music in the Age of Buxtehude* (Oxford: Clarendon Press, 1996).

Weeda, R., *Le Psautier de Calvin* (Turnhout: Brepols, 2002).

Weeks, A., *German Mysticism from Hildegard of Bingen to Ludwig Wittgenstein – A Literary and Intellectual History* (New York: State University of New York Press, 1993).

Wendel, F., *L'Église de Strasbourg. Sa constitution et son organisation 1532–1535* (Paris: Presses Universitaires de France, 1942).

Weyer, M., 'L'*Apologie chrétienne* du réformateur strasbourgeois Matthieu Zell ("*Christeliche Verantwortung*", 1523)', 3 vols (Doctor ès Sciences Religieuses thesis, Université des Sciences Humaines de Strasbourg, 1981).

— 'Martin Bucer et les Zell : Une solidarité critique', in Krieger, C. and Lienhard, M., eds, *Martin Bucer and Sixteenth Century Europe – Actes du colloque de Strasbourg (28–31 août 1991)*, 2 vols (Leiden: Brill, 1993), vol. 1, pp. 275–95.

Willis, J., *Church Music and Protestantism in Post-Reformation England: Discourses, Sites and Identities* (Farnham: Ashgate, 2010).

Wilsdorf, C. et al., *La Musique en Alsace, hier et aujourd'hui* (Strasbourg: Istra, 1970).

Wilton, P., 'Hymn', in Latham, A., ed., *The Oxford Companion to Music* (www.oxfordmusiconline.com) (accessed 23 March 2010).

Wolff[-Hoffmann], A., 'Le recueil de cantiques de Catherine Zell 1534–1536', 2 vols (Master's diss., Université des Sciences Humaines de Strasbourg, 1986).

Wolff-Hoffmann, A., 'L'Influence de l'hymnodie strasbourgeoise sur l'Eglise d'Angleterre à ses débuts, par l'intégration de mélodies dans des recueils de cantiques publiés entre 1535 et 1610', 2 vols (Master's diss., Université de Paris X Nanterre, 2006).

—, 'Which Texts for Travelling Tunes? The Metrical Psalms which Crossed the Channel from 1535 to 1603', paper presented at the Society for Reformation Studies 18th Annual Conference (Westminster College, Cambridge, 13–15 April 2011).

Wright, D. F., ed., *Common Places of Martin Bucer* (Appleford, Abingdon: Sutton Courtenay Press, 1972).

Wycliffe, J. (Loserth, J., ed.), *Opus Evangelicum*, 4 vols (London: Trübner, 1895–96).

Young, C. W., 'School Music in Sixteenth-Century Strasbourg', *Journal of Research in Music Education*, 10.2 (1962), pp. 129–36.

Young, W., 'Effects of the Reformation on Church Music in 16th-Century Strasbourg', *Church Music*, 69.2 (1969), pp. 16–24.

— 'Music Printing in Sixteenth-Century Strasbourg', *Renaissance Quarterly*, 24 (1971), pp. 486–501.

Zahn, J., *Die Melodien der deutschen evangelischen Kirchenlieder*, 6 vols (Reinheim: Lokay, 1889–93; repr. Hildesheim: Olms, 1968).

Zorzin, A., 'Andreas Bodenstein von Karlstadt (1486–1541)', in Lindberg, C., ed., *The Reformation Theologians: An Introduction to Theology in the Early Modern Period* (Malden, MA: Blackwell, 2001), pp. 327–37.

Zwingli, H. (Egli, E. et al., eds), *Huldreich Zwinglis Sämtliche Werke*, 14 vols (Berlin: Schwetschke; Leipzig: Nachfolger; Zurich: Berichthaus; Zurich: Theologischer Verlag, 1905–56).

Zwingli, H. (Schuler, J. M. and Schulthess, J.), *Huldrici Zuinglii Opera*, 8 vols (Zurich: Schulthess, 1829–42).

Chronicles

Dacheux, L., ed., *Annales de Sébastien Brant (suite)*. Fragments des anciennes chroniques d'Alsace, IV (Strasbourg: Schultz, 1901) (also published in *Bulletin de la Société pour la conservation des monuments historiques d'Alsace*, 2nd series, 19 (1899), pp. 33–260).

— *Fragments de diverses vieilles chroniques*, Fragments des anciennes chroniques d'Alsace, IV (Strasbourg: Schultz, 1901) (also published in *Bulletin de la Société pour la conservation des monuments historiques d'Alsace*, 2nd series, 18 (1897), pp. 1–181).

— *La Chronique strasbourgeoise de Sébald Büheler*, Fragments des anciennes chroniques d'Alsace, I (Strasbourg: Schultz, 1887) (also published in *Bulletin de la Société pour la conservation des monuments historiques d'Alsace*, 2nd series, 13 (1887–88), 'Mémoires', pp. 21–150).

— *La Petite chronique de la cathédrale*, Fragments des anciennes chroniques d'Alsace, I (Strasbourg: Schultz, 1887) (also published in *Bulletin de la Société pour la conservation des monuments historiques d'Alsace*, 2nd series, 13 (1887–88), 'Mémoires', pp. 3–20).

— *Les Chroniques strasbourgeoises de Jacques Trausch et de Jean Wencker. Les Annales de Sébastien Brant*, Fragments des anciennes chroniques d'Alsace, III (Strasbourg: Imprimerie Strasbourgeoise, 1892) (also published in *Bulletin de la Société pour la conservation des monuments historiques d'Alsace*, 2nd series, 15 (1892), 'Mittheilungen', pp. 1–280).

Fritsch, P., ed., *Die Strassburger Chronik des Johannes Stedel* (Strasbourg: Sebastian Brant-Verlag, 1934).

Meister, A. and Ruppel, A., 'Die Strassburger Chronik des Johann Georg Saladin', in *Bulletin de la Société pour la conservation des monuments historiques d'Alsace*, 2nd series, 23 (1911), pp. 182–435.

Reuss, R., ed., 'La Chronique strasbourgeoise de Jean-Jacques Meyer', *Bulletin de la Société pour la conservation des monuments historiques d'Alsace*, 2nd series, 8 (1872), pp. 121–289.

— *Les Collectanées de Daniel Specklin, chronique strasbourgeoise du seizième siècle*, Fragments des anciennes chroniques d'Alsace, II (Strasbourg: Noiriel, 1890) (also published in *Bulletin de la Société pour la conservation des monuments historiques d'Alsace*, 2nd series, 13 (1887–88), 'Mémoires', pp. 157–360, and 14 (1889), 'Mittheilungen', pp. 1–178 and 201–404).

— *Les Éphémérides de Jacques de Gottesheim, docteur en droit, prébendier du grand-chœur de la cathédrale (1524–1543)*, Fragments des anciennes chroniques d'Alsace, IV (Strasbourg: Schultz, 1901) (also published as *Bulletin de la Société pour la conservation des monuments historiques d'Alsace*, 2nd series, 19 (1899), pp. 261–81).

— 'Strassburg im sechszehnten Jahrhundert, 1500–1591: Auszug aus der Imlin'schen Familienchronik', *Alsatia*, 10 (1873–74), pp. 363–476.

Schmidt, C. G. A., 'Note sur le couvent et l'église des dominicains de Strasbourg jusqu'au seizième siècle', *Bulletin de la Société pour la conservation des monuments historiques d'Alsace*, 2nd series, 9 (1874–75), pp. 161–222.

Stenzel, K., ed., *Die Straßburger Chronik des Hieronymus Gebwiler* (Berlin and Leipzig: Grunter, 1926).

Straub, A., *Geschichtskalender des Hochstiftes und des Münsters von Strassburg* (Rixheim: Sutter, 1891).

Select Bibliography of Fifteenth- and Sixteenth-Century Publications (see also Appendices A and E)

Note This list is in order of chronology, then name. Libraries and classmarks are shown when they are known. These details are not intended to be exhaustive, but merely provide an indication of where such items can be consulted, in the UK if possible, and elsewhere if not.

von Simmern, R., *Breviarium Argentinense* (Strasbourg: Reyser, 1478; Grüninger, 1489; Prüss, 1511).
D Mbs – 2 Inc.c.a. 741 m-1/9 and online at http://daten.digitale-sammlungen.de/~db/0002/bsb00026250/images (1478 edition);
D Mbs – Inc.c.a. 63-1/4 and online at
http://daten.digitale-sammlungen.de/~db/0002/bsb00026672/images (1489 edition)

Brant, S., *Das Narrenschiff* (Basel: Olpe, 1494; reprinted many times thereafter).
D Dl – Ink.394.4 (and online at http://www.slub-dresden.de/sammlungen/digitale-sammlungen/werkansicht/cache.off?tx_dlf[id]=11823&tx_dlf[page]=1&tx_dlf[pointer]=0
Uor sant Ursulen schifflin (Strasbourg: Küster, 1497). **GB Lbl – Hirsch III.1065**

Agenda siue Exequiale sacramentorum. Et eorum que in ecclesiis aguntur (Strasbourg: Prüss, 1505; Beck, 1508; Beck, 1513).
F Sn – R.102.393 (1513 edition)

Erasmus, D., *Moriae Encomivm Erasmi Roterodami Declamatio* (Strasbourg: Schürer, 1511).

Virdung, S., *MVsica getutscht vnd auszgezoge[n] durch Sebastianu[m] virdung Priesters von Amberg vnd alles gesang ausz den note[n] in die tabulature[n] diser benante[n] dryer Jnstrume[n]te[n] der Orgeln: der Laute[n]: vnd d[er] Flöten transferieren zu lerne[n]* (Strasbourg: n.p., 1511).
GB Lbl – K.8.c.9

Adelphus, J., *Seque[n]tiarum lucule[n]ta interpretatio: nedu[m] scholasticis / sed & ecclesiasticis cognitu necessaria* (Strasbourg: Schürer, 1513; repr. Knobloch, 1519). **GB Cu – Norton.d.111** (1513 edition)

Adelphus, J. *Hymni de tempore & de sanctis: in ea[m] forma[m] qua a suis autoribus scripti sunt denuo redacti* (Strasbourg: Knobloch, 1513; repr. 1516, 1518, 1519). **GB Cu – Norton.d.111** (1513 edition); **F Sn – R.101.969** (1513 edition); **D Mbs – Rar 357**, and online: http://daten.digitale-sammlungen.de/bsb00012214/image_278 (1513 edition); **D Mbs – 4 Liturg. 8**, and online: http://www.mdz-nbn-resolving.de/urn/resolver.pl?urn=urn:nbn:de:bvb:12-bsb10164179-8 (1519 edition)

Piccolomini, E. S. and Wimpheling, J., *Germania Enee Silvij, in qua, candide lector, continentur. Grauamina germanicę nationis. Confutatio eorundem cum replicis* (Strasbourg: Beck, 1515).

Die zehe[n] gebot in disem büch erclert vnd vßgelegt durch etlich hochberümbte lerer (Strasbourg: Grüninger, 1516).

Luther, M., *Ad Leonem X. Pontificem Maximvm: Resolutiones disputationum de uirtute indulgentiaru[m]* (Strasbourg: Schürer, 1519).

Luther, M., *Ein Sermon von dem Gebeet vnd Procession. yn der Creützwochen: auch sunst on allem gebet durch dz ga[n]tz Jar wie sich der me[n]sch darin halte[n] sol, allen christen me[n]sche[n] nützlich vnd selig zü wissen* (Strasbourg: Knobloch, 1519).

Eeyn new lyed von den falschen Preedigern. jn des Binzenawers thon (Strasbourg: Flach, 1520).

Murner, T., *Ein christliche vnd briederliche ermanung zu dem hochgelerten doctor Martino luter Augustiner orde[n] zu Wittemburg* (Strasbourg: Grüninger, 1520).

Murner, T., *Antwurt vnd klag mit entschuldigung doctor Murners wider bruder Michel stifel weyt von eßlingen da heim, vff das stüfelbuch so er wider meyn lied gemachet hat, daruß er des lieds den rechten thon erlernen mag* (Strasbourg: Grüninger, 1522).

Murner, T., *Von dem grossen Lutherischen Narren wie in doctor Murner beschworen hat. &c.* (Strasbourg: Grüninger, 1522). **Gb Lbl – 11517.c.33**

Murner, T., *Ain new lied von dem vndergang des Christlichen glaubens Doct. Murner. jn[n] Brüder Veiten ton* (Augsburg: Steiner, 1523). **D Mbs – Res/4 P.o. germ. 229,52**

Stiefel, M., *Von der Christfoͤrmigen / rechtgegründten leer Doctoris Martini Luthers / ein überuß schoͤn kunstlich Lyed / sampt seiner neben vßlegung* (Strasbourg: Schott, 1522).

Stiefel, M., *Wider Doctor Murnars falsch erdycht Lyed: von dem vndergang Christlichs glaubens* (Strasbourg: Beck, 1522). **GB Lbl – 3905.d.107**; **D Mbs – Res/4 Polem. 3341,38**, and online: http://daten.digitale-sammlungen.de/bsb00052091/image_2

Fisher, J. (Cochlaeus, J., trans.), *Uon dem hochgelerten vn[nd] geistlichen Bischoff Johannes von Roffa vß engeland / seynes großen nutzlichen bůchs CXXXIX. artickel wid[er] M. Luther sein hie verteütscht zů nutz dem christlichen volck zů bedencke[n] irer selen selikeit* (Strasbourg: Grüninger, 1523).

J. Graff, *In disem tractetlin sind drey | hübsche lieder new gemacht in Christus namen | vo[n] Bapst Cardinal Bischoff prelate[n] / Pfaffe[n] | vnd Münch / darumb ich Joͤrg Graff be- | gnad bin mit einem priuilegio solchs mir | nit nach zů drucke[n] / wer solchs überfür | wolt ich beklagen nach lautung mei | nes priuilegiums* (Strasbourg: Prüss, 1523).

Zell, M., *Christeliche vera[n]twortung M. Matthes Zell von Keyserßberg Pfarrherrs vnd predigers im Münster zů Straßburg / vber Artickel jm vom Bischoͤfflichem Fiscal daselbs entgegen gesetzt / vnnd im rechten vbergeben* (Strasbourg: Köpfel, 1523).

Etlich Cristlich lider | Lobegesang / vn[nd] Psalm / dem rai- | nen wort Gottes gemeß / auß der | heylige[n] schrifft / durch mancher- | ley hochgelerter gemacht / in der | Kirchen zu singen / wie es dann | [z]um tayl berayt zu Wittenberg | in ubung ist (Nuremberg: Gutknecht, 1524). Facsimile published as an insert to *Jahrbuch für Liturgie und Hymnologie*, 2 (1956).

Facsimile of: *Eyn Enchiridion oder | Handbuchlein, eynem ytz- | lichen Christen fast nutzlich bey sich | zuhaben / zur stetter vbung vnd | trachtung geystlicher gesenge | vnd Psalmen / Recht- | schaffen vnd kunst- | lich verteutsch* (Erfurt: Loersfeld, 1524), published as *Das Erfurter Enchiridion* (Kassell: Bärenreiter, 1983). **GB Cu – MR250.e.95.9**

Facsimile of: *ENCHIRIDION | Oder eyn Handbuchlein / | eynem yetzlichen Christen fast nutzlich bey sich zuhaben / zur stettervbung | vnnd trachtung geystlicher ge- | senge / vnd Psalmen / Recht- | schaffen vnnd kunstlich | vertheutscht* (Erfurt: Maler, 1524; facs. repr. Erfurt: Gerhardt & Schreiber, 1848). **GB Lbl – 3456.aaa.64(1)**

Bucer, M., *Grund vn[nd] vrsach ausz gotlicher schrifft d[er] neüwerungen / an dem nachtmal des herren / so man die Mess nennet / Tauff / Feyrtagen / bildern vn[nd] gesang / in der gemein Christi / wan[n] die zůsamen kompt / durch vnnd auff das wort gottes / zů Straßburg fürgenomen* (Strasbourg: Köpfel, 1524).

Capito, W., *Verwarnung / der diener des worts / vnd der brüder zu Straßburg. An die Bruͤder von Landen vnd Stetten gemeiner Eidgnoßschafft. Wider die Gotslesterige Disputation Bruͤder Conradts Augustiner Ordens Prouincial* (Strasbourg: Köpfel; Augsburg: Ulhart, 1524).

Capito, W., *Was man hal- | ten / vnnd Antwurtten | soll / von der spaltung | zwischen Martin | Luther / vnnd | Andres Ca- | rolstadt* (Strasbourg: Köpfel, 1524).

Luther, M., *DAS ALTE Testament deutsch nach vrspringlicher Hebreischer warheit. Mit schöner / der schwersten oͤrter außlegung* (Strasbourg: Knobloch, 1524). **GB Lbl – 1407.g.19**

Luther, M., *DAs neuw Testament, recht grüntlich teutscht. Mit schoͤnen vorreden / vnd der schweresten oͤrteren kurtz / aber gůt / ausslegu[n]g* (Strasbourg: Knobloch, 1524). **GB Lbl – 3035.c.13**

Luther, M., *Der Psalter Teutsch. durch D. Martinus Luther* (Strasbourg: Knobloch, 1524). **GB Lbl – 3089.a.9**

Müntzer, T., *Deutsch Euangelisch Messze* (Allstedt: Müntzer, 1524). **D HAu – Pon Vg 646, QK**, and online at http://nbn-resolving.org/urn:nbn:de:gbv:3:1-120114

Das Tauffbuchlin / nach rechter Form vff Teütsch zu Tauffen (Strasbourg: n.p., 1524). **F Ssp – 16. 87, 4** (Wilhelmitana collection)

Manuel, N., *Eyn schön reygenlied im thon / Rusticus ambilem, Neüwlich geschmidet durch Meyster Hemerlin jm berg Ethna* (Strasbourg: Schürer Erben, 1524).

Zütphen, H. von (Müller, H.), *Eyn schön neüv Lied vom glauben vnnd Testament / auch von der bereytung zů dem tysch Gottes / zů nutz den vnerbauwenen / von eynem liebhaber Göttlicher warheit zů Straßburg gesungen vnd gedicht. Jn der Flam[m] weyß / oder in Hertzog Ernsten melody* (Strasbourg: Schürer Erben, 1524).

Zütphen, H. von (Müller, H.), *Jn disem lied wirstu verston | Wie allweg die geystlichen hon | Die krancken in der letsten not | Gefuͤret hand so ferr von Gott | Mit erschröcklichen worten vil | Aber yetz nůn zů disem zil | Finstu die rechte troͤstung gar | Jn disem dicht so nym du war | Wie man die krancken trösten sol, o Cristen mensch, betracht das wol, Das du die krancken troͤstest schon, und syngt man es ins Speten thon* (Strasbourg: Schürer Erben, 1524).

Das die papistische[n] opffermessen abzuthun: vnd dagegen das nachtmal Christi: Christlicher weisz vffzurichten sey Sampt eim kurtzen bericht: wie das zů der Apostelzeyten gehalten / vnd durch welche es zů solchem mißbrauch des opfferns kommen sey (Strasbourg: n.p., c. 1525). Available through H-J. Köhler's IDC microfiche series, fiche 1946, no. 4959.

Enchiridion geistlicher gesenge / so man yetzt (Gott zů lob) yn der kirchen syngt. Getzogen auß der heyligen geschrifft des ware[n] vnd heyligen Euangelions / welches jetzt von gottes gnaden wider auffgange[n] ist / vnd mit etzlichen gesenge[n] Gemehrt / Gebessert / vn[nd] mit fleyß Corrigyert / mit einer Vorrede Docto. Martini Luther (Strasbourg: Schürer Erben, 1525). **F Ssp – 16. 87, 12** (Wilhelmitana collection)

Gernoldt, W. *Das Aue Marie außgeleyt. | Der Engelisch grůssz würt außgeleydt Wie Gott Maria die reyne Meydt | Gegroͤsset hat in allen sachen | Dz sye Gott wolt groͤsser vn[nd] heylger mache[n] | Ir somen ist so gwaltig kummen Hat der Schlangen das haubt genum[m]en* (Strasbourg: Frölich, 1525?). **GB Lbl – 11517.aa.25**

Vogtherr, H., *Ein neuwes Euangelisch Lied in allem creütz Jedem Christenn gantz tröstlich Auß göttlicher schrifft gezogen. Jm Jar da man zalt tausent fünff hundert vnd. xxvj. &c.* (Strasbourg: Kornmann, 1526).

Psalter Teutsch mit M. Buceri vorrede 1526 (Basel: Petrus, 1526). **GB Cu – BSS.228.B26**

Warer verstand / von des herren Nachtmal. Vff die weyß zů singen / Es ist das hayl vns komen her. &c. (Strasbourg: Prüss, 1527). **CH Zz – Res 1041** (Alte Drucke collection). N.B.: This is mistakenly classified as a hymn book by *RISM DKL* (no. 1527^{10}).

Brunfels, O., *CATECHESIS PVERORVM, IN fide, literis & moribus. Ex probatißimis quibusq[ue] Authoribus* (Frankfurt: Egenolph, 1529). **GB Lbl – 3505.cc.22**

Bucer, M., *S. PSALMORVM | LIBRI QVINQVE AD EBRAI- | CAM VERITATEM VERSI, | ET FAMILIARI EX- | PLANATIONE | ELVCIDA- | TI | PER ARETIVM FELI- | NVM. THEOLO- | GVM* (Strasbourg: Ulricher, 1529; repr. 1532, 1547; Geneva: Stephan, 1554).

Bucer, M., *The Psalter of Dauid in Englishe purely a[n]d faithfully tra[n] slated aftir the texte of ffeline: euery Psalme hauynge his argument before / declarynge brefly thentente & substance of the wholl Psalme* (Antwerp: Keyser, 1530). **GB Lbl – C.17.a.2**. Facsimile published with the same title (Appleford, Abingdon: Sutton Courtenay Press, 1971).

Bucer, M. et al., *Bekandtnuß der vier frey vn[nd] Reichstatt / Straßburg / Costantz / Memmingen / vnd Lindaw* (Strasbourg: Schweintzer, 1531). [The Tetrapolitan Confession] **GB Lbl – 853.H.7**

Bucer, M. et al., *Schriftliche Beschirmung vnd verthedigung der selbigen Bekantnusz / gegen der Confutation vnd Widerlegung / so den gesandten der vier Stätten / vff bemeldtem Reichstage / offenlich fürgelesen / vnnd hie getrewlich einbracht ist* (Strasbourg: Schweintzer, 1531). [The Apology to the Tetrapolitan Confession] **GB Lbl – 3505.e.35**

Ein New Geseng buchlen (Bohemia: Buntzel & Wylmschwerer, 1531). **GB Lbl – C.61.f6**; microfilm: **PB Mic 39916**. Facsimile published as: Ameln, K., ed., *Gesangbuch der Böhmischen Brüder, 1531* (Kassel and Basel: Bärenreiter, 1957).

Dachser, J., *Form vnd Ordnung gaystlicher Gesang vnd Psalmen: mit sonderm Fleiß corrigiert auch zu rechtem Verstand punctirt und virguliert, welche Got dem Herren zu Lob und Eer gesungen werden* (Augsburg: Ulhart, 1533). **D Sl – R 16 For 2**

Epicedion Thomae Sporeri Musicorum Principis, Modulis musicis à Sixto Dittricho illustratum (Strasbourg: Schöffer & Apiarius, 1534). **D As – Tonk Sch 520–522**

Wittenbergische Gsangbüchli durch Johan. Waltern / Churfürstlichen von Sachsen senger meystern vff ein newes corrigiert / gebessert vnd gemeret (Strasbourg: Schöffer & Apiarius, 1534; repr. 1537). **Gb Lbl – K.1.c.15** (1534 edition); **D Mbs – Mus.pr.3** (1537 edition); **D As – Tonk Sch 520–522** (1537 edition)

Coverdale, M., *Goostly psalmes and spirituall songes drawen out of the holy Scripture, for the co[m]forte and consolacyon of soch as loue to reioyse in God and his worde* (London: Rastell & Gough, *c.* 1535).

Frosch, J., *RERVM MVSICARVM OPVSCVLVM RARVM AC INsigne, totius eius negotii rationem mira industria & breuitate complectens, iam recens publicatum* (Strasbourg: Schöffer & Apiarius, 1535). **GB Lbl – Hirsch I.183**

Ein nüw Lied von der vffrůr der landtlüten zů Jnderlappenn in der herschafft Bern in üchtlandt beschehen Jm[m] M. D. XXVIII. Jar (Strasbourg: Apiarius, 1536).

Fünff vnd sechzig teütscher Lieder / vormals im[m] truck nie vßgangen (Strasbourg: Schöffer & Apiarius, before 1537). **GB Lkc – mf062** (Maughan Library, Chancery Lane) (microfilm). N.B.: This is mistakenly classified as a hymn book by *RISM DKL* (1537[02]).

AVLCVNS pseaulmes et cantiques mys en chant (Strasbourg: Knobloch, 1539), facsimile published as: Terry, R. R., ed., *Calvin's First Psalter [1539]* (London: Benn, 1932).

Gesangbuch / darinn | begriffen sind / die aller | fürnemisten vnd besten | Psalmen / Geistliche Lieder / vnd | Chorgeseng / aus dem Wittem- | bergischen | Strasburgischen / vnd anderer | Kirchen Gesangbüchlin zůsamen | bracht / vnd mit besonderem | fleis corrigiert vnd | gedrucket (Strasbourg: Köpfel & Messerschmidt, 1541). **D Iek; D PA**. Facsimile published with the same title (Stuttgart: Evangelischen Verlagswerk, 1953). **GB Cu – MR250.a.95.1**; **GB Lbl – 3438.p.1**

Wied, H. von, *A simple, and religious consultation of vs Herman by the grace of God Archebishop of Colone, and prince Electour* (London: Daye, 1547).

Pseaumes Octantetrois de | Dauid, mis en rime Francoise. A sauoir, qua- | ra[n]teneuf par Clement Marot, auec le Canti- | que de Simeon & les dix Commandemens. | Et trentequatre par Theodore de Besze, de Vezelay en Bourgongne. || Auec priuilege pour les Pseaumes dudict de Besze (Geneva: Crespin, 1551).

Bucer, M., *De Regno Christi* (Basel: Oporinum, 1557). **GB Cu** (3 examples) – **Peterborough.A.10.18**; **Rel.a.55.3**; **D*.3.13(C)**.

Sturm, J., *Classicarum epistolarum Lib. III. Siue Scholae argentinenses restitutæ* (Strasbourg: Rihel, 1565).

Archival Material Consulted

Archives d'Etat de Genève:
  Pièces Historiques (PH)

Archives de la Ville et de la Communauté urbaine de Strasbourg:
  1 AST
  90Z
  II
  IV
  V
  VI
  VIII
  AA
  LDA
  MR
  R

Index

St Andrews Studies in Reformation History

Seminary or University? The Genevan Academy and Reformed Higher Education, 1560–1620
Karin Maag

Marian Protestantism: Six Studies
Andrew Pettegree

Protestant History and Identity in Sixteenth-Century Europe
(2 volumes) edited by Bruce Gordon

Antifraternalism and Anticlericalism in the German Reformation: Johann Eberlin von Günzburg and the Campaign against the Friars
Geoffrey Dipple

Piety and the People: Religious Printing in French, 1511–1551
Francis M. Higman

The Reformation in Eastern and Central Europe
Edited by Karin Maag

The Magnificent Ride: The First Reformation in Hussite Bohemia
Thomas A. Fudge

Kepler's Tübingen: Stimulus to a Theological Mathematics
Charlotte Methuen

The Reformation and the Book
Jean-François Gilmont, edited and translated by Karin Maag

'Practical Divinity': The Works and Life of Revd Richard Greenham
Kenneth L. Parker and Eric J. Carlson

Frontiers of the Reformation: Dissidence and Orthodoxy in Sixteenth-Century Europe
Auke Jelsma

The Jacobean Kirk, 1567–1625: Sovereignty, Polity and Liturgy
Alan R. MacDonald

The Education of a Christian Society: Humanism and the Reformation in Britain and the Netherlands
Edited by N. Scott Amos, Andrew Pettegree and Henk van Nierop

Tudor Histories of the English Reformations, 1530–83
Thomas Betteridge

Poor Relief and Protestantism: The Evolution of Social Welfare in Sixteenth-Century Emden
Timothy G. Fehler

Radical Reformation Studies: Essays presented to James M. Stayer
Edited by Werner O. Packull and Geoffrey L. Dipple

Clerical Marriage and the English Reformation: Precedent Policy and Practice
Helen L. Parish

The Faith and Fortunes of France's Huguenots, 1600–85
Philip Benedict

Penitence in the Age of Reformations
Edited by Katharine Jackson Lualdi and Anne T. Thayer

The Sixteenth-Century French Religious Book
Edited by Andrew Pettegree, Paul Nelles and Philip Conner

The Bible in the Renaissance: Essays on Biblical Commentary and Translation in the Fifteenth and Sixteenth Centuries
Edited by Richard Griffiths

Music as Propaganda in the German Reformation
Rebecca Wagner Oettinger

Christianity and Community in the West: Essays for John Bossy
Edited by Simon Ditchfield

John Foxe and his World
Edited by Christopher Highley and John N. King

Obedient Heretics: Mennonite Identities in Lutheran Hamburg and Altona during the Confessional Age
Michael D. Driedger

Reformation, Politics and Polemics: The Growth of Protestantism in East Anglian Market Towns, 1500–1610
John Craig

Usury, Interest and the Reformation
Eric Kerridge

Confessional Identity in East-Central Europe
Edited by Maria Crăciun, Ovidiu Ghitta and Graeme Murdock

The Correspondence of Reginald Pole: 1. A Calendar, 1518–1546: Beginnings to Legate of Viterbo
Thomas F. Mayer

The British Union: A Critical Edition and Translation of David Hume of Godscroft's De Unione Insulae Britannicae
Edited by Paul J. McGinnis and Arthur H. Williamson

Self-Defence and Religious Strife in Early Modern Europe: England and Germany, 1530–1680
Robert von Friedeburg

Penitence, Preaching and the Coming of the Reformation
Anne T. Thayer

Huguenot Heartland: Montauban and Southern French Calvinism during the French Wars of Religion
Philip Conner

Reforming the Scottish Church: John Winram (c. 1492–1582) and the Example of Fife
Linda J. Dunbar

Baptism and Spiritual Kinship in Early Modern England
Will Coster

Charity and Lay Piety in Reformation London, 1500–1620
Claire S. Schen

Cultures of Communication from Reformation to Enlightenment: Constructing Publics in the Early Modern German Lands
James Van Horn Melton

The Construction of Martyrdom in the English Catholic Community, 1535–1603
Anne Dillon

Sebastian Castellio, 1515-1563: Humanist and Defender of Religious Toleration in a Confessional Age
Hans R. Guggisberg, translated and edited by Bruce Gordon

The Front-Runner of the Catholic Reformation: The Life and Works of Johann von Staupitz
Franz Posset

The Correspondence of Reginald Pole: Volume 2. A Calendar, 1547–1554: A Power in Rome
Thomas F. Mayer

William of Orange and the Revolt of the Netherlands, 1572–1584
K.W. Swart, translated by J.C. Grayson

The Italian Reformers and the Zurich Church, c.1540–1620
Mark Taplin

William Cecil and Episcopacy, 1559–1577
Brett Usher

A Dialogue on the Law of Kingship among the Scots A Critical Edition and Translation of George Buchanan's De Jure Regni Apud Scotos Dialogus
Roger A. Mason and Martin S. Smith

Music and Religious Identity in Counter-Reformation Augsburg, 1580–1630
Alexander J. Fisher

The Correspondence of Reginald Pole Volume 3. A Calendar, 1555–1558: Restoring the English Church
Thomas F. Mayer

Women, Sex and Marriage in Early Modern Venice
Daniela Hacke

Infant Baptism in Reformation Geneva
The Shaping of a Community, 1536–1564
Karen E. Spierling

Moderate Voices in the European Reformation
Edited by Luc Racaut and Alec Ryrie

Piety and Family in Early Modern Europe
Essays in Honour of Steven Ozment
Edited by Marc R. Forster and Benjamin J. Kaplan

Religious Identities in Henry VIII's England
Peter Marshall

John Jewel and the English National Church
The Dilemmas of an Erastian Reformer
Gary W. Jenkins

Catholic Activism in South-West France, 1540–1570
Kevin Gould

Local Politics in the French Wars of Religion
The Towns of Champagne, the Duc de Guise, and the Catholic League, 1560–95
Mark W. Konnert

Enforcing Reformation in Ireland and Scotland, 1550–1700
Edited by Elizabethanne Boran and Crawford Gribben

Philip Melanchthon and the English Reformation
John Schofield

Reforming the Art of Dying
The ars moriendi *in the German Reformation (1519–1528)*
Austra Reinis

Restoring Christ's Church
John a Lasco and the Forma ac ratio
Michael S. Springer

Catholic Belief and Survival in Late Sixteenth-Century Vienna
The Case of Georg Eder (1523–87)
Elaine Fulton

From Judaism to Calvinism
The Life and Writings of Immanuel Tremellius (c.1510–1580)
Kenneth Austin

The Cosmographia *of Sebastian Münster*
Describing the World in the Reformation
Matthew McLean

Defending Royal Supremacy and Discerning God's Will in Tudor England
Daniel Eppley

The Monarchical Republic of Early Modern England
Essays in Response to Patrick Collinson
Edited by John F. McDiarmid

Adaptations of Calvinism in Reformation Europe
Essays in Honour of Brian G. Armstrong
Edited by Mack P. Holt

Johann Sleidan and the Protestant Vision of History
Alexandra Kess

The Correspondence of Reginald Pole
Volume 4 A Biographical Companion: The British Isles
Thomas F. Mayer and Courtney B. Walters

Life Writing in Reformation Europe
Lives *of Reformers by Friends, Disciples and Foes*
Irena Backus

Patents, Pictures and Patronage
John Day and the Tudor Book Trade
Elizabeth Evenden

The Chancery of God
Protestant Print, Polemic and Propaganda against the Empire, Magdeburg 1546–1551
Nathan Rein

The Impact of the European Reformation
Princes, Clergy and People
Edited by Bridget Heal and Ole Peter Grell

Patents, Pictures and Patronage
John Day and the Tudor Book Trade
Elizabeth Evenden

The Reformation in Rhyme
Sternhold, Hopkins and the English Metrical Psalter, 1547–1603
Beth Quitslund

Defining Community in Early Modern Europe
Edited by Michael J. Halvorson and Karen E. Spierling

Humanism and the Reform of Sacred Music in Early Modern England
John Merbecke the Orator and The Booke of Common Praier Noted (1550)
Hyun-Ah Kim

The Idol in the Age of Art
Objects, Devotions and the Early Modern World
Edited by Michael W. Cole and Rebecca Zorach

Literature and the Scottish Reformation
Edited by Crawford Gribben and David George Mullan

Protestantism, Poetry and Protest
The Vernacular Writings of Antoine de Chandieu (c. 1534–1591)
S.K. Barker

Humanism and Protestantism in Early Modern English Education
Ian Green

Living with Religious Diversity in Early-Modern Europe
Edited by C. Scott Dixon, Dagmar Freist and Mark Greengrass

The Curse of Ham in the Early Modern Era
The Bible and the Justifications for Slavery
David M. Whitford

Dealings with God
From Blasphemers in Early Modern Zurich to a Cultural History of Religiousness
Francisca Loetz

Magistrates, Madonnas and Miracles
The Counter Reformation in the Upper Palatinate
Trevor Johnson

Narratives of the Religious Self in Early-Modern Scotland
David George Mullan

Church Music and Protestantism in Post-Reformation England
Discourses, Sites and Identities
Jonathan Willis

Reforming the Scottish Parish
The Reformation in Fife, 1560–1640
John McCallum

Commonwealth and the English Reformation
Protestantism and the Politics of Religious Change in the Gloucester Vale, 1483–1560
Ben Lowe

Heinrich Heshusius and the Polemics of Early Lutheran Orthodoxy
Confessional Conflict and Jewish-Christian Relations in North Germany, 1556–1597
Michael J. Halvorson

Humanism and Calvinism
Andrew Melville and the Universities of Scotland, 1560–1625
Steven J. Reid

The Senses and the English Reformation
Matthew Milner

Early French Reform
The Theology and Spirituality of Guillaume Farel
Jason Zuidema and Theodore Van Raalte

Catholic and Protestant Translations of the Imitatio Christi, *1425–1650*
Maximilian von Habsburg

Getting Along?
Religious Identities and Confessional Relations in Early Modern England
Essays in Honour of Professor W.J. Sheils
Edited by Nadine Lewycky and Adam Morton

From Priest's Whore to Pastor's Wife
Clerical Marriage and the Process of Reform in the Early German Reformation
Marjorie Elizabeth Plummer

George Buchanan
Political Thought in Early Modern Britain and Europe
Edited by Caroline Erskine and Roger A. Mason

Censorship and Civic Order in Reformation Germany, 1517–1648
'Printed Poison & Evil Talk'
Allyson F. Creasman

Private and Domestic Devotion in Early Modern Britain
Edited by Jessica Martin and Alec Ryrie

A King Translated
The Writings of King James VI & I and their Interpretation in the Low Countries, 1593–1603
Astrid Stilma

A Linking of Heaven and Earth
Studies in Religious and Cultural History in Honor of Carlos M.N. Eire
Edited by Emily Michelson, Scott K. Taylor and Mary Noll Venables

Worship and the Parish Church in Early Modern Britain
Edited by Natalie Mears and Alec Ryrie

Baal's Priests
The Loyalist Clergy and the English Revolution
Fiona McCall

The Early Reformation in Germany
Between Secular Impact and Radical Vision
Tom Scott

The Search for Authority in Reformation Europe
Edited by Helen Parish, Elaine Fulton and Peter Webster

Practical Predestinarians in England, c. 1590–1640
Leif Dixon

Following Zwingli
Applying the Past in Reformation Zurich
Edited by Luca Baschera, Bruce Gordon and Christian Moser

Andrew Melville (1545–1622)
Writings, Reception, and Reputation
Edited by Roger A. Mason and Steven J. Reid

Metrical Psalmody in Print and Practice
English 'Singing Psalms' and Scottish 'Psalm Buiks', c. 1547–1640
Timothy Duguid

Andrew Melville (1545–1622)
Writings, Reception, and Reputation
Edited by Roger A. Mason and Steven J. Reid

Public Religious Disputation in England, 1558-1626
Joshua Rodda

The Sacralization of Space and Behavior in the Early Modern World
Studies and Sources
Edited by Jennifer Mara DeSilva